The Complete

A doption Book

The Complete Adoption Book

Laura Beauvais-Godwin
& Raymond Godwin

Adams Media Corporation
Holbrook, Massachusetts

Published by
Adams Media Corporation
260 Center Street, Holbrook, MA 02343

ISBN: 1-55850-644-6

Printed in the United States of America.

J I H G F E D C B

Library of Congress Cataloging-in-Publication Data
Beauvais-Godwin, Laura.
The complete adoption book : choosing an agency, independent adoptions, international
adoptions, state-by-state requirements / Laura Beauvais-Godwin & Raymond Godwin.
p.   cm.
ISBN 1-55850-644-6 (pb)
1. Adoption—United States. I. Godwin, Raymond. II. Title.
III. Title: Everything you need to know to adopt the child you want in less than one year.
HV875.55.B45   1997
326.7'34—dc20   96-43250
CIP

The authors have made every effort to ensure that the information contained in this book is
current and up to date; however, matters relative to adoption often change quickly. Because
adoption involves people and changing information, the authors have found that each
adoption scenario is unique and different to some degree. This book therefore should not be
a substitute for an adoption professional's involvement in your specific adoption matter.

This publication is designed to provide accurate and authoritative information with regard
to the subject matter covered. It is sold with the understanding that the publisher is not
engaged in rendering legal, accounting, or other professional advice. If legal advice or
other expert assistance is required, the services of a competent professional person should
be sought.
— From a *Declaration of Principles* jointly adopted by a Committee of the American Bar
Association and a Committee of Publishers and Associations

This book is available at quantity discounts for bulk purchases.
For information, call 1-800-872-5627 (in Massachusetts, 617-767-8100).

Visit our home page at http://www.adamsmedia.com

*We dedicate this book to our dear children, Erika and Elizabeth,
who have taught us that a true family is one based on love, openness,
and honesty. We also thank their birth mothers, who made this all possible.*

Contents

Acknowledgments

This book could not have been written without the many professionals who provided us with their expertise. We would like to thank the staff at Adoptive Families of America, the Child Welfare League, National Adoption Information Clearinghouse, and the North American Council on Adoptable Children. Thanks also to the professionals at the South Carolina Department of Social Services, Area III Adoptions, and Linda Williams at Seedlings, who have provided immeasurable information regarding children with special needs. Thanks to Judith Paris at South Carolina Department of Social Services and Steven Humerickhouse for providing extensive information on the funding available for these special children. We also thank Julie Wilson, congressional aide to Rep. Bob Inglis (SC), for her diligence in obtaining information from the Immigration and Naturalization Service.

We appreciate the many attorneys who provided us with legal and practical advice regarding their states' laws. Also, several therapists have given us insight into issues that must be faced by all involved in adoption.

Thank you, David and Mary Mexcur at New Hope Adoption Agency for sharing with us your international adoption experiences as professionals and as parents.

Pam Liflander and Elise Bauman, our editors at Adams Media, were committed to this book and provided much inspiration and support. Their suggestions helped to make the technical information more palatable and kept what is truly important in perspective. Thanks for all your encouragement and hard work.

Our very special thanks goes to the countless friends, adoption professionals, adoptive parents, birth parents, and adoptees whose lives have demonstrated that adoption is a loving choice and have made so many dreams come true.

Preface

In America today there are about 200,000 couples who want to adopt. This dream is said to be very costly and difficult to achieve. Yet nearly all the people we know who have actively and diligently sought to adopt had a baby or child in their home within eighteen months.

Nine years ago my husband and I did not know this. In fact, we were not aware that there were choices in the area of adoption. We did not know that a couple could adopt and have a baby within months. When we seriously began to consider adoption, we gave little thought to independent adoption. The idea of advertising for a baby made us uncomfortable; more important, we did not know anyone who had adopted independently. We had heard that independent adoption was risky and that it usually required the assistance of an expensive attorney.

So for a couple of years we pursued adoption through more traditional channels. Like many prospective adoptive parents, we spent years examining applications, and finally completed the forms for a few adoption agencies. This was a rather complicated process, as some applications were quite lengthy, and even after completing forms and sending in application fees, we had no guarantee of becoming parents. After attending a meeting conducted by an international adoption agency, we finally decided that we would adopt through an agency that placed Korean babies in a matter of months.

Then, on the day that we mailed our final application to the international agency, an acquaintance called us and asked whether we would be interested in meeting with a pregnant woman who wanted to place her baby for adoption. We were stunned. In a reversal of all our expectations, we became parents in four short months through independent adoption.

Moving from that fateful phone call to our daughter Erika's arrival was trying, despite the fact that our adoption was relatively simple and uneventful. So after we became adoptive parents, my husband decided to use his experience in family law and his personal experience as an adoptive parent to provide independent adoption services. Two and a half years later after Erika was born, an agency for whom Ray worked as a consultant asked whether he would be interested in adopting a baby that was soon to be born. Three weeks later, Elizabeth was in our arms.

Our goal in writing this book was to provide you, the prospective adoptive parent, with a step-by-step resource to guide you through a process that can sometimes feel overwhelming. Couples often tell us that they feel bewildered—that they do not even know where to begin. We have been there, too. In fact, when we were researching the adoption laws and practices of Canada, we were reminded of what it was like to begin the adoption process for the first time. When we started to look at adoption, we were helped tremendously by adoptive parents associated with a local chapter of RESOLVE, an infertility support and referral organization. They understood adoption issues and knew how to give us good, practical advice. Simple things like encouraging the birth mother to stay on a nonmaternity floor if she wished was invaluable information at a time when our emotions were running high. In fact, knowing people who had experienced all the emotions that we were about to embark upon was very comforting.

Still, even with this advice we often felt unsure about how to handle certain situations. Unfortunately, we knew of no book that could help us with issues like talking with birth mothers, meeting with obstetricians, and when to pay medical expenses. Nor did we know of a book that could prepare us for the perplexing situations that my husband and I would encounter: the obstetrician who told my daughter's birth mother that the adoption was illegal, or the hospital staff who made insensitive remarks.

Our experience has taught us that nearly every adoption unfolds a little differently from what is expected. Adoption—like all other miracles—has its quirks and unpredictable moments. Nevertheless, there are some constants in the process, and preparation can alleviate a great deal of uncertainty. If you follow our advice, there's no reason pursuing adoption shouldn't be a positive experience for you, and for the birth parents too, if they are involved in the process.

As with any process, the more you know about adoption at the outset, the more confident you can be. There is a lot of information contained in the following pages, and a lot of choices to make. Do not become overloaded. Find what is best for you. As you will see, adoption can be broken down into manageable steps. In the chapters that follow you will find much of the legal and practical information you will need to make you comfortable with the process. We have experienced many different adoption situations and learned a great deal about the nuances of the process. We also remember how *we* felt when we first got involved in adoption. We hope this book reflects that.

All information offered in this book is true to the best of our knowledge. Information, however, especially legal information, can change rapidly. Rely on an adoption attorney for updates.

Names have been changed throughout, unless otherwise stated, and certain facts altered to protect anonymity.

Attorneys, state agencies, newspapers, support groups, books, newsletters, professionals, and organizations mentioned in this book *are not* endorsed by Laura Beauvais-Godwin or Raymond Godwin. It is up to the reader to investigate the credentials of any person or organization before using its services.

Chapter One

Is Adoption for You?

If you are reading this book, chances are you are considering adoption. Perhaps you are in the middle of infertility treatment, or nearing the end of that treatment and wondering, "Where do I turn now?" Or it may be some time since you ended your treatments, and now you are ready to proceed with adoption. By now you know that the world of adoption is far from simple. There's a lot to learn. The good news is, that also means a lot of choices.

At the beginning, the process will probably seem confusing. Should you hire an attorney and adopt independently, or go with an agency? Is it better to adopt internationally or simply go through the local social services department? No one can answer these questions for you. You must consider the advantages and disadvantages of each route and decide which risks you can live with and which ones you cannot.

Even after you have decided on the method you want to pursue, approaching the adoption itself can feel overwhelming at first. There are so many fees and unknown expenses, so much paperwork. You have to think about getting through a home study, possibly meeting a birth mother, or even traveling to another country. You may create worries of your own by presuming that you must look a certain way, weigh a certain amount, and earn a certain income.

All adoptive parents go through this process, and they should. After all, this is a major life decision. With so many avenues to explore, it is important to take your time and ask as many questions as you can. Emotionally, you are bound to have a lot at stake, so proceed cautiously; get all of your facts in order and try not to let your feelings run ahead of your wallet or reality. Remember, proceeding cautiously does *not* mean proceeding slowly.

Many couples spend a year or two or three just "thinking about adoption" and making a few contacts. Some are still trying to conceive; others are just not quite ready to make the decision. It is very easy to fall into this routine. Each month may hold some promise that you may conceive, making it difficult to commit wholeheartedly to the adoption process. Without the actual promise of a real live baby, you may find it hard to put much effort into completing forms, getting the paperwork together for a home study, and writing out your life stories. The thought of talking to a birth mother may unnerve you, and when you consider traveling to another country, you remember the friend who got malaria while in Africa.

And so you say to yourself, "Let's wait another couple of months and see whether anything happens." This is understandable. What we hope to do in this book is show you that the tasks are not insurmountable. Sure, it is unfair. Biological parents do not have to go through the research, assemble documents, submit to a home study, or pay the fees. But if you are considering adoption, it is worth it. There are babies and children to adopt, and it does not take years to do it or tens of thousands of dollars. Most adoptions cost under $10,000 and take a matter of months. You do not have to be perfect, either—just normal and stable and loving.

THERE *ARE* CHILDREN TO ADOPT

There is a widespread myth that adoption choices are limited because there are too few babies and children to adopt. It is true that a few years ago your options were more limited. Things have changed: There are many babies and children available. In fact, when international as well as domestic adoptions are considered, there are far more babies and children available than there are parents seeking to adopt.

So how many parents *are* looking to adopt? You will sometimes see the figure of two million couples being bandied about. That figure, though, really relates to the number of infertile couples, not all of whom are pursuing adoption. Elizabeth Bartholet, author of *Family Bonds*, writes that at any given time there are approximately 200,000 women looking to adopt, while two million have at least investigated the process. This figure seems closer to the true number of prospective adoptive couples. That means that in any given year about one prospective couple in three will adopt. Those are very promising numbers.

The number of adoptions by nonrelatives has fluctuated over the years. In 1951 there were 33,800; in 1961, 61,600. Adoptions reached a peak of 89,000 in 1970, then fell to 47,000 in 1975. Today there are probably about 63,000 adoptions by nonrelatives every year. However, there is a real lack of concrete data regarding numbers of couples hoping to adopt and numbers of children placed for adoption. Even the numbers of adoptions taking place can be hard to measure. Intrafamily adoptions (grandparents adopting grandchildren, aunts adopting nieces and nephews...) and stepparent adoptions account for about half. Because many such adoptions are private, the exact number is not known, but it is estimated to be about 50,000. Many other adoptions may go unrecorded as well. For example, if an independent international adoption is finalized in another country, there may be no record of it here in the United States. The Immigration and Naturalization Service has the data but no method for passing it on to the states. All that is really clear is that adoption figures vary dramatically from state to state—influenced not only by population but by the various state laws surrounding adoption. So hard numbers are elusive. We do know this, however: People *are* adopting. Statistics prove it.

WHO CAN ADOPT?

Nearly anyone who can provide a child with a stable, loving environment can become an adoptive parent. You do not have to be under thirty-five, have a large income, own a home, have money in the bank, or be married, childless, or infertile. Unlike any other group of parents, however, you will be required to provide information that indicates that you are stable and loving; that you are not too old to adopt; that you have a normal life expectancy; that you have a sufficient income to provide for a child; that you have adequate space for the child to live; if you are married, that your marriage is healthy and that you do not have an extensive divorce history; and if you do have children, that they are not exhibiting problems related to poor parenting.

Many people worry that they will not be approved to adopt. Most states do require that you be evaluated by a social worker or caseworker, who will then prepare a preplacement report known as a *home study*. Regulations as to what is included in this study are established by each state, but the basic standard is really one of common sense. What does it take to be a fit parent? Basic financial wherewithal, stability, and love. The home-study process is designed to screen out those who would not make suitable parents because of serious medical problems, mental illness, insufficient income, criminal history, a record of child abuse, or a current drug or alcohol addiction. Unless you have a serious problem, chances are good that you will be able to adopt.

You may run into other restrictions, depending on what avenues you decide to explore. Some licensed agencies have restrictions as to who can adopt as a means of limiting the number of prospective adoptive parents. Public agencies have requirements that those adopting children with special needs be able to meet the challenge of raising a child who has physical, mental, or emotional disabilities or illnesses. Every foreign country has its own guidelines as to who can adopt.

HOW TO BEGIN

Many people begin investigating adoption by looking under "Adoption" in the yellow pages of their telephone book and calling up the agencies listed, both public and private. Initially, this can be very discouraging. If you are looking to adopt a healthy infant, most social services departments have years-long waiting lists. Private agencies may also have long waiting lists, and they may have in addition many requirements and restrictions, not to mention high fees. For many the next step is to call an attorney's office, where they are asked to advertise for a birth mother, meet her, and possibly pay her living expenses for several months. Those who then turn to an international adoption agency learn they must travel to a foreign country and stay there for at least two to three weeks. All these options seem to have a downside. All you want is a baby or child, and suddenly you must consider what route you want to take, whether you will be accepted, whether you can afford it, and whether you are ready to take the risk. For many, it can feel overwhelming.

No matter what avenue you choose, there will be risks, whether they are financial risks, risks relating to the child's health, or risks associated with birth parents' rights. But these are calculated risks—not blind risks. For some, the risks associated with certain kinds of adoptions are enough to keep them away from that route. Others decide to go ahead. Only you can make the choice.

WHAT KIND OF CHILD DO YOU WANT?

In deciding which route to take, you may first want to consider what kind of child you want to adopt. Initially most people think of adopting a healthy newborn infant or a very young baby of their own ethnic background. But as people begin to consider adoption, the categories of adoptable children they will consider can broaden. This does not mean that a couple who had their heart set on a healthy Caucasian infant but could not afford the fees decides to "settle" for a two-year-old of another ethnic background. It is far more complex than that. All adoptive parents must carefully consider their background, resources, family, neighborhood, church, and available schools in considering what kind of child would be best suited for their family.

WHAT ROUTE DO YOU WANT TO TAKE?

There are two broad categories of adoptions: domestic and international. Within each of those two categories there are two general types of children to be adopted: those who are healthy and those who have special needs.

When adopting domestically, most people are interested in adopting healthy infants. There are two routes taken toward achieving this goal. One is private, or independent, adoption. This entails hiring an attorney who will either locate a birth mother for you or instruct you on how to find one yourself through advertising or networking. The other route is to go with an agency, either public (a state agency) or private. The advantages, disadvantages, and legal issues associated with these two routes are discussed at length in the chapters that follow. For now, you may simply find it helpful to know that state agencies do have some healthy children to place for adoption—that applying to a state agency does not necessarily mean applying for a child with special needs, as many people believe. Many couples begin as foster parents and then learn as much as possible in order to be in the right place at the right time for a permanent placement. The success of this approach depends on the state and the timing. Not many infant adoptions take place through these state agencies, but your local state agency may present an opportunity. Some attorneys specialize in representing foster parents who aggressively push for adoption.

Most state agencies and a few private ones focus on placing children with special needs in the homes of adoptive couples. The special needs category includes both physical and psychological needs, with the label "physical needs" covering a wide range of medical conditions. Special needs children often come from abusive homes. Having been surrendered voluntarily by dysfunctional birth parents or taken from such homes by court order, they have usually been placed in foster homes for a time. The state agency operating the foster care system also has an adoption unit, which attempts to place the children for adoption. Again, the severity of the "need," whether physical or psychological, varies greatly.

MOVING FROM INFERTILITY TO ADOPTION

Before you begin the adoption process, you will want to explore your feelings about infertility and adoption. If you have been undergoing infertility treatment, you have probably felt out of control. Not only have you not achieved a successful pregnancy, but other areas of your life have probably been very much affected. You may not have taken the vacation you wanted because it conflicted with your infertility treatment. Or infertility has affected the way that you relate to others. For example, you may find it difficult to be around pregnant women, while attending a baby shower has become nearly intolerable. The self-doubts and out-of-control feelings that accompany infertility may remain with you as you approach the adoption process.

It is important to try and resolve some of the negative feelings associated with infertility, and also to examine your true feelings toward adoption, both positive and negative. Infertility treatment is an exhausting, time-consuming undertaking, and you may feel that you do not have the emotional energy to pursue these issues diligently. If you choose adoption, however, now is the time to begin resolving your feelings. If you pursue a private adoption, you may be parents quickly—perhaps even before you have had time to search within yourself and feel whole again. On the other hand, couples pursuing agency adoptions may be required to attend infertility and adoption workshops for several weeks. They also may be on a waiting list for three to five years—plenty of time to explore their feelings.

Adopting a baby does not necessarily alleviate all the insecurities that accompany infertility. We recommend that you join an adoption support group or an infertility support group, such as RESOLVE, to learn more about infertility and adoption issues. Read this and other books that deal with adoption after infertility. Not only will you be better prepared to be in charge of your adoption plans, you will be more comfortable in talking with others about your desire to adopt.

ARE YOU READY TO ACCEPT PARENTHOOD THROUGH ADOPTION?

You have probably invested much time, money, and energy in attempts to have a biological child. Somewhere in the middle of your infertility treatment, you probably began to ask yourself why you so desperately wanted to have a child. As you thought about that question and underwent more invasive procedures, you may have been more convinced than ever that you wanted a biological child. As a successful pregnancy began to seem less and less likely, however, you had to move from your dream of having a biological child to considering child-free living, or adopting. Now, as you think of beginning the adoption process, you need to establish your reasons for becoming parents and to realize that an adopted child can fulfill your need to be parents. The first step, then is to explore why you really want to be a parent.

Life is a constant series of decisions. Some are minor, such as what to have for breakfast; some are major, such as choosing a college or a partner, or deciding to have children. Nearly all the decisions we make are reversible. We can change our job, get a divorce, or transfer to another college. But one decision is never considered reversible, and that is the decision to have children.

That is why it is crucial to answer the question, "Why do we want to have children?" Although your reasons do not have to be completely logical, they should be defined, because of the tremendous responsibility and expense that come with being a parent. You need to establish some rational and sensible motives for having children, if you are about to adopt.

People who set out to have biological children have many reasons for doing so, some more important than others. Here are the most common reasons people give for wanting children. Each is followed by a response suggesting why an adopted child would most likely meet a couple's needs.

To have the perfect child. Many people fantasize about having the "perfect" child. They think, "He will have my nose, my hair, my husband's eyes and lashes, my family's mind, and his family's language skills."

Response: Now imagine the worst possible genetic combination and ask yourself how "perfect" such a child would be. Don't forget to consider the worst traits of your family and in-laws. In other words, the "perfect" biological child might not be so perfect. There are many genes your child could inherit.

To continue your family lineage. Some people do not want to create the "perfect" child; rather they feel the need to perpetuate the "perfect" family. Perhaps your family is one that believes that "blood is thicker than water." In fact, you may feel a great responsibility to pass on certain characteristics of your family or yourself to a child.

Response: Again, children can draw from a very large gene pool. There is no guarantee of passing on any single characteristic to your child. It may be that the characteristics you want to perpetuate have more to do with your values than with your family genes, however, and these are passed on to your child through your nurturing, not your genetic role. An adopted child will have the same opportunity to develop strong, positive values that a biological child would.

To have a child with your interests, talents, and abilities. The reasons for wanting a child who shares your interests are similar to those for wanting the "perfect" child: your desire to pass on the best of the family's traits. For example, you may be a wonderful pianist. Music may always have been a great love in your family. You might fear that an adopted child would not have the same innate musical ability that a biological child would have.

Response: First, acknowledge that even a biological child will not necessarily inherit your musical abilities. Second, be aware that you can seek out and select a birth mother who is musically inclined, if you believe that musical ability is inherited. Finally, remember that even a child born without innate musical ability can be coached to play a musical instrument and to appreciate fine music.

Of course, we must accept our children for who they are, not for what we want them to be. Whether our children are born to us or adopted by us, they are ours to love for themselves, not for what they do.

To pass on the family name. When people think of perpetuating a family heritage, the "family name" is often the first thing they think of. Viewed in this light, it becomes almost an obligation to keep the family name moving.

Response: If you are a Louis Johnson III, can you feel comfortable naming an adopted child Louis Johnson IV? Some people's initial response is negative. Yet when they think further about what it means to name a child after themselves or another family member, they realize that it does not really matter whether the child is biological or adopted. The feelings that parents have for their adopted children are the same as for biological children. Feelings of love make the connection between the parent and the child; the name can just be an extension of that connection.

To have your child accepted by other family members. Many couples fear that other family members will not love and accept an adopted child, particularly one of a different ethnic background.

Response: Research indicates that even relatives who are opposed to the adoption develop very strong feelings for the child once the child is placed.

To experience pregnancy and birth. Some women believe that to feel truly feminine, they must experience pregnancy, giving birth to and breastfeeding a baby.

Response: If these reasons for having a child are very important to you, then you need to grieve the loss of these opportunities. If you cannot move past the grieving stage, then perhaps you need to continue infertility treatment.

Joining an infertility support group, such as one offered by RESOLVE, can help you through the grieving process, as well as assisting you and your spouse in deciding when to continue infertility treatment or when to end it. Knowing when "enough is enough" can help you and your spouse move toward resolving your infertility and accepting adoption or child-free living.

Control of mother's health during pregnancy. Another reason to want biological children is to have as much control as possible during your pregnancy. As a conscientious person, you would eat well, take prenatal vitamins, avoid alcohol and drugs, and seek proper medical care.

Response: Adoptive parents are right to be concerned about the birth mother's well-being and health during her pregnancy, since we know that her health can influence a child's development. Actually, depending on what route to adoption you follow, control of the birth mother's health is not entirely out of your hands. Nevertheless, for some couples considering adoption, the risks are too great. Perhaps you and your spouse need to put your fears into words. Sometimes identifying fears can help you face them. Then you can determine what risks you are willing or not willing to take. For more about medical issues, see chapter 18.

To rear a child that you love. This should be your number-one reason for wanting to be a parent: to provide a loving and stable environment for a growing child. To make this investment in a life, you want the child to be truly yours. Indeed, some people believe that the love you have for a child is a result of the biological connection and not the relationship; therefore, an adopted child can't be truly theirs.

Response: Adoptive parents, some with both biological and adopted children, unanimously say that they love all their children the same.

For most, the decision to adopt follows infertility treatment. You may take comfort in knowing that although adoption may be your second choice, it is not second-best.

WHAT ARE YOUR REASONS FOR WANTING A CHILD?
Having thought about some of the things that motivate people to have children, you and your spouse need to explore your reasons for wanting to be parents. Here is an exercise designed to help you do just that.

1. Working independently, write out the reasons you want a child.
2. Now identify the reasons you have in common. Are there answers that are important to both of you? Is there one that is very important to you but not to your spouse?
3. Now write out the needs that you believe having an adopted child can fulfill.

Chapter Two

Agency Adoption

A n adoption agency is a business incorporated as either a nonprofit or a for-profit entity. It is licensed by its state to place children for adoption and to conduct home studies; some agencies only conduct home studies. The director of the agency must also have certain qualifications, such as a master's in social work and several years' experience in the adoption field.

The social workers or caseworkers working for the adoption agency generally have at least a college degree, if not a master's in social work. Sometimes years of experience in social work or adoption will allow someone to work for the agency without having a specialized degree. Being qualified by state standards, however, does not guarantee that the worker is knowledgeable about adoption issues or highly sympathetic to your concerns and needs. Like many attorneys, adoption caseworkers may have no clue, for example, about how to interact with birth parents or what to look for in discussing adoption with a birth mother.

Fortunately, there are numerous directors and social workers involved with adoption agencies who *are* highly qualified and professional. Many are themselves adoptive parents, and so can bring a special touch of empathy to the process.

Each state has its own laws and regulations as to who can form an agency and what guidelines must be followed to maintain an agency license or certification. Remember, just because an agency is incorporated as a nonprofit entity does not mean that the owner of the agency is not profiting from the organization; the owner will profit by drawing a salary. Nor does another's agency's for-profit status imply that those who operate the agency are money-hungry and unscrupulous. Whether an agency is nonprofit or for-profit has more to do with tax and legal considerations than anything else.

Some people still believe that operating as a nonprofit organization gives an agency the appearance of being more ethical, since almost all well-known charities and religious organizations are nonprofit entities. No matter what your take on this issue, it is important to question an adoption agency about its experience and professionalism, no matter what umbrella the agency is incorporated under. The agency's written policy and the way it really functions can sometimes be quite different.

Most agencies have a policy stating that their purpose is to provide suitable homes for children—not to find children for couples. Their focus is often on the birth mother, with the agency in essence acting as her advocate; the agency does not represent the adoptive couple, nor are the couple's interests as highly regarded as they may believe. To use an extreme illustration, in one case an agency informed an adoptive couple on the weekend they were to pick up their baby, that the birth mother wanted an open adoption after placement, and that the couple had no choice in the matter. This would mean visits with the birth mother on a regular basis. The agency director informed the couple, who had received no prior warning about open adoption and had been given no information about their rights, that this was the way adoptions were done in the 1990s, and that if the couple could not consent to such an arrangement, they were not ready for adoption. The couple declined to go forward with the placement.

Birth mothers and children do need advocates. But adoptive parents also have rights and feelings. An ethical agency will be clear as to its purpose and up front as to its policies from the very beginning.

PUBLIC ADOPTION AGENCIES

Public, or government-operated, agencies are usually a part of the state social services department. Most states operate several adoption agencies, generally on the regional or county level. To locate the public adoption agency in your area, contact the adoption specialist in your state (see the Appendix) or look in the government section of your telephone directory.

Couples seeking to adopt will often begin their adoption research by opening up the telephone directory and calling their social services department. If they are looking for a healthy Caucasian infant, they may be discouraged to be told that the wait is seven to nine years. For those who are truly flexible, however, who have researched the possibility of adopting a child with special needs or one of another ethnic background, going through a state adoption unit may be a very good choice. It is estimated that there are at least 50,000 U.S. children in need of adoptive homes; these are children placed in the states' foster care systems.[1]

AVAILABLE CHILDREN

Public agencies primarily place children who have been in the foster-care system, even if the children have no physical health problems. These children have often been abused or neglected; many have been in multiple foster homes. Their biological parents' rights have usually been involuntarily terminated because of the abuse or neglect.

Many of the children placed for adoption are older. However, as more laws are passed to get children into permanent homes at a faster rate, more babies and preschool children are becoming available. Many of these children are physically healthy. If the children are young, they are less likely to have the depth of emotional scars found in older children. If you are willing to be a "foster-adoptive" parent and to have a child in your home who is considered a moderately high legal risk (because of issues such as the biological parents' rights), you may also have more opportunity to adopt a child at a younger age.

Although the trend in government is to provide permanency for children instead of allowing them to go from foster home to foster home, it may still take months or years before both biological parents' rights are terminated and the actual adoption can go through. The length of the waiting time varies from state to state and according to individual circumstances. In any case, you can be the child's foster parents until the adoption is finalized.

PUBLIC AGENCY ADOPTION: PROS AND CONS

Few of life's accomplishments provide the same level of reward as adopting a child with special needs. Also, you can adopt quickly—in six to twelve months—if you desire to adopt a minority or school-age child. Another important advantage of using a public agency is cost. Adoption expenses are usually minimal, and often state and federal subsidies are available. Support services are usually available and public agencies usually network with other government agencies to provide counseling services to children and adoptive parents.

Concerning the disadvantages of using a public agency, several important—but not insurmountable—challenges must be highlighted.

1. There's no denying that working with the bureaucracy can be difficult. You may agree to take a child who is considered a moderate-to-low legal risk and find that because of the law it takes years to terminate a missing parent's rights. You may also have to interact with social workers who have a bias against transracial adoptions. In one case, two African-American children were kept in foster care for a full year after the rights of the birth parents were terminated because the social worker involved

was seeking only a college-educated African-American couple with a certain income as the prospective adoptive couple.

2. The agency may expect you to attend twenty-five hours or more of pre-adoption seminars.

3. The public agency's home-study process may be more demanding than a home study done for a private placement. Because you are requesting a child with special needs or of a different ethnic background from your own, the agency may ask you numerous personal questions about your upbringing and your attitudes on many issues. These questions may be necessary, but they can also feel invasive.

4. The child that you are adopting will not be a newborn, and the quality of care he or she received during the first year or more of life may be relatively unknown.

5. You will need to become educated about the kinds of emotional problems the child may suffer as a result of his past experiences.

STATE- AND FEDERALLY FUNDED PRIVATE AGENCIES

Some agencies operate much like public adoption agencies, receiving government monies, networking with their state's social services department, and placing exclusively special needs children. Such agencies usually accept children for adoption and assume legal responsibility for them. Often they will function to fill a need not covered by the public agencies. For example, a specialized agency may place older African-American children, whereas a social services department might not have the resources to reach out aggressively to the African-American community for potential adoptive parents. Such agencies do not usually charge a fee, because they are serving waiting children, but if they do charge one, it is made considerably lower by the provision of government grants.

Sometimes an older or special needs child may be placed with a private agency that is working with the biological parent or guardian of the child to keep the social services department from getting involved and placing the child in foster care. In cases like this, the agency itself may be hindered by the bureaucracy in attempting to establish a permanent placement.

RELIGIOUS AGENCIES

Some agencies providing adoption services have a specifically religious affiliation. These include Catholic Charities, Lutheran Social Ministries, and Bethany Christian Services. From this group, some take applicants only from certain religious affiliations, while others have more flexible policies, especially for special needs or minority children. These agencies receive charitable donations and so can often keep their expenses lower. Moreover, they often do not charge directly for the birth mother's expenses, because so many birth mothers change their minds when working with these agencies. (Religious agencies are more likely to counsel birth mothers to raise their own children.) These agencies usually have a set fee. If the birth mother changes her mind, you are not charged for her living expenses. Sometimes services are provided to the birth mother through the agencies' own organizations. For example, they may allow or require her to live in a home for unwed mothers or with a family who will care for her during her pregnancy.

Religious agencies network with churches, synagogues, crisis pregnancy centers, hospitals, private religious schools, and other organizations that often refer birth mothers to them. Because some of these agencies are well-known names, they are often the first place a birth mother will go when she learns she is pregnant.

Other religiously affiliated adoptions agencies are offshoots of homes for unwed mothers. These homes may have been created as conscious alternatives to abortion, and their staffs may provide career training and counseling services. Such agencies often provide strong emotional support for choosing an adoption plan. When a woman places a child for adoption, the fees to the adoptive parents often pay for the upkeep of the home and services to other pregnant women.

Like birth mothers, many adoptive couples often turn first to an organization affiliated with their religion. This can work to your advantage if the agency is selective and you meet its requirements. Some religious agencies, however, can be overly controlling in their approach to adoptive parents, insisting on significant paperwork, attendance at several workshops, a home study that can feel invasive, and excessive initial fees. These requirements can limit the number of applicants and slow down the adoption process so that it takes six months to a year just to complete all the requirements. But if you are patient, you can adopt.

PRIVATE AGENCIES THAT PLACE INFANTS

For years private adoption agencies that placed primarily infants were the chief vehicle for couples seeking a placement. Indeed, up until the mid-seventies, private agency adoption was virtually the only system used. Things have changed now, but many of the old impressions and fears about private agencies persist. Birth mothers worry that an agency caseworker will interrogate them and pass judgment about their unplanned pregnancy, or that their baby will be placed in foster care for a week or more, then adopted by a couple they know little about. Some adoption agencies still do operate like this, but not many.

Adoptive couples may suffer from equally outmoded ideas. They may think that all they have to do is apply to an agency, and after a short time, they'll receive a phone call that a baby is waiting to be picked up. This picture no longer matches reality. Today, the birth mother's cooperation is often actively sought during the process of making a placement. Couples applying for adoption compile portfolios about themselves, complete with photographs and a letter to the prospective birth mother, on the basis of which she makes the selection. Some agencies may allow the birth mother to meet with the couple before the birth. Thus, the decision as to placement is very often left up to the birth mother, not the agency. Of course, the agency controls which portfolios it presents to the birth mother. But placements are no longer simply made on the basis of first come, first served.

Agency adoptions take several different forms. Let's begin with the traditional agency adoption.

TRADITIONAL ADOPTION

Traditional adoption is a closed adoption in which the birth and adoptive parents never meet. An agency calls you to take home a baby who has been released for adoption. This often means that the child has been in foster care for a few weeks. Why? Because depending upon the state, the birth mother may have a set period of time after the baby is born in which to change her mind about placing the baby for adoption. This waiting period may be anywhere from ten to ninety days, and some agencies will not permit a child to be placed in an adoptive home before the waiting period has elapsed. In some states, in fact, it is against the law to do so because the child is considered a "high legal risk." If he or she is permitted to go home with the adoptive parents, they may be referred to as the "foster parents" until the waiting period has elapsed and the birth parents' rights are terminated. Unquestionably the worst-case scenario is for an infant to be placed in a couple's home, only to have one of the birth parents change his or her mind and remove the child. This happens only rarely, but when it does, the heartache is immense.

The scenario just described occurs only in states in which birth parents' rights are not terminated when they sign the consent to the adoption. (The consent is usually signed a few days after the child's birth.) States have such laws for a reason. Their point is not simply to favor birth parents but to avoid the often thorny legal challenges associated with adoption. However, they can have unintended consequences. Birth mothers find themselves in a dilemma: Should their child be placed in foster care or not? Most birth mothers do not want their babies in foster care; they very much want the baby to go home from the hospital with the adoptive couple. Because agencies are usually not willing to place a baby with a couple until the birth parents' rights have ended, birth mothers often end up avoiding agencies altogether. Agencies that are able to comply with the birth mother's wishes by making the adoptive couple the foster family until the birth parents' rights are terminated probably offer the best solution.

FACILITATED AGENCY ADOPTION

With a facilitated agency adoption, the agency introduces you to a birth mother before the baby's birth. This option is much like a private adoption (see chapter 3) and therefore is now much more prevalent than a traditional agency adoption. You take on essentially the same involvement that you would in a private adoption, and unless the agency receives outside funds, you will be paying the birth mother's legal, living, and counseling expenses in addition to the agency fee.

Some agencies now require their clients to advertise for their own birth mother. Once you find a birth mother, the agency will handle her concerns, provide her with counseling, and sometimes make arrangements for her housing and medical care.

The chief difference between this type of agency adoption and private adoption has to do with cost. The up-front costs of the agency adoption may be much higher—in many cases, several thousand dollars before you even start. Moreover, once you make such an investment in an agency and locate a birth mother, you and the birth mother are pretty much committed to working with this agency.

There are risks with this approach. If a birth mother changes her mind and decides to keep her child, the couple are not only heartbroken, they may be several thousand dollars out of pocket as well. If a child is placed with you as a result of your finding a birth mother on your own, and for some reason the birth mother cannot or does not want to work with the agency, the agency may require that you forfeit all of your initial fees. This arrangement is usually spelled out in the agency-client contract. Be very cautious of such a contract; it means that you can lose substantially. Some agencies will allow you to put the money toward a second adoption, while others will not.

THE MIDDLE ROAD

With the third option you are informed that a birth mother has chosen you after viewing your portfolio, and you wait to pick the baby up from the agency immediately after the birth mother has signed the documents terminating her parental rights. Like a traditional agency adoption, the fees are generally higher than if you find the birth mother yourself.

Many agencies have taken this middle road, as it were, between an independent adoption, in which you meet the birth mother, and a traditional agency adoption, in which the placement is completely anonymous. Taking this in-between route can protect the emotions of both the birth mother and the adoptive couple, in the event that the birth mother changes her mind.

The caveat with this method of adoption is that you must be very careful in working with an agency that requires large payments for a specific birth mother's living and counseling expenses. If she changes her mind, you will probably not be reimbursed for the monies paid to her and for her benefit. Since this middle approach does not normally include your meeting the birth mother, you will not have the opportunity to evaluate her sincerity and resoluteness about placement.

You will want to confer several times with the social worker assigned by the agency to work with the birth mother. An agency will often assign one social worker to work with you and another to work with the birth mother. The two social workers will confer together about the birth mother, but there may not be an opportunity for the adoptive couple to meet with the birth mother's social worker unless they insist upon it.

Even if they do, if the social worker is inexperienced, he or she may not know what to ask a birth mother in order to gauge her resolve in placing her child for adoption or to spot warning signs that certain issues have not been addressed. Unfortunately, it is too easy for an agency to charge its nonrefundable fees for matching you with a birth mother that the agency should have had reservations about. If you do not meet with the birth mother, you will not pick up on the warning signs. Meeting you, furthermore, can force a birth mother out of denial and lead her to make a concrete decision about an adoption plan. Otherwise she may continue to draw monies from the agency as she works through certain issues about the adoption—at your expense. If you know that there is some hesitation, articulated or not, then at least you can make the decision whether to risk your money and your emotions. The same scenario can also happen with attorneys who match couples with birth parents.

IDENTIFIED AGENCY ADOPTION

Identified agency adoption, also called designated agency adoption, is essentially an independent adoption that becomes an agency adoption. Usually the prospective adoptive parents and a pregnant woman have made some form of contact with each other before involving an agency. An identified adoption proceeds much like an independent adoption, except that the agency provides guidance and support. Also, the laws governing an agency adoption are followed, rather than those governing an independent adoption.

Agencies recognize that more and more people are choosing independent adoption, and are therefore providing more identified adoption services. Actually, this compromise can offer the best of both worlds: the personal control the birth and adoptive parents seek in an independent adoption, and the emotional and sometimes legal advantages permitted in an agency adoption. Some agencies even counsel prospective adoptive parents on how to proceed with an independent adoption.

In the four states where private adoption is illegal, an identified adoption is one of the few options available. In a few more states it can be advantageous (see the Appendix). In most states, however, an identified adoption offers limited benefits.

WHY CONSIDER AN IDENTIFIED ADOPTION?

If you are thinking about private adoption, there are a number of reasons why an identified adoption could make sense. For instance:

1. *Counseling for birth and adoptive parents.* The counseling that birth parents receive through an agency can help determine whether they are quite sure of their decision to place the baby for adoption. Counseling can also help prepare them for the feelings they will experience once the baby is born. Adoption creates many highs and lows for everyone, birth and adoptive parents alike, and it can be reassuring to have a counselor on hand to provide support and encouragement, to give the feeling that someone is "holding their hand" throughout the process.

2. *Birth mothers' expenses.* Expenses that adoptive parents cannot legally pay for in an independent adoption, such as rent, may be permitted in an agency adoption, although state laws vary considerably on this point. Paying expenses can help facilitate the adoption process and provide an incentive to the birth mother to work with you. But be careful! You do not want to fall into the trap of paying for excessive expenses.

3. *Fewer legal complications.* In some states the birth parents' rights are terminated earlier in an agency adoption than they would be in an independent adoption. This provision usually prevents the removal of a child from a couple's home if a birth parent changes his or her mind, saving much heartache for everyone involved.

   Knowing that her parental rights are terminated once the baby goes home with the adoptive couple can actually give a birth mother greater peace of mind. There is no temptation to second-guess her decision or agonize about whether to change her mind. She is also more secure knowing that the birth father's rights have been terminated and that he cannot interfere with the adoption plans.

Although placing a child for adoption can be very sad for birth parents, having the process reach closure allows them to grieve their loss and then to get on with their lives.

4. *More legal options.* In states in which independent adoption is illegal, a couple can essentially pursue a private adoption and then contact an agency to make it into an identified/agency adoption. An agency can also serve as an intermediary in states where intermediaries are not permitted. This means contracting with an agency so that an intermediary or a birth mother can contact the agency instead of you. For example, you may wish to write to obstetricians and enclose your adoption business cards. Instead of putting your name and telephone number on the card, you can supply the agency's name and telephone number, along with your first names.

5. *Protection of privacy.* When advertising in newspapers and through adoption cards, you can use the agency's name and phone number instead of your own. By doing so, you remove some of the anxiety associated with screening phone calls, especially prank calls.

   Note: This does not always work to your advantage. Many birth mothers will not want to deal with an agency. *Be sure to specify in your ad that the phone number belongs to an agency. Birth mothers will hang up if they feel they are being deceived*—and rightfully so. No birth mother wants to hear "Happy Land Adoption Agency" when she is expecting to reach Arlene and Peter at a private home.

6. *Support system for birth mother.* For adoptive couples who do not wish to meet and talk with the birth mother on a weekly or even a monthly basis, the agency social worker assigned to the birth mother can "hold her hand" in a positive sense.

IDENTIFIED ADOPTION—SOME DISADVANTAGES

With an identified adoption, problems sometimes arise if you or the agency are not clear in your expectations. As identified adoptions become more common, long-established traditional agencies that primarily place babies may decide to go along with the trend and offer identified adoption services. The problem is that such agencies are historically biased against independent adoptions, and this strong bias can eventually show.

An example of agency bias has to do with foster care. Some agencies will encourage a birth mother to place the baby in foster care for six weeks or longer. Even if you have met the birth mother yourself and have begun to work out an arrangement, the agency may have its own agenda, insisting, for instance, on repeatedly contacting the birth father and getting him to relinquish his rights even when the father is completely unresponsive and the state laws provide an adequate way to terminate his parental rights without his having to formally sign them away.

Another bias of some agencies is to bar communication between birth and adoptive parents during the birth mother's pregnancy. One very traditional agency forbids you to talk to the birth mother after the initial contact until she has placed the baby with you. Not surprisingly, about 80 percent of the birth mothers who enter this agency's doors end up deciding to raise their babies themselves. It is our hunch that when the agency discusses with the birth mother her decision to place the baby for adoption and to look at all of her "options," it is strongly encouraging her to consider raising the child herself. The 80 percent statistic is so unlike the figures of most other agencies that we wonder whether guilt is used to make birth mothers feel like monsters for wanting to "give their babies away."

Most states require that agencies discuss alternatives to adoption with the birth mother whether she wants to or not. That's not necessarily bad. A woman seeking to place a baby for adoption has a right to consider all her options. When she does so and still chooses adoption, she is less likely to change her mind after the baby is born. However, if you have met with a birth mother who is resolute in her decision to place the baby for adoption, she may feel very uncomfortable having to discuss in detail why she is not planning to raise the child, or even why she is not considering an abortion. Repeated probing about feelings and family backgrounds can make a birth mother feel she is guilty of something. Understanding counselors will respect a woman who is very firm in her decision and not press her for an elaborate explanation.

Before committing yourself to an identified adoption, *find out what the expenses will be.* The cost of this kind of adoption varies greatly from one agency to the next, as do the billing systems used. Some agencies charge one fee; others bill by the hour. Circumstances make a difference: If you meet a birth mother when she is nearly nine months pregnant, she will probably not receive as many hours of counseling as a woman who contacts you when she is three months pregnant.

Other factors that can increase the cost include the level of birth father's involvement, his counseling, the distance the social worker has to travel to meet with the birth mother and father, and whether she communicates with the birth mother and father by long-distance telephone.

Watch out! If you have not personally met the birth mother, an agency may want to charge you for a direct placement instead of an identified adoption. One couple had spoken with a birth mother and then contacted an agency to conduct an identified adoption. The cost was $2,000 one day, $14,000 the next. Because the couple had not met the birth mother face to face, the agency wanted to charge them the higher rate.

In states in which private adoption is illegal, such as Massachusetts, agency fees for an identified adoption can be astronomical—$4,000 just for the home study. It may be less expensive to adopt in another state. Even if you have to live in a hotel for two weeks after the baby is born, it will still be much cheaper than an agency fee of $10,000 plus the birth mother's expenses.

Finally, find out whatever you can about an agency's reputation. Some agencies will "steal" a birth mother from you and steer her to one of its own couples. A dishonest agency would find this very profitable, because when an agency finds a baby for someone, the fee is almost always more than for an identified adoption. Consult your attorney before making a commitment. Be aware, however, that some attorneys discourage identified adoptions, since they usually make less money when an agency takes on more responsibility.

IS AN IDENTIFIED ADOPTION FOR YOU?

Now that you know the pros and cons of an identified agency adoption, the question becomes one of individual circumstances. For some situations an identified adoption may be the best way to go. Consider the following scenarios:

Scenario A. You live in a state in which the birth parents' rights are terminated at a later date in an independent adoption than they are in an agency adoption.

For many couples this is the most important reason to go with an identified adoption. They could not bear to have a birth mother change her mind after the baby is already placed with them. In New Jersey, parental rights can be terminated only two to three months after placement if the birth mother does not appear in court shortly after birth. The agency's involvement, however, ensures that rights are terminated earlier, usually within days after birth, providing security for the adoptive couple and closure for the birth mother.

Scenario B. You want to adopt a baby from another state, and the law requires an agency in an out-of-state placement.

If you adopt a baby from Florida, for example, and you are not a Florida resident, the baby must be released to an agency before he is given to you. Even in states that do not require an agency, you may want to use one as a security measure. You want to make sure everything is signed and sealed before the adoption proceeds through Interstate Compact (the branch of the state department of social services that oversees interstate adoptions). Also, having a sensitive, knowledgeable social worker in the same city as the birth mother can be a comfort to her, especially if you live miles away yourself.

Scenario C. You are unsure about a birth mother and believe that counseling will help her become more secure in her decision.

Of course, an agency is not necessary for a birth mother to receive counseling. If everyone agrees, a social worker or therapist not affiliated with an agency can counsel birth parents.

Scenario D. A birth mother needs to have more expenses paid than are permitted by law in an independent adoption.

Some states restrict the expenses that a couple can pay in order to prevent the practice of "buying" babies by paying excessive expenses. For example, until recently, in North Carolina an adoptive couple could not even pay for the medical expenses of a birth mother. Such laws usually allow agencies to pay for more of the birth mother's expenses than are permitted in an independent adoption. The couple is in essence paying for the birth mother's expenses; the monies are just going through the agency first.

A final note before moving on to agency services. An agency, as has been pointed out, can represent both adoptive parents and birth parents. Many will make it clear that they do not represent the interests of the adoptive couple; others give the appearance of regarding the concerns of the adoptive couple by assigning them a social worker separate from the one assisting the birth mother. Because of some of the financial and emotional risks discussed earlier, it is suggested that a couple hire an attorney to represent them even if they are seeking a placement through an agency. The attorney will be the couple's advocate, emphasizing the concerns of the couple and seeing to it that an inexperienced social worker does not disrupt an adoption plan. Also, the attorney will be needed to process the adoption paperwork with the courts after placement.

WHEN AN AGENCY TURNS YOU DOWN

Agencies do not have an unlimited number of children for placement; therefore, some establish criteria for adoptive parents beyond what is mandated by the state. These criteria may be related to geographic area, age, marital status, educational level, and religion, and must be applied equally and without bias to all applicants.

Some agencies also have a screening process separate from the mandatory home study. *Remember, being refused by an agency that makes direct placements and conducts home studies is not the same thing as not having an approved home study.* You may simply have failed to get through the agency screening for direct placement purposes.

Once the screening process is completed, the agency will conduct a home study, if one has not already been conducted by another agency. If an applicant is rejected, the agency should provide detailed information as to why. In New Jersey, for example, the agency must offer services to help the couple adjust to the decision, as well as give information about the agency's grievance procedure.

ADOPTIVE PARENTS' RIGHTS: GETTING ALL THE INFORMATION

As prospective adoptive parents, you do have certain rights, and one of the most important is the right to information, especially about the adoptive child. Agencies are required to provide any medical information about the child that is available, as well as any genetic and social background. Sometimes this information will be part of the placement agreement; at other times it will be a separate document. Some states require in-depth information, including the child's diet and feeding habits. If the child has special needs, the agency may be required to provide the applicant with a list of long-term needs and available community resources for coping with them.

Remember, clients have the right to refuse a child. This is not so adoptive parents can "shop"—that is, pick and reject children; it is to encourage them to make an intelligent decision, based on full information, as to whether they can appropriately meet a child's needs.

Sometimes couples will state that they are open to adopting, say, a toddler with certain physical disabilities, when what they really want is a healthy infant. Do not try this. There's no point in going through an agency that places many special needs children unless you are willing to be honest about what kind of child you can care for.

PRIVATE AGENCIES: WHAT TO LOOK OUT FOR

Although there are many excellent agencies that truly support both the birth parents and the adoptive parents, some agencies are set up in a way that makes the process difficult for everyone involved. Here are some of the problems you could find yourselves running into:

1. *The agency is not sufficiently aggressive in recruiting birth mothers.* Many adoption agencies are not even listed in the yellow pages. Some long-

established traditional agencies do not appear to be what one might expect. We did consulting work for one agency that gave no indication that it was in the adoption business. Because the agency also provided a broad range of social services, a birth mother coming into the office would be hard-pressed to find brochures or other information that explained the advantages of adoption. This agency, like many others, simply did not emphasize adoption services.

2. *The agency expects you to find the birth mother.* Some agencies require you to pay a sum of money up front—up to $10,000, in some cases, and the couple must then find their own birth mother! The agency fee is for taking care of all the details and some of the expenses after a couple finds the birth mother.

3. *The agency does not encourage adoption.* In an October 14, 1991, article in *Forbes* magazine, William Pierce of the National Committee for Adoption noted that many social workers appear to do as much as possible to talk a woman out of placing a baby for adoption. This is a common bias among social workers and religious counselors. The question is, Does it have any place in an adoption agency?

You might suppose that adoption agencies would have to place a certain number of babies each year in order to stay in business, but this is not necessarily so. Agencies have other ways to raise funds, including donations, conducting home studies, and requiring couples to attend adoptive parenting classes and counseling. Charging prospective adoptive couples a fee, as some agencies do, to have their portfolio placed on file and shown to birth mothers generates further income. Once a birth mother selects a couple based on their portfolio, the couple may be responsible for paying all of her medical expenses, counseling fees (for counseling provided by the agency), and the agency's administrative costs, even if the birth mother changes her mind.

Adoptive parents may also be allowed to use an agency's phone number in their newspaper ads—for a fee. The agencies may charge for the service, as well as for each phone call made to the office.

All of this is not to say that agencies that provide such services do not support adoption—usually they do. Just be aware that the cost of the actual adoption is only one means of collecting revenue. It is important to note that although thousands of agencies conduct home studies and provide other adoption-related services, only about 250 are directly involved in the majority of placements that occur each year in the United States.

Some social workers are paid a salary regardless of the number of adoptions they oversee. Often working on a limited budget, they have neither the time nor the resources to market the agency and its services. Furthermore, some social workers who work for an agency that provides many social and charitable services often do not take a positive view of adoption. They look on it as a last resort, believing that there are enough social programs available for single mothers. Also, women who choose adoption may be viewed as "unfit mothers"—either because they have not accessed the available social programs or because they have the audacity to choose not to parent, and to move on with their lives.

4. *The agency has restrictions regarding who can adopt.* Agency restrictions usually relate to age, religion, weight, ethnic background, income, educational level, marital status, and an infertility diagnosis. Some agencies are so restrictive that they have two applications: one to determine whether you meet the initial standards, and a second for the adoption itself. Even when a couple meets all the standards, success is not automatic.

5. *The agency permits limited contact, if any, between adoptive parents and birth parents.* Some agencies still take the old-fashioned approach to arranging adoption. Many, however, are beginning to allow more communication, so that the birth mother and adoptive parents may meet in person or through pictures and biographical sketches. Most parents see this as a step in the right direction.

6. *The agency has a long waiting list.* An agency may claim that the wait is two to three years, but this may be after the home study is completed—and you may wait six months to a year for the home study. One agency is listed as having a waiting time from application to homecoming as two to four years. Yet I know couples who waited four to five years for the arrival of their baby. Not surprisingly, the waiting period for special needs children and non-Caucasian infants in the statistics is often much shorter than that for healthy Caucasian infants.

CONTRACTING WITH AN AGENCY: WHAT TO ASK

Before you decide to use an agency, you will want to investigate it thoroughly. Talk with the staff; if you can, talk to other parents who have dealt with them. Many agencies will provide the names and numbers of couples who will gladly talk with you about their experience.

Before you visit an agency, call and ask the counselor or secretary about its philosophy on adoption. What you ask will depend on what kind of child you are seeking to adopt. If you are looking for a healthy infant, and the agency requires that you do at least part of the work of advertising and networking for a child, then you will want to ask questions about their relationships with birth mothers and what support systems they provide. If you want to adopt a toddler-age child with special needs, you may want to ask questions about what birth family background they usually provide and what services and subsidies are available to meet the child's special needs.

Trust your instincts. If you call an agency and feel that you are being treated as an irritant, even though you are asking the questions very politely, take it as a warning. Remember, a birth mother is going to feel even worse if she contacts the agency. On the other hand, do be reasonable; agency personnel have a limited time to talk on the phone.

Some of your more in-depth questions might better wait for an initial interview or for one of the seminars that the agency gives on a regular basis.

No matter what kind of agency you are contacting, you will want to ask these questions:

1. *What are their requirements and restrictions?*
2. *What kinds of children does the agency place?*
3. *How many children did the agency place last year?*
4. *What are the agency's fees?* If there is a standard flat fee, ask:
   - What is the payment schedule?
   - If the birth mother changes her mind, is any money refunded?

   If the fee is based on the number of hours the parties spend in counseling and on the nature of the adoption, then ask:
   - Is there a cap on the fees?
   - Do the fees include the birth mother's living and medical expenses?
   - How much do the home study and postsupervisory visits cost? An agency's adoption fees may sound reasonable, until you hear that the agency requires a social worker to visit your home eight times at a cost of $2,000, when your state requires only two visits. A reasonable fee would be well under $200 for each visit.
   - What is the initial fee? Some agencies charge large up-front fees and then expect you to play an active role in finding your own birth mother. Retaining an agency the way you retain an attorney is fine. However, paying $10,000 or more to an agency and still having to find your own birth mother is too risky. If an agency asks you for more than $1,000 up front, ask whether that money is returned if it turns out you do not need the agency.

6. *What is the agency's home study process like?* If you have already had a home study completed, ask whether the agency accepts home studies conducted by other agencies.

7. *Does the agency provide you with a copy of the home study?*

8. *Does it release the home study to attorneys or other agencies upon request?* If so, ask whether there is a fee. A small fee is reasonable—$100 per copy is not.

These are the questions that are appropriate to ask at the beginning of your investigation. Once you get more serious about an agency that places infants, you can schedule an interview to ask more in-depth questions. For example:

1. *What roles do the agency and the birth mother play in selecting a couple?*

2. *Do you get to meet the birth mother during her pregnancy?*

3. *How does the agency feel about dealing with an attorney or another agency, if you find a birth mother in another state?* (If you find a birth mother on your own in another state, there may be no need to use the agency.)

4. *Does the agency discuss all of the woman's options with her?* You want a birth mother who is firm in her decision to place the baby for adoption. You want her to feel comfortable, not pressured to make a decision or to defend her choice.

5. *How does a social worker determine whether the birth mother is sincere?* This is especially important to ask if an agency identifies a birth mother for you and then asks you to pay her living expenses and counseling fees.

6. *If the agency senses that the birth mother is uncertain about her adoption plans, how does it respond?*
   - Does it notify the adoptive parents of the apparent uncertainty?
   - Is it made clear to a birth mother that to have a couple pay for her medical and other expenses when she has no real intention of placing the baby for adoption is fraud, and that she could be prosecuted?

7. *At what hours are agency personnel available?* If you are working directly with a birth mother, and the agency is involved, it is very important that you be able to reach someone at the agency during nonbusiness hours. What if the birth mother goes into labor earlier than expected? What if the hospital personnel are giving you problems about visiting the birth mother or baby?

8. What if the birth mother wants to meet with you immediately, along with a counselor? Many agency personnel believe that phone calls after

five P.M. are an intrusion and that few emergencies warrant this invasion. For the most part this is true. Be reasonable. But remember, you are paying for a service.

When investigating an agency that places special needs children, other questions and concerns arise. Begin by telling them what kind of child you are interested in adopting. If you are very specific, saying you want a one-to-two-year-old blind Asian girl, the agency staff person may offer to put you on the waiting list; however, the opportunity to adopt such a child may range between limited and nonexistent. If you are very specific about the kind of child that you want to adopt, you should apply to many agencies and work with the large adoption exchanges.

Here are some important questions to ask.

1. *How many and what kinds of legally free (or almost legally free) children are in the agency's caseload?*
2. *Does the agency place children only from its county (or other geographic region), or does it place children from other parts of the state?*
3. *What is the average wait for a child?* Is this from the time of the home study or from the time the application is completed?
4. *What kinds of pre- and postadoption services does the agency provide?*
5. *If the child is in foster care, would you be allowed to visit the child there once he or she was assigned to you?*
6. *What is the agency's policy toward adoption subsidies?* Are most of the children it places eligible for federal or state subsidies?
7. *If you decline a child that is offered, what is the agency's policy about future placements?*
8. *What if a situation does not work out; how is this handled?*
9. *What level of openness is expected with the birth family?* You will want to raise this question before committing to an agency. If the agency believes that birth families and adoptive families must maintain some level of openness no matter what the circumstances, then you will want to find out what they mean and whether they have any exceptions. Or you may find an agency that wants to bar all contact; this, again, is not an appropriate response.

INVESTIGATING AN AGENCY'S REPUTATION
Except with some international adoptions, agencies have legal custody of the child until the adoption is finalized and can use this as leverage with the adoptive parents

before and after placement. Expenses are one area in which they can exert control—occasionally through deception. No matter how many questions you ask the agency staff directly, one of the best ways to find out about an agency's reputation is to ask others about the agency and how it handled their adoption. Joining a RESOLVE support group or an adoption group is one of the best ways to find out about an agency's reputation. Don't ask just the support group leadership. Ask couples who have worked with the agency what their experience was.

You can expect to hear from people who are somewhat disgruntled. Adoptive couples sometimes complain about costs even when they knew up front what the expenses were going to be. And couples who have sought to adopt a child with special needs may not have "heard" the agency staff tell them all the possible legal risks involved or the child's potential problems.

Chapter Three

Independent Adoption

A lthough independent adoption has been legal in most states for the last ten or twenty years, only recently has it begun receiving public attention. Over the past five years, stories on adoption have finally begun appearing prominently in newspapers and magazines like *Time* and *Forbes*, especially during November, national adoption month. *Immediate Family*, a film about independent adoption, generated much interest in how a couple finds a birth mother without waiting for years on an agency list, while more recently, the film *Losing Isaiah*, with Jessica Lange, explored the theme of an independent interracial adoption.

Many people have at least an idea about what independent adoption is, without quite understanding its legal and practical meaning. Some people think it is baby buying or black-market adoption. After watching some talk show segments on the topic, viewers across the nation become convinced that every other independent adoption fails, leaving a devastated couple in its wake. The reality is, if every talk-show host presented a success story a day, they would still not run out of happy placements to share.

In an independent adoption—also called a private, or self-directed, adoption—the birth parents and the adoptive couple find each other through advertising, through a personal referral—usually by a mutual friend or acquaintance—or through an adoption attorney. There is no agency involved.

Often the birth parents and the couple will meet to become acquainted and discuss the adoption. For birth parents or adoptive couples who do not wish to meet, communication can take place by telephone or letter; or it can be handled by a third party, provided this is legal in their state. From these contacts an understanding develops that the birth parents' child will be placed with the adoptive parents. The adoption statutes of various states refer to this kind of adoption as a nonagency adoption, to distinguish it from an agency or stepparent/family adoption.

The time frame is the most dramatic difference between an agency and a nonagency adoption. In an independent adoption you can start the adoption process immediately and have a newborn baby in your arms within several months. Things do not always go this smoothly, of course, and yet we know many couples who have adopted within three to six months after beginning their adoption endeavors. Whether it works this way for you will depend on certain factors outside your control. There are couples whose adoption search has taken much longer than months, and in some cases has been totally unsuccessful. But with independent adoption you are in charge of the process, and the effort you put forth will largely determine how much time it takes before you become a parent.

To get started, contact an adoption attorney to make sure you are on the right legal track. Do not worry that you will have to fill out mountains of forms; your attorney will take care of the paperwork. While you are waiting for an appointment with your attorney, read chapter 4 of this book and begin to follow some of the steps it outlines for getting the word out. Write your broadcast letters. Assemble your portfolio. Install a second phone line. Your adoption adventure is underway!

THE INDEPENDENT ADOPTION PROCESS

The first thing to know is that independent adoption is illegal in some states. Laws regulating adoption vary considerably from state to state; you will therefore need to find out what your rights are before proceeding.

Where independent adoption is legal, the basic steps are as follows. A couple hires an attorney. This attorney will act as an unpaid intermediary; that is, she will charge fees for legal representation but not for serving as an intermediary. The couple may give her a portfolio containing photographs of themselves, a letter, and other material that gives a picture of their lives, which their attorney can then show to birth mothers.

At this point a couple will often have a second telephone line installed in their home to take phone calls from prospective birth parents. They may begin advertising in newspapers and networking with friends and family to try to meet a prospective birth mother.

If they have not already done so, they may arrange for a home study at this time. Every state requires that adoptive parents undergo a home study to determine their parental fitness. In most states the task is delegated to licensed adoption agencies and independent social workers, who then submit the home study to the court. To initiate this process, contact an agency or social worker.

In nearly all states the home study is conducted before the child is placed in your home; in a few states, you can wait until afterward. If you live in a state in which a home study is required beforehand, you should probably have it done when you first start to seek a birth mother. If you network or advertise out of state for a birth mother, then you should begin the home study process, regardless of whether your state requires a home study prior to placement. Any interstate placements are governed by the Interstate Compact Act, which requires a home study prior to placement in any state.

The next thing that is likely to happen is that a pregnant woman (or a parent with a child) will call in response to your advertisement or letter to discuss her intentions to place her child for adoption. If you and she are comfortable about meeting, you discuss this possibility. If one of you is not comfortable with meeting face to face, you will talk about keeping in touch by telephone, letter, or through your attorney, who will most likely meet with the birth mother.

Next, the birth mother or birth parents meet with you at a restaurant or other public place or at your attorney's office. If both of you are comfortable with each other, you and she will probably make a verbal commitment to each other. If you do not meet, this commitment will take place by telephone.

Depending on the circumstances, you and the birth parents will decide whether the adoption is to be an independent or an identified agency adoption. An identified agency adoption is one in which an independent adoption is converted into an agency adoption. The agency may provide counseling for the birth parents, in addition—at least in some states—to obtaining surrenders of parental rights in a shorter time frame than with an independent adoption. Because an identified adoption is considered an agency adoption, the laws that govern agency adoptions apply. Your attorney can help you sort out the pros and cons of either choice.

Be careful not to discuss the possibility of agency involvement with the birth parents until you have built a relationship with them. Many birth mothers do not want a third party, such as an agency social worker, asking them a lot of questions.

If you and the birth parents agree to an identified agency adoption, contact an agency that provides such services. The one you choose will probably conduct your home study too, if you have not already done one.

Again, discuss your choice of agencies with your attorney. It is vital that the agency staff work well with birth parents. Birth parents know that they have choices; the newspapers are full of adoption advertisements. If you have not built a solid rapport with the birth parents, and the agency staff are condescending or lacking in sensitivity, the birth parents may well go elsewhere.

If you do not get an agency involved, then you or your attorney should discuss with the birth parents the advantages of counseling. The benefits are twofold: (1) Some states require birth parents to have counseling or at least be offered counseling; and (2) more important, counseling may assist the birth parents in understanding adoption issues and their feelings about them.

Also, your attorney should discuss with the birth parents the opportunity to be represented by their own attorney. In some states, such as New York, a birth parent must be represented by an attorney who is not representing the adoptive couple.

Now you or the birth mother will contact an obstetrician or clinic and the hospital where the baby is to be delivered, if this has not been taken care of already. Finding a physician who is open to adoption is very important. It is also important, if possible, that your attorney become involved in choosing the hospital, as some are actually hostile toward adoption; he will contact the hospital's social services department to determine its policy on adoption.

Next, depending on where you live, the birth parents will give up their parental rights by signing legal documents referred to as "surrender of parental rights." This is different from a consent-to-adoption document, which is not a surrender of rights but simply indicates the birth parents' approval of you as adoptive parents. Confusingly, some agencies and attorneys refer to the termination document as a consent form, so you must ask what purpose the consent document serves in your state. Depending upon state laws, the documents may be signed either before the baby's birth or in the hospital after birth. Each state has different laws as to when birth parents' rights can be terminated, how long birth parents have to change their minds and revoke their surrenders, and whether the birth parents must also appear in court to have their rights terminated officially (even after signing the surrender documents). Check with your attorney, since these laws can change.

Now the baby is born. Your attorney may visit the birth mother in the hospital so that she can sign legal forms. Before the birth you should find out what documents are needed by your insurance company to ensure immediate coverage for the baby.

You and possibly your attorney go to the hospital, where the baby is given to you. Often a birth mother will discharge herself before the baby goes home. In this case she must sign documents allowing the baby to be placed directly with you. Many hospitals, however, require the birth mother or her relative to place the baby in your arms. If the birth mother does not wish to see the baby, and the hospital requires her to be there at the baby's discharge, then your attorney can arrange legally for her to avoid this situation by filing legal documents in the county court.

Your attorney next files the adoption petition, or what is sometimes called an adoption complaint, with the court. Some time later, depending upon the state's regulations, you go to family court to gain parental rights to the child (an adoption hearing). Unless the parental rights of the birth parents have already been terminated, they must be provided notice of this hearing, but they are not usually required to attend unless they have changed their minds about the adoption.

If you reside in one state and the baby is born another, then your attorney must also complete Interstate Compact forms and file them in both the "sending state" (the state that the child was born in) and in the "receiving state" (the state where you reside). There are several other forms that the birth mother and the adoptive parents must sign for interstate purposes.

As a final step, your attorney accompanies you to court and presents your testimony, including how you came in contact with the birth parents, what monies you have paid, and why you wish to adopt the baby. The adoption agency or social worker (independent investigator) that conducted your home study will have provided your home study to the court, including a favorable recommendation as to your fitness as parents. The judge hearing the adoption will generally review the home study to ensure that the agency has recommended you as adoptive parents.

Each of these steps will be discussed in detail in the chapters that follow, so if you have any questions, just read on.

WHY PURSUE AN INDEPENDENT ADOPTION?

Adoption can be a wonderful experience for the birth parents who are placing the baby in a loving home, for the baby who is going there, and, of course, for the couple who has longed for the baby. With an independent adoption, the experience can be especially positive. Both sets of parents can feel more in control, because they are the decision makers. They meet and decide together what is best for the baby. A birth mother feels very secure in knowing and approving of the adoptive parents. The decision about the couple is made by her alone, not by an agency. Although she will still feel sad about placing her child for adoption, she will have seen firsthand that the child will be reared by a mother and father she has chosen and who can provide love and stability, an impression she will carry forever.

Indeed, independent adoption is usually a birth mother's first choice. Twice as many birth mothers choose independent adoption as agency adoption. Birth mothers choose this approach because they want to be in control. They do not want agency personnel questioning their motives for choosing adoption or explaining their "options" to them. Often they have already made an adoption decision and are ready to go ahead. They want to choose the adoptive parents themselves. In fact, the level of control a birth mother has is often what determines whether she will place the infant for adoption.

Most birth mothers select adoption because they are young, are in school, know they can provide little for themselves and the child at this point in their lives, and want a better future for everyone. They're not after a better career for themselves or a swimming pool and trips to Disney World for their child. They want the child to have a stable, loving home life. A nineteen-year-old woman with few resources in her second year of college cannot provide a home for a child if she must work full-time in a minimum-wage job. Most birth mothers care enough to make a decision that is best for themselves and the baby. A birth mother chooses adoption because of her love for her child.

Many adoptive couples start out believing a certain stereotype of the birth mother: that she is ignorant, unfeeling, on welfare, and basically a "low life." The reality is, the average birth mother is "the girl next door who got pregnant." No one kind of person is more likely than another to be a birth mother. Almost all, however, want what is best for their child, and direct involvement in the decision making.

The second argument for private adoption is this: It's fast. In *The Adoption Resource Book,* Lois Gilman quotes a study conducted in California that found that of all the couples who adopted, more than 90 percent had done so privately. Of these, most had a baby *within four months* of actively pursuing adoption. All but 2 of the 105 infants were placed in the couples' homes within a year.

Empirical data on private adoption are difficult to find, partly because states are not required to keep track of how many adoptions take place, and so many do not. But based on the data from the National Council for Adoption, it would appear that at least two-thirds of the infant adoptions finalized in the United States each year are independent adoptions. Some believe the figure is closer to 80 percent.

In any case, in the majority of situations that we have known, couples who pursue independent adoption have a baby in about one year or less. The process takes commitment, but once a couple commits, they become parents. If you work diligently, very likely you will have a baby in your home sooner than you thought possible. The advantage of private adoption is that it works, and it works quickly.

Here are some other advantages to think about:

- *The infant is placed directly with the adoptive couple.* In traditional agency adoptions, an infant will often be placed in a foster home for a period of time, weeks or even months. Many birth mothers strongly oppose this arrangement. An independent adoption satisfies the birth mother's concern for her child's welfare and allows an adoptive couple to experience the first days of infancy with their child.

- *The adoptive parents may share in the pregnancy experience and in the baby's delivery.* If a birth mother lives nearby, the adoptive mother may take her to doctor appointments and may even act as her coach during labor and delivery. A birth mother may want the adoptive parents to be a part of her life. This can often help her to see past her own difficult circumstances and focus instead on the benefits of her unplanned pregnancy.

- *An adoption agency is not in control.* Independent adoption increases the likelihood that a pregnant woman will choose adoption. Between 50 and 80 percent of pregnant women using an agency do *not* release the baby for adoption, whereas 75 to 90 percent of pregnant women using private channels do. A very active agency in Arizona (now out of business) arranged for the adoptive parents and the birth parents to meet when the birth mother was eight months pregnant. This meeting reduced the risk that a couple would meet a birth mother who would change her mind. Even then 50 percent of the birth mothers changed their minds.

  In states that do not permit independent adoption, the number of adoptions per capita is usually lower. In 1960, when Connecticut outlawed independent adoption, the number of adoptions taking place dropped by half.

- *Independent adoption is less expensive.* In an article in *Forbes* magazine entitled "How Much Is That Baby in the Window?" an independent adoption is stated to cost about $50,000, while Cynthia Martin, a California psychologist and adoption expert, is quoted as saying that adoptions for healthy Caucasian infants cost about $20,000. Our experience is that few adoptions in which the couple find the birth mother cost anywhere close to $20,000. *The total expenses for an independent adoption, including medical expenses, attorney fees, and some living expenses, need not be more than $10,000.* In an article in *Smart Money* (April 1993), a couple quotes their total expenses for private adoption at $6,000. (The magazine mistakenly said that $6,000 was the attorney's fee. These fees were actually $3,200.)

  The administrative and personnel costs involved in a single agency adoption can range from $10,000 to $15,000, and that may not cover the birth mother's medical, living, counseling, legal, and transportation expenses. One very popular agency that places about sixty babies each year uses an attorney who charges $5,000 per adoption. Even adoption attorneys who handle the process from beginning to end do not usually charge this much.

Some agencies have the adoptive parents pay a birth mother's expenses indirectly as part of the agency's fees, in which case the fee will range from $20,000 to $30,000. In an independent adoption, it is often possible to find a birth mother who has her own medical insurance or who qualifies for Medicaid coverage and so does not need living expenses. In such cases the adoptive couple pay only for the medical expenses of the baby and any counseling requested by the birth parents, in addition to necessary living expenses. In many adoptions the couple's medical insurance will cover the baby's hospital costs.

INDEPENDENT ADOPTION—SOME DISADVANTAGES

Not every couple has a positive experience with pursuing independent adoption. Sometimes the problem is the attorney. Although most adoption attorneys are straightforward and reasonable in their fees and practices, there are some dishonest ones around. Some will charge for expenses never incurred by the birth mother and engage in other illegal practices. In other cases, the attorney is honest but does not assist his client with sufficient one-on-one attention; he does not get directly involved with the birth mother or hospital or agency (if one is needed). Basically, the couple is on their own. Needless to say, this gives independent adoption a bad name.

For other couples the personal involvement in an independent adoption is simply too difficult. Putting in a phone line and waiting for "that call" is too intense an experience, while actually talking to or meeting with a birth mother is more than some couples can take on emotionally. This may be especially true for a couple who has been through the wringer of infertility treatment or experienced multiple miscarriages.

One other potential difficulty with independent adoption is that birth parents who could really use some counseling may not get it. Even in an independent adoption a birth mother has every right to receive counseling. Of course, most adoptive parents will pay for a woman's counseling expenses if she requests it. She does not have to go to an adoption agency to receive counseling. Call your local adoption support groups for the names of therapists, counselors, or social workers specializing in adoption.

An attorney is not, of course, an adoption counselor. Nevertheless, a compassionate attorney should be able to discuss with a birth mother her reasons for placing the baby for adoption. This will give him a sense of whether the woman is sincere or whether she is being coerced by someone or is emotionally confused. A sensitive attorney can also determine how well she is coping with her adoption plans. These discussions help a woman verbalize her feelings, helping her further solidify her reasons for making adoption plans. Again, an attorney should never be a substitute for competent counseling. Your attorney must make sure a birth mother has access to counseling. Any attorney involved with adoption has a list of capable therapists.

Note: In nearly every state you are permitted to pay for counseling fees, but double-check to be sure it is legal before you do so.

IS AN INDEPENDENT ADOPTION FOR YOU?

Agency adoptions are not suited to everyone, any more than independent adoptions are. Many people assume that couples who pursue independent adoption do so because they've been rejected by the agencies, perhaps because of their age or personality. This is unfounded. People who have difficult personalities or overwhelming problems are usually no better candidates for independent adoption then they are for an agency adoption. After all, in most states, in either independent or agency adoption, adoptive parents must undergo a home study conducted by a licensed adoption agency or certified social worker to determine their suitability as parents.

Some people, it is true, do pursue independent adoption because an agency will not accept them, especially when age is an issue. Others, however, never decide whether independent or agency adoption is right for them. They just happen to learn of a pregnant woman, sometimes through a mutual acquaintance, and the parties come to an agreement. In such cases they may have no contact with an agency, except perhaps during the home study.

Following is a list of some of the tasks and stresses associated with independent adoption. Discuss with your spouse how each makes you feel. If you feel negatively about one aspect of independent adoption, do you believe that you can overcome these feelings?

1. *Placing an advertisement telling of your desire to adopt in various newspapers and responding to calls the ad generates.* (Note: Not all states that allow independent adoptions allow such advertisements.)
2. *Having a special "baby telephone line" placed in your home and waiting for it to ring.*
3. *Receiving prank phone calls.*
4. *Speaking articulately and compassionately with a woman who calls in answer to an advertisement or letter.*

5. *Meeting with a birth mother.* Most couples who pursue adoption do meet with the birth mother to share some information. In some states, such as Virginia, identifying information (complete names and addresses) must also be shared between the adoptive and birth parents.

    At first many couples are afraid of that initial meeting. Yet no adoptive couple we have ever known was sorry they met with their child's birth mother. Most likely you will be glad you did, not only before the baby is born but long after.

6. *When you meet the birth mother, presenting yourselves as "normal" people.* Many kinds of people meet with birth mothers and complete the adoption. However, there are special considerations to be aware of and adjustments that may have to be made if:

    ■ *The prospective adoptive parent has an obvious disability.* We know of one wonderful man who lost his legs in military service. Despite his disability, he and his wife had no problem getting a birth mother to select them. In fact, they now have a beautiful baby boy. If you have an obvious disability, tell the birth mother before you meet her, but do not mention it immediately in your first conversation.

    ■ *The husband has long hair and earrings and dresses for shock value.* Some birth mothers are looking for the home with the "white picket fence." On the other hand, if the husband has long hair because he is, for example, a musician, and in your newspaper ad you state, "professional jazz musician" or "nature lover," a birth mother probably will not expect a couple dressed like June and Ward Cleaver. In fact, many birth mothers would find long hair and an earring appealing and would be delighted by a "funky couple." In general, however, a man with shorter hair and no earring has a better chance of appealing to a birth mother—even a birth mother who likes to dress in the latest fad.

    ■ *The husband or wife is obese.* Unless the birth mother is a real fitness or sports buff, she will probably not care if one of you is overweight. Yet we must all acknowledge that people do discriminate against overweight individuals, and a birth mother could be turned off if you are extremely overweight. If this is your situation, you may want the birth mother to know your positive attributes before she meets you in person. And before you do meet, you may want to mention that you are working hard to lose weight.

    We know of women and men who were overweight, however, who have adopted without their weight ever being an issue. In two of the cases the birth mothers themselves were overweight. Moreover, being overweight appears to be less important if one spouse is of average weight. In short, do not wait until you lose the weight to pursue an adoption.

7. *Meeting with a birth mother and making arrangements with her, knowing that she may change her mind.*

8. *Taking a limited financial risk with a birth mother, such as paying some of her medical expenses and/or living expenses.*

9. *Becoming emotionally involved with one or both birth parents.*

10. *Pursuing an adoption in which the baby may be born with medical problems; if it is, deciding whether you can go through with the adoption.*

11. *"Working" with more than one birth mother at a time.* Making arrangements with two or more birth mothers, knowing that you want only one baby, can be very emotionally taxing.

INDEPENDENT ADOPTION: ONE COUPLE'S STORY

My husband Richard and I were happy with the differences in our ages and our religious and ethnic backgrounds. We had been married for four years. I had been married before, and that marriage had ended in divorce. My marriage to Richard signaled a new beginning, a chance to have a family, even though I was now older than I would have preferred to be as a prospective mother.

Sadly, nature and the state of technology at the time of my experience were defeated by my "advanced" age. I was in my early forties. A biological child seemed an impossibility, and we were unsure about taking the step toward adoption. Even if we decided to adopt, agencies might turn us away for having an unconventional profile.

Richard felt that I needed to be absolutely sure about the decision to adopt, since he would undoubtedly be content without children. This placed the responsibility for making the "right" decision on me, and I lingered for months with the possibilities, the fears, and the longing, while becoming more and more discouraged by the imagined failure ahead.

At last, after reading an article in their newsletter about independent adoption, I called RESOLVE of Central New Jersey and spoke to a woman who was planning an independent adoption information session. She spoke at length about her own experience, which seemed miraculous.

Feeling a burst of hope in spite of my misgivings, I announced tearfully to her, "We're thinking about adoption, but I'm afraid we won't qualify because I'm too old, we're of different religions, and I've been divorced."

"It only matters to the birth parents," the woman said. "If they like you and want you to be their child's parents, then you won't have any other significant barrier." My uncertainty disappeared with this new information. "I'm now sure that we should try to adopt a child," I told Richard that evening. "I don't look forward to the next twenty years without a child."

"Are you really sure?

"Yes!"

Within two weeks my friend phoned me with the news that someone knew a pregnant woman who wanted to place her baby with a nice couple.

This was too much good fortune to be believed. Yet later in the week, the young woman, Linda, called and confirmed that she hoped to find a nice couple for her baby, since it was too late in the pregnancy to have an abortion.

She was nineteen. She had had another child whom she relinquished to her in-laws when she and her husband divorced. Because of her pregnancy they had had a "shotgun" wedding when they were sixteen. Things had gone from bad to worse, and she did not want to repeat her mistake this time with another man.

Richard and I met Linda in person. We reviewed her health history with the aid of a questionnaire supplied by our attorney. Linda and I went to the obstetrician together. We also went to a social service agency in case Linda wanted counseling, financial support, or Medicaid.

Linda called frequently. She used me as her lifeline, she said, and she was very appreciative of my time and the monies spent on her medical care. I felt that I had developed enough of a relationship with Linda that I would be alert to a difficulty or a change of heart. When she told me that she had located the address of her boyfriend's parents in New York, an alarm went off.

Would Linda actually make contact with them or with her boyfriend with the idea of reuniting and keeping the baby, perhaps even using the pregnancy as leverage (again)? While such a plan seemed foolhardy, it was entirely possible, given Linda's past experience.

Was she feeling reluctant to part with this potential bundle of love, silky skin, and gurgles that was growing inside her? Did she wish that her boyfriend would see the error of his ways and love her again?

Sure enough, with just two weeks remaining, Linda phoned to say, simply, "I've decided not to give you the baby, so I won't be talking to you again." Good-bye, little love. Good-bye, hope. Good-bye to the settled situation.

Richard cried with grief, surprising me with the intensity of his feelings, since I had been the one to initiate the adoption and carry on the relationship with Linda. He said that somehow his stake in adoption had crept up on him, with its promise that he would soon be a daddy, that we would experience the joy that a new baby brings, that this long wait would finally end. He had been unprepared emotionally to feel much one way or another. Now he could see that this unexpected disappointment could happen again and again, even if we found another birth mother.

With renewed determination, I proposed contacting the attorney about this change in plans and about placing ads in the newspaper. Using suggestions from the attorney and from people at a RESOLVE meeting, I phoned in the first of several advertisements to run in New Jersey newspapers, while Richard made arrangements to install another phone line in our home.

The ad read "Everything is ready for a baby." I didn't see any other ads like that. Maybe it would catch someone's eye.

The ad appeared the following weekend. Nothing happened. I used call forwarding during the days that I went to work. My new friend Karen from RESOLVE, who had recently adopted, had agreed to take calls during those times. She had a vibrant phone personality and was deeply sensitive and caring. She was so kind to do this for us. However, no calls came.

Three days later, when I arrived home, I phoned Karen just to check in.

"You just got a call!" Karen said. "You better call back fast before she calls someone else!"

"Hello. This is Ellen," I said. "I understand you just called about our ad in the paper. . . . Yes, we are ready to adopt a baby immediately. How wonderful! A baby girl!"

Richard and I brought home our little girl within a week. She was born the weekend our ad ran, and her birth mother, Sandy, still had the newspaper.

Sandy had made earlier adoption plans with an agency but changed her mind because of a negative experience with a social worker. Ultimately she had resolved her problem by requesting information about independent adoption. Her requirements were to have the adoptive parents pay for medical expenses, since she did not want to involve an agency of any kind, and to have the adoptive parents—us—take the baby home right away without resorting to foster care, despite the sixty to ninety days that would elapse before she could surrender her parental rights under New Jersey law.

Sandy was delighted that we resided in a certain county in New Jersey because she knew it from her childhood experiences with her family. She was going back to college and wanted no further contact. She preferred not to meet with us prior to our taking custody of the baby because she wanted to protect herself from additional involvement.

Her mother and sister wanted to speak to me on the phone. It felt like the embrace of a family.

"What a great family our daughter comes from," I said to Richard later. The miracle of adoption had happened to us too, just nine months from the start of our quest. Would it last? It did.

A beautiful resolution for all concerned. In fact, Richard and I are sure that the reason it took nine months was that we had to wait for our daughter to be born!

Chapter Four

Choosing an Adoption Attorney

I f you decide you want to adopt through private channels, one of the first steps is to contact an adoption attorney. Your attorney is by far the most important professional in the adoption process. He or she will guide you through your state's adoption laws and provide you with practical tips. Your attorney is also someone the birth mother can contact to discuss legal and financial matters.

Many people have a trusted attorney who has completed their wills, conducted the closings on their homes, and provided legal advice on other matters. He may be likable and competent in the areas of wills, real estate closings, and general law; he may even have assisted others with one or two agency adoptions in the past. However, this is not necessarily the same attorney you want to guide you through a private adoption. Not only must an adoption attorney be very knowledgeable about your state's adoption laws and the nuances of Interstate Compact requirements, he must also have a comfortable manner with clients and people in general. This is especially important because the attorney will be talking (and often meeting) with birth parents, social workers, and sometimes the parents of birth parents. It is better to find a good adoption specialist.

Perhaps you've had the experience of engaging a professional (a doctor, a dentist, an infertility specialist, a CPA) who was extremely competent but not very personable. You may have overlooked any boorish or rude behavior because she was a "good doctor" or an "excellent endocrinologist." The adoption attorney *must* be someone you like and feel genuinely comfortable with. If you like him, the birth parents will probably also like him and feel comfortable with him. This cannot be emphasized strongly enough. Adoption plans have ended because an attorney was condescending or rude to a birth mother. A birth mother wants to be treated with respect and sensitivity and will look for another couple if your attorney is lacking in these areas.

If you have friends or acquaintances who have hired adoption attorneys, ask for a recommendation. RESOLVE or an adoption support group is an even more likely source. If you are not involved with your local RESOLVE chapter, call the national number at (617) 643-2424 or write to 1310 Broadway, Somerville, MA 02144. Staff members can give you the names of attorneys listed in the American Academy of Adoption Attorneys, as well as the address and phone number of the RESOLVE chapter nearest you.

SERVICES AND FEES

In states where this is legal, an attorney can serve as an intermediary, matching a prospective adoptive couple with a birth mother. In California, for example, which permits attorneys to bring birth mothers and couples together, birth mothers as well as adoptive parents often hire attorneys as intermediaries. Not surprisingly, California has one of the highest numbers of infant adoptions each year compared with other states, most through private placement.

Attorneys who work as adoption intermediaries often advertise in the yellow pages under "Adoption," using ads explicitly directed at birth mothers. Some advertise in states where intermediaries are permitted, even if their practice is not in that state. It is not unusual to find a California attorney placing an ad in a Louisiana newspaper.

An independent adoption always begins with finding a birth mother. In some states this task may be carried out by an adoption attorney for an additional fee, but many other states forbid the practice, regarded as too much like "baby selling." Find out what the rules are in your state and make sure your attorney's fees are in accordance with them. Of course, even assuming that they are, you will do well to remain cautious—especially of an attorney who claims he has located a birth mother and then immediately asks for monies related to the woman's needs, such as traveling, hotel rooms, rent, food, medical fees, and counseling. Remember, *at this point your emotions and your checkbook may not balance.* At the very least, obtain documentation for all expenses before paying for anything. Not only is it unethical for an attorney to ask you to pay for a woman's gynecological visits without proof of a bill, it is also illegal. Once you have dispersed substantial expenses and lawyers' fees "up front," you may feel compelled to continue sending more money; otherwise, you will have forfeited your initial investment. Find out your attorney's total fees before committing, including the expenses you will be reimbursed if no birth mother selects you within a reasonable period of time—usually eighteen months.

THE ATTORNEY AS INTERMEDIARY

How does an attorney arrange for birth mothers and adoptive parents to select one other? An ethical attorney usually uses the same system employed by many adoption agencies, allowing a birth mother to select adoptive parents from an assortment of portfolios. A portfolio is a three-ring binder containing biographical information, pictures, a letter to the birth mother, and sometimes your home study (no last names or other identifying information). For advice about putting together a portfolio, turn to the end of this chapter.

Once the birth mother has decided upon the couple or couples she may be interested in, the attorney may suggest that she meet them. If she prefers not to meet with anyone, the attorney will simply contact the couple himself and describe the birth parents to them.

Sometimes a birth mother will want to meet more than one couple before she makes up her mind. Of course, only one couple will ultimately be selected, which can lead to disappointment.

Some attorneys are unethical. Be cautious of the following scenarios:

- *An attorney places several prospective adoptive couples in one room at the same time and then allows a birth mother to pick one.*
- *You are at an introductory session with other prospective parents to find out about an attorney's services, and the attorney suddenly states, "A birth mother has just called, and someone will soon receive the infant."* This actually happened to a friend of ours!
- *The attorney claims that a birth mother is interested in you, then asks you for money for her expenses.* Although this is not necessarily a sign of trouble, the couple may find themselves paying money for weeks before their attorney tells them that the birth mother has "changed her mind." The attorney gives no explanation about your money. You just lost a few thousand dollars. Unfortunately, this experience is not uncommon.

During the year after one couple first retained an attorney, for example, he "found" them two birth mothers. The first time he immediately asked the couple to send money for expenses. They sent $3,000. A few weeks later the couple received a call from the attorney's office telling them that they would not have wanted this birth mother, because she was using drugs. (The couple never met the birth mother.)

A few months later the couple received another phone call from their attorney about a second birth mother. Of course they were expected to send more money, which they did. By this time, with the attorney's expenses continually rising, they were borrowing money from relatives. (Once someone spends $6,000, it is hard to say, "I do not want to go through with this adoption.") A few weeks later they were once again told, "The birth mother changed her mind." The couple is not even sure whether these birth mothers ever existed. They had only one "documented" adoption expense from their attorney—furniture for the birth mother. (Incidentally, it is usually considered illegal to pay this kind of expense.)

If anything like this should happen to you, call the State Bar Association or State Supreme Court immediately and file an ethics complaint against the attorney. Then call the attorney and demand your money back—*all* of it.

One final note of caution. When an attorney is acting as an intermediary to link you up with a birth mother, the usual wait for a placement is a year to a year and a half. If the attorney says, "I can guarantee you a baby within three months," be very careful. It is nearly impossible for an attorney to do this. Remember, price does not guarantee success.

YOUR ATTORNEY'S ROLE IN A DOMESTIC OR INTERNATIONAL AGENCY ADOPTION

In an agency adoption, the attorney's role is more limited than in an independent adoption, but not less important. Normally, the attorney will not interact with the birth parents or assist you when the baby is placed in your arms at the hospital. However, your attorney is a resource person and must be aware of state laws regarding agency policy and procedure. Your attorney should review all documents that the agency has you sign, including the application, placement agreement, and especially the surrender documents to ensure that they comply with state law. For example, you want your attorney to make sure all paperwork is filed with the local court in states where parental rights are revocable until filed. This is particularly important if you are dealing with an out-of-state agency. Also, the attorney will assist the agency in complying with Interstate Compact requirements. In addition, an attorney can often get through the bureaucracy and confirm that all necessary paperwork is filed.

Remember, an agency is usually representing the birth mother and child; you need an attorney to represent you. Therefore, share with your attorney your interactions with the birth mother and agency social worker. The attorney's goal is to determine if the agency is doing its job. For example, one agency never asked the birth mother's mom how she felt about the adoption—a critical question, especially if the unborn child will be the first grandchild.

Your attorney's role in an international adoption is usually limited and may be unnecessary when working with very large agencies such as Holt International—an agency with years of experience and an excellent reputation. However, if you are dealing with a small agency or with an intermediary, your attorney can ensure that the foreign translation of the Judgment of Adoption or the termination of parental rights documents contain correct legal jargon to satisfy your local court. Also, your attorney can help you complete the various international documents and put you in touch with the right person.

In any adoption—domestic or international—your attorney can also guide you so that you pay only expenses that are permitted by law.

PUTTING TOGETHER A PORTFOLIO: A QUICK OVERVIEW

A portfolio is a picture story of your life as a couple or as a family with children. It is like a scrapbook or picture album containing pictures of you, any children, close relatives and friends, pets, your home, important occasions, and favorite activities. Its purpose is to tell your "story" to a birth mother.

Even if you plan to do your own advertising and are not expecting your attorney to find a baby for you, a potfolio can be a useful thing to have. It can be shared with your birth mother at any point to give her an idea of who you are and what your lives are like.

One couple met a birth mother just after she gave birth. When they went to the hospital to meet her, they were able to present their lives very succinctly by showing her their portfolio. Once the baby is placed with you, a birth mother may want to keep the portfolio as a keepsake.

Portfolios are *not* beauty contests. They are not designed so that a birth mother can select the family with the largest home, nicest furnishings, or prettiest smiles. They are meant to provide a picture description of you as a couple and family. If your home is very large or elegant, try to minimize this. It may only intimidate a birth mother.

Designing Your Portfolio

Choose an album book in which pages can be rearranged and added. Avoid bulky, fabric-stuffed books, which are difficult to store and mail. We recommend using low-acid paper for the original to ensure that it will last a lifetime—or several lifetimes. Someday it will be a precious keepsake for your family.

Once you have your album, you may wish to select a theme, usually one related to childhood. For example, the cover may have motifs of Beatrix Potter, Disney, Winnie the Pooh, or other storybook characters; or baby animals such as bunnies, ducks, or teddy bears. These motifs may then be sparingly placed throughout the rest of the album. Avoid motifs involving babies—booties, diaper pins, pacifiers, etc. These are *not* appropriate.

The next step is to place pictures of yourselves, special people in your lives, and important life events in chronological or thematic order. You might include pictures of your wedding; holidays with family and friends; vacations, outings, and picnics; your home; and favorite activities or hobbies, such as your art collection, crafts, woodworking productions, or activities like horseback riding, skiing, and gardening.

Select photographs that are homey and provide a feeling of comfort, warmth, and responsibility. Do not include pictures of the two you in your bathing suits or in skimpy outfits, or pictures that show alcoholic beverages. If your favorite cousin looks as if he belongs to a motorcycle gang, you may want to leave him out. Not all birth mothers and fathers care about issues like smoking, drinking, or style of dress; but even if they do not, the birth mother's parents might see the portfolio and influence the birth mother to select a more "wholesome" couple. Play it safe. No one is *not* going to select you because you weren't pictured drinking alcohol, but they may exclude you if you were.

Place no more than six to ten pictures on a page. This may sound like a lot of pictures, but if you trim them, you can fit about eight comfortably. Using heart-shaped, round, and oval cookie-cutters as stencils makes for nicely trimmed pictures.

Write captions for each picture or set of pictures. It is better to write or print, if your handwriting is legible; otherwise, type your labels and attach them to the pages. When referring to yourselves, use your first names. Personalize the information as much as possible while still maintaining your anonymity. Be creative but not too cutesy.

Include no more than twenty pages of pictures in the book—ten pages front and back.

The next item to prepare is a "Dear Birth Mother" letter. This letter describes your feelings toward the birth mother who is reading the letter and also how you feel about the decision she is making. It says something about the two of you and why you want to adopt. The letter goes on the first page of the portfolio. A sample birth mother letter can be found on pp. 59–60.

These are the essential features of the portfolio. Many couples also include a copy of their home study. Home studies usually highlight people's positive characteristics. If yours is like this, place what is called a "sanitized" home study (with all identifying information taken out) in the back of your portfolio. Accompanying your home study are letters of reference; these add a nice touch to your portfolio as well.

If you do not include a home study, an alternative is to write a one-page "resume," or biographical sketch, that highlights your life and some of your positive assets, such as your stability, love, financial security, home, family, hobbies, and favorite activities. In fact, even if you do include a home study, a birth mother may be more likely to read a one-page outline of your life than a multipage home study. Place the biographical sketch in the front of the portfolio, after the "Dear Birth Mother" letter.

Now your portfolio is finished. But can you be sure it looks right? Have a few trusted friends look it over and give their feedback. If you can, send a copy to your agency or attorney's office for suggestions.

When you are satisfied with your finished portfolio, take it to a shop that does color copying and have two copies made. Keep at least one copy at home and send one or more to your attorney. Remember, if you or your attorney identifies a potential birth mother and a portfolio is mailed to her, you may never get that portfolio back again. Keep the original at home. Once you adopt a child, the portfolio makes a lovely beginning to a baby book! That's one reason why doing a portfolio is never a waste of time. You can always use the original to tell your child the story of how you adopted him.

Some people like to include a video with their portfolio. If this appeals to you, the guidelines are fairly simple. Share the kind of information you included in your birth mother letter and biographical sketch. In other words, talk a little about yourselves and her. You may also want to include a special occasion that captures you at your best. Keep the video short—about five to ten minutes.

Chapter Five

Finding a Birth Mother

Now that you have decided to adopt, should you share your desire to find a baby with people you know? Telling others about your decision essentially means publicizing your infertility, and that makes many people uncomfortable. Try telling a few people in your "safe zone" first—people that you trust, like close friends or relatives. Later you may feel ready to share your plans with coworkers or acquaintances.

If you are truly serious about adoption, however, it is best to tell nearly everyone. The more people you inform, the more you will increase your chances of finding a birth mother. As you explain your situation, never sound desperate. Let people know that you and your spouse have chosen to go on to this next step in your lives, emphasizing your interest in adoption in a casual, matter-of-fact tone. Most couples are rewarded with sincere empathy.

Sharing your desire for children often opens the doors of people's hearts, leading them to go out of their way to pass on the word about your adoption plans. Do, however, be prepared for a few negative reactions. Some people will respond with surprising ignorance. Fortunately, this group is likely to be in the minority.

Your job is to throw the "pebble"—the news that you want to adopt—into your "pond" of friends and acquaintances, and wait for the ripple effect to take place. Your friends and acquaintances will tell their friends and acquaintances— often people you do not even know—who will tell their friends and acquaintances, resulting in your contact with a birth mother. Perhaps you have had this experience when searching for a job. If you tell 25 people that you are interested in adoption, and they each tell another 25, you will have "told" 625 people. This "ripple effect" does work.

NETWORKING

Establish a network for spreading the word about your decision to adopt. Remember, though, that a contact from a birth mother usually comes from the most unexpected sources, not necessarily from your "planned" efforts.

Here are some good places to start your networking campaign.

People in Adoption or Infertility Support Groups or Organizations

Infertility and adoption support groups can provide a strong network of people who are also pursuing adoption. At first you may be tempted to view these couples as your competition. Sometimes, though, they may have contact with more than one birth mother and will be able to refer one to you. We know of a couple who had contact with three birth mothers. After adopting two of the babies themselves, they referred the third birth mother to another couple, who adopted a beautiful baby boy.

In another situation a woman named Michelle casually mentioned at a RESOLVE board meeting that she would like to adopt an older baby. A few days later, an adoptive mother named Betty, who had also attended the meeting, received a phone call from a birth mother who had an eighteen-month-old baby. Betty told the birth mother that although she was not interested, she knew of someone else who might be. Two days later the birth mother contacted Michelle and her husband. Ten days later Michelle and her husband brought home a baby girl.

Another benefit of knowing other prospective adoptive couples is being able to make referrals to them. If you are not interested in adopting a particular baby, it is comforting to be able to give the birth mother another couple's name. Betty, for example, did not have to just say "no" to the birth mother. She successfully referred her to another couple.

Friends and Relatives

Telling friends and relatives, especially those far away, that you want to adopt can extend your likelihood of locating a birth mother by tapping resources that you would otherwise not have been able to reach. One couple's friend was at her obstetrician's office for a routine visit when she struck up a conversation with a pregnant woman. The woman was experiencing a crisis pregnancy and intended to place the child with an adoption agency. The friend referred the birth mother to the couple, who successfully adopted her baby.

In another example, a couple's friend's cousin knew a nurse who knew a birth mother. The nurse referred the birth mother to the cousin's friends—the adoptive couple. The adoption was a success. Yes, it sounds confusing, but this is how you make contact with birth mothers. The moral of a complicated story? Don't overlook anyone.

Coworkers, Clients, and Customers

Telling coworkers, colleagues, and sales representatives, for example, can also provide you with a far-reaching network. However, a woman who plans to remain at home once her baby arrives should be cautious about broadcasting this information too freely. She does not want to jeopardize her job or career advancement.

If your job involves routine contact with clients or customers, mention that you are seeking to adopt when they ask, "Do you have children?" Ray was weary of the "You've been married ten years and still no kids?" comment from those at his office. He finally told them that we were infertile and hoped to adopt soon. Not long after that disclosure, a secretary telephoned him with a birth mother contact that resulted in our adopting Erika.

Hairdressers, Manicurists, and Barbers

Consider the broad range of people you come into contact with each week. Your hairdresser probably sees hundreds of clients a month. One of these contacts just might be a pregnant woman, her mother, or her friend, who happens to share information about her adoption plans while getting her hair cut. Do you think this couldn't happen? It does.

Your Dentist or Other Health Professional

Medical forms include questions about your general health and whether you are taking any medication. These may provide an opening for you to share your situation with the health care professional.

Some people try to adopt through obstetricians, sending countless letters to every ob-gyn in the yellow pages. This effort is usually in vain. In some states it is even illegal for a doctor to assist a nonfriend in meeting a birth mother. In any case, ob-gyns are inundated with letters from couples hoping to adopt. Unless you know a physician personally or are in the medical field yourself, you will seldom get a lead in this department.

If you are in the medical profession, however, you will probably have some opportunities for adopting a baby. One physician and his wife adopted a baby just three days after they first began to consider adoption seriously. This came about because the wife had casually mentioned to one of her husband's colleagues that they were now considering adopting. "That's interesting," the physician said. "I know of a baby who was just born who is going to be placed for adoption."

Clergy

If you are religiously affiliated, the network you maintain through your denomination or affiliation can be a wonderful way to find a prospective birth mother. There are many birth mothers who want to select a couple of a particular faith.

Talk with your pastor or clergy person. Explain your infertility and your desire to adopt. (Do not be surprised if he or she is unaware of the emotional impact of infertility.) Let the clergy person know that if he learns of a pregnant woman from another church who wishes to have her child adopted, you would be glad to be contacted. He may be able to spread the word to his colleagues and associates.

Pastors, priests, and rabbis need to know about potential adoptive parents, since they are often the first to counsel a family whose daughter is experiencing a crisis pregnancy. How reassuring it would be for a pastor to tell the parents of a pregnant teenager, or the teenager herself, that he knows of a wonderful couple who could provide a secure and loving home for the baby.

Ask your clergy person for the names of other clergy who may be interested in talking with you or receiving a letter from you. Send them each a letter (see examples on pp. 60–61), enclosing copies of letters that can be given to birth mothers.

If your faith places an emphasis on the sanctity of unborn life, let the woman know this in your letter. Emphasize the attributes of your faith that will make you a better parent. One note of caution about discussing your faith, however: Do not assume that the birth mother places a great emphasis on her religion or that she expects you to do so just because the referral was through her clergy person. A birth mother's main concern is probably that appropriate family values are taught to the child—the kinds of values that often come through religious teachings.

BROADCAST LETTERS

Sending out letters is a relatively inexpensive way to make contact with a birth mother. Although writing one takes time and forethought, once one letter is written, duplicates are the easiest things in the world to produce. Here are some likely people to send letters to:

- *Friends.* When you send out your holiday cards, you may want to share with your friends your desire to adopt. Of course, you do not have to do this at Christmas time, but the holidays are a time for children and babies, and people tend to be extra responsive.
- *Professional or volunteer associates.* If you belong to a professional or volunteer organization, you may consider sending letters to some or all of its members. There are print shops listed in the yellow pages that handle

mailings if you give them your organization's list. In one situation, two birth mothers contacted a couple who used this method. Apparently, people are very receptive to these letters.

- *Clergy.* As noted earlier, contact with clergy can be a good way to locate a birth mother. Sometimes it is better to contact a clergy person outside your own church or synagogue. You probably do not want to adopt a baby whose birth mother attends your church or synagogue.

Here's a list of where *not* to send letters. Although sending letters to the these organizations will not do any harm, the likelihood of finding a birth mother this way is next to zero.

Crisis Pregnancy Centers (CPCs). At first CPCs might seem like a likely source for pregnant women seeking to place their babies for adoption. However, the staff at these centers are usually not permitted to give birth mothers the names of couples who are interested in adoption. CPCs get many letters from couples who want to adopt, which they have no choice but to throw away. When a woman considers adoption, they usually send her to an adoption agency of the same religious affiliation as the center.

If you know someone who works at a CPC, you may mention to her your desire to adopt. She might be able to provide your name to a pregnant woman, if this is not viewed as a conflict of interest.

Planned Parenthood. Planned Parenthood and other clinics already receive many letters from prospective adoptive parents. Even if they had a policy of responding to them, they wouldn't have the resources to.

Obstetricians. Ditto. Don't waste your time.

Writing the Letters

Separate letters should be written for friends, associates, clergy, and potential birth mothers. Examples of three letters can be found on pp. 59–61.

Make sure that your letter to the birth mother expresses your special understanding of what she is experiencing, and also that it tells her something about you: your hobbies, home, talents, interests, and positive attributes. Follow these guidelines:

- *Keep it easy to read.* Remember, she may be a teenager. Keep the language simple and the sentences short. You are trying to impress her not with your command of the English language but with your genuine desire for a child and the love that you can provide to that child.

- *Be sensitive to her needs.* Let her know that you are sympathetic about her unplanned pregnancy and that you realize she does care about her unborn child. This woman did not choose abortion. Without directly saying so, let her know that you respect her for choosing to carry her pregnancy to term.

- *Mention your infertility.* You do not have to mention your specific infertility diagnosis, but vaguely addressing the problem can help a birth mother feel for your situation as well. Never say, "We cannot have children of our own." Adopted children *are* your own.

- *Mention your livelihoods.* It is fine to state your professions, but keep the reference to it general. Notice in the letter on p. 59 that the husband's profession is not specified.

- *Mention your favorite hobbies and activities, especially ones that a child may enjoy.*

- *Share the positive points of your marriage.* For example, you may want to mention long walks and talks, suggesting a warm and communicative relationship.

- *Share your religious faith.* When talking about religious involvement, however, it is usually best not to mention your denomination, unless you are targeting pregnant teenagers or women who share that denomination or belief. If you are not part of an organized religion, then you will want to share the values that will make you a good parent, such as commitment to family and community, honesty, hard work, and acceptance of others.

- *Show that you are willing to have some level of "openness" in adoption.* Suggest your willingness to maintain an "open" relationship. If you are not willing to see the birth mother after the baby is placed, do not mention this. Please note, however, that most birth mothers do not expect to see you or the baby after placement. Whatever degree of openness you are comfortable with, let her know. Every birth mother should at least be given the opportunity to receive pictures and progress notes about the baby. Do let her know that you will send these to her. It is very comforting to a birth mother to know that she is not just handing a baby over to someone, never to hear about the couple or the baby again.

- *Make it personable.* Do not greet the birth mother as "Dear Birth Mother." Just say hello, or use some other informal salutation. Use your first names in letters and portfolios. Do not refer to yourselves as Jane and John Doe or "The Adoptive Couple." You are two real, living human beings with feelings: Let this come through.

SAMPLE LETTER TO BIRTH MOTHER

Hello,

You and I are in very different circumstances, and yet in some ways we are in very similar circumstances. We both find ourselves in a situation that we wish we could change. You have an unplanned pregnancy, yet love the child that you will give birth to. I cannot bear a child, but would love to have a baby for our family. My husband and I have longed for a child for three years. But I had four miscarriages, and the doctors cannot give me any treatments that will help me carry a child to term. Like you, I value unborn life and do not feel that it is right to keep trying to give birth to a baby while risking another miscarriage. My husband also cares about my health and that of the unborn child. Besides, our goal is to be parents, and through adoption we can love and cherish a child.

Just to let you know a little about us, I will tell you about our home and our activities. We live in a lovely ranch home with four bedrooms. Outside is a large yard with apple trees. There are two parks within walking distance of our home. My husband has a management job with an oil company. He was recently promoted. I am a third-grade schoolteacher. I enjoy my job, but I would like to be home with a child. If we are blessed with a child, I plan to stay home full-time. Both my husband and I love snow skiing and take about four or five trips to Vermont each winter. During the year we enjoy bike riding and long walks and talks together. Sometimes we take a picnic basket to the beach or park and then walk for hours. We also love to socialize with our friends. Many of our friends have small children. David and I both teach Sunday School at our church. Our lives are very full. There is only one thing missing—a child.

We would love to meet with you, if that is your desire. Or if you are more comfortable, we could exchange information over the telephone or through letters and pictures. David and I are also willing to maintain a relationship with you, even after the baby is born. If you select us as parents, we would be happy to send you pictures and letters to let you know what the child is doing at each age. We would even consider a more open relationship if you are comfortable with that. Of course, we also want to respect your privacy and the life ahead of you.

We also could pay for your medical expenses if you do not have insurance. All information between you and us would remain confidential. We have an attorney so that everything is legal.

Please let our friends who have given you this letter know what you would like best. They can then contact us. Or you can contact us directly at (800) 123-4567.

We wish you the best, whatever you decide. I know it is a difficult time in your life. We do care and are willing to help.

Susan and David

SAMPLE LETTER TO FRIENDS

Dear Friends,

As you may already know, David and I have longed to have children and have been unable to do so. This time of year is especially hard for us, as we would love to have presents under the Christmas tree for our child.

Recently we have decided to adopt and are letting all of our friends know in case they may know of someone who wants to place her baby for adoption.

We have everything that a child could want. Most of all, we want to provide a child with love, stability, and acceptance.

Our jobs are going well. In fact, David was recently promoted to northeast director of marketing. I do enjoy my job, but I would rather be at home with a child.

If you hear of anyone who is pregnant and knows this is not the best time in her life to raise a child, please let her know that we would be interested in meeting with her, talking with her, or making whatever arrangement she finds comfortable. Our number is (222) 555-1234.

Dave and I have also enclosed some "Adoption" cards. If you feel comfortable with distributing them, you could help us by placing them by public telephones and in the women's rooms at shopping centers.

We appreciate your help, and we'll keep you posted about our progress.

Wishing you all a Joyous Christmas and Happy New Year,

Sue and Dave

SAMPLE LETTER TO COLLEAGUE OR ASSOCIATE

Dear Fellow Rotary Member:

This may seem like an unusual appeal, but I hope you consider it seriously. As a fellow volunteer, I know that you are in contact with many people, and therefore may know of a woman who is experiencing a crisis pregnancy and is interested in placing the baby for adoption.

If you do, my wife Gloria and I would be most interested in contacting her. For five years now we have longed to become parents but cannot. Our lives have gone well, and sometimes it seems as if we have everything—everything except a child to love.

Please contact us at (555) 123-4567 (collect) if you know of someone who is considering adoption. If you can, please pass the enclosed letter on to her.

Thank you.

Terry Harkins

BUSINESS CARDS AND FLIERS

Business cards are yet another way to get the word out. They can be designed so that the front of the card presents a colored photograph of a baby and the word "Adoption." Or you could place a picture of you and your spouse on the front of the card. On the back of the card, write a message similar to one that you would put in a newspaper advertisement (see p. 66). As with an ad, you also include an 800 number or "Call collect." Place these cards in malls, rest rooms, restaurants, and other public places. You also may want to mail several to each of your friends with the letters described earlier.

Because fliers are larger and inexpensive—you pay only for paper and photocopying—you can add more information than you would in a classified advertisement. Fliers can be placed at bus stops, college campuses, and other public places where young women may be.

NEWSPAPER ADVERTISEMENTS

The most common way for adoptive parents and birth mothers to make contact is through newspaper advertising. Writing an advertisement for a newspaper takes a little work, but the rewards can be great. Like all ads, adoption ads should be short, convey an important message, and immediately attract the reader. You are not only presenting yourselves, you are seeking a most important person—your baby. Your ad should display warmth and compassion as well as your unique characteristics.

Listed below are some tips on writing an advertisement. But before you write your own, read other adoption advertisements. Which ones grab your attention? Decide why that advertisement makes a positive impression on you. If you can, fashion your ad in a similar way, yet make yours unique. You want a birth mother to see your ad and say to herself, "They sound like a nice couple who could provide a good home."

What should you include in your ad? Following is a list of what to cover—and what not to cover.

1. *What kind of child you are interested in adopting.* How much should you say about what kind of child you would like to adopt? Most couples seeking to adopt through private channels are interested in a healthy Caucasian newborn infant. If these are the limits you are placing on the child you seek to adopt, you should *not* mention it in your ad. Most birth mothers who are calling you will be Caucasian and pregnant and planning to place the baby with you immediately after birth. If you state that you are willing to pay for medical expenses, you are in essence saying you want a newborn baby.

    Here are some other issues parents have to consider in wording their ad:

    ■   The child's health status. Don't mention that you want a healthy baby. A birth mother may think you are looking for a "doll" and not a real child who will get sick throughout his life. Most birth mothers who respond to advertisements are pregnant and believe that the baby is healthy.

    ■   The child's racial/ethnic background. Many newspapers have policies that prohibit you from mentioning ethnic background or age. The best thing to do is wait until you talk with the woman on the telephone to determine her ethnic background and that of the birth father. If you are interested in adopting an African-American or biracial child, you may choose to mention this in your advertisement. Part of your ad may read, "interested in infant of any racial background."

        If you are of a specific nationality and state that you want only a child from that ethnic background, you may find yourself waiting a long time for a birth mother to respond. Instead of stating that you want, for example, a baby of Irish descent, you may say in your ad "Irish-American couple seeking to offer a child happiness." You may also want to advertise in a newspaper that targets those of your specific nationality.

Some couples do not want to adopt a child of a certain ethnic heritage. Even if you feel strongly about this matter, do not mention it in your ad. Screen your telephone calls to find out what the birth parents' ethnic backgrounds are.

■ The child's age. If you want an older baby or young child, placing an advertisement in the newspaper probably is not a good way to find such a child. Yet if you are willing to adopt a child from birth to three years of age, your ad may read like this: "Couple seeks child for adoption."

2. *Your first names.* We advise against using false names. In the first place it is unethical, and in the second, impractical. Once you meet with the birth parents, it will be very difficult for you to keep calling your husband "Harry" if his name is "Massimo," and for him to call you "Sue" when your name is "Angelina." On the other hand, a birth mother may not respond to an ad if she has never heard of your first names before. She may feel more comfortable calling a Mary and John than a Xenia and Archibald. If your names are particularly ethnic-sounding, you *may* want to Anglicize them a bit. "Mordecai" could become "Mort," and "Raymondo" could become "Ray."

If your name comes from another language, just change it to English. Instead of being "Jose," call yourself "Joseph." Then if you inadvertently call your spouse by his or her more ethnic-sounding name in the presence of the birth parents, at least your spouse can honestly say, "That's what my family calls me."

The point is not to misrepresent yourselves. If you are Jewish and your names are very ethnic, you would not want to select names traditionally Christian like "Mary" and "Christopher."

Some adoptive parents are very concerned about retaining their anonymity and do not want a birth mother to find out their full identity. If your names are "Archibald" and "Penelope," you may fear that a birth mother will be able to figure out who you are. "How many couples are there named 'Archibald' and 'Penelope' in the State of Iowa?" you may be thinking. Or you may fear that your specialized profession will be a dead giveaway to a birth mother intent on finding out who you are. After all, how many "Samantha and Jacks" are there in which the wife is an orthopedic specialist?

The truth is, no combination of first names is either common or unique. We do not know any other "Ray and Laura" combinations, although neither of these names is unusual. What you should really consider is what you could lose by using an alias. It is too easy for you or your attorney, legal secretaries, physicians, or anyone else involved in the adoption to make a mistake and call you by your "real" names. If this happens, the whole adoption could fall through.

Apart from that, it is morally wrong to try to deceive a birth mother about your names. When the truth is discovered—and it probably will be—the birth mother's trust will be diminished, if she does not immediately change her mind about placing her baby with you. Besides, you may have an ongoing relationship with this woman for the rest of your lives, even if just through letters and pictures. If your child seeks out his birth mother when he is eighteen years old, how will everyone feel when it is discovered that you had lied about your names all these years?

3. *Your unique characteristics.* Nearly every couple who advertises claims to be "a loving, happily married couple who will provide a child with much security." You therefore want your advertisement to stand out. Emphasize some unique characteristics that make you special. For example, if you are gifted as an artist, musician, baseball player, or tennis pro, you may want to include these details in the ad. One prospective adoptive father was a mechanic and did not want to include this in his ad. It turned out he had many interesting hobbies, such as hiking and woodworking. The couple included this information in the ad instead, and soon had a response from a birth mother. They are now parents.

Your profession is a unique characteristic that can serve to your advantage, and sometimes disadvantage. Birth mothers seem to respond most favorably to teachers and nurses, and less favorably to physicians and attorneys.

Activities that revolve around animals, beaches, mountains, and other outdoor activities are especially appealing.

Be careful of setting yourself too far apart from a birth mother. You may be very well educated, have a large home, and take many vacations, but don't call attention to it. The following will *not* do: "Harvard graduates who love tennis, golf, and yachting in the Caribbean seek to provide a child with much love. Call Biff and Buffy." Most birth mothers are intimidated by such a show of education and wealth.

4. *Your religion.* Again, your religion, or a profession that may suggest your religion, can work either for or against you. In many cases, however, mentioning a religious affiliation will only serve to screen out birth mothers. Use your judgment.

Many Jewish couples worry that they may have difficulty finding a birth mother who will work with them, since very few birth mothers are Jewish. Actually, experience shows that this is not an obstacle. Birth mothers are usually more interested in whether you practice a religion and will make good parents.

5. *Your financial status.* If you are financially comfortable or a member of a respected profession, you may *discreetly* mention these facts in the ad.

6. *Medical expenses.* If you are willing to pay for medical and other expenses, instead of directly stating this in your ad, simply say, "We care and want to help."

7. *Legality of independent adoption.* Even in states where it is legal, which includes most, you will be surprised how many people think that independent adoption is illegal. You may want to mention that the adoption plans are *legal* and confidential if no other adoption ads are in the newspaper.

8. *Your telephone number.* At the same time that you plan to place an ad in the newspaper, have a separate phone line installed in your home for responses from birth mothers. Order an 800 number from the telephone company, or state in your ad that the birth mother can call you collect. *Do not place ads in newspapers that permit only a PO box number and no phone number. Birth mothers will not write to a box number.*

OTHER CONSIDERATIONS

Start your ad with the letter A or with the word "Adopt." This will put your ad at or near the beginning of the adoption ads or "Personals" column of the newspaper. One couple told me that a birth mother confessed to them, "I called you because your ad was one of the first of thirty ads, and I am not going to call all thirty ads." We do suggest that you not compete with more than four other adoption ads. Although having other adoption ads can be a good sign—it probably means this is a newspaper in which adoption ads are read by and responded to by birth mothers—it is hard to make an ad stand out. Make sure yours is unique.

Be succinct. Cut superfluous words and phrases. Just don't go overboard! Saying that you are a loving couple sounds superfluous, but you must say it. Leaving it out is like not putting "attractive male/female" into a singles ad; if you do not say it, it is assumed you are unattractive.

The truly adventurous may want to experiment with a very unusual ad, testing it out in one newspaper to start with. Make sure the newspaper or magazine fits your style. Do not say you are a Rush Limbaugh fan in the "Personals" section of *Rolling Stone* magazine.

SAMPLE ADVERTISEMENTS

ADOPT Manager and piano teacher want to share the love that we have for each other and our joy in music with a child. We care and want to help. Fred and Wilma at (800) 123-4567.

ADOPT Professional yet fun-loving couple desires to share our love of life with a child. We enjoy camping and horseback riding. Call Martha and Harry at (800) 333-4444.

An accountant and teacher—financially secure—want to offer child a wonderful home by the beach, but most of all—lots of love. Call Blair and Lois collect at (333) 123-4567.

A successful broker and loving at-home artist seek infant. We can provide child with many blessings, but most important, lots of love and happiness. Call Steve and Jane at 1-800-123-4567.

Physician and nurse who cherish quiet walks, friends, and family want to share our love with a child. Dave and Sue, at 1-800-123-4567.

We want to share our large home and small farm in the country—but most of all our love and happiness with a child. Call Susan and Jim at 1-800-555-6543.

Teacher dad, loving at-home mom, and big sister long to share our love with a child. Call Tony and Pam at 1-800-123-4567.

Adoption is a loving choice, as three-year-old brother knows. Dad, loving at-home Mom and Grandma and Grandpa all can't wait. We care and want to help. Call Mike and Lisa at 1-888-765-1234.

Loving dad and mom want to provide a child with strong family values and security plus fun days at the beach with lots of cousins. Call Mark and Pam at 800-123-4567 PIN 1234, or our attorney John Smith at 800-555-1313.

WHERE SHOULD YOU ADVERTISE?

Perhaps you've been wondering how far from home it is best (and safest) to advertise for a child. Here are some options you may or may not have thought of already.

Out of State

As a general rule, the state where you advertise is the state where the baby will be born. (Note: Not all states that permit independent adoptions allow advertising. See the Appendix.) This means that if you live in New Jersey and advertise in Iowa, you must correspond with someone in Iowa and possibly visit the birth mother there at least once before the baby's birth, in addition to the trip to Iowa to receive the baby. Of course, many trips to another state can be expensive. Laws differ from state to state, too, resulting in possible complications. But even without complications you will need to either retain an attorney or engage an adoption agency in each state. Before you decide to advertise in a state other than your own, therefore, ask yourselves these questions:

- Am I willing to travel there at a moment's notice?
- Can I afford to make more than one trip to that state?
- Am I willing to incur the expense of living in a hotel before and after the baby is born? (You will usually live in a hotel from one to two weeks while all the Interstate Compact paperwork is filed.)
- Am I willing to incur the expenses of maintaining a long-distance relationship by telephone?

If you decide that advertising out of state is still a good idea, then the question becomes "Where?" Some couples find that they get a better response advertising in less densely populated areas of the United States, like the Midwest and the South, than they do in the Northeast. A couple seeking a Caucasian infant is more likely to find a birth mother in a rural area than in a cosmopolitan or urban area.

In Your Own State

If you advertise in your own state, select a small hometown newspaper about fifty miles away from where you live. Do not advertise in a newspaper that is distributed too close to your home. You probably do not want to live in the same town as the birth mother.

Although birth mothers and adoptive parents and children are maintaining closer relationships these days, living in the same area and having mutual acquaintances may infringe on everyone's privacy.

What Kinds of Newspapers?

Once you have decided which state(s) to advertise in, decide which area of the state to target. Some say the best place is near a college campus or military base. In other words, advertise in a community where there is a high concentration of young women.

This does not necessarily mean a college newspaper, although you might assume this would be the perfect place to advertise. Unfortunately, these young women often choose abortion over adoption. However, there are couples who have advertised in campus newspapers and received positive responses.

If you do choose a campus newspaper, select a college that is rural and, if possible, of a religious affiliation that does not condone abortion. If you think of this newspaper as one means of locating a birth mother but not your only means, you will have nothing to lose.

What about a large daily paper? It is true that a large newspaper goes to more homes. However, the "Personals" section of a small newspaper is more likely to be read by a birth mother or her friend or family member. Weekly newspapers are also more likely to stay in the home longer than a large, daily newspaper; and since advertising in a small newspaper is usually less expensive, you can afford to do it more often.

Call the various newspapers to determine their rates. Ask to have the papers mailed to you so that you get a "feel" for the area and so you can see how many other couples are advertising in each paper.

Remember, with a daily newspaper it is best to place your ad every day. If this is too expensive, try placing it twice a week and once on the weekends. Similarly, if you place the ad in a weekly newspaper, plan to do so for a few weeks running.

Newspaper Networks

If your finances are limited, you can still get broad coverage in some states by advertising in the Newspaper Network Association in your state. Then your ad will go in both daily and weekly newspapers. For $100 to $250 per week you can place an ad of twenty-five words or less (extra for each additional word) in all the newspapers that belong to that association. About 90 percent of the newspapers will place your specific ad.

In New York only 50 percent of the newspapers in The Classified Advertising Network accept adoption ads. However, the response you receive from birth mothers can still be very good, depending on what region of New York State you choose. By selecting, for example, only the Metro, Western, or Central region, you may pay less than $150 to have your ad placed in thirty-five to sixty newspapers.

For a larger sum of money you can place your ad in several networks simultaneously, giving you multiple-state coverage. Again, this can be done with one call to a local network association. For more information, see the Appendix.

An obvious but important note: If you have invested several hundred dollars in placing ads, you, the wife (birth mothers are more comfortable talking woman-to-woman), should either have a cellular phone and much privacy at work, or stay home for a week or two to answer the phone. That's too much money to spend only to have a prospective birth mother reach an answering machine.

Finally, if you want to go nationwide, advertise in *USA Today*. Yes, it is expensive (about $1,500 a week), but you will probably find a birth mother in a matter of two or three weeks. Again, if you do this, *stay home to answer the telephone.*

Note: If you advertise in a national newspaper or in a different time zone from yours, you may receive phone calls at odd hours. For most people this poses only a minor inconvenience.

How Long Should You Run Your Ads?

It is easy to be discouraged if you place an ad in a weekly newspaper and have not heard from a birth mother in a month. If you still have not had any calls after two or three months, this may not be a good source.

If you do get a few phone calls from one newspaper, continue advertising, even after a birth mother contacts you and decides that she wants to place the baby with you. If you have paid for a certain period of time, such as a month, keep the advertisement for that time period. You could get a call from another birth mother. It can sometimes help to have more than one option.

INTERNET ADOPTION SERVICES

On-line listings for adoptive parents, and hundreds of Web sites by adoption agencies and support groups, are among a number of Internet services now available. Adoption Online Connection is the first Internet listing service that offers in-depth national exposure for prospective adoptive parents. Listings go primarily to adoption agencies, hospitals, and organizations offering services for unwed mothers. The fee is about $40–65 if a photo is included—plus a monthly fee of $25. The listing you submit resembles a portfolio and includes a birth mother letter, your 800 number, and possibly your e-mail address. The Online Connection cannot serve as an intermediary, so an agency, service, or birth mother must contact you directly.

The advantage of the service is that it reaches states where adoption advertising is not permitted. As with any advertising, however, there is potential for prank messages and calls.

Will you find a birth mother through this method? Perhaps. As the Internet becomes more popular and user-friendly, the potential of finding a birth mother increases. You may not find a birth mother directly this way, but you could find out about other people who are also looking to adopt, and by connecting with them as you would with an adoption support group, you may find a child another couple is not interested in adopting.

Resources:

The Yahoo Internet directory has a section linking to adoption classified advertisements on the Internet at **http://www.yahoo.com/ Business and Economy/Classifieds/Adoption/**.

SETTING UP A TELEPHONE LINE ("BABY PHONE")

Most couples pursuing private adoption have a telephone line installed in their home just for calls from birth mothers. Your first contact with a birth mother, after all, is usually by telephone. Having a separate telephone line can provide you with some emotional control as well. Every time your regular phone rings, you will not assume it is a birth mother. If you are seeking a birth mother by the means of advertising, sending out "adoption cards," or letters to acquaintances, you will definitely want to set up a special line.

When you contact your telephone company to install the line, you may want to explain why you are installing a second line and ask that the second line be billed to your original phone number so that the telephone company has no separate record of the second phone line, and so that your address is not connected with the second line. The representatives are usually very understanding, although some personnel at the telephone company are not knowledgeable about adoption and think that "baby phones" are illegal.

Also ask for a "lock" to be placed on the number. That way a birth mother cannot call the phone company when she gets her phone bill and ask for the name of the person associated with your number. *A second telephone line is no guarantee, however, that a prospective birth mother will not detect your last name and address;* computerization of data means that this information is available to marketers and others. A birth mother who lived in the Midwest, whose parents had access to a large computer system, was able to learn a couple's last name and address in the Northeast.

Installing a telephone is a moderate expense and well worth your peace of mind. According to a representative from New Jersey Bell, installing a private line to your "phone box" costs $42. Labor for wiring inside your home costs approximately $64 per hour. The representative also said many people can do their own "inside" wiring. The monthly charge to maintain a second line is between $11 and $12.

Following are some other phone options you might consider.

- *An 800 number.* A birth mother is more likely to call an 800 number. Many long-distance carriers such as EXCEL now allow you to order an 800 number without installing a second line. The 800 number simply overrides your regular line. The cost is about $3 per month, and all incoming phone calls on the 800 line are billed at the regular long-distance rate and not a collect-call rate.

- *Voice mail and answering machines.* If you use an answering machine, be sure the outgoing message tells the birth mother the best time to call back. Don't state that collect phone calls are permitted unless your machine is the kind that allows the caller to leave only a three-minute message. Otherwise, prank phone callers can use all the recording time available at your expense.

- *"Identa Ring."* Another option is "Identa Ring," which costs about $4.50 per month. This system allows you to have up to three different telephone numbers and three different ring patterns on one line. If you have "Call Waiting," a special tone that matches the special ringing pattern assigned to each telephone lets you know which number the caller is trying to reach. All outgoing phone calls, however, are from your main number.

- *Phone block.* Using "Caller ID," a new technology that identifies an incoming call by phone number, a birth mother could potentially learn your main home number. To avoid this you might consider having a block placed on your number, especially if you are using an 800 number that rides over your existing telephone number. Then your number will not be traceable.

- *"Call Forwarding."* "Call Forwarding" can be used to send calls from your home to a friend's or relative's home. This may be something to consider if both of you are going to be away from home all day. The friend or relative can take messages and have you contact the birth mother in the evening.

- *Cellular phones.* Cellular phones are very inexpensive, and you may want to purchase one and obtain an 800 line so that you can be reached nearly anywhere you go.
- *Attorneys and agencies.* Attorneys and agencies can also take phone calls for you. If you arrange this, make sure you list the attorney's or agency's number in the ad along with your own.

We should say that the advice offered so far about how to maintain your anonymity is not intended to imply that having a birth mother know your telephone number and address is risky or even inappropriate. These measures are really for protection from pranksters and criminals, not well-meaning young women. We should note that none of the adoptive couples that we know have had any problems with criminals and pranksters beyond an occasional crank call. Once you establish a relationship with a woman and are certain she will place her baby with you, you may choose to share more identifying information.

SEARCHING FOR A BIRTH MOTHER: ONE COUPLE'S STORY

The quest for a birth mother can sometimes involve a few unexpected twists and turns, as Leslie and Paul discovered. Here's the way Leslie tells the story.

> It seems as if a large chunk of my life was spent thinking about getting pregnant, trying to get pregnant, and then worrying about it— I'd been an infertility patient for more than eight years. At last my husband Paul and I decided to end the treatments and focus our energies on adoption. Reaching this decision lifted a huge burden from our shoulders. Finally we could share our secret.
>
> Apart from our immediate families, no one was aware of our situation. We had felt it would be easier to keep our infertility under wraps. That way there would be no pressure and no nosy questions from well-meaning friends and acquaintances.
>
> The response to our adoption plans was wonderful. I'll never forget how immensely pleased our families were when we broke the news. Until then they had just figured we didn't want to have children. It's funny—I went from telling no one to telling everyone. When people would casually ask, "So, do you have any children?" I'd say, "No, but we're hoping to adopt." Even on airplanes I started asking other passengers how many kids they had. Invariably they'd turn the question around and ask me, which was the perfect entree.

We had already decided to pursue an independent adoption, for several reasons. Because Paul was in his early forties, and because I was in my late thirties when we started the process, we would probably not have met the age requirements for many agencies. In addition, a number of agencies are religious based, usually Christian. We're both Jewish, so this would not have worked for us. We also considered an international adoption, but dismissed the idea after speaking to our rabbi and other Jewish friends. We agreed that it would be difficult for a child of a different ethnicity to fit into the Jewish community.

Having made this decision, though, we barely knew where to begin. We figured it was best to speak with an attorney first and proceed from there.

Unfortunately, the first attorney we talked to left us cold. We were uncomfortable with what we perceived as her lack of integrity. I feared that if we used her, some day down the road someone would knock at our door and demand our baby back because the adoption wasn't conducted legally. So I found another attorney who seemed much more credible and kept him on retainer. He immediately recommended that we install a separate phone line and begin our newspaper campaign. We placed ads in papers all over the country. Our ad was short, and we ran it daily for thirty days in roughly four to six papers a month.

It worked. We received calls from all twelve states in which the ads appeared. The calls ranged from the serious to the ludicrous—like the man who guaranteed that I'd become pregnant if I spent a week with him! After all, when your phone number is appearing all over the country, you are bound to attract some weirdos. But we attracted serious callers, too. Like the Louisiana college students, newly married and shocked to discover that the young wife was pregnant. Knowing that they couldn't possibly raise a child now, they began seeking out adoptive parents. They said they were instantly drawn to our ad.

In fact, after I'd spoken to the young woman a few times, she asked for more information about us—what we were like as a married couple, our careers, and what we'd be like as parents. She also wanted to speak to our attorney. Things were looking quite promising, and I was starting to feel excited. So was Paul. With the Louisiana woman five months pregnant, we might have a baby in four months! Shortly after we sent them our biographical sketches, however, the couple called to say they could no longer work with us. They didn't like the abrupt manner with which our attorney treated them on the phone. They felt he was unsympathetic and brusque. I was stunned. They also admitted they'd been in contact with other couples, and, frankly, why should they deal with a condescending attorney when plenty of other couples out there have warm and thoughtful attorneys?

At first, I didn't know whether their concerns were legitimate or whether they were politely refusing us. Of course I was upset; it was very discouraging. Yet I had been warned that these things happen. Paul and I continued on. We placed more ads and took more calls.

I had decided early in the process to quit my engineering job and concentrate on the search. Paul's job as a marketing analyst would allow me to be a full-time mom once the baby arrived. Since the adoption process required so much energy, it made no sense to keep working. It was far better for me to be available to answer the baby phone myself than hook it up to a phone machine. What birth mother wants to pour her heart out to a machine?

Certainly not Annie, a sixteen-year-old Iowa girl who was expecting twins. Annie liked our ad, called us, and struck up a friendly rapport with me. A needy young woman, Annie would sometimes call me as often as three times a day. I spent hours and hours on the phone with her. We discussed virtually everything. After several months of dialogue she verbally committed to placing her babies with us. Naturally, Paul and I were elated! Not one, but two babies! It seemed too good to be true. It was.

The first setback came after Annie talked with our attorney. There was a mix-up with some paperwork, and she said the attorney was so mean and rude to her on the phone, she never wanted to speak to him again!

This was the second time we had heard negative remarks about our attorney. It was the last straw! If you are going to be an adoption attorney, you have to be prepared to do a lot of hand holding for young girls who are nervous, even hysterical. Our attorney's abrupt "New York" manner was not what these Midwestern girls wanted to hear. We immediately fired him.

Not long afterward, Annie confided that she had severe epilepsy. This did not pose a problem, until she mentioned that she was taking an antiseizure drug on a daily basis. I immediately phoned my pediatrician and discovered that there was a very high chance that the twins would be born with multiple birth defects—spina bifida, a cleft palate, even brain damage.

Could we take this chance? Paul and I were forced to do some serious soul-searching. What would it be like to care for not one but two babies, possibly with very high needs? Could we do it? In the end, we decided we could not take the chance. Birth defects are a terrible thing. When it's your biological child, you cope wonderfully because you have to, but Paul and I felt that we had a choice.

Then came the hardest part of all—telling Annie that we changed our minds. It was one of the most difficult things I've ever had to do. We had developed a very close relationship over the phone, and I knew she was going to be devastated. She was. I tried to be as gentle and as loving as I could. I did not mention the possibility of birth defects. I felt this information should come from her doctor. Instead, I told her we were simply not equipped to care for twins.

We both cried on the phone. Annie sobbed uncontrollably. I tried to reassure her that with hundreds of couples out there looking to adopt, surely she would find someone to provide a loving home for her babies.

As it turned out, Annie went into labor the very next day, six weeks before her due date. She delivered a girl and a boy. Sadly, the boy died a month later. Annie ended up raising the girl herself. Surprisingly, she continued to call me from time to time. We had a strong emotional connection, and she looked to me for support. She ended up going away to college, only to become pregnant again within five months! Since then I have not heard from her.

After Annie we had a few calls, but nothing promising. The next few months were totally uneventful. I was feeling discouraged and wondered whether it made sense to continue the ads. I questioned what we could have been doing wrong.

Around this time we hired a new attorney on the recommendation of the state agency that handles adoptions. The new attorney, Ray Godwin, suggested advertising in a newspaper in an urban area about forty miles from our home. I was skeptical, but figured we should give it a try.

Within three days after the ad ran a pleasant, articulate woman named Hayley phoned us. Unlike the other callers, Hayley was not a birth mother. She was the best friend of a woman who was due in exactly two days. This young woman wanted very much to place her baby for adoption, yet could not bring herself to make the calls or even talk about the situation. Hayley was very generously acting on her nineteen-year-old friend Diana's behalf.

Well, Hayley and I just hit it off fantastically. Here we were, two strangers talking on the phone, yet it felt as if we were old friends. At the end of our conversation Hayley said she felt as though we had just gone out together for a long, chatty lunch. More important, she couldn't wait to tell Diana about us!

Later that night Hayley called again and spoke to Paul. Initially, he'd been skeptical, but like me he started to get excited about the possibility. Things were looking very promising—yet I didn't want to get my hopes up too high. I'd already seen how easily things can fall through.

The next step was to speak to Diana herself. Hayley warned us that Diana was a very shy, very insecure young woman. She was a bank teller who lived at home with her mother and brother, neither of whom had been supportive of her decision. She had a long-term boyfriend who had fathered the child, but they were not ready to marry or raise the child themselves.

Hayley was very much on target—her friend was extremely shy. Our phone conversation was strained. I tried to get as much detailed information from her as I could the two times that we spoke: Was she right, or left-handed? What were her likes and dislikes? What did she and her family members look like? During our second talk she agreed to place her baby with us!

We were thrilled! Soon, very soon, we'd be parents. Paul assembled the crib, relatives loaned us a bassinet, we bought diapers, formula, and bottles. The anticipation, the excitement, the thrill of it all were just overwhelming. In a matter of days we'd actually have our baby! Or so we thought.

About a week later (like many first-time moms, Diana was late), Hayley called with some grim news. Another couple had offered Diana $10,000 for her baby. (Although it's illegal to "buy" a baby, many desperate couples are said to do so.)

Paul and I thought long and hard before we came up with a strategy. We got Diana on the phone and asked her outright, "Is your child's life worth money?" And, "Do you really want to turn your baby over to a couple who would buy him?"

Our tactic worked! A day later Hayley called to say that Diana definitely wanted us as parents. Whether the other couple had ever existed, we'll never know. Needless to say, these ups and downs were emotionally draining. We were exhausted.

A few days later, on a Thursday—it was the first day of Rosh Hashana, the Jewish new year—Diana delivered a healthy baby boy! We were ecstatic. We had a son! Ray Godwin assured us our baby would be home within a few days.

Once again, however, trouble loomed. Mysteriously, the hospital staff would not allow Ray inside to see the baby. The staff began pressuring Diana to turn the baby over to Catholic Charities and telling her they would not release her unless she carried the baby out herself.

Like most birth mothers, Diana had been under the impression that the adoptive couple would be taking the baby home directly. Neither did she expect to have to feed and change the baby, which the hospital required her to do.

In the meantime, we were at home, pacing, worrying, and praying, waiting for Diana to call. Ray urged us not to panic or lose faith. Diana would call us. We kept hoping in our hearts that he was right. But Saturday came and went with no calls. We called it Black Saturday—it was a horrible day. Late that night, truly alarmed, we slowly began resigning ourselves to the reality that we'd lost another baby.

When Ray called the hospital on Sunday, he found that both Diana and the baby had been discharged. No one answered when he phoned her home. We had no idea where she might have gone. Did she take the baby and flee? Did she accept the $10,000 offer from the other couple? By Sunday afternoon Ray still hadn't had any contact with Diana. Gently, very gently, he told us that we might as well just forget it.

Paul and I couldn't stop crying. We knew in our hearts this was *our* baby. We had already named him David. How could this be happening? To be so very close and have the baby just slip away was devastating.

Sunday, ironically, was sunny and crisp, an absolutely gorgeous day. We drove to the beach, where we walked for miles and miles, all afternoon. At times I would just collapse in a heap and cry. Paul would stop and console me, and I did the same for him.

As the afternoon went on, we decided to take a few weeks off, go away somewhere, grieve a little, and then renew our energies. We'd come back and resume our search.

When we finally got home from the beach that night, I couldn't even bear to walk past the baby's room. I asked Paul to take down the crib and bassinet and put them away in the basement. I didn't want to look at them.

I had started to prepare some dinner when the phone rang. It was Hayley.

"What's the matter?" she asked. "Don't you want the baby?"

I was speechless.

"I've been calling you all afternoon, and no one's been home," Hayley explained. "Diana figured it would be easier for her to just go home, rather than deal with the hospital. She's staying here at my apartment."

This was unbelievable! These two young girls had simply brought the baby home and were playing "Mommy" for a day.

While I kept Hayley on the "baby phone," Paul called Ray Godwin on the other line. Ray, his wife, Laura, and daughter Erika were at a party that afternoon, and we reached him through his beeper. He told us to get to Hayley's apartment immediately. He'd follow with all the paperwork.

I'd been crying all day and I looked terrible. I needed a complete makeover, but there was hardly enough time to change clothes. Instead, we sped off to Hayley's to pick up our baby. Everything had an edge of unreality to it. Just hours earlier, we'd phoned all our relatives with the bad news.

Paul and I kept each other calm during the thirty-minute drive. I hoped and prayed that nothing would go wrong this time. Ray did warn us about one thing. Diana did not want to meet us face to face. Although she would be there in Hayley's apartment, the thought of meeting us was overwhelming, too much for her to handle. But she did want to see what we looked like.

It would have been wonderful to meet her, to be able to thank her for all she'd done for us. But we understood how she felt.

When we arrived at the apartment complex, Ray, Laura, and their daughter had already gotten there. Diana had completed all the paperwork.

Just as we stepped into the apartment, Hayley slowly walked out of the bedroom, holding a tiny baby swaddled in a blanket. "This is your son," she said, and handed David to me.

When I saw the baby's beautiful little face, tears flowed down my cheeks.

It was wonderful, it was all you could imagine. Hayley and I gave each other a huge hug. But there was no time for heavy emotional exchanges. Ray had urged us beforehand not to dilly-dally. He recommended keeping the exchange as brief as possible.

As we bundled the baby into the car, I glanced back up at the window and saw the curtains fluttering. I knew Diana was watching us.

David, now nearly three years old, is a happy, rambunctious toddler who brings great joy to his proud parents.

Chapter Six

Who Are Birth Mothers, Fathers, and Grandparents?

Exactly who are birth mothers, and why do they place their babies for adoption? As you begin your search for a birth mother, you'll probably be wondering about what kind of person she might be, and why she has chosen to place a child with an adoptive family. You might be anxious about meeting her. But the more you know about the birth mother, the more comfortable you will be when you do meet each other. Even more important is the fact that usually, if the birth mother is comfortable with you, she will be more likely to go through with the adoption.

In most independent adoptions, the prospective adoptive couple will meet with the birth mother, and possibly the birth father, before the baby's birth. Most encounters that we know of go very smoothly. The personal contact that you have with her is one of the main reasons that a birth mother chooses the independent adoption route. You are not adopting an anonymous woman's baby; you are meeting a person who will give birth to your child. A birth parent deserves much respect. She is not a commodity or merely a person who is a means to an end—a birth mother is a woman who has gone through nine months of pregnancy, labor, and birth and has probably agonized over her decision.

A HISTORICAL PERSPECTIVE

Adoption has not always been viewed in a positive manner. It was once a solution for "bad" women who got pregnant, for couples who could not "have children of their own," and for "illegitimate" children. In other words, it was considered a second-rate choice for all parties involved. While adoption has certainly become more mainstream, the myths of the birth mother still linger. The following are examples of reasons why birth mothers have been stereotyped. As you read them, keep in mind the impact that such attitudes could have on the adoption process.

1. Birth mothers were told to "forget" their babies. Pregnant women were told to have their babies, surrender the child to the agency, go home, forget what happened, and get on with the rest of their lives.

2. Birth mothers were treated as though they were shameful. Some were sent away to a home for unwed mothers, so that no one would know about their pregnancy and adoption plans.

3. Birth mothers did not see their babies at birth or ever again. In the delivery room, physicians sometimes instructed nurses to cover the birth mother's eyes so that she would not see the baby.

    Once the baby was relinquished, a woman did not know what gender the child was or what he looked like, much less what happened to him. She also had to bear a secret for many years in her attempt to "forget it all." This level of secrecy led to much anguish.

4. It was believed that a birth mother was a poor judge of what was best for the child. Not only was it assumed that the less a birth mother knew, the better, but it was also assumed that a woman who allowed herself to get pregnant could not possibly be a good judge in selecting adoptive parents. Therefore, agency workers selected the best parents for the child.

5. It was believed birth mothers cared very little about their children. This attitude is probably best expressed in the term "unwanted child," but birth mothers in general do care very much about their children.

Today, we know that many birth mothers are simply women whose birth control method failed. These women believe that their child can be given a better life with other parents than with themselves or their families. Generally, they have chosen placing their child for adoption over abortion or the possibility of raising the child alone without financial support.

PREDICTING THE LIKELIHOOD OF PLACEMENT

Only a few studies have been conducted to determine the likelihood that a birth mother will actually proceed with adoption plans after the baby is born. These studies have examined birth mothers who have used agencies. Yet, for the most part, the same factors that determine if a woman is more likely to place her baby with an agency for adoption can also be applied to an independent adoption.

According to studies conducted in the late 1950s and 1960s, birth mothers who placed their babies for adoption were primarily white, middle to upper-middle class, with white collar or professional employment. They generally lived in a shelter for unwed mothers during their pregnancies, where they received group counseling.[1] A 1971 study analyzed data from 1967 to 1968 and came to similar conclusions—birth mothers with fewer emotional, social, and economic resources were more likely to retain their babies.

In a study published in 1988 by Steven McLaughlin, birth mothers who chose to give their children to adoptive parents were more likely to marry later, and less likely to be unemployed. These findings are confirmed by Christine A. Bachrach of the National Center for Health Statistics. She stated that birth mothers who retained their children had fewer educational or career goals, whereas birth mothers who placed their babies for adoption had significant life goals. Bachrach also found that birth mothers who made adoption plans were similar in income and education to birth mothers who married before giving birth or who had abortions. More often, it was middle-class women who were more likely to place a newborn for adoption, contrary to the popular opinion that only lower-class women place babies.[2]

According to a 1993 study done by Medoff, it was found that women who were also religious fundamentalists and had a high school education were more likely to place a child for adoption, whereas women receiving Aid to Families with Dependent Children (welfare) were less likely to place a child for adoption.

In applying these statistics to private adoptions, there are certain "red flags" that can indicate whether or not a birth mother will relinquish her baby. Usually, these women who ultimately decide to keep their child are on public assistance, or have unmarried friends who have children and are also on public assistance. On the other hand, women who are likely to place a baby for adoption communicate frequently with the adoptive parents beforehand and have family members who are supportive of the adoption.

Six percent of women who have children out of wedlock place them for adoption. One study has indicated that over 12 percent of white birth mothers place their children for adoption, while less than 1 percent of black birth mothers choose this option. However, other studies have shown that black women are not more or less likely than white women to place a child for adoption.[3] In our experience, black women will consider adoption but seldom go through with the decision. Therefore, it is very difficult to adopt a black newborn through a private agency or attorney. However, white women expecting biracial children frequently place their children for adoption.[4]

The women who choose to place their babies for adoption are generally sixteen to twenty-nine years old. Many of them already have children. A birth mother may already have had two children in or out of wedlock, is now single, and just cannot afford or manage another child.

CHOOSING TO PLACE A BABY

In general, birth mothers care very much about their children. It takes a lot of love to make adoption arrangements to ensure that a child goes into a loving, stable home in which her emotional and material needs can be met. Birth mothers do not make their decision lightly. Even the woman who knows right away that she cannot have an abortion or rear the child usually spends time soul-searching and agonizing over her decision.

According to Anne Pierson of LOVING AND CARING, INC., a Christian organization that provides counseling for birth mothers considering adoption, the advice her clients would give to others in the same situation includes the following:

1. Make a decision that benefits the child as well as you.
2. Look at the future and outline your goals and plans.
3. Think of the consequences of your decision.
4. Pray and seek God's help.
5. Think of the adoptive couple.
6. Never forget your child and always think of him/her.
7. Choosing adoption with the right intentions is positive and rewarding.

In Pierson's 1989 book, *Helping Young Women Through the Adoption Process*, she lists some conditions and attitudes that help birth mothers:

1. The knowledge that the child is going to a parent or a couple who would love the child as much as the birth mother would
2. Loving support from friends and relatives
3. Faith in God
4. Counseling
5. Having much information about adoption and the adoptive couple
6. Exchanging letters, gifts, and pictures with the adoptive couple
7. Surrounding herself with understanding people who do not condemn her
8. Being able to see the baby and say good-bye
9. Meeting other birth mothers and adoptive couples
10. Having her physical needs provided for (e.g., clothing, medical)

However, Pierson also mentions some experiences that birth mothers say are not helpful:

1. Acquaintances approaching them and confiding in them that they would have adopted the baby
2. Not being treated with the same respect as other mothers in the hospital
3. The awkwardness they encountered with friends and acquaintances when discussing the baby
4. Being told, "You're doing the best thing"
5. Not being given enough time to say good-bye to the baby, and being ignored by the adoptive couple once the baby is placed

Qualities Birth Mothers Look for in Adoptive Couples

Because most birth mothers care about their children, they want to be part of the adoption process. A birth mother usually wants to know the couple and wants some contact after placement to assure her the baby is doing well.

Pierson's book lists certain traits birth mothers seek in adoptive couples:

1. Financial security and good jobs
2. Some type of spiritual commitment to provide the child with a religious upbringing and strong family values
3. Emotional stability and readiness for a child
4. A strong marriage of at least four to five years
5. No history of substance abuse
6. Nurturing and loving qualities
7. Being supportive of the birth mother
8. Willingness to send letters and pictures to the birth mother
9. Willingness of adoptive mother to stay home with the child
10. Infertility
11. A good sense of humor

For more on the kinds of questions birth mothers will ask you, see Chapter 7.

BIRTH FATHERS

A survey completed by the Catholic Charities Adoption Services found that

1. Most birth fathers (81.8 percent) are more than "casually" involved with the mother.
2. Most (62.5 percent) are committed to the relationship.
3. Most (52.3 percent) dated the birth mother for more than six months.
4. Most (73.9 percent) acknowledge paternity.

Based on our experience, these statistics are representative of birth fathers involved in independent adoption.

However, the birth father is often not part of the adoption decision. Frequently, the birth mother and her family do not want him to be part of the process. Usually, the less romantically involved the birth mother is with the birth father, the more likely she is to place the baby for adoption.

Until 1972 birth fathers had no legal rights. Today birth fathers can gain custody of their child based on their emotional and financial commitment to him or her. (See Chapter 8: "Birth Fathers and Their Rights," and the Appendix for the laws of each state that relate to birth fathers' rights.)

BIRTH GRANDPARENTS

Prospective adoptive parents may find themselves dealing with not only the birth parents but with the birth grandparents. If the birth mother is living at home, it is more likely that her parents, particularly her mother, will want to meet with you and discuss the adoption plans. Jeanne Warren Lindsay, in her book *Parents, Pregnant Teens and the Adoption Option*, cites cases that describe the experiences and emotions that birth grandparents often have throughout the process.

1. When parents hear of their daughter's pregnancy, they are usually in shock. Then they often react with anger and bitterness before they move to the next stage of love and acceptance.
2. Many parents of pregnant teenagers never consider adoption. Most parents believe they and their daughter must rear the baby.
3. Birth grandparents feel very alone in what is happening to their family. Some want to talk with friends and family, while others want to be left alone.
4. Of those families that consider adoption, the birth grandparents need to allow the birth mother to feel secure in her own decision. Although it is difficult for birth grandparents not to give advice, the birth mother must ultimately be the decision-maker.
5. No matter what the birth mother's age, by law she has the right to have an abortion, to select adoption (in some states if she is under eighteen, a guardian is appointed), or to rear the child herself. This can make the birth grandparents feel very powerless, especially when they are still responsible for many of their daughter's other actions.
6. No matter how disturbed the birth grandparents are about the pregnancy, their daughter and the baby's father need much support during this time.

7. When parents say to their teenage daughter, "You can keep the baby, but you cannot live with us," they are, in essence, not giving her a choice.
8. Often the baby is their first grandchild.
9. When adoption is the choice, the birth grandparents need to grieve, just as the birth parents need to grieve, for the loss.
10. Birth grandparents need to consider the hopes and dreams they have for their daughter as she considers whether to raise the baby or to make adoption arrangements.
11. Often the younger the birth mother, the more difficult it is for the birth grandparents to go through with an adoption plan, as they feel more compelled to raise both their daughter and the baby.

    In fact, most birth mothers that Ray talks with are between nineteen to twenty-four years of age. Other statistics also indicate that most birth mothers are between these ages.
12. Often the birth grandparents are younger than the adoptive parents. This can cause the birth grandparents to feel guilty, for if the adoptive parents can rear the child, they ask, "Why can't we?"
13. Some birth grandparents do help their daughters interview prospective adoptive couples. The questions they ask are often more sophisticated than a teenager's would be.

    Lindsay recommends that the birth grandparents receive counseling as well as the birth parents.

Talking with Birth Grandparents

The ideas listed above can provide you with some understanding about birth grandparents. By recognizing their situation, you can better communicate with them if the occasion or need arises.

These pointers will help you talk with birth grandparents:

Provide a listening ear. Unfortunately, they may not have many other people who are supportive of their daughter's/son's decision. Often people seek counseling from those who are most understanding of their situation. You may be the most understanding person in their lives.

Let them talk out the option of rearing the child. As they discuss this option and the details involved, they probably will realize that adoption is the best plan. If they do not bring up the subject, you may ask, "Why did your daughter choose adoption instead of deciding to raise the child herself?"

At first this may seem like a question that could cause the family to change their minds, but actually their answers will reinforce their reasons for making adoption plans. The reasons birth grandparents and birth parents give you for making adoption plans will later provide them with rational guidance once the baby is born—a time when everyone's emotions take over.

If they really have no reasons for adoption, then perhaps they may be considering raising the child. It is better to find out during the pregnancy than afterward.

Discuss with them their hopes and plans for their daughter. When birth grandparents begin to discuss their children's college education and other matters, they realize that she would have difficulty achieving her goals while raising a child.

Let them know that you appreciate their involvement and commitment as well as their daughter's. Everyone wants to be appreciated and understood. Also, this is an opportunity to let them see that an unplanned pregnancy can touch other lives in a miraculous way.

By understanding the families' feelings about adoption, you have a better idea of whether the birth parents will go through with the adoption plans once the baby is born. For example, if a birth mother wants to place the baby for adoption, but the birth father is ambivalent and the birth grandmother thinks the baby should not be placed for adoption, there could be trouble ahead.

In situations in which an adoption is questionable, counseling could be useful. It could help guide all the parties involved so that they can manage their emotions and understand the facts. Also, counseling will assist all the family members to consider their options and find out who is going to be emotionally and financially responsible for the child if she is not placed for adoption.

Ray always counsels a birth mother that family pressure should not influence her ultimate decision. The decision to rear a child, or to place a child for adoption, must be made by the birth parents.

In some states birth parents' rights are terminated shortly after birth, whereas in others it could take months. If birth parents can change their minds after the baby is with you, you may not want to take the baby home unless the birth parents and other family members are secure in their decision. The birth grandparents and other family members can strongly influence a woman who has just had a baby and may convince her to change her mind. Perhaps if the family seems uncertain, ask your attorney about the possibility of foster care placement until the birth parents' rights are terminated.

If you are older than the birth grandparents, do not make an issue of it. Explain your situation. Tell them how you tried for years to conceive a child and how much you long to become parents. If you are wealthier or have a position with more status, do not flaunt this. Let the birth grandparents know that you want to provide the child with the best in life, especially time and love.

Because birth grandparents can ask sophisticated questions, be prepared. Often the birth grandparents are looking for the same traits in adoptive parents that more mature birth parents look for: a stay-at-home mom, financial security, lots of love and warmth, a stable marriage, and some commitment to a religious faith.

Chapter Seven

Meeting the Birth Mother

n most cases the first contact with a birth mother is by telephone. This is an emotionally fraught moment for everyone. You and she will both have many questions; both of you will be wanting to present yourselves in a favorable light. After all, this could be the beginning of an important relationship.

The birth mother is considering you to be the parents of her child, and so she is likely to be curious about your home, other family members, your religion, and your employment. Answer her questions honestly, but do not feel you have to provide more information than is necessary. For example, she may ask if you go to church. If you do, say yes. You do not need to go into detail about your religion and the tenets of your faith.

If you get the feeling that one of your answers is not the "correct" one, and you cannot change the situation, then ask her if the issue is a problem. For example, perhaps she asks whether you have any other children, and you say yes. If you sense that this is not the answer she wants to hear, then simply ask her kindly, "Is that a problem?" You cannot change certain factors in your life, such as your religion, your age, or where you live, but depending on how she responds when you ask, "Is that a problem?" you may be able to tell her other things that help her feel more comfortable.

WHAT TO TELL HER, WHAT TO ASK

Early on you will want to let the birth mother know what your level of openness is toward an adoption arrangement. A birth mother usually cares very much about the child's welfare, although she may not know how to express that she is interested in knowing about the baby after it is born. You may want to offer to send photos and letters to her.

Do share a special interest, hobby, or sport. Sometimes one common interest is the reason a birth mother pursues you as parents.

There are several things you will probably want to ask a birth mother in your first conversation with her. For example:

Why she wants to place the baby for adoption. She will probably confide her reasons before you even ask. If she does not, try to determine her reasons and whether they appear to be valid.

Her health history. It is not easy to ask someone outright, "What is your medical background?" You may instead ask, "How is your pregnancy going?" Be cautious in asking direct questions. Your attorney will also be asking her these questions, and you may want to wait for him to do so.

Needless to say, asking someone point-blank about possible drug use is not tactful during a first conversation. Asking about school, work, hobbies, and interests may help you get a sense of how well this birth mother is caring for the unborn child. If she says she spends most of her spare time in pool halls with the guys in a rock band, or at bars, you may have cause for concern. On the other hand, if she says she spends her time studying, swimming, and participating in a church youth group, she is probably living a clean life.

Asking someone about her life without prying also demonstrates that you are a caring person. Your concern for this unborn life can indicate that you will care about the baby later.

The birth parents' ethnic backgrounds. If you want a Caucasian infant, or any other kind, then it would be appropriate to find out early on about the parents' ethnicity. You may simply ask, "What ethnic background are you and the birth father?" Don't make this your first question, but do raise it the first time you talk with her.

Money. Do not bring up the subject of money unless she does. A woman who is just looking for someone to pay her medical and living expenses and has no plans for adoption will probably ask for money in the first conversation. A woman who mentions that she does not have insurance and would like to receive money for medical care, on the other hand, is not necessarily insincere.

When you are ready to end the telephone conversation, you might say something like, "I've really enjoyed talking with you, Jane. Perhaps we can meet each other so that we can talk further and you can get to know us a little better. Would you like to meet in a diner somewhere between our location and yours or at our attorney's office?"

Here are a few more pointers about telephone contacts with birth mothers.

Don't pose questions as if you are reading from a list; ask in a conversational manner, and listen to her responses carefully and thoughtfully. It is a good idea to practice this with a friend before you actually talk with a birth mother.

Jot down any questions that occur to you while she is speaking so that you are not tempted to interrupt her. You will probably be nervous (and so will she); however, give her time to complete her statements before you ask another question.

Maintain good records so that you can give any information you have to your attorney.

Do not expect to complete a full interview with every birth mother. Some women call many ads. Some are "just thinking" about adoption and are still unsure. Other calls will be pranks.

Always ask the birth mother for her phone number. This is a good way to find out whether the person is sincere or just someone making prank phone calls. Most genuine callers will leave a phone number, whereas most prank callers will say they can't or that they are calling from a phone booth.

If a woman gives you a phone number, call her right back after you end your conversation with "just one more" comment or question. This lets you know whether she really is at that number. When you do call back, you may say, "I just wanted you to know my lawyer's number in case you also wanted to talk with him. Or if you would prefer, I can have him call you at a convenient time." (Of course, if she is very far along in her pregnancy, she *must* talk to your attorney as soon as possible. Most birth mothers are unsure of the legal process and do want to know what to expect.)

Following is a list of questions you will want to ask in your first few telephone conversations with a birth mother. It is a good idea to copy this list and post it near your baby phone so that you will not have to think about what to ask when you are under pressure. Do not try to ask every question on the list during your first conversation. Concentrate on the ones that seem the most important, and be sure she has a chance to ask all her questions, too.

1. Birth mother's name _____ (She may choose to give just her first name.)
2. Why do you want to place the baby for adoption?
3. How do you feel?
4. How did you find our number? (Friend, ad, business card? If newspaper, which one?)
5. How old are you?

6. Is the birth father involved in your life?
7. How does he feel about your adoption arrangements?
8. Does your family know that you are pregnant?
9. [If yes] How does your family feel about your adoption arrangements?
10. How many months pregnant are you?
11. Where do you live? (state or general area of a state)
12. Where do you plan to deliver the baby? (hospital and state)
13. What medical care have you received? Did it include an ultrasound?
14. What other results did you get from the obstetrician?
15. Are you taking any medications?
16. How has your pregnancy gone? Are there any complications?
17. Do you live with your family, by yourself, in a dormitory, with friends…?
18. What nationality are you?
19. What ethnic background is the father?
20. May I call you back? (if she is comfortable giving you her phone number)_____
21. Where can we meet? (if she wants to meet)
22. Other relevant information:

MEETING

Once a birth mother has called and seems sincere, arrange to meet her, if this is what everyone wants. You will probably not agree to meet after the first phone call—more like the second or third.

You will need to decide *where* to meet. If you made contact through a mutual friend, relative, or acquaintance, then you may want to meet at that person's home for the first time. For more confidentiality, meet at a park, library, or restaurant. Make sure you describe yourselves on the phone so you can identify each other easily. If you meet at a restaurant, pick up the tab!

If she selects a place that is familiar to her but not to you, visit the destination (if it is not too far away) so that you know that the place really does exist and so you will not get lost when it comes time to meet her.

You could agree to meet at your attorney's office, but this might be a bit intimidating for a first meeting.

Overcoming Your Fears about Meeting

Meeting a birth mother is important for your peace of mind. It will give you at least a sense of the kind of person she is. If she is neat, clean, and dressed in a turtleneck, khaki jumper, and penny loafers, chances are slim that she is taking drugs. If she is disheveled and smells of tobacco and liquor, she is probably not taking care of herself, and she may be taking other substances. Seeing her and speaking to her will go a long way toward allaying your anxieties—or may warn you if something isn't right.

There's no question, however, that meeting a birth mother face to face is difficult for all parties. Everyone is nervous. To relax yourself, think of all the other firsts in your life and how nervous you were: your first day of kindergarten, your first date, your first good-night kiss, and so on. This is just another first—the first time you have ever met a birth mother. For additional reassurance, talk to other people who have met with a birth mother and adopted.

Be yourself. Isn't that what your mother told you as you went on your first date with the guy that you were crazy about? But being yourself and knowing what to say are not always easy.

Birth mothers are no different from other people: Some are talkers and some are quiet and reserved. If the birth mother is shy, making conversation can be difficult. Do not feel that you have to make great conversation. It should be pleasant and polite.

You could start the conversation by asking her how she is feeling. If you begin to feel comfortable with her, and you both agree, you can go on to give identifying information such as your place of employment, the town you live in, and your last names. If you've met through a mutual acquaintance, she may already have this information.

Some birth mothers have no idea what to ask. You may have to take the initiative. Explain why you want to have a baby, and ask her why she is making this decision. A teenage mother may be accompanied by one of her parents, who will usually know what to ask, even if the teenager does not. Be aware of the birth mother's behavior if she is young and accompanied by her mother. Sometimes the adoption is her mother's idea, not hers, and she does not want it to happen.

If you have talked on the telephone with a birth mother, you have probably already shared some facts about your lives. As birth parents become more sophisticated about adoption, seeking greater control, some will want to know very specific facts about you. Naturally, you will present your finest points and discuss your interests. Be honest but not controversial. Birth mothers are looking for assurance that you will be a good parent—not that you are a Democrat or a Republican.

Here are the questions about your life that birth mothers usually want answered:

- *What is your family like? Your parents, brothers, sisters, etc.?*

- *How do you spend the holidays?* Birth mothers find it reassuring that the child will be in a home in which extended family members share important occasions together and where warm traditions are carried on.
- *What activities do you enjoy?* Sharing your interests in sports, music and community activities indicates that you will probably share these interests with a child.
- *What kind of a community do you live in?* The kind of community you live in says something about what kind of life a child will have. Talk about any parks, beaches, mountains, or other recreational sites close by. Tell her that there are other children in the neighborhood.
- *Will a parent be staying home with the baby? For how long?* Some birth mothers feel that if you are going to place the child in a day care center, she might as well raise the child herself and make the same arrangements. No matter how untraditional her life may be, chances are she wants a traditional home for the baby. A birth mother wants to know that the mother (or father) is going to be home to care for the child for as long as possible. If you know that staying home full-time is not possible, you may want to share your intention to have the child cared for at your home by a motherly figure or a relative of yours. Never lie about your plans. If you are unsure, tell her that you plan to stay home as long as possible. If you tell the birth mother that you plan to stay home full-time to care for the baby when you really plan to go back to work, you will probably feel guilty once you return to work. Going back to work and leaving a baby in someone else's care can be difficult enough. Do not add extra guilt to the situation.

Remember, if you choose not to meet face to face, you will want to keep in contact through telephone or letters. This happens often. Some birth mothers avoid emotional involvement by making all arrangements through a third party—the person who told you about each other or an attorney. You will simply want to do your best to stay aware of how she is feeling about her adoption arrangements, and whether she is getting the care and counseling she needs.

TALKING TO BIRTH MOTHERS

When talking to a birth mother, take cues from her about her conversational comfort level. If she is a soft-spoken Midwesterner, do not overpower her with your Northeastern accent. If she is animated and lively, then you will want to be positive as well.

It is appropriate to ask questions and make statements like these:

- What plans do you have for your future?
- Why do you want to place the baby for adoption?
- Have you discussed your plans with anyone else? What do they think?
- Why do you think adoption plans are best?
- I understand that placing a baby for adoption is a difficult decision; if you need counseling, we will be glad to assist you financially.
- I believe that you want what's best for the baby. As a couple, we want what's best for the baby too.
- It must be difficult not to have your parents support your decision (if this is the case). Is there anyone else who supports you? (If not, then offer to provide her counseling from a professional, if she so desires.)
- We will be praying for you as you go through this difficult time in your life.
- From what I understand, placing a baby for adoption can be painful and fulfilling at the same time. I know of a group of other women who are facing the same issue. I can give you the phone number of this support group.

Such statements acknowledge that the adoption decision is difficult, while offering her constructive means for making and accepting that decision.

SUPPORTING A BIRTH MOTHER EMOTIONALLY

You may well become part of the birth mother's support system, and you do want to be a considerate, thoughtful friend. As with any relationship, however, there are appropriate limits. You may not mind becoming "counselors" for the birth mother—many couples do—but you will not want to provide a twenty-four-hour-a-day counseling service. That can drain you and make you feel negative toward the birth mother. If you begin to dread the ringing telephone for fear that you will have to listen to a birth mother's problems for another two hours, you will need to set limits. Similarly, if you are uncomfortable about the discussions you are having, perhaps you can offer to pay for counseling for the birth mother.

Let her know that you will do what you can to make each part of the adoption process as easy as possible. If you can, help her set up her doctor and counseling appointments. If she needs transportation, make arrangements for this as well. Let her know that you understand her need to get on with her life while demonstrating that you are willing to maintain a certain level of openness within the relationship.

SUPPORTING A BIRTH MOTHER FINANCIALLY

Expenses that an adoptive parent legally can pay for vary according to state law, so you may be limited by more than your own finances. Even if there were no such limits, however, you would not want to be taken advantage of by an insincere woman who has no plans to place a baby for adoption, or one who believes that doing so entitles her to a nine-month luxury vacation.

Living Expenses

Paying for a birth mother's living expenses is a very delicate balancing act. Some couples resent paying anything, making the adoption process difficult. Some attorneys offer birth mothers excessive living expenses, making it difficult for couples who cannot afford to pay, for example, $1,000 a month in living expenses for seven months.

Some birth mothers ask, while others expect, to be assisted with rent, phone, utilities, food, gas, car repairs, and so on. All such financial assistance should be handled through your attorney or agency. Your attorney should give the final approval, with funds coming through his trust account. In most states a judge must approve these expenses, usually at the time of the adoption hearing. You do not want your adoption questioned because living expenses were excessive or inappropriate. Having your lawyer handle the finances also keeps you from having to say no to a birth mother when expenses cannot be paid. Instruct your attorney to contact you before sending out monies that were not prearranged. One attorney sent a birth mother in California $1,500 to have her car fixed without first asking the couple whether it was all right.

Medical Expenses

It is appropriate to support a birth mother by allowing her to see a private physician (if she has no health insurance or does not qualify for Medicaid) or by purchasing vitamins and healthy foods. It shows you care about her and the baby.

Counseling

Paying for counseling also shows that you care about her emotional needs. Sometimes a birth mother has more difficulty after she places the baby than before. Many adoptive parents pay for her counseling fees during this time.

Legally, most expenses can be paid only up to six weeks after birth. Yet counseling may be required for an extended period of time. If your birth mother needs counseling, try to see whether you can get special court approval through your attorney to pay for counseling beyond six weeks if necessary.

Lost Wages

In some states birth mothers are permitted to be reimbursed for lost wages resulting from pregnancy and postnatal recuperation. This can be very expensive and is sometimes used as a "legal" way "to pay" a birth mother for placing her child with you. If a birth mother earns, for example, $300 a week and is out of work for six weeks before birth, some attorneys will tell her that she can be given $1,800 at birth and another $1,800 after if she is out of work for another six weeks—possibly even on top of whatever she receives in living expenses.

This is an area where paying lost wages can look like baby selling. If you are giving a birth mother this kind of assistance, be sure she is not also receiving disability or paid sick leave.

RELATING TO MORE THAN ONE BIRTH MOTHER

What do you do when you receive calls from more than one birth mother? If you have advertised diligently, especially in the newspapers, you can have more than one birth mother who is interested in placing a baby for adoption. This offers you more options but also means you must make some difficult choices. It is not unethical to be making arrangements with more than one birth mother for a very short time period without disclosing that to both birth mothers; you have the right to change your mind, just as she does. However, it is unfair to string someone along for more than a couple of months. Here are some scenarios that could arise, and some suggestions for handling them:

A birth mother calls you on Tuesday and another calls you on Wednesday. One has a delivery date of two weeks; the other is due in six months. If both women seem sincere, agree to meet both of them. If both agree to place a baby with you after meeting with you, your choices are as follows:

a. Decide which birth mother you would rather deal with based on her background and interests.
b. Select between the birth mothers based on the earlier delivery date. All other things being equal, if one birth mother's due date is in two weeks and the other's is six months away, it is best to make adoption arrangements with the former while maintaining communication with the latter. If the first birth mother changes her mind, you can then make arrangements with the birth mother whose delivery date is in six months.
c. Agree to make arrangements with both women, and if neither changes her mind, be ready to have two babies—five to six months apart. Good luck!

Two birth mothers call, and each one has a delivery date about five to seven months away. You meet each birth mother and agree that you like both equally.

a. Continue arrangements for a few weeks with each woman until you sense which one you would prefer and which seems most sure of her decision.
b. Make arrangements with both birth mothers, and if both place the babies, be prepared to have two babies a few weeks apart!

Here are some general guidelines for relating to more than one birth mother at a time. *Note*: Should you become pregnant while pursuing adoption, you may want to use similar strategies, given the uncertain outcome of your pregnancy.

1. While you are still choosing between two birth mothers, never let one know about the other.
2. If you cannot bear to call a birth mother to tell her that you did not choose her, have your attorney do so for you.
3. Have a network of other prospective adoptive parents so that you can give their names to a birth mother if you are not going to commit to her. Alternatively, if your attorney is permitted to act as an intermediary, he can provide another couple.

Chapter Eight

Birth Fathers and Their Rights

The moment Mary and John had long awaited finally arrived when they took home their beautiful baby girl. They had not expected problems, since both of the sixteen-year-old birth parents supported the adoption. In fact, both the birth mother, Sally, and her ex-boyfriend, Tom, had responded well to counseling. Then Tom unexpectedly threw a wrench into the works. He decided that the only way to win Sally back as his girlfriend was to insist upon having the baby back. Surprisingly, Tom's mother supported his wish, even agreeing to help raise the baby. Tom hired a high-profile attorney he had seen on television who argued that the "natural" parents are always best for the baby.

Sally knew that Tom's family had many problems and that this was not the ideal household for the baby. Her only choice was to raise the child herself. Naturally, it was not her first choice. Sally had hoped to go to college. Nor were her parents able to help. Her mother worked full-time, and her father was partially disabled.

Ray and I will never forget having to pick up the one-week-old infant from John and Mary's home and take her back to Sally. Of course, Ray could have brought the case to court. But with no guarantee of winning their case, the adoptive parents would have risked losing the baby after she had been in their home for nine months or more, an even worse scenario.

Ironically, two weeks later, Sally, the baby, and her family moved to a new city 800 miles away from Tom. Now Tom has visitation rights that he has yet to exercise. The baby is with the birth mother, and her life goals have been severely limited. If Tom's goal was to punish Sally, he succeeded.

LAWS AND PRECEDENTS

These events took place in New Jersey, where Tom has the same right to change his mind about an adoption as Sally does, provided he has a means of caring for the baby. Birth mothers in New Jersey do not have the right to say they want their child to be placed for adoption instead of being raised by a birth father, even a birth father who has not been supportive of her during the pregnancy. The story illustrates the impact of various state laws on adoption outcomes. Had Sally agreed to take part in an identified adoption, working with an adoption agency, she and Tom would have been asked to sign a termination of rights seventy-two hours after the baby's birth. If Tom had refused, the baby would never have gone to Mary and John's home, saving them untold heartache.

If Mary and John had lived in South Carolina, the birth parents' rights could have been terminated immediately after birth in either an agency or private adoption. Across the border in North Carolina, on the other hand, where parental rights are terminated twenty days from birth whether the adoption is agency or private, getting an agency involved would not have changed the circumstances. There is no "national policy" on adoption. Every state has its own laws, and invariably there are unintended consequences.

One area in which state adoption statutes have been affected across the board, however, is that of birth fathers' rights. Until 1972, "unwed" or "putative" (meaning "supposed" or "presumed") fathers had relatively few rights. States did not include an unwed father in the definition of "parent," meaning that his consent was not needed for adoption placements. These laws cut both ways. An out-of-wedlock child could not demand support or inheritance from his birth father; the birth father had no legal status to influence the child's upbringing. Not only was the birth father's consent not needed in many states, but he was often not even entitled to notice of any adoption hearings or proceedings. Unless he took the extraordinary step of asserting his paternity, an adoptive couple had no need to worry about the birth father. An adoption was routinely initiated and finalized without any regard to him.

Since 1971, however, the Supreme Court has rendered several decisions that provided, under certain circumstances, the same rights to a birth father as are given to a birth mother. All state adoption statutes must provide these rights so long as the birth father meets certain conditions or takes certain steps to establish his paternity. Usually this means taking one or more of the following actions:

1. Establishing paternity by obtaining a court order
2. In states with a putative father registry, submitting his name to the registry
3. Having his name placed on the child's birth certificate or similar document
4. Maintaining a relationship or attempting to maintain a relationship with the child to be adopted—including providing financial and emotional

support. New Jersey law, for example, emphasizes maintaining an emotional relationship with the child. Many state laws stipulate that this relationship must be maintained during the six months (or some part thereof) following birth.

Which of these steps are regarded as indispensable varies from state to state, but in most, if the birth father puts his name on a putative father registry or on the birth certificate without attempting to "act like a father," it will probably not be enough to prevent an adoption. Similarly, if he tries to establish paternity just prior to or just after the adoption finalization, his rights are limited unless he can show that his inability to assert his parental rights was the result of circumstances beyond his control, such as being incarcerated in a state prison. A birth father who "sits" on his rights as time goes by and fails to show paternal interest weakens his position to contest the adoption.

In 1979 the United States Supreme Court stated that an unwed father who has "manifested a significant paternal interest in the child" must be allowed the right to veto his child's adoption. What constitutes "significant paternal interest," of course, is left to the interpretation of the states. Let's consider a 1983 case involving a New York birth father. In *Lehr v. Robertson*, a putative father attempted, after the fact, to contest the final adoption of his daughter by the birth mother's husband. The birth mother consented to the adoption. The case went all the way to the Supreme Court, which stated that an unwed father who had failed to establish and maintain "any significant custodial, personal, or financial relationship" with his daughter was not entitled to notice of the adoption proceedings.

The birth father had lived with the birth mother before the child's birth and had visited the hospital several times after birth. However, he provided no financial support, nor did he offer to marry the birth mother. Of equal importance, he did not take the steps required under New York law to establish his paternity, which included putting his name on the birth certificate or mailing in a postcard to New York's putative father registry. Noting further that the birth father did not live with the birth mother and child after birth, the Court declared that "the mere existence of a biological link does not merit" constitutional protection when the birth father in essence "sat on his rights." This decision incorporates the principles of all recent Supreme Court decisions pertaining to the putative father's rights to contest an adoption. As Justice Stevens noted in the *Lehr* decision, "The rights of the parents are a counterpart of the responsibilities they have assumed."

These principles have been incorporated into the laws of every state. In any adoption situation, the adoptive couple and attorney must determine what role the birth father desires to play, if any, and to what extent he will be involved. His involvement should be addressed at an early stage to avoid any "surprises" at the time the baby is discharged from the hospital. Many birth mothers, of course, do not want the birth father to be involved, particularly if they have parted ways. However, once a birth mother learns that the birth father has equal rights and could cause the adoptive couple problems, she will usually agree to provide information about him. She, a family member, or the adoptive couple's attorney must then approach him, perhaps for the first time, with the issue of his interest in the child to be born.

The couple's attorney must be aware of the state statute and case law dealing with the birth father's rights. In situations like the *Lehr* case, where state law and the facts allow, the attorney and couple can abide by the birth mother's wishes not to notify the birth father of the adoption proceedings because the birth father has not asserted his rights by following state law.

Unless an adoption has a *Lehr* birth father, the United States Supreme Court has required in general that if a birth father's rights are to be terminated, he must receive notice of the adoption proceedings. The notice must provide in clear language that unless the birth father communicates his opposition to the court, his rights will be forfeited forever. It must state how much time he has to act and how he can communicate his opposition. The time period in which to respond is usually ten to forty-five days, depending on the state. If he is opposed to the adoption, he must usually communicate this in writing to the court or appear at the adoption hearing. At this point the adoption is classified as a contested adoption.

WORST-CASE SCENARIOS

Most adoptions go through smoothly. Sometimes, however, questions about the identity or whereabouts of the birth father can lead to serious complications. One—fortunately rare—illustration has to do with the naming of the birth father. A birth mother can name any man as the birth father. So long as he signs the consent or surrender, and the true genetic father is not in the picture, there is no problem. But if she or the real birth father changes her or his mind, the birth mother who has given an irrevocable surrender (or whose rights have been terminated in court) can ask the "real" birth father to come forward and ask for the child back. In other words, a dishonest birth mother can ask her cousin Vinny or some friend to say he is the birth father, use his name on the birth certificate, and ask him to give consent or sign surrender documents. Then if she changes her mind, all she has to do is ask the true birth father to identify himself and say that the birth mother miscalculated her menstrual cycles and that he would like the child back. The birth parents' surrenders mean nothing if the genetic father is not the person giving surrender. This situation does not often come up, but it high-lights the need to focus on a birth mother's honesty.

Another scenario that can create problems is when there is an unnamed "out of the picture" birth father. This is usually a man who had sexual relations with the birth mother but has had no more contact with her and did not know she was pregnant. If, fourteen months after conception, he suddenly finds out the child was placed for adoption, he may decide that he wants to raise the child himself.

This came up in New York in the case of *Robert O. v. Russell K.* The birth father had learned two years after placement that the birth mother, with whom he had sexual relations, had become pregnant, delivered the baby, and placed the child with an adoptive couple. He brought the matter to court, stating that had he known she was pregnant, he would have wanted to parent the child. The court ruled that a birth father's "opportunity to manifest his willingness" to parent a child after his birth must be of short duration because of a societal need for adoptions to be finalized promptly and efficiently. It further declared that "promptness is measured in terms of the baby's life, not by the onset of the father's awareness" that a child was born to a woman with whom he had sexual relations. In *Robert O.* the court stated the birth father was too late; he had an obligation to confirm whether the birth mother became pregnant after the relationship. Since he did not, it was in the best interests of the child to remain with the adoptive couple.

In sharp contrast is a 1990 North Carolina case, *Adoption of Clark,* in which the birth father was in a Marine boot camp in another state and did not know of his child's birth and placement. The agency, which knew his identity but not his whereabouts, did not attempt to locate him and notify him of the proposed place-ment. The court recognized that the birth mother had withheld information from the adoption agency as to the birth father's whereabouts, but ruled that the agency had failed to exercise "due diligence" in seeking out the birth father and notifying him of the adoption proceedings. In other words, the agency hadn't tried hard enough. The horror of this case, as pointed out by one of the justices who disagreed with the decision, is that the litigation had lasted six years, during which time the child lived with his adoptive parents. The ruling did not consider whether it would be in the child's best interests to remain with the only parents he had ever known. Sadly, North Carolina is not the only state that fails to consider the child's best interests if the birth father's rights have not been properly termi-nated under state law, even when it can be shown that a child has bonded with a couple and will suffer psychological and emotional harm by being taken from his home. It seems to defy logic when a child who is flourishing with an adoptive couple for several years is turned over to a birth father she knows hardly, if at all.

The California courts have articulated a standard that a birth father's parental rights cannot be terminated if he is exercising due diligence in pursuing custody of his child, unless it can be shown that he is an unfit parent. In one case the California Supreme Court stated that it would not presume "either as a policy or factual matter, that adoption is necessarily in a child's best interest," going on to say that a child's best interest is not automatically enhanced because a birth mother places him with an adoptive couple instead of the birth father (*Kelsey S.*, 1992). Having made this judgment, however, the court then goes on to say that all factors must be considered in deciding whether a birth father is fit, including a father's actions prior to and after birth. At the time he knows or should have known about the birth, he must present himself as one who can and will assume full custody. If there is any hesitation or lack of ability to parent, this will be held against him. Practically speaking, this covers most cases.

Nevertheless, it is clear that the birth father's rights cannot be ignored and that his status must be resolved as expeditiously as possible. Although his rights are as viable as the birth mother's, they weaken with time if he does not assert them or act upon them either during the pregnancy or after the birth of his child. As the Arizona Supreme Court stated, "an unwed father's parental rights do not attain fundamental constitutional status unless he takes significant steps to create a parental relationship...for, in the child's eyes, a valiant but failed attempt to create a relationship means little" (*Appeal in Pima County Juvenile Severance Action*, 1994).

Chapter Nine

Openness in Adoption

O penness in adoption means communication between you and the birth parents, primarily after placement of your child in your home and after finalization of the adoption. This can range from sending your attorney pictures and progress notes about the baby for him to forward to the birth mother, to having the birth mother visit you and the baby at your home and perhaps even celebrate holidays with you. Openness can consist of contact for a very short period of time—six months—to contact for a period of several years.

In most adoptions openness is fairly minimal, but attitudes are changing. More adoptive couples are becoming comfortable about sharing the details of their child's life with the birth mother. There are, it is true, situations in which openness would not be appropriate, some of which are discussed in chapter 14, "Special Needs Adoption." And for many children who are adopted internationally, there is little, if any, possibility of maintaining an open relationship with the birth parents. But in most other cases, open adoption is coming to be seen as a healthy alternative to the anonymity and secrecy of the past.

IS OPEN ADOPTION FOR YOU?

Couples involved in an open adoption will want to attend workshops and read books to learn as much as possible. Although it is important to agree on a plan for openness before the adoption takes place, adoptive parents must be willing to allow the openness to be an evolutionary process and not a specific set of terms. In most cases the adoptive couple and the birth parents get together more when the children are young; the need for openness usually dissipates over time. You may want to ask yourself how you would feel if the birth mother visited the child the first year and then did not visit after that. Or, to turn the question around, how would you feel if the birth mother wanted to visit more often than originally planned? Will you feel a sense of entitlement to your child? Would you worry that the birth mother might interfere too much?

OPEN ADOPTION—ADVANTAGES

Open adoptions are a relatively new phenomenon, and we lack models for them. Advocates point out that the secrecy associated with closed adoptions has been detrimental to all involved—concluding that if closed adoption is bad, open adoptions must be good. However, there is more anecdotal information than hard evidence to back this up. Indeed, there is no question that open adoption can sometimes be difficult. The fact that a birth mother chooses you does not guarantee that you and she will have a wonderful, communicative relationship, even if you all initially agree on the level of openness you want.

This is why it is best to allow the relationship to evolve. For example, you may initially agree that you will talk on the phone and send letters and photographs. If you and she find that the relationship is very comfortable, you may want to meet without the baby. From that meeting you may decide that she can come to your home to meet the baby.

Open adoption offers psychological advantages for everyone concerned: birth parents, adoptive parents, and child. To the birth mother, for instance, it offers the opportunity:

- To resolve many of her feelings as she grieves placing her child for adoption
- To have peace of mind
- To see firsthand the kind of family the child lives in
- To know the status of the baby's health
- To minimize her fears and insecurities
- To be part of the adoption process
- To have an honest and realistic picture of the child, not an idyllic fantasy

It allows the adoptive parents:

- To see the birth parents' traits firsthand, including physical appearance, intellectual abilities, personality, and skills
- To assess the birth parents accurately instead of fantasizing about them
- To have fewer fears and insecurities about the birth mother
- To answer the child's questions about why the birth mother placed the child for adoption and about the birth mother's love for her child

Finally, it allows the adoptee:

- To understand her biological roots.
- Not to feel that her life is filled with "secrets."
- To know the circumstances surrounding her placement. This allows her to move beyond the sense of rejection that can occur in a closed adoption.
- To grieve the loss of biological parents. Unlike adoptive parents, who choose to adopt, the child does not choose to have no biological link with her family. It just happens.
- To have a more realistic picture of the birth parents instead of fantasizing about an ideal parent.
- To know that she was born and did not just arrive on planet Earth. This may seem simplistic, but it is very important for a child to know that she was born as well as adopted.
- To have a medical family history. As the birth parents' families age, their medical histories can give the adoptee a better picture of her genetic history. The child's birth parents and grandparents will probably be healthy at the time of the child's birth, because they are young. But they may later develop genetically linked health problems. This knowledge could help save an adoptee's life down the road.

OPEN ADOPTION—DISADVANTAGES

Given the emotional factors associated with adoption, it is not surprising to learn that there may be stress in most open adoption relationships. Expectations, for example, can sometimes evolve to an uncomfortable point. You and the birth parents may both agree to one set of expectations at the baby's birth, only to find the birth parents pushing for more openness than you want later on. Especially if the birth mother is a teenager, she may have unrealistic expectations about her role in your family, expecting in some way to become a part of your family—to be "adopted." These expectations may be more apparent in girls who have families with profound problems and who view the adoptive couple as the perfect family.[1]

Another problem associated with open adoption is that the birth mother may not properly grieve for the loss, because she does not fully experience the adoption as a loss.[2]

Of course, there is always the possibility that the birth mother will not want an open relationship; many do not. If so, you cannot coerce her into one. A birth mother does have the right to place a child for adoption, grieve the loss, and move on with her life. In fact, in a survey of fifty-nine biological mothers (aged sixteen to forty-five years) who placed a child for adoption through an agency, it was found that those who chose an open adoption felt *more* social isolation and despair, and expressed more dependency, than those who opted for a confidential adoption.[3] Although it could be that these particular women simply had more difficulties, it could also be that open adoption prevented them from "moving on" in their lives.

Finally there's no denying that some birth mothers are more "together" than others. Although we have enjoyed working with nearly all of our birth mothers, not all have been stable people. Having said that, not one who knew the address and phone number has ever yet shown up at the adoptive parents' home. One birth mother, who does have a mental illness, did call the adoptive parents once and harass them, but after that incident, all other limited communication between them was cordial.

In other words, even when there was a history of mental illness or instability, no birth mother has ever caused problems in any of the adoptive couples' lives. Even so, just knowing that a birth mother's mood can swing can cause some people so much consternation that they find themselves living in a state of "what if."

LEGAL CONSIDERATIONS

In most states a signed agreement between you and the birth parents to maintain an open adoption is not legally binding. Where states have addressed the issue of open adoption rights, only one-third have held that open adoption agreements are valid and that they do not go against public policy so long as the openness is in the child's best interest. The cases in which openness was allowed came as a result of a lawsuit in which birth parents wanted to challenge the adoption. In these cases visitations were allowed in exchange for dropping the lawsuit.[4]

HOW OPEN IS OPEN?

When you first make contact with a birth mother, all you will know about each other is your first names. As you become more comfortable with each other, you and she may want to share last names too. Then, if you decide to correspond directly with each other, you will exchange addresses and perhaps telephone numbers. (Note: In a few states you are legally required to reveal your last names and addresses to the birth parents, in which case anonymity is no longer an issue.)

If you are not comfortable sharing such information, or if the birth mother is from another state, you may arrange for all contact to be handled through your attorney's office. Your attorney may include this service as part of the adoption arrangement, or he may charge extra each time his staff handles correspondence and telephone calls. The fee for such services should be reasonable.

Remember, no matter how careful you and the birth parents are about retaining your anonymity, it is all too easy for a professional to slip and reveal your last names. If your attorney's staff is accustomed to addressing you as Mr. and Mrs. Sanders, for example, they will have to change gears to refer to you as Chuck and Doris when speaking to the birth mother. Forgetting to conceal last names on documents is another common slip. Mistakes do get made. We've often known the judge who presides over the court hearing to reveal the last names of the birth parents.

STAYING IN TOUCH

There are various ways to maintain openness in an adoption arrangement. Here are some of the most common.

Correspondence

Many couples exchange letters and photographs with birth mothers. Most birth mothers want to maintain some level of correspondence, at least for the child's first year of life. Letters telling of the baby's progress are usually sent at Christmas and the baby's birthday. You may want to send a note once a month along with a picture, especially during the baby's first year.

Sending Pictures

Nearly all birth mothers want pictures and letters sent to them. Even those who did not make an adoption decision but had the child removed from them want to know that the "child is all right," and pictures are the most obvious way— short of seeing the child in person—of knowing that she is alive and well. Videotapes are very easy to produce, and a growing number of adoptive parents and birth parents exchange them.

The birth mother may likewise send you pictures of herself, her family, and the birth father. These can be important keepsakes for your child.

Telephone Calls

Calling the birth mother, or having her call you, will probably occur more spontaneously than an arrangement to send letters and pictures, but adoptive parents could agree to call the birth mother once a month or so to let her know how they and the baby are doing. The birth mother could also have permission to call the adoptive parents for information about the baby. If this is too personal, she could call your attorney's office for information about the baby; then the attorney's office personnel could call you and get a verbal progress report to pass along.

Sometimes a birth mother just does not want to communicate with the adoptive parents. Perhaps she is living with a boyfriend or husband, someone she does not want to know about her past. In such cases it is sometimes a relative of the birth mother who stays in touch.

Exchanging Gifts

A birth mother or her family may want to give the baby a special gift, perhaps one with sentimental value. This can be a special keepsake to share with your child to let her know that the birth mother cared very much about her.

After the adoption is finalized, you are permitted to send the birth mother a gift. (It may be illegal to do so before then in your state.) You may want to give her a token to remember you by.

Exchanging Other Mementos

Some birth mothers may request other sentimental tokens from you. Our younger daughter's birth mother asked that we send her a lock of hair when she got her first haircut. Other personal tokens can be the child's "artwork," or one of the child's favorite dolls or rattles after she has outgrown it. Some people like to send a special book, a Bible, or jewelry.

Sample Letters

Following are samples of the kinds of letters that you or your child's sibling may want to send to the birth mother. *Always respond to a letter sent to you from the birth mother.*

LETTER FOR BIRTH MOTHER WHEN SHE RELINQUISHES CHILD TO YOU

Dear Cindy,

Thank you so much for all that you have done for us. Your love and commitment to David's well-being are magnificent, and the joy that he will add to our lives is immeasurable.

We loved David before we even met him, and we look forward to caring for him and sharing our lives with him. He will truly be a special person—not just for the love that we will provide him, but for the love that you have expressed in making plans for his life.

Christopher is already so excited about the campsites and ball games that he wants to take David to. I have to remind him that it will be a few years before David will be playing ball and camping.

Cindy, Christopher and I wish you well in your education. You have been so diligent in all that you have done. I trust that you will find just the right job when you graduate from school next year.

You will certainly always be a part of our lives and in our prayers. We truly love you for all that you have done. Do keep in touch. As we have promised, I will send you lots of pictures of David each month. (I can hardly wait to start photographing our beautiful baby.)

Do take care, Cindy, and I will write to you next month.

All our love,

Sharon, Christopher, and David

LETTER TO A BIRTH MOTHER WHEN CHILD IS SIX MONTHS OLD

Dear Jenny,

I can hardly believe that James is six months old. He is now starting to creep and to make the funniest sounds. He is very alert and loves to watch his older sister play. James especially loves music. When Jodi's singing her favorite nursery rhymes, he nearly hums along with her while his body rocks back and forth. Sometimes I play some lively classical music, and again, his body sways to the music. Everyone says James is very good-natured.

Enclosed are pictures from Thanksgiving. We had a wonderful day at my parents' home in the country. All thirteen of James's cousins were there. My favorite picture is Tom holding James next to the turkey. The turkey and James weighed about the same—20 pounds.

We and all the relatives will be back at my parents' house again for Christmas. As soon as we get pictures of James's first Christmas, I will send them to you.

Jenny, I trust you are doing well. I was very pleased to hear about your new adventures. Please continue to keep us updated about your activities and plans.

Thank you so much for the letter and pictures you sent James. We will keep them in a very special place for him. Someday James will know how blessed he is that you loved him enough to make adoption plans for his life.

John and I trust that you will have a warm and special Christmas. We understand that this time of year may be difficult for you. You have made a very difficult but loving decision, and I hope you are especially comforted knowing that James is loved immensely by us and his relatives.

We'll look forward to hearing from you.

Love,

Sandy and John

LETTER FROM CHILD'S SIBLING TO BIRTH MOTHER

Dear Stephanie's birth mother,

Thank you for giving us a baby sister. She is so cute. We love her and we love you. Mommy and Daddy said you are a really nice person. We will take good care of her.

Love,

Jason and Brian

Resources:

The Adoption Connections Project is a group of women dedicated to bringing together birth mothers, adopted daughters, adoptive mothers, foster mothers, and stepmothers. They have a Web site at **http://www.sover.net/~adopt**, or you can contact Susan Wadia-Ellis at **adopt@sover.net**.

To subscribe to the Open Adoption Mailing List, address your message to **majordomo@chrystal.com**. In the body of the message put: subscribe openadoption. The mailing list is a friendlly, informative place to discuss various issues related to open adoption, and should be of interest to people who are involved in open adoption.

Chapter Ten

Single-Parent Adoption

I f you have made the decision to become a single parent, you are not alone. In 1990, 170,000 single women over the age of thirty gave birth. Most were in their mid-thirties, well-educated, financially secure, and concerned that they had few years left in which to have children. They often planned for a baby for several years by saving, buying a house in a neighborhood with a good school system, and even changing jobs so that they could spend more time with a child.[1]

According to Shirley Roe, a single mother who adopted from China and the former copresident of RESOLVE of Greater Hartford, Connecticut, adoption is now very possible for single people, even adoption of young babies. Whereas in the past unmarried individuals may have been restricted to adopting older children, new flexible policies in China and other countries mean that babies are available to single parents. Even domestic agencies are broadening their policies and allowing singles to adopt.

At least one study suggests that being single has little, if any, effect on adoption outcome. Single-parent families were shown to be as nurturing and viable as dual-parent families. In fact, without the demands of a marital relationship, a single parent may be better equipped to give the level of involvement and nurturing needed by a child who has had severely damaging experiences. Mature single parents can offer a child many benefits.

Having said that, no study is needed to highlight the fact that being a single parent has many drawbacks as well. Juggling a full-time job and a child is a daunting task requiring both maturity and resources. Single parents can often provide these things, and certainly from the child's standpoint having one stable, loving parent is better than living in an orphanage or institution, or being bounced from one two-parent foster home to another. But the challenges are considerable, and it is essential to consider them carefully before taking this step.

WHAT TO ASK YOURSELF

Jane Mattes, founder of Single Mothers by Choice, recommends that you begin by asking yourself whether you are ready to become a parent and whether you are seeking parenthood for the right reasons. The following questions are ones she has drawn up to help singles explore these issues. Answering them will also help to make you more prepared for the home study process.

1. Have you accomplished all the personal and career goals that are necessary for you to feel good about yourself? How will you feel if you are not able to achieve some of these goals?

2. How will you feel about some people being critical of your decision to be a single parent?

3. Are you able to support yourself and a child emotionally and financially?

4. Do you have elderly parents who may need your assistance just at the time that you will be devoting yourself to a baby or young child?

5. Do you understand why you are not with a partner, and how this will affect your relationship with your child?

6. If you still feel the need to date often, how will you feel about working, dating, and caring for a child? How will a child affect your likelihood of finding a mate? Can you make a distinction between which needs can be fulfilled by a child and which ones can be fulfilled only by a spouse?

7. Do you have a good support system of friends, family, church/synagogue, and work to help you during stressful times? If you do not have family who can care for the child, are you prepared for the twenty-four-hour-a-day responsibility of caring for a child with no assistance except from friends and paid child care?

8. Is your job flexible enough so that you can meet the child's needs when he is sick, has a special event, or needs extra attention?

9. How do you handle stress? Will you be able to meet the challenge of caring for a baby while working? Will your coping skills enable you to deal with the stressful situations that having a child will bring, like a baby crying all night, ear infections, etc.?

10. If you are considering adopting an older child, are you prepared to meet the child's special emotional needs and issues? Do you have time to take a child to a therapist in addition to Girl Scouts and other school and community activities?[2]

OPTIONS FOR SINGLE PARENTS

Although some courts have stated that to promote the welfare of the child, parents should be married, most agencies and courts do not make marital status alone the basis for assessing parenting skills. More than 15.5 million children in the United States are being raised by single-parent families, and although a societal goal may be to promote two-parent families, without evidence that children are harmed by unmarried adopters, states should not discourage single-parent adoption.

Yet adoption professionals do have difficulty placing children in single-parent homes. One reason is that statistically, single-parent families produce children who have far more problems than children who are raised by a mother and father. Although these statistics are based on the experiences of poor, undereducated teenage moms with minimal parenting skills and inadequate plans for the future, rather than those of older, well-educated women with well-paying jobs, experience with children, and goals for the future, they can make it hard for a birth mother to accept a single woman as a potential adopter. After all, if the agency professional has been making the case that the birth mother's child needs to be raised in a more stable environment with a mother and father, how easy will it be for her to turn around and present a single mother as a potential adopter?

The argument about whether a child is better off with an adoptive mom than his teenage birth mother has become a class issue, diverting participants from focusing on what is better for the child. Many articles have been written to suggest that adopters are in a class tug-of-war with women who cannot afford their children. From the agency's standpoint, presenting a two-parent family to a birth mother is a way of staying out of this battle. The practical reality, however, cannot be glossed over by talk of "class tug-of-wars." More often than not single adoptive mothers do have the maturity, the financial wherewithal, and the support system to provide a healthier environment for a child than a teenage mother.

Of course, even if the single adoptive mother has these things, a birth mother is still likely to be concerned. If she has had lots of boyfriends—no matter how destructive or otherwise unsuccessful the relationships were—she will wonder, "What's wrong with this woman, and why couldn't she find a husband?" Birth mothers are more open to a single adoptive mother if she is divorced, widowed, or presently involved with a man. If the birth mother senses that the adoptive mother will eventually marry, she may be more open to placing her newborn child with her.

Agency Adoption

In *How to Adopt a Child*, Connie Crain and Janice Duffy warn that some domestic agencies will accept the single person's up-front fees and then stall the adoption process. They will seldom show your profile to birth mothers, so that there will never be an opportunity for a birth mother to select you. Duffy and Crain suggest talking to other single parents who have adopted through the agency you are considering to see how long it took them to adopt.[3] Lois Gilman further cautions that "Singles often find that agencies will not allow them to apply to adopt healthy infants and younger children. Many agencies will tell them bluntly that these children are reserved for two-parent families and will encourage them to consider special needs children instead."[4]

Independent Adoption

Single adoptive mothers will encounter roadblocks in the independent adoption process as well. In this country most birth mothers do not choose to place their children with single parents. Their attitude is, "If she (the adoptive mom) can raise a child by herself, then so can I." When a birth mother makes the decision to place a child, she wants a home with more resources than she can provide, and to her this means a father and a mother.

Some birth mothers, however—especially those who grew up in single-parent homes or who already have one child and are able to maintain a family life of sorts—believe that the stability of family life is determined solely by the issue of income. Their experiences tell them that a single mom can provide a suitable home for a child if her income level is adequate to do so. In fact, many birth mothers' experiences are positive enough that they would parent the children born to them if their cash flow warranted it.

The reality is that very, very few successful agency and independent adoptions involve single mothers. Although it is not impossible, prospective adoptive mothers need to know that the image of a "June and Ward Cleaver" family strongly dominates the typical birth mother's thinking.

Special Needs Adoption

It should surprise no one to learn, however, that agencies that place children with special needs are usually very accepting of single adoptive parents, so long as they have an income sufficient to meet the child's needs. Most social services departments will not allow you to adopt if the child's monthly subsidy from the state is going to be your main source of income.

Single people parenting special needs children may have fewer resources than a two-parent family, and yet these children usually require extra resources.

Many single people, however, can meet the demands of a special needs child very well, especially one whose behavior improves as a result of the one-on-one attention and understanding single parents can provide. Indeed, children who come from chaotic backgrounds and have been physically and sexually abused often do better in single-parent homes where the family dynamics are simplified.

International Adoption

The great majority of adoptive single parents have adopted internationally. Many countries now permit single people to adopt, especially women thirty-five and older. As with any adoption, you must prove to the Immigration and Naturalization Service that you can afford the child and provide adequately for him.

THE HOME STUDY PROCESS

If you are a single person about to arrange for a home study, you can expect to be asked to address issues related to marriage, including what plans if any you may have for marriage, how marriage would change your relationship with the child, and how being a single parent might change your prospects for marriage. If you answer that you would consider marriage, the caseworker may want to know what kind of a person you would seek to marry. Or you may be asked about your living arrangements and whether you are gay or lesbian.

It is crucial that you understand as quickly as possible during the home study process what bias the caseworker may have against you as a single prospective adoptive mother. Tune in to any common theme in the caseworker's questions. General questions about your employment, for example—hours, responsibilities, stress level, etc.—may lead to the all-important issue of child-care arrangement, and you may be expected to address arrangements in greater detail than a married couple, even where both of them plan to work. The caseworker will want to know whether you will have any time and energy left over from the workday for your child.

ADOPTION FOR SINGLE MEN

Crain and Duffy write that men have a much more difficult time than women adopting children. In the first place, they are not perceived as nurturing, and in the second, their motives are questioned. Simply put, they are suspected of being child molesters. (After all, most known child molesters are men.) Single men over thirty years of age are often assumed to be gay. To get around this, Crain and Duffy suggest that you take a personality test so that you can prove you are "normal." They point out that boys who need a strong male role model, firm discipline, and guidance have been proven to do well with single fathers—especially boys with emotional problems.[5]

The discrimination is most apparent in international adoption, since many countries that permit single women to adopt will not permit single men. Check with an international adoption agency or attorney to find out what countries will accept single men.

Resources:

Committee for Single Adoptive Parents
PO Box 15084
Chevy Chase, MD 20815

National Council for Single Adoptive Partents
http://www.adopting.org/ncsap.html
Provides help and support for single women and men looking to adopt.

Single Parents Adopting Children Everywhere (SPACE)
6 Sunshine Avenue
Natick, MA 01760
(508) 655-5426

Single Mothers by Choice
PO Box 1642
New York, NY 10028
(212) 988-0993

This national organization provides support and information to single women. It publishes a quarterly newsletter and local membership directories.

SingleMOTHER
PO Box 68
Midland, NC 28107
(704) 888-KIDS

Publishes a bimonthly newsletter for divorced, widowed, and never married mothers. Has local chapters.

Single Parents with Adopted Kids
Dannette Kaslow—SWAK
4108 Washington Road #101
Kenosha, WI 53144

A newsletter for singles with adopted children that is produced four times a year.

Curto, Josephine J. *How to Become a Single Parent: A Guide for Single People Considering Adoptions or Natural Parenthood Alone*. Englewood Cliffs, NJ: Prentice-Hall, 1983.

Mattes, Jane. *Single Mothers by Choice*. New York, NY: Random House, 1994.

ADOPTION FOR GAYS AND LESBIANS

Court cases involving adoption by gays and lesbians have been making news headlines. Most of these situations involve one partner adopting the biological child of the other. Some courts have ruled, for example, that a lesbian may adopt the child of a partner who became pregnant through donor insemination. In fact, it is very rare for two same-sex partners to adopt a child of no biological relationship. In the first place, gays and lesbians make up only about 2 percent of the population, and couples only a fraction of this group. Among couples, only a small percentage is interested in adopting.

Although most states do not permit unmarried couples to adopt, only two states—New Hampshire and Florida—have an outright ban on gay adoptions. South Carolina is also considering a ban. Some states, like New York, New Jersey, Vermont, Minnesota, and California, allow gay adoption, but most cases involve the partner of a biological parent. Although some gays and lesbians adopt children as single parents—usually harder-to-place children—their partners usually do not adopt the children.

Most agencies that place infants with adoptive parents allow the birth mothers a role in the selection of the adoptive parents, and most birth mothers want a traditional two-parent family for their children. An agency whose policy is to present a few prospective adoptive parents' portfolios to a birth mother will hesitate to offer a portfolio of a gay or lesbian couple, for fear of giving offense. It is a rare birth mother who walks into an agency and says that she wants to place the child with a gay couple. The few agencies that still place infants with adoptive parents without much input from the birth mothers are traditional organizations, usually ones with a strong religious orientation. This kind of agency is not likely to approve a gay or lesbian couple to adopt a child.

Attorneys who do direct placements will experience the same kinds of responses from birth mothers. Finding a birth mother who feels enthusiastic about gay or lesbian adoptive parents is difficult. Sometimes gay and lesbian couples place ads in some of the more avant-garde newspapers, hoping to attract a birth mother, and this is not a bad strategy, although probably still a long shot. But they will encounter other obstacles besides finding a birth mother.

First the couple will have to find an agency/social worker willing to approve their home study. Second—if the case law permits such an adoption in their state—the judge who conducts the adoption must view the adoption as being in the best interest of the child. If the couple is in one state and the baby is in another, Interstate Compact approval will also be necessary, which means getting two states involved.

In most states gays and lesbians can adopt through a public agency, though an exception would very likely be made with a child who had a history of neglect and abuse, including sexual abuse. Then an agency may feel that the child would be better off in a traditional two-parent home or a single-parent home, so that as he deals with the difficulties in overcoming his abusive background, he does not also have to deal with the issues of coming from a lesbian or gay home. In all cases, the agency will want to consider the impact living in a nontraditional family will have on the child. Special needs children have usually lived chaotic lives filled with emotional pain. To place them in a gay or lesbian home may mean more emotional challenges as they seek to integrate their home experience with their lives in the world at large.

What about international adoption? At first this might seem like an option for gay and lesbian couples, since there are so many children who need a home and since single parents are now permitted to adopt in many countries. However, many countries will not permit this. Certainly there are lesbian women who adopt children without disclosing their sexuality in the home study. If their partner wishes to adopt the child, however, they must seek a joint readoption once the child is in the United States.

ADOPTION FOR UNMARRIED COUPLES

Except in rare cases—Woody Allen and Mia Farrow come to mind—unmarried couples are usually not permitted to adopt. Unlike gay and lesbian couples, for whom marriage is not an option, marriage for heterosexual couples usually is as simple as getting a license and saying "I do." For this reason, even where unmarried couples are permitted to adopt, the question of why two people do not get married will be a focal point in the home study process, and the commitment level of the two prospective adoptive parents closely scrutinized. Because the stability of the couple's relationship is essential to approving a home study, an agency caseworker would find it difficult to approve such a home study. A social worker conducting a home study for a private adoption, however, may simply write up the home study without strongly addressing these issues.

However, courts are beginning to allow unmarried couples to adopt in certain situations. This is particularly true in states that recognize common-law marriages; that is, if a couple has been together for a certain time period, then the state recognizes their relationship as a marriage. The key components in evaluating an unmarried couple's fitness for adoption are the longevity of their relationship and whether they are stable people and committed to each other and to having children. For example, one court judge in South Carolina approved an adoption of a hard-to-place child with an unmarried couple who had lived together for seven years.

Chapter Eleven

Relative and Stepparent Adoption

The most common form of adoption in the United States is a stepparent adoption, in which the child of the biological parent is adopted by that parent's spouse. A relative, or "intrafamily," adoption is usually defined as one close relative, and possibly that person's spouse, adopting another relative. This child can be related to the wife or the husband (as is the case with a niece or nephew) or to both (as with a grandchild). The degree of relationship permitted varies from state to state.

Unlike other adoptions, in general, one does not plan to become a parent through stepparent or intrafamily adoption; the adoption occurs because of other circumstances in your life. Neither do people set a goal for themselves of becoming stepparents. Instead, marriage to a particular person is a package that includes children. A stepparent often wants to make an investment in the child's life, and the child and parent believe that it is important to cement that commitment through adoption.

About 8 percent of all adoptions in the United States are relative adoptions. According to statistics gathered from the National Center for State Courts, 42 percent of all adoptions are stepparent adoptions and just over 50 percent are either stepparent or intrafamily adoptions.[1] The two kinds, although quite different from each other, follow similar laws within each state.

In many states a home study is not required for a relative or stepparent adoption. When one is required, it is often conducted in a simplified form and is mainly intended to confirm that the placement was voluntary and that the adoptive family is functional and can provide for the child. The adoption is viewed as a family matter. Having children is a fundamental right that extends to family members who adopt the child, so long as the child is not abused or neglected. However, one very important component of the home study is educating the adoptive couple about adoption-related issues. If the home study is not done, the educational opportunity is missed. That education may be all the more important in a relative or intrafamily adoption because the adoption issues may be more complex. Since families involved in stepparent and intrafamily adoptions do not usually seek out adoption information, there may be no other such opportunity.

ADOPTION BY RELATIVES

As a rule, the relatives included in the definition of an intrafamily adoption are the child's grandparents, aunts, uncles, and siblings. Children are placed with relatives at different ages and for different reasons. Often a girl or woman becomes pregnant and wants to place the child for adoption, and another family member who cannot have a biological child adopts him. As with any other infant adoption, in this situation the birth mother (and perhaps the birth father) makes a decision to place a child for adoption because her life circumstances make it difficult to raise a child.

There are obvious advantages and disadvantages to relative adoptions. One long-term benefit is that the child can grow up with his biological relatives and have a stronger connection to his genetic background—so long as the child is aware that he has been adopted within his biological family. It may also be easier to have more consistent contact with the birth mother so that the child can know his birth mother's health history.

A legal advantage to a relative adoption is that the adoption itself is usually less complicated than an independent or agency adoption, and in some states the laws are more lax. In the four states where independent adoption is illegal, it is all right to pursue a relative adoption, although a home study may be required, and if the child is born in one state and you live in another, you will not have to go through Interstate Compact.

The disadvantages of relative adoption can be more or less pronounced depending on the birth mother's location and situation and how the rest of the family handles the adoption. If she is a close relative and lives very close by, you may be concerned that she will want to share in parenting decisions. If you have a difficult relationship with her, you may worry about her interfering or saying inappropriate things to your child. A woman's reasons for placing a child for adoption can also influence how she feels about setting boundaries. For example, an older sister who is divorced and already has four kids would probably have a very different attitude from the fifteen-year-old cousin who places a baby with you. Your sister, because she is older and a mother already, may feel that she has a right to give input about the raising of your adopted child—her birth child.

If you have such concerns, they need to be discussed up front. Sometimes attitudes can be deduced from comments by the birth mother and other family members and from the way the birth mother has handled other situations. If she is very unstable, you may need to create some distance between her and your immediate family once the child is born. Remember, unlike other birth mothers, she will probably always know where you live.

Other family members may feel the need to give their advice as well. You may find yourself pressured by suggestions and negative comments made by other family members. Although you want your family's support in your adoption decision, all communication should be between you and the birth mother. For example, if your mother tells you that she was talking to your Aunt Edna, and Aunt Edna mentioned that her teenage daughter, your cousin Tracy, is pregnant and wants to make adoption plans, and your mother told Aunt Edna that you may be interested, your Aunt Edna and Mom may feel that they should be privy to all future conversations between you and your cousin. It is nice that your mom took the initial step to "feel out" the situation, but the remaining communication needs to be between you and your cousin. Of course, her parents, your aunt and uncle, may be involved because of the birth mother's age. This no longer is an issue between your mother and aunt, however; it is between you and the birth mother.

If you were adopting a nonrelative, you might well share with your parents details of your conversations with a birth mother and how all the plans were going. In an intrafamily adoption, you need to protect your privacy as well as the birth mother's. This means setting up very clear boundaries, if possible without hurting anyone's feelings. Let family members know, very tactfully, that you are glad they are concerned but that you want your cousin Tracy to be able to make her plans as she sees best. You would not want to say anything to anyone that would influence her decision or make her upset. Remind them that it is important to protect Tracy's privacy. If she wants to share information with others, that is her decision.

You will also want to establish some boundaries with the birth mother if she does live close by and if you normally see her for family gatherings and holidays. Having her remain in your life as much as she was before the child was placed with you can be appropriate, but because you will need to feel entitlement to the child, there may need to be limited contact initially.

What if the birth mother changes her mind? A woman named Katie who was in her late thirties wanted to have another child with her second husband, but infertility problems prevented her. When her son's girlfriend became pregnant, it was decided that the child would be placed with Katie and her husband. Toward the end of the pregnancy, however, the birth mother changed her mind. Katie and her husband were very disappointed. It was difficult, because they felt they could not express their disappointment to the girlfriend since they wanted to have a relationship with the child as the child's grandparents. They had already prepared a nursery in anticipation of adopting the child. They kept the nursery instead in anticipation of their grandchild. Once the child was born, the grandparents had to be careful that they maintained appropriate boundaries. Otherwise, in time, the child's mother might have come to see the grandparents as full-time babysitters, rationalizing leaving the child with them for extended periods by saying to herself that they were going to adopt the baby anyway.

How to Tell Your Child

Unfortunately, because a relative adoption is so close, some adoptive parents do not share with the child that he is adopted. Perhaps they assume it is not important, since the child is already "family" and he already "knows" his birth mother—even though he does not know, for example, that his older sister is also his biological mother. Or they tell the child that he is adopted but leave out the fact that his aunt Jane is also his biological mother. However, this can create problems in the future, since the lie conceals the child's genetic background.

When children are adopted, a birth mother has a dual role: one of biological parent and one of relative. According to Sharon Kaplan Roszia, it is best in these cases that a child call the adoptive parents "Mom" and "Dad' and the birth mother "Aunt" or whatever relation she is to the child based on the child's adoption.[2]

Using a Private Attorney

Nearly all stepparent and intrafamily adoptions are handled independently. An agency cannot file papers for you, so most people file the necessary legal documents through their attorney. Because most stepparent and relative adoptions are uncomplicated, nearly any competent attorney can facilitate the adoption. However, if you think that the adoption may be contested, you will want to retain an experienced adoption attorney. These are the steps that must take place before the adoption can be finalized:

1. Depending on what state you live in, you, the adoptive parents, may need to have a home study, a child abuse clearance, a criminal clearance done by your local police department or your state agency, and possibly an FBI clearance, carried out through a fingerprinting check.
2. If you are adopting an infant who will be placed with you upon her release from the hospital, the biological parents must sign consents that terminate their parental rights.
3. If the child is older and you have been caring for her but the birth parent(s) have not signed consents, they must be contacted for their

consent or at least notified of an adoption hearing so that they have the right to object to the adoption if they so choose. You may need to employ a process server to serve the papers on the biological parents. They do not have to sign anything; the papers are simply to inform them that their rights are about to be terminated and an adoption is about to take place, and that they can contact your attorney or be at court if they want to contest the adoption. Some states would require consents unless the child has resided with you for at least six months.

4. Legal papers, including a Judgment of Adoption, is filed with the courthouse in your county. A date is then given to your attorney as to when the adoption will take place.

5. You go to court to adopt the child.

Young and Older Child Placements

Most adoptions among relatives start as informal arrangements. A relative may serve as a guardian for a time, then eventually adopt the child. Knowing each other and having a blood connection can make intrafamily adoptions both easier and harder. The common heritage, family lifestyle, and traditions are already known to the child, smoothing the transition; however, in most situations in which a young or older child is placed with a relative, it is because of the parent's inability to care for him. The birth parent may be viewed negatively in the family, an attitude that can extend to the child. The relationship can be even more complicated if, for example, the husband has a very negative attitude toward his wife's sister—the biological mother of the child. When a woman adopts her incarcerated sister's baby, for instance, the husband may have ambivalent feelings over the decision, a tension that will be heightened if the wife adopted her sister's child because it was the "right" thing to do—not because she especially wanted to expand her family.

Why Relatives Choose Adoption

Adoption is not always a choice, especially in cases where it will be difficult to terminate the parents' rights. However, if the parents are willing to have their rights terminated, or if their lives are in such disarray that they would have trouble making a case for their suitability as parents, or if the social services department has declared that the relatives are the permanent foster parents, then adoption may be considered. The great advantage of adoption is permanency. Permanency not only benefits the child; the relatives are also reassured to know that the parents, whose lives are not together, cannot, on a whim, remove the child from the home. If the child was removed from his biological parents because of neglect or abuse, and the parents have not complied with the requirements for getting him back, adoption can be a message to the child that someone is going to take care of him and love him unconditionally. It also means an end to intervention by the social services department, which will no longer have the power to separate the child from the relative's home or otherwise interfere in the life of the family.

Because adoption is permanent, it usually means a severing of relationship between the child and his biological parents. Depending on the situation, this step may be too extreme. A *kinship adoption* can allow some aspects of the birth parent and child relationship to stay intact, if appropriate, by establishing a certain level of openness between the child and biological parents.

Kinship Adoption

"Kinship adoption" is an informal term used when a parent can no longer parent a child and a relative takes over that role. When children are removed from their homes because of abuse or neglect, for example, and relatives who can adequately care for the child are called upon, the term "kinship adoption" comes into use. Usually a kinship adoption is an informal arrangement between the parent and the relatives; sometimes the arrangement is more formal. For example, a social service agency will often seek out relatives to care for a child instead of placing her in a foster home. Often this makes a great deal of sense, especially if the child has had regular contact with the relatives. According to a study by the National Black Child Development Institute in 1986, when an agency asked relatives to care for the children, more than 50 percent said yes. The care of children by relatives helps preserve families, traditionally one of society's most important support systems. "Traditionally grandparents have been viewed as the keepers of the family culture and the thread that ties the family together, by providing the wisdom and emotional support that serve as the forces for continuity."[3] When it comes to adoption, however, it is important to realize that relatives are no longer automatically awarded first preference. Although the courts may decide that a family relationship best fulfills the child's interests, the family relationship itself will not be the deciding factor. The ruling is based solely on what appears to be best for the child.

According to Ann Sullivan of the Child Welfare League of America, more and more children are living with relatives in general and grandparents in particular. The reasons for this go beyond parental divorce and death to reflect a range of social ills: teenage pregnancy; joblessness; child neglect, abuse, and abandonment; incarceration of the parent; drug addiction; and diseases like AIDS. Sullivan says that only 15 percent of relatives legally adopt the children who are placed into their custody by social services departments. Many family members believe that to adopt another family member's child would cause great conflict in the family, so they do not take this step. In informal situations, in which the family is being assisted by social workers but the child is not in the custody of the child welfare agency, adoptions are particularly rejected. Most relatives see adoption as unnecessary, since the child is already with family.[4]

If you have been caring for a relative's child because the child was abused or neglected, and you decide you would like to adopt her, the public agency that first got involved in the placement can usually handle the adoption. This agency and the court must believe it is in the child's best interest for the parents' rights to be terminated and for you to adopt the child. Talk with your caseworker about the possibility of the child becoming your full charge instead of the state's responsibility. You may need to hire your own attorney to get the process moving faster and to see that your and the child's rights are fully protected.

If the agency has legal custody of the child and you have been a foster parent and receiving subsidies, you most likely will be eligible for subsidies even after the adoption takes place.

Grandparents

"In 1990 more than three million children under the age of 18 lived with their grandparents." In a third of these cases, the grandparent provided care without the assistance of the parents. One study found that 50 percent of the relatives caring for the children were grandmothers.[5]

If a girl has a child at the age of sixteen, and her parents are about twenty-five years older than she is, that means that her parents are in their early forties—an age when some couples today are beginning (or continuing) to have children. As lifestyles have changed, many grandparents in their forties and early fifties are able to take on the responsibility of caring for young children. Sometimes grandparents deliberately plan to adopt the child who is about to be born out of wedlock; for others, the decision evolves out of circumstances. If a daughter has a child at sixteen and over time realizes that the task is more than she can handle, her parents may assume more and more responsibility until they are making the major life decisions for their grandchild. At this point the grandparents may decide that adoption would be in their and the child's best interest. At least it would mean that the child could be covered by their health insurance and could receive benefits like social security.

One set of grandparents, for instance, adopted their fifteen-year-old daughter's infant, initially for legal reasons (the family was traveling internationally), even though both mom and grandparents were sharing in the parenting role. Over time, however, the grandparents took full responsibility for the child because the daughter—the child's biological mother—was doing other things in her life. Now the child is seven years old, and the grandparents are still his primary parents. He knows that he is adopted and that his "sister" is his biological mother. He calls his grandparents "Mom" and "Dad," and his birth mother by her first name.

Nancy, who is in her late thirties, says her grandparents adopted her because her mother was only fourteen years old at the time of her birth. Although her birth certificate was changed to name her maternal grandparents as her parents, her mother maintained a relationship with her, mostly by telephone, and she called her mother "Mommy." As Nancy got older and her mother matured, her mother was able to communicate with her and help Nancy make decisions. Today the two have a close relationship. They live near each other and see each other regularly.

ADOPTION BY STEPPARENTS

As divorce and out-of-wedlock rates rise, stepparenting is becoming more common. Remarriages accounted for nearly 46 percent of all marriages in 1990, compared with 31 percent in 1970. Every year more than one million children are involved in a divorce, and in several million families at least one spouse has had an out-of-wedlock child before getting married. As a result, more and more families will be made up primarily of a biological mom and stepdad. Today, nearly seven million children live in stepfamilies, making up 15 percent of all children living in a two-parent household.

Only a fraction of these stepchildren, however, are ever adopted. Why? One reason may be the ways in which general adoption laws are applied to stepparent adoptions. One study, for example, found that stepfathers wanted to adopt but thought it would be impossible because of the biological fathers' involvement in the children's life.[6] As the courts allow more flexibility in stepparent adoption, we may find more stepparent adoptions taking place.

Stepmothers/Stepfathers

Most stepparent adoptions are cases of stepfathers adopting their stepchildren. In 1988, only 11 percent of stepfamilies were made up of the biological father and the stepmother. Custodial stepmothers seldom adopt their stepchildren—even when the father is widowed.[7] Perhaps this is because the children and the stepmother all share the same last name, meaning that the stepfamily does not appear any different from a fully biological family. One study found that children tend to do better in mother/stepfather homes rather than in father/stepmother homes. Also, girls do not appear to be more disturbed than boys. The same study demonstrated that the stepparents' interpersonal relationship with the child played a crucial role in the child's academic achievement.[8]

Why Adopt Stepchildren?

Here are some of the reasons to consider adopting your stepchild or stepchildren:

1. *You will still be the child's parent should the biological parent die, become disabled, or divorce you.*
2. *Should you die or become disabled, the child will be entitled to social security benefits.*
3. *You can feel like a real parent.*
4. *The child can have a sense of permanency.* Children's security is often tied to being in a "forever" family. The adoption by a stepparent can provide this "foreverness." Adoption can provide other emotional benefits, too, if your child is from a previous marriage or relationship and you now have another child with your husband. In a situation like this, your older child may feel "second-best" because he is not your husband's child. Adoption can help him feel that he belongs permanently to both you and your husband.
5. *The child can take on her parents' last name.* If you are a woman and have taken your husband's last name, your children may still have your last name (if they were born out of wedlock) or their father's last name. Adoption means the whole family can have the same last name. If adoption is not feasible because your ex-spouse objects, you can still consider a name change. Conversely, if the child is older, she can be adopted without a name change. If the biological father has died, the child may see a name change as disloyal to the deceased parent.
6. *The child's birth certificate changes.* Unlike the simple name change that sometimes occurs in stepfamilies, with adoption the birth certificate changes to indicate the stepparent as the original parent. If the child is older (usually ten years and up), the child's permission is needed to do this.

Disadvantages of Stepparent Adoption

Here are some concerns to consider before taking the step to adopt:

1. *The stepparent may have to make child support payments in the event of a divorce.* If you are the primary wage earner and you and your spouse

divorce, you will probably be responsible for child support payments if the child lives with her mother. If your spouse were to leave you for someone else and take the children, you could still end up being responsible for child support payments.

2. *The child may feel disloyal to her noncustodial parent.* She may feel that if she is adopted she can never have a relationship with her other biological parent, and that to proceed with the adoption would be to reject that parent. Such feelings are not easily overcome.

3. *The noncustodial parent could interfere.* Trying to gain the cooperation of the noncustodial parent could turn into litigation if the parent contests the adoption. Your family also runs the risk of counterclaims by your ex-spouse if you mention your adoption plans to him.

   Contrary to what many assume, adoption does not necessarily cut off all relationship with the parent who is not living with the child. The other parent can still have visitation rights as part of the adoption agreement. Indeed, most couples who want to proceed with a stepparent adoption are not trying to get the other biological parent out of the picture. Usually the father is already out of the picture and is not paying any child support.

   Many stepparents say that they want to adopt but believe that it is impossible because of the previous spouse's interference. Check with a lawyer in your state or where the parent lives to see what his rights are. Bear in mind, however, that no matter what those rights, there is always the possibility of a dragged-out family conflict in which the child will be exposed to the problems of both of his parents.[9]

4. *Any child support being paid by the noncustodial parent would stop.* A parent who is faithfully paying child support usually cares very much about his child and is involved in her life. Many stepparents prefer not to assume full financial and legal responsibility while the noncustodial parent still has this close relationship, especially if the parent and ex-spouse have had a bitter divorce.

Grandparent Issues

You and your children may have a relationship with their grandparents even if they have little contact with their noncustodial parent. This may be especially true if the parent lives in another state while his parents live close to you and your children, or if your first spouse has died. In either case, but especially the latter, the grandparents may feel that your husband's adopting the children is removing your late husband's place in the family. It would be wise to discuss the adoption plans with them before you proceed—not to get their permission but to reassure them of the important role that they will continue to have in your children's lives.

Parent-Stepparent Issues

If a stepparent has been married to the biological parent for a year or more (in some states six months), and the other biological parent is essentially not in the child's life, you can consider adoption. If the other biological parent is involved in the child's life, the adoption can be finalized only with that parent's consent.

Children in stepfamilies are likely to have known and to have had an emotional relationship with the parent who is not living with them. In such cases there is a strong argument for establishing what is called an "open arrangement"—proceeding with adoption, but continuing at least limited contact with the noncustodial parent. This allows children to express their preference for being adopted without breaking allegiance to the biological parent who no longer lives with them. Of course, if the child has not known the biological parent, if the biological parent abused or neglected the child, or if the biological parent has never paid any child support or provided any emotional connection to the child, then an open arrangement may not serve any purpose.

If parents are pressing for an adoption, the child may feel ambivalent and confused. You will want to discuss both sides with your child, even though you may feel strongly about proceeding with the adoption. A child over the age of eight should have freedom of choice about the adoption and what last name he will use, unless the adoption is sought in an emergency. An example of this is if the mother has a life-threatening illness and wants to solidify the legal relationship between her spouse and her children in the event of her death.

If the biological parent will not consent to the adoption, you may need to wait to find grounds for termination. If several years of non–child-support payment and lack of contact are grounds for involuntary termination in your state, it would be better to wait out the time period than to initiate an adoption that might only serve to draw the biological parent back into your lives.

The best stepparent adoptions occur when the whole family wishes for the adoption as a legal means of expressing their emotional security. The least successful are those in which a child has been coerced into the decision. Sometimes when there is friction between the stepparent and child, families may suggest adoption as a way of solidifying the relationship. This is a mistake. Adoption should take place when the relationship between the child and stepparent is positive, and always with the agreement of the child.

When a child reaches adolescence, as with any child who is adopted, he may want to reexamine his adoption and ask questions about his origins, identification, and original name. He may also want to search for his biological parent. During this time it is important for his parent and adoptive parent to reassure him of their commitment to him while allowing the child to explore his identify.

For a child, living in a household with only one biological parent represents a loss. Despite the commonness of divorce and remarriage, children are well aware that the "ideal" family is made up of two parents who stay together. The divorce itself is a loss for children. If the original marriage was horrible and the noncustodial spouse was abusive or deserted the family, divorce for the child represents the lost possibility of a good biological parent. Even if the next spouse is "Mr. Wonderful" and loves the child and wants to adopt him, the child may still need to grieve for the "lost" parent, the lost marriage, and possibly the lost "ideal" parent.

You may have very negative feelings toward the parent, and your child may share those feelings. Remember, however, that just as you may have wished that your first marriage could have been better, your child will probably wish the same thing. Try to acknowledge his loss. You may say, "I wish that your dad could have been more caring, and I know it hurts you that he was not kinder. One thing that I am glad about is that you are my child and that you have another dad who really does care about you."

If your child has never met her biological parent, then she may have a need to know about him as well as a desire to meet someday. This desire on the part of a child is comparable to what is felt by those conceived through donor insemination. It is not that she wants to change anything; rather, as she matures, she may need a greater understanding of her genetic background. She needs to know "who I am."

If a woman has a child out of wedlock and marries a man who is not the child's biological father when the child is still very young, and he adopts the child, then this adoption needs to be explained to the child from the earliest age possible, whether or not the birth father is in the picture. This may not feel comfortable at first. You may begin by saying to a one-and-a-half-year-old, "Mommy and Daddy love you so much, and Daddy adopted you because he loves Mommy and you so...o...o...o much..." This may feel contrived and awkward, but the alternative is not saying anything until the child is older, which can be damaging. Finding just the "right" age may be awkward. If you wait until she is old enough to "understand" that she is adopted, she may have already found out through documents or through others' comments.

If your husband has legally adopted your child, you may want to place the paperwork and pictures associated with the occasion in the child's baby book. If you can find other mementos surrounding the adoption that demonstrate your husband's commitment to and love for the child, include these as well.

Resources:

> **Stepfamily Foundation**
> 333 West End Avenue
> New York, NY 10023
> (212) 877-3244

> **Kids 'n' Kin**
> Philadelphia Society
> 415 South Fifteenth Street
> Philadelphia, PA 19146
> (215) 875-3400

> **Brookdale Grandparent Caregiver Information Project**
> Center on Aging
> 140 Warren Hall
> University of California
> Berkeley, CA 94720
> (510) 643-6427
> fax (510) 642-1197

The Stepparent Adoption Process

Here are the basic steps toward a stepparent adoption:

1. *Depending upon the state and county in which you live, you may have to have a home study and a criminal and child abuse clearance conducted.*
2. *The other biological parent's rights must be terminated, or he must sign a consent to an adoption.* If the biological parent has been out of the child's life, he may be served legal papers (the adoption complaint or petition) informing him of the adoption hearing. If he objects, he can contact your attorney or show up at court to contest the adoption. If he does not respond by a specified number of days, usually twenty to thirty-five, he is presumed to have waived his right to object to the adoption.
3. *A hearing is held, usually two to six months after the filing of the adoption petition.* At the hearing the adopting parent must say why he wants to

adopt the child; testify that he contributes to the financial stability of the home or that he and the biological parent together can provide financial support the child; and state his belief that it is in the child's best interests to be adopted by him. The biological parent must testify that she consents and that she feels it is in the child's best interests to be adopted. If the child is over the age of ten (in some states twelve or fourteen), he is questioned by the judge either in the courtroom or in her chambers to confirm that he wants to be adopted. At the hearing the attorney must present to the court either the signed consent of the noncustodial parent or proof that he was served the legal papers and did not respond.

If the noncustodial parent cannot be found, the attorney must place a legal notice of the adoption proceedings in a newspaper published in the last county in which the parent is known to have lived. If he does not respond, the effect is the same as if he had been served personally.

Chapter Twelve

International Adoption

M illions of children around the world need a family, not just for their emotional well-being but often for their very survival. Although only a fraction of these children are legally free for adoption, this fraction still translates into tens of thousands of children being available and waiting for adoption. During the 1980s the number of international adoptions rose from 5,700 in 1982 to nearly 10,000 in 1987. The numbers dropped in the early nineties, mostly because South Korea reduced the number of children available. In 1992 about 6,500 orphans were adopted from other countries. In 1994 the number rose to 8,200, a 12 percent increase over 1993, and it appears that the numbers are continuing to grow, largely because of an increase in adoptions from China, Russia, and the countries of Eastern Europe. Today international adoption makes up more than 10 percent of the roughly 60,000 adoptions by nonrelatives in the United States every year and is the fastest-growing area of adoption.

INTERNATIONAL ADOPTION: ADVANTAGES
The advantages of international adoption are considerable. Here are several:

1. *There are plenty of children available.* There are significant numbers of healthy babies and children available, many more than there are in the United States.
2. *Adoption requirements are often less restrictive.* Adopting from other countries is a more viable choice than domestic adoption for many couples, especially for those who are single or have other children. The requirements on such issues as number of children, age, and marital status are usually less stringent than in a domestic agency adoption. Singles can adopt, as can those over forty. China, for example, prefers couples over

the age of thirty-five. Other countries set very broad age ranges for prospective adoptive parents.

3. *The wait can be shorter.* Because of the abundance of children available, a baby or child can be adopted as soon as your paperwork is completed. The paperwork usually takes three to four months to complete.

4. *Once you have an approved home study, you are virtually guaranteed a child.* Unlike adopting in the United States, where you can comply with all requirements and still not have a child, when you are adopting internationally, you are almost guaranteed success. You are not counting on a birth mother selecting you; instead, you and a child are matched, either through your own resources or through an agency or organization.

5. *The cost of adoption is well defined.* The cost of an international adoption usually ranges from about $10,000 to $20,000. Although the cost is fairly high, principally because of the traveling that is usually required, you know what to expect. With a domestic adoption, you can pay for a birth mother's living expenses, and if she changes her mind, those expenses are not recouped. With international adoption, expenses may unexpectedly increase but you are almost certain to end up with a child. True, there are horror stories of those who have gone overseas—to Eastern European countries in particular—and been swindled out of large sums of money. The laws have been changed, so now there is less opportunity for exploitation, but always consult with others who have used the agencies or organizations you are considering using before paying any fees.

6. *Healthy children are available.* Most of the medical problems children have are related to living in an impoverished country, and these conditions are treatable. The children, even if older, do not usually display the same depth of psychological problems as do children who are adopted at an older age in the United States.

Adoption attorney Melinda Garvert, who has conducted more than 600 international adoptions, says that although you cannot expect a child who has been living in an orphanage to fall in line with American standards for growth and development when he is first adopted, he will usually catch up. In a matter of weeks such children "snap back" and begin to flourish. Indeed, notes Garvert, children who are raised in orphanages and receive routine, even if custodial, care, have far fewer emotional problems than the children in the United States who are adopted after being in foster care. In the fifteen years that she has been placing children internationally, no family has called to say, "It's not working out."[1]

INTERNATIONAL ADOPTION: DISADVANTAGES

Having considered the advantages of international adoption, let us turn to the disadvantages.

1. *You will probably have to travel to another country.* Couples with busy schedules often consider this a great disadvantage. If they already have children, staying a week or more in another country can mean making extensive child care arrangements or taking their children along. Traveling by plane and staying in hotels can also be expensive.

   However, traveling can be an advantage as well. It is an opportunity to learn about your child's country. While you are there, you can press the orphanage caretakers and medical personnel to give you more medical and social information than may be in the documents accompanying your child. Immediate adjustment issues can be handled by finding out little details, such as the temperature your child likes his bottle, his sleeping habits, and his food likes and dislikes. Also, some orphanages will allow you to feed, dress, and otherwise interact with your child during the time you wait for approval to leave the country.

2. *You cannot bring home a newborn infant.* The "infants" that are available are usually between a few months and one year old at the time of placement. Although many children are abandoned at birth, the complications of international adoption make it difficult for a child to be placed with a couple right away. China is one of the few countries in which children in orphanages—invariably girls—are placed as soon as possible.

3. *The child's background is uncertain.* There is usually a gap in the information available about the child and his family background. Even in domestic adoptions the child's biological parents' full medical background is often unknown; yet most couples in the United States have at least some medical and social background on the birth mother and could perhaps track down the birth father if necessary. Studies of adopted children do show that it is important for parents and professionals to obtain accurate and detailed information on the child's background whenever possible. Finding your child's birth parents in another country may be next to impossible.

4. *The child is unlikely ever to know her birth parents.* Openness in adoption is considered an advantage to the child, especially when she comes to inquire about her genetic background. In an international adoption, no matter how much you share the child's culture with her, she will probably

know little about her biological parents and will probably never have the opportunity to meet them.

Some people say that they chose international adoption because they did not want to "worry" about the birth parents interfering with the adoption. Although it is true that no birth parent has ever come back to the United States to take back a child in an international adoption, it is also true that fewer than 1 percent of all American-born children are removed from their adoptive homes by a birth parent. Furthermore, although the birth parents cannot interfere in an international adoption, an adoption agency can. We know of two cases in which a large international adoption agency removed an international child from a couple's home because they did not believe that the placement was appropriate. In one case the parents got their child back; in the other they did not. A disreputable agency may even attempt to remove a child from a home so that the agency can charge another couple to readopt the child.

Not wanting to involve yourself in a legally risky adoption is understandable no matter what route you take. Many couples choose international adoption in order to avoid dealing with birth parents before and after the placement of their child. If this is how you feel, you may need to give some more thought to the roles the birth parents will play in your child's life, whether or not they were directly involved with him or you. Birth parents matter to children, and this is true even in the thousands of adoptions in which there is no contact with a birth mother or father.

5. *The wait for a child, once he is identified as your child, can be very emotionally taxing.* Waiting for a child is always difficult, and in some countries it can take months before your identified child can come to the United States. Knowing that your child is in a foster home or in an orphanage with less than optimum care is difficult for you as a parent. Your child is somewhere where you cannot help him. Some adoptive parents go to the country beforehand and care for the child themselves until the paperwork is completed.

If you must wait for your child while she is one country and you are in the United States, you can comfort yourself with the knowledge that she is going to get the best possible life once she comes home to you. You did not do anything to cause your child to be in an orphanage, but you are doing something to bring her out of it. If you had never made plans to adopt her, and you did not allow yourself to experience the emotional agony of being separated from your child-to-be, then she might never have had the opportunity to live with a family.

6. *The paperwork and repetitive procedures can be difficult.* The hardest requirement in adopting a child from another country may be completing what appears to be endless paperwork and dealing with bureaucracies both at home and abroad. This endless paperwork limits the number of parents and children available for adoption and elevates the cost beyond the means of those who would like to add more children to their family.

Nevertheless, it is doable. One adoptive mother whose child is now twenty-three years old says that when she began to inquire about the process twenty years ago, she was told by a legal secretary that the paperwork was so overwhelming that she should not even bother to proceed. This mother thought that if a legal secretary, who deals with paperwork and forms all day long, found the paperwork burdensome, then she was in no position to tackle such a task. Then she met a woman who belonged to an adoption support group, Latin American Parents Association, who was planning to adopt in Colombia. This woman had done her paperwork and was so confident that she would be returning from South America with a child that she was already decorating the nursery. The prospective adoptive mom thought that if this woman could do it, so could she. And so can you! (Incidentally, both woman adopted within months of their meeting each other.)

Fortunately, some countries, like China, have made the process very easy. To help minimize your paperwork, Melinda Garvert recommends that you ask the attorney or agency what paperwork will be completed and processed for you.

BEFORE YOU ADOPT

The first thing to do is join a support group of parents who have adopted internationally and those looking to adopt. (See the Appendix for a list of support groups.) These are some of the greatest advocates of international adoption. Find out how people in the group adopted their children. Not only can they tell you the best agencies or facilitators to use, they can also fill you in on all the little things you need to know about the process, the trip to the foreign country, what you need to pack, and what costs can be expected.

Often support groups will have speakers come in and discuss various aspects of international adoption. Agency personnel, for example, can offer very practical advice while promoting their services.

The more information you gather, the better. Contact several agencies and ask them to send you their literature related to their program. Attend a few different agency meetings to find out what kinds of programs they offer and what countries they operate in.

From the time that you decide to adopt internationally, it is important to have a complete understanding of the adoption procedure. Your agency, facilitator, or attorney will guide you. Each country will be somewhat different, but many of the steps and documents required will be the same everywhere. You may be handling much of the paperwork yourself, so regardless of what agency or attorney is responsible for it, you must keep close track of who has your paperwork, where it is, and where it must go. This does not mean that you call your agency or attorney every day to check on everything; it means you take responsibility for getting your paperwork done and seeing that whoever is supposed to receive it has actually gotten it. You must be an advocate for yourself and your child.

There are hundreds of agencies and child-placement entities in the United States that handle international adoptions, as well as a number of attorneys. *You may want to decide which countries you want to adopt from before you decide on an agency.* Most agencies or entities work with at least a few countries, because one country may suddenly ban adoptions; no one agency, however, can handle adoptions from every possible country. If you decide you want to adopt an Asian boy between the ages of three and five, you will not want to work with an agency that conducts adoptions only in China, which releases mostly infant girls. If you want a Caucasian child, you will want to work with an agency that conducts adoptions in Russia and Eastern Europe, where countries tend to open and close their doors to adoptions on an almost monthly basis.

Except in cases of direct placement by agencies, most international adoptions are essentially independent adoptions and are accomplished in one of these ways: through an agency, through child-placement entities and attorneys, through parent initiation, and through Americans living overseas.

TYPES OF ADOPTIONS

International Agency Adoption

Agencies in the United States can take one of two roles. One kind places a child with you directly—usually a large, very well-established agency with a long history of placing children internationally. Another kind simply helps you facilitate an adoption by providing guidance, direction, and contact people overseas.

Direct-placement agencies are licensed in the United States and maintain a direct relationship with foreign placement services. Their function is to place international children directly with American families or to refer these children to

American agencies. Korea, for example, permits only licensed agencies who have a formal agreement with the country to conduct adoptions there. If you want to adopt from Korea, you must go through a licensed agency that has a relationship with that country. That agency places the child with you directly.

A direct-placement agency handles the paperwork, including the foreign application; assigns a child to you; and communicates with those in the child's country by coordinating state, foreign, and emigration procedures. Once the child is assigned to you, the foreign child-placement organization sends the birth mother's relinquishment or abandonment decree and the child's birth certificate to your agency, which sends these documents on to the Immigration and Naturalization Service. Without these two documents, the adoption cannot take place.

If the foreign country permits, the child may then be escorted to the United States. Although the child is in your home, the agency will continue to be responsible for her until she is formally adopted by you in the United States.

If the agency is located in one state and you live in another, the paperwork regarding the child must also go through two Interstate Compact on the Placement of Children (ICPC) offices: the one in the agency's state and the one in your state. This is true even if the child was escorted directly to your state or if you personally received the child in her country of origin. This ICPC approval is necessary only if the American agency has legal custody of the child and ultimate responsibility for her, even though you have physical custody, until the final adoption. If the child is adopted in her country of origin, or an American agency does not have legal custody, then ICPC approval is not necessary. After ICPC has approved the proceedings that have taken place, you can initiate a U.S. adoption of your child.

A direct-placement agency will generally charge more, since they are taking a more active role in the whole adoption process.

Some agencies do not place children directly but simply help facilitate the adoption. In these adoptions you may do more of the paperwork and take more responsibility for the procedure. Since there are many agencies that serve as facilitators, you may find one in your own state. This agency will probably conduct your home study and see that all the required documents are together. Once the home study is completed and the documents are together, the agency will assist you in putting together a dossier to send to the foreign country.

Agency personnel invest a great deal of time and money in paving the way for adoptions to proceed in a particular country. The fees you pay to the agency are for their knowledge and expertise in the culture, laws, procedures, and required paperwork of a given country. Generally, the service fees are about $4,000.

Remember: If you live in a state like Connecticut or Colorado that allows only agency-placed adoptions and only by approved agencies, make sure that the agency you are going to use can legally place children or help facilitate an adoption in your state. Remember too that just because you are using a licensed agency does not mean that the people operating the agency are knowledgeable, scrupulous, and ethical. Some states are more lenient than others about issuing licenses to agencies. There's a chance that the licensed agency taking your money for an international adoption does not have the contacts and the expertise to facilitate an international adoption successfully.

Child-Placement Entities and Attorneys

Some organizations, individual liaisons, and attorneys have contacts, or sources, in other countries and know how to proceed with an international adoption. Agencies cannot conduct adoptions in certain countries, so an independent adoption is your only choice. According to attorney Melinda Garvert, an international adoption attorney serves as your advocate in conducting an adoption, whereas an agency may be advocating more for the adoption program itself.

Some of these liaisons are people who have adopted independently themselves, have learned what must be done, and are now assisting others to take the same route they have taken. They have established and maintained strong contacts in the foreign country and may work with contacts who prefer to work with an individual rather than an agency. Like agencies, these organizations handle the red tape, have contacts in other countries, and can help with the language barrier.

Sometimes a liaison organization is in the process of getting an agency license from its state. States can make it difficult to get a license until you can prove that you have children available and can show some record of success. In order for an organization to do that, it may have to coordinate several adoptions before it can become licensed.

A child-placement entity can be less expensive than an agency. Remember, though, always to get their fee schedule in writing. Licensed agencies, adoption organizations, and law firms are operated by individuals: Some are honest and some are not.

Parent-Initiated International Adoption

Some people do not use an agency or facilitators, but instead conduct parent-initiated adoptions, also called "direct" or "independent" adoptions. The prospective parents have a home study conducted by an agency or certified investigator, then take full responsibility for adopting a child. This kind of adoption occurs frequently in Latin American countries and may be the only way to adopt a child when there is no U.S. agency interacting with a particular foreign child care agency.

Some people like the high level of personal control they have with this method of adoption. It can actually speed up the procedure when you do not have to rely on agency personnel who must divide their time among many clients. You may also have greater control over the health, ethnicity, age, and gender of the child, though not necessarily. An agency or attorney will also give you the power of selection by providing you with a picture of the child and as much background information as possible; after all, they want the adoptions to be successful as well.

A parent-initiated adoption can be less expensive than an agency adoption. However, if you make mistakes along the way, the financial and emotional costs can be far greater. Remember, no matter which method you select, you will have certain expenses: processing fees, a home study, translations, a donation to the orphanage in some cases, foreign attorney fees, air fare, and so on. If you are going to invest that much money, you may want to be assured that everything is going smoothly and to spend the few thousand dollars more to have an agency or attorney handle the red tape. If you do decide to conduct an adoption independently, make sure you seek guidance from others who have preceded you. There are plenty of horror stories circulating about bribes being taken and children being sold on the black market. The best way to avoid this is to join a support organization and talk to the people in it.

Before you proceed, you should certainly write to the U.S. State Department, to the Immigration and Naturalization Service (INS), and to the embassy of the country where you are thinking of adopting and find out what the requirements are for adopting a child from that particular country. If you have a particular child in mind, make sure she is legally eligible for adoption.

Here is the process you will probably follow. First, you will deal directly with a foreign child-placement source. Your responsibilities will include fulfilling your state's requirements and getting a home study, sending your home study and documentation to the international source, assuming full responsibility for your child, and complying with INS regulations, which are discussed later in this chapter.

Next you will legally adopt your child in the foreign country. This is done in cooperation with the international child-placement entity and with the laws of the foreign country. You must then also comply with INS regulations before you can bring the child to the United States. To satisfy INS regulations, you must have personally seen the child before and during the adoption procedure. If you did not adopt the child in his country, you could bring the child to the United States and legally adopt him in your own state. However, *it is much better to adopt a child in his own country.*

Before the child can emigrate to the United States, his birth parent must provide a written, irrevocable relinquishment and release, or it must be found by a court or other authority that the child has been abandoned by his birth parents.

Adoption for Americans Living Overseas

If you live overseas, an adopted child may also enter the United States if she is under the age of sixteen and has lived with you for at least two years. No home study is required, and the child does *not* need to meet the INS definition of being an orphan. This method of adoption is often used by Americans who are working overseas, including missionaries.

SELECTING AN AGENCY, ORGANIZATION, OR FACILITATOR

To be sure of a given agency's or facilitator's credibility, call the adoption unit of your state and ask about the agency or the organization; if you can, talk to members of an adoption parent support group.

Agencies range in size from small local organizations to large national ones. As a rule, the safest and easiest way to adopt a child from another country is to involve an adoption agency in your state and to adopt the child through that agency. Of course, this is not always possible, since some international adoption agencies handle only certain countries. If you want to adopt a child from a certain region of the world and the agencies in your state do not handle them, or if the agency is very expensive, you will want to go through another agency, organization, or facilitator. There are many agencies, so gather lots of information from several of them before you decide.

When you call an agency, do not expect the staff to have time to cover every last question. Begin with general questions and ask to receive their literature. Once you decide you would probably like to use a particular agency or organization, then you can begin to ask more in-depth questions that are not covered in its literature.

Here are some questions to ask:

1. *What countries does the agency work with,* and what kinds of connections do they have with that country?
2. *What criteria must you meet?* (List the specific countries you are interested in adopting from.)
3. *What services does the agency offer?* Get very specific information. Some agencies actually assign and place children with you; others just help facilitate the adoption and guide you along the way.

4. *Does the agency provide help with the paperwork*, putting together a dossier, finding a translator, and making travel arrangements? What services does it help you obtain in the foreign country? Finding an interpreter and a lawyer? Finding the embassy? Getting the child's visa and passport?

5. *How is the agency aware of the children who are available?*

6. *What are the adoption laws of the country?*

7. *Can the agency provide you with the names of families who have adopted there?* With the names of professionals who work with the agency?

8. *How many adoptions has the agency conducted in that country?* (If you are looking to adopt in Korea, and you are dealing with a large organization such as Holt, this is an unnecessary question.) Also, some programs are just opening up in certain countries. The key is for the agency or facilitator to be honest with you in stating what she does and does not know.

9. *What are the fees and other expenses?* Agency quotes can often vary by thousands of dollars. Some of this discrepancy can be explained by what the agency includes in the cost and what it omits. Part of the cost is often a "donation" to the orphanage. Find out how much the donation is to be. If it is $3,000, this adoption can end up being almost $25,000, once you add in all the other hidden expenses.

10. *How are monies for in-country expenses and fees handled?* Foreign country fees should, as a rule, be deposited into a separate escrow account and released when the adoption is completed. There should be no need to take large sums of cash with you.

11. *What can be known about a child's health and background?* In certain countries, such as China, little may be known about the child's family. If this information is not usually available, the agency should say so.

12. *Must you and your spouse travel to the country, and if so, for how long?*

13. *Once you complete your paperwork and receive approval from the INS, how* long can you expect to wait for a child to be assigned to you?

DECIDING ON A COUNTRY

Because you must meet the requirements of a particular country, you will want to begin by investigating which countries will accept you and what kinds of children are available. At the end of this chapter is a list of countries that permit people from abroad to adopt their orphans. The list of countries that permit international adoptions may vary from year to year, so be flexible and decide on more than one country, if at all possible.

A country's status can change quickly, so getting up-to-date information is crucial. The agency or attorney that you are working with should be able to provide the information you need.

International Concerns for Children publishes an excellent resource called the *Report on Intercountry Adoption,* which comes out once a year and includes ten updates annually. This book provides excellent information about international adoption and a country-by-country description of what is required to adopt and which agencies are assisting in the placement from that country. Contact:

International Concerns for Children
911 Cypress Drive
Boulder, CO 80303-2821
(303) 494-8333 (Voice and fax)

The State Department lists the laws, requirements, and procedures for adopting from different countries on the Internet. The URL is **http://travel.state.gov/children's_issues.html**.

As you contemplate international adoption, keep several things in mind. If you are Caucasian, adopting a child from another country—unless it is a European country—probably means that the child is not going to look at all like you. If you adopt a child from Asia, for example, your family is entering into a transracial adoption. For a Caucasian couple, adopting an Asian child is certainly a different cultural experience than adopting an African-American or biracial child, yet there are many similarities. You and your spouse need to review some of the issues involved in entering into a transracial adoption before deciding to adopt a child from another country.

Expenses can be another issue. Sometimes the cost of the adoption has little to do with the agency's fees; it arises from the fees of the country in question, the orphanage fee, traveling expenses, and the required length of stay in the country. However, agency and attorney fees can also vary quite drastically. Make sure you get an itemized list of all fees, including traveling and lodging expenses.

The ages of the children available may vary widely by country. Some countries, like Romania, do not allow children to be adopted until they are at least six months old. If you want a very young baby, you will want to choose a country that has a policy of releasing children as soon as the mother relinquishes the child, or as soon as the child is abandoned.

Also variable is a country's policies regarding who can adopt. Agencies may have few requirements, but the country from which you seek to adopt may impose restrictions related to age; marital status, including number of years you have been married; number of previous divorces; weight; and the number of children you have. Find out whether you will be accepted before you set your heart on adopting a child from a particular country.

Finding a reputable agency or facilitator to handle the adoption is crucial. If you can't find such a person or entity for a particular country, you will be better off looking elsewhere.

To obtain the most comprehensive information about a country, you will need to make use of several resources. First, get advice from other adoptive parents: Join an active international adoption support group. Chances are that you will find members of the group who are current on a country's situation. Find out what the country is like, what it is like to travel there, what to expect once you get there, and how easy it is to process the adoption papers once you are in the country. Second, read. Visit your library and go through the guide to periodical literature to find out whether there is political unrest or other factors that may make adoption difficult. Your reference librarian will be happy to help. Borrow a few books and read up on the country's history and culture. The more information you get, the better!

Following is a list of countries that permit people from abroad to adopt their orphans. Bear in mind as you read this list that adoption laws in a particular country can change quickly. Countries are often criticized for "not taking care of their own," prompting them to close down their adoption programs. This happened in the case of Korea, whose adoption program drew much attention. After receiving a great deal of criticism from other Asian countries, Korea sharply cut back on the number of children available.

Latin America

Bolivia. Infants and older children are available, as well as sibling groups. Couples should be infertile and at least thirty years old, but not more than forty-five years older than the child. It takes about four months' time to get a child after INS approval. One family member must stay in the country from two weeks to two months. Cost: about $11,000.

Brazil. There is a large biracial population in Brazil, and many of the children available are black or of mixed race. Couples do not have to be married for a prescribed length of time when adopting a child under two years of age. Brazilians are given first priority and prefer to adopt Caucasian newborns. Judges do not like to split sibling groups. If you are willing to adopt more than one child, an older or non-Caucasian child, or one with medical problems, you have the greatest chance of adopting. Cost: $12,000 to $18,000. The following restrictions also apply: You must be at least twenty-five years old; the husband and wife must stay with the child in Brazil for two weeks before beginning the adoption process (a month, if the child is over the age of two); and only approved agencies can represent adopting parents.

Chile. Couples should be twenty years older than the child and have been married for at least three years. Singles are seldom accepted. Nonresident foreigners cannot adopt, so they are given guardianship and authority to take the child out of the country; you cannot finalize an adoption there. The system is handled by private attorneys. Adopting parents must appear before a judge in Chile (sometimes only one spouse must appear). Cost: $12,000 to $25,000, including travel.

Colombia. Couples should not be more than thirty-five years older than the child. Toddlers and siblings are available. Children must stay in the country until the final adoption is completed. Both parents must stay for about one to two weeks; then the mother must stay for another one to two months before the child can be brought home. Families are randomly assigned to one of twelve family courts; the wait is between three and eight weeks before a hearing is scheduled.

Only sources licensed by the Colombian Family Welfare Institute and licensed Colombian adoption agencies can offer children for adoption. The Colombian Family Welfare Institute and most private agencies will work only with United States adoption agencies, not individuals. Casa de la Madre y el Niños, however, will place children directly with couples.

It takes about eight months to get a child after INS approval. Cost: starts at about $8,000.

Dominican Republic. Couples must be married for at least ten years, and one spouse must be thirty-five years or older. Biracial infants are available. Private adoption attorneys can arrange adoptions as well as agencies. Traveling to the country is required: You may also have to wait three to six weeks after placement to come home.

Ecuador. The wait for a boy is very short. The husband must be between the ages of thirty and fifty-five, and the wife must be between twenty-five and forty. You must have been married at least five years; no previous divorces are permitted. The wait between getting an assignment and receiving the child is about a week. Travel time spent in Guayaquil is between ten days and two weeks, though some agencies estimate it at more like three or four weeks. Agencies may have motel rooms for adoptive parents. Adoption can take place from either an Ecuadorian or an American-based agency.

El Salvador. At present there is political unrest, and adoption plans could be abruptly halted.

Guatemala. Christian singles or couples between the ages of twenty-five and sixty are eligible. Children are fair-skinned and have dark hair and eyes. Mostly healthy infants—more boys than girls—are available. Abandoned children or those whose parents have died can also be adopted.

In a private adoption, the biological parents release the child to an attorney, who represents both the biological mother and the adoptive parents. The private adoption must take place in Guatemala. According to attorney Melinda Garvert, when adopting a newborn independently, the wait is about five months from the time you receive INS approval to the time you receive your child. In an agency adoption the wait is six to eight months. The adoptive parents do not have to stay there the entire time. Newborns are registered with adoptive parents at birth but cannot be taken back to the United States until they are about five months old. If you want, you can care for your child in Guatemala until you leave, but you are required to stay in the country only three to seven days. Sometimes an escort can bring the child to the United States. Cost: $12,000 to $17,000.

Honduras. At least one spouse or single person must be at least twenty-five years old. Both spouses must be there for the initial assessment. After this session, the prospective adoptive parents may leave the country and let the attorney handle the final adoption, which takes eight to ten months. You then return to get your child, since he cannot leave the country until a final adoption decree is issued. Only licensed agencies may place children from Honduras.

Jamaica. Singles may adopt. The wait for a child is about eight months. Black infants and older children are available. Travel is optional. Cost: $2,000 for foreign fees, not including escort service.

Mexico. This is a very limited program. Travel time can be a few months. Judges like the child to be with adoptive parents in Mexico for six months for a "trial" period.

Because adoption procedures vary widely through the thirty-one Mexican states, the time required to complete an adoption can be anywhere from one month to two years. The cost can also vary widely. Using a private attorney is more costly but usually less time-consuming.

Nicaragua. Singles and those who have been married for one year may adopt. Applicants must be between twenty-five and forty years old. Children are between three months and six years old. Placement takes about six months. Parents must stay in the country about two weeks. New programs are opening up.

Panama. Travel is usually four to six weeks, or two trips.

Paraguay. Single women and couples who are at least thirty-five years old or who have been married five years or more are eligible. This is a very active program. Many healthy infants and toddlers in foster care are available, as are children up to fifteen years old. Some agencies allow skin and hair color preference. The only age limits are those imposed by the agencies. Travel is for about four weeks, or two trips. Cost: about $15,000, not including travel. Other agencies list $21,500, including travel and local service.

Peru. Couples and single women may adopt. The country's programs work with licensed agencies only. Two parents must usually stay two weeks, and one spouse must stay for six weeks.

Africa

About seventy children from Africa are adopted each year. Many are older and have lived through war or refugee camps; some have experienced sexual abuse and have chronic hepatitis B (see chapter 18, "Healthy Mothers, Healthy Babies").[2] Cost: about $5,500, not including travel.

Americans for African Adoptions, Inc., is the primary agency placing children from Africa.

Asia

Asian children account for 75 percent of all international adoptions in the United States.

Cambodia. Single woman who live alone or with relatives, and couples married at least two years, may adopt if they are twenty-five to fifty years of age. Christians, nonsmokers, and small families are preferred. One parent must be at home at least six months after placement. Travel is optional, and if you do go, you need stay only one week.

China. A new adoption law in China went into effect in April of 1992, and in October of that year the China Centre for Adoption Affairs was created in Beijing. It is through this center that agencies send applications to prospective adoptive parents. The center tells the agency of your approval and then selects which province your dossier will be sent to. The translations of the dossier must be done in Beijing by the China Translation and Publishing Corporation. It is illegal to work directly with welfare houses.

An assignment letter is sent from the Ministry of Justice in Beijing telling your agency, attorney, or facilitator about the child who has been assigned to you. This assignment includes medical information and a small black-and-white photo of the child. You must accept the child in writing before traveling. After arriving in Beijing, you then travel to meet your child the next day. After completing the paperwork necessary to finalize the adoption, you and other families with their newly adopted children go to Guanzhou to obtain the children's visas. The following day the families go to the medical center, where the children are examined. Next you obtain photos for your child's visa and then go over to the American embassy for the visa interview. The visa is issued in a few hours, and you can be on your way home the next morning.

Adoptions are finalized directly in China, and at least one parent must travel to receive the child and finalize the adoption. The stay is about two to three weeks. There are facilitators in the country to guide you through the process. Some organizations arrange for groups of parents to go to China and then help that set of parents adopt their children.

Overall, the Chinese government has been very cooperative about adoptions, and the paperwork required is relatively easy to understand and follow. For the most part, the children are healthy: Chinese women usually do not smoke, and AIDS and other sexually transmitted diseases have not been a concern so far. Because the children live in poor conditions in orphanages, however, they may be malnourished.

The children available are for the most part infant girls. Sibling groups are not available. Childless singles and couples over thirty-five years old are generally eligible. If the child has health problems, is older (two to four years old), or is an orphan—both of her parents have died—you can be under thirty-five years old or have other children and still qualify. Also, the fees for the adoption are reduced.

It takes about four months to get a child after INS approval. Cost: $12,000 to $17,000, including travel.*Hong Kong.* Hong Kong officials give priority to Chinese applicants.

India. Parents do not necessarily have to travel. If you do travel, the stay is one to two weeks.

Japan. Japan prefers couples of Asian descent, but the law does not prohibit foreigners from adopting. There are no specific government regulations. Traveling is optional. If you do travel, plan to stay anywhere from three days to three weeks. Visas are issued only on Tuesdays, so paperwork can be delayed by a week. The waiting period for a placement can vary from a matter of months to four years, depending upon what program is used. It is best to work directly with an orphanage. Costs vary widely but can be over $25,000. Having a personal contact can reduce costs considerably.

Korea. The following regulations apply: no single parents; American agencies with Korean contracts cannot place outside of their service areas (this usually means their own state); couples may not have more than four other children, unless they are adopting a special needs child; and children who are classified as abandoned must stay in Korea for six months in case a family member comes forward, unless one or both birth parents have signed relinquishments. Some agencies require that prospective adoptive parents not weigh over 30 percent of ideal weight for their height.

Koreans are beginning to adopt within their own country, meaning that fewer children are available. Nevertheless, large numbers of orphans are still adopted in the United States every year. The children are brought to the United States, so traveling is unnecessary. Cost: about $10,000.

Korea works only with adoption agencies that have child-placement contracts with Korean agencies, and only those U.S.-based agencies in each state can place children in that state. Unlike most other international adoption agencies that help couples all over the United States, the agency can place only in the state where it is licensed. If you are seriously considering adopting from Korea, you will also want to get your home study done by the agency that is licensed in your state.

Nepal. This country is very flexible about the age of the prospective adoptive parents; it simply states that you cannot have a combined age of more than 100. Childless couples are preferred, and you must submit a letter from your physician stating that you are infertile. The children are Indo-Asian; newborn infants are available.

The wait for a child is between six months to two years, depending upon the agency used; according to Mary Mexcur of New Hope Christian Services, however, the wait can be much shorter. Mrs. Mexcur also points out that Nepal has one of the lowest in-country fees. Parents must stay in the country for thirty days at a cost of about $30 per day. Other expenses can vary considerably depending upon the agency used. Cost: $7,000 to $12,000.

Philippines. Mostly boys, aged one month to fifteen years old, are available. Rules are fairly flexible as to parents' ages. Travel is usually for three to nine days, but sometimes escorts can be arranged. The usual wait for a child is six months to two years, depending upon the agency. Cost: $5,000 to $10,000.

Taiwan. Healthy infants who may have some previous medical problems are available. Couples twenty-five to forty-five years old with one or no children are eligible. Wait for INS approval is one to two years. Traveling is not always required; if you do go, plan to stay two weeks.

Because the United States does not recognize Taiwan as part of China, all visas are issued by the American consulate general in Hong Kong.

Thailand. Children available are zero to five years old. Preferably childless couples thirty to fifty-five years old are eligible. Adoptive parents are allowed to express a gender preference. One parent must travel for about two weeks.

Vietnam. Many children are available, including infants. The wait for a child is about three months for a child under three years old, six to twelve months for an infant. Usually you must wait three to four months from the time a child is assigned to you until the time she emigrates to the United States.

Europe and Russia

Belarus. Single women and couples may adopt; the mother must be under forty-five years old for a child under five years of age. Many boys six months and older are available, of whom a number are of mixed ethnic background or have correctable medical problems. The wait is about one year. Cost: $13,000 to $15,000. Parents must stay in the country for one to three weeks.

Bulgaria. Children ages one through seven years old and older are available. Regulations prohibit foreigners from adopting children under the age of one. Most of the children available are over the age of four, especially those with minor physical problems and those of Romany (Gypsy) descent. The wait for a child is about six months. Cost: about $13,000. Escorting is possible, for a fee (usually about $1,200). If you do travel, it takes about two weeks.

Georgia. Singles and couples can adopt. Children of all ages are available, but mostly infants two to six months old, according to one agency. Travel (usually to Moscow) is for about one week. Cost: about $15,000.

Greece. The Children's Home Society of Minnesota is the only agency listed as conducting adoptions in Greece. Children available are toddlers and older. The wait is twelve to eighteen months after the child is identified for you. This is a very small program. Guidelines are flexible if you are adopting a disabled child. Greek parents are preferred. Two trips are required, lasting seven to ten days each. Cost: about $5,000, not including local service or travel.

Hungary. Singles and couples may adopt. Parents must be no more than forty-five years older than the child. Toddlers and older children are available— especially boys. Some are part Gypsy. Orphanage conditions are good, and children come with thorough health records. The wait for a child is about six months. Travel is required for both spouses. One may leave after one week; the other must stay two to four more weeks. Cost: $15,000 to $20,000.

Kazakhstan. Singles and couples who have been married at least two years may adopt. One parent must be under forty-five. Children available are between newborn and twelve years old. The wait for a child is about six months. One parent must travel for two weeks. Cost: about $11,000 plus travel. Families are needed.

Latvia. Singles and couples married at least one year and under the age of fifty-five may adopt. Children available are between one month and fifteen years old. The wait is usually four to nine months after INS approval. The stay in the country is for ten to twenty-one days. Cost: about $14,000, including travel.

Lithuania. Singles and couples married at least one year can adopt. They must be under forty-five to adopt an infant. Children available are between one month and twelve years old. The wait is usually four to nine months after INS approval. Travel is for about ten to fourteen days. Cost: about $12,000, not including travel.

Moldova. Single women and couples may adopt. Most of the children available are healthy toddlers. The wait is about six months. One parent should be at home at least three months after placement. Travel for one parent is about three weeks. Cost: about $13,000—possibly less if the child has medical problems.

Poland. Children four and older and many sibling groups are available. Regulations, the kinds of children available, and the required length of stay are all subject to change. Poland works only with licensed agencies. Catholic couples no more than forty years older than the child with strong Polish background are preferred. The wait can be less than six months. Both parents must travel for one week; the other can then stay for three more weeks. Cost: about $9,000, plus travel.

Romania. Single women and couples who have been married for at least three years can adopt. The mother must be no more than thirty-five years older than the child, the father no more than forty years older. There can be no more than two children in the family already. Children must be considered abandoned for at least six months before adoption proceedings will begin. Birth mothers cannot directly place their children with couples.

Escort service for the child is now available; otherwise, the parent who travels stays about two weeks, mostly in Bucharest. Priority is given to those of Romanian descent. The wait for a child is about eight months. Cost: about $21,000, including travel. Expenses vary considerably from one agency to another.

Russian Republic. Couples should not be more than forty-five years older than the child. Singles may adopt. In 1995 the children available were mostly from Moscow and St. Petersburg, because these cities have ignored the acting prosecutor general's order to stop all adoptions. In March of that year, however, president Boris Yeltsin signed a new law that allows international adoption and establishes Russia's commitment to continue placing children internationally. A search must be made to find Russian adoptive parents first, however, before a child is available to foreigners. Children who are three or under must be registered for three months so that a Russian family can have the first opportunity to adopt the child. If the child is older, he must be registered for six months.

Infants and up and many sibling groups are available. Most of the children are between six months and six years old. Tens of thousands of children are in institutions, but many do not fit the INS "orphan" definition. It is estimated that over 100,000 children will be abandoned in Russia in the next year.

It takes four to eight months to receive a child after INS approval. You must take at least one trip, sometimes two, depending upon the program, for about one week each. Cost: $15,000 to $20,000, including travel. Very young children are generally in good health and are well cared for. If you adopt a child with a medical condition or disability, or a black or biracial child, expenses will be about $6,500 to $10,000.

Ukraine. Singles and couples married at least two years may adopt. The children available are between zero and fifteen years.

Resources:

Precious in His Sight maintains an extensive photolisting of children available for international adoption through a variety of agencies. Countries of origin include Russia, China, India, and Korea. The photolisting is updated at least once a month. You can reach this Web site at **http://www.adoption.com**.

Latin American Adoptive Families sponsors the Internet Resource Project Web site at **http://nysernet.org/cyber/adoption/laaf/**.

Ichild is an Internet mailing list for families who have adopted children from India. To join the list, send a message to **ichild@ibm.net** with "subscribe" on the subject line.

Adoption in China has a Web site at **http://www.tiac.net/users/sunny/**. This site contains links to other China and adoption sites, and information on the China's Children adoption agency.

Families with Children from China, an adoptive parent organization, has a Web site at **http://www.catalog.com/fwcfc/**.

The Web site **http://www.itginet.com/ksloan/triplist.html** contains many useful travel tips for adoptive parents who are planning a trip to China.

East-West Concepts., Inc., the American Hungarian Adoption Center, has been facilitating Hungarian adoptions since 1989. Their Web site and photolisting can be reached at **http://world.std.com/~AdoptHun**.

Families for Russian and Ukrainian Adoption is a support group for adoptive families. They have a Web site at **http://www.serve.com/fredt/adopt.html**.

Adoption InterLink UK provides information about adoption in the United Kingdom. The Web site address is **http://box.argonet.co.uk/users/adopt/**.

WHEN A CHILD IS ASSIGNED TO YOU

Depending upon the program or agency you are using and the country from which you are adopting, there are different methods of having a child assigned to you. The countries placing these children want to make sure you want the child you are adopting. That is one reason, for example, that in Russia one of the adoptive parents must visit the child before proceeding with the adoption. As with any adoption, the older the child, the more you will want to know about him in order to be fully aware of his physical and emotional needs.

Years ago prospective adoptive parents would go into an orphanage and select the child they would like to bring home. This is not the way adoption happens today—not even when there are scores of children in one orphanage. A child is generally assigned to you *after* all your paperwork is done and you are approved to adopt but before you actually travel to the country.

Sometimes adoptive parents go to an adoption agency's workshop and see pictures of children available for adoption. They may want to know whether they can adopt a particular child. The child cannot be held for a family, however, while they are completing their paperwork and waiting for approval from the INS.

If you see a picture of a child who is waiting to be adopted and have some facts about her, go ahead and get all your paperwork done. The child may still be available; if she is not, there will be others.

As a rule, expect younger children to be assigned to you. The younger the child, of course, the less you will need to know about her. In a country like China, where most of the children placed are girls ages three to six months, you will just be given a picture of the child and as much information as possible about her and her parents' medical history.

People often worry about how they will react when they receive an assignment. They think, will I like the baby? Will she be cute or ugly? *Remember, you do have a choice.* And yet, of all the infant placements we have ever heard of, we have never known of parents who did not like the child that was assigned to them. The adoptive parents we have known have all been pleased with their child and considered him the most wonderful child ever.

If the child is older, profiles of various children will be offered to you; or the agency may call you and say that a five-year-old girl is available for adoption, and ask whether you are interested. This can be a similar process to adopting an older child in the United States. You will see a picture of the child and possibly a videotape. Once you select a child, he will be tentatively assigned to you before you travel to the country. At that time you will be told more about him—his likes and dislikes, his temperament, his learning ability, and any health problems. The older the child, the more you will want to know about him.

Some parents do not want to proceed with the adoption of a particular child once they meet him; this usually occurs when the child is older and turns out to have more medical or emotional problems than the parents had anticipated. For that reason, more care is taken in matching an older child with a family.

Sometimes before or at the time a child is matched with you, you will receive a referral packet that contains pictures and whatever information is known about the child's background and present condition. The level of medical information available varies. Most adoptive parents will present the information they have to a physician for interpretation. Remember, the physician can describe a disease or condition and possible problems associated with a given condition, but do not expect her to make a full evaluation based on the notes presented.

If the child is very young, making an assessment is relatively easy; most problems, if they exist, are medical, not developmental. True, infants in orphanages often do not receive the emotional love and stimulation that they need, which can cause some developmental delay. However, most catch up quickly. A child under the age of one will not have moved from one caretaker to another. Nor will he suffer from the emotional problems associated with orphanage neglect, fending for himself on the streets, or abuse at home; and the physical examination he will have before leaving the country will tell you whether he has any congenital health problems or other medical conditions. The major risk is that of unknown genetic factors, which is often true with domestic adoptions too—especially when a birth father is not identified.

Adopting an older child is invariably more of a challenge. For one thing, it can be difficult to make an accurate assessment, since her exact age may not be known. Malnutrition and lack of emotional attention can influence growth, so that tooth eruption and head circumference are sometimes the only measurements available to estimate age. If the child was abandoned, moreover, her history before being placed in an orphanage or with a foster family can be completely unknown.[3]

If you choose to adopt an older child, you will want to know more about her environmental background. If she has been raised in an orphanage, she may be very developmentally delayed and may even have an attachment disorder. Such a child may have a host of emotional and behavioral problems and may never develop properly. Unlike with the adoption of a child with special needs in the United States, where his background is likely to be well documented, with international adoption the child's background will probably remain unknown or undisclosed.

Many couples seeking to adopt never "hear" what the social worker is telling them about the child's problems. They see the beautiful child's picture and "fall in love with her face." As difficult as it may be, try to be objective. Listen carefully and understand what problems the child may have. Yes, you can make a difference in a child's life, but a very disturbed child can also make a difference—for the worse—in your life. You must be prepared to handle the potential problems.

For example, even very young children who have grown up in poorly staffed orphanages may have attachment disorders. This condition is not going to be doc-umented, and the only way you may be able to tell whether the child is going to be able to bond with you is by visiting him and seeing what he is like. Such a child will generally not respond to you, and when you look at him, his eyes will appear to be "hollow." Agencies may gloss over such conditions, insisting that within a few months of living with you, the child will be very "normal." However, attach-ment disorders are very difficult to treat, and the course of treatment can be extensive—and expensive.

If you were to adopt such a child in the United States through a social ser-vices agency, the child would probably be entitled to special services paid for by Medicaid and other funds. Not so with an international adoption; if your health insurance does not cover extensive mental health counseling, the cost can be very high, although there are limited state funds available. (See chapter 14, "Special Needs Adoption.")

AFTER A CHILD IS ASSIGNED TO YOU
Once a child is assigned to you and you accept the child, the care of the child in a foster home or orphanage may become your responsibility. In some countries it can take several months before the child is actually placed with you (depending upon the country's regulations), so in the meantime you want to make sure that your child is as well cared for as possible. Make sure the amount being requested to care for your child is in accord with the country's average wage. If the average family income is $150 per month, you should not be sending $500 per month to a family or orphanage to care for the child.[4] If you are concerned about poor foster care, make sure your facilitator or agency knows how you feel and that you want to make sure that the monies you are sending for the care of your child are doing just that.

SPECIAL NEEDS CHILDREN
Just as there are thousands of special needs children in the United States waiting to be adopted, so it is in countries around the world. The International Concerns Committee has a photo listing from several international and domestic agencies of children who are looking for homes. Many international adoption newsletters also feature special children waiting for a special home.

There are three basic criteria that will qualify a child as special needs:

1. *The child is preschool age—at least four years old.* Again, the age of the child is less of a determinant of the child's adjustment than her early experiences. Early neglect, abuse, and repeated changes in the care-taking environment increase the risk for later maladjustment.[5]

2. *The child is part of a sibling group.* Some may consider adopting, say, a brother and sister. Sometimes children are available only as siblings, since an agency, orphanage, or government may be opposed to breaking up the family unit. There are distinct advantages to adopting sibling groups: The children may have an easier time adjusting because they "have each other," and you can grow your family faster than if you adopt singly. Adopting more than one child at a time can be far less expensive in the long run, too, especially when you consider traveling expenses.

    If you are considering adopting siblings or more than one child at the same time while you are in another country, your home study must qualify you for the exact number of children you wish to adopt. Just because you are qualified to adopt one child does not mean you are qualified to adopt three. A social worker doing the home study will want to know how many other children you already have, what experience you have with children if you do not have any children, how large your home is and how many bedrooms it has, and whether your income can support a larger family.

    If you have no children, you may be tempted to adopt two or three young siblings. You may have longed for children for some time, and now you feel you are ready to settle down into a large family. However, you need to think hard about the impact this decision will have on your life. Adding just one child to a childless home changes life completely. Babies are a lot of work, but they do sleep a lot, and it is possible to adjust to their schedule. If you suddenly find yourself with a nine-month-old baby, a two-year-old, and a three-and-a-half-year-old, you will have three children all going through a cultural adjustment while you yourself are going through a major life adjustment. If you plan to be a stay-at-home parent, staying at home and caring for children will be pretty much your life. Lots of people, of course, have three children close in age, but they've had time to "grow" with the job— and their children are not making the cultural and emotional adjustments that yours will be.

This is not to discourage you from considering siblings, but only to help you think about what it might involve. Actually, the decision to adopt sibling groups can be good for you and certainly for the children. A study shows that international children who are adopted as siblings actually have fewer disruptions and behavior problems than those adopted singly.[6] If you are seriously considering this option, we suggest you offer to have two or three of your nieces and nephews over for a few days or more and see how you cope. If it feels manageable, and you have good support systems and the financial resources to meet their needs, ask your social worker to approve you for up to the number of children you want to adopt at the same time. The INS does not place restrictions on the number of children you can adopt.

3. *The child has a correctable or noncorrectable medical condition.* "Correctable" covers the following:

- club foot
- cleft palate/cleft lip
- need for open-heart surgery
- malnourishment
- medically controlled epilepsy
- scars from burns
- cataracts
- tumors or cysts
- delayed development

Noncorrectable conditions include:

- postpolio effects
- cerebral palsy
- spina bifida
- blindness and deafness
- unknown prognosis—child may be "slow"

In some countries the stipulations as to who can adopt may be very narrow, and only those adopting a child with a medical condition may have the restrictions broadened. If the country happens to be one where there are far more children than adoptive parents, however—meaning that officials are eager to find placements—the definition of "special needs" may be very broad, covering such conditions as chronic ear infections. If you want to adopt in a particular country and you do not qualify because of an arbitrary guideline, you may indicate that you are willing to adopt a child with a "minor, correctable disability or health condition."

Sometimes it turns out that children have been classified as "special needs" so that they can be placed for adoption. In the former Soviet Union children were not allowed to be released unless they had a health problem. (In certain sections of Eastern Europe this could still be true.) To get around this rule, the officials in charge of the orphanages would classify the child as having a health problem just so he could be released for adoption.

Remember, fees can be reduced if you adopt a "special needs" child. Many countries and orphanages charge a fee to adopt in their country. Those adopting a child with a health problem may pay at the lower end of the range. Also, in countries like Romania and Russia, children of certain nationalities or ethnic backgrounds are not as "adoptable," meaning that those adopting such children will pay a lower in-country fee.

Resources:

> To subscribe to the Deaf Adoption News Service (DANS), a text-based e-mail mailing list of deaf/hard-of-hearing foreign children who are available for adoption, contact Jamie Berke at **sberke@netcom.com**. DANS also has a Web site at **http://www.erols.com/berke/ deafchildren.html**.

SATISFYING THE ADOPTION AND IMMIGRATION REQUIREMENTS

When adopting, you must satisfy the requirements of your state, the agency (if you are working with one), the foreign country, and the United States government. You cannot change the requirements that your state places on you, unless you move to another state, and you have no say in the requirements imposed by the United States. But you do have a choice in the country you adopt from and the agency that conducts the adoption.

The following must be satisfied in order for you to adopt:

An approved domestic home study. You must have a home study conducted by a *local* agency or social worker. Generally your state's and agency's requirements will be met through your approved home study and the appropriate documents. International agencies, unlike domestic ones, do not have to create artificial barriers in order to decrease the number of applicants.

United States approval, which comes through the Immigration and Naturalization Service. This is the office that handles all immigrations. The INS wants to ensure that the following requirements are met: first, that you are following your state's laws and the laws of the foreign country; second, that you are suitable as indicated by your home study and that you have no criminal or child abuse history; and third, that the child you want to adopt is an "orphan" as defined by United States immigration law. Also, at least one parent must be a U.S. citizen, and both parents must officially reside in the U.S.

The criteria of the foreign country. Nearly all countries require a dossier, which consists of many documents. These documents are essentially the same ones that accompany your home study and immigration forms. Each country will have its own set of rules as to who can and cannot adopt. These rules, which tend to reflect the country's culture, usually relate to age, marital status, number of previous divorces, and number of children already in the family.

MEETING THE REQUIREMENTS OF YOUR STATE, AGENCY, THE INS, AND THE FOREIGN COUNTRY

The section that follows describes as comprehensively as possible the paperwork involved in international adoption. (Of course, not every item on this list will necessarily be required by your agency, your state, the INS, or the country where you are adopting.) If you find yourself feeling overwhelmed and discouraged as you read, remember two things: first, a child is there for you, and second, you can succeed. Yes, you will have to wait for others to do their part, but if you are committed and persistent, you can move the process along quickly.

Few people really *like* to complete forms. If you are someone who cannot even stand to complete a credit card application, you will want to select an agency that leads you through the process, reviews your forms, and handles much of the processing for you.

Except for the home study itself, *try to obtain four sets of every document.* It will cost a little extra, but there is no more effort involved in getting four birth certificates than in getting one. Keep a set of originals in your possession at all times. If a set gets lost, you always have the extra set, and you won't fall two or three months behind in the adoption process.

The various documents you gather will be sent to the following:

1. A local agency or social worker conducting your home study (Only copies are needed for a home study.)

2. The agency, facilitator, or attorney handling your adoption (Only copies are needed.)
3. The Immigration and Naturalization Service
4. The overseas agency or court (papers in your dossier)
5. The United States consulate
6. The court in your state (if the adoption will be formalized in the United States)

The Home Study

When pursuing an international adoption, you may end up with two home studies: one that meets the requirements of your state and the INS, and another, shorter version for the country in which you will be adopting. Why is the export version shorter? First, because it must be translated, and second, because a home study that has too much "psychological" information in it may cause some foreign officials concern. On the other hand, the shorter version may address an issue or two of concern to the specific country that may not be asked on a standard United States home study. An international adoption home study also needs to include a child abuse clearance through your department of social services, in addition to a criminal clearance through the F.B.I.

The INS requires that your home study indicate whether or not you or your partner have a history of substance abuse, sexual or child abuse, or domestic violence, even if no arrests have been made. If there is a history, the issues must be addressed. The home study must also include whether or not you have been rejected as a prospective adoptive parent or had an unfavorable home study in the past. If you have, these also must be addressed. If you seek to adopt a child with special needs, your home study must state that fact. Finally, a summary of the preadoption counseling you have received must be included in the home study. It should state that the counseling included a discussion of the international adoption process, and its possible expenses, difficulties, and delays.

Assuming that the international child placement agency will not be conducting your home study, begin your home study process as soon as possible; it can take a long time to complete, especially if there are only a few licensed agencies in your state that can conduct home studies. If your state permits individual licensed social workers to conduct home studies, make sure that the country from which you are adopting and the child-placement agency will accept a home study from a nonagency professional.

In selecting an agency or certified home study investigator, check that the person doing the home study is familiar with the requirements of the Immigration and Naturalization Service, of the agency you will be working with, and of the country you will be adopting from. The agency hired to conduct your home study will not usually place restrictions on you beyond those imposed by the INS and your state. If you are forty-five years old, for example, and both the country from which you are adopting and the child-placement agency accept applicants of this age, then the agency doing your home study should not say that you are too old to adopt.

Often, indeed, the child-placement agency will be able to do the home study. You may be charged more for the home study because the agency is also handling the checklist of twenty or more documents that accompany your home study and are placed in your dossier. Don't forget that for every hour you spend with a social worker, she may be spending ten or more hours doing paperwork and making telephone calls on your behalf.

The INS will accept only a home study that has been completed within the last six or twelve months. If you already have a home study, the original agency or investigator may have to be contacted to update the study, adding whatever information may be required by the country to which you are applying for adoption. Although there is a charge to do this, it is not the same cost as a full home study. It is *not* legal for another agency simply to add information and then "sign off" on another agency or investigator's home study.

Certified Birth Certificates

You will need four certified copies each of your birth certificate, your spouse's, and your children's. Call the library to get the address of the vital statistics department of the state in which each person was born. Be sure to order at least one long-form birth certificate (be sure to specify "long form" as opposed to "short form") for each person in the family in case the information contained in the long form is wanted by another country. Obtaining a birth certificate can sometimes take several weeks, especially if you are not sending the department of vital statistics a copy of one that you have at home. Going in person is the fastest route, although some offices allow you to order the certificate using a credit card. If you must send the request in writing, sending it Priority Mail with a self-addressed, stamped Priority Mail envelope enclosed can expedite things.

Certified Marriage License

You will need two copies of your (current) marriage certificate. One each will go into your foreign dossier and one will be sent to the INS.

Divorce Decree and Certified Death Certificate

Order an existing divorce decree from the clerk of court where the decree was issued. If a former spouse has died, order a death certificate from your state's vital statistics department. These also go to the INS and in your dossier.

Life Insurance Policies

Include only the page or pages showing the name of the company, the beneficiary, and the amount. For security purposes, white out a portion of the policy number.

Medical Statements

Medical statements should include the dates of your last physical exams, one for each member of the household. Most countries are looking for a simple statement from your physician that you can expect to have a full life span; that you have no communicable diseases; that you are not infected with the HIV virus (you may have to take an AIDS test); and that you do not use drugs.

If you are just beginning to gather all of your documents and are still exploring options, you may want to wait until you have gathered all your other documents before getting a medical exam. When you do, ask the physician to have it notarized if possible.

Some agencies or countries may require a letter indicating that you are infertile.

Police Clearance Letter

Your agency or state may require that you get this from your local or state police system confirming that you and your spouse have no criminal records. When requesting this letter, ask that it also be notarized. This is *not* the same as being fingerprinted.

Child Abuse Clearance

Your social worker will ask you to sign a form, which she will process with the social services department in your state. As of October 1995, the Immigration and Naturalization Service requires child abuse clearance on all adoptions.

Fingerprints

Some adoption agencies now take fingerprints. Have the fingerprints placed on the FD-258 Fingerprinting Chart, which is ordered from the INS office when you order your other forms. Order two charts for each spouse, in case your fingerprints smear. The INS requires that fingerprints be taken only by designated trained personnel or by INS staff, meaning that some police departments may not have the staff and record-keeping system to comply. Fingerprints are sent on to the FBI. *Get these done right away,* as some fingerprints cannot be read properly the first time and must be redone, a process that can take a few months. In many domestic adoptions, the placement of a child in your home can proceed so long as the fingerprints are being processed. *In an international adoption, the child cannot enter your home without the fingerprint clearance, even if it is because the fingerprints cannot be "read" properly.* Unlike other documents and the home study itself, fingerprints are valid for fifteen months.

If you have a criminal history, no matter how minor, tell your caseworker. If you are unsure how she will feel about the matter, discuss it with her *before* you pay for a home study. Most caseworkers will approve your home study if you have small violations in your past, especially related to teen drug or alcohol use or shoplifting. She will not be likely to approve you if it turns out after the FBI matches your fingerprints that you lied to her. A past arrest does not necessarily disqualify you as an adoptive parent. If your home study agency approves you in general, so will the INS.

Letters of Reference

You will need to assemble letters of recommendation from at least three different people. Foreign officials often like to see letters of reference from professionals and leaders, so try to have at least two letters of reference on professional letterhead from a lawyer, city council member, minister, teacher, or business owner, and at least one from a friend who will write a warmer, more descriptive letter. Ask each person to have the letter notarized.

Most other countries do not have a computerized system for checking on someone's credit history and possible criminal and child abuse record. Officials will be looking for documentation to confirm that you are an upright citizen. In the United States, where your history can be checked, references are much more personal and directed more toward your child-rearing abilities than your good citizenship.

Pictures of Applicants

The INS wants pictures of the applicants in front of their home, as well as individual, close-up photos of each member of your family. Passport photos are fine. You will also need two family pictures and two of your home for your dossier.

Letter to the Agency or Entity Who Is Finding Your Child

Write a brief description of yourselves, any children you may have, and the kind of child you wish to adopt, including their age, sex (if you have a preference), and any medical conditions you are willing to accept. If the agency that does your home study is the same agency that will be making arrangements for you to find a child, it will probably have you complete this information on their forms.

Affidavit of Support Form I-134

As long as you are collecting information about your financial status, make sure you get the documents that must accompany INS Form I-134 showing that you can support a child. This form is needed later to obtain the child's immigration visa, which you will get when you order your other forms from the INS. At the very end of the form you will find a list of all the supporting documents you must attach. Obtain four copies of each: one for the dossier, two to accompany the affidavit of support for the INS, and one for yourself.

The documents include:

1. A statement from a bank officer or officer of another financial institution in which you have deposits, providing the following details:
   - The date the account was opened
   - The total amount deposited during the last year
   - Your current balance

2. A statement from your employer on business stationery that tells the following:
   - The date and nature of your employment
   - Your salary
   - Whether your position is permanent or temporary

3. If you are self-employed, you must include the following:
   - A copy of last year's income tax return (filed)
   - A report of commercial rating
   - A list containing the serial numbers and denominations of bonds and the name of the record owner

INS APPROVAL TO ADOPT

Before you can adopt a child from another country, you must get permission from the INS both to adopt and to bring a child who truly is an "orphan" into the

United States. You can order the necessary forms by calling 1 (800) 870-FORMS—or the agency, organization, or attorney you are working with may have them.

If you must talk with someone at the INS, call the office of your U.S. representative or senator and ask a staff member to contact the INS for you. If you call the INS yourself, you will talk to a machine, not a person. Try to make a personal contact at your legislator's office if you think you will be dealing directly with the INS in the future. You will probably be calling this person at least a few times to double-check on everything.

Order the INS forms at the same time that you are having your home study completed. The INS requires the same kinds of supporting documents as your home study agency. There is no need to have your documents verified, translated, or authenticated to receive approval from the United States INS office to adopt. Your INS application can be processed while these other things are going on.

Note: When you send documents to the INS, send them Federal Express instead of certified mail. It is well worth it. *Enclose a full set of copies of your INS forms, home study, and other documents with a request that the INS send you back all of your originals.* It is wise to enclose a large, self-addressed, stamped Priority Mail envelope for this purpose. The INS does not make copies, so they will keep your originals in a file unless you make copies for them; do make copies, since you will want your originals for other purposes.

Resources:

The U.S. Department of Justice has a Web site at **http://gopher.usdoj.gov/offices/ins.html**, where you can find more information on the INS.

INS Application for Advance Processing (Form I-600A)

If you plan to adopt but do not have a specific child designated for you yet, you can have the immigration paperwork done much faster by "advance processing" the I-600A form. It is filed along with your fingerprints and other documents and fees to the local INS. The one-time filing fee is $155. Process yourselves for approval now; then, when the child is identified, you can process his paperwork for his approval. At the time a child is assigned to you, you must process the I-600 form, which is also known as an "Orphan Petition." Advance processing can also be done when the prospective adoptive parents are traveling to a country that has no INS office and they want to file the Orphan Petition at a United States consulate or embassy there.

Here are the documents that must accompany the I-600A form:

1. Your home study
2. Evidence that you have met your state's preadoption requirements (This statement can be included in the home study.)
3. Birth certificate for each spouse, or current United States passport
4. Marriage certificate (if applicable)
5. Divorce decree (if applicable)
6. Fingerprint charts, Form FD-258 (Order these from the INS.)
7. Form I-134 Affidavit of Support

INS Approval to Adopt (Form I-171H)

Once you have sent all your documentation to the INS, the office will send back to you Form I-171H, Notice of Favorable Determination Concerning Application for Advance Processing of Orphan Petition. If you have a child already selected, the INS may also cable preapproval status to the consulate in the child's country. If it is necessary for the INS to cable the preapproval, make sure they have done so; call your senator's or representative's office and ask him or her to check on the matter.

Form 1-171H indicates that once a child is assigned to you, it is acceptable for you to proceed with an adoption by filing the Orphan Petition (I-600 form), so long as the child qualifies as an orphan. As a rule, if your home study approves you as adoptive parents, the INS will approve you too. The document is valid for eighteen months, instead of twelve, except for the fingerprints, which are valid for only fifteen months. This means you have an extended period of time before your permission expires.

COMPLETING YOUR DOSSIER

Your dossier includes documentation required by foreign officials. Almost everything needed for your dossier you will already have collected for your home study, the agency, or the INS. Therefore, keep a notebook or an accordion file folder that is clearly labeled and contains all your documents. This minimal organization step can save you hours of time of looking for the same document over and over.

Unlike a standard U.S. home study, in which photocopies of important documents are perfectly acceptable, the documents that go into a dossier must be original or certified copies, and often they must have a series of authorizations placed on them to indicate that they are legitimate.

Listed are the following documents that most countries require:

- Your home study and the documents that accompany it
  (Remember, the home study most likely will be an abbreviated version—about four to eight pages long. It may need to be translated.)
- Affidavit of Support for the INS (Form I-134) and the documents and forms that accompany it
- Letter to your agency or facilitator describing yourselves, the children in your home, and the type of child you want to adopt
- Two pictures of your family and two pictures of your home
- If you have adopted previously, a copy of the child's final adoption decree and possibly an updated report on the child's well-being

Verifying or Certifying Your Documents

Some countries require that each document's notary public signature be verified, or certified. Find out the rules for the country you will be working with: The process is expensive, and you do not want to do it unless it is required. Your agency or facilitator should let you know exactly what must be done. In some instances, he or she can help you complete the process.

Verification sheets can be obtained from the county clerk or secretary of state to verify that the notary publics' signatures are valid. Each document needs to be verified, even if the same notary public signed each one. In some states you do not need to send the actual document but just a typed sheet that includes the name, county, and expiration date of the notary as well as the fee for *each* document. Then just order verification seals for the number of documents the notary signed. The verification seal can cost from $5 to $25 per document, depending upon which state you live in.

Translating Your Documents

Before you send documents to the consuls of certain countries, it is required that the documents be translated. The official seal of the translation service on each translated document may be required. The service should also provide a cover letter certifying that the translator is licensed. Notarize and verify this letter as well.

This means, of course, that a single document may have been notarized, verified, certified, and translated; then the cover letter for the translation must be notarized and sent off to be verified. To speed up the process of completing your paperwork, if possible, get the notarized cover letter that indicates the competency of the translator, and send this along with your other documents to be verified *before you begin the translation*. Obviously, you will have to know which country you wish to adopt from before you can find a translator.

The Apostille, or Legalization and Authentication

After the documents are notarized, verified, and then translated, most countries that are part of the Hague Convention require that certain documents no longer be authenticated by a consul but rather have an apostille attached. An apostille is a paper that bears your state's official seal and has the word "apostille" on it. It indicates that the county and its seal are legitimate. Usually the apostille is obtained at your lieutenant governor's office, and there is usually a fee for each document requiring an apostille.

The apostille is a further step in the verification process: Your signature is verified by a notary; the notary's signature is verified or certified by your county clerk. So far so good. What is not clear is that the county clerk's verification of the notary's signature and her status as a notary will contain the county court seal or be on the letterhead of the county court. Thus, the apostille verifies that the county court is legitimate.

If your country of adoption has not signed the Hague Convention, your documents will need a *legalization* from your lieutenant governor's office instead of an apostille. The statement serves the same purpose as the apostille. Your documents may all also have to be *authenticated* by a consul who is in the United States representing the foreign country. The consul's seal, stamps, and signature attest to the documents' authenticity. Call your U.S. representative for the consul closest to you. If the consulate is close to you, you may be able to go in person. If you do so, dress and act as if for a day in court. The cost per document is about $10 to $30.

Once your documents have been notarized and have had other verifications attached, make a copy of each one before you send them to the foreign country. Take these copies with you when you go to your child's country.

Note: In 1993 the Hague Conference on Private International Law adopted the Convention on Protection of Children and Cooperation in Respect of Intercountry Adoption, covering all adoption between countries that are members of the convention. As of June 1995, twenty-two countries signed the Convention, including the United States; but it has not yet been ratified. The Convention states that the best solution for an orphan is for the child to be adopted within her own country, but that international adoption is preferable to foster care or institutionalization in the child's country of origin.

DOCUMENTS FOR TRAVELING

Once your paperwork is complete, you will need to be ready to travel at short notice. Make sure you have all the proper documents, including:

A *current passport*. An adult passport is valid for ten years, so you will want to get one while you are completing all the other paperwork. In many countries your passport number is your identifying number; therefore, both spouses should get a passport, even if only one spouse will be traveling. If you travel together, always travel with a copy of the other's passport as a precaution in case one of you loses a passport. If your spouse is not traveling with you, take a copy of his or her passport's vital page as identification. If you are just thinking about adopting an international child, get a passport now. They're valid for ten years, and it's one less piece of paperwork to obtain when you do adopt.

A *tourist card or visa*. Some countries require adoptive parents to have tourist visas, while others require business visas. Contact the consulate of the country you will be adopting from and find out what documents are needed. You may want to call a travel agency or airline for this information first. Verify what the cost and procedure are for yourself and your child, if he will also be traveling. If you or your spouse is not a citizen, tell the consulate. Visas are usually attached to your passport, so the consulate will need your passport to issue the visas. Find out the best way to get it to them directly—Federal Express is usually the safest.

First find out how long you can have the visa before it expires. Get it for at least three to six months in case of a delay. If it expires in a matter of months, you may not want to get one until your flight reservations are made. In this case, obtain visa application forms, but do not complete them until you have made all your reservations for the trip.

Identifying photos.

Power of attorney. If you are not traveling with your spouse, you will need a legal document giving you power of attorney on behalf of your spouse. It is best to have this power of attorney document prepared by your attorney.

You may need to get vaccinated against certain diseases. Vaccination certificates are not necessary, however, unless a traveler is coming from an area that is experiencing an epidemic.

DOCUMENTS NEEDED TO ADOPT THE CHILD

Once you have been approved to adopt a child and a child is identified for you, you must file papers to make sure that the INS approves the child for you to adopt. This is the I-600 form, or Orphan Petition. Sometimes this is handled in the United States before you leave, sometimes in the child's country. Your agency or facilitator should be guiding you through the whole process.

If you are adopting without the assistance of a child-placement agency, you need to make sure the child is truly an orphan. The federal definition of an orphan is very narrow and somewhat ambiguous. An orphan is a child whose parents have both died or a child whose "sole parent" is placing the child for adoption. Under United States law, a "sole parent" is an unmarried person. This single parent can sign a release of parental rights for his or her "illegitimate" child to be placed for adoption. However, the other parent must have severed all ties to the child. If the child has two parents, her parents must abandon her, as two parents cannot sign a relinquishment.

Another complication is that the U.S. Immigration and Naturalization Service makes a distinction between children who were born "legitimated" and those born "out of wedlock." In many countries, however, there is no distinction made between "legitimate" and "illegitimate" children. Children born to unmarried parents may be considered both "legitimate" and also "born out of wedlock." If a child is considered "legitimate," even though he was born out of wedlock and has only a mother, he is not considered to be an orphan unless his mother abandons him.

In general, children are matched with parents by an agency; or the parents may have seen pictures of children and identified one they want to adopt. Once you accept a child, the adoption process in the foreign country can begin. You may have to give power of attorney to a foreign lawyer who will represent you in the other country's court. You are not responsible for obtaining these documents, only for processing them later.

The major documents needed to prove that the child you are adopting can come to the U.S with you, or to you, include the following:

The orphan's birth certificate. If this cannot be obtained, an explanation of circumstances needs to be submitted. The birth certificate should show the date and place of the child's birth. Some countries change the certificate to show the child's new name and the names of the adoptive parents. **Make sure you get at least two sets of certified copies—one for the INS and one to use in applying for the child's visa.**

Statement of release of child for adoption. **Again, get at least two sets.** The statement of release shows that the orphan's only surviving parent cannot provide for the child and has forever and irrevocably released the child for adoption and emigration. The release must state why the mother (or possibly the father) relinquished the child. If the birth father's name is known, it should be listed. Certified copies of this form must be retained to use in adoption proceedings in the United States.

Certificate of abandonment (if the child has not been relinquished). **Get at least two sets.** This document is issued by the court after publishing for the child's parents. If the child was in an orphanage, it must show that she has been unconditionally abandoned to the orphanage. The certificate grants custody to an agency, legal placing entity, or the adoptive parents.

Death certificate of orphan's parents (if applicable).

Adoption decree, permanent guardianship, or custody transfer to adoptive parents. This should confirm the child's legal status as an orphan. **Get at least two sets.** A resolution is sometimes given instead of a final decree, which is issued later. The resolution is as acceptable as an adoption decree and will give the adoptive parents custody of the child.

The above documents represent the necessary evidence to substantiate the child's status as an orphan, which is required for processing the I-600 form. The complete list of documents needed for the I-600 is described below.

BRINGING THE CHILD BACK TO THE UNITED STATES

Certain documents must be completed before a child can be brought into the United States. Your agency can instruct you as to which forms must be submitted to the INS and which should be sent to the U.S. embassy or consulate in the child's country of origin. Not all states require all documents.

A number of documents are required for INS approval to bring the child into the United States.

INS Petition to Classify the Orphan as an Immediate Relative (Form I-600)

If you will be traveling to the child's country, you will take the I-600 form with you so that you can get the child a visa. Leave the child's name blank on the form and complete that information once the child is definitely going to be placed with you. If your spouse is not traveling with you, have him or her sign the document and have it notarized before you leave. *Always take two copies with you, with your spouse's signature on each, in case one is lost or the wrong information on the child is entered.*

Once you have adopted the child, the petition must be filed *immediately*. One petition is necessary for each child adopted. If more than one petition is filed on behalf of siblings, there is only one application fee. The I-600 form is often filed in the same INS office as the I-600A form.

All of the documents that support the child's status as an orphan must be typed and translated into English. An affidavit affirming that the translator is qualified to translate from the given language to English, and that the translated document is accurate, complete, and true, must accompany the translation.

Supporting Documents for Form I-600

The requisite supporting documents include the following:

1. *The child's birth certificate, or proof of the child's age*
2. *Statement of Release of Child for Adoption or Certificate of Abandonment*
3. *Background information on the child's biological parents*
4. *Death certificate of orphan's parents* (if applicable)
5. *Adoption Decree, permanent guardianship, or custody transfer to adoptive parents* (Must be translated into English. **Get at least two sets.**)
6. *An agreement signed by you that any charges for long-distance phone calls will be paid by you*
7. *A filing fee of $155* (unless you have already sent the fee in when filing the I-600A form)
8. *The home study and other documents that were required for filing the I-600A form, if not already submitted*
9. *If the child is not already adopted in another country, a statement that pre-adoption requirements are fulfilled* (This includes notification that a home study is approved, and other appropriate documents. In some states the social service department must send this to the INS. *Make sure this has been done.*)
10. *INS Approval Form I-171H* (The INS requires that the orphan's documents be in duplicate, each of which is either an original or a certified copy. Send them an additional set of copies too, so that they can return the original to you and you will have another set for the child's adoption. The U.S. consular offices in other countries have the power to certify copies.)

At this point you are notified that the petition for the child has been approved via Form I-171, Notice of Approval of Relative Immigrant Visa Petition. Another copy will be cabled to the foreign consulate. You can now travel to the country to pick up your child, if you are not already there.

GETTING A VISA FOR YOUR CHILD

Once the consulate receives approval from the INS, it conducts an orphan investigation to make sure that the child is truly an orphan and does not have a significant illness or disability not listed on the I-600 form. The consul will require a completed INS Form 157, Medical Evaluation of the Child. The U. S. embassy in your child's country will provide you with the names of U.S.-approved clinics or physicians who can complete this form. The consulate wants to make sure that the parents are fully aware of the child's medical problems or disability and are going to take full responsibility for the child. Once your child is examined, you will receive a medical form enclosed in a sealed envelope. Do not open the envelope; it will be given to the consulate when you apply for the child's visa.

Some consuls require additional documents, so call the consulate to make sure you have all needed documents.

The documents needed to obtain a visa are similar to the ones needed to get approval from the INS when you submitted the I-600 form. Give the United States consulate the certified set of documents and file the copies. After applying for the child's United States visa, make sure the original set of documents are sent back to you so that you will have them when you adopt your child in the United States. Remember, they may not get returned; that is why it is necessary to have at least two copies of everything.

Following are the documents necessary to apply for a visa:

1. *Visa Application Form OF-230 or FS-510*
2. *Pictures of the child for the visa* (This means three color photos on a white background. The photo must be one and a half inches square, the head size must be about one inch from chin to hair, and the child should be shown with three-fourths frontal view, with right face and right ear showing. Lightly print the child's name on the back of each photo and sign your name on the front side using pencil or felt pen.)
3. *Child's birth certificate*
4. *Country's adoption decree*
5. *Death certificates of biological parents* (if applicable)
6. *Passport* (You will need to obtain a passport for your child.)
7. *Child's medical records*

ADOPTING YOUR CHILD IN THE UNITED STATES

Once your child is in the United States, you will want to adopt her officially regardless of whether you officially adopted her in her country of origin. You will be required to have postplacement studies and file for adoption in accordance with your state laws. Please be aware that your child will not automatically be a United States citizen once she is adopted in the United States.

Here is the procedure you will probably follow:

1. *You will contact a knowledgeable attorney to file papers for adoption.* The cost of this adoption is a fraction of an independent adoption. The attorney is simply filing the appropriate papers. Some couples do this work themselves, but getting a birth certificate can be difficult unless all the papers that should be submitted are exactly the way they should be. Be prepared to provide the attorney with one or possibly two copies of your home study (one for state approval and one for foreign country approval), the child's birth certificates, documents indicating parental abandonment or relinquishment, and the adoption decree from the foreign country.

2. *You will arrange with an agency or independent home study investigator to conduct postplacement visits.* This is not required in all states.

3. *You will go to court for the child's final adoption.*

4. *Your attorney or the court submits a Judgment of Adoption* to your state's department of vital statistics to obtain a birth certificate. Make sure the Judgment of Adoption lists your child's date and place of birth. Vital statistics offices do not like to have to look at any other paperwork.

5. *You obtain a copy of the child's birth certificate.* The new birth certificate will include the child's new adoptive name, you as his parents, and his date and place of birth. In some states, such as New Jersey, when a child is adopted internationally as opposed to domestically, the birth certificate says "Adopted" right on it.

6. *You apply for the child to become a citizen.*

7. *You may need to communicate with the child's country of origin.* Many countries require that follow-up documentation be sent to the foreign courts to monitor the child's progress. These reports and documents, and especially photos (send photos even if not asked), allow the placing organizations to prove to the courts and authorities that this child is in a wonderful environment and is not being exploited. Sending this documentation can mean the difference between a country's keeping its adoption policy open or closing the doors. Even if the courts do not

mandate that you send documentation, send letters, small gifts, a few dollars, and photographs to your child's caregiver or orphanage. In some countries you should not send large packages, since corrupt mail carriers and others will open packages that appear to have valuables in them. Keep your child's orphanage address on your Christmas list, and send photos and a letter at least once a year.

Resources:

International Adoption Consultants provides help with the paperwork needed to complete an international adoption. You can reach them via their Web site, **http://www.adopting.org/Adoption_consultants.html**.

ISSUES RELATED TO HAVING INTERNATIONAL CHILDREN

Because children adopted internationally often look different from their parents, you may be subject to such unintentionally insensitive questions as, "Where did he come from?" "When did you get her?" or "How old was he when you got him?" Holly Van Gulden and Lida M. Bartels-Rabb suggest giving answers like, "We come from New Haven," "I pick her up after school," or "It seems she's been with us forever."[7]

When we are on the playground and spot a family that appears to have adopted children, because of our interest in adoption, we too are tempted to ask such questions. In adoption play groups, where some of the children are adopted and some biological, such questions are considered perfectly acceptable. And sometimes people ask such questions because they are genuinely interested in adoption. Gulden and Bartels-Rabb emphasize the importance of answering such questions so that your child feels like a part of the family and to give examples to your child of setting appropriate boundaries. In doing so, you never want your answer to be sarcastic so that it makes your child and others uncomfortable about adoption.

Insensitive questions can happen to any parent of a child who is "different." When adopting internationally, you inevitably will be exposed to some racism. Gulden and Bartles-Rabb write, "Regardless of how you interpret such situations, your first response must be to validate your child's feelings." They suggest making the following points: that comments will happen and do hurt; that your child is worthy and good and does not deserve the comments; and that people who make such comments do not know your child and have no right to say such things.[8]

ῃg to Another Country

ɪ ιιe main reason many Americans do not want to adopt a child from another country is fear of travel. People will cite the usual disadvantages of traveling—being away from your job, traveling with your children, or making child care arrangements. The real reason, though, has more to do with fear of the unknown. If you are traveling to another country to get your child, you will want to make sure that you are as prepared as possible.

If possible, go during "tourist season." Tourists are particular and want to be comfortable—you will also want to be as comfortable as possible, especially with a new small child.

If you are staying less than three weeks, your chances of getting ill are slight. Most parents travel for less than two weeks, and they stay in large city hotels and eat at better restaurants. This minimizes the likelihood of contracting illness. It is certainly essential, however, to get whatever immunizations are recommended for the country you will be traveling to. Start by making sure your childhood immunizations are all up-to-date. In addition, we recommend the following:

Diphtheria. If you have not had a diphtheria/tetanus booster in the last ten years, get one. Diphtheria is a major health problem in all of the former Soviet Union.

Cholera. Cholera is an ongoing epidemic in Latin America and much of Africa, as well certain parts of Russia. Because cholera vaccine is not very effective and has side effects, it is not recommended if you are traveling for a short time.

Typhoid. Typhoid has been reported in many parts of the former Soviet Union. New typhoid vaccines—both injectable and oral—are available, have few side effects, and are effective in preventing 50 to 75 percent of cases.

Other vaccines are recommended to those who expect to be staying for a long time under adverse conditions:

Hepatitis A. Nearly everyone in the developing world has had it, and about 50 percent of American adults have been infected. If you are going to be in contact with a baby or will be eating in questionable places, get a shot of immunoglobulin, or ISG. This immunization is partially protective for several weeks and is very safe. Unfortunately, the dose is so big that you will have to get it in the thigh or buttocks, and you will be in some pain for a few days.

Hepatitis B. Hepatitis B vaccine is not usually considered necessary unless your child has the virus or you will be caring for children who carry it. There are two kinds of vaccines, each of which costs about $110 for three doses. Even one provides some protection if you do not have time to complete the series before traveling.

Influenza. The "flu" can be prevented by taking amantadine for the whole trip. If you are at risk for other diseases associated with the flu, get immunized instead.

To prevent serious illness and the gastrointestinal problems caused by viruses, bacteria, and parasites, you will have to take certain commonplace precautions. Needless to say, do not have unknown sexual contact, blood transfusions, or contact with animals. Avoid mosquito-ridden areas, and use mosquito repellent if necessary; mosquitoes can carry malaria, Japanese encephalitis, yellow fever, and dengue.

Malaria is a significant problem in many areas. Every year between 200 and 300 Americans contract the disease. If you are going to an area that has a high incidence of malaria, especially in the rainy season, you may need to take an antimalaria drug, starting one week before you leave and continuing for six weeks after your return home. Depending upon where you are going and what kinds of malaria strains are present, you may have to take more than one drug. All can cause severe reactions, so you will want to discuss with an expert whether they are necessary.

If you are going to a big city and will not be going out much at night, your risk for getting a mosquito-carrying disease is very low. Even travel to the countryside poses little risk during the day. Stay in a hotel with air conditioning, and to be extra safe, bring an insect repellent and wear long pants and sleeves.

Contaminated food and water pose the greatest risk. Remember this motto: "Boil it, cook it, peel it, or forget it!" Always ask for *carbonated* bottled or canned beverages or boiled water. (If these are not available, use purifying tablets, which can be bought at camping stores.) Use the boiled water for making hot drinks and formula. Rinse out the cup or container first with the boiled water (preferably while the water is still hot). You will also need boiled water for brushing your teeth. Beer and wine that have not been mixed with another beverage are safe. Do not use ice cubes.

As for food—if it is not steaming hot or peelable or dry (cereal, bread, crackers), you should probably not eat it. Eat hot dishes that have been made up fresh. Food eaten in a private home is usually safer. You may ask your hostess how she prepares such a wonderful dish before you eat it.

Finally, avoid contact contamination. Wash your hands, wash your hands, wash your hands.

Drive carefully! Accidents are the major cause of death and disability for travelers.

For more information on international travel, try the following resources:

HHS Publication No (CDC) 85-8280/Superintendent of Documents
United States Government Printing Office, Washington, DC 20402

According to Dr. Jeri Ann Jensita, this is a very authoritative book and the most accurate source of information regarding immunization and malaria risk. It is organized first by country, then by disease.

CDC's International Traveler's Disease Hotline: (404) 332-4559

To obtain specific health documents call (404) 332-4565. Call this number for information on disease risk and prevention for every country. Your requested information is faxed back to you within minutes.

Consular Information Sheets: (202) 647-5225; or FAX (202) 647-3000

State Department/Electronic bulletin board modem at (202) 647-9225; the Web site at **http://www.stolaf.edu/network/travel-advisories.html** also can provide this information.

Steps to Take

So you are definitely interested in pursuing an international adoption? Congratulations! Following is a checklist of all the steps involved, from start to finish. You may find it helpful as you embark on this complicated but very worthwhile endeavor.

1. Join a support group.
2. Decide which countries you want to adopt from. (Always have a second one in mind in case one closes for unforeseen reasons.)
3. Find an agency or facilitator that conducts adoptions from those countries.
4. Determine the requirements of that country and agency.
5. Begin to gather paperwork— birth and marriage certificates, 1040s, etc.
6. Arrange for a home study.

7. Schedule a physical examination for every family member.
8. Call the INS and order your adoption forms; ask for at least two. (You can order up to five sets.)
9. Begin to have letters of reference done.
10. As soon as your fingerprint chart forms come from the INS, complete them and send them off for FBI clearance.
11. Complete all remaining INS paperwork (I-600A) and wait for their approval to adopt.
12. Have all other documentation verified and certified, if necessary. Also obtain the Apostille.
13. Have translations done, if necessary.
14. Wait for a child to be assigned to you by your agency or facilitator.
15. Make sure the child is truly an orphan. Complete the I-600 form.
16. Travel to the child's country and adopt the child in that country.
17. Process INS Form I-600 to get your child a visa to come to the United States.
18. Take your child to the U.S. embassy for a physical examination.
19. Bring the child home.
20. Have the child adopted in the United States.
21. Arrange for the child to become a United States citizen.

INS Offices:

Western Region
24000 Avila Road
PO Box 30080
Laguna Niguel, CA 92607-0080
Attn: Gustavo De La Vina

880 Front Street
Suite 1234
San Diego, CA 92101-8834
Attn: Mark K. Reed

Appraisers Building
630 Sansome St., Rm. 232
San Francisco, CA 94111-2280
Attn: Thomas J. Schiltgen

815 Airport Way, South
Seattle, WA 98134
Attn: Richard C. Smith

District Offices
620 E. 10th Avenue
Suite 102
Anchorage, AK 99501
Attn: Robert C. Eddy

595 Ala Moana Blvd.
Honolulu, HI 96813
Attn: Donald A. Radcliffe

300 N. Los Angeles St.
Los Angeles, CA 90012
Attn: Richard Rogers

2035 N. Central Avenue
Phoenix, AZ 85004
Attn: Roseanne Sonchik

Federal Building
Portland, OR 97209
Attn: David V. Beebe

Central Region
7701 North Stemmons Freeway
Dallas, TX 75247
Attn: Michael S. Williams

2800 Skyway Drive
Helena, MT 59601
Attn: Donald M. Whitney

509 North Sam Houston
Parkway East
Houston, TX 77060
Attn: Robert A. Wallis

9747 N. Conant Avenue
Kansas City, MO 64153
Attn: Michael Heston

3736 S. 132nd Street
Omaha, NE 68144
Attn: Dnnies Peruzzini

8940 Four Winds Drive
San Antonio, TX 78239
Attn: Richard M. Casillas

2901 Metro Drive
Suite 100
Bloomington, MN 55425
Attn: Dean Hove

10 W. Jackson Blvd.
Suite 600
Chicago, IL 60604
Attn: A.D. Moyer

8101 North Stemmons Freeway
Dallas, TX 75247
Attn: Arthur E. Strapp

4730 Paris St.
Denver, CO 80239
Attn: Joseph R. Greene

1545 Hawkins Blvd.
Suite 167
El Paso, TX 79925
Attn: Kenneth L. Pasquarell

Eastern Region
70 Kimball Ave.
South Burlington, VT 05403-6813
Attn: Carol D. Chase

District Offices
970 Broad Street
Peter Rodino Federal Bldg.
Room 1633
Newark, NJ 07102
Attn: Warren A. Lewis

26 Federal Plaza
Room 14-102
New York, NY 10278
Attn: Edward J. McElroy

1600 Callowhill St.
Philadelphia, PA 19130
Attn: J. Scott Blackman

739 Warren Ave.
Portland, ME 04103
Attn: Eugene M. Fitzpatick

Carlos Chardon St.
Hato Rey, PR 00917

GPO Box 365068
San Juan, PR 00936
Attn: John Abriel

4420 N. Fairfax Dr.
Arlington, VA 22203
Attn: William J. Carroll

77 Forsyth St., SW
MLK Federal Bldg.
Room 117
Atlanta, GA 30303
Attn: Thomas P. Fischer

Nationsbank Center
12th Floor, Tower One
100 S. Charles St.
Baltimore, MD 21201
Attn: Benedict J. Ferroi

Government Center
JFK Federal Bldg.
Room 1700
Boston, MA 02203

130 Delaware Ave.
Buffalo, NY 14202
Attn: Kpojn J. Ingham

A.J.C. Federal Bldg.
1240 E. Ninth St., Room 1917
Cleveland, OH 44199
Attn: Robert L. Brown

333 Mt. Elliot St.
Federal Building
Detroit, MI 48207-4381
Attn: Carol Jenifer

7880 Biscayne Blvd.
Miami, FL 33138
Attn: Walter D. Cadman

701 Loyola Ave. Room T-8011
New Orleans, LA 701113
Attn: John B. Z. Caplinger

INTERNATIONAL ADOPTION: ONE COUPLE'S STORY

For seven long years my husband and I tried thermometers, surgery, syringes, and just about everything short of swinging chickens over our heads. Still, we had no children. Our doctors had no idea why I couldn't get pregnant. They still don't, but now we have children. They came a year ago from Korea—according to our youngest son, "born on the Christmas airplane when I was three and my brother was five."

How did we come to be at BWI airport that night? It started four months earlier in August with the blinding realization that what we wanted was not to get pregnant but to be a family. Our first thought was to adopt an American infant with high APGAR scores. After all, one agency was ready to give us just such a child, so long as we paid them $16,000 and didn't ask any questions. But in the end we did something very different. We applied to Catholic Charities' international program on August 21, requesting an infant girl.

In September, two days before completing our home study, we called our caseworker and said we'd done some thinking about diapers and drool and would consider an older child—say, a girl about two years old. After all, we'd waited long enough for a family and didn't really see the point of waiting still longer for a child to gurgle, "Mama, Da-da." That was when the caseworker showed us the picture— two little brothers, three and five, looking impossibly dirty and infinitely sad. Days later we were petitioning the INS for visas for these two little boys, whom we were about to adopt from 12,000 miles around the world.

Our families were enthusiastic—my mother pointing out that adoption was infinitely better than pregnancy because you got pictures. We were euphoric—finally able to prowl the children's department at Garfinkel's and Lowen's in preparation for their arrival. We never regretted the decision, but we did get chills.

After all, these were older children. They were probably a little hardened. Bonding certainly wasn't going to be an issue; what we were worried about was, "Why can't we have more treats?" They'd probably test us and be suspicious.

By December we'd reached such a state that we fully expected them to arrive with beards, smoking cigarettes and cursing. When the caseworker called my husband at work to say they were to arrive in just five days, he said, "How nice," and threw up in his wastebasket.

So there we were at BWI, ready to face two sullen boys who by that time we imagined as six feet tall and ready to form an alliance against us. Instead, two tiny, terrified children walked haltingly down the ramp and reached out their hands. What we never anticipated is that our sons wanted a family as much as we did. Their need, like ours, was to love and be loved, and to build a future. And from the moment they put their small hands in ours, that's what we've been doing.

There was never any of the struggle we'd expected. We found ourselves the parents of children who were inexpressibly joyful to have a mama and a papa. They were untiring in their desire to please, expansive in their appreciation of our attempts to please them.

After our son's birthday party in September, we were tucking the boys in, and my husband said, "I'm sorry we weren't together for your first three!" Our older son touched his arm and said, "It's okay, Papa, we're together now." It is okay. We've learned to carpool, bake brownies, make valentines, and clean mud off tiny soccer shoes. I've also learned that the most wonderful part of the whole day can happen unexpectedly—anytime a small pair of arms reaches up to give a hug, or a small voice says, "Mama."

Hardened? Our six-year-old got into a fight at school because a boy was teasing a little girl. He explained that the girl didn't know it was just teasing and that she felt scared. He knew how that felt, he said, and wanted to help her. Hardly dog-eat-dog.

Are they like us? I don't know anymore. I know we fit together tightly, but I'm not sure who changed, or whether we were alike from the start.

They're teaching us to see our entire world with new, gentle, and eager eyes. Labeled as "hard-to-adopt" because of their "advanced ages," these two children are teaching us to find blessing wherever we look, and to know that even when sneakers have "accidentally" been glued to the refrigerator, we're happier than any of us would have dreamed before that night when the "Christmas airplane" landed.[9]

Chapter Thirteen

Adopting in Canada

J ust as in the United States, there are three basic routes for nonrelative adoption in Canada. First there is public adoption, in which primarily children who have been removed from their parents' care are placed with the state. Because of the abuse or neglect these children have suffered, they are generally considered to have special needs. This is very different from the way things were in Canada in the early eighties, when 78 percent of adopted newborns were placed through public agencies. Since 1988 most newborns have been placed privately, generally by an agency or an attorney.

At present there is a trend in Canada away from attorney-conducted adoption toward more agency-conducted ones. The laws vary from province to province, and each is considering changes. It is essential to obtain current information so that you can comply with the laws. Contact an adoption support group in your province to see what changes may be taking place.

The rights of birth fathers are another area of change. Until recently, unmarried birth father's rights have been negligible. Birth fathers are beginning to gain some recognition, and they may soon gain more rights.[1]

PRIVATE ADOPTION

In 1990 a total of 2,836 children were placed for adoption, of which 39 percent were private. Private adoption is not a uniform term in Canada. There are three kinds of private adoptions: independent, or self-directed, in which an attorney is used; licensee, in which a licensed agency or person conducts the adoption; and identified, in which you find the birth mother while working with an agency.

Independent Adoption

In an independent, or self-directed, adoption, you contact a birth mother, who chooses to place the child directly with you without the assistance of a licensee or an agency. This usually means finding the birth mother yourself. Some provinces have a few unlicensed agencies that can conduct an independent adoption, and these can help you find a birth mother. However, make sure paying such an intermediary is legal in the province in which the adoption will take place.

Independent adoptions are not allowed in Ontario, PEI, and Quebec. In Ontario and PEI, however, you can find a birth mother and work with an agency or licensee. If you live in Quebec, you must find a birth mother in another province; then the adoption is classified as an international adoption. For those adopting domestically in Quebec, only public agency adoptions are allowed.[2]

Licensee Adoption

A licensee is an adoption professional, either an agency or person, who has met certain requirements set by the provincial government. Licensed agencies employ social workers to coordinate the adoptions and a lawyer to conduct the legal work; licensed individuals are usually lawyers, social workers, or physicians. Licensee adoptions are legal in four provinces: Alberta, Ontario, Prince Edward Island, and Saskatchewan, and will become legal in most of the provinces before very long. According to a spokesperson at the British Columbia Adoptive Parents Association, the laws in British Columbia and in other provinces are changing so that agency placements will become legal and private-attorney placements illegal.[3]

Identified Adoption

In identified adoptions, a birth mother chooses you, but a licensee conducts the adoption. Identified adoptions can be quicker than independent adoptions, because the agency you are working with may find a child for you while you are also doing your own search for a birth mother.

Private adoption also includes stepparent adoptions, intrafamily adoptions, and international adoptions, in which children who were brought to Canada are then adopted. The number of children placed through private means has remained fairly constant from 1981 to 1990. Most of the children placed privately (82 to 94 percent) are infants.

According to a national adoption study conducted in 1993 (Kerry J. Daly and Michael P. Sobol: *Adoption in Canada*), the average waiting time when using a paid adoption professional to conduct a private adoption is between 20 and 21 months. There were 2.7 applicants for every private adoption in 1990.

Private adoptions in general are more costly than public adoptions.[4]

If you are interested in adopting an infant, the least expensive way is to pursue a private adoption in Canada rather than in the United States. In Canada you can pay only for professional, legal, and counseling services, which generally total about $5,000. In the United States, at least in many states, birth mothers can be paid living expenses as well as medical expenses—although most birth mothers use Medicaid, a government-paid program. Such costs can easily add $2,000 to $5,000 to the cost of the adoption. You will also have to hire two attorneys or agencies, one in the United States and one in Canada to proceed and finalize the adoption. This can then add another $4,000 to $6,000. Such expenses do not include traveling or the costs of conducting an international adoption.

On the other hand, the adoption laws in the United States do tend to be less restrictive and can make finding and assisting a birth mother easier than it is in Canada.

Adopting in Other Provinces

Most Canadians who pursue a private domestic adoption adopt a child who is born in their own province. Canadians can adopt in any other province, however, except for Quebec, whereas those living in Quebec who want to adopt privately must go to another province.

Adopting a child in another province means you must take two sets of laws into consideration and engage an adoption professional in each province. Often there are no clear-cut guidelines as to which province's laws you follow. You will also have to travel to the other province twice, once to meet the child and again to pick her up.

Finding a birth mother can be complicated, since in many provinces you cannot advertise. Advertising in a province where it is not permitted is considered a serious violation of the law. In the provinces where you can advertise, research the best newspapers. There are more than 400 community newspapers in Canada. The Canadian Federation of Students publishes a Student Association Directory, which includes a list of contact people for every college newspaper. Contact your library for the telephone numbers of newspapers in which you are thinking of placing adoption ads.

Those living in Quebec—where you can adopt only through a public agency or internationally (which means adopting not only from another country, but also from another province)—and in Newfoundland cannot advertise in their own provinces. In Newfoundland, however, a birth mother can contact you if she has a personal relationship with you, and it is all right to let people know you are looking into adoption.

Networking means telling everyone you know that you want to adopt. For Canadians this is a *must*, simply because Canadians have so few ways to find a birth mother. Even if you are considering adopting internationally or through a public agency, let every last person know. Someone may know of someone else who is interested in placing a child for adoption, which could mean you will be able to adopt faster and less expensively.[5]

PUBLIC ADOPTION

In 1981 most Canadian adoptions were public adoptions; now most are private. Although public adoptions are less expensive than private adoptions, the average wait for a child is six years, and as of this writing the government is considering contracting out all adoptions to private agencies. Waiting lists are closed in many public agencies. The typical child placed is either over the age of one or has physical or mental challenges. Placement statistics for Alberta for 1991 illustrate this point:

Government Placements	233
Healthy Infants	54
Special Needs	179
Private Adoptions	328
Direct Placements*	
(87 percent infants/babies)	179
Licensed Placements	
(99 percent infants/babies)	149

(*These include intrafamily/stepparent adoptions, which explains the lower percentage of infants and babies.)[6]

INTERNATIONAL ADOPTION

It is estimated that between 2,000 and 5,000 Canadians are actively seeking to adopt internationally. How many children have been adopted from other countries is not known, because until late 1991 no data were collected on these adoptions. International adoptions are very popular with Canadians, especially those living in Quebec. One reason is that Canadians are less interested in open adoptions than Americans and would prefer to avoid contact with birth parents.

All children entering Canada must be "sponsored," which means you need to complete a form called Undertaking of Assistance. This form can be obtained from your local Canada Employment and Immigration office. Once the form is returned, the immigration office contacts the provincial government and asks for a letter of no-objection regarding the adoption. The letter states that your adoption plans are known and that they have no objection. Your provincial minister should already have a copy of your home study and other documents that indicate that you are eligible to adopt. This minister's permit is valid for one year.

The provincial letter and sponsorship forms are then sent to the Canadian consulate or embassy in the child's country or in the country closest to the child. An immigration visa is issued that permits the child to enter Canada once the embassy is satisfied that the immigration requirements are met. To meet these requirements the child must have a physical examination and a passport as well as other documentation that proves that he was legally freed for adoption. If visa requirements cannot be met, a minister's permit may be given allowing the child to enter Canada; from there the child must become an immigrant.[7]

Most countries allow you to finalize the adoption in the child's original country. The Canadian government, unlike the United States government, recognizes virtually all adoptions finalized in other countries. It does not place a restrictive terminology on the word "orphan." Often, in fact, when a child is not able to come into the United States because she is not an "orphan" as strictly defined by the U.S Immigration and Naturalization Services, an immediate search will begin for a Canadian couple instead.

The cost for an international adoption, measured in American currency, is about $15,000.[8]

There are two kinds of international adoptions: public and private. A public adoption is one conducted by the National Adoption Desk in Ottawa—referred to as "the Desk." The Desk was formed in 1975 and serves as consultant and coordinator for international adoptions, tracking the adoption laws and policies of other countries so that the information given to the provincial governments can be shared with prospective adoptive parents. The Desk also develops programs with other countries so that Canadians can adopt from that country. All provinces, except Quebec, allow residents to use some or all of the Desk programs. Guidelines vary from province to province.

Prospective adoptive parents learn about each country and the programs available and select one or two countries they are interested in. From there they apply to the country through their provincial government. Depending upon the program and the child requested, you may wait anywhere from several months to several years. Adopting through the Desk takes longer than a private international adoption, as a rule, but is usually less expensive. There are newer programs in which children are being placed more quickly.[9]

Adopting privately is similar to adopting publicly, in many ways. You must meet the requirements of the country, and Immigration Canada must issue a visa to the child entering the country. Here's how the process works: First you contact a private agency or facilitator in Canada or the United States. Some provinces impose no restrictions as to what kinds of agencies and facilitators can be used. If the adoption is completed in the child's country of origin, many provinces do not regulate the process, and some do not even require a postplacement report after the child arrives. The country from which you are adopting may require a report, however, so make sure you arrange for the agency that conducts your home study to write one.

You will probably have more control if you pursue a private adoption, especially over the speed at which you can adopt.[10]

Adopting in the United States

Adopting in America is like any other international adoption in most ways. You will have to follow three sets of laws and regulations: those of the state in which you are adopting, Canadian immigration laws, and the laws of your province regulating international adoptions. If you are interested in adopting a biracial or African-American child, you may consider adopting either independently or through an agency. If you seek to adopt only a Caucasian child, independent adoption will probably be your best route.

THE HOME STUDY

The home study process in Canada is similar to the one described in chapter 16, "The Home Study." In some provinces a home study must be conducted before the child is in your home, while others accept postplacement studies. Many of the documents required for the home study must be submitted to the government during the adoption process. Check with your adoption professional as to which documents you will need and which you must file with the government.

The home study must be done in Canada and is generally valid for one year. Check with your ministry and follow any guidelines. How extensive the study is depends on the social worker, the agency, and the province. You might wish to contact another adoptive family and find out from them what the social worker was like and how the process went.

QUEBEC—SPECIAL CONCERNS

The government and culture of Quebec frequently set it apart from the rest of Canada, and adoption laws are no exception. In Quebec there are no private or agency adoptions; you can adopt only through the public social services department called the Association des Centre de Jeunesse du Quebec. The social services department is known to be so invasive and so difficult to work with that few Quebecois are willing to deal with it.

If a birth mother chooses you to be the adoptive parents, everyone would have to go through the social services department. Since neither birth mothers nor adoptive parents want to deal with the department, adoptive fathers will sometimes claim to be the birth father so that the baby can go home with the adoptive couple. Later the adoptive mom will adopt the baby as would be done in a stepparent adoption. This kind of deception is an appalling way to go about an adoption, of course, but people feel forced into such situations when the regulations are so restrictive. New legislation has declared an amnesty for all those who have adopted using false information.

Because adopting through the social services department is so unpopular, and because the wait for a newborn baby is eight years, many in Quebec are adopting internationally. (As mentioned previously, a child adopted from another province is also considered an international adoption.) The disproportionate number of international adoptions conducted by Quebec residents reflect this. Quebec has a population of only seven million people, yet last year Quebec residents adopted more than 1,000 children internationally. In the United States, where the population is thirty-five times that of Quebec, there were only 10,000 international adoptions. In France—a country with a population of fifty-seven million—there were only 3,000 international adoptions.

According to Claire-Marie Gagnon, an adoption advocate and former president of the Federation des Parents Adoptants du Quebec, Quebec has established excellent contacts in China and other countries. Follow-up studies have found that the adoptive parents were well prepared and had postadoption support systems in place.[11]

Quebec offers two ways to adopt a child outside of Canada: through one of the sixteen licensed nonprofit agencies called organismes, or through the secretary of adoption. The secretary is there to conduct adoptions in countries such as Peru and Taiwan, where the foreign government wants government-to-government adoptions instead of agency adoptions.[12]

Resources:

Adoption Council of Canada
PO Box 8442
Station T
Ottawa, Ontario
KIG3H8
(613) 235-1566

Open Door Society of Canada
(613) 827-3532

Adoptive Parents Association of B/C
Suite 205
15463 104th Ave.
Surrie, BC V3R1N9
Attention: Helen Mark
(604) 588-7300 or
(604) 588-6111

Adoption Council of Ontario
(416) 484-7454
(416) 482-0021
Provides workshops for adoptive
parents.

Vanier Institute of the Family
120 Holland Ave., Suite 300
Ottawa, Ontario
K1Y 0X6
613/722-4007
FAX 613/729-5249
This group publishes a
French/English newsletter cov-
ering many family issues,
including adoption.

**Adoptee and Birth Parent
Reunification**
Colleen Elizabeth Clark,
MSW, RSW
Alberta Adoption Council
8116 187th St.
Edmonton, Alberta T5T1K3
(403) 245-5005

**Ms. Clark is also the director of
Imagine**
705 1520 4th WW
Calgary, Alberta T2SOB5
Imagine provides reunification
counseling for adoptees and birth
parents seeking to find each
other.

Parent Finders
613/730-8305

**Quebec: International
Adoptions**
Secretariat à l'adoption
3700, rue Berre
Montreal, Quebec H2L 4G9
(524) 873-5226 or
(800) 561-0246
FAX 514/873-1709

Association of Parents
(514) 271-8297
(May reach member who speaks
only French, but other members
also speak English.)

Claire-Marie Gagnon
4264 Ferncrest Rue
Pierrefonds
H9H 2A1
Quebec, Canada
(514) 696-0508

Toronto Free-Net, whose Internet site can be reached at **telnet://torfree.net**, offers online adoption information provided by *Adoption Helper,* Canada's national adoption magazine. The adoption area holds about 1 MB of information in 60 files, and is updated quarterly. To reach the adoption area, type GO ADOPT. It covers all aspects of adoption, including how to adopt, postadoption issues, and infertility information. The emphasis is on information and resources available in Canada; however, some U.S.-related information is also available.

Child and Family Adoption Services Society places both domestic and international children with Canadian families. Their Web site may be reached at **http://www.maple.net/ads-online/CFAS/cfas.html**.

Adoption Information for Canadians includes listings of Canadian agencies, general adoption information for Canadians, a book list, and more. Its Web site address is **http://www.ri-studios.com/my/my.html**.

Chapter Fourteen

Special Needs Adoption

S pecial needs" is a general term for children whose special characteristics can make them more difficult to place for adoption. Sometimes they are also called "waiting children." This grouping encompasses older children, children of certain ethnic backgrounds, sibling groups, and children who have a disability, medical condition, or psychological problem that either makes them less likely to be adopted or means that their adoptive parents must be equipped to handle the challenge of caring for them. Some special needs children can be adopted through private agencies or independently, and these children as a rule have physical handicaps or are mentally retarded. They are available because their birth mothers make the decision to place them. However, most children with special needs are adopted through state-run public agencies, and most of these children are placed because of parental abuse or neglect.

According to the Department of Health and Human Services, two out of three waiting children have medical, developmental, behavioral, or psychological special needs, and most have more than one condition. About 41 percent of the children are part of a sibling group, making them particularly hard to place.[1]

Often children with special needs also have a complex relationship with birth parents because of a history of parental abuse or neglect. Usually, the birth parents' rights have been terminated only after considerable disruption and pain in the children's lives. Although the biological parents may be out of the children's lives, their influence on the children can still be very intense. Children with special needs are often older, and often remember living with their biological parents as well as with previous foster parents, and, of course, they remember being placed for adoption. Often, indeed, what makes a special needs child "special" is the fact that he has suffered so much.

About one-third of the children who are in the foster-care system and then become eligible for adoption are victims of overt abuse. All neglected and abused children are also emotionally abused. Virtually all children who are removed from their homes must be placed in foster care before their biological parents' rights are terminated. The trauma of being abused and then going to one or more foster homes can have a profound emotional impact on the child. In addition, some children, especially those placed in group homes, become the victims of sexual abuse. The perpetrators are usually older children who themselves were victims of sexual abuse. The child who has gone through one caretaker after another may have deep-seated psychological problems, often expressed in attention deficit disorder, hyperactivity, daytime wetting and soiling, sexual acting out, detachment, and a host of other behavior problems.

Those considering adopting neglected or abused children must go through extensive preparenting classes and may also be required to get counseling so that issues they have within their own family systems can be clarified and dealt with before they adopt. Couples who have not had to face family-of-origin issues because they have experienced no real crises may suddenly have to face these issues once a difficult child enters their lives. Adding a child to a family always changes its dynamics; adding a child with psychological scars can change the dynamics in the family dramatically. Being prepared to parent an emotionally abused child and having realistic expectations of yourself and the child are musts. Unlike medical conditions, which tend to fit more or less into textbook models, the emotional problems that these children have can be varied, and the outcome is far less predictable.

TYPES OF SPECIAL NEEDS

Physical and Medical Problems

Physical disabilities can include in utero exposure to drugs and alcohol, sensory disabilities such as blindness and deafness, and diseases such as epilepsy. Although the outcome for certain conditions, especially those related to exposure to drugs and alcohol, is uncertain, most conditions have a predictable course. You may believe you have the background and skills to help a child with a particular kind of physical problem. Of course, if you are considering an older child with a medical condition, you must also recognize that any child who is older will most likely also have some emotional problems. But studies show that those who do adopt such children have a high degree of satisfaction. The placements with the best outcomes were ones in which adoptive mothers were not depressed, had few reservations, were married, had experience with disabling conditions, and had strong religious beliefs.[2]

Learning Disabilities

There is a much higher-than-average incidence of attention deficit disorder (ADD), attention deficit hyperactivity disorder (ADHD), and other learning disabilities among adopted children, even among those adopted at birth. Poor parenting, abuse, and neglect can interfere with the child's ability to attach and to learn. Prenatal exposure to drugs and alcohol also increases the likelihood of a child's developing a learning disability.

Emotional and Behavioral Problems

Many children who are removed from their parents as result of abuse or neglect will display a variety of emotional and behavioral problems as a direct result of their traumatic backgrounds. These problems can be further exacerbated by the loss of their biological parents and possibly their foster parents. This means that nearly all adopted children, except those adopted at birth and not exposed to drugs or alcohol, are at risk for emotional problems, although many will not have such problems. Unlike physical conditions, emotional problems are not easily diagnosed and can have uncertain behavioral outcomes. Typical emotional problems for these children include fear, anger, low-self-esteem, anxiety, depression, lack of trust, and developmental regression. The problems a child has may be known at the time you plan to adopt her and may subside as a result of her being in your loving and nurturing home environment. On the other hand, a younger preschool child may not have any notable emotional or behavioral problems, but she may develop problems later on.[3]

Many of the behavioral problems children have often resolve themselves after the child feels secure within the adoptive home. Helping a child overcome her emotional problems and the behaviors that accompany them can be very rewarding. It requires a great deal of patience and understanding and realistic expectations.

Knowing what problems you can and cannot accept is very important. One behavioral problem, even if minor, that one parent can overlook can cause havoc in another family. Also, the child's age can play a role in the parent's attitude. For example, most parents adopting a five-year-old would accept the fact that she wets the bed; however, some parents cannot cope with bed-wetting in a twelve-year-old. The same is true for lying. A four-year-old who lies may seem cute; a twelve-year-old with the same behavior is often viewed as cunning and manipulative. As will be discussed later in the chapter, know what you can handle and what you cannot. Also, even though you may be able to accept a wide variety of behavioral problems, this does not mean that you are willing to accept a child with many behavioral problems.

The following description includes the behavioral characteristics often associated with children who have been abused, neglected, or have moved from one caretaker to another:

- *Delayed development.*
- *Aggression and hyperactivity.*
- *Indiscriminate affection.* These children have not attached to one particular person. Although overly friendly when they are small, as they grow older they may be cold, aloof, demanding, and manipulative.[4]
- *Lack of self-awareness.* The child is not aware of his own needs, including the need to eat or use the bathroom.
- *Control issues.* The child who has had no normal boundaries set for him may try to set his own boundaries.
- *Wetting and soiling clothes.* A child who tries to control his environment may not go to the bathroom and then become constipated or soil or wet his pants during the day.
- *Food hoarding.* A child who has not been able to depend on adults to meet his needs may hide food in his bedroom because he has learned to be self-sufficient.
- *Lying.* The child lies indiscriminately, that is, when the lie is obvious or when telling the truth would not normally lead to punishment.
- *Profound emotional problems, including attachment disorders.*

Attachment Disorders

Attachment disorders are a different classification from the usual emotional and behavioral problems a child may have. They are a group of serious, hard-to-treat, and often misdiagnosed conditions. Because they are so difficult to treat, knowing whether a child has an attachment disorder is crucial in making the decision to adopt. And if you do decide to adopt, you need to know how to get help for the child.

Some children who have been grossly neglected or have gone from one caretaker to another without "bonding" with anyone will probably never bond with anyone without intensive treatment. Such children do not respond to standard therapy because they cannot "connect" to the therapist. As a general rule, the earlier the abuse and neglect, the more likely the child will have an attachment disorder. This is one of the most difficult emotional disorders to handle, because the child may never respond to your love and affection.

Fortunately, most children who have the risk factors for an attachment disorder—primarily abuse and neglect—will *not* have one. How a child has responded to abuse and neglect is what determines whether she will have an attachment disorder. Children who can learn to gratify themselves when their needs are not met will usually have fewer symptoms, and when placed with proper caretakers, they are more likely to bond with them. The greater the degree of abuse and neglect, by and large, the greater the chance that the child will have an attachment disorder. Yet some children who have more risk factors will have a greater ability to overcome their backgrounds, while other children who were not as severely abused or neglected may display gross behavioral and emotional problems.

For a diagnosis of attachment and bonding disorders, one or more of the following must have been present:

- *Prenatal exposure to drug or alcohol.* This causes the most permanent damage.
- *Lack of early bonding with caretaker and lack of love and nurturing.* The child cries for food or for a diaper change. When he is not fed or changed, he rages. After a cycle of crying and then raging, the child learns self-gratification and to trust only himself.
- *Multiple foster care placements.* When a child has multiple caretakers, he learns not to "bond" with anyone, knowing that if he does, the pain will be heightened when he leaves that person's home.
- *Other interruptions such as hospitalizations, or going from one relative to another.*
- *Abuse and neglect.* A history of mistreatment, including physical or sexual abuse before adoptive placement, affects the child's level of attachment.[5] The younger the child, the more impact the trauma has on him.
- *Painful medical conditions.* A child who has pain that the parent cannot alleviate may detach.
- *Chaotic family life.* For example, a mother who is on drugs or who suffers from mental illness.

It is important to be aware of the symptoms associated with attachment disorder, not only so that a diagnosis can be made but so that you can decide whether this is the kind of child you want to adopt. If you are adopting a child from another country, you may have a very sketchy background on her, making it difficult to know whether she has been grossly neglected or abused. One way to tell is by looking for the signs associated with an attachment disorder. If she does display the signs, finding resources to help may be very difficult, especially if you have adopted internationally.

Here are some of the symptoms of an attachment disorder:

- *Poor eye contact.* The child may be aloof, make little or no eye contact, and appear to have no conscience. Some people describe such a child's eyes as "hollow." For those who are adopting internationally, this may be the only symptom that can be observed. If the child cannot connect his eyes with yours, he may very well have an attachment disorder.
- *Can be delightful initially.* These children have moved from one household to another and learned to "adjust" to many different people and situations.
- *Emotional withdrawal.* The child does not respond to affection and will not snuggle with you if you touch her. Or she may display indiscriminate affection with strangers but not be cuddly or affectionate with parents.
- *Overcompetency.* The child may not allow anyone to help him. He may refuse any help with getting dressed or any other activity. This is a very serious problem that is often mistakenly viewed as independence.
- *Aggressive behavior.* A child who is defiant and hyperactive is usually diagnosed with attention deficit disorder. If he improves while taking Ritalin, then the diagnosis is considered to be attention deficit disorder and probably not an attachment disorder.
- *Frequent accidents.*
- *Cruelty to animals, fire setting, bed-wetting.*
- *Lying.* Crazy lying for no apparent reason; stealing to get caught.
- *Idiosyncratic speech patterns.*
- *Delayed learning; wanting to act "dumb."*
- *Lack of cause-and-effect thinking.*
- *Lack of conscience.*

History of Sexual Abuse

Many children who are removed from their parents have been sexually abused. The factors that led to their removal from their families are the same factors that increase the risk of sexual abuse. For example, lack of parental protection, parental drug use, and parents socializing with other drug users, all increase the likelihood of sexual abuse. Also, children who are neglected or abused are often more passive and emotionally vulnerable, making them easier targets for perpetrators.

Adults are not the only perpetrators. Children also abuse other children. This is particularly true in foster or group homes in which younger children are in contact with older children. Some older children, who are usually themselves victims of sexual abuse, abuse younger children. Ironically, a child who has never been sexually abused may be the victim of such abuse once he is removed from his birth family and placed in a foster care setting. The emotional scars from sexual abuse from a child's peers can be just as damaging as those caused by sexual abuse from an adult.

Contrary to popular opinion, sexual abuse is not restricted to males exploiting girls and boys. Children are also abused by women and older girls. However, when women are the perpetrators, determining sexual abuse is even more difficult to diagnose because of the nature of the abuse and also because boys, especially older boys, may not view the exploitation as offensive.

Overall, diagnosing sexual abuse is difficult because the abuse can be subtle and may never involve actual physical contact with the child. For example, the child may have viewed actual sexual acts or X-rated films and have been the target of inappropriate gestures and comments. Second, if the child was abused, he may not view it as abuse but as a display of affection and a way of gaining approval. Children often try to "normalize" such behavior if the behavior is done by a parental figure. If the child does view the abuse as wrong, he may have so much shame that he will not discuss it. Also, children often do not discuss the abuse because their two main fears are that they will not be believed and that nothing will be done. These fears are reinforced only if therapy and other interventions do not take place.

Even if no one knows if a child has been sexually abused, the child's behavior may be an indication. Children, even young children, who have been sexually abused are generally more sexually knowledgeable, may act out sexually, and may be sexually provocative around adults as a way of getting attention. Many victims also struggle with such emotional problems as guilt, depression, anger, fear, and inability to trust. Depression in particular appears to be present in nearly all victims.[6]

You may feel that you cannot handle the issues associated with raising a child who has been sexually abused. This is understandable. However, do be aware that *any* child who has been removed from his home may have a history of being sexually abused. Usually the problem behaviors will diminish once the child is in a stable environment in which proper guidelines and trust are established. As with any child who has been abused, the child will require some therapy to deal with her past. Also, adoptive parents who were also the victims of sexual abuse may need to resolve their own issues through therapy before adopting.

The most sensible approach to adopting a child who may sexually act out is to adopt only a very young child or one who is significantly younger than any children already in your family. You certainly would not want an eight-year-old who may sexually act out if you already have a five-year-old. This is not to say that every child who has been sexually abused is going to be a perpetrator, but taking such precautions can help the placement of a child in your home go more smoothly.

If you do adopt a child with a history of sexual abuse, remember: A victim may say or do things that are viewed as perverted. Do not regard the child as a deviant but as one whose actions are a result of his background. Helping a child show affection appropriately and express his anger and hurt can assist him or her in healing.

The treatment for attachment disorders must usually be intense. Generally the therapy is to help the child rework her negative life experiences and help her reduce anger, resentment, fear, and rage. As she lets go of these negative feelings, the child learns to experience trust and closeness so that she can bond with others. Some children and their adoptive families may be helped through weekly therapy, whereas other children may require an intensive inpatient therapy. Parent participation is crucial to the child's success, so much so that confidentiality between the child and therapist is secondary to having the parents' full understanding and input.[7])

Resources:

For further information about attachment disorders, contact:
Attachment and Bonding Center of Ohio
Dr. Gregory C. Keck, Ph. D.
12608 State Road
Cleveland, OH 44133
(216) 230-1960

Forest Hill
Evergreen, Colorado 80439
(303) 674-6681

The Institute for the Prevention of Child Abuse
can be reached at **http://www.interlog.com/~ipca/ipca.html**.
They have a catalog of publications to help adults handle
the needs of abused children.

The National Data Archive on Child Abuse and Neglect
has a Gopher server at **gopher://gopher.ndacan.cornell.edu/**.
This site mainly contains professional research on child abuse but
some may be helpful to adoptive parents or foster parents of abused
children.

Sibling groups

For a sibling group to be considered "special needs," usually there must be three or more children who all need to be placed in the same family. Again, if such children are available, it is usually because they have been removed from their home because of neglect or abuse. These children are also likely to have emotional problems due to their backgrounds.

When abuse or neglect occurs, usually all of the children in the home are removed. These brothers and sisters are often very bonded to each other and may have learned to meet their needs through each other.

Therefore, when adoption is the plan, agencies try to find a family who can adopt all of the children. However, while the children are initially in foster care, they are often separated because it is difficult to find a foster home that can accommodate three or more children. Sometimes one child may become very attached to his foster parents, who may want to adopt him but not his siblings. Such a scenario further complicates the emotional issues these children face as a result of being separated from each other during foster care, being removed from their foster family, and then reunited once again in an adoptive home.

Finding an adoptive home can be difficult for sibling groups if one of the children has a more serious medical condition or behavioral problem. This may mean, for example, that an adoptable four-year-old may wait a long time for a family because she must be placed together with her eight-year-old brother, who has serious emotional problems. However, it can be difficult for social workers to decide when siblings should be separated so that an adoption for at least one of the children is feasible.

The dynamics among the siblings need to be understood before adopting. Often the older child has been the caretaker of the younger children. The older child may have been playing this role for so long that she may find it difficult to relinquish it even after she and her siblings are placed for adoption. If you adopt such children, you will need to help each child learn new family roles. The oldest child will have to learn that her and the other children's needs will be met by you, and that she can be a child again. Although the children must learn new roles, the children's transition to a new home can be eased by the fact that they have a connection with each other.

Initially, the concept of having an instant family of more than one child can seem very attractive. However, be aware that meeting the needs of multiple children requires a great deal of time and commitment. If you already have one or two children, you probably have a more realistic understanding of the responsibility involved in caring for two or more additional children.

In some states, if the number of children in your home is greater than six, then you will need to be licensed as a group home. Once your home is licensed, you will be required to maintain a certain level of fire and safety precautions.

There are funds available for those adopting sibling groups. Generally, these children already qualify for subsidies because they are at risk for emotional problems.

African-American and Racially Mixed Children

Sometimes a child's racial or ethnic background makes it more difficult to find her a home. A child of mixed racial background is usually African-American and Caucasian. Although "Hispanic" is not a race, a child who is both Hispanic and Caucasian may be classified as racially mixed. A child who is two years old, healthy, and seems to be developmentally and emotionally on target may still be considered "special needs" because of her racial background.

Older Children

Defining "older" children is difficult. Some agencies call any child over a year old an "older child." One thing is certain: The older the child, the more emotional problems he is likely to have.

Of the hard-to-place children, 85 percent are over five years old, and 43 percent are over eleven years old. Although most children classified as "special needs" because of their age are five or older, any child over the age of two who has suffered abuse or neglect, and often younger children too, are going to bear the scars of that trauma in their early lives. If you are considering adopting an older child, you are considering adopting a child who has lost at least one caretaker. The process of going from one caretaker to another can have a great psychological impact on the child. So if you are adopting an older child, you must be prepared to face special emotional problems that may also cause behavioral problems.

In a study of adoptions that were and were not successful, the child's age was the single best predictor of disruption. Older, more troubled children not only entered the foster care system at a later age but remained in foster care longer and waited longer to be freed for adoption and to be placed.

ADVANTAGES OF SPECIAL NEEDS ADOPTION

As explained, there are often challenges associated with special needs adoption. What are some of the advantages?

1. *Expenses can be minimal.* In many cases, in fact, the child may be eligible for monthly subsidies. Depending on what state you live in, the child's age, and the severity of his problems, you could receive $200 or more per month. These subsidies do not add to your income; they are simply meant to defray the costs of raising a child who requires extra parental care and possibly such specialized services as physical therapy or psychological counseling.

2. *Children are available.* According to the Department of Health and Human Services, in December 1990 there were 69,000 foster children in the United States who needed to have an adoption plan. Today about 30,000 to 50,000 children are legally free to be adopted, and of these, about 15,000 are actively searching for a family. About 50,000 are not legally free for adoption because their parents' rights have not been terminated, but they need a "permanent" home in the meantime.[8]

3. *The wait for a child can be a matter of months.* If you are diligent about getting a home study completed through your social services department, you could have a child in the time it takes to complete a home study and be approved. Sometimes the wait for a child will be directly related to how long it takes you to complete a series of workshops on adoption, and the social services department to come to your home to conduct a home study, complete the paperwork, and file all the correct papers.

4. *You can know about the child you are going to adopt.* Unlike most other domestic or international adoptions, you get to meet the child before you adopt him. For some people, the certainty of meeting a child before making the decision to adopt is paramount.

5. *You will have specialized training and workshops as well as pre- and post-adoption support from the agency.* Sometimes the requirements may seem

arbitrary or invasive, but most people can benefit from the opportunity to learn more about parenting. Also, once the child is in your home, before and after the adoption is made legal, your agency may provide extensive services to help you meet your child's needs.

6. *You have an opportunity to make a difference in the life of child.* Many people who are able to have biological children also choose to adopt children with special needs because they want to expand their families and make a contribution to the lives of children. Few other achievements can have such an impact on an individual life, and offer you such a reward.

DISADVANTAGES OF SPECIAL NEEDS ADOPTION

What are some of the disadvantages of special needs adoption? For many people, working with the system heads the list. Most children with special needs are adopted through the social services department, and working with a government bureaucracy can be frustrating. The staff may be small and overburdened, and the rules they must follow may seem arbitrary. Having to get supervisor after supervisor to sign off on form after form can slow the process. Take the case of John, who is ten years old. He has been waiting for a home nearly all his life. When he was a toddler, his drug-addicted mother lost her parental rights; his father was unknown. Although John has been legally free for adoption since he was three years old, he has lived in foster and group homes while social workers decide on his best interests and the services that will help him the most. "I'm all wrapped up in programs," this child says. "What I need is a mom."

According to the American Public Welfare Association, the number of children in substitute care is growing thirty-three times faster than American's child population in general. Although the Child Welfare League of America says that more resources are needed, the government is already spending ten billion dollars a year on foster care and adoption services through public agencies. Federal money now accounts for nearly one-third of all foster care funding. According to the ACLU, each child in foster care costs $17,500 per year, including payment made to the foster families. It is clear that the funding system provides incentives to keep adoptable children in state care. It is not clear whether there is sufficient financial incentive to recruit adoptive families.[9] Private adoption agencies are paid to find adoptive families. Public agencies are "paid" for the number of children in the system, not in adoptive families. Caseworkers' hands are often tied, however, because judges are reluctant to terminate parents' rights. More legislation is needed to limit the time allotted to biological parents to get their lives together before their children can return to live with them. Fortunately, special private grants made to state agencies are beginning to speed up the adoption process.

Here are some other disadvantages of special needs adoption:

Special needs children often require special services. This means that you need to live in an area where such services are available. If you live on a large ranch in Wyoming and the closest large city is three hours away, regularly getting your child to a psychologist or an occupational therapist may be very difficult.

Adoptions can disrupt. Those adopting older children with special needs have the highest rate of adoptions not working out. The adoption disruption rate of adolescents can be as high as 25 percent; for older children overall, it is about 10 percent. One study looked at the records of 1,500 children over the age of six. It found that children between the ages of six and eleven years old disrupted at a rate of 10.2 percent during a two-year period, children over eleven at a rate of about 8 percent. The success rate was higher when children were placed with their own siblings. Children who were placed alone but had a sibling living elsewhere disrupted at a rate of 20.6 percent. This could either mean that one or more of the siblings had such profound problems that no family could take on the responsibility of all the children, or that the separation was part of the problem.

Another study found that disruptions were lower in homes where there were biological children already in the home, but still another found that more than 50 percent of the cases of disruption involved serious conflicts between the adopted children and the nonrelated children in the home. A history of previous disruptions is a high indicator for another disruption. The behaviors associated with disruption included cruelty, fighting, and vandalism. Parents who were the most informed about the child, had prepared for the child, and had adoption subsidies were the most likely *not* to disrupt. Psychotherapy also helped families avoid disruption.

A research study lists the following stages of adoption disruption:

1. *Diminishing pleasure.* The joy of taking care of the child becomes outweighed by the burden.
2. *The child is perceived as a major problem.* The parents can't cope with the child. They want change, but the child does not change.
3. *The parents complain to others about the child.* They are urged by friends and family members to vacate the adoption.

4. *The turning point.* A specific event leads the parents to believe they can no longer tolerate the child's behavior. The parents look to life without the child and no longer try to assimilate him into their family.

5. *Deadline.* Either the child is given a "shape-up or ship-out" message, or the parents decide that if the behavior occurs once more, they will vacate the adoption.

6. *Giving up.* The parents give up and return the child to the agency.[10]

The psychological factors can be unpredictable. If the child needs counseling, the costs can be very high. The home study process may also be quite a bit more rigorous. Public agencies and private agencies that place special needs may be flexible about the size of your home, but they are likely to question you extensively about your attitudes toward marriage, child rearing, adoption, adjustment to stress, and counseling for your children. After all, the caseworker wants to know how you will be able to handle a child with special needs. She may expect you to understand issues related to the separation and loss the child has probably experienced. The home study is not just to see whether your lives are stable but whether you can adjust to having a child who may be very disruptive.

GETTING STARTED

If you are ready to go ahead with a special needs adoption, the first thing to do is join an adoption support group in which a good number of members have adopted children with special needs. Those who have adopted through the Department of Social Services or through a public agency will know what works with the system and what does not. Next, call your local public adoption agency. Find out whether they have upcoming workshops for those who are interested in adopting a child with special needs. These multisession workshops usually cover the legal issues, the kinds of children available and their special needs, and the relationships these children have with their birth families and foster care parents. Your attitudes about adoption, the kind of child you can accept, emotional problems, and similar issues will also be addressed. Many people "screen" themselves out of the process after going to these workshops.

The next step is to check out local special services in your area. If you want to adopt a certain kind of special needs child, find out what services you'll have access to, what expenses are involved, and whether those expenses are covered by Medicaid. Remember, be realistic about what kinds of children are available and about how much impact you can have on a given child. If you want an essentially healthy but older child, for example, you must recognize that any child who has been removed from his home because of abuse or neglect is likely to have some emotional or developmental or learning problems. If you have successfully raised children through the teenage years, you may feel that you would like an older child. However, the way you measured "success" in raising your children, who came to you at birth or at a very young age, will probably not be the standard for success in raising a child from a troubled background. You need to explore how you feel about dealing with a child's emotional problems, the behavior that may accompany the problems, and going with your child to a counselor.

Sit down with your spouse and discuss what you can and cannot accept. Your spouse may be unwilling to care for a child who is mentally retarded but feel very different about adopting a bright child with fairly serious learning disabilities—in other words, one whose problems appear more "correctable." Again, be sure that your expectations are realistic.

Beware of social workers pushing you to accept more than you can handle. Sometimes well-meaning social workers who want children to be placed in a good home will recruit families by showing one set of children on television programs or in special "waiting children" photolisting books; however, these children may not be available. When the family calls to inquire, they are told they cannot adopt the child they had in mind and are encouraged to adopt one of the other children available instead, often one who is older or part of a sibling group. Or a family who plans to adopt a seven-year-old child may be told there are children available in this age bracket. After going through classes and a home study, the family is then encouraged to adopt a twelve-year-old or a sibling group. Social workers are "stretching" the family expectations, a practice Christine Adamec calls unfair.[11] Most caseworkers who handle adoptions, however, do not take this approach. They want families to be fully informed, not only about the child's positive and negative attributes but what may be anticipated down the road. Having realistic expectations is the best insurance against an adoption disruption.

Be especially careful about "broadening" your level of acceptance because you find a child so attractive. Sometimes a prospective adoptive family will see a child or a picture of the child and "fall in love" with his cute face and charming personality. At this time the couple may not "hear" what the caseworker is telling them about the emotional, physical, and/or behavioral problems the child has or is at a high risk of having. They see only the adorable four-year-old who, with enough love, will overcome all his problems. One caseworker says that when families change their minds and "broaden" their level of acceptance, they usually have problems with their adopted child in the specific area they stated on their initial application they would not be able to accept.

Although the overall tone of special needs adoption seems to focus more on what is wrong with the child than what is right, this is done to increase realistic expectations. However, once parents adopt these children, like all parents, they also focus in on the children's positive traits and accomplishments. These parents, like most adoptive and biological parents, find the experience rewarding and have felt the same pride in their children.

The Child's Background

The previous list of traits that describes the various types of special needs children is not meant to dissuade you from considering such a child. Rather, it is provided so that you can have a fuller understanding of the issues involved and what you may have to deal with. That is why it is very important to get a child's full social, medical, and psychological history. Of course, it is not always possible to know everything. Ask the caseworker what her "sense" is if the record is not complete. In particular, be sure to ask the following, if you feel that the whole background is not presented to you:

- What kind of foster homes was the child in?
- What kinds of emotional, social, or behavioral problems can you expect, based on the child's history?
- What kind of counseling and other medical or special services will the child require?

Choosing the Best Route

If you are pursuing special needs adoption, you may want to try various routes at the same time, especially if you want to adopt an infant or small child. Often there is no application fee to adopt a child with special needs. For example if you want to adopt a blind infant, you may send letters to attorneys and private agencies telling them of your desire to adopt such a child. You may also want to contact crisis pregnancy centers and let them know that if any woman is carrying a child with a defect, you may be interested in adopting that child. In the meantime, you may want to get your home study done by your public agency. They will usually not charge you for the service.

HOW TO ADOPT A CHILD WITH SPECIAL NEEDS

Most children with special needs are adopted through a public, or state, adoption agency. Some are adopted through private agencies that specialize in placing children with special needs, and others are listed through adoption networks or exchanges. Few are adopted through private means.

Independent Adoption

If you adopt independently you will probably receive an infant, because most independent adoptions involve birth mothers placing their children at birth. The baby you adopt will probably have been designated for another couple originally, and the couple changed their minds because of the child's disability.

If you are interested in adopting a child with special needs, write to every adoption attorney in your area who serves as an intermediary and let them know that you are interested in adopting a child who may be difficult to place. Be specific about the disabilities you are willing to accept—Down syndrome, cocaine or other drug exposure, cleft palate, etc. Here is an example of such a letter.

> Dear Mr. Smith:
>
> My husband and I are interested in adopting an infant or very young child with a physical disability or impediment. These disabilities may include deafness, blindness, cleft palate, or inability to walk.
>
> We know that an opportunity to adopt such a child is limited, so we are sending this letter to several attorneys and private agencies to let them know that in the event that a child with a disability is born, and a couple decides not to adopt the child, we are more than willing to adopt this child.
>
> Enclosed please find copies of our completed home study, including a "sanitized" version you can show to a birth mother. Attached to the home study are two pictures of our family and home.
>
> You can reach us at (800) 123-4567 at any time. Our pager number is (704) 555-1234/PIN 2345. Please feel free to call us at any time. Thank you.
>
> Sincerely,
>
> Tom and Judy Cook

Here is another broadcast letter, this one addressed to a birth mother.

Dear Friend:

My husband and I both want very much to adopt a child that perhaps other couples may not want to adopt. We want to give a child with special needs the extra care, time, and attention required. We both are very experienced in dealing with children with disabilities. My husband, Brad, teaches at a school for the deaf and blind. I am a special-education teacher by training and teach part-time. My sister, who is six years younger than I am, has cerebral palsy. In my family I often had the responsibility of taking care of her. Although my sister cannot walk and has limited speech ability, she is a successful accountant for a large corporation.

My husband and I both believe that regardless of a child's physical disability, he or she needs a great deal of love and attention as well as a well-structured environment. We are very committed to our marriage and to loving a child.

We have many resources, including a large extended family that is looking forward to a new addition to the family. Although we are not rich and live in a modest home, my husband's position provides us with excellent medical benefits. This means the child will have access to the best medical care.

We are very open to meeting with you. We would also be glad to share pictures and letters of the child with you so you see how well the baby is growing and developing.

Please feel free to call us so that we can talk further. We know this is a very difficult time for you, and we want to provide the reassurance you need. We can be reached at (800) 555-1234.

Very warmly yours,

Melinda and Brad

With independent adoption, very often the "special needs" of this child will be a physical or mental disability or problems related to in utero drug exposure. If you are willing to adopt a child who has been exposed to drugs, you may also end up dealing with the Department of Social Services, unless the birth mother places the child immediately after birth. The medical personnel in the hospital usually are required to alert the Department of Social Services if a child or mother tests positive for drug exposure. Because drug exposure is often considered child abuse, the child may be removed from the biological mother and placed in foster care. If this happens, even if the birth mother wants the child to be placed with you, and even if you have an approved home study, DSS may say that you need to become a foster parent first. They may also tell you that other parents are in line waiting for an infant, and that you will just have to wait in line like all other foster-adoptive parents—even if you have been helping to pay for food and housing for the birth mother for the last several months. If, however, the birth mother relinquishes the child to the adoptive family before DSS becomes involved, the placement will usually be allowed. The hospital staff may also be more cooperative about having the child go home with an adoptive family.

By the way, if you adopt privately, you are *not* eligible for federal or state adoption subsidies.

Private Agency Adoption

Some private agencies receive grants to place children with special needs. These agencies may offer special programs to screen families, help them prepare for adopting a child, and help the child prepare for being placed in a new family. The children available through these private agencies are generally eligible for state and federal subsidies. These agencies often work in conjunction with the state agency. The process involved in adopting a child through a private agency that places such children is very similar to that of a public agency, as explained in the following pages.

Public Agency Adoption

Every state has at least one agency that handles adoptions, usually an extension of the state's social services department. There are over 2,000 such agencies in the United States. In some states there is one agency; in others there is one in every county. (Consult your state directory for the name of your state's adoption specialist; this office can direct you to the agency in your county or district.)

In the United States at least 50,000 children are searching for a family. These children are in the custody of the state and are often taken from foster home to foster home—even if they are free for adoption. Unlike Baby Jessica or Baby Richard, there are no cameras, no six o'clock news coverage for these children. Yet they hurt deeply because they are caught up in the bureaucracy and have no permanent home.

Contact your state agency to see how to apply. They may send you a preliminary questionnaire and ask that you attend a series of training or workshops. Public agencies conduct workshops not only to educate prospective adoptive parents about issues involved in adopting a child with special needs but also to screen out prospective adoptive parents who are unready to deal with the emotional and behavioral problems of children in the system.

Resources:

> **Adoption Online Connection at**
> **http://www.clark.net/pub/crc/open.html**
> is a Web site registry of waiting adoptive families hoping
> to connect with birth parents. AOC represents an alternative
> to newspaper advertising.

THE HOME STUDY

Next, complete your home study. If your state agency conducts home studies, this is a good place to start, because they will usually not charge you if you are interested in public agency adoption. The home study they conduct can also be used to adopt a child through a photolisting service. Remember, a home study conducted by a public agency may be more stringent than a standard study, because the social worker is looking for more than good health, a clean record on child abuse, and financial stability. She wants to find out how you cope with setbacks and how you deal with frustration and anger, because these relate to the kind of special needs child you want to adopt. The caseworker will also want to see how flexible you are. If you say you are a childless couple and enjoy traveling all around the world, yet you are willing to adopt a child who is in a wheelchair, the caseworker is going to ask how such a child is going to fit into your vacation routine.

In addition to the basic documents required for a home study (see chapter 16), a state agency may ask for certain kinds of information. For example, if you have had any kind of counseling, even for infertility, the agency may ask for a letter from your counselor or therapist. They will also have forms for your physician and your references to complete, where a private agency would simply request letters. A standard form can be helpful, actually, because it assures you that most of the information needed will be addressed by completing the forms.

For the most part, the home study for a special needs adoption will be like any other, except that the caseworker may ask you more in-depth questions, especially as certain issues relate to the kind of special needs child you hope to adopt. The questions will have to do with family values, what you learned from your parents that you want to pass on to your children, how you cope, how you and your spouse deal with disagreements, how accepting of the particular child your family and community would be, what support systems you have to care for a child, your attitudes toward the birth parents, how siblings are going to react, and your attitudes toward counseling. Unlike a standard home study, the caseworker may want you to discuss your attitudes toward sex, what you consider sexually age-appropriate behavior in a child, and how you feel about caring for a child and not receiving much appreciation and affection in return. If both of you work, the caseworker will probably go into depth about your child care arrangements. If the child will need special services, the caseworker will also want to know about the availability of these services in your area. One question that may also be asked involves who would care for your child in the event of your death. If you have other children without special needs, and you have appointed legal guardians for them in the event of your death, remember that these same people may not be open to adopting a child with special needs.

Be prepared to explain just what kind of child you want, how much openness with the birth family you are willing to accept, and what legal risk you feel you can handle if the parents' rights have not been terminated. You will probably be asked to fill out a special needs acceptance list, checking off what factors you can accept in a child or in her family background, and to what degree you can accept these characteristics. Before answering this section, you may want to do some basic homework to determine what is meant by such terms as "deformity," "physical disability," or "learning disability." These are broad terms, and you may want to attach a sheet of paper explaining exactly what you can accept. The social worker who comes into your home will also want to explore this with you. For example, if you answer that you can accept no sexual abuse, they may ask you how you will feel if you find out later that the child was sexually abused. Sexual abuse is a very sensitive topic, and the caseworker may want to find out whether there are any underlying reasons why you would not accept this kind of child.

When you have finally attended all the workshops and completed all the paperwork, the agency has a matching system based on the type of child you want. As children become available, you may be selected to adopt a particular one. You will be presented a child or sibling group that the agency thinks matches the kind of child you are willing to accept. You do not have to accept the child. If you feel that the child is not one that you are prepared to parent, tell the agency. You may need to work with them to clarify what kind of child you wanted. In some cases, of course, parents will say they are willing to accept a child with certain characteristics, but then when they are presented a child who has these characteristics, they are disappointed. It is clear they were secretly hoping to adopt a healthy child with few problems. They should have been honest at the outset.

Assuming you approve the child, however, the next thing that will happen is that she will be placed with you. At this point she may or may not be legally free for adoption. If she is not legally free, and the birth parents are not making any progress, then you must wait until their rights are terminated. (In some cases the parents' rights are terminated at the adoption.) Legal adoption can take between several months and several years to accomplish, although there is now a big drive underway to move adoptions through faster.

THE LEGAL RISKS OF SPECIAL NEEDS ADOPTION

Nearly all adoptions are "legal risks," but ones in which an involuntary termination of parental right is concerned or ones in which the birth mother may have given false information about the birth father are considered especially "risky." Although the media has created much of a sensation regarding this matter, the reality is that a child who has been abused or neglected and cannot go back to his original family is not a high legal risk even if no one can find the child's birth father.

Let's look at three categories of risk: low risk, moderate risk, and high risk.

Low risk. A low-risk adoption means that the consent of the birth mother, the birth father, and any alleged fathers have been given, or their parental rights have been terminated. If there is no consent from the birth father because he cannot be found, then there is documentation to support that efforts were made to find him and tell him of his rights. If the agency says that a child is a low legal risk, ask whether documentation is there to show that both parents' rights have been terminated or that efforts were made to contact the birth father so that he could not contest the adoption if he chose.

Moderate risk. An example of moderate risk would be a situation in which the birth mother's rights have been terminated, but the birth father cannot be found and there is sketchy documentation regarding the state's effort to find him.

High risk. High-risk adoption is not adoption—it is foster care, called foster-adoptive placements. It means the birth mother's and probably the father's rights have not been terminated. Do not necessarily rule out taking a high-risk child initially as a foster-adoptive child; it may be that the birth mom and dad are never going to get their lives together, but that not enough of a paper trail was left to prove that efforts were made to find them and explain their rights. Babies are often high legal risks simply because not enough time has passed to allow their birth parents to do a turnaround. If you find out that no other family member is available to care for the child, and the parents are not making any effort to follow their court-ordered plan, you may want to consider this situation.

OPEN ADOPTION

Openness in a special needs adoption can be very similar to openness in a standard infant adoption, with letters and pictures being exchanged with the birth mother every six months or so. Or it can be quite different. Children with special needs are often old enough to remember their parents or relatives, and, therefore, more openness may be advised. On the other hand, parents who may pose a danger to the child should not have contact with the child.

Where possible, a certain level of openness is now commonly viewed as beneficial to the birth parents, the adoptive parents, and most of all the child. Although the birth parents and the child probably gain the most advantage from openness, adoptive parents and the agency usually have the most control over the matter. Because you will ultimately set the tone for the level of openness that will take place in an adoption, the caseworker will want to know what your comfort level is and also under what circumstances you may or may not be comfortable with openness. Whether or not contact in person or through letters with the biological parents is advised, the caseworker will probably expect that you remain in contact with the child's previous foster parents for at least a few months to make the child's transition easier.

Here are some of the different levels of openness and the times when each kind may be appropriate:

1. *Personal visits with birth parents, extended family members, or foster family members.* No one wants to see a child abruptly removed from his home and placed with a new set of parents, never to see his biological parents or caregivers again. We have all heard about children being taken from the only home they have ever known and sent to live with their biological parents. No matter what we believed was the right legal decision, our hearts ached for the children. Yet every day, 2,000 children in the United States and Canada are separated from their parents and placed in another home.[12] Often they are placed with foster parents with whom they become attached before they move on to be with their adoptive parents. The trauma of separation from parent(s) and other relatives is added to the trauma of the neglect and abuse. That is why social service agencies work so hard to reunite children with their parents or to have a relative care for the child if the parent cannot.

   Not all children's parents who have neglected them are malicious. Cocaine and crack have disrupted the lives of many parents who come from seemingly stable family backgrounds. A child of such parents may have aunts and uncles and grandparents who lead normal lives. These extended family members may love the child very much, and although they lack the resources to care for her, may desire to see her at least a few times a year. Since they did not neglect or abuse the child, they may be the ideal people to provide her with the link to her birth family and allow her to feel connected to her original family in a positive way.

Other children have parents who have a mental illness or a level of retardation that makes caring for the children very difficult, causing the parents' rights to be terminated. A child may have parents who truly care about him and wish him no harm, but just cannot provide the day-to-day structure needed. He may well benefit from having contact with his parent(s), especially if he has strong memories of them and knows that they care about him. Having contact with the birth parents can give him a sense of continuity and connectedness to his biological roots.

Of course, if you adopt an older child—one who can remember phone numbers and make phone calls—openness may not be an option—it may just be a fact. Children can and will make phone calls to relatives.

The child's response to seeing his biological parents or other relatives when they visited him while in foster care should be taken into consideration when deciding whether such visits are appropriate. Depending upon the situation, it is best for such meetings to take place in a public area, such as a restaurant. You probably do not want the family to know exactly where you live.

2. *Letters and pictures.* Sometimes children are placed with adoptive families who live so far away from their birth parents and relatives that personal contact with the birth family is nearly impossible, even if it is appropriate. Sometimes parents' lives are too chaotic, or the abuse they inflicted on the child was too severe, for visits to take place. In such situations, cards, letters, and pictures may be appropriate. Again, the child's age and history should be taken into consideration. If the child is very young, contact with the birth family is for the birth family's benefit. As the child matures, the contact can be for his benefit.

If the child's parents' rights were involuntarily terminated, you will probably not want the parents to know your address. All correspondence should go through the agency.

3. *No contact.* Children who were grossly neglected or abused may be traumatized by any contact. The parents can continue to abuse the child psychologically in letters, even if the content of the letters is not overtly abusive. Parents who used code words when they abused the children

could still continue to use those terms in a letter. A letter may remind a child of past trauma in a way he is not ready or capable of dealing with; it may even cause flashbacks that may retraumatize the child.

Of course, even if minimal contact with the parent is not appropriate now, some level of contact may be appropriate in the future. If the child is in therapy and needs to confront his abusers on some level, making contact with his parents may be part of his healing process. He may also have to make contact with his biological relatives to understand his genetic background, especially as it evolves over time.

Finally, the child may desire and need to continue contact with the foster parents. Sometimes, however, it is not appropriate for children to have contact with the foster parents if they are trying to sabotage the adoption or are causing the child to have conflicting loyalties.

ADOPTING BY SPECIAL NEEDS CATEGORY

If you are specifically interested in adopting, for example, a blind, deaf, or mentally disabled child, or an orphan child of a parent who died from AIDS, you might begin by contacting support and referral organizations that address the specific concerns of the illness or disability. If you take this approach, getting state and federal adoption subsidies may be difficult, since these children may not be in the foster care system and are probably not receiving foster care subsidies. However, children with profound problems will be eligible for Supplemental Security Income (SSI) and other benefits that are provided to any child with a disability regardless of whether the child is adopted or biological—though she may not receive the benefits if your income is too high. However, if an agency handles the adoption, you very likely could receive subsidies.

Before considering adopting a child with a specific disability or health condition, it is best to find out from those who have children with the condition what issues must be addressed, and what the day-to-day responsibilities will be.

AIDS

It is estimated that by the year 2000, 82,000 children will be orphaned as a result of their parents' death from AIDS.[13] (Of course, this may change as better drug therapies delay or possibly even halt the disease's progression.) Programs are now being developed so that prospective adoptive parents can become involved in the lives of children whose moms and possibly dads have AIDS or are HIV-positive. The biological parents care for the child as much as possible, but as their health deteriorates, the prospective adoptive parents take on a more active role.

When the parent dies, the child, who then lives with the adoptive parents, has already formed a close-knit relationship with his new family. The adoptive parents can also have the opportunity to know and share in the child's life before placement.

Families adopting HIV-positive children struggle with many problems, including uncertainty and a lack of resources. Social workers can be instrumental in evaluating family needs and in orchestrating and managing resources to fit the legal, foster care, or adoption needs of families with afflicted children. Common issues faced by these children and their families include the need in some cases to keep the child's disease secret.[14]

Resources:

CDC Hotline (800) 342 AIDS

Children with AIDS Project of America
1414 W. Bethany Home Road, Suite 5
Phoenix, AZ 85019
(800) 866-2437 or (602) 973-4319
E-Mail jjenkins@indirect.com*
http://www.aidskids.org/index.html

This organization recruits families from all fifty states to adopt HIV children, AIDS orphans, and drug-addicted infants and refers the families to private and public adoption agencies. If you register with them, your name and background will be shared with agencies. The organization maintains a database that includes children, recruited families, and adoptive families. There is no fee for the service.

Tanya's Children (213) 730-8202
This organization places independently infected
and noninfected children whose parents have died from AIDS.
For California residents only.

Down Syndrome

If you wish to adopt a child with Down syndrome (DS), it is best to go through a DS support and resource organization, especially if you desire to adopt a newborn or young child. Few very young children with Down syndrome are available through adoption exchanges.

The Down Syndrome Center, an organization that provides education and support to families with children who have DS, also provides an informal network to bring together prospective adoptive parents with infants and children who have DS. Some infants become available for adoption because the biological parents discovered at birth that the child has DS. Other times the birth mother is making adoption plans and the initial prospective adoptive parents did not want to adopt a child with DS.

For every child born with DS, at present there are about forty-five families in the United States waiting to adopt him. Because there are more prospective adoptive parents than children available, birth parents can select the family, and in general want to see a short biography of the adoptive parents, to meet with them, and to maintain a certain level of openness after the child is placed with the couple. Robin Steele, an adoptive mother actively involved with the DS Center, says that couples can expect to wait at least six months before an infant becomes available. Because many couples request a girl, if you have no gender preference, you can adopt sooner.

Steele suggests the following guidelines:

- Gather as much information about DS as possible.
- Get involved in a DS support group and an adoption support group.
- Get your home study completed.
- Send a general letter to as many agencies as possible describing yourselves and expressing your desire to adopt an infant/child with DS. Agencies will often waive their initial fee, because they are pleased to keep a list on file of prospective adoptive parents who desire to adopt a child with special needs.
- Contact the DS Center and complete their two-page form. The form asks what agency and caseworker conducted your home study; what age, ethnic background, and gender you desire; and what level of openness you are willing to maintain with the birth family.
- Get an agency involved so that you will be eligible for state funding.

Resources:

Down Syndrome Association of Greater Cincinnati,
Adoption Awareness Committee
(513) 761-5400

Knowledge and Information for Down Syndrome A-KIDS
(914) 428-1236
This is an adoption exchange program.

ADOPTION NETWORKS OR EXCHANGES

Adoption networks are photolisting services that present children who have not been able to be placed by their own social services department. Such children are usually more difficult to place, and therefore need a broader exposure to potential adoptive parents. An adoption exchange is not an agency but a networking system where public and sometimes private agencies can register children who need homes. The exchanges do not have custody of the children; they are merely facilitators in bringing children who are in the custody of an agency or foster care system together with prospective adoptive parents. Exchanges often will try, using a computer, to match prospective adoptive parents with children.

You may be very excited about the number of children available in a photolisting, but remember that many other prospective adoptive parents may be inquiring about the same children and that the children may be in the process of being adopted even as you are beginning plans to find out more about them. As you pore over these books, try not to raise your hopes too high. Prospective adoptive parents have often reported much disappointment.

Rita Laws suggests the following tips for making photolistings work for you:

1. Get a home study completed if you are not already approved. Be sure to use an agency that will give you copies of your study so that you can send them out to the exchanges.

2. As soon as you complete your home study, get a personal subscription to a photolisting, because the children in the updates can be placed very quickly. Call on new listings the day you receive them.

3. Fax or send overnight a copy of your home study as soon as the social worker requests it. Address it to the correct social worker and include a cover letter that tells why you would be the ideal parent for a particular child.

4. Call the exchange the next day to be sure that the correct social worker received your home study. If the home study is being sent out from the agency that conducted it, you will want to be doubly sure that all the paperwork has been sent out.

5. To expedite the process, send out home studies for several children at the same time.

6. Invest in a good medical encyclopedia or computer program. Learn the terminology and what treatments will be necessary. If you have access to medical personnel, review the child's conditions with them. (If the child is available and you are definitely interested in her, you will want your pediatrician to review her medical records.)

7. Keep your photolisting book up-to-date as new pages are sent to you. If most of the children in the new pages are already placed when you call, the listing is not up-to-date. Subscribe to a different listing.
8. Once you have selected a child, ask lots of questions.

The photolisting book is one of the most creative and effective ways available to recruit families for waiting children. Each listing includes the following information:

- The child's first name, month and year of birth, state of residence, and ID number, and the date on which he was added to the photolisting book
- The child's likes and dislikes
- A brief medical and social history
- The kind of foster home the child lives in
- The kind of adoptive home that would best suit the child's needs (single woman, married couple with no children, etc.)
- A contact person and number

Because photolistings must present a lot of information in a small space, certain key phrases may suggest much more than they say. Just as "cozy" describes a small home, assume that certain words can be taken literally and that others have deeper meanings. Rita Laws gives some examples:

- "All boy, very active, impulsive, needs a lot of attention, acts out"—may mean the child has attention deficit hyperactivity disorder (ADHD).
- "Requires lots of structure, needs constant supervision, manipulative, has experienced several losses, has experienced many moves"—may mean the child has emotional and/or behavioral problems, including attachment disorder (AD).
- "Neglected"—may mean the child was malnourished, and may also mean attachment disorder.
- "Developmentally delayed, immature, delayed speech"—may mean child has mental retardation or even attachment disorder.
- "Has difficulty in school"—may indicate that the child has learning disabilities and/or emotional and behavioral problems including attachment disorder.
- "Moody or sad"—may mean child has depression and/or other emotional problems.

- "Prenatal exposure to drugs/alcohol"—may indicate problems related to cocaine or fetal alcohol syndrome or effects.[15]

Note: A child's history of sexual abuse is not included in photolisting books or other public media; this information will not be provided to you until you become a serious inquirer.

It is best to place yourself on a few adoption exchange lists to increase your opportunities for adopting a child. Different lists cover different geographical territory: Some cover a single state, some a region, and some the entire country:

State. It is probably best to begin your search for a child in your own state. First, you are more likely to be selected than an out-of-state parent, because some social workers are opposed to sending a child a long distance away, especially if the child needs a more gradual transition from his foster home to his adoptive home. Second, the adoption process can usually go more smoothly because the Interstate Compact is not involved. Third, it is easier to visit the child before the adoption takes place if you live within a few hours' driving distance.

Regional. A regional exchange lists children in a multistate area. You do not necessarily have to live in the region to adopt a child from this exchange. It is up to the social worker whether to allow the child to go outside the region.

Resources:

Rocky Mountain Adoption Exchange
925 South Niagara Str.
Denver, CO 80223
(303) 333-0845
This exchange lists children from Colorado, Missouri, Nevada, New Mexico, South Dakota, Utah, and Wyoming but places children throughout the country.

National. A national exchange certainly allows you to select from a greater number of children. Remember, however, that any time you adopt a child from a distance, you must consider the cost of transportation. You will probably be expected to visit the child a few times before making a permanent adoption plan. Traveling can be expensive and time-consuming Your library, a local adoption agency, or adoption support group in your area may subscribe to these listings. Check to see before you invest in your own copies.

Resources

National Resource Center for Special Needs Adoption
16250 Northland Drive
Suite 120
Southfield, MI 48075
(810) 443-7080 x295

The CAP Book, Inc.
700 Exchange Street
Rochester, NY 14608
(716) 232-5110

The CAP Book is a national register that provides a photolisting of hard-to-place children. Only children who legally can be placed with out-of-state adoptive parents are included. The book costs $75 per year, lists hundreds of children, and is updated every other week.

The National Adoption Center
1218 Chestnut Street
Philadelphia, PA 19107
(215) 925-0200
(800) TO ADOPT

The National Adoption Center operates the National Adoption Exchange, which also provides a computer matching service for waiting children. You must contact an adoption caseworker to access the computer system for you. The center also provides information and training for those adopting.

Aid to Adoption of Special Kids (AASK)
657 Mission Street
San Francisco, CA

North American Council on Adoptable Children (NACAC)
1821 University Avenue
St. Paul, MN 55104
(612) 644-3036

This organization provides materials and videos for a fee and maintains a listing of local adoption support groups. NACAC also maintains an up-to-date listing of adoption professionals and organizations listed on the Internet.

Faces of Adoption provides a photolisting
of available children with special needs,
as well as adoption-related information,
on their Web site at **http://www.adopt.org/adopt**.

The Adoption Exchange Web site
at **http://phoenix.uchsc.edu/rmae**
links prospective adoptive families
with waiting children.

The Placenet Web site
at **http://www.adopting.org/placenet.html**
lists information about waiting families.

FOSTER CARE

Couples often ask whether foster care is a good strategy for those who want to adopt a child. As a rule, the answer is no. Taking a foster child into your home can be a wonderful, challenging opportunity; it is not a means in itself to adopt a child. However, there are opportunities to become a foster parent as a means of adopting. *If you are becoming a foster parent as a step toward adopting a child, make this very clear to the state social worker who will be licensing you.*

At one time social workers would not allow foster parents to adopt the child they were caring for. The child would be adopted by another family, even if she had been in the foster home from a young age and her foster parents were the only parents she had known. The rationale was that a couple who takes on a foster child in the hope of adopting the child will wish for the termination of his biological parents' rights. Although foster care can be a temporary place for a child whose family is in crisis, it is often a place where a child stays while one or both of his birth parents get their lives together, a process that can take years, if it happens at all. This can be frustrating to the foster parents, who love and care for the child as they live in a state of limbo wondering whether the parents are ever going to pull it together. Biological parents may meet marginal requirements, keeping their rights from being terminated, but not meet enough requirements to parent the child fully. Even when one of the biological parents begins to take appropriate actions so that she can resume full responsibility for the child, the foster family can be heartbroken at seeing the child go from a stable situation to a home that is less than stable.

Many foster parents do eventually adopt the children who have been in their home. In some states they are allowed the first opportunity to adopt the children if the children are not going back to their biological families. For the foster parents to qualify, the child must usually have been in the foster home for at least six months.

Foster/Adoption

Foster/adopt does *not* mean becoming foster parents as a way of caring for children who "might" become available for adoption. It means taking a child into your home who will probably become available for adoption. Although 50 to 70 percent of the children in foster care return to their biological families, others will never go back to their biological families and are not being adopted quickly enough. Many could be eligible for adoption, but the legal steps have not been taken to terminate the parents' rights (TPR), or a certain time has not lapsed until the parents' rights can be terminated, and so the children are technically not available for adoption. While these children are waiting for a TPR, it is best if their foster home is also their potential adoptive family.

About half of these children are already in foster homes in which the foster parents want to adopt them. The others need to be. However, the time of placement in the adoptive home to the time of adoption can be lengthy, and the paperwork extensive. When social workers have limited time and resources and many emergencies to deal with, pushing through the adoption of a child who is in his loving and stable foster/adopt home is not a priority. The actual adoption is important for the child and parents, however. They need to know that this is forever.

Caseworkers know it is important for children to be placed in permanent loving homes, and there is a trend in the United States to approve more foster/adopt homes. However, you may find some resistance by your state agency if your intention is to be an adoptive, not a foster, family. Some public agencies do not want to expend the effort to license a home in which only one child or sibling group will stay—even though this means a permanent plan for the children. This, of course, puts you in a bind: You cannot adopt the child until the parents' rights are terminated, the parents' rights cannot be terminated until the child has found a foster family that wants to adopt him, and you cannot be that foster home because your intention is to adopt. This kind of catch-22 may explain why seemingly very adoptable children can wait so long for a permanent home.

To become a foster/adopt parent, you must meet requirements both for becoming a foster parent and for becoming an adoptive parent. This process can take a long time, which can be frustrating if you have a particular child in mind. Depending on the requirements of your state for becoming a foster parent, more emphasis may be placed on the safety of your home, compared with adoptive parent requirements. Therefore you will probably need a safety and fire prevention inspection, and any lead paint in your home (common in older homes) may have to be covered or removed.

Resources:

> **The Foster Parent Home Page**
> at http://www.worldaccess.com/~clg46/
> contains the most extensive listing of foster parenting resources
> on the Internet, and provides links to many other
> foster parenting sites. It is also useful for adoptive parents
> who have adopted children out of foster care.

> **The Usenet newsgroup,**
> **alt.support.foster-parents,**
> is dedicated to the exchange of ideas
> and experiences involved in foster parenting.

SPECIAL NEEDS ADOPTION SUBSIDIES

Expenses for adopting a child with special needs can be minimal. In fact, if your employer offers funding for adopting children, the cap on what the employer will pay is often higher for a child with special needs.

Years ago children remained foster children because foster parents who were receiving monthly payments could not afford to lose those benefits if they adopted the children. Other parents interested in adopting a child with complex medical needs, or a sibling group, could not afford to. Now, thanks to the Adoption Assistance and Child Welfare Act of 1980, a whole new pool of parents can consider special needs adoption. This act mandated that all states establish a Title IV-E adoption subsidy program for children previously eligible for funding while in foster care. Title IV-E monies come from both federal and state dollars. Each state also administers other subsidies that come solely from state dollars. (As of this writing, some states are considering limiting or omitting state subsidies.) In 1992 more than $219 million supported over 66,000 children. Unfortunately, many adoptive parents are not even aware of the subsidies—sometimes because social workers neglect to make them aware. In some states adoptive parents may have to go to court to make sure that their state provides them with the funds that are due them. Read on to find out who is eligible for subsidies.

Title IV-E

The first thing to know is that in order to be eligible for subsidies, a child must be under the guardianship of an agency. Children adopted through an attorney are *not* eligible. In about fifteen states, some international adoptees are eligible for one-time reimbursements of up to $2,000.

In general, for a child to receive federal monthly adoption subsidies from Title IV-E, he must have sufficient medical, developmental, or psychological problems or disabilities to be eligible for Supplemental Security Income (SSI), or he must meet the state's criteria for having special needs, and he must come from a birth family or relative's home that was receiving or was eligible to receive Aid for Families with Dependent Children. If the child has special needs but does not meet the other criteria, he may be eligible for an equal state subsidy.

Children who are receiving Title IV-E federal foster care maintenance payments are eligible for federal adoption assistance benefits. Many foster children are receiving state and not federal funds, however, so the child may or may not be eligible for federal funding once adopted. Children who are receiving SSI benefits at the time of adoption are financially and categorically eligible for adoption assistance; in fact, even if they have been not receiving SSI benefits, if they meet SSI criteria at the time of adoption, they are eligible for adoption subsidies. With SSI benefits, however, the adoptive parents' income is taken into consideration, which means that most children are not eligible for SSI once adopted.

Even if your income is too high, determining whether a child is eligible for SSI is still a wise idea. First, the child can receive SSI before the adoption is finalized. Second, if she does qualify for SSI, she will qualify for adoption assistance subsidies after finalization, since these are not determined by your income. Remember, prospective adoptive parents cannot receive the maximum amount of federal support from both SSI and the adoption assistance program, even if the child is eligible for both programs.

Following are the general categories of SSI eligibility. This is not a comprehensive list, so be sure to contact your local Social Security office at (800) 772-1213 for more complete information on eligibility criteria and application forms.

- Growth impairment of the musculoskeletal system (e.g., arthritis, disorders of the spine)
- Blindness or hearing impairment
- Respiratory problems (e.g., asthma or cystic fibrosis)
- Cardiovascular problems
- Digestive system disorders

- Malnutrition
- Endocrine system (e.g., thyroid) disorders
- Diabetes
- Blood and lymph disease (e.g., sickle cell disease)
- Cancers
- Multiple body defects
- Down syndrome
- Immune deficiency
- Neurological problems (e.g., cerebral palsy)
- Mental and emotional problems
- Attention deficit hyperactivity disorder
- Developmental and emotional disorders of newborns and infants
- Genito-urinary problems

If a child is not receiving federal foster care maintenance payments or is not eligible for SSI, two categories must be met in order for her to be eligible for the federal adoption assistance program. The state must determine that the child has special needs, and the child must meet the financial and categorical criteria of Aid to Families with Dependent Children (AFDC) both at the time she was removed from her parents' custody and at the time of adoption

Each state establishes specific guidelines as to what defines a "special needs" child. In one state a child may have to be six years old to be considered special needs, while in another she must be ten years old. A child who is African-American or of mixed ethnic background will have a lower age requirement than a Caucasian child in order to be considered special needs.

A child is considered to have special needs when she has met these three factors:

1. She cannot or should not be returned to her biological parents. This includes children whose parents have voluntarily released them for adoption.
2. The child has a specific condition, including minority ethnic background, age, being part of a sibling group, or having a medical, mental, or emotional disability or being at risk for one, that would make adoption difficult without a financial incentive.
3. Except where it would be against the best interests of the child to place him, efforts to place the child without offering medical or adoption assistance have been unsuccessful. Federal officials have finally recognized that a focus on "shopping" a child until adoptive parents who do not

need the subsidy can be found is contrary not only to sound adoption practice but to the intent of the adoption assistance program.

If parents cannot or will not adopt without the subsidy, then the requirement is met. Asking parents whether they are willing to adopt without subsidies does not put the placement at risk for them.[16] As a practical matter, however, children with special needs who are easily adoptable, such as a cocaine-exposed Caucasian six-month-old, can easily be placed without subsidies. A few couples will usually be considered for the child, and the one willing to adopt without subsidies will be selected.

Foster parents who have had a child in their home for a significant time do not need to consider whether they are willing to take the child without a subsidy. Because of the emotional ties involved, this requirement is waived.

Aid for Families with Dependent Children

There are two classifications of AFDC requirements: need and deprivation. Deprivation requirements are met if a parent is absent or if parents' rights have been terminated. To qualify for the need category, a child must have been eligible, even if an application was not made for AFDC, at the following times:

- In the month that a petition was filed with the court for the removal of the child from his home, or six months before
- In the month before the child's parent voluntarily signed an agreement for the child to be placed outside the home, or six months before

In other words, even if the child was not receiving AFDC at the time he was removed from his home, if his biological family qualified for it, he still will meet the AFDC criteria. He must also be eligible when the adoption is petitioned. Children who meet the AFDC requirements at the time they are removed from their parents' custody may or may not meet the criteria when the adoption proceedings are initiated.

Requiring children to be AFDC eligible seems arbitrary, and as of this writing, federal lawmakers are reconsidering the requirement. Meeting the AFDC requirement is not as simple as it may look. More and more children entering foster care who then become eligible for adoption are not coming from welfare homes but from working families. Moreover, even if the child's biological family was AFDC eligible at the time he was removed from his home, his family's work status may change from the time he was removed from the home to the time the adoption petition was put into place. Often the employment status of one of the biological parents does change between the time the child is removed from the home and the time the adoption petition is filed. The biological mother may have gotten a job, making the child ineligible for AFDC status.

Note: A child who is receiving Title IV-E foster care payments at the time the adoption petition is filed meets the AFDC relatedness test.

Resources:

> Information on the **Federal Adoption Assistance Program**,
> which offers financial assistance in domestic special-needs adoption,
> can be found on the Children Youth Family Education Research
> Network (CYFERNet) gopher at **gopher://cyfer.esusda.gov:70/00
> /CYFER-net/funding/faprs/f209**.

State Adoption Subsidy Programs

Most states have an adoption subsidy program for children with special needs who do not qualify for federal adoption assistance under Title IV-E—usually because they do not meet the SSI/AFDC requirements. In many states the IV-E adoption assistance and state payment subsidies are administered as the same program, with the same payment rates for families. If a child meets the criteria for special needs but not for the SSI/AFDC requirements, the payments come from state instead of federal funds. Most states have fairly broad standards for defining "special needs." Some even say that if a child has been in your home for eighteen months as a foster child, she qualifies as special needs because of the emotional trauma that would be caused if she was removed from your home. Just be aware that as federal and state dollars become tighter, fewer benefits may be offered.

Monthly cash benefits. Once a child is considered to have special needs, she is eligible for monthly assistance, usually in the amount you would receive if you were foster parents. Each state sets up its own fee schedule. As a rule, the higher the cost of living and the older the child, the higher the payments. Some states provide a higher foster care rate for children who require special care: This is called *specialized or accelerated care rates.* If the adopted child was eligible for specialized care rates when she was in the foster care system, the rates would stay higher after the adoption.

Medical assistance. Children in the federal adoption assistance program are automatically eligible for Medicaid benefits. Many states also choose to provide

Medicaid coverage for children who are receiving benefits from state or local (nonfederal) adoption assistance programs. Although states have broader standards in defining who is a special needs child, the definition for special needs is directly related to having a special medical or psychological need, as opposed to being in a certain age or ethnic background category. A healthy two-year-old African-American child would not necessarily qualify.

Minimum Medicaid benefits for children include inpatient hospital services (except for tuberculosis or mental disease), outpatient hospital services, laboratory and x-ray services, screening and diagnosis, and medical and dental services provided under state law. Children are also entitled to optional services to correct or lessen the effects of physical or mental illnesses or conditions discovered during a health care screening under the Early and Periodic Screening, Diagnosis and Treatment Program (EPSDT). These services include home health, private duty nursing, clinic services, dental services, physical therapy, prescription drugs, dentures, prosthetic devices, eyeglasses, inpatient psychiatric services, respiratory services, and other medical care.

Even if you have comprehensive health care insurance, you may want the extra security of Medicaid in case your situation changes.

If your child has special mental or physical needs and is to receive Medicaid, try to negotiate as much other assistance as possible. Many physicians will not accept Medicaid, which can be difficult, especially if you have other children who are already going to a particular physician.

Medicaid is especially useful when you are using specialists and not general practitioners and for getting specialized hospital care. You can also request that the state pay for psychological counseling and for one-time medical needs and equipment, such as a wheelchair ramp.[17]

Social Security Block Grants (formerly called Title XX) govern the social services grant, which gives federal money to states to use for helping families maintain self-support, remedying neglect and abuse, and preventing or reducing the need for institutional care by providing these supportive services to adoptive families.

These funds have not been actively promoted by child welfare workers, and the individual states have much latitude in designing the programs. Each state has an outline for services and established activities to be supported and who will be served. Types of services vary from state to state. Potential services include day care, respite services, in-home support services such as housekeeping and personal care, and counseling.

Unlike the Medicaid program, SSBG is not given automatically to dependent children or children eligible for AFDC. However, the program is designed to make sure that children in the adoption assistance program will not be excluded from services that the state provides children who do receive AFDC. For example, if the state operates a day care program funded by these block grants and gives preference to AFDC children, then a child in the adoption assistance program will have the same preference regardless of the adoptive parents' income.

Other Services and Assistance

The federal law also requires that the adoption assistance agreement include any additional services that are needed for the family or child. Prospective adoptive parents should closely monitor their child's needs and anticipate any future needs. For example, a family may have to change their home to accommodate the physically challenged child now or in the future.

Service subsidies. Many states provide medical, mental health, and other postplacement services that are not covered by the adoptive family's health insurance or by Medicaid. Service subsidies should be established before the adoption is finalized. Some states do provide service subsidies to adoptive families after finalization.

Education. This may include speech and physical therapies.

Reimbursement for nonrecurring adoption expenses. Since 1987 the federal adoption assistance law has required states to pay nonrecurring adoption expenses in the adoption of children with special needs through a state or nonprofit private agency.[18] The cap is usually $2,000 per child. A child need only meet the Federal IV-E definition of a special needs child to qualify for this one-time subsidy; he does not have to meet SSI or AFDC eligibility. You must apply for reimbursement of these expenses in the state where the adoption assistance agreement is signed. If you are not receiving adoption assistance, you must apply in the state where the adoption will be finalized.[19] The subsidy covers:

- Adoptive parents' home study, medical exams, and postplacement supervisions
- Legal and court costs
- Transportation, meals, and lodging
- Adoption fees

Subsidies for International Adoptions

The following states will consider reimbursing nonrecurring adoption costs for international adoptees.[20] If your state is not on the list, check with your state adoption specialist to find out whether reimbursement is a possibility.

Alabama	Kansas	Nebraska
Alaska	Kentucky	Ohio
Hawaii	Maryland	Oklahoma
Idaho	Mississippi	Utah
Iowa	Missouri	Vermont

Adoption Assistance Checklist

Whenever a family receives adoption assistance, a written adoption assistance agreement between the adoptive parents and the state agency will be provided. These agreements vary from state to state, but there is a model adoption assistance agreement available that contains the requirements under Title IV-E, useful for adoptive families who move across state lines. The agreement should state that a commitment is made regardless of where the adoptive parents live and should specify the kinds of care and services that will be provided. It should be specific enough to ensure future enforcement but flexible enough to allow for new provisions if circumstances change. For example, if your child is receiving physical therapy, the agreement should describe the services in detail and state that if the provider can no longer offer services or if you move, equal services will be provided. Services should be described in very specific terms: not just "therapy will be provided" but "individual and family therapy will be provided for at least one hour per week by a licensed child psychologist or social worker." The agreement should also state the date on which each benefit will start and the circumstances under which it can be terminated.

Following is a checklist of questions to refer to when reviewing your adoption assistance agreement:

1. Does the agreement clearly state all the responsibilities of the prospective adoptive parents? Are financial reporting and recertification requirements explicit?
2. Is the agreement signed by someone with proper authority to bind the state agency?
3. Are all necessary agencies parties to the agreement?
4. Does the agreement specify the amount of cash assistance to be provided?
5. Does the agreement state all necessary services to be provided?
6. Does the agreement give the date when each benefit and service will begin?
7. Does the agreement clearly list the conditions under which benefits and services may be terminated?

8. Does the agreement specify the condition under which benefits and services can increase or decrease? Is there any clause that restricts the prospective adoptive parents' authority to negotiate changes in the future?
9. Do the services end when the child turns eighteen or twenty-one?
10. Does the agreement specify what will happen if the adoptive parents die?
11. Does the agreement specify that the agreement itself will still be in effect and that the benefits will remain in effect if the adoptive family moves out of state?
12. Does the agreement provide for Medicaid eligibility?

If you believe your child has special medical or psychological needs that will not be adequately met by the subsidies and services outlined in your agreement, it would be wise to take the child to a specialist of your choosing (orthopedic, neurological, psychiatric) to obtain the clearest prognosis possible so that you can negotiate the best possible agreement for your child. Even if this means taking your child to a specialist who does not accept Medicaid, in the long run it may save you both money and time.

Negotiating an Agreement

Federal policy requires that the child's and the family's circumstances be taken into consideration in establishing an adoption assistance agreement. For example, although there are written state guidelines as to the maximum amount of monthly payments in each age category, the state and the adoptive parents can negotiate the amount. Your goal as adoptive parents should be to provide comprehensive support. Follow these steps:

1. Obtain complete information on the child's family background and medical history, including current health status, psychiatric and psychological evaluations, if necessary, and the current physical, intellectual, and emotional needs of the child. State agencies do not always collect all the essential information about a child, and the information is not always in one place. Nor does the agency always provide prospective adoptive parents all the information available. Federal law, however, requires that the following be in the child's foster care plan:

    ■ The names and addresses of the child's health and education providers
    ■ The child's grade-level performance

- The child's immunization records
- The child's medical problems
- The child's medications
- Other relevant health and educational information

2. Based on the child's medical needs, and on his social and educational background, a discussion of services may be needed.
3. Give thorough consideration to your resources and ability to meet the child's needs so that he will successfully be incorporated into your family. Take into account not only your income but your other expenses, the number of children in your home, and the circumstances of these children.
4. Compile complete information about the federal and state adoption assistance programs available, including service and medical subsidies.
5. Negotiate a support plan that combines all appropriate programs.
6. Negotiate *specific* guidelines for services to be provided in the event that you move to another state. Although federal law requires federal adoption assistance agreements to state that subsidies remain in effect regardless of where you move, some services may not be specifically addressed in the agreement.[21]

Remember, federal adoption assistance agreements remain in effect regardless of the state in which you live. If you live in South Carolina and your child receives $200 per month in subsidies, and you move to New York City, where the cost of living is much higher, you will still receive only $200 per month.

Enforcement

Most of the disagreements that arise over the negotiation or enforcement of an agreement can be handled on an informal basis. When they cannot, federal law requires that states provide prospective adoptive parents a "fair hearing" before the appropriate state agency to contest the agreement or petition for its enforcement. Some states have special review panels to hear adoption assistance appeals. A fair hearing can also be helpful if a caseworker is not responsive to the adoptive parents' requests.[22] There are separate fair hearings for Medicaid and Title XX services.

Fair hearings are informal occasions, and the rules of evidence do not strictly apply, so many adoptive and prospective adoptive parents represent themselves instead of hiring an attorney. The fair hearing officers can decide about the fact that is in dispute and order the agency to follow state statutes and agency guidelines. We strongly recommend, however, that you hire an attorney to work with you throughout this process. An attorney can help the family by establishing the eligibility of the child for benefits, by helping plan the negotiation of the adoption assistance agreement and future changes, and by taking legal steps to enforce the agreement if the family does not receive the proper benefits and services. Often additional benefits such as speech therapy, psychological counseling, and equipment for disabilities can be negotiated. Why shortchange yourself or your adopted child? Have an attorney negotiate as much as possible in your favor.

Prospective adoptive parents who are presented with a standard agency form that sets forth the terms should negotiate an individual agreement that meets the child's needs. Except for legal restrictions, there is no requirement that the adoption assistance agreement follow any particular format.

Sometimes foster parents are told that they will not receive adoption assistance if they adopt their foster child, or prospective adoptive parents who want to adopt a particular child are informed that the child will not be eligible for subsidies. In these situations the prospective adoptive parents can request the agency to reconsider the decision, and if necessary can demand a fair hearing. Have your attorney provide the state agency with the information necessary to establish the child's eligibility. If the state criteria are too strict, they may be challenged as not conforming to federal law.

Note: If you adopt a child whose parents signed a voluntary consent, you will need to have a judicial determination that the adoption is in the child's best interests or that remaining with the birth family is contrary to the child's welfare. *This needs to be done within six months of the parents' signing the consent,* because you will not be able to go back later and obtain subsidies should the need arise.[23]

Title IV-E for Child's Blood Relatives

In order for a child who is to be adopted by relatives to meet Title IV-E requirements, the court must usually state that it is against the child's welfare for him to stay in his biological parents' home, or that placement in the adoptive home is in his best interest. There is no need to discuss the manner in which the child came into care. The child must also have been AFDC eligible at the time the adoption petition was filed.

PREPARING FOR YOUR CHILD

There are a number of ways to prepare for your special needs child. This section outlines the most important.

Gathering Information

Carol McKelvey and Dr. JoEllen Stevens suggest you compile the following before the adoption placement takes place:

Complete background information, including:
- Full disclosure of the child's social and family background
- Full medical and psychological reports, including those that may result from psychological tests
- Personality and temperament testing of your family, including the Steven Adopt-Match Evaluator
- Disclosure of any problems[24]

Life Books

A life book is a pictorial and descriptive history of a child's life. Like any scrapbook, it can be put together at one time; but it is better if it is made over time. Usually a caseworker assists a child in completing the pages, but a dedicated foster parent may also put in entries.

The older the child, the more important the life book. A child in the foster-care system often has had a fragmented life and may have difficulty knowing where he was and what he was doing at various times. The life book can help put the pieces together. Unlike a regular photo album, the life book provides more than pictures of the child's past; the book can also fill in gaps that even his current social workers may not be able to tell him about. Also, the life book can help a child express his feelings about different points in his life.

Ideally, a child or his caseworker has a regularly updated life book from the time he enters foster care until the time he is adopted. However, this probably will not be the case. First, many children enter foster care with no pictures of themselves, and second, foster parents often do not take pictures. Also, social workers may have limited opportunities to take meaningful pictures of the child, so the pictures may be only of the child's foster home, his church, and his school.

If your child comes with a life book, do treat it as a special object. Go through it with your child so that he can share his past with you. Do this more than once. The child may tell you more and more each time. You will want to add pictures of your child with your family. The life book is the child's personal history, so don't put the book on the coffee table—or in the attic, as one adoptive family did, sending a message to the child that his past was not significant.

Below is a listing of what goes into a life book, but your child's life book may not contain all of these items. You may want to add some of these entries yourself.

- Information about the child's biological family, along with pictures and letters from or about family members
- The child's birth certificate and social security card
- A family tree
- A page about the child's nationality
- A list of relatives, including parents, grandparents, and siblings
- Birth and death dates
- Pictures of your child's family of origin, the homes they lived in, and the pets they had
- The child's health records
- Any family history of diseases
- The child's immunization records
- A record of childhood illnesses and health problems, including injuries
- An education page, including a list of schools the child has attended, photos of teachers, and a list of things the child enjoys
- Pictures of special foster family members and any notes from them you might have
- Illustrated stories by you about funny experiences related to the child
- A letter about why you like and love the child
- A "Heart" page where the child describes with words, magazine pictures, etc., how he likes to show feelings and affections and what makes him feel loved
- A "Bug" page where you or the child draws or writes down all the things that "bug" him (Put a picture of a big bug on this page)
- A page about church/temple and Sunday school experiences, including pictures of a favorite teacher
- Information gleaned from social workers or the child's previous foster family about his day-to-day routine, the foods he likes, his sleeping habits, favorite toys, books, and blankets, and the kinds of clothes he likes.[25]

Telling Others About the Child's Arrival

Share with your close relatives what the child is like and what may be expected. If they live nearby, their assistance could be very important, especially if you have other children in the home.

Finding Professional Assistance

Begin by asking a pediatrician who is very competent in treating children with special needs to review the records. You may also want to ask other appropriate professionals, such as psychologists, to review them. Make it very clear that the review is not to determine whether you want to proceed with the adoption but to get a complete picture of the situation you and the child will be entering. Once you feel you have a clear picture, you can begin to arrange for physicians and other professionals who accept your insurance or Medicaid coverage.

THE CHILD'S ARRIVAL AT YOUR HOME

Depending on the child's age, very likely a child will visit with you a few times and spend a weekend before coming to live with you. It is best if you visit her at least once or twice in her foster home first. You and your spouse may want to go visit the first time; then the second time you may want to take your other children with you, if you have any, and perhaps plan a fun outing all together. The third time you all meet, the child will come to your home, and the fourth visit will probably be a weekend overnight. Again, depending on the child's age, this process should take about two to three weeks.

Before the child arrives at your home, she will have to leave at least one, possibly two, families behind: her immediate foster family and her biological family. Even if she has not lived with her biological family for years, she may still need to "leave" the dream of living with her biological parents. This transition can be very difficult for a child, especially if she has feelings of mixed allegiance to her foster and birth families. If she is older, you or the caseworker may want to arrange a special ceremony in which the birth parents say good-bye to the child. If this is not possible or appropriate, a birth parent will sometimes write a letter wishing the child well in her new home. The child needs to feel that it is all right with her birth parents for her to move on to another home; she may need their "permission." If birth parents are not available, you may want to arrange a special ceremony. Buy some helium-filled balloons, one representing the child, one for each of her birth parents, one for each of her foster parents, and one for each of you. You can write each person's name on a balloon and then have the "persons" talk to each other. In the end, the child can hold on to the balloons representing herself and you and release the birth and foster parent balloons into the air.

Learning the Child's Routine

The small things in life can go a long way toward making a child's placement successful. If a child needs a lot of structure and routine, that needs to be established before he arrives. If he is very controlling, you will need to decide what is important and what you need to overlook so that everything does not become a power struggle. Often adoptive parents get upset over minor irritants—how much toothpaste is used, food "stealing," eating habits, and so on. A parent who can handle the child's learning disability may get quite upset if the child is clumsy. Issues such as space, sharing, meals, favorite foods, television time, and how to get along should be thought through as much as possible beforehand, and the child's day-to-day activities, preferences, and interests learned. Your caseworker should be able to give you practical tips in dealing with the child.

Depending upon the child's nature and background, you may want to keep things fairly calm the first few days after the child's arrival and not have many people to your home, so that the child does not feel more like a specimen than a new arrival.

Making It Work

Once a child is in your home, the experience can be wonderful. However, after the child arrives—usually about three to six months later, and often even sooner—the relationship with the child may begin to deteriorate. Caseworkers see this as the end of the "honeymoon" period, when the reality of the child's problems begins to hit. Before the child comes to live with the adoptive parents, they may not have fully heard what the caseworker was saying to them about the child's needs and problems.

Although most parents of kids with special needs experience a great deal of joy and personal satisfaction despite the extraordinary demands, many adoptions do disrupt. Planning ahead and having realistic expectations can help reduce the likelihood of an adoption not working out. Here are some suggestions for making the experience as positive as it can be:

Join a support group of parents with special needs kids. If you did not do this before you adopted, do it now. The more information you can gather from others, the more prepared you will be for whatever postadoption issues you will have to face.

Research the special characteristics of your child. Read, read, read. Once you decide on a particular special need you would be comfortable handling, do as much research as possible on the subject. Get to know other parents who have a child with that particular medical, psychological, or disability problem. Visit them at their home, if possible. See how day-to-day family life goes with such a child.

Get a support system in place. No parent can care for a child twenty-four hours a day, seven days a week, and a child who has many needs can be emotionally and physically draining. Get someone to help you and give you a break. If you are reluctant to have yet another person taking care of your child after all the caretakers he has experienced, hire someone to come into the home and help you while you make yourself a cup of tea and go through the mail or read a book.

Studies show that in families in which the father played a significant role, the parents were able to stay far more committed. Make sure that you have support from friends and family as well. If you are functioning well now, that is a good predictor that you will perform well with an additional child.[26]

Hire an attorney. It is very important for a child to feel that he is in a "forever family" and not in legal limbo. If your child's adoption finalization is taking longer, you may need the help of your own adoption attorney. An attorney can review all legal documents and adoption subsidy agreements and can expedite the adoption process, especially if one or both of the birth parents' rights have not been terminated.[27]

TALKING TO YOUR CHILD ABOUT ADOPTION AND HIS PAST

When you adopt a child with special needs, you are likely to be dealing not just with adoption issues but with issues of why the child's parents could not care for him and perhaps why they abused or neglected him. This kind of abandonment is different from the "abandonment" that occurs in other countries, in which a child is left in an orphanage. "Abandonment" in the United States usually involves overt neglect. Similarly, if the child was abused, he will not understand why his parents would do this to him.

Although hearing about the neglect and abuse and why he was placed for adoption is very painful for the child, at some point he will need to know the details surrounding his placement. Children have a right to know their pasts—it helps them understand why they feel what they feel. Without this information, the child may feel like a partly blank slate.

Of course, children do not need to know all this information at an early age or all at the same time. Telling your child the truth is a process that may parallel the discussions you have with him about adoption. Just as you do not explain adoption all at once when the child is four years old, never to bring up the subject again, you would not think of sharing the child's past with him all at the same time. Sharing the past is a process in which information is gradually revealed in ways that the child can understand.

Many adoptive parents feel as if they want to protect the child by withholding some of the grimmer details of her abuse or neglect. This is understandable, but they should know that the child may find out elsewhere. It is better if the information comes from you.

As your child asks questions, try to answer her honestly, providing only as much information as she is seeking and as is appropriate for her age. When she asks about her birth parents, try to tell the facts without making a judgment. Do not be overtly condemning of her birth parents. The child may feel she needs to "defend" her biological heritage, and she may become uncomfortable about sharing her feelings or memories if you use those occasions to bad-mouth her biological parents. Be careful, too, of the way you talk about her biological parents in front of others. Your attitude will come through.

Although it is best, in discussing the child's past, to state the facts without adding a negative interpretation to it, there will be times when a judgment will be needed to let the child know that what was done was wrong. To say, "Your mother was a wonderful woman who drank too much alcohol, and that is why she couldn't keep you" may confuse the child. The child may think, "Why do you think she was so wonderful when I remember going hungry when she was drunk?" or "If she was so wonderful, why didn't she just stop drinking so that I could live with her?" It might be better to say, "Your first mother loved you, but she drank too much alcohol, which made her do bad things like not feed you often enough." The child will understand that he was not necessarily rejected, but that his mother chose not to get help for her alcoholism and therefore was not able to provide for him. Similarly, if a birth mother was a prostitute or the birth father sold crack, you do not want to excuse their lifestyles and diminish the reality of what the child went through. You cannot say that a certain behavior is unacceptable and at the same time that the birth parents were honorable people.

Here are some organizations you may want to contact for referrals for special needs children:

Alliance of Genetic Support Groups
38th and R Streets NW
Washington, DC 20057
(202) 331-0942

Association for Retarded Citizens
2501 Avenue J
Arlington, TX 76006
(817) 588-2000

Cystic Fibrosis Foundation
6931 Arlington Road
Bethesda, MD 20814
(301) 951-4422

Epilepsy Foundation of America
4351 Garden City Drive
Landover, MD 20785
(301) 459-3700

March of Dimes
1275 Mamaroneck Avenue
White Plains, NY 10605
(914) 428-7100

Muscular Dystrophy
Association
3561 East Sunrise Drive
Tucson, AZ 85718
(602) 529-2000

National Down's Syndrome
Adoption Exchange
56 Midchester Avenue
White Plains, NY 10606
(914) 428-1236

National Down's Syndrome
Congress
1800 Dempster Street
Park Ridge, IL 60068
(708) 823-7550

National Association for
  Perinatal Addiction
Research and Education
11 East Hubbard Street, Suite 200
Chicago, IL 60611
(312) 329-2512

Spina Bifida Adoption
  Referral Program
1955 Florida Drive
Xenia, OH 45385
(513) 372-2040

Spina Bifida Association
1770 Rockville Pike, Suite 540
Rockville, MD 20852
(800) 621-3141

United Cerebral Palsy
Association
7 Penn Plaza, Suite 804
New York, NY 10001
(212) 268-6655

Chapter Fifteen

Transracial Adoption

wo years ago on the day before Christmas, we brought home a healthy eight-week-old female puppy. We knew nothing about her background, but she seemed to be part Labrador and part chow. Her breed didn't matter to us; all we wanted was a dog with the temperament to tolerate the poking, pulling, and petting our three- and five-year-old daughters were sure to inflict upon her. If breed could predict the level of a dog's tolerance for small children, we were betting on the most gentle breeds.

When Pepper arrived at our home, we were all instantly taken by her. While I snuggled next to her, I thought about the decision-making process we had gone through in selecting an animal, and how different it was from the process we had entered into when adopting our children.

Like us, most folks select a dog based on its breed's temperament, intelligence, hunting ability, looks, and size. With dogs we can sort and choose. There's even a book that lists the world's dumbest dog breeds. Who on earth wants a dumb dog?

In adopting a child, we may seek certain characteristics, but humans are complex creatures, and we cannot select a child's characteristics based on its ethnic background. You cannot request an Italian infant because Italians are intelligent, obedient, and hardly ever shed, or a German child because Germans are good-looking and quick runners and never grow above 200 pounds. Every child has her own unique characteristics that need to be valued and cultivated. Children will be who they will be, a fact of life that is as true when adopting as when you have a biological child. And yet with adoption you do have some control in the selection process.

One example has to do with the child's race or ethnic background. This does not predict the child's outcome the way breed, or species predict behavior in animals, but it may well predict the reactions of others. That is why the first question that often comes to mind when you consider adopting a child outside your racial background (a transracial adoption) is often "What will my family think?" And perhaps you do need to consider the responses of family and friends, especially if you think your family would have difficulty accepting such a child. Often the "lack of acceptance," however, has more to do with what your mother's aunt Edna *may* think rather than what your immediate family *will* think. Sometimes people use nonacceptance by family as a way to cover up the fact that they would find it difficult to raise a child who does not look like them or who belongs to a certain race or ethnic group.

If you are truly comfortable with a transracial or international adoption, expecting acceptance from every last relative, including those you see once a year, is unrealistic. If you are concerned that closer family and friends may have difficulty, you may want to discuss some of their concerns with them and let them know that you want to consider their feelings. Your parents may have to go through the stages of grief related to the loss of having biological grandchildren, and from there they may need to come to terms with having grandchildren who do not look like them. It may have taken you months or years to process the decision to adopt transracially; expect your family members to need some time to process their feelings as well.

Remember, though, that grandparents and other close relatives who say they cannot accept a baby of a certain racial or ethnic background will probably be enthralled with him once he arrives. We have heard countless stories of relatives who opposed the adoption of a child outside the family's ethnic background; yet once the child arrived, the grandparents could not wait to care for her. And if they can't accept the child, you may ask yourself, in the words of one adoption attorney, "Do you really want to be around someone who cannot accept a sweet innocent baby because of the color of her skin?"

WHAT TO CONSIDER

If you are Caucasian, for example, and are considering adopting an African-American, biracial, or international child who will look very different from you, here are some questions you may need to ask yourself:

1. How do I feel about raising a child and providing him with a sense of his heritage?
2. How would I handle the comments from others about how my child looks different from me?
3. How would I feel about my child marrying someone of the same racial or ethnic background and having grandchildren of that heritage?

4. How would I feel about my child marrying someone of a different race?
5. Do I have friends or relatives outside of my race or culture?
6. How will I feel if people tell me how lucky my child is to be adopted by an American family?
7. Will my expectations for the child be based on his race or culture?
8. Do I feel differently about adopting a black or Asian girl versus a black or Asian boy?

If you did not answer the questions "correctly," relax. These questions are not designed to trap you; they are there to help you explore your feelings and what biases you may need to overcome.

Some of our biases are sexist as well as racial. For example, there is such a disproportionate number of couples who want to adopt Korean girls, that at least one agency will not allow couples to request a girl unless they already have a son. Why the desire for a girl and not a boy? Perhaps it is because we perceive Asian girls and women, who generally are petite, as fitting into our American stereotype of what is feminine, or maybe it is because we have difficulty thinking about having sons, who are supposed to pass on the family name and traits, who do not look like us.

Even if you have worked through any sexist or racial biases you may have, you may believe that because you live in an all-white neighborhood and did not sign up to lead the diversity weekend retreat at work that no agency is going accept you for a transracial adoption. One Caucasian couple said they considered adopting a biracial or black child, but decided against it after an agency sent them a list of questions regarding the racial makeup of their neighborhood, friends, church, employers, and so on. You should not be intimidated by such questionnaires. If you are open-minded, you can change your lifestyle so that an international child of another race or a black child can feel comfortable with your family and friends while retaining a sense of his heritage and culture.

Broadening Your Options

Just as people dream of the ideal biological child, so you may dream about the ideal adopted child. At first this fantasy may be to adopt a child who looks like you and your spouse. Expecting a child to look like you, however, even if you were to find biological parents who resembled you, is unrealistic. Even to expect biological children to look like you is unrealistic. Accept the likelihood that a child will probably *not* look like you—although, when it comes to that, we've seen lots of children who look like their adoptive parents, even those of a different race or ethnic background. Once you arrive at this realization, you may find yourself expanding your ideas about what kind of a child you would be able to accept.

This is not to say that someone who is uncomfortable with adopting a child from outside his or her race is nonaccepting. There are many things to consider when adopting a child, including the child's age, health background, and prenatal exposure to drugs and alcohol. Sometimes, though, looking at what you can accept emotionally, culturally, and financially allows you to move beyond preconceived ideas about what your child will be like and challenges you to consider adopting a child who does not fit into your original, often unrealistic, fantasy.

Regardless of background, every child needs to be loved and accepted for his unique qualities. We do not adopt children to make a social statement, out of pity, or because we feel some kind of social guilt. We adopt because we want children and because children need a loving and supportive home. The positive environment you provide may not compensate for every challenge your child may face, whether she is biological or adopted, but we know that regardless of their backgrounds, children do better in stable, loving homes.

WHAT IS TRANSRACIAL ADOPTION?

Transracial adoption is adopting any child outside of your racial background. Most international adoptions are transracial adoptions, because most of the world's children who are available for adoption are from Asia. Indeed, most transracial adoptions involving Asian children are international, since only 15 percent of Asian births in this country take place out of wedlock. For this reason, this chapter is primarily about Caucasian parents adopting biracial or African-American children. Many of the studies cited and issues discussed, however, could also apply to those adopting Asian and other international children. However, in the U.S. the experience of being an Asian raised by white parents is very different from being black and having white parents. Historically, overall race relations between Asians and Caucasians has been more positive than those between blacks and whites. Asians and whites also tend not to segregate socially as much as whites and blacks. For example, Asians are less likely to live in racially distinct neighborhoods, except in very large cities.

Also, the adoptive couple's extended family members may initially be more accepting of an Asian child than a black child. Perhaps this is because interracial marriages between Asians and Caucasians have been historically more acceptable. In addition, many may feel that only African-Americans should adopt black children, a view regrettably shared by some social workers.

Biracial Adoption

For those who are Caucasian and are considering adopting a biracial child of white and black heritage, there are some considerations that need to be explored.

First, according to Beth Hall of Pact, An Adoption Alliance, Inc., which places children of African, Asian, and Latino heritage, children are identified by the racial background that they most resemble. Most biracial children appear to be black and will therefore be identified by others as black. In our culture, which is very race conscious, to be identified as black is a very different experience from being identified as white.

Hall asks prospective adoptive parents to explore their reasons for wanting to adopt a biracial child, as opposed to one who is fully black. Perhaps, she says, it is because a white couple has difficulty accepting the "blackness" of that child. If a family has difficulty with the "black" part of the child, that message is going to be sent to the child in some form.

Hall's organization does not permit couples to select a birth mother who will deliver a biracial instead of a black child. She believes that to accept a biracial child is to accept his black and white background equally, meaning that parents should feel comfortable adopting either racial background. Some biracial children, after all, look fully black. A white couple needs to be willing to accept the biracial child regardless of what she looks like.[1]

When adopting a biracial child, some adoptive parents plan to wait until after the child is born to determine how "dark" she is before they proceed with the adoption. Such parents have clearly not accepted the child's black heritage. Yes, some biracial children will look nearly entirely African-American. Biracial siblings with the same two biological parents can, like other siblings, look very different.

Beth Hall is right that prospective adoptive parents need to think through why they want to adopt a biracial child and not a black child. However, it is not necessarily right to say that parents need to be willing to adopt a black child if they plan to adopt a biracial child. Parents have different reasons for wanting to adopt a biracial child. Biracial children are both black and white, and some white parents want the child to match part of their heritage. Other parents are attracted to the "distinct" look that can characterize a biracial child. And what about couples who are multiracial themselves? They may want to adopt a child who resembles them. One African-American couple who describe themselves as being "light-skinned" said that they would prefer to adopt a biracial child so that the child would resemble them.

We believe that to say biracial children are black because they are perceived as black by society detracts from who the child is. Is a child more what he is perceived to be or what he identifies himself to be? Indeed, because biracial children are neither fully black nor fully white, some do have difficulty in how they identify themselves. Biracial children who do not try to be either black or white, but both, tend to have the strongest sense of identity.

THE ADOPTION PROCESS

When you adopt an African-American or biracial child, the same laws and methods apply as with any other adoption. The only difference is the time line for finding a child—about three to six months.

If you want to adopt an infant, it is best to contact several agencies and private attorneys who are permitted to do direct placements. If you have your heart set on a newborn baby, you should plan to wait three to six months, although most couples who are serious about adopting don't wait that long. If you are an African-American or interracial couple, you may not wait long at all before the attorney or agency calls to tell you that a child is ready to be placed.

PRIVATE ADOPTION

If you live in a state where it is legal for an attorney to place a child directly with a couple, the first thing you may wish to do is find a reliable attorney and get yourselves on her waiting list. Some attorneys may waive or lower the retainer fee for placing your name and home study with their office if you are seeking to adopt a black or biracial child. Like many agencies, attorneys like to have couples on hand who are ready to adopt a black or biracial child, because many attorneys have too few prospective adoptive parents to present to a birth mother.

What happens next, as with any independent adoption, is that a birth mother either contacts the attorney directly or calls the office after being referred by adoption clients. These are clients who have placed adoption ads and are seeking to adopt a white child. When a birth mother expecting a biracial child answers an ad, the clients refer her to the attorney's office to find another couple.

In general, our experience is that more biracial babies than African-American babies are available through private adoption. Few African-American birth mothers place their children for adoption through an attorney. The pressure not to is great, not only from her own family but from the birth father's family. We have seen two recent situations where African-American birth mothers chose to raise the child in order to keep the birth fathers' families from taking the children. On the other hand, Caucasian women who are expecting a biracial child will often choose private adoption. They like the control that they can maintain in selecting a couple.

Private adoption expenses are the same regardless of the child's racial background. Sometimes an attorney will reduce her fee when placing an African-American or biracial child, sometimes not. This is not always possible, especially if the adoption is a complicated one.

Advertising

Most advertising is done by Caucasian parents looking to adopt Caucasian children. In fact, years ago a typical ad would read, "Couple looking for healthy white newborn." Most ads today are not so candid, and many couples get calls from birth mothers expecting African-American and biracial children. If you know of someone advertising who wants only a Caucasian child, let that person know that you are interested in phone calls from other birth mothers.

Even if your attorney cannot legally serve as an intermediary, he can tell his clients who are advertising to call you if they receive a call from a birth mother expecting an African-American or biracial child. Joining a local adoption support group or a RESOLVE group can also help you hook up with couples who are advertising.

AGENCY ADOPTION

An agency adoption of an African-American or biracial child will be handled much the same way all other adoptions are handled. However, the agency policy may require you to attend classes so that you can understand some of the issues related to adopting transracially. Also, many agencies have different standards about matters such as age or length or marriage for those adopting transracially.

Private agencies want to place the babies born to birth mothers who come to them. They do not want to send a birth mother away, and are usually more than willing to place transracially.

Most private agencies, like all attorneys, permit the birth mother to select the couple. One agency reports that most of their birth mothers expecting biracial children want to place the infant with an interracial couple. Many other birth mothers do not care what ethnic background the parents are. Sometimes a birth mother will specify that she wants to place the child only with an African-American or Caucasian couple. In these agency adoptions, the birth mother's wishes are respected. Sometimes it is difficult, however, to find the match that she desires, since there is often not a large pool of prospective adoptive parents.

Some agencies have a different fee scale for those adopting African-American and biracial children, especially agencies of a religious affiliation that raise support. A private adoption agency without outside support will generally charge you its standard fee plus birth mother living expenses, though it may reduce the application fee to increase the pool of applicants.

There are not as many African-American and biracial newborns available as there are Caucasian newborns, but there are also far fewer couples seeking to adopt these newborns—although the number is growing very quickly. The best way to adopt quickly is to make as many contacts as possible. Join an adoption support group and let people who are in adoption circles know of your desire. It often happens that a couple is sought out suddenly to adopt a new baby, and you could be that couple.

PUBLIC AGENCY ADOPTION

Adopting through your social services department essentially means adopting children in the foster care system. If you are flexible and are willing to adopt a toddler-age child or older, you can have a child fairly quickly. Although dealing with the bureaucracy can sometimes be very frustrating, the fees for the adoption service are minimal, and in some cases the state may provide monthly subsidies if the child is considered to have special needs. In some states, coming from a minority ethnic background is considered in itself to be a "special need."

Although no social services department or agency that accepts federal funds can discriminate against you because of your ethnic background if you are seeking to adopt a biracial or black child, many of the public agencies have had policies against transracial adoptions in the past, and because of this, their staffs may make the process more difficult for you. You may be asked numerous questions about your neighborhood and your ability to provide the child with a sense of his culture, as well as the acceptance level by your friends and family. Although yours and other people's attitudes are important to explore, you do not want to be excluded just because you live in an all-white neighborhood. People's acceptance level has more to do with their attitudes than with where they live. Nor does every last relative have to favor your decision. If you live close to parents who will be involved in the child's life, you will certainly want your child to feel as loved and accepted as any other grandchild, and if this seems to be a serious issue, it makes sense to think carefully before insisting on more flexibility than your parents are capable of. But if their hesitation is a normal one of getting used to a new idea, this should not be a serious obstacle.

It is generally difficult to adopt a newborn child through social services, but get your name on their list just in case. This will mean attending a series of classes and having a home study conducted and approved by your social services department.

THE CONTROVERSY OVER TRANSRACIAL ADOPTION

Why was transracial adoption prohibited in the past?

During the 1950s and 1960s, transracial adoption increased sharply as a result of the rise in the number of children in the social service system and the lack of minority homes in which to place minority children. In 1972, however, the National Association of Black Social Workers (NABSW) came out strongly against transracial adoption. Within a year the number of transracial adoptions was cut in half to 1,569, and by 1975 the number was down to 800.[2]

The NABSW policy was and still is that a black child needs to be raised by black parents in order to develop a positive racial identity, and that only black parents can help the child develop skills for coping in a racist society. This view, seconded by many others, has had an unintended side effect: children languishing in foster care because no family of like ethnic background can be found. Until recently, many state agencies simply would not place African-American or biracial children with Caucasian parents.

Waiting Children

Despite this, the NABSW continues to argue that black children in white homes is black cultural genocide. But does this really make sense? Are there really enough transracial adoptions to wipe out black culture? And even supposing there were, shouldn't the child's best interests prevail over a culture's interests? As Peter Hayes observes, "To compromise a child's welfare in the name of culture, especially when the cultural benefit is slight or nonexistent, is inimical to the purpose of child placement and violates the best-interests standard mandated by law."[3]

Consider these statistics. African-Americans and people of color make up 12.3 and 17 percent of the total population, respectively; yet African-American children and children of color make up 34 and 47 percent of the children waiting for homes. According to research by Elizabeth Bartholet, nearly half of the 100,000 children in the United States waiting for homes are "children of color." In Massachusetts, for example, about 5 percent of the population is African-American, yet nearly half of the children in need of foster or adoptive homes are. In New York City, 18,000 children are awaiting adoption, of whom 75 percent are black. These children generally wait for two to five years, about twice the average wait for a white child. The numbers alone suggest that even if more recruitment efforts were made to find African-American parents, there would not be enough such parents to fulfill the need.[4]

The number of children in foster care has gone from 276,000 in 1986 to 450,000 in 1992. This tremendous breakup of families is the result of parental poverty, crime, and substance abuse. These statistics hit minority children the hardest.[5]

Bartholet's research into the practices of adoption agencies responsible for placing African-American children shows that agencies do typically practice racial matching, leading to delays in permanent placement. The costs to the children are great—too great. Six months may be a short time in the life of a bureaucracy, but for a small child it can have significant impact. Racial preferences can also mean that a two-year-old child can be torn from the foster parents who want to adopt him so that he can be placed with parents of the same ethnic background. There are many cases where foster parents have gone to court to contest such disruptions.[6]

It is useful to remember that racial discrimination is against the law. Since the Multiethnic Placement Act, effective as of October 1995, ethnic background can be *a* consideration for placing a child with a family, but it cannot be the *only* consideration. Some felt that allowing ethnic background to be a consideration slowed the process of placing African-American and biracial children into families, so this law has been further strengthened. As of January 1, 1997, a child's or adoptive parents' race or ethnicity cannot be a consideration if it delays the placement of that child. The new law is so strict that it appears that transracial adoptions must take place. However, a child's cultural needs will still be considered as a factor in deciding what is in his or her best interests.

In short, the harmful consequences of transracial adoptions remain merely speculative, while the social and economic costs of keeping children in the foster care system are obvious and monumental.

TRANSRACIAL FAMILIES

What can be said in answer to the argument that only same-race placements give a child a positive racial identity? Our response is that it is not necessary for a child to identify with his entire cultural system whether he is black, Asian, Latino, or white. Many white adoptive parents successfully teach their children about their ethnic/racial culture and help foster in them a sense of ethnic pride.

How well white parents do in raising children transracially has been researched for more than twenty-five years. According to Elizabeth Bartholet, however, few of these studies were designed to look at the positive aspects of transracial adoption, and virtually none were set up to assess the negatives associated with same-race placements only. No studies have been done to compare the experience of children placed immediately with white families to those of children held in foster or institutional care while they waited for a same-race home.[7]

In a long research study on transracial adoptions that focused on African-American, international, and Native American children who were placed transracially, adoptees have been found after twenty years to be stable, emotionally healthy, and comfortable with their racial identity and to have positive relationships with their parents.[8] Most of the children in the study were adopted before the age of one.

According to Elizabeth Bartholet, there are no data to demonstrate that transracial adoptions have a harmful effect on children. On the contrary, the evidence is that those who were adopted as babies into transracial homes do as well as those adopted in same-race homes. In an extensive twenty-year study, 90 to 98 percent of transracial adoptees were found to enjoy family life, were well adjusted, and had a strong sense of racial pride. Another longitudinal study also showed positive results. In 1970 the Chicago Child Care Society began a study of the family lives of African-American and biracial children adopted by Caucasian families, and African-American and biracial children adopted by African-American families. The following conclusions are drawn from thirty-five transracial adoptees, twenty intraracial adoptees, and their parents when these adoptees were seventeen years old. It was found that: (1) the children's developmental problems were similar to those found in the general population; (2) most of the adoptees had good self-esteem; and (3) 83 percent of those adopted intraracially said they were black, 33 percent of those adopted by white parents said they were black, and 55 percent said they were of mixed ethnic background.

Some other interesting facts emerged. Among those with white parents, 73 percent lived in primarily white neighborhoods, while 55 percent of those with black parents lived in primarily black neighborhoods. Those with white parents had primarily white friends, while those with black parents had primarily black friends. Of the adolescents with Caucasian parents, the girls were more likely than the boys to date African-Americans. All those adopted transracially knew of their adoption before they were four years old, while 80 percent of those adopted intraracially did not learn about their adoption until after they were four. Finally, 83 percent of those adopted transracially and 53 percent of those adopted intraracially had interest in meeting their biological parents.[9]

PROVIDING YOUR CHILD WITH A POSITIVE ETHNIC IDENTITY

One of the arguments against transracial adoption is that black children need a cultural history. It is logical that a black child should have a positive racial identity; however, it is not necessarily true that black culture is the only route to that positive identity. Several studies have indicated that Caucasian parents of

African-American or biracial children usually offer those children a healthy sense of racial identity. Studies conducted by both black and white researchers, proponents and opponents to transracial adoption, show much evidence that adoptees have a strong sense of racial identity while being fully integrated into their families and communities.[10] The studies' positive outcomes also apply to those adopting internationally.

Caucasian parents can support African-American culture and ethnic pride in their children by providing books and music about black culture, encouraging friendships with other African-American children, and participating in African-American cultural events. These activities appear to be associated with being middle-class, whether African-American or Caucasian. It is questionable whether a black single parent living in poverty can provide a child with the same positive black cultural background as a white family, though a black middle-class family could probably provide more cultural opportunities and more of the subtle day-to-day experiences distinct to black communities.

What of the argument that only black parents can teach the survival skills needed to be in a racist society? It is believed that a child's racial identity can affect his ability to cope with the world, and it is true that transracial adoptees are generally less comfortable with African-American children than are intraracial adoptees. However, transracial adoptees associate more comfortably with Caucasian children and do as well as same-race adoptees in interpersonal relationships. African-American children who identify with the dominant cultural values also have higher levels of academic achievement, and transracial adoptees are statistically more likely to get better grades in school than intraracial adoptees.[11]

Children can learn to cope with racism. Caucasian parents who adopt transracially are in general less race conscious than those who adopt intraracially and so are at an advantage to teach children to be less race conscious. The message from the Caucasian parents that all ethnic backgrounds are equal can carry more weight than the same message coming from an African-American parent, who may seem to have more personal interest in protecting her status as a black person.

Professor Joan Mahoney, who has adopted transracially, reports that she and her daughter have African-American friends, that she sends her daughter to integrated schools, and that she provides the child with books and toys that will help relate to her culture. Mahoney recommends investigating your neighborhood for black role models, for churches and other cultural institutions, and for postadoption counseling.[12]

ADOPTION POLICIES AND PRACTICES

The Adoptive Families of America, like the North American Council on Adoptable Children, believe that a child should be ethnically matched when possible, but that children should not have to wait for long periods of time to find a same-race family. How long is too long is not an exact science. The detriments associated with being in foster care while waiting for a family must be weighed against the advantages of ethnic matching.

Some assert that if immediate placement is given automatic priority over ethnic matching, not enough effort will go into recruiting African-American families to adopt. Others believe that agency standards for adoptive parents are biased in favor of Caucasian parents. If more single parents and those with lower incomes could adopt, they say, then more African-American parents would do so. This may be true, but a child or a sibling group may need the energy of two parents, not just one. Humans are finite, and sibling groups probably need the financial security and time that only two parents can provide.

Still, greater efforts need to be made to recruit African-American families and to build trust in the African-American community so that more African-American families will adopt. Agencies need to do more through training and literature to educate prospective adoptive parents about adopting transracially.[13] In the meantime, Caucasian children are primarily going to Caucasian families, and biracial and African-American children are going to both Caucasian and African-American families. Children are adopted because they need love, and parents adopt because they want to extend their love to the next generation. No child should have to wait for a home because of the color of his skin.

Chapter Sixteen

The Home Study

Although each state has its own laws regulating adoption, nearly all require adoptive parents to complete a home study. In a home study a social worker gathers information about you and your spouse and your backgrounds by asking you direct questions about your family, your marriage, and your attitudes about parenting and adoption. Do not confuse a home study with the kind of investigation the FBI conducts when screening applicants for certain jobs. This is a meeting between you and a social worker to discuss the attributes that will make you a good parent.

Historically, a home study was a written investigation conducted by a state's department of social services to ensure that adopting couples were suitable to be parents. Today most states have delegated this responsibility to licensed adoption agencies or to specially authorized social workers. Some agencies perform only this service and do not place children for adoption. Agencies that do place children do not necessarily impose the same restrictions when conducting a home study for an independent adoption, even if the agency itself restricts applications according to age, marital history, etc., of prospective parents who apply for direct placement.

Most states require that a home study be conducted before the baby is placed in your home. If you are adopting a baby from another state, you *must* have the home study conducted beforehand to comply with the Interstate Compact Act. In other states, however, the home study is not required until the baby is placed in your home; then it is called a postplacement investigation or an adoption complaint investigation. This is permitted only in independent adoptions, and only when the baby is born in the same state as the adoptive parents.

Whether you have a preadoption home study or a postadoption investigation, once a child is in your home, all states require postplacement supervisory visits—brief visits with a social worker whose job is to note the child's progress and your family's adjustment. The caseworker will visit with you and your baby at least once, if not more often, until the adoption is finalized. These visits usually take place at your home and are conducted by the same agency that handled your home study.

The home study is designed to protect children from going into the homes of unfit parents, to assess your ability to raise an adopted child and deal with adoption issues, and to introduce you to the caseworker—your advocate and an invaluable adoption resource. A caseworker is there to help you as a couple develop a philosophy of child rearing and to provide you with information so that you can learn more about the issues related to raising an adopted child. Some agencies require that you attend adoption seminars or workshops, some of which may be especially designed for those in the home study process, while others address general adoption issues.

Another of the caseworker's tasks is to obtain information about your adoption process. If you have already found birth parents, for example, or if the child has already been placed with you, the caseworker will ask how you met the birth parents and what expenses you paid for. Usually there are two or three interviews. At least one will take place at your home, and the other may be at the agency's office.

WHEN TO HAVE A HOME STUDY

As a rule it is best to have the home study done just before you begin seeking a birth mother. If an FBI clearance is required, you will need to be fingerprinted; this can take up to a few months to get processed, so start the process as soon as possible. If you are planning to adopt in your own state, however, and the home study is not required until after the baby is placed in your home, you can relax. You do not want to have a home study done too soon, because it is usually valid for only twelve months, after which a small fee is charged for updating it.

Various states have different regulations concerning who needs to undergo a home study and when. Find out which of these apply to your state:

- In some states a home study is not required for those who are adopting independently.
- In some states a home study is not required until after the baby is placed in your home.
- In some states a home study is required before a baby is ever placed in your home.
- In some states you must have a home study conducted before you can advertise in that state.

Remember, if you are adopting a baby from another state, *you must have a home study done before you can take the baby across state lines.*

One reason it makes sense to start the home study process as soon as you begin looking for a birth mother is that it will help prepare you for meeting one. Many of the questions posed in a home study are the ones you can expect a birth mother to ask. Birth mothers tend to be interested in the same character traits a social worker is looking for in a couple: stability, a good marital relationship, love of children, and strong family values. A birth mother will also be reassured to know that you have met certain state requirements by completing your home study.

Remember, too, that even if you advertise only in your own state, a birth mother from another state may contact you. It is wise to have your home study finished and out of the way in case of the unexpected. Think of it as one fewer hurdle to jump! With your home study complete, you can focus your attention on pursuing an international adoption or on finding a committed birth mother and getting to know her. Otherwise you might find a birth mother and then also have to think about gathering the documents for the home study, instead of focusing on the birth mother and the baby.

If you are considering adopting a child with special needs, a child outside your race, an international child, or a sibling group, be sure that your home study addresses the issues surrounding such an adoption. For example, your home study may approve you for only one child, but you may then have an opportunity to adopt a sibling group of three. You cannot adopt more than one child until you are approved for more. In one situation, a Caucasian couple wanted to adopt a black or biracial child or a sibling group. However, their home study did not address the couple's attitudes about a transracial adoption, and when a sibling group became available through an agency, their home study could not be updated quickly enough to include this information. Another couple ended up adopting the children.

If your home study will be sent out to other agencies, remember that an agency that did not conduct your home study may be reluctant to place a child with you until they have updated information about the type of child you want to adopt and how ready you are to face the issues associated with the adoption.

WHO QUALIFIES TO ADOPT?
Nearly everyone who seeks to adopt is qualified. Not one of our private adoption clients has ever been rejected. Yet many couples worry about supposed "skeletons" in the closet. Remember, you are not running for president. No one is going to ask your former college roommates whether you ever smoked marijuana.

When a social worker conducts your home study, she is not looking to disqualify you; she simply wants to know that you are capable of providing a child with a loving and secure environment. Most couples who seek to adopt privately are in their late thirties to early forties and often have accomplished other life goals that lead to being good parents, such as emotional and financial stability. When an agency caseworker writes your home study, she is usually acting as your advocate. As honestly as possible, the caseworker is there to present you in the best light.

If you think something in your past may present a problem, talk with your attorney about the matter and get his advice. Some people worry needlessly about arrests made when they were much younger, such as for shoplifting. Other problems are more serious, such as repeated divorces, a recent recovery from alcoholism, or a criminal history. Your attorney may call an agency, explain your situation, and see how the staff would handle it. For example, if you were treated for alcoholism, an agency may simply require that you have a letter from a counselor explaining your situation and stating that you have not had a drink since your treatment five years ago. If a caseworker believes that a couple may have some emotional or psychological problems, she will usually recommend counseling.

Sometimes couples will ask what they should and should not discuss with a social worker. Our guideline is simply this: There is no need to bring up issues that serve no purpose. If you had a difficult relationship with your parents during your teen years and, as a result, spent most of your summers with your grandparents, then you can state these facts in positive terms. For example, you might say, "I had wonderful summers at my grandparents' farm milking the cows and tending a large garden. I learned to be very resourceful during these years."

Even a very difficult situation need not be discussed. If a teacher or scout leader sexually abused you when you were young, and you have received therapy for this or have dealt with it through counseling or self-help books, telling the caseworker may not serve any purpose. Some caseworkers may ask you directly, however, if you have ever been emotionally, verbally, physically, or sexually abused. This is usually a question on a home study for a public agency adoption. If you must answer in the positive, explain how you have overcome this abuse. *You are not disqualified for having experienced it*; but you should be able to demonstrate how it may have affected you and how you have dealt with it. The purpose of this question is to make sure that you are emotionally stable in spite of being abused, that you are not going to abuse a child in the same manner, and that a child from a difficult background is not going to "push your buttons" and perhaps trigger problems in your life that you have not sufficiently resolved.

The following "problems" will *not* disqualify you as adoptive parents:

- *You have been married only a short time.* So long as you are married, you have every right to pursue an independent adoption. Some agencies, for direct placement purposes, may require you to have been married a minimum period of time.
- *You are not married.*
- *You are divorced.* If you have been divorced (even more than once), you are still permitted to adopt. A caseworker will ask you about your previous marriage(s), but the agency's main concern is the stability of your current marriage. If someone has gone through multiple marriages because he is unstable, this instability will probably manifest itself in other areas of the person's life as well.
- *You are in therapy.* If one of you has been in therapy individually, or if you have had therapy as a couple, your chances of being approved may not be lessened. In fact, most agency personnel view counseling as a sign of strength. The reasons you give for your counseling are what matter. For example, if you were in counseling to deal with issues related to infertility, communication, or family of origin, this will be considered very normal.

  Some agencies may require a letter from your therapist stating why you are in therapy and that you are stable and capable of caring for a child. Some agencies may even require a copy of the therapist's case notes. If they do, you will have to sign a letter of release before the notes are sent to the agency. You should review all notes before allowing them to be sent to another party.

  Do some research first to find out what the agency's policy is on such matters. A policy of requiring people to submit their case notes can encourage people to be dishonest about their counseling histories. Suppose you have suffered from depression. Instead of revealing that to the caseworker and letting her know that, thanks to medication and counseling, you are doing well, you may be tempted just to skip the issue and say that you have never sought counseling. You should not have to face this moral dilemma; finding out the agency's policy will prevent you from being placed in this position.
- *You have a history of drug or alcohol abuse.* If you used illicit drugs in the past, there is no need to mention this to a social worker. If you have been treated for abusing drugs or alcohol, however, you will need to tell the social worker. It will not disqualify you, but the agency will

want evidence from a treatment counselor that you have resolved this problem and that the risk that you will become a substance abuser again is minimal. Most agencies will require a letter stating that you are no longer addicted to drugs and alcohol and that you are doing well. Some agencies may want more information—why you entered treatment, what the course of treatment was, and whether you followed the treatment plan.

■ *You have a history of psychological problems.* If you have been treated for a psychological disorder such as depression or anorexia, and it has not been a life-dominating problem, then you do not need to mention it. If you are still in treatment, however, and the problem interferes with your life (you are not able to work, say), then you will probably have difficulty being approved by an agency immediately.

■ *You have a chronic health condition.* People with physical disabilities should not be disqualified from adopting so long as they can care for a child. Neither should a chronic disease like diabetes disqualify someone, provided it is well controlled. What could disqualify someone is a life-threatening condition like cancer. The purpose of the medical report in the home study is to determine that the parent is expected to have a normal life span and be able to care for a child.

■ *You come from a dysfunctional family.* If you have come from a grossly dysfunctional family and have dealt with the issues appropriately, and other facets of your life are in order, then a social worker will minimize your family's past and focus on your life now. If you were physically or emotionally abused as a child and recognize that such behavior is inappropriate, and you can state reasonable measures for disciplining a child, then a caseworker will simply say so in your report.

If you have a criminal history, are grossly dysfunctional, or display other attitudes or behaviors that would make you unfit as a parent, a caseworker cannot recommend you as an adoptive parent. Here are some examples, usually based on law, of what can disqualify you. If any pertain to your situation, talk it over with an attorney. He will not reveal what you tell him with an agency, because he is required by law to maintain client confidentiality.

■ *You or someone who lives in your home has committed a felony.* If you have been arrested for a crime, even if you were found not guilty, this information may be part of the police department's records. Find out before you begin a home study. Any adult living in your home must undergo the same police and FBI screening you do. If your parents live with you, and one of them has a criminal history (at least one conviction, not just an arrest), you may be disqualified because that person is living in the home. Convictions for certain felonies (burglary, forgery, etc.) that occurred over ten years ago are often noted but disregarded if there are no other legal violations.

- *You have been convicted of child abuse.* Even an unfounded investigation for child abuse with no convictions may still be in your record. If you think there may be such a problem, have your attorney contact the police department or other government agency from which you may need clearance to see whether there is any record. Any unfounded investigation should be discussed with a caseworker. Again, anyone living in your home will have to undergo the same child abuse clearance you do. If that person has a history of documented child abuse or neglect (not just allegations), that person will have to move out, or you may be disqualified to adopt.
- *You are still in treatment for substance abuse.*

SELECTING AN AGENCY OR INDEPENDENT INVESTIGATOR

Agencies are required by state law to obtain specific information from couples seeking to adopt. Some agencies, however, require more extensive information than others. Agencies can also vary widely in their fee structures.

Call several agencies before making a decision. Ask specifically about their fees and requirements. Most agencies have forms that you must complete before a caseworker meets with you. Your attorney should advise you about an agency's minimum legal requirements. Some agencies may require more frequent meetings between the couple and the caseworker, or psychological evaluations or participation in parenting classes. Although a more extensive home study may have its merits, the more services an agency provides or requires, the more costly the home study.

Before you select an agency or social worker, you should also ask whether you are permitted to have a copy of your home study, and what the agency's or person's attitude is toward issues like divorce, a limited income, inactive church membership, and a minor criminal history—whatever your concerns are. Try to get a sense of the social worker's background. If she is an adoptive parent, chances are she is more understanding of how you feel than an unmarried twenty-five-year-old who may have little experience with children.

THE HOME STUDY

Relax. The caseworker is not coming in with white gloves, armed with a psychological examination. If possible, talk with her on the telephone before you meet in person. It might help you feel more comfortable when you do meet.

Prepare for the home visit by making the mood as comfortable as possible. Have some light refreshments such as tea and cookies ready. If you have no children, have your home comfortably clean and tidy. You will be more relaxed. Do not apologize about anything related to your home. If you are in the middle of a move, just say, "We moved here two weeks ago and the boxes in the dining room are waiting to be unpacked."

Turn off all distractions like the TV or radio—perhaps even the telephone. Do not set your appointment so that you are squeezed for time. Put pets outside, or confine them elsewhere. For some caseworkers there is nothing worse than a dog jumping on them or cats crawling around their legs.

If you have children, arrange for them to be there so that the social worker can interview them. If you need to discuss sensitive information, you should also arrange for them to be gone part of the time. Renting a video they have never seen is one way of keeping them occupied while the rest of the home study is conducted.

Remember, the caseworker serves as your advocate. Caseworkers have different personalities and styles; you may or may not feel comfortable with someone. Regardless of how well you "connect" with the caseworker, however, she has specific guidelines to follow and cannot subjectively reject a couple based on personality differences.

A progressive adoption agency will have clear objectives and will focus its questions on your attitudes toward each other and on your parenting style, especially as it relates to an adopted child. The agency will be concerned about adoptive parenting issues and will want to provide you with resources: book titles, the names of adoption support groups, and the names of contact people for play groups once the baby arrives.

Preliminaries

Before you have a home study done, the agency will usually send you an application with questions like the ones the caseworker will pose. Don't be intimidated. Some of the questions may seem invasive or difficult to answer, and you may feel resentful having to answer questions that other parents never have to consider. Such feelings are normal.

When you receive the application, you will also be asked to produce the following documents. It is best (even if not required) to have these ready before you meet the caseworker.

1. *Birth certificates.*
2. *Marriage certificate.*
3. *Divorce decree (if applicable).*
4. *Death certificate (if former spouse died).*
5. *Military discharge (if applicable).*
6. *Photographs of you as a couple or family (if you have children) and pictures of your home.*
7. *Income verification (W-2 or income tax statement).*
8. *Health status statement from physician.* Some agencies may require a complete physical that is no older than one year.
9. *Personal references from friends.* Usually three to five references are required. Some agencies stipulate that one reference must come from a friend, one from a clergy member, one from an employer, and one from a neighbor. (If one partner, particularly the wife, plans to quit working after adopting, using her employer is not wise.) One agency that places 200 to 250 babies a year requires applicants to supply *eight* letters of reference. This is too many. Look for another agency.

   Good references are important in establishing your character. Their purpose is to tell how these people feel about you as potential parents and your readiness to have a child. Of course, every reference is going to be good, because you will select only people who like you. But they will prove that you have the ability to establish solid relationships.
10. *FBI, police, and child abuse clearances indicating no record.* These requirements vary from state to state. In some you must receive a report from your local police department or from the state police. The FBI clearance is done through fingerprints and can hold up the process by up to three months. If you must get FBI clearance, begin this process before or as soon as you start your home study. Once the clearance comes back, have the caseworker finish and date the home study using the date on which the fingerprints were issued, if possible, so that the home study stays current as long as possible.
11. *Statement from each of you declaring that you are not addicted to drugs or alcohol, nor have you been treated for a drug or alcohol addiction.*

As part of the study, you will be asked to provide identifying information such as your name, address, telephone number, and citizenship. You will also be required to answer questions about your history, lifestyle, and attitudes.

Autobiographical Information

Autobiographical information includes a physical description and information about where and how you were raised. Did your parents teach consistent values? Did they emphasize education or sports? Were they very involved in your life; did they encourage independence; were they domineering? Did they abuse alcohol, or were they violent or undisciplined in lifestyle? How was love demonstrated, and what was the method of discipline? You will be asked to provide background information on your parents, including their names, ages, professions, and work histories, and to say something about your relationship with and attitude toward them, both when you were a child and now.

The names, professions, and ages of any siblings will be requested, along with a description of your relationship with them. Other questions will cover your schooling and education level, your social life as a child and teenager, your interests and hobbies, your profession and work history, your personal strengths and weaknesses, and any history of psychological counseling.

Your Marriage

Considerable attention will be devoted to your marriage. You will be asked about your premarital relationship (how you met, when you were engaged), how you resolve differences, how your relationship has grown and changed over the years, and your spouse's assets and liabilities, including his or her overall emotional stability and maturity as a person and a marriage partner. It is not appropriate for a caseworker to question you about your sex life.

Your Religious Background and Values

Another part of the study will look at your values and religion. You may be asked about your religious tradition, your church, temple, or synagogue attendance, your religious faith as a child, and your current religious beliefs and what impact they have on your life. If you and your spouse practice different faiths, the caseworker will want to know whether this will create a conflict in raising a child. If you do not participate in an organized religion, highlight your strong family values and whatever beliefs provide inner strength and comfort.

Some of the questions in the home study will have to do with character. What are your goals and how do you set and reach them? What are your values and where do they come from?

Parenting Issues

Be prepared to talk at length about parenting issues. Why do you want to be a parent? Why do you want to adopt? What do you see as an appropriate method of discipline? (Some states require a declaration that you will not use corporal punishment.) Some people feel pressured to say that they will not spank their child, even though they know in their hearts that occasions may arise when they will do so. Nearly every adoptive couple we have talked with believes that at some point a spanking may be appropriate, and most social workers will agree. However, there is no point in discussing with the social worker why you think that a spanking should be given at certain times. If you think it would be false to say that you will never spank your child, tell the caseworker that you will focus on passive forms of discipline and not on corporal punishment. Instead, you would remove the child from the dangerous situation. If the child is unruly, you would remove him, take away a favorite toy, or place him in a "time out" chair.

Other parenting questions will concern the parenting styles of each partner, and how your own styles will be the same or different from your parents'. What attitudes and values do you hope to pass on to your child(ren)? What parenting and child care skills do you already possess, and what is your willingness to acquire new skills? Will one parent be home to care for the child? If not, who will care for the child? How much experience have you had with children? Are you able to give and receive affection? If you have children already, what is their attitude toward the idea of a new sibling?

Infertility Issues

Another area the home study will certainly explore will be your attitudes toward infertility and adoption. You will be questioned about the following:

- Your infertility diagnosis and treatment(s)
- Your infertility resolution
- The impact of infertility on your marriage
- How you came to choose adoption and what resources you used to come to that decision
- What parenting an adopted child means to you (How will this differ from parenting a biological child?)
- What kind of child you seek to adopt (Caucasian newborn, etc.)
- What your attitudes toward birth parents are
- How you feel about the idea of your child seeking his birth parents
- What adoption resources you have access to, including others you know who have adopted

Your Home

The caseworker may ask what you paid for your home and its current value, and what kinds of neighborhood and community resources you have access to—parks, schools, libraries, museums, etc.

Don't go crazy trying to get your home into "order." If anything is clearly a potential danger (no cover over the fireplace, frayed wires, clutter that is a fire hazard), take care of it before you have a home study. Have a fire extinguisher and other safety features present in your home. But don't act as if your house is about to be photographed for *Better Homes and Gardens*. The social worker is primarily interested that the home can accommodate a baby or older child. In her report, she will comment on the bedroom or area of the home where the child will sleep.

Don't worry, especially if you already have a child, if your home is not spotlessly clean. Social workers are not looking to see whether Mr. and Mrs. Clean live at your home; they just want to make sure that your home is a safe and healthful environment. If life is getting a little crazy, of course, you could always treat yourself to a housekeeping service before your home study appointment. You will be much more at ease knowing that the cobwebs have been dusted away.

Your Finances

You will be expected to disclose your salaries, savings, and other resources, as well as your debts, health insurance, and life insurance. Your financial status should indicate that you have enough discretionary income each month to meet the needs of a child. However, a large savings account and a substantial stock portfolio are not necessary for you to "pass" a home study. A social worker will instead look for savings of perhaps two or three months' salary set aside for emergencies, and a general sense that you and your spouse manage your money sensibly.

SAMPLE HOME STUDY

Following is a mock home study to use as a guide. Although it may seem overly "perfect," remember: Most home studies are written to show your best assets. This one is very similar to ones used in actual adoptions.

SOCIAL HISTORY

John Smith is a Caucasian American male, born July 4, 1960, in Cape May, New Jersey (verified). Mr. Smith is six feet one inch tall, weighs 190 pounds, and has brown hair and eyes.

John is warm, sincere, and genuine. He openly expresses his desire to adopt a child and raise a family.

John was born and raised in Cape May, New Jersey. In 1978 he graduated from Cape May High School and attended Rutgers University in New Brunswick, New Jersey, where he received a degree in accounting in 1983.

John states that his family was very traditional. His father is vice-president of a bank in Cape May, New Jersey, and his mother is an innkeeper, also in Cape May. Although his father worked hard, he still managed to spend time with John and took him to the shore and on skiing trips. He describes his mother also as hardworking. He vividly describes the fun he and his cousins had living at the shore. Both of his parents are described as people who emphasized values and were fair and consistent.

John and his three siblings hardly presented any discipline problems to their parents. When John had to be disciplined, both of his parents were fair and consistent. Very infrequently did they spank him, but rather talked to him about what he had done wrong.

John has two older sisters and one younger brother. All of his siblings live within the Cape May area. He maintains a warm, close relationship with all three.

Upon graduation from college, John took a job with a real estate firm in Cape May. He worked as an accountant for two years. In 1975 he worked with an accounting firm as an auditor. He took time away from this job to travel through the United States. He states that he was feeling restless and did not want to spend his youth behind a desk working with numbers. He feels that the two and a half years he spent traveling have now helped him to feel more settled. If he had not taken this adventure, he would never have met his wife, Carol.

After traveling, John came back to Cape May and joined an accounting firm in 1990. In 1995 he was named a partner. He says he enjoys his job, but sometimes finds the work tedious and exhausting. He jogs and plays tennis to release his stress.

John and his family are still very close and enjoy activities together. His father has assisted him in business. They still enjoy playing golf together as well as working on home projects. It is clear that his desire to have children is based on his happy childhood as well as his love for his nieces and nephews.

SOCIAL HISTORY

Carol Jones-Smith is a Caucasian American of Irish background who was born on January 16, 1966, in Philadelphia, Pennsylvania (verified). She is five feet five inches tall and weighs 125 pounds. She was reared in the suburbs of Philadelphia, Pennsylvania. Carol's mother stayed at home to rear her children while her father worked as a plumber. Carol's parents and one of her two sisters reside in Pennsylvania. Her other sister lives in California.

Carol is very sociable, warm, and easygoing. Carol desires to be a full-time homemaker and stay at home until the child is at least two years old.

Carol states that her family is loving. She is close to both parents and believes that they taught her values such as respect and honesty. Although she was never a difficult child, she states that at times she was mischievous. She believes her parents raised her well and disciplined her fairly. Her parents usually took away privileges as a means of discipline.

Carol was very sociable growing up and was involved in Girl Scouts and church activities. She believes that her association with her church instilled many positive character qualities. She enjoyed the many church-related activities as well as camping with the Girl Scouts. Her mother volunteered for the Scouts as well as the PTA and the school library. After high school she went to Pennsylvania State University where she graduated with a degree in elementary education in 1978.

For two years after graduating from college, she substitute-taught, because no full-time teaching positions were available. She and John maintained a long-distance relationship until she could find a job in Cape May.

In the fall of 1991 she took a position as a second-grade teacher. She enjoys teaching and says that second-grade children are old enough to learn, yet young enough not to be a discipline problem.

Carol's hobbies include reading, golf, music, and home projects. She and John enjoy day trips, long walks, and bicycle rides. For special occasions, such as Christmas and baby showers, she enjoys making gifts. She loves having the summers free to focus on such activities.

MARITAL RELATIONSHIP

John and Carol were married on June 10, 1992, in Philadelphia, Pennsylvania (verified). They met in the summer of 1989 while she was visiting her sister in California. He was attracted to her right from the beginning. She was a little bit unsure of a man who was taking such an extended "vacation." After talking to and then maintaining a long-distance relationship with him, she began to understand his commitment to a secure lifestyle while still having a spirit of adventure. In 1990 they became engaged. In the fall of 1991 she took a position as an elementary school teacher in Cape May.

In the initial stages of their relationship, Carol's parents were concerned about the age difference between them (six years) and his job situation. But after he went back to work for a large accounting firm and seemed settled, they soon began to like and trust John. Today they have a comfortable relationship with all four of their parents. John and Carol enjoy spending the holidays with family members. In fact, they say that the more extended-family members present for celebrations, the better. Birthday parties for family members are celebrated by parents and siblings.

The Smiths' good relationships with family are also expressed in their marriage. John and Carol state that they communicate well and often have deep discussions while taking long walks on the beach. They seldom argue, and when they do, they usually compromise until the difference is resolved. They state that their marriage is excellent.

Carol and John appear to be thoughtful of each other's needs. For example, John did not want Carol to continue infertility treatment that would cause her emotional or physical discomfort or to take medications that could have adverse side effects.

VALUES AND RELIGION

Both John and Carol attended church as children and believe it is important for children to receive a solid religious upbringing. As children, John attended a Lutheran church and Carol attended an Episcopalian church. John and Carol are currently visiting churches and believe they will select a Lutheran church in Cape May that is very family oriented and provides special programs for children.

The Smiths both value family life, marriage, and hard work and commitment. They say that they get these values from their family and from their friends. John and Carol also have seen the problems in children's lives when parents are not fully committed to the responsibility of parenting or to the marriage.

The Smiths have set several goals that they have reached, including purchasing a home, planting a vegetable garden, and establishing a savings account for a child. Each year they sit down on January 1st or the weekend of the holiday and set individual goals, and goals as a couple. This year they decided that they will each read a good book a month. They also want to "finish the basement" and have already made arrangements with a contractor. Their primary goal is to adopt a child, and they have set aside money to begin the process.

PARENTING ATTITUDES

John and Carol believe they will raise their children according to the positive set of values that helped to shape them. They love children and often care for their siblings' children. This love for family makes them long even more for a child of their own.

In disciplining their children for wrong behavior, they plan to use "time-out" or take away a favorite activity or toy.

ATTITUDE TOWARD ADOPTION

John and Carol have undergone about four years of unsuccessful infertility treatment. Carol has endometriosis, and John has a low sperm count. Carol has had surgery and has taken infertility drugs while having intrauterine inseminations done. They decided that more advanced treatment would be too financially and emotionally draining for them. Carol and John both state that the hormonal therapy has not caused any adverse physical or emotional reactions.

They have chosen to end infertility treatment, since successful pregnancy is very unlikely. Also, they decided that they were not seeking a pregnancy but wanted a child, and that adoption would provide them with this opportunity. Both John and Carol feel adoption is a very positive alternative to biological children.

The Smiths have read a number of books about the adoption process as well as the raising of an adopted child. They appear to have a good understanding of adoption. For example, they both agree that openly sharing information with a child about her adoption is important. Yet they state that they do not want to overemphasize the difference and perhaps make the child feel out of place. John and Carol are comfortable in communicating with a child's birth parents (i.e., sending photos and letters). Also they recognize that their child may someday seek her birth parents, and understand that this would not be a negative reflection on their relationship with their child.

Carol said that once she adopted, she would want to communicate with other adoptive moms. The Smiths are members of RESOLVE. If they have a child, Mrs. Smith plans to join a play group in which many of the children are adopted.

FINANCE AND THE HOME

John and Carol live in a lovely, well-maintained Victorian house that is within walking distance of the beach. The home has a large eat-in kitchen that John completely renovated. John also renovated a playroom/den. The child's bedroom is spacious and comfortable. In this room there is already a child's toy cradle filled with stuffed animals.

The home is valued at about $160,000, and as John continues to make further improvements, the home may increase in value.

John earns about $60,000 per year, and Carol earns $22,000 per year (verified). The Smiths have no debts except their mortgage payment of nearly $900 per month and property taxes at $300 per month. He has a life insurance policy worth about $150,000, and she, through work, has one valued at $35,000.

TYPE OF CHILD REQUESTED AND FROM WHOM

The Smiths are interested in adopting a healthy Caucasian infant. They have sent letters to friends expressing their desire to adopt. Many people have responded, wishing them well. Next week an advertisement will be placed in a small newspaper in Central New Jersey. An attorney, John Johnson, has been retained by the Smiths.

REFERENCES

Each reference (verified) cites the Smiths as a couple who would provide a loving, moral, stable home for a child. Those who know them say that they are respected by friends and family, are committed to each other, and are energetic, fun-loving people who would provide much happiness to a child.

HEALTH STATUS

Both Carol and John are in good health, according to Dr. Laura Jones, and are able to care for a child and are expected to live a normal life span (verified). Neither person is a smoker.

RECOMMENDATION

John and Carol Smith appear to be open, expressive, and caring individuals who have strong family relationships. It is clear from the love that they express for each other and for their family members that they would offer a truly loving home to a child. They are recommended as adoptive parents.

POSTPLACEMENT SUPERVISORY VISITS

Postplacement supervisory visits are a series of visits made to your home by a case-worker or social worker to ensure that the family is adjusting well to the child and that the child herself is doing well. Supervisory visits are simply a time for you and the caseworker to share how the baby is developing.

Information gathered at a postplacement supervisory visit will begin with the child's medical progress. You should keep a record of his doctor's appointments, illnesses, and routine vaccines. Most people will simply tell the caseworker when the child had his last well-baby checkup and whether he had any reaction to the vaccines.

The caseworker will ask about the child's eating and sleeping patterns, which will change as the child progresses. If the caseworker visits you when the child is two months old, you may share, for example, that he is taking about six four-ounce bottles per day of Similac with iron, and that he generally sleeps from eight P.M. to six A.M., wakes up once in the middle of the night, and during the day has a morning nap, an afternoon nap, and a later afternoon nap. When the caseworker visits you again in two months, you will tell her that the baby is now having apple sauce and rice cereal twice a day, goes to bed around eight P.M. and gets up at six A.M., seldom wakes up in the middle of the night, and generally sleeps for two hours in the morning and an hour and a half in the afternoon.

At each visit you will share with the caseworker the progress your child is making. For example, if the caseworker visits you when the child is two months old, you will probably say that the child smiles and responds to facial expressions. At four months old you will say he can play with his feet and hold an object in his hands. At six months old he may be crawling, sitting up, and cooing.

Some agencies focus on you and your child's appearance as well as the appearance and cleanliness of the home. If you are feeling overwhelmed, hire someone to clean your home before each visit. The investment is well worth the expense, simply because you will feel so much more comfortable during the case-worker's visit.

Finally, the caseworker will want to know how your family is adjusting to the child's arrival. Both of you will be required to be present for at least some of the visits. Sometimes husbands, either because of nervousness or because they do not want to steal the limelight from their wives, do not interact with the child during a caseworker's visits. However, it is very important that the social worker see *both* parents holding and feeding a baby, or attending to the needs of an older child.

The question of how much time the adoptive parents spend with the child will probably come up. The only wrong answer is "none." Social workers are aware that one spouse may work ten- or twelve-hour days, and that both parents may work outside the home. Again, a commonsense approach is all that is required.

Chapter Seventeen

Adoption Expenses

Money is often an emotional issue, and the way you feel about it can affect the way you approach adoption. Most people become involved with adoption after expending years and thousands of dollars on infertility workups and unsuccessful treatments. Often there is a sense of anger about spending more money on another procedure—adoption—that, like infertility treatment, has no guarantee of success.

Paying out thousands of dollars with no tangible return makes a person feel victimized and out of control. Feelings of "Why me?" are natural and common, as are feelings of anger and a sense of futility. The question is, how do we cope with them? Some people cope by developing an unhealthy defensiveness and extreme skepticism toward the idea of adoption. Such attitudes will need to be dealt with and worked through before you take any steps toward adoption. If you do not work through them, they will end up being communicated to the birth mother; you will not be comfortable meeting her, and she will know this. She will feel your angst and your defensiveness. Many adoptive couples have indirectly projected their insecurities and defensiveness onto the birth mother. She will not understand the uneasiness she feels about you as a couple, of course; all she will know is that she has "bad vibes" about you.

Even more self-defeating than this projection of feelings by the adoptive couple is their direct discussion with the birth mother of their fears of losing money or making an emotional investment in an unsuccessful adoption plan. One birth mother let a prospective couple know that she did not want to hear about the adoptive mother's disappointments with unsuccessful infertility treatments and other previous adoption plans. This birth mother felt that she had enough of her own problems; she really did not need to hear the adoptive mother pour her heart out about the lost money and failed attempts.

It may be appropriate and even necessary for the adoptive couple to share their feelings about their emotional and financial investment later in the relationship; however, several birth mothers have felt this sharing as attempts by adoptive couples to "lay a guilt trip" on them. Remember, a birth mother usually assumes you are middle or upper-middle-class in lifestyle and finances; she assumes your life is structured and in control. It is her life that is out of control, and placing her child for adoption is a way of regaining control. The last thing she wants and needs is to feel that you doubt her honesty or her motives, and that is what will be portrayed if you have not worked through your feelings of victimization.

Adoption author Patricia Johnston writes that finances can be a most uncomfortable issue for everyone involved in the adoption process. Prospective adoptive parents do not like to think about the costs because it reminds them further of how they are different from those who can give birth to a child. Professionals who have to ask clients directly for fees are sometimes uncomfortable charging them, although they rely upon these fees for their livelihood and the functioning of the agency or office. Nor does the issue of fees end when you receive your child. Feelings about the adoption process, including the costs, can color our attitudes for a long time. Confronting your feelings of victimization helps minimize any anger or bitterness. It is also important to make sure there is clarity between you and the agency or attorney about what fees and expenses are your responsibility. To maintain a good attitude throughout the whole adoption process, you want to make sure not to let misunderstandings get in the way or questions go too long unanswered.

One understanding that needs to be established, of course, is that no matter which route you take, all adoptions, except some public agency adoptions, will involve expenses. If you are pursuing a public agency adoption or a private agency adoption of a child with special needs, plan to spend between zero to $2,000; for an independent adoption, $5,000 to $13,000; for a domestic agency adoption, $7,000 to $25,000; and for an international adoption, $7,000 to $20,000. Fortunately, there are now adoption tax credits available, and your employer may offer adoption benefits.

Be aware that some attorneys and agencies do overcharge. As Christine Adamec writes in *There ARE Babies to Adopt*, a higher fee does not mean a "better" baby or a better quality of service. She notes that in 1994, one agency was charging about $30,000 per adoption, yet was withholding important birth parent background information.

In this chapter we will discuss the basic expenses associated with various kinds of adoptions, and what it will be helpful for you to know about them. First,

however, a word about birth mother expenses. Many birth mothers begin interacting with an adoptive couple with no desire or need to accept monies for
living expenses. During her pregnancy, however, a birth mother's circumstances
will sometimes change, giving rise to a need for assistance. When a birth mother
requests help at that point, couples are often quick to feel taken advantage of.
They should know that most birth mothers, at least in our experience, are really
reluctant to ask for and accept money and do so only in time of great need. If
that need arises shortly after a couple begins working with a birth mother, a
couple must be careful not to overreact. Any rapport that exists between the
birth mother and the couple could be ruined if the couple suddenly becomes
defensive about money.

And then there is the birth mother who asks for money up front, sometimes in large amounts. One birth mother told an adoptive couple that she
wanted $12,000 as soon as the baby was born. The couple was speechless, but
was able to refer her to their attorney to discuss the amount requested. When
asked why she chose $12,000, the birth mother replied that she knew that was
the amount adoption agencies were paid, and she assumed she would be paid
the same thing, since an agency was not involved. Once it was explained that
such an amount was not legal to pay and that only reasonable living expenses
were allowed, things were fine. She did place her baby with the couple, and she
received reasonable living expenses as allowed by law. We will be saying more
about how to handle this kind of situation later in the chapter.

INDEPENDENT ADOPTION

Almost every step of the adoption process requires money. An independent adoption, however, is usually less expensive than an agency adoption. Expenses you are
likely to incur include the following (amounts are approximate):

Attorney's fee: $4,000
Advertising costs: $250 to $450 per month.
The low figure is the approximate cost of placing an ad in a daily newspaper (usually for a small or average-size town) twice a week. The high figure
is the approximate cost of placing an ad in two big-city newspapers twice a
week.

Telephone installation: $150
You might also consider the "Identa Ring" option at about $4 per month.

Telephone calls: $50 to $100 per month.

The figure depends on the number of calls you receive. Add to this the expense of having an extra line. Once you make contact with a birth mother, she may want to talk with you at length, thus increasing your telephone bill.

The home study: $400 to $1,200.

In states like Massachusetts, where independent adoptions are illegal, the home study could be as high as $4,000. A $4,000 home study is not necessarily more comprehensive than a $500 home study; some agencies simply take advantage of your need for one. Call around to find out about fees.

Counseling for birth mother: $50 to $100 per hour.

Many birth mothers do not ask couples to pay for counseling, but it should be offered by the agency social worker or the attorney representing you. The birth parents often receive counseling if the adoptive couple wants to pursue an identified/agency adoption.

Birth mother's obstetrical and delivery bill: $2,000 to $2,700.

Most birth mothers are covered by their own insurance or Medicaid, so you will seldom have to pay this cost. You may need to help her pay her insurance premiums, however.

Birth mother's hospital bill: $3,500 to $7,000.

Without complications. Again, most birth mothers are covered.

Infant's hospital nursery bill: $1,000.

Many hospitals will not process the infant's bill under the birth mother's coverage (private or Medicaid) once it is disclosed that the baby will be placed for adoption. Your own insurance should pay for this bill. The key language in your medical insurance benefits booklet is the definition of "dependent," which should include the child to be adopted, over whom you have "dominion and control" (meaning coverage should be automatic). Some booklets still specify that coverage begins upon the finalization of the adoption. This simply reflects the drafter's ignorance of the adoption process, since finalization can occur up to one year after placement. Your attorney should provide an explanation to your benefits office or to the insurance company.

Infant's medication, pediatric exam, and circumcision.

Again, your insurance should cover this.

Keep close track of all your expenses. You may be eligible for a tax credit (see p. 299).

AGENCY ADOPTION

If an agency places a healthy infant directly with you—if, that is, you did not find your own birth mother—their fee may range anywhere from about $7,000 to $35,000. The agency may have a standard fee regardless of what the birth mother's needs are: It may charge you a fee of $12,000 to $15,000 and then add on to that the birth mother's medical, living, and counseling expenses, as well as attorney fees. It is crucial that you understand whether the fees quoted to you by the agency include the birth mother's medical, living, and counseling fees. It would be easy to misconstrue the agency's quoted fee of $12,000, for example, as being your total cost. More than one couple has been surprised when presented with doctor and hospital bills after having already paid the agency fees. If you hire your own attorney to represent you, that will be an additional fee.

In states in which only agencies can legally conduct an adoption, it is not uncommon for agencies to charge an outrageous amount.

IDENTIFIED AND FACILITATED ADOPTION

Some agencies specialize in identified adoptions and even provide workshops on how to find a birth mother. In this kind of adoption, the agency will generally charge a standard identified adoption fee of $4,000 to $12,000, in addition to legal fees and birth mother expenses, usually putting an identified adoption in a higher range than an independent adoption.

INTERNATIONAL ADOPTION

The cost of an international adoption can vary widely, depending on how you go about it. If you have connections to an orphanage in another country, perhaps through a missionary or a religious organization, your only expenses may be $155 to the Immigration and Naturalization Service, the cost of your home study, the child's transportation costs, your transportation and lodging expenses, if you travel, and a donation to the orphanage, plus about $1,500 for legal fees to have the adoption refinalized in the United States. This may total well under $5,000.

If you do not know of someone in another country but you want to facilitate your own adoption instead of hiring an agency or facilitator to help you, you may be able to save $4,000 or more in administrative costs. You may, however, encounter many roadblocks that can add to the cost of the adoption.

If you are dealing with a large agency, the costs are generally well defined and payments expected at regular intervals. The fee will vary depending upon the country from which you are adopting. Expect to spend between $7,000 and $25,000.

When you hire an independent agency, attorney, or facilitator, you should be charged in the range of $4,000 for their services—again, based on the country's fees and the cost of transportation and lodging.

HOW TO KEEP YOUR EXPENSES TO A REASONABLE LEVEL

Like any other legal process, adoption requires professional assistance, and medical, legal, and adoption specialists deserve to be paid a reasonable fee for their services. There are professionals, however, who prey on the emotions of desperate couples, claiming that if they do not pay a certain amount of money immediately, they will lose this once-in-a-lifetime opportunity to have a baby. Sometimes you need to rely on your instincts to tell you whether an attorney or an adoption agency social worker is pushing too hard or seems overly concerned with money. Here are some guidelines you may find helpful:

1. *View with caution any agency or attorney who asks for more than $1,500 up front without any service being rendered.* Having said that, you should know that there are several reputable agencies that are charging up to $4,000 to initiate your application. These agencies have written refund policies stating that the bulk of the monies will be refunded to you in a year or so if no placement occurs. Have your attorney check the agency's references, and telephone other couples who have obtained placements from the agency to find out whether they were satisfied with their experience.

2. *Make sure that any agency or attorney who charges you gives you an itemized bill.* An attorney may say that her fee is $3,000 for all services. This is fine. But if the bill keeps getting higher as the attorney does more work, or because new "expenses" keep popping up, make sure you receive an itemized bill. There is one well-known adoption attorney in the eastern United States whose bill almost always ends up somewhere around $6,000 to $7,000. A couple obtaining a baby through his office is shocked, of course, but they pay. Why? Well, they are getting a son or daughter, and who wants to quibble about a few thousand? That this should happen a few times a year is conceivable; that it should happen to three out of four couples interviewed leaves no doubt as to the attorney's honesty. Before hiring an attorney, contact your local RESOLVE chapter and try to find out what his reputation is.

3. *Find out whether there will be any additional charges for birth father issues.*
    This is one aspect of adoption procedure that many attorneys and agen-
    cies do not make clear. Find out whether there will be an additional fee,
    for example, if a birth father's rights must be terminated in court by a
    separate proceeding. Many agencies state that the adoptive couple's
    attorney must take care of any birth father rights if he does not sign an
    agency surrender. Again, ask for a written schedule of fees.

If your funds are very limited, you may want to consider adopting through a
public agency. The fact that you cannot afford another route should not, however,
be your primary motivation for selecting a public agency. You must be prepared
and have a strong support system to handle the special needs a child adopted
through this avenue may have.

If you want to adopt a child from a minority ethnic background, adopting
through a public agency will probably be your least expensive route. However,
there is no guarantee that you will be chosen when a committee meets to select a
family for the child. You may end up waiting a long time.

PAYING FOR A BIRTH MOTHER'S LIVING EXPENSES

Most states permit an adoptive couple to pay for the birth mother's living
expenses. The amount paid may have to be preapproved by a judge, however, to
ensure that there is no appearance of "baby buying." Some judges are very particular about this matter. Your attorney should guide you so that you do not pay
extensive living expenses. Document all payments. It is best if all monies go
through your attorney's escrow account to avoid any appearance of impropriety.

Legal living expenses usually include a few months of average rent (about
$400 per month), food ($50 per week), and transportation to the doctor's office.
However, what is deemed reasonable depends on the state and even the region of
the state. The cost of living in a given place is what determines the appropriate-
ness of expenses. It would be difficult to obtain a decent apartment in southern
New Jersey for less than $500 a month, for example, while in northern New Jersey
you will pay more like $750. The standard of reasonableness will also change if the
birth mother has one or more children to care for.

Birth mothers do have crises—emergency car repairs and other unforeseen
expenses. These should be dealt with on a case-by-case basis. Always have your
attorney get your permission before advancing money that was not already agreed
upon beforehand.

Sometimes a birth mother will request money for placing a baby. Perhaps a
friend or relative told her that this was a common practice, or perhaps she saw a

television program or a magazine article about attorneys and agencies charging $25,000 to $50,000 for an adoption and asked herself, "If the attorney gets that much money, why can't I?" After all, she is the one going through pregnancy, labor, and delivery.

If a birth mother asks you for "placement money" or tells you of another couple who has offered her $10,000 for the baby, tell her that you do not want to jeopardize the baby's welfare. Tell her you would hate to see the baby removed from your home because the authorities discovered that you had paid her monies that are not allowed by law. Emphasize that you are willing to pay what is legal and that you would want to help in her time of need (assuming this is true), but that your attorney must approve everything involving money. You should ask the birth mother to contact your attorney to discuss the money issue further. One couple asked a birth mother who said she had had an offer for $10,000 from another couple, "Would you really want your baby to go to a couple who is willing to pay you $10,000 illegally?" The birth mother placed the child with the honest couple.

Some people can afford to take risks and others cannot. If a birth mother is asking for $1,000 a month in living expenses for herself and her three children, and you make contact with her when she is three months pregnant, these expenses alone will be $6,000—money that you could lose if she changes her mind. Some people can afford to lose this kind of money and move on to another adoption. If you are not among them, you may need to forgo that situation and look for a birth mother who is further along in her pregnancy or has fewer living expenses.

The problem of risk is one of the things that can make international adoption so attractive: You are not dependent upon the birth mother. Unless a country suddenly closes its doors to adoption, if you work with a reputable agency you are virtually guaranteed that your money will pay for what it is intended to. If you have access to $17,000, for example, you can put that money toward an international adoption and be fairly certain that in a matter of six to eight months you will have a baby. In addition, your tax credits can be applied for years to come if the costs of the adoption exceed $5,000—which most likely they will. Also, many international children are considered to have special needs, and you may qualify for an additional $6,000 tax credit each year.

ADOPTION INSURANCE

Some couples purchase "adoption insurance" to protect them in the event that a birth mother changes her mind. It is available from Fireman's Fund in California and is administered nationwide by Jardine Insurance Brokers in California. To be eligible, you must be working with an attorney who is using the insurance program. The premium should be low and cover a few thousand dollars in expenses. In the past, the insurance required very high premiums and covered large birth mother expenses, which only served to encourage couples to take on riskier adoptions and pay expenses indiscriminately. You should not be paying $4,000 in insurance premiums to cover $25,000 worth of expenses.

PAYING FOR YOUR ADOPTION

Needless to say, not everyone has $20,000 in the bank. Indeed, even a relatively inexpensive adoption will stretch most couples' resources. In her book *There ARE Babies to Adopt*, Christine Adamec discusses various techniques for meeting these expenses, from asking relatives for help to taking out a second mortgage. There is nothing shameful about taking out a loan to adopt a baby, but the bank may not approve you because there is no "collateral," except the world's most valuable possession—your baby. You may find yourself thinking along the same lines as your bank, at first—a baby is not a financial investment. But if you consider that an adoption costs less than many new cars, you may gain a different perspective. Why not ride around in your old '87 car a few more years instead of spending $15,000 on a new one? Then you can take the payments that you would have used for a car and pay back your "baby loan" for the next five years.

Compare adoption expenses with the costs of infertility treatment. Some infertility treatment is covered by a third party—your insurance company. When another party is paying the bill, the costs do not seem so bad. But many insurance companies do not pay for certain treatments, especially high-tech reproductive procedures such as in vitro fertilization. These kinds of procedures can cost $6,000 to $10,000 per cycle. And, of course, only a certain percentage of couples will achieve a successful pregnancy. Although you cannot chose adoption over having a biological child merely for economic reasons, you need to weigh whether one kind of investment is really more worth it to you than the other. If you were to take the money for two in vitro fertilization cycles, you could easily adopt a child from, for example, China, and probably in less time than it would take you to conceive and carry a child to term.

The truth is, people often decide they cannot afford adoption before they have really explored their options. Even if you have only a few thousand dollars in the bank, you can easily proceed with an adoption. Most attorneys and agencies do not ask for all the adoption fees and expenses upfront—and if they do, you should probably not be dealing with them anyway. As you look through the expenses associated with an independent adoption, you will see that you are not required to pay a lot of money upfront. You start by advertising, then you may begin helping a birth mother with living expenses, which can be paid monthly, and along the way you may be paying the attorney or agency its fees. If your budget does not allow you to pay an agency or attorney $5,000 to $10,000 up front, then don't. Most agencies charge $1,000 to $4,000 to begin processing your application, then ask for the next installment when a birth mother is matched with you. Adoptions usually take place in stages, allowing a couple time to save.

ADOPTION ASSISTANCE AS AN EMPLOYEE BENEFIT

Just as you must decide when to use limited resources toward an adoption instead of toward infertility treatment, some companies are beginning to see the financial value in providing adoption coverage to their employees. If an employee decides to adopt, that person (or the employee's wife) is probably not going to be accumulating the medical expenses associated with having a baby. For companies that are self-insured (meaning that the company and not a medical insurance company covers its employees and their families' medical bills), the decision to provide adoption assistance can be even more of a financial incentive. If a self-insured company pays all or part of the costs associated with infertility treatment, as well as the medical costs associated with pregnancy, labor, and delivery—about $7,000 to $10,000—the company may view adoption assistance as a very worthwhile—and less expensive—benefit. Instead of paying what can be at least $20,000 in infertility and birth-related expenses, the company can have a policy of paying, for example, up to $5,000 toward an adoption. In South Carolina, as of this writing, state employees can be reimbursed $5,000 in adoption expenses for a healthy child and $10,000 for a child with special needs. As politicians begin to see the value of adoption, perhaps more states will be offering their employees such benefits.

For more information about companies that provide adoption assistance, contact Adoptive Families of America. If your company does not offer adoption assistance, you may want to advocate for such a policy. If you talk in terms of what a company can save, those who make such decisions may see the benefit.

Resources:

> **Adoptive Families of America**
> 3333 Highway 100 North
> Minneapolis, MN 55422
> (800) 372-3300
> (612) 535-4829
> Adoptive Families of America also has a Web site at
> **http://adoptivefam.org/.**This group is the largest nonprofit organization

in the United States, providing resources and support to people interested in adoption.

THE ADOPTION TAX CREDIT

The 1996 federal Minimum Wage Bill contains an adoption tax credit for expenses paid after January 1, 1997, for adoptions finalized after that date. Expenses incurred during 1996 but not paid until 1997 are also given tax credit. Qualified expenses include adoption fees, court costs, your attorney's fees, and other adoption-related expenses such as travel.

There is also a separate $6,000 tax credit for adopting a child with special needs. Check how your state defines special needs; your child may be eligible if he is, for example, biracial. However, most special needs children are placed through state agencies, and usually there are no expenses incurred, and therefore, no tax credit eligibility.

If a child is adopted internationally, the adoption credit is available only after the adoption if finalized or refinalized in the United States. For example, if you incur expenses in 1997 and the child's adoption is not finalized until 1988, you may not claim a tax credit until you file your 1988 tax return.

A tax credit is not the same as a tax deduction; a credit is far more generous. If, for example, you paid $15,000 in adoption expenses in 1997, and in 1997 you owe $7,000 in taxes, then once you apply the $5,000 credit, you will owe only $2,000 in taxes. Also, in 1998 and 1998 you can get an additional $5,000 tax credit each year for the other $10,000 in adoption expenses that you incurred back in 1997.

You can only take the full credit if your family's adjusted gross income is less than $75,000. Partial credits are available for those earning up to $115,000. The IRS is also developing guidelines to address the income qualifications of unmarried adoptive parents.

If your employer provides adoption benefits, these benefits—up to $5,000 for an adoption and up to $6,000 for a special needs adoption—are not taxed. Plus, you can use the tax credit in addition to your employer's benefits if your expenses exceed the employer's benefits. For example, if your adoption costs $15,000 in 1997 and your employer provides you with $5,000 toward the adoption, you can still take a tax credit for the remaining $10,000.

Relative adoptions, except for stepparent adoptions, appear to be covered by this legislation. However, how the IRS will interpret this is still not fully clear.

This tax credit is in effect only until 2001, but remains permanent for special needs adoptions.

Chapter Eighteen

Healthy Mothers, Healthy Babies

I f you are adopting independently or through a domestic agency, you may be actively involved in the birth mother's prenatal care. The level of medical attention a woman receives while pregnant can greatly influence both her and the baby's health. Not surprisingly, adoptive parents are usually very concerned about the quality of medical care a birth mother receives. Often, indeed, a birth mother has not had any prenatal care before she contacts a couple. Perhaps she did not know she was pregnant at first, and when she found out, she immediately began to make adoption arrangements before doing anything else.

You and your attorney will often make the initial medical arrangements, if a birth mother has not already done so. Here is some advice about how to find an obstetrician.

FINDING AN OBSTETRICIAN

First, try to get as much information as possible. It is best to have more than just a list of names from the telephone book. Find out whether the birth mother prefers a male or a female doctor, and do your best to honor that preference. Contact an adoption support group or the RESOLVE chapter closest to where the birth mother is going to deliver her baby, and ask for names of physicians who understand what is involved in an adoption and what special needs a birth mother may have before, during, and after the baby's birth.

A physician should be sensitive and recognize that each birth mother has different needs. Some, for example, may show detachment toward the baby in utero, while others may be very interested. One birth mother may want to see the baby's image on the ultrasound screen, while another does not. Some women want to go to prenatal classes; others do not. After the birth, some birth mothers want to see and care for the baby while in the hospital. Others do not.

If you can't find the right physician through a support group, there are other sources to try. An adoption agency in the birth mother's area may know of some obstetricians who support adoption. Try contacting them. Another person to ask is your gynecologist or infertility specialist. Then there's your attorney, who has handled many adoptions and may even have a list of names on hand.

Some HMOs will pay for a birth mother's expenses if she uses a doctor who is on the adoptive parents' insurance plan. This is not the case with conventional insurance policies. If the HMO pays for the obstetrician's bill, it will pay for the participating hospital's bill as well. Just remember, whether or not you find a doctor who can be paid through your insurance program, the most important criteria for selecting her is that she is supportive of the birth mother's adoption plans.

All this being said, however, most birth mothers will be using Medicaid, which just a few years ago was not the case. Using Medicaid means that you and the birth mother will have much less say in selecting a physician. At a clinic a birth mother may see several different health practitioners, each of whom may have varying views on adoption. Birth mothers are generally very savvy and know how to handle this situation.

Ask the birth mother whether she has any preference about where she receives treatment. The advantage of using a clinic is that they frequently offer prenatal care free or at minimal cost, based on a sliding scale; also, she and the baby will both be covered in the hospital. Even if your insurance is supposed to cover the expenses of the child, there is sometimes some ambiguity in this area, so it is reassuring to know that in the event of a medical problem, Medicaid will cover the child's medical bills.

To find a prenatal clinic, call the state Medicaid office in the state where the birth mother will deliver and get information from a staff member. In some states a woman who has no medical coverage whatever can go to a prenatal clinic without paying anything under a plan called "presumptive eligibility." The purpose of this plan is to encourage women to seek prenatal care regardless of their financial status. At this first visit the clinic staff will determine, based on the woman's financial resources, what assistance programs she may qualify for. In New York State, for example, if a woman qualifies for Medicaid, the clinic staff can assist her in completing the forms right there instead of at a Medicaid office.

Some states have special prenatal programs like the "Healthy Mothers, Healthy Babies" Program. To find the coordinator in your state, contact:

Healthy Mothers, Healthy Babies
409 12th St., SW Washington, DC 20024-2188
Phone: (202) 863-8444, ext. 2458 Fax: (202) 484-5107
They will send you a free newsletter.

Contacting the Obstetrician

Before deciding on an obstetrician, you will need to call and ask some questions. For example:

1. *What are your fees?* The physician may want payment up front to protect himself in case the birth mother changes her mind. If she does, she may not be able to pay for the services rendered, and the adoptive parents will not want to. Although the physician's viewpoint is understandable, you certainly do not want to end up paying for a woman's medical bills, only to have her change her mind. If a physician does ask for payment up front, and you truly believe that the birth mother is going to place the baby with you, then go ahead and pay. But *never* pay the doctor more because this is an adoption. That is unethical.

2. *What kind of insurance does the office accept?* When it comes to medical insurance, ask the doctor's office the following questions: (a) Do they accept Medicaid payments? (Most private physicians do not accept Medicaid payments.) (b) Do they expect payment up front before the insurance carrier has reimbursed them? (Some physicians want to be paid up front; the insurance company then reimburses the patient.)

3. *If a woman has no insurance, what is her payment schedule?* If you will be paying for the birth mother's medical expenses, try to set the payment schedule. Try to pay as little as possible before the baby's birth in case the birth mother changes her mind. These medical expenses cannot be recouped. Have the monies put in your attorney's escrow account; if the woman changes her mind about the adoption, the monies will not be sent to the physician.

   The practice of placing the woman's medical expenses in escrow may be deemed illegal in some instances. Some authorities believe the practice should be prohibited when payment is contingent on the birth mother's placing the child for adoption. Never pressure a woman to place her baby for adoption by telling her that her medical bills will not be paid if she does not. Payment arrangements are between you and the doctor.

4. *Will the clinic staff or physician give medical treatment to a woman who will be placing her baby for adoption?* Even before making the first appointment, let the obstetrician know right away of the woman's adoption plans. This is better than finding out later that the obstetrician or the support staff has a negative attitude toward adoption. When you call, you may start by saying, "I am a prospective adoptive mother and am helping a woman find an obstetrician. This woman is planning to place this baby for adoption through private channels with my husband and me. I want to know whether your staff will care for a pregnant woman placing a baby for adoption." If the person answering the phone says that the obstetrician will accept a woman placing her baby for adoption, ask the following questions:

- *Has the obstetrician treated other women who were placing the baby for adoption through private channels?* If the staff says yes, you may want to ask whether everything went well.
- *Does the office have a policy about treating birth mothers?* Most offices will not have a written policy, but by asking the question you let them know that you expect professional protocol to be followed in treating the birth mother.
- *Will the obstetrician permit the adoptive parents to be in the delivery room with the birth mother?* If you and the birth mother are very sure it is in everyone's best interest for you to take her to prenatal visits and to be present in the delivery room, discuss this with the obstetrician right away. Even if you do not have plans to be in the delivery room, this is still a good question to ask. If the obstetrician says yes, this probably signals that she has positive views about adoption.

You might consider having your attorney's staff screen obstetricians before you or the birth mother calls for an appointment. By doing so you can be saved some awkward moments on the telephone. After the attorney's staff has screened various obstetricians' offices, you can then call the office yourself and simply make an appointment for the birth mother.

In the past few years there has been a marked improvement in the attitudes of physicians, nurses, social workers, and others who may be involved in caring for the birth mother, but you could still encounter a lack of understanding and discretion. The obstetrician's staff should be aware of the birth mother's situation, however, in case she wants to make special prenatal arrangements. For instance, she may not want to attend birthing classes that include discussions on baby care. Whether you want to let the health care staff know that you are the prospective adoptive parent is a matter of personal preference. If you will be accompanying the birth mother to her prenatal visits, you will probably want to say who you are, but be prepared for the possibility that although they support the birth mother, they see you as an intruder.

5. *Does the obstetrician have a midwife or nurse practitioner on staff?* If the obstetrician happens to be male, the birth mother may feel more comfortable being treated by a female nurse. Nurse practitioners and midwives often have broader views on women's issues, moreover, and may be more supportive of women who choose adoption.

6. *At what hospital(s) does the obstetrician deliver babies?* This is an important question, because the social services departments of certain hospitals are known for their negative attitude toward adoption.

Determining the Staff's Attitude Toward Adoption

Based on the responses to your questions, you may have a good idea about the staff's attitude already. If you are still not sure (and this is not unusual), you, the wife, may want to go with the birth mother to her first obstetrical appointment.

If you are dealing with a clinic, there may be counselors who will try to talk her out of her decision to place the baby. Be honest with your birth mother and tell her this. Ask how she would handle this situation.

In all fairness, most obstetricians and their staff have a positive attitude about adoption and will provide a birth mother with proper health care and respect. There are doctors, however, who look on independent adoption as a quasi-legal activity, or at any rate an inappropriate choice for a woman to make.

One doctor told my daughter's birth mother during her first visit that after the baby was born, while she was still in the hospital, the state agency that deals with child abuse cases would visit her to determine why she was not caring for the baby properly. After a few weeks of treating her at our expense, the obstetrician said that he could no longer be her doctor because the adoption was illegal. Needless to say, he lacked even basic knowledge about private adoption.

In another situation an adoptive mother named Linda took her own mother to the doctor's office for an appointment. After her mother was examined, the doctor said hello to Linda and her four-month-old baby. Linda casually mentioned

ıdopted her baby. The doctor responded, "The [birth] parents
."

ɔfessionals oppose adoption. If the obstetrician you select turns out
to be one ơ ınem, the earlier you find it out, the better.

PRENATAL CARE

Prenatal health care should be comprehensive and should include the following:

1. *Medical history and complete physical examinations*
2. *Laboratory and diagnostic procedures*, including:
   - Blood pressure
   - Hemoglobin and hematocrit (to test for iron-deficiency anemia)
   - ABO/Rh typing (to determine blood kind and Rh factor)
   - Sexually transmitted disease cultures
   - Hepatitis B surface antigen
   - Urinalysis for bacteria in urine

For high-risk groups:
   - Hemoglobin electrophoresis
   - Rubella antibodies
   - Chlamydia testing
   - HIV testing and counseling

3. *Nutrition assessment and counseling* and, if appropriate, a referral to the government's Woman, Infant, and Children's (WIC) program. Entry into a WIC program is based upon financial and nutritional status. The guidelines are very broad, and a woman who is well above the poverty level may still be eligible. WIC centers have nutritionists and dietitians who counsel women and give them vouchers for specific food items, like milk, cheese, nutritious cereals, and iron-rich foods.
4. *Health education*, including information about fetal development, preventive health care, and preparation for labor and delivery
5. *Basic psychological assessment*. In particular, anyone suspected of substance abuse should receive special attention and referrals. (See pages 316–330.)

Although the problems associated with alcohol and drug abuse can be profound, do *not* expect an obstetrician, especially one in private practice, to do a thorough investigation of a birth mother's possible substance abuse. The most the average physician will do along these lines is ask the woman whether she uses alcohol or drugs, and she'll probably just answer no, even if she does. There are ways, however, through careful, appropriate, and tactful questioning, to elicit honest answers from a pregnant woman about her history of drug and alcohol use.

6. *Screening for environmental health hazards* common in the community or work site (pesticides, radiation, parasitic infections, etc.). Many birth defects can be associated with environmental exposures.

THE BABY'S BIRTH AND HOSPITAL STAY

Once you have selected an obstetrician and know the hospital where the baby will be born, either you or your attorney should contact the hospital to find out about its adoption policy. Ask whether you can speak with a social worker. It is likely that a social worker will meet with the birth mother while she is in the hospital.

Here are some questions you will want to ask:

1. *Does the hospital have a policy regarding independent adoption?* If so, is the policy enforced, or do the personnel practice a more flexible policy? (Some hospitals have archaic written policies that are no longer followed.) Based on the way the policy is explained by employees, you will probably discover their attitude toward adoption.

2. *Can adoptive parents be in the delivery room if the birth mother authorizes their presence?* (Ask the obstetrician first.)

3. *Can the adoptive parents visit the baby and birth mother in the hospital?*

4. *If so, can the adoptive parents dress, and feed the baby if the birth mother permits?*

5. *If the birth mother does not want to see the baby, what arrangements are made for the baby to be fed, dressed and bathed?* In one hospital the social workers threatened to call a state agency that deals with child abuse to claim that a birth mother was neglecting the baby. In another case, a nurse forced a birth mother against her will to dress the baby before the woman and child were discharged. Through her tears, this poor woman had to fully dress the infant she did not even want to see.

6. *If the birth mother chooses, can she be placed on a medical/surgical floor after delivery instead of the maternity floor?* Many birth mothers, even those who desire to see the baby, do not want to be on the maternity floor facing questions from other new mothers and nurses.

7. *What hospital personnel are allowed to talk to the birth mother about her decision to adopt, and what are they allowed to say?* Find out whether the hospital has a policy about the kinds of questions and comments that nurses, social workers, and other hospital personnel are permitted to

make to a birth mother about her decision. You will also want to find out whether the hospital has a policy dealing with tactless, unsolicited advice from hospital personnel. Some people feel they have a right to comment about a woman's choice to place a baby for adoption, saying things like, "How can you give away your own baby?" These comments can come from the nurses, social workers, or housekeepers. If you sense that the social worker will not prevent unsolicited advice from hospital staff, then ask how the administrative staff would handle such remarks.

Even more alarming are hospital personnel who know "the perfect couple" to adopt the baby and try to persuade the birth mother to place the baby with a couple other than you. These solicitations can come from anyone, from a physician to the person who delivers meals. Be honest. Warn your birth mother that people may make negative comments or that they may try to get her to place the baby with another couple. Ask her how she would handle such a scenario. Mentally rehearsing her response can help her deal with insensitive people, especially at a time when her emotions are very strong.

8. *Does hospital policy allow direct placement of the baby with the adoptive couple at the hospital?* Some hospitals do not allow anyone except the birth mother or an adoption agency to leave with a baby. Find out whether the adoptive parents and attorney can leave the hospital with the baby if the birth mother has signed the consent forms, or whether the birth mother must leave the hospital with the baby.

If the hospital does not allow you or your attorney to leave with the baby, and if a birth mother does not wish to see the baby, discuss the possibility of having a friend or relative hold the baby and leave with her, or hiring a private-duty nurse to carry the baby out. As the adoptive parents, you can then meet the person carrying the baby outside the hospital.

Financial Arrangements

By law, any woman can walk into a hospital and deliver a baby. She cannot be turned away. Therefore, you are not responsible for paying the hospital bill before the baby's birth. In fact, if the birth mother has no insurance, and she is not able to pay, have the hospital send her the bill. There may be special funds that assist those in a low-income category without insurance, and if you do pay the bill, it will be based on the birth mother's income and not yours. Chances are likely that the hospital bill will be less expensive if it is based on the birth mother's income.

Make all arrangements through your attorney's office. He or she can find out how much the hospital charges for delivery, the mother's care, and the nursery. Make sure he examines all the bills! We have twice caught hospitals charging an adoptive couple $4,000 more than they should have. Apparently, because no insurance carrier was paying the bill (and therefore questioning it), the hospital billing department sought to collect extra revenue. These are *not* isolated examples. *Some hospitals will try to charge extra if an adoptive couple is paying the bill.* (When a hospital bill is excessive, your attorney can often negotiate to have it reduced.)

What if the hospital bills are excessive because of medical complications? A premature baby with many medical complications can run up a medical bill well over $100,000. Needless to say, even a $20,000 hospital bill can be beyond the means of many couples. (Hospital bills generally run about $1,000 a day for patients.)

How unfortunate that a loving couple with limited means may have to reconsider an adoption if the baby's hospital bill is beyond their financial ability. After all, if the birth mother changed her mind and decided to raise the child, the hospital would have to absorb the bill anyway. If it is impossible for you to pay for the hospital bill, these are some strategies to consider:

First, see whether your health insurance policy will pay for the baby's expenses. Technically, if you are legally bound to pay the bill, then your insurance company is required by law to cover it. This is a "gray" area, however, and you want to be extra sure. You will probably have to make the decision whether to proceed with the adoption before you get a firm (*and written*) commitment from the insurance company. Some health maintenance organizations (HMOs) will now pay for the infant's medical expenses if the child is born at a participating hospital and is attended by a participating physician.

Second, make sure your insurance company will pay the baby's medical expenses once she is home with you. You are *not* obligated to tell your insurance company (although most ask) whether the child is adopted. Do not allow the insurance company to stall you. Call your state health insurance commissioner. Document all phone calls. Federal legislation now requires insurance companies to pay for the medical expenses of an adopted child at placement.

Third, see whether the birth mother qualifies for Medicaid. Medicaid funds will cover the hospital bill. A birth mother can usually obtain Medicaid coverage retroactively up to ninety days after birth.

If the birth mother cannot take responsibility for the bills, have her claim herself as an indigent. Her hospital bills may then be absorbed by special state funds designated for this purpose.

Never allow the hospital billing department to send you bills directly.

If the birth mother will be "paying" the bills, have your attorney send her the money to send to the hospital. *Carefully document all paperwork. Save all your canceled checks.*

Document every transaction you make and what you have paid, no matter how little or how much you have spent.

The Baby's Delivery

The birth of a baby is one of life's most wonderful events. You and your spouse may want to share in this experience with the birth mother. Of course, there are many factors that can keep you from doing so. But if it is possible to be there, the birth mother may appreciate your support.

Several factors will help determine whether you can be present at the birth, beginning, of course, with the birth mother's preference. She may want the adoptive mother to be there to give support and encouragement, or she may want this to be "her time" with the baby. She may have other support to help her through labor and delivery—the birth father, a family member, or a special friend.

Some hospitals have a policy about nonfamily members being present at the delivery. In others, as soon as hospital staff hear "adoptive parent," red flags start waving and a "policy" is suddenly established that forbids your presence. If you and the birth mother are determined that you will be there, you will have to be the birth mother's "friend" or coach, and simply not reveal your status to hospital personnel. Some hospitals are very cooperative, while others are very uncooperative. If possible, find out what you can expect *before* the baby's birth.

Do take your comfort level into consideration. If you nearly faint when you have blood drawn, then you may not be a good candidate to view a baby's delivery, especially if it turns into a cesarean section birth. If a birth mother really wants you there, perhaps you can compromise and hold her hand and look at her face during delivery.

The Length of the Hospital Stay

A mother who has given birth vaginally will generally stay in the hospital about one to three days. Most newborns are also released after a couple of days. A woman who has had a cesarean section may stay in the hospital a few days longer than the baby. Or if a baby has a medical problem, such as jaundice, he may remain in the hospital after the mother is released.

Usually these circumstances present no problem. If the baby is released after the birth mother is, she must sometimes come back to the hospital so that the hospital staff will permit the baby's release.

The Baby's Medical Records

Once the baby is born, you should receive all relevant hospital records. Like any other parent, you should know your child's health history. This information may be important for future use.

A baby who is released from the hospital is generally a healthy child. However, do not expect the hospital to send any records home with the birth mother or you. You may want to have a pediatrician, whom you should already have selected, contact the hospital to receive all medical records. It is best if you can get the birth mother to sign a release to have all medical records sent to your pediatrician or attorney. Some hospitals will not release the medical information without the birth mother's signature, or will insist on adoption documents before they will release the information.

The Release of the Baby and Birth Mother from the Hospital

For the birth mother, going home from the hospital usually means separation from the baby. This can be an especially emotional time for the birth mother. If you know her address, you may consider sending her flowers or some other small token of caring at her home. If not, have your attorney's office arrange for the delivery of some special small gift and card. Ask your attorney what is an appropriate amount to spend without appearing cheap but remaining within the confines of the law.

The baby will need clothes to wear home from the hospital. You will probably want to bring these to the hospital after the baby is born or send them through your attorney or the birth mother's friend or family member.

We have often encountered the unexpected during our involvement in adoptions over the years—including a wonderful adoptive couple who sent used, stained clothes to the birth mother's attorney. The couple reasoned that there would be no loss in case the birth mother changed her mind. Fortunately, the attorney was sensitive enough to buy new clothes to send to the hospital.

We suggest you purchase a lovely new baby outfit and wash it carefully to protect newborn skin before taking it to the hospital—or borrow an outfit that looks brand-new. If you find shopping for baby clothes too difficult, have a friend shop for you. Also, have a clean, sturdy car seat to take the baby home in. Many hospitals will not allow you to leave without a seat. In fact, it is illegal for a child to ride in a vehicle without an infant restraint system.

Potential Problems at the Hospital

By this time you may well be wondering why some hospital staff seem so hostile toward adoption. In all fairness, hospitals are simply trying to stay out of legal difficulties. Hospital attorneys, social workers, and administrators know little if anything, as a rule, about adoption and the legal process. Each state has very different laws, and sometimes within a state the laws can vary county by county. To expect hospital staff to have a complete grasp of the law may be expecting too much. Hospitals want to maintain a good public image, moreover, and fear that if an adoption situation is handled improperly, they could be sued, or, worse, receive bad publicity. Unfortunately, it often happens that in trying to "keep their hands clean," hospitals end up taking away a birth mother's basic rights.

Of course, these reasons do not explain all the problems at hospitals. Social workers also have their agenda. They have been trained to "preserve" the family unit, meaning that some view adoption as the last option for very desperate women. Some social workers feel they must "counsel" a birth mother and insist she explain her reasons for wanting to place the baby for adoption. No other patient is required to endure such pressure before she makes a personal, nonmedical decision.

Then there are the nurses and other health care professionals, who may not want to deal with a birth mother who will probably not be caring for the infant. In the first place, it may mean more work for the nurses: After all, they, instead of the mother, must feed and change the infant. Second, nurses view the maternity floor as a happy place, and they may not want to see someone leave without her baby. Finally, professionals are accustomed to handling every situation according to a routine, and adoption may mean they have to rethink how they will handle a birth mother and child.

HEALTH RISKS

To cover every possible health problem a child could have would require a whole medical book. Yet as adoptive parents you do want to know the possible genetic and environmental factors that could influence your child's health, so that you can make informed decisions. You need this information, first, to assess the medical risks and decide whether you can accept a child with these risk factors. Second, if you proceed with the adoption, your child's medical background may be crucial to his well-being.

It is your attorney's responsibility to do a thorough investigation of the birth parents' medical backgrounds and those of their families. Most birth parents will reveal basic health history information (such as a family history of diabetes or heart disease) to a physician or lawyer. Getting a birth mother to admit her drug and alcohol use during pregnancy is a much more difficult task, and yet obtaining this information is absolutely essential. The consequences of substance or alcohol abuse on the child's development are often profound.

A pregnant woman's use of tobacco, alcohol, or drugs is only one of many risk factors associated with defects in the child. Other risk factors that should be assessed include:

1. *A family history of reproductive problems.*
2. *Multiple previous pregnancies within a short time span.*
3. *Medical problems concurrent with the pregnancy,* such as sexually transmitted diseases, diabetes, and health, liver, or kidney disease.
4. *Obesity, poor eating habits, or signs of poor nutrition.*
5. *Poor living conditions and lack of education.*
6. *Excessive stress.*
7. *Inadequate prenatal care.* In 1983 one woman in four had no prenatal visits in the first trimester of pregnancy. It is not unusual for birth mothers to wait until the second or third trimester. Many are not aware of their pregnancy, or are in denial.
8. *Repeated exposure to environmental hazards such as lead, pesticides, or x-rays.*
9. *Being younger than fifteen years old.* Teenage mothers are twice as likely to have low-birth-weight babies and have a higher incidence of obstetrical complications. Low-birth-weight infants are forty times more likely to die during the first eight days of life and twenty times more likely to die during the first year of life than other infants. Those who live often have developmental problems. Teenage mothers are also more likely to have sexually transmitted diseases like hepatitis B, because they are more likely to have had multiple sexual partners.

Genetic diseases

Whether adopted or not, everyone has the right to know his or her genetic background. Indeed, a thorough genetic history may be essential in preventing certain diseases. For example, adult-onset diabetes has a strong genetic component; yet 80 percent of those who have this kind of diabetes are overweight. If you know that diabetes runs in your family, you can significantly decrease your likelihood of getting the disease by keeping your weight in the normal range. Other genetically linked diseases, such as breast and other cancers, should be screened for more frequently if they run in your family.

Simple precautions can prevent the occurrence of other genetic diseases. In one adoption a hospital failed to perform a simple PKU test on an infant. This is a routine test for phenylketonuria, a genetically carried disease. If diagnosed properly, it can easily be treated by altering the child's diet. The child then developed

PKU, which led to profound mental retardation. It was extremely unfortunate that the agency social worker involved failed to notice the omission of the test.

Some basic questions should be posed to get a genetic history of the birth parents. The Children's Home Society of Minnesota, with the assistance of geneticist Dr. V. Elving Anderson, University of Minnesota, has developed a comprehensive, twenty-six-page form for gathering birth parents' genetic histories. It covers 138 medical conditions thought to be genetically linked. The form is $3.50 (prepaid—make the check out to the Children's Home Society) and can be ordered from Ann Meagher, CHSM, 2230 Como Avenue, St. Paul, MN 55108. The phone number is (612) 646-6393. For further information consider purchasing the book *Genetic Background History*, by Maretta Spener, also from the Children's Home Society of Minnesota.

If possible, have the birth parents, or their parents, describe their traits and those of other family members (parents, grandparents and siblings), including:

- Physical characteristics
- Educational experience
- Religion
- Nationality and racial background
- Employment history
- Social adjustments (the way they relate to friends, coworkers, community)
- Interests, hobbies, talents, skills, recreational activities
- Intelligence, aptitude, temperament, personality
- Medical history

Hepatitis B

The two sexually transmitted diseases adoptive parents need to be aware of are AIDS (Acquired Immune Deficiency Syndrome) and hepatitis B. Babies are now routinely screened for HIV infection, the virus that causes AIDS, and adoptive parents will be told immediately if the screening is positive. All babies in the United States now also receive hepatitis B immunoglobulin (in case the child has the disease) and HBV vaccine to prevent getting the disease in life (such as through sexual contact). Studies have shown that immediate treatment beginning two to twelve hours after the baby's birth, with injections of hepatitis B immunoglobulin and hepatitis B vaccine, is 85 to 95 percent effective in preventing hepatitis B virus chronic carrier status in childhood.

For more information on hepatitis B, see pages 336–338.

HIV and AIDS

An estimated 7,000 infants in 1993 were born to women who carried the AIDS virus. Of these 7,000 infants, between 1,000 and 2,000 are HIV infected, based on a transmission rate of about 15 to 30 percent. If a woman takes zidovudine (ZDV) while pregnant, she can reduce the risk of passing the AIDS virus to the fetus by as much as two-thirds—which means that if all pregnant HIV-positive women took the drug, only about 300 to 600 babies would be born HIV positive.[1]

About 77 percent of the mothers of those 7,000 infants were African-American and Hispanic. The rate of AIDS infection in non-Hispanic Caucasian women was 3.8 per 100,000 population; for non-Hispanic blacks, 62.7, for Hispanics, 26.0, and for Asians, 1.3.[2]

This means that if your birth mother is Caucasian, the chance is less than 1 in 800 that she is HIV positive, and if she is, there is only a 15 to 30 percent chance that the child will contract the disease—5 to 10 percent if she takes ZDV during her pregnancy. Even if a child tests positive at birth, moreover, that does not necessarily mean that she is HIV positive. It could just mean the child carries the HIV antibody. (It is through the presence of the antibody, not the virus, that the diagnosis is made.) These antibodies can remain in the child's blood until he is fifteen months old. Such babies are tested regularly to see whether the antibodies have left the blood. If they do, the child does not have the virus for AIDS.

For further information, contact:

CDC National AIDS CLEARINGHOUSE
PO Box 6003
Rockville, MD 20849-6003
(800) 458-5231

CDC National AIDS Hotline
1(800) 342-AIDS

Poor Nutrition

Malnutrition is a major cause of low-birth-weight babies. These babies are ten times more likely to be mentally retarded. A 1972 study found nearly half the children who were underweight at birth had an IQ of 70, well below the normal rating of 100. This is not surprising, considering that the baby's brain develops the most during the last trimester of pregnancy and the first month after birth. A birth mother who is undernourished can cause irreversible neurological and brain underdevelopment. Lack of oxygen, birth injuries, and respiratory distress, more-over, mostly affect babies who weigh less than five and a half pounds.

Most women should gain at least twenty-four pounds during pregnancy. Studies have shown that a thirty-five-pound weight gain produces babies who weigh an average of eight pounds. These larger babies are more active, mentally more alert, and generally healthier than five-pound babies.[3]

Substance Abuse

Certain medical problems can arise if a birth mother uses drugs, alcohol, or tobacco during her pregnancy. Although the problems associated with these substances are not always apparent at birth, they may, for example, develop into a learning disability when the child reaches age five.

And yet a birth mother's use of these substances does not guarantee that the child will have problems. Only 30 percent of babies born to mothers who used crack or cocaine, for example, display health or learning problems. Most birth defects are not attributable to maternal drugs and alcohol use but to genetic or other factors.

If you suspect that a birth mother is using drugs or alcohol during her pregnancy, find out as much as possible about the effects of what she is taking may have on the unborn child and the problems that may arise as the child matures.

You may be under the impression that middle-class white women do not use drugs to the extent that poor black women do. If so, you are mistaken. A study conducted in 1989 by the National Association of Perinatal Addiction Research and Education (NAPARE) found that pregnant, middle-class Caucasian women in private care used drugs nearly as much as women in public health clinics. The women's urine was screened for cocaine, alcohol, marijuana, and opiates to test who had used drugs in the last forty-eight hours and who had consumed alcohol in the last eight hours. The results were startling: 16 percent of the women in the public health care centers tested positive, as did *13 percent of the women in the private obstetrical offices*. Ethnic background and economics are not necessarily risk factors for drug use.

If a birth mother is Caucasian and middle class, it is very unlikely that she will be screened appropriately for substance abuse. In one study, physicians were asked to report drug use based on the women's urine at the time of delivery, or on the infant's urine. The study found that African-American women were ten times more likely to be tested and reported than Caucasian women. Questioned about this, physicians explained that Caucasian women stop using drugs when pregnant, whereas African-American women do not. As we have seen, this is simply not the case.

Studies show that the pattern of drug use among pregnant women is as follows: A woman decreases her drug use immediately after finding out she is pregnant. By the second trimester, her rate of drug use is similar to what it was before she was pregnant. During the third trimester, the rate may be higher than her pre-pregnancy rate because of the stress of pregnancy.

Some believe that adopted children are more likely to have been exposed to drugs than nonadopted children. According to Dr. Ira J. Chasnoff, who heads Northwestern University's Medical School Perinatal Center for Chemical Dependence, adopted children are more likely to be exposed to drugs and alcohol in utero, because birth mothers are young and are likely to be risk takers. Often they do realize that they are pregnant when drinking alcohol or using drugs. Dr. Chasnoff says that drug use peaks in the twenty-five to thirty-five-year-old age group and that alcohol use is very high among college-age women.

What You Need to Know

You will want a detailed list of any over-the-counter and prescription medications or illicit drugs a woman has used during her pregnancy. Certain medications, whether prescribed by a doctor or not, can have a detrimental effect on the fetus.

To find out about a birth mother's possible tobacco, drug, and alcohol use, a doctor, lawyer, or adoption counselor needs to ask the appropriate questions. Unfortunately, although the doctor is certainly the most appropriate person to raise this issue, few doctors know how to ask a pregnant woman about her drug history in a way that elicits an accurate response. Sometimes a woman is simply not honest; other times she just does not know how to answer a direct yet vague question like "Do you use drugs?" Her idea of what constitutes a "drug" or "drug use" may be different from the doctor's.

If you are involved in an identified adoption, the agency, by law, is responsible for investigating and evaluating the medical condition and background of all children to be adopted, and to communicate that information to the adoptive parents. It is up to the agency, therefore, to ask appropriate questions. Certainly an adoption counselor, like a physician, is in a better position than you or your attorney to raise these sensitive questions. If you are using an agency, make sure that the counselor investigates all avenues to determine any medical problems or history of drug or alcohol use.

In the case of an independent adoption, however, because you cannot depend upon the birth mother's obstetrician, you may have to ask your attorney to collect this sensitive information as part of the woman's medical background. It may be a little more difficult for an attorney to find an appropriate way to ask a woman about her alcohol and drug use. After all, he is representing the couple, and the birth mother may see these questions as a threat. He must, however, carefully and tactfully pose the questions to elicit a truthful response; it is his legal responsibility to obtain all information important to a child's health and to share this information with the adoptive parents. Make it clear to your attorney that you want this information. If you are working with an agency, that also means he should check to make sure the agency has investigated the drug-use issue thoroughly.

Of course, you may be the person most likely to see the birth mother on a regular basis. However, it is a very delicate matter for adoptive parents to ask questions that relate to substance abuse. You cannot come out and bluntly pose such a question, but through discussion and other leading questions, you may be able to elicit some honest responses.

All of this raises thorny ethical issues. A professional's interest in maintaining a woman's right to confidentiality must be weighed against the unborn child's right to medical intervention if the mother is abusing drugs or alcohol. These issues are further complicated when adoptive parents want to know whether a woman is using drugs and alcohol. For this reason it is not surprising that some health professionals may be more comfortable than others about revealing a woman's drug use, even to prospective adoptive parents.

In asking a woman whether she is using tobacco, alcohol, or drugs, the following techniques can be helpful. The first is to frame questions about substance abuse within the context of another questionnaire. A medical or dietary intake form, for example, can ask, "What do you like to drink: water, milk, juice, beer, soft drinks, wine, iced tea?" That way the woman's drinking history is asked matter-of-factly, minimizing any embarrassment.

Another technique is simply to ask the woman about substance abuse, but to keep your tone casual. Ask whether she ever used illicit drugs in the same sentence, if possible, in which you ask her about prescription and over-the-counter drugs. You might say, "Are you taking any medications or drugs such as aspirin, cold medications, vitamins, or prescription medicines like Phenobarbital; or other drugs such as cocaine, crystal, speed, barbiturates, or heroin?" Notice that this question moves from over-the-counter medications to prescription medications to illicit drugs. Or you could ask whether she has ever used stimulants or tranquilizers. Use the specific brand names of the drugs. For example, ask, "Do you take Valium?"

If she answers yes to any of these questions, then in the same casual tone, ask what her approximate maximum use or consumption is. Try to "normalize" immoderate consumption so that she does not feel ashamed. When a woman answers, for example, that she drinks beer, ask, "How much do you drink—two or three cans or about one or two six-packs a day?" If she sees that you are comfortable discussing these amounts of alcohol consumption, she is more likely to be honest with you. When asking about consumption, it is important to follow up by asking, "Do you ever use more?" The purpose of this question is to determine whether the woman ever binges on alcohol or drugs or both.

If direct questions do not seem appropriate for any reason, asking a woman about how she relaxes, deals with stress, and handles her emotions can be a good way to lead into questions about alcohol and drug use. Ask questions like these:

"How do you usually relax when you are tired or stressed?"
"Do you find that smoking a cigarette helps you to relax?"
"Do you talk with a friend over a drink or take some time out for yourself?"

You can also ask whether she has ever used drugs in the past. A woman who is too embarrassed to tell you that she is using drugs during her pregnancy may be willing to reveal that she has used them just before pregnancy. If so, this is a strong indicator that she is still using them or at least used them before she found out she was pregnant. Many birth mothers do not know they are pregnant until three to four months into their pregnancy. So even if she states truthfully that she did not use drugs or alcohol after she found out she was pregnant, she may still have used them up to her second trimester. If a woman admits that she has used tobacco, alcohol, and drugs in the past, try to get as much detailed information as possible about previous use.

Physicians are in a position to administer questionnaires about drug use and to include a drug screening as part of a routine urine test. The questionnaire may even state, "Your urine will be tested for diabetes and for drug use. Do you know of any drugs that may be in your urine?" Women often provide very accurate answers to such questionnaires. A skilled physician may know how to ask a woman directly about her drug and alcohol use in a way that gets an honest response. He or she might say, for example, "Alcohol and other drugs, even over-the-counter drugs, may make pregnancy more difficult or harm the baby. Because many women drink or use drugs, it is important to know exactly which ones are used. Many women do not fully understand that using alcohol or drugs while pregnant may cause problems. We need complete information from every pregnant patient so we can give you the personal advice you need." The physician should explain that all information is helpful and that all answers are held in strictest confidence, but that under the law, professionals are required to tell adoptive parents about any significant information related to the baby's background and health. He also needs to explain some of the reasons why it is important for adoptive parents to know this information.

Signs of Substance Abuse

Sometimes simple, careful observation of a birth mother can provide information about possible substance abuse. Here are some of the clues and symptoms associated with various substances:

Tobacco

- Dry coughing, yellow stains on fingers and teeth, "tobacco" breath.
- Jitteriness. If you meet with her for an extended period of time, you may notice that after an hour or so she has to use the ladies' room or go outside.
- A sibling who smokes. According to our research, the strongest indicator of a teenager's being a smoker is if an older sibling smokes.

Alcohol

- History of low-birth-weight delivery. If a woman had a previous pregnancy, find out the child's weight and whether the birth mother had any problems in delivery, particularly placental abnormalities.
- The smell of alcohol on her breath.
- A family history of alcohol abuse.
- No prenatal care.

Drugs

- Disease. Diseases that are spread through intravenous use, like hepatitis B, can be one indication that a woman has used drugs.
- Malnourishment. Drug abusers often eat poorly, leading to malnourishment.
- Nasal inflammation, track marks. Evidence of snorting cocaine and drug injection.

Helping Women with Substance Abuse Problems

Physicians, agency caseworkers, and other professionals have an obligation to talk to birth mothers about substance abuse and its consequences for the developing fetus. Many women, when told of the harmful effects that tobacco, alcohol, and drugs can have on the unborn child, will stop using these substances. Such information must be given in a simple and positive manner so that it is clear and well understood. If the risks associated with a certain drug are exaggerated, the birth mother may dismiss the message to quit. For example, it would be inappropriate to insist that a woman stop drinking all caffeinated beverages. Here are examples of positive language:

If you stop drinking now, you will have a better chance
of having a healthier baby.
You and the baby will feel better if you are sober.

If gentle encouragement is not enough incentive for her to quit smoking, drinking, or using drugs, the woman is addicted and cannot quit without help. She will need to be referred to a treatment center. Making a good referral, however, is not always easy. Some treatment centers will not accept pregnant women. And although women who use one drug often abuse another, treatment centers often focus on only one substance. (Most people in treatment centers are also smokers, yet smoking as an addiction is seldom addressed.)

Ideally, a pregnant woman should receive comprehensive treatment both for her dependency and for her pregnancy. A multidisciplinary approach employing social workers, nurses, doctors, and counselors would best meet a woman's needs.

CONSEQUENCES OF PRENATAL DRUG AND ALCOHOL EXPOSURE

According to Dr. Chasnoff, it is difficult to determine the specific prenatal effects of any one drug apart from alcohol, whose effects have been well documented. Drug abusers tend to use more than one substance. Alcohol and marijuana are the two drugs most commonly used together. The worst combination is that of alcohol and cocaine, which forms byproducts harmful to the child. These are also believed to be the only two drugs that can produce physical abnormalities.[4]

Dr. Chasnoff lists the following essential information in assessing a drug-exposed child:

- Birth weight
- Head circumference
- Physical examination
- Tests for syphilis and HIV
- Neurological and behavioral state[5]

For more information contact:

National Association for Families and Addiction Research and Education (NAFARE) at (800) 638-BABY
Dr. Chasnoff of NAFARE will consult with you via telephone. The thirty-to-forty-five-minute call is $100. Call (312) 541-1272.

Nicotine

Although most people do not view it as a drug, the nicotine in tobacco is as addictive as heroin. Because tobacco has so many toxins and is so widely used, it is one of the primary causes of infant mortality in the United States Nicotine is associated with low-birth-weight babies, and the complications that accompany low birth weight are the leading causes of infant death. Prenatal exposure to nicotine is also strongly associated with sudden infant death syndrome (SIDS), the number-one cause of death in infants under the age of one.

Although the problems associated with prenatal tobacco exposure are not always obvious, such exposure often means that the child does not have the same full potential he could have had if not exposed to tobacco. Tobacco use can mean a newborn weighs six pounds at birth instead of, for example, seven pounds. In fact, years ago physicians encouraged pregnant woman to smoke and to restrict their diets to produce smaller babies. Tobacco use is also associated with a decrease in a child's academic potential, but this is difficult to evaluate. A bright child could perhaps have been even smarter if his mother had not smoked during pregnancy.

Here are some of the possible effects of nicotine on a newborn infant:

- *Low birth weight.* Low birth weight babies are forty times more likely than normal weight babies to die before they are one month old. Those who do survive may have health problems, including mental retardation, cerebral palsy, and hearing and visual problems.
  - *Increased risk of physical abnormalities.*
  - *Malformations such as heart defects, cleft palate, and hernias.*
  - *Central nervous system defects.*
  - *Threefold risk of sudden infant death syndrome (SIDS)*

As the child grows, the following problems may arise:

- *Hyperactivity and lack of self-control*
- *Decreased attention span*

- *Irritability*
- *Decreased language development*
- *Decreased academic ability*

Alcohol

Among the health problems associated with prenatal alcohol use, fetal alcohol syndrome is the most serious. Indeed, prenatal exposure to alcohol is now considered more dangerous to the health of the child than cocaine. Its consequences include:

- Growth retardation (decreased weight, height, and head circumference)
- Specific facial abnormalities (the eyes are almond-shaped, the nose is short and upturned, the upper lip is thin, and the area between the mouth and nose is flattened)
- Decreased intellectual and motor abilities, as well as microencephaly (small head and profound mental retardation)

Long-term problems include such psychosocial problems as poor judgment, short attention span, and inability to pick up social cues and form friendships. These problems are evident into adulthood even in those with normal IQs. They interfere with learning, and most of the children cannot live or work independently. Children who were in foster care or adopted do not do better than those raised by their birth families. *FAS is the third leading cause of mental retardation after Down syndrome and spina bifida in the United States, and the leading cause of mental retardation in the world.* Unlike these disabilities, however, FAS is completely preventable.

It is difficult to recognize FAS in a newborn. Small size and abnormal behavior in the newborn can result from any number of factors, including prenatal exposure to cigarettes or drugs. The "typical" FAS facial features may not be apparent.[6] In an international adoption the diagnosis may be even more difficult, especially when no maternal history is known, no growth and developmental records are available, and poor growth and development may be attributed to living in an orphanage and poor nutrition.

A physician diagnosing FAS must recognize three problem areas: pre- or postnatal growth deficiency, central nervous system abnormality, and facial signs. When a child has abnormal findings in one or more of these areas with a suspected history of prenatal exposure, the term "fetal alcohol effects" or "subclinical FAS" is often used. Research in animals shows that just one-fifth the amount of alcohol needed to produce the obvious problems associated with FAS can cause learning problems in the offspring. Such problems are not obvious, but the effects can manifest themselves as the child grows.

Heavy drinking is defined as having two or more drinks per day, or fourteen or more per week. A drink is equal to one twelve-ounce beer; one 4-ounce glass of wine; or one 1-ounce glass of distilled spirits such as vodka, whiskey or scotch.[7] Problems associated with heaving drinking include:

- Classic FAS
- Partial FAS
- Sleep disturbances
- Jitteriness
- Poor muscle tone
- Poor sucking response
- Minimal brain dysfunction
- Slight malformations
- Behavior problems such as hyperactivity, decreased alertness, disrupted sleep patterns, feeding difficulties, and decreased intellectual capability

As the amount and frequency of alcohol consumption increase, so do the likelihood and extent of medical problems. Even two drinks a day can cause growth retardation. Fetal alcohol effects can occur in babies whose mothers have two to four drinks a day about 10 percent of the time during the pregnancy. This means there are potential problems for the baby if a pregnant woman has two drinks, three or four days a month.

Studies demonstrate that pregnant women should not consume any alcohol. The American Council on Science and Health (ACSH) recommends that women avoid alcohol completely throughout their pregnancies.

Alcohol can have different effects at different stages of fetal development. In the beginning stages of pregnancy, about six drinks per day is too much, even if the woman stops drinking after she learns that she is pregnant. Alcohol can impair or halt the delivery of oxygen through the umbilical cord. During the first months of pregnancy, even a few minutes of oxygen deprivation can have negative effects on the fetus's brain. Alcohol can also interfere with the passage of nutrients through the placenta to the fetus.

How does one decide whether to adopt a baby who has been prenatally exposed to alcohol? First, it is important to recognize that the likelihood of a birth mother having consumed some alcohol during pregnancy is very high, especially if she is a young woman enduring an unplanned pregnancy. Working with a birth mother who has taken a few drinks at the beginning of her pregnancy is probably not taking an unnecessary risk. Most of our mothers probably had a few drinks during their pregnancies. (Back in the 1950s and 1960s there was no established correlation between alcohol and birth defects.) With evidence now indicating that the higher the birth mother's level of alcohol intake, the more likely the child may be to develop learning or other medical problems, however, adoptive couples will want to know about a birth mother's drinking patterns during her pregnancy. The more you know, the more informed a decision you can make.

Knowing that a woman drank alcohol during her pregnancy should not necessarily disqualify her as a birth mother for you. Instead, you will want to find out how her habits may have affected the child's health. If you do know that a birth mother has drunk heavily at any point in her pregnancy, especially in the beginning, you will want to decide what disabilities and learning problems you can accept. Even if the likelihood of the child's having fetal alcohol syndrome or its effects is low, you should think carefully beforehand about the possibility. If you feel you cannot accept the risk of problems that may not even manifest themselves until the child is in school, then you should not continue dealing with this birth mother. Perhaps you are willing to accept a child who has been exposed to alcohol, but not if the child has profound problems. In some cases the problems may be apparent at birth. An infant with profound FAS will probably display the facial characteristics associated with the syndrome. If so, you may decide at birth whether or not you want to rear a child who may also be mentally retarded or have a lower-than-average IQ.

Resources:

National Health/Education Consortium.
Fetal Alcohol Syndrome: The Impact on Children's Ability to Learn.
(202) 822-8405
A summary of knowledge, misconceptions, and strategies in the education of a child with FAS.

The Fetal Alcohol Syndrome/Effects Information Homepage at
http://www.kumc.edu/instruction/medicine/genetics/wwwgene/fashome. html offers information and resources for families affected by FAS.

Cocaine

Cocaine can pose a great threat to unborn babies, beginning with its tendency to cause a decrease in the mother's functioning—leading to increasing drug exposure and poor prenatal care.[8] Some of the other effects include:

- Threefold risk of premature birth.
- Increased risk of a stroke (caused by increased fetal blood pressure). This is rare but can cause permanent brain damage.
- Smaller head circumference, which may mean child will have a smaller brain.
- Increased likelihood of low weight at birth. Low birth weight babies are forty times more likely than babies with a normal weight to die before they are one month old. Those that do survive have increased health problems, including mental retardation, cerebral palsy, and hearing and visual problems.
- Tenfold risk of sudden infant death syndrome (SIDS).
- Increased likelihood of genito-urinary defects that can cause life-threatening infections.

A cocaine-exposed infant may display some or all of the following symptoms at birth:

- Decreased scores on motor ability reflexes, attention, and mood control
- Low response to human faces or voices
- Jitteriness and irritability
- Sensitivity to any stimuli, including the slightest touch or sound
- Withdrawal and unresponsiveness
- Avoidance of stimuli by staying in a deep sleep most of the day

As with any drug exposure, the most significant long-term effects of prenatal cocaine exposure is on a child's behavior. About 20 percent of the children studied have had significant behavioral problems, and another 15 percent showed less severe but similar problems.[9] As cocaine-exposed children mature, they are at a much higher risk for incurring developmental and learning problems, according to Dr. Ira J. Chasnoff of the National Association for Perinatal Addiction Research and Education. And Dr. Dan Griffith, developmental psychologist at Northwestern University, says a baby's neurological problems show up later as hyperactivity, learning disabilities, and difficulty focusing.

In one study, foster toddlers who had been prenatally exposed to cocaine were compared to those who had not. Those who had been prenatally exposed to cocaine had more risk factors at birth and experienced more illnesses after; they scored lower on conceptual development but excelled in areas of expression of feelings and peer interaction. They also displayed more physically violent behavior than those not exposed. All scored below normal in most areas of development.

According to Jane Schneider, a physical therapist at Children's Memorial Hospital in Chicago, cocaine-exposed children are forty times more likely to have delayed motor development,[10] including delayed language development. Drug-exposed children often have difficulty expressing language. Although they can understand what they hear, speech production is delayed. In fact, 70 percent of three-year-old cocaine-exposed adopted children are in some kind of speech therapy.[11]

According to Dr. Chasnoff, the question that parents ask is, "Are these children adoptable?" He answers with an emphatic yes. True, they may need a few extras, such as speech therapy and maybe some learning disability classes early on. They may also need a little extra love, because they can test your patience. An infant going through withdrawal from drugs can be difficult, but with the right help, the child has a very bright future. Even with some of the potential problems associated with maternal drug use, cocaine-exposed infants are adoptable. In fact, in a study in which 1,269 adoptive families completed questionnaires, almost all the parents of drug-exposed children were highly satisfied, almost as satisfied as those whose adopted children had not been exposed. Overall, the idea that drug-exposed children are significantly different from non-drug-exposed children and that adopting them is less satisfying received no support.[12]

Most children are unharmed by prenatal cocaine exposure. According to Dr. Chasnoff's research, about 70 percent of the cocaine-exposed children seem to develop normally, while the remaining 30 percent have a range of developmental, behavioral, and attention span problems. Many of these can be minimized through a good environment. As can be expected, for example, drug-exposed infants who are adopted early have significantly higher IQs at age three than those reared by their biological mothers—higher than children who were not exposed but who live in deprived conditions.

If you are planning to adopt a baby who has been exposed to cocaine, understand that he may need special attention, particularly during the first eight to ten weeks, when he may be extremely sensitive to stimuli. Even eye contact can overload the child's system, causing him to close his eyes. Often the baby is either crying or in a deep sleep, making it difficult to bond with him. Parents may be convinced that the child simply doesn't love them. The problem is not psychological, however, but physiological. With early intervention, says Dr. Chasnoff, children can develop normally and can even be mainstreamed.

Of course, not only are adoptive parents likely to provide a more stimulating environment for these children, they may also be saving many of them from abuse. Experts believe that the rise in cocaine-exposed babies being placed with their cocaine-abusing mothers has probably accounted for a 27 percent increase in child abuse and neglect. It is very difficult for a woman with few support systems to care for even a healthy infant. Complicating the mother's situation is her own drug use, her lack of resources, and an infant who alternates between a shrill cry and a "shutting down" of his system. This can lead to an explosive situation.[13]

Heroin and Opiates

Heroin and opiates belong to a group of drugs called opioids and are natural and synthetic drugs that act primarily on the central nervous system. They include such therapeutic medicines as morphine, opium, codeine, meperidine (Demerol), oxcycodone (Percodan), and methadone (Dolophine), which is used in treating heroin dependency.

Heroin can be taken in different forms, but mostly it is injected. Pregnancy complications for heroin addicts include early separation of the placenta, premature labor, and ruptured membranes. Toxemia during pregnancy affects 10 to 15 percent of addicts, resulting in high blood pressure and even seizures. About half of infants born to heroin-abusing women with no prenatal care were of low birth weight, and 80 percent had serious medical problems. The chaotic lifestyles of addicts also increases their chances of contracting AIDS through sex or needle sharing.[14]

Heroin readily crosses the placenta. If the mother suddenly stops taking the drug while pregnant, the fetus can experience withdrawal and die.[15] Although opioid exposure before birth is not associated with an increased risk for physical malformations, one in four infants born to mothers in a methadone treatment program had strabismus, a visual disorder in which the infant's eyes cannot focus properly. It was unclear whether the heroin or other drugs had caused the disorder.

Between 60 to 90 percent of these newborns develop withdrawal symptoms and require special, gentle handling and medication. Like the jittery cocaine babies, they are challenging to care for. Withdrawal symptoms can include high-pitched crying, fever, irregular breathing, and seizures within forty-eight to seventy-two hours after birth. Occasionally these symptoms do not begin until two to four weeks after birth. Irritability resulting from overarousal usually ends in about one month but can last up to three months or more.

After these babies are a month old, however, only subtle differences can be observed between them and those not exposed to narcotics in utero. Muscle development may be uneven, and coordination may be impaired. Studies are difficult to conduct, as mothers often drop out of the studies, and the home environments are usually such as to make it difficult to distinguish problems associated with drug exposure from those stemming from poor parenting. Like the cocaine-exposed children, physical and psychological development seem to be within normal ranges, but speech development may be impaired.

In another study, heroin-exposed babies at age one tended to be impulsive, were easily upset, and had sleep disturbances and temper tantrums. Between twelve to eighteen months they were hyperactive. At age one the most distinguishing characteristic for these children was an early separation from their biological mothers. Only 8 percent of three-year-old children had contact with their mothers. Either these mothers could not care for their children, or the children were removed from their homes.[16]

These points are made not because an adopted child will display these tendencies but to show what lives these children may lead when not placed for adoption. Again, the problems associated with any drug exposure are inseparable from parental influence unless studies are conducted with children who have been adopted into stable homes.

PCP

PCP (Phencyclidine) is a synthetic drug with no clinical use. Very little research has been conducted on prenatally exposed infants, because women who take PCPs often take other drugs as well.

Like infants born to mothers who use cocaine or heroin, PCP-exposed newborns were jittery, had poor visual coordination, and were difficult to console. Although these babies alternated between restlessness and calm, they did not have withdrawal symptoms. Animal studies suggest that PCP at very high doses may cause birth defects.[17]

Marijuana

There is limited knowledge about the long-term effects marijuana has on the developing fetus. It is known, however, that its primary component easily crosses the placenta. Marijuana use may be associated with low birth weight and birth defects similar to those with fetal alcohol syndrome and depression of the central nervous system in the newborn.[18]

Sedatives and Tranquilizers

All minor tranquilizers have been associated with increased fetal malformations if used during the first trimester of pregnancy. These birth defects are similar to those of babies with fetal alcohol syndrome. Nearly all the infants were also significantly below normal birth weight.

Valium (diazepam). When taken in the first trimester, Valium increases four-fold the likelihood of a cleft palate, lip anomalies, and malformations of the heart and arteries. This risk increases when Valium is combined with smoking and alcohol. If it is taken within the last two to four months of pregnancy, even in low dosages (ten to fifteen milligrams), the infant may suffer from tremors, lethargy, and other symptoms associated with withdrawal in newborns.[19]

Barbiturates. Barbiturates are commonly used drugs that include sedative hypnotics and antiseizure medications. They are associated with birth defects similar to fetal alcohol syndrome. Infants born to mothers who use barbiturates can suffer from tremors, restlessness, high-pitched crying, and convulsions.[20]

Prescription Drugs

Accutane (isotretinoin). Accutane, an antiacne medication, is associated with major abnormalities such as microencephalus (small head with severe mental retardation) and external ear and cardiovascular defects.[21]

Antibiotics. Some antibiotics, including tetracycline and some sulfanilamides, when taken during the last four to five months of pregnancy may cause permanent discoloration of the child's teeth. For the most part, antibiotics are considered safe.[22]

Anticonvulsants. Anticonvulsants have been associated with an increase in heart defects, cleft lip and palate, microencephaly, mental deficiency, and impaired growth. However, even with this risk, doctors often recommend that the mother continue taking the drug, as withdrawal may cause seizures, resulting in oxygen reduction and threat to the fetus.[23]

WHAT RISKS CAN YOU ACCEPT?

Before you adopt, you and your spouse will want to decide what conditions you can and cannot accept in a child. Your decisions will also influence the kind of adoption that you will choose. For example, you may be able to accept a problem if it is present right at birth (such as cleft palate), and you know the exact treatment that the child will receive (e.g., surgery and speech therapy). However, you may not be able to accept a child who may develop learning problems later on because the birth mother used cocaine occasionally during her pregnancy. Often an agency will ask you what problems you can or cannot accept, and to what degree.

Most doctors do not routinely screen women, and even if the birth mother is screened, the results may not prove anything. Drugs stay in the system for a period of time only and cannot be detected in the mother's blood or the infant's meconium (first stool sample). You may therefore have to "assume" on some level that a birth mother may have drunk at least some alcohol, taken some over-the-counter medicines, and perhaps even used illicit drugs. You may have to base your decision on your gut feelings and the actual health of the baby at delivery.

With your spouse, list the medical conditions you could accept and those that you could not. In each case, ask yourselves, could you truly accept a child with this disease? Could you live with the condition and all it may entail? Would you be looking for any sign of the disease to the child's detriment? For example, a professional psychologist and her husband were told of a birth mother who had a three-generational family history of clinical depression. Knowing this, the couple felt they would be watching for signs of depression at all times.

Based on the conditions you agree you can accept, ask yourselves next what resources you have that can enable you to handle each condition appropriately. Include financial resources, time, personal strength and patience, support systems, and access to care.

What if you cannot accept the child's health status?

The choice is yours. Do not feel guilty if you cannot accept certain medical problems. You have the right to choose, just as the birth mother has the right to select you as parents and then to change her mind. Remember, many couples are willing to adopt newborns with physical problems and mental retardation.

One day a birth mother contacted our office and said that she had a one-week-old baby who had a 95 percent chance of developing muscular dystrophy (MD)—a condition in which the child can have profound disabilities and an early death. The child's MD status could not be determined for sure until he was three months old. We contacted a couple that same day, the couple said they were interested, and that day the child went home with his adoptive parents.

Another couple was ready to adopt a baby through private channels. After the baby was born, the birth mother revealed that she had used cocaine during her pregnancy, having previously stated that she was not using drugs. The couple decided that they did not want to take any chances, yet they felt very guilty because they had visited the baby in the hospital and were concerned about her overall future, especially if the birth mother decided to raise the child herself. An agency was contacted and the child was immediately placed in a loving home. Fortunately, the baby is perfectly healthy and at this point shows no adverse effects from drug exposure.

Adoption is a positive choice in our society, although, sad to say, it is not always viewed that way. As a prospective adoptive parent, however, you should not make the decision to adopt based on your concern about the negative environment the child may encounter if you do not. This is not a good reason to adopt a child. Children have the right to be loved for themselves, not because someone felt sorry for them. No adoptive parent should be a martyr, and no child should be considered a burden.

If you decide that you cannot go ahead with an adoption, refer the birth mother to another couple or to an agency with the resources to place the baby with a loving couple. Virtually all babies, no matter how severe their condition, can be placed in an adoptive home.

Genetic Illness

Should you proceed with an adoption if genetic illness is in the family?

When agreeing to commit yourself to a birth mother, even one who does not use alcohol, tobacco, or drugs, you know that the baby has at least the same risk of medical problems as if you yourself had given birth. None of us lives in a risk-free world, even in the best circumstances. Some risks, however, are known and calculated. If a birth mother tells you that a certain kind of genetic illness has been diagnosed in her family, then you must decide whether you can accept a child who may have the genetic potential for it.

If a baby is to be born with a genetic disease like hemophilia, you must first decide whether you can accept a child who has this disease. If you cannot and you know it, be honest with the birth mother and tell her so. You may know of other couples who are interested in adopting a child with this disease. It is comforting to be able to give a birth mother the name of a couple or an adoption agency. If you are uncertain about accepting a particular medical condition, tell the birth mother that your acceptance depends upon how profound the problem is. You could wait until the child is born or ask for amniocentesis, if appropriate, then tell the birth mother whether you are interested in adopting the baby. If you can accept the disease, start to research what help you could provide the child to minimize the impact of the disease.

Mental Illness

In some ways it is harder to accept a child who *may* develop a disease later in childhood. For some the uncertainty is worse than dealing with the disease itself. You may feel as if you are living with a time bomb, particularly if the child has a genetic predisposition to certain mental illnesses.

One couple had agonized over whether to adopt a baby whose family has a history of schizophrenia. They decided that they would find it very difficult to raise a child who might develop the disease in early adolescence. In some ways they wished they had not known, since their knowledge meant that they would always be looking for a sign of mental illness in the child. This watchfulness could cause them to overreact to any emotional problems the child might have. After much discussion, the couple decided not to adopt this baby.

Very often the birth mother's genetic history is known, but not the birth father's. Had it been the birth father who had a family history of schizophrenia, it is likely that no one would ever have known, and the couple would have adopted the baby. Someone with one manic-depressive parent has about a 20 percent chance of inheriting the disease. If the birth father is very young, he may not even have begun to display the behavior associated with manic depression. No one would know that he would someday have the condition or that he is a genetic carrier.

HOW TO ACCEPT A CHILD WITH A MEDICAL CONDITION

Just as people dream of the ideal biological child, those who are infertile resolve to adopt and then begin to fantasize about the ideal adopted child. If a problem does arise, you can go through another stage of resolution and accept the condition. Some people are better suited than others to deal with a child's medical condition or disability. You may not know how strongly you may feel for a child, and you may find yourself willing to rear a child who has limitations.

Get all the information you can. If a problem does arise during pregnancy or right after birth, your attorney should get hold of the birth mother's and child's medical records so that he and you can discuss the possible problems with the attending physicians.

For further information about drugs and the impact they may have on the child, contact:

> **National Association of Perinatal Addiction and Research and Education/The Child Study Center.** (312) 329-2512 or (800) 638-BABY.
> 200 N. Michigan Avenue, Suite 300
> Chicago, IL 60601
> (312) 541-7553
> (800) 638-2229
> fax (312) 541-1271

For information on fetal alcohol syndrome and fetal alcohol effect, contact:

The National Resource Center for Special Needs Adoption
PO, Box 74612
Fairbanks, AK 99707
(907) 456-1101

Let your child know that you accept him. A few years down the road, a child who is different will know it. To show your child that you accept him, demonstrate that you accept all kinds of people. This can mean that you participate in intercultural events, that you restrict your comments about other people's habits and characteristics, and that you show an interest in a broad range of subjects and ideas. Accepting a child who has a medical or behavior problem or the potential of one is like accepting any other child—adopted or biological. We accept a child for who he is—not what we want him to become.

Know your financial limitations. A child born with an acute medical condition needs care that may not be covered by your insurance. Hospital bills, for instance, can be tremendous. Have your attorney make arrangements so that if you do proceed with the adoption, you are not responsible for the child's medical bills. One way of doing this is to use an adoption agency, which may then be able to apply for Medicaid to finance the child's hospital costs. Another is to get state funds to support the child. For more about financial assistance for special needs children, read chapter 14, or contact:

Program Operations Division, U.S. Children's Bureau
Administration on Children and Families
PO Box 1182
Washington, D.C. 20201
(202) 245-0671.

North American Council on Adoptable Children
970 Raymond Avenue
Suite 106
St. Paul, MN 55114-1149
Jeanette Wiedemeier
(800) 470-6665

You may find, however, that your insurance will cover all the child's medical needs. Adopted children can now have the same medical coverage that biological children have. The Omnibus Budget Reconciliation Act of 1993 mandates that so long as your insurance covers dependents, then adopted children are covered by the same standards as soon as they are placed with you. There cannot be restricted coverage because the child has a preexisting condition. Only those whose insurance is subject to the Employee Retirement Income Security Act of 1974 (ERISA) are exempt from this new law. Check with your employer if you are not sure.

This new legislation may benefit the child and your pocketbook before the child even comes home. For example, if a newborn baby has surgery while in the hospital, and the birth mother is not permitted to sign a consent terminating her rights until three or more days after birth, your insurance company is probably obligated to pay for the baby's surgery. In fact, it should probably pay for the birth mother's medical expenses as well, if you are legally obligated to pay for them.

If a child is covered by Medicaid and has complications after birth requiring expensive medical intervention, check with your insurance company first to see what it will pay for once the consent for adoption is signed. You may want to delay having the birth mother sign a consent while the child is in the hospital, if you are not sure your insurance company will pay all medical expenses. Often Medicaid coverage does not extend to the child once the baby is placed for adoption—even if he is still in the hospital. You do want to be in a situation where you are morally or legally obligated to pay tens of thousands of dollars because you were in health insurance "limbo."

For help in obtaining government funding or health insurance coverage for medical expenses, contact:

> **Steve Humerickhouse of Adoption Advocates.**
> This is a telephone information service at (612) 521-1098 in
> Minneapolis, Minnesota. The fee for assisting adoptive parents in
> obtaining state or federal funding or insurance coverage is about $300.
> Mr. Humerickhouse is one of the nation's foremost experts on these
> issues and has lobbied in Washington, D.C. for adoptive parents' med-
> ical coverage rights.

SPECIAL HEALTH CONCERNS FOR THE INTERNATIONAL CHILD

Your child will have an in-country medical clearance exam before she can come to the United States. Although this exam is usually comprehensive, your child may have a condition that is not properly diagnosed. Therefore, as soon as your child arrives in the United States, she will need a complete physical exam by a pediatrician who is familiar with parasitical diseases and other conditions not commonly seen in American children. Most conditions are easily treatable, but correctly diagnosing the condition, and therefore prescribing the right medication, is not always accomplished at the first doctor's visit.

The following evaluations are recommend by the American Academy of Pediatricians specifically for internationally adopted children of all ages and from all countries:

- Complete hepatitis serology
- TB evaluation
- Stool exams for ova (eggs) and parasites
- Syphilis
- HIV screening (Screening for the AIDS virus is very carefully done in foreign countries; therefore, this is most likely unnecessary.)
- Complete blood count
- Urine analysis
- Review of immunization status
- Growth and development
- Age-appropriate screenings such as vision and hearing
- Monitoring for medical and psychological problems that may be due to the child's life circumstances[24]

The following are a description of the more common diseases that the child may have that can also pose a threat to others if proper precautions are not taken. The descriptions are not meant to alarm you—you are not at high risk of "catching" a deadly disease from an international child. If your child is treated and you and your family take necessary safeguards, you and others can be protected.

Hepatitis B

Hepatitis B is a viral infection of the liver. There are two types: active and chronic. With chronic hepatitis B the person is a carrier but has no liver damage. Of the children who get hepatitis B in the first year of life, 90 percent will develop chronic hepatitis B and therefore be carriers. Hepatitis B is the most common chronic viral infection in the world.

It is important to have your international child tested for hepatitis B, because the tests done in other countries are often unreliable. Unless the screening shows that the child is definitely infected or is immunized, she should be given a routine series of hepatitis B vaccine. If your child is positive, no matter whether he is acute or a carrier, everyone in your household should be immunized. The disease is not spread through urine or stool but through other body secretions including blood and saliva. Those who will be giving the child a lot of affection, like grandparents, should also be immunized.

The only FDA-approved treatment as of January 1996 for hepatitis B is alpha-interferon. This stimulates the immune system and encourages the body to recognize and get rid of the virus. In adults, 30 to 50 percent of patients benefited after six months of treatment. In studies of Asian children who took interferon there was no sustained improvement, perhaps because the booster seems to offer the most benefit to children who acquired hepatitis B after their first year of life. In children from other countries, however, the treatment seems more promising. Children do better with the drug if they have had the infection for fewer than two years.

The interferon treatment is still controversial, and the long-term benefits and possible harmful affects are not fully known. Other drugs, such as lamivudine, currently licensed only for use in HIV infection, may offer much hope in treating hepatitis.[25]

A child who is a carrier of the disease can lead a normal life, although hepatitis can lead to liver disease. Regular exams and follow-up are important. In the meantime, letting every last person your child comes into contact with know that she carries the hepatitis B virus is not necessary. Because all children born in the United States since 1991 have been immunized, infecting other children is not a concern. Those in the medical professions are immunized against the disease, and those who do not have daily close contact with your child do not need to know, unless an exposure of blood or saliva occurs.

According to the Center for Disease Control, hepatitis B carriers should not be prohibited from pursuing any career. However, schools for professional health care providers may refuse infected candidates. Your child does need to know at an appropriate age that a sexual partner must be informed of his carrier status, because the disease is spread sexually. However, since all children born after 1991 are immunized against the disease, the child's future partner will probably be immune. Finally, an infected person can never donate blood or an organ.

You will probably have to educate yourself and the child's pediatrician about hepatitis B. As long as liver function tests are normal and the child is growing well, experts recommend the child have a yearly exam covering the entire initial medical evaluation, except for the hepatitis D screening. After she is ten years old, the child should have a blood test and ultrasound to screen for liver cancer. Some professionals believe that Asian children should be screened in the first decade of life, non-Asian children in their early twenties. Most people who are carriers of the disease, however, suffer no consequences. The long-term effects are known for those who stay in their own country, but not for those who receive the excellent medical care and nutrition available here. It appears that the lifetime risk of some complication is about 25 percent. Complications include an active case of hepatitis B, chronic liver infection, and a two-hundred-fold risk of developing liver cancer. Alcoholism, viral infections like HIB and HIV, and hepatitis C or D could lead to serious and even fatal complications. These statistics have been gathered from older subjects in other countries, but we now have better medicine, and the outlook for today's children is much improved. If it is detected early, even liver cancer is highly curable.

For more information on hepatitis B, contact:

The Hepatitis B Coalition
1573 Selby Avenue, Suite 229
St. Paul, MN 55104
(612) 647-9009

Centers for Disease Control and Prevention Hepatitis B
Hotline: (404) 322-455 code 234. Provides up-to-date information on the spread of disease and its prevention.

Hepatitis B Foundation
PO Box 464
New Hope, PA 18938
(215) 884-8786

Dr. Hari Conjeevaram
National Institute of Health
Liver Diseases Section
Building 10, Room 9C 103
Bethesda, MD 20892
(301) 496-1721

Intestinal Parasites and Bacteria

If the child has a history of parasites, has bloating, diarrhea, or weight loss, or if the child was walking before being abandoned to an agency, he should have repeated stool examinations for intestinal parasites. Intestinal parasites include roundworms, ringworms, pinworms, and tapeworms and are picked up from contaminated food or water. They can affect your child's nutritional status. Finding the exact kind of "worm" through a microscopic examination is the only way to give the child the right medication.

If your pharmacy does not have the medicines needed, your physician can order them from the Tropical Disease Center of the Tulane University Medical School, New Orleans, Louisiana.

Salmonella. Salmonella is a bacteria infection that affects the stomach and intestines. Symptoms include vomiting, diarrhea, fever, and severe abdominal pain. If the child got the disease from contaminated food, she can be excreting the bacteria in her stool for up to two months. Dispose of diapers properly and make sure you wash your hands thoroughly. If the child is older, make sure he washes his hands very carefully after going to the bathroom. The treatment for salmonella is Ampicillin or sulfa drugs.[26]

Tuberculosis. The American Academy of Pediatrics recommends that the Mantoux intradermal skin test be used to screen children from other countries. A candida control should be in place when this is administered, since the presence of candida (yeast infection) may give a false negative. Most children are not given the TB vaccine, but if it was given in the last year for any reason, the child will have a false-positive reading.[27]

Cytomegalovirus. Cytomegalovirus, or CMV, is a viral infection that is part of the herpes simplex 1 and 2 categories. It is the most common cause of congenital birth defects acquired during pregnancy. How it is transmitted is not completely understood, and although not highly contagious, it can be transmitted through sexual contact and contact with body fluids. CMV is chiefly found in poorer women in the developing countries of India, Africa, and Asia. It is a common medical diagnosis in international children, especially those from Asia, Africa, and India.

Symptoms are vague and include low-grade fever, sore throat, and swollen glands. Few cases are ever diagnosed. The disease itself poses no real problem to the child, and if you were to get it from the child, you would not have any serious consequences either. However, if a woman gets the disease for the first time and becomes pregnant in the next six months, the condition can cause hearing and vision loss and mental retardation in the child, especially in the first trimester of pregnancy. Therefore, if you have even a slight possibility of getting pregnant, and your child carries the antibodies for CMV, you will also want to be tested to see whether you are immune to CMV. Only 50 percent of women in upper- and middle-income groups are immune. If you have not built up enough CMV antibodies, you may want to consider using birth control, however strange it may seem to have to worry about getting pregnant after adopting a child.

Nutritional Concerns

Over 80 percent of today's internationally adopted children have spent most of their lives in an orphanage or hospital. Most of these child have been eating very simple diets and many of them have never had enough food. As a result, they may be small for their age, but often can "catch up" if given a proper diet.

You will want to find out from your agency the types of food the child is accustomed to and gradually add more American-type foods into the child's diet. Also, be aware that your child may need to be assured that food will be readily available all the time. Do not use food as a bribe or for punishment—food has far too much significance to a child who has never had enough.

If you are adopting a baby, she also may not have had enough formula, and when you start to feed her, she may drink so quickly that her stomach can actually "explode." Also, babies in some foreign countries are not started on solid foods until they are one year old. Author and adoptive parent O. Robin Sweet states that her daughter drank ninety-two ounces of formula every day for four months until she caught up to her age-appropriate weight. She also mentions that her son, who was adopted from Russia, was addicted to strong tea because it was readily available in his orphanage, unlike milk.

Many of these children cannot tolerate milk because their bodies cannot digest the sugar, lactose, that is found in milk and many milk products. This intolerance to lactose can cause diarrhea, vomiting, and excessive gas production. Asian children and infants who have been raised on vegetable-based formulas or goat's milk have the highest incidence of lactose intolerance. If your baby is lactose intolerant, she will require soybean-based formula such as Isomil or Pro-Sobee, which are readily available wherever formula is sold. An older child can get his calcium from lactose-free milk (such as Dairy-Ease) or from yogurt containing live acidophilus (such as Dannon).

When feeding your baby or small child, also realize that no one may have looked at your child while feeding him in the orphanage, and he may have to become accustomed to your looking and smiling at him when you feed him.[28]

For more on the health concerns of children adopted internationally, see:

Adoption Medical News by Adoption Advocates Press
1921 Ohio St. NE
Palm Bay, Florida 32907
407/724-0815

An excellent newsletter, written by a physician, that addresses health-related issues of adopted children.

Chapter Nineteen

Preparing for a Baby's Homecoming

In preparing for a new baby's homecoming, one of your first tasks will be to select a pediatrician. As an adoptive parent you will probably have special considerations. The first thing you will want to know is, what is the pediatrician's attitude toward adoption? When you interview a pediatrician, explain that you will be adopting a baby and would like to have the child examined a few days after birth. Ask whether the baby's medical records can be sent to her, since most hospitals will not give them to you directly. The doctor's response should give you a good idea of her attitude about adoption. Most pediatricians understand the situation and do not expect you to have the child's or birth parents' complete medical histories. If you are adopting a newborn infant, also ask whether the pediatrician would be willing to call the hospital physician who treated the baby to discuss the baby's overall health, since the records may not arrive for weeks.

If your child is born in another state, you may have to select a pediatrician there for the child's first visit. Call an adoption support group in that area for a recommendation.

Since many hospitals will probably give you a full medical history of the infant, you will want to have him examined within a day or two of his release from the hospital, not to determine whether he is healthy enough to proceed with the adoption but simply to reassure you that all is well. If there are any medical problems, they are almost certain to be minor ones, since no infant with a serious illness or condition would be released from the hospital. At this first visit you can begin to establish a rapport with the doctor, who may need to be called from time to time for general information or in case of an emergency.

Most pediatricians will tell you the baby's APGAR scores. This test, which is administered one and five minutes after birth, measures color, pulse rate, muscular tone, respiratory rate, and reflex activity, with a possible score of 0, 1, or 2 in each category. Ten is a perfect score.

INFANT CARE

Like any first-time parent you will want to know how to care for an infant. Most couples get some of this training in childbirth classes, but some hospitals, agencies, and adoption support groups now offer infant care and parenting classes. Call a local chapter of RESOLVE or some other adoption support group or for information. Classes usually cost about $25 to $50 for five sessions.

In addition to taking classes, it is a good idea to buy or borrow from the library a general baby care book such as Penelope Leach's *Your Child from Birth to Five Years Old*. Such books can be found in any general bookstore.

Breastfeeding/Bottle Feeding

You may have heard that adoptive mothers can breastfeed their children. This is true. And because there are many advantages for the child in receiving breast milk as opposed to formula, you may want to consider breastfeeding. Approach it realistically, however. Most women who have nursed an adopted infant did so for less than a month. It is difficult, tiring, and even at maximum milk production supplies only 25 percent of the milk your child needs. The rest must come from formula. Of course, getting some human milk, with its natural antibodies, is better than formula alone.

If you decide to pursue this option, your doctor may offer to prescribe hormones—prolactin and oxytocin—to cause milk production. Debra Stewart Peterson suggests in *Breastfeeding the Adopted Baby*, however, that you not take these drugs. She says the baby's regular nursing will send the message to the pituitary gland to produce these hormones naturally, stimulating milk production. Also, some women experience fatigue with these medications.

To prepare for nursing an adopted child, Peterson suggests wearing nipple shells to stimulate the hormone oxytocin, instead of pumping your breasts before the baby is placed with you. Once the baby is with you, you can start using a supplemental device called Supplemental Nutrition System (R) or Lact-Aid (R). These involve tubes that connect a bottle of formula to your nipples. Every time the child is fed, she is nursing at the same time she is getting formula from a bottle. The more relaxed you are, writes Peterson, the easier it is to build up your own milk supply. Of course, you may find it difficult to get the formula warmed up and attach the nursing tubing to your breasts while your infant is crying for milk, especially in the middle of the night.

Even if you know ahead of time that you would like to try nursing your infant, you may not want to pump your breasts, wear nipple shells, or take hormones before the child's birth in case the birth mother changes her mind or the adoption does not proceed as quickly as you had anticipated. And one final note:

Although you can produce breast milk, you cannot produce colostrum, a thin, yellowish fluid that is secreted by a woman in the first days after childbirth and that is present in the milk for weeks afterward. Colostrum is rich in antibodies and minerals and is considered very beneficial to infants. You can get colostrum from other nursing mothers, if you can find someone who is willing to pump; just make sure the woman is someone you know well, because drugs, alcohol, bacteria, and viruses can be passed to the baby through her milk.

Resources:

For further information, contact the **La Leche League**. They publish *Nursing Your Adopted Baby* for $4.95 including shipping and handling. Call 1 (800) LA LECHE.

Debra Stewart Peterson's book *Breastfeeding the Adopted Baby* is published by Corona Publishing Company, San Antonio, TX, 1994. For a copy of that book and supplies such as a breast pump, supplemental feeding system, and breast shells, call (801) 392-9074.

Ross Laboratories, the producers of Similac baby formula, sponsor a **Welcome Addition Club**. Call 1 (800) BABYLINE to register. You can receive a free twelve-can case of ready-to-feed formula, coupons, printed material, and baby gifts. You can also request the "Adoptive Gift Package."

Infant Equipment

Of course you will be excited about preparing a nursery. We recommend, however, that you not set up a nursery until you actually have the baby. Just keep the room in reserve, ready for a baby, and if you like, cover the walls in a color scheme that will coordinate with baby decor. We decorated what was the nursery in yellow wallpaper—just in case we ever had children. When selecting the pattern, we knew we could not stand to look at teddy bears or other baby motifs until we actually had a child.

You may want to ask some friends or family to hold on to a few basic items, such as undershirts and one-piece pajamas, a bassinet or cradle, and a car seat. You might make arrangements with a friend whose child has outgrown his infant gear and clothing to use some of these items until you purchase them yourself or receive them as gifts. As soon as you take the baby home, your friends and family will probably inundate you with gifts. In any case, the only items you will really need to begin with are some warm blankets and a few outfits. The hospital usually sends the child home with formula and diapers, and you will not need a crib until the child is about two or three months old. In fact, if you suddenly get a call to pick up a baby, there's nothing wrong with taking a drawer out of the bureau and lining it with blankets for a cradle.

NAMING THE CHILD

Selecting a name for an adopted child is not very different from selecting a name for a biological child. Sometimes, however, there may be special considerations.

In years past the birth mother selected the child's name, and the adoptive parents called the child by that name. During the last few decades, however, the birth mother has selected a name to go on the original birth certificate, and the adoptive parents have selected another name that goes on the child's permanent birth certificate. Now, as open adoption becomes more acceptable, a birth mother may request that you give the child a name she has selected, or you may request that she put the name you have selected on the original birth certificate. Why? Because when you communicate with the birth parents, it is easier and less awkward for everyone to refer to the child by the same name. You do not want the birth mother referring to the child as Melinda when you named her Catherine. By keeping the names similar or the same, you preserve the child's original identity instead of taking it away. When older adoptees meet their birth mothers, the first two questions they often ask are "What did you name me?" and "Why did you place me for adoption?"

If your birth mother asks you to give the child a name you do not like, consider using it as a middle name. Sometimes, however, you may need to suggest that she reconsider the name she has chosen. If the birth mother tells you that she is giving the child a name she has always loved, or is naming him after a dear cousin who died, or is selecting a name for some other very strong reason, suggest that she not do so. Encourage her to choose a name that she truly loves but to save the "special" name for later when she is married and prepared to raise a child. If she gives the child a name that has a strong sentimental association, she may identify the adoption with that person or tragic event. For example, she does not need to be reminded of her adoption plans every time she hears her deceased father's name mentioned.

If your child is of a certain nationality, such as Spanish, and clearly looks Spanish, and you and your spouse are of Norwegian extraction, giving your child a very Nordic family name may cause comment: "How did such a dark-haired boy get the name Leif?" Try not to select a name that will make the child feel he must continually explain that he is adopted.

Once you have selected a name, discuss your choice with the birth mother, if you feel it is appropriate to do so. Perhaps together you can agree on a name for the baby.

T he names, addresses and telephone numbers of each state's adoption specialist, state bar association, and Interstate Compact on the Placement of Children Unit are listed, as well as adoption attorneys, private adoption agencies, and adoption support groups. How each can be of assistance to you is briefly discussed below.

THE STATE ADOPTION SPECIALIST

The adoption specialist is usually in the state's social services office (or Office of Children's Protective Services). Sometimes this person also serves in the office of the Interstate Compact on the Placement of Children (see below). This specialist should have a comprehensive view of the state's adoption system and may provide statistical data, the names of licensed agencies, details about adoption statutes, subsidized adoption programs, and other information.

The specialist's staff may also be able to recommend attorneys who are thorough and who submit paperwork in a timely manner.

If you feel that an agency or attorney is not handling your case ethically or properly, you can call the state specialist to question the procedure. Do not report any unethical practices to this office, because complaints of this nature should be directed to the attorneys' ethics office of the state bar association or the state Supreme Court. Complaints concerning agencies should be directed to the adoption agency licensing office in the state's department of social services.

THE STATE BAR ASSOCIATION

Most bar associations will refer you to attorneys who practice family and adoption law. Be aware that an attorney listed as practicing family law most likely handles divorces and not adoptions. If the attorney indicates that he does handle adoptions, make sure he has experience handling your type of adoption, as many attorneys have only handled agency or stepparent adoptions. When you receive a referral, check the attorney's credentials with another source (e.g., a member of an adoption support group or RESOLVE).

The state bar association may also give information about appropriate legal fees.

In discussing your specific adoption with an attorney, do not hesitate to ask the attorney detailed questions, such as whether he will interact directly with a birth mother in a private adoption (and if he has done so in the past), or with the agency social worker in an agency adoption. Also, will the attorney review agency surrender documents or international adoption decrees before an adoption is finalized? Many attorneys who indicate they do adoptions simply mean they will file the court documents at the time you are ready for court. The involvement of these attorneys is quite limited and can be inadequate; for example, we have had many couples tell us that a particular attorney was "an adoption attorney," and yet, the same attorney never assisted with picking the baby up from the hospital nor in interacting with the hospital social worker prior to delivery or the discharge of the birth mother from the hospital.

THE INTERSTATE COMPACT ON THE PLACEMENT OF CHILDREN (ICPC)

Because adoptive couples and birth parents often live in different states, the need to regulate the interstate movement of children was recognized as early as the 1950s. The Interstate Compact on the Placement of Children provides such a mechanism, and also outlines the procedure for the orderly transfer of children across state lines. The ICPC states that each state must have an office (or a separate unit of its social services agency) to monitor the individuals, organizations, or other entities involved in the placement of children in other states.

These include:

- The birth mother and birth father
- The adoption agency
- Any other person having custody of the child, including grandparents and other relatives
- Any corporation or association
- A court
- The state or the appropriate agency, or a subdivision of a state agency

The Compact does not involve the placement of a child by a family member into the home of another close relative, unless the child is in the custody of the state social services department. It only covers children placed through the foster care system, court-ordered placements of children, and children placed for adoption into the homes of nonrelatives.

Within the legal language of the Compact, the birth mother of a child to be placed is called the "sending agency," and the state from which the child comes is called the "sending state." (Note: If a birth mother's rights have been terminated and an adoption agency is involved, then the agency is known as the sending agency.) The sending ICPC office or unit retains jurisdiction over the child when he or she crosses a state line to the "receiving state." Keeping jurisdiction means that the ICPC unit receives supervisory reports and other regular reports detailing the child's adjustment to the new home and general progress. (Generally, this information comes from the post-placement supervisory visits, which are similar to a home study.) It also means that if the sending ICPC unit or sending agency (birth mother or adoption agency) believes that the adoptive family is not providing a home in "the best interests" of the child, then the sending ICPC unit or sending agency has the right to petition the court to have the child removed from the home.

The sending ICPC unit must be given the adoptive couple's approved home study before the child is placed with the adoptive parents. Until an adoption is finalized, the sending agency is technically responsible for the legal and financial protection of the child.

States began participating in the Compact beginning in 1960. New Jersey was the last state to join in 1990. All states now participate in the Compact and have enacted similar Compact laws.

While ICPC laws in each state are generally the same, certain guidelines vary. For example, some states require that the home study include a criminal and child-abuse clearance provided by the appropriate state law enforcement agency, while others simply request a letter stating that the couple has no criminal history from the couple's home town police department.

Connecticut residents are required to use only an "approved" agency in the state in which the child is born. In fact, many states' ICPC guidelines mandate that a couple's home study be completed only by an approved adoption agency, and not by a certified social worker, who is normally allowed to provide home studies for instate adoptions.

If you are adopting a child from out of state, it is critical that your attorney know the regulations for both the sending and the receiving states. Sometimes the guidelines for each state can appear contradictory. For example, in Virginia the adoptive and birth parents must know each other's names and addresses, while another state may require that all information be kept confidential. Also, sometimes the ICPC guidelines or state laws can change. Therefore, your attorney should talk with the correct personnel in the ICPC units for exact regulations and procedures. He should do this even if you have retained an attorney in the sending state. Unless your attorney has dealt extensively with the attorney in the sending state, he or she should not simply assume the other attorney knows his own state adoption laws and ICPC regulations.

Each state has a compact administrator, as well as one or more deputy administrators, who are responsible for day-to-day tasks. The deputy compact administrator generally handles all telephone calls and correspondence, and grants the necessary approval to place a child with an out-of-state couple.

Contacting the right person at the ICPC office and having your attorney(s) quickly submit the correct paperwork is very important when the child you are about to adopt is in another state. Until all the required documents are submitted to and approved by the ICPC offices of both the sending and receiving states, the adoptive couple is not allowed to cross state lines with the child.

For example, if you are from New York and you locate a baby born in Utah, you will most likely go to Utah once the infant is discharged from the hospital. However, you cannot leave the state with the child until the ICPC offices in both Utah and New York give you permission. If the paperwork is not processed properly, you could find yourself living in a hotel for a couple of weeks with your new baby while you wait for approval from the ICPC offices. Of course, you want an attorney who will process all paperwork very quickly so that you can return home as soon as possible.

Do not depend on the ICPC personnel to fully assist you. Many ICPC offices are very helpful and do take the time to provide information; most are particularly helpful in dealing with attorneys who want a list of that state's ICPC requirements. However, many of the units are understaffed, so your lawyer should develop a good relationship with the adoption attorney in the state where the baby is born so that he or she can monitor the flow of paper and any new requests for information put forth by the ICPC offices.

ADOPTION ATTORNEYS

The adoption attorneys listed are either members of the American Academy of Adoption Attorneys or attorneys who have conducted a significant number of adoptions and are well versed in adoption law. In some states in which the population is very low, an attorney may conduct only a few adoptions, but the attorney should still be very knowledgeable. None of the attorneys are endorsed by the authors. Call a local RESOLVE support group or adoption support group members to determine if other people have used the attorney. Also, you can telephone the ICPC office and ask for names of attorneys who practice adoption law regularly in that state.

ADOPTION LAW: QUESTIONS AND ANSWERS

This section is provided to answer some of the most commonly asked questions about adoption law, primarily for those adopting independently or through a private agency. We have not attempted to address the laws and regulations relative to adoptions in which the birth parents' rights have been terminated due to abuse or neglect. However, some of the laws we do discuss can be applied to such situations.

Laws are subject to change, and even within a state, there can be county-by-county differences based on the way a judge interprets the law.

Several guides were considered in addressing the questions, including *Adoption Laws: Answers to the Most-Asked Questions*, published by the National Adoption Information Clearinghouse. In addition, scores of attorneys were interviewed, as well as the state adoption specialists and/or staff at ICPC units in nearly every state to determine how the law is actually practiced there.

Can an attorney serve as an intermediary?

This question asks whether an attorney can "find" a birth mother for an adoptive couple. In most states this is permissible as long as the attorney is not paid for her role as the intermediary. In several other states, an attorney technically is not even supposed to tell an adoptive couple about a birth mother. In many states that permit intermediaries, an attorney cannot directly place the baby with a couple. He may refer the birth mother to the adoptive couple, and the parties must then communicate with each other, either face-to-face or through letters or telephone calls.

In these states, an attorney cannot operate like an agency. The birth mother cannot place the baby first with the attorney and allow him or her to then select the adoptive parents. The attorney also cannot present information about and pictures of several couples to a birth mother and let her choose the couple.

Also, in many states the attorney cannot charge a fee for assisting a couple with finding a birth mother. Some judges will not even allow an attorney to charge an hourly rate for the services involved in finding and making arrangements to match a birth mother with an adoptive couple. Instead, the attorney may only charge a flat rate related to legal services provided, regardless of whether the couple finds a birth mother or not. Sometimes an attorney who does locate birth mothers for couples will have a higher fee than one who does not.

Is advertising permitted?

In most states and Washington, D.C., you can place an adoption advertisement in a newspaper. Some newspapers may have their own restrictions and may require you to have a letter from your attorney verifying that your interest in adoption is legitimate.

The *Gale Directory of Publications and Broadcast Media* provides a state-by-state listing of newspapers and magazines in the United States and Canada. This can be found in your library's reference section.

To obtain an up-to-date list of more than 700 newspapers and magazines that accept adoption ads, send a $10.00 check to:

Adoption Home Study Services
307 Sassafras Drive
Taylors, SC 29687

Who must consent to the adoption?

In almost all states, if a birth mother does not sign a surrender, then she must at least provide a written consent to the adoption. A consent or surrender is not necessary in those situations in which her rights are terminated because of mental illness, child abuse, neglect, etc. State laws vary on the circumstances in which a birth father's consent is required. A small number of states do not even require a birth parent's written consent before placement; the birth parents must, however, receive notice of the hearing that terminates their parental rights. It is a wise practice, however, to have in writing the birth parents' consent to the adoption (at the very least, that of the birth mother's) to avoid any later allegations of wrongdoing or kidnapping.

When a birth parent is under 18 years of age, a parent or court-appointed guardian may also have to consent to the adoption.

Again, after consent is given, the birth parents usually must be notified of the court hearing that will terminate their rights.

What is the difference between a birth mother's consent to adoption and the surrender or relinquishment of her parental rights?

A document that indicates that the birth mother is consenting to the adoption of her child by the adoptive couple is often referred to as the birth mother's consent to adoption. The birth mother's rights are not terminated by her signing this consent document; it is simply a statement by her that she is agreeable to the placement of her child with the adoptive couple, knowing that the couple will start legal proceedings to adopt the child. It is written evidence that the adoptive couple has physical custody of the child with the birth mother's approval.

A document which, if signed by the birth mother, terminates her parental rights, is known as a surrender or relinquishment of parental rights and is often referred to simply as a surrender or relinquishment. Most states allow only an approved adoption agency to "take a surrender" after several hours of counseling with a birth mother and birth father. Obviously, signing such a document is a serious matter and all attempts must be made to ensure that the birth parents really want to place the baby for adoption and understand fully the consequences of their actions. As an aside, the counseling provided must also inform the birth parents of state financial assistance available to them if they decide to keep the child. Some states allow an attorney or certified social worker to take a surrender without involving an adoption agency.

Some states allow the surrender document to be signed in front of a notary or an attorney, but some require that it be signed in court before a judge. Many states specify that the birth parent's rights are terminated immediately upon signing the surrender documents, while other states have a revocation period that allows the birth parents to revoke their surrender of parental rights within a specific amount of time. Such revocation periods are noted where applicable.

Because most of the state laws we reviewed referred to the surrender document as a "consent," the section on surrender of parental rights also uses "consent" to describe the termination of parental rights. Many attorneys and agency social workers also refer to the surrender as the consent. In discussing the termination of parental rights with an attorney or ICPC staff, it is wise to confirm that the consent referred to has the same legal effect as the surrender of parental rights.

What is a notice of an adoption hearing?

Notice of the adoption hearing must be given to the birth parents unless they waive their rights to this notice, which some states allow, or unless, as indicated before, they have already signed surrender documents. The notice document states that the adoptive couple (usually first names only) desires to adopt "Baby Boy Smith" and a hearing will be held on the matter; the time, date, and place of the hearing are also stated. Some states require that the adoption petition or complaint be served on the birth parent by a process server. Most states, except Virginia, allow all confidential information about the adoptive couple to be "whited out." Usually the birth parents must be given notice within a specified time period (usually between twenty to thirty days) prior to the hearing. How this is given varies from state to state. Sometimes notice is given in person (which means that a process server or law enforcement officer personally hands the legal documents to the birth parent), while other states allow the notice to be provided by certified mail. If the birth parent cannot be found or their identity is not known, notice is given by publication in a newspaper. Exactly what is published depends of course on the state; the notice is placed in the legal notes section of a newspaper along with notices of foreclosure actions and local zoning board applications and meetings. The basic contents of such a notice are that a baby was born on a certain date to the birth mother, the birth father is alleged to be the father of the child, and if he desires to assert his parental rights to the baby before the adoption is finalized he must do so within a certain time frame.

Several states, such as North Carolina, allow birth parents twenty-one days after signing a surrender to revoke it. In many states such as New Jersey and South Carolina, the surrender is not revocable unless the birth parents can show they were coerced into signing, or that they did not understand the seriousness of their actions because they were taking medications at the time that affected their judgment.

A small number of states require the birth parents to testify in court that they signed the surrender documents with full knowledge and understanding and that it was their intention to place the baby for adoption; until this is done, the surrenders can be revoked within a certain time period (ten to forty-five days). In lieu of the birth parents' attending a court hearing, some states allow the adoptive couple's attorney to present to the judge the signed surrender documents for the judge's inspection and approval.

Again, if an attorney or ICPC staff member discusses adoption law and practice with terms such as "consent" or "surrender," be sure to ask for definitions. It is important to know whether "consent" as used in that attorney's state means termination of parental rights or simply the birth mother's written statement of approval that the adoptive parents have custody of the baby with the intentions to adopt him or her. Ask whether there is a time period for revocation; also, ask if the birth parents must go to court to finalize the surrender in front of a judge.

What is a petition or complaint for adoption?

To schedule an adoption hearing in court, the attorney for the couple files with the clerk of the court (usually the family court clerk of court) an adoption petition or complaint, usually in the county in which the couple lives. The petition tells the court the adoptive couple's desire to adopt the baby placed with them. The identities of the birth mother and birth father are disclosed; if the identity of the birth father is not known or the birth mother refuses to name him, then this is stated. The petition for adoption also requests that the judge terminate the birth parents' rights (if they have not already been terminated) and finalize the adoption. The information most often required in a petition is:

- Identifying information about the adoptive parents, including names, ages, and addresses
- The relationship between the adoptive parents and the child
- The legal reason that the birth parents' rights are being terminated
- An explanation of why the adoption is in the child's best interest
- Proof that the adoptive parents are fit to adopt the child
- The name of the guardian appointed for the child, if required, and
- The name of the adoption agency or certified social worker chosen by the court to conduct post-placement supervision and to provide a written report to the court.

Some states require that only one hearing be held to terminate birth parents' rights and to finalize the adoption. Other states have a two-step process. The first hearing, scheduled ten to ninety days after placement, is known as a preliminary hearing, which allows the judge to terminate the rights of the birth parents (assuming they have no objections) and to review the home study report. The final hearing is scheduled months later and simply allows more time for the placement to be reviewed by the court vis-à-vis the post-supervisory visit reports. The preliminary hearing is the critical one; the rights of the birth parents are terminated and the adoptive couple acquire "the legal rights of parents" but not the legal title of parents. The purpose of the final hearing has nothing to do with the birth parents' rights, because these have already been terminated. Rather, it is to allow the state to further evaluate by home visits the fitness of the adoptive couple as the parents of the child to be adopted. It is at the final hearing that the adoptive couple acquire the legal title of parents.

The judgment of adoption or order of adoption is signed by the judge holding the hearing and is the legal document that states the adoptive couple have legally adopted the child. This document allows the birth certificate to be revised showing the adoptive couple as parents as of the date of birth of the adopted child.

When can consent be taken from birth mother (father) and how long after the consent is signed can it be revoked?

In most states, a birth mother cannot sign a surrender form until after the baby's birth. In states in which she can sign it before the birth, it is not valid until after the birth. In many states, the surrender cannot be signed until seventy-two hours or more after the baby's birth.

In some states, a birth mother can also revoke her surrender within a certain time period (such as ten to thirty days after signing). If this happens, the court usually must then determine what is in the child's best interest.

A birth mother's surrender in some states, such as South Carolina, automatically terminates her rights. In other states, a birth mother signs a surrender, but her rights must also be terminated by a judge (e.g., Colorado).

What are the birth father's rights?

See Chapter 8 for more information on this issue.

What fees can the adoptive parents pay?

In most states, adoptive parents are allowed to pay reasonable fees associated with the adoption so that placing a child is not financially burdensome to a birth mother. However, direct payment to the birth mother for placing a child for adoption is illegal in all states. State laws vary as to the penalty for this crime, but in nearly all states, baby-buying is grounds for a birth mother to revoke her consent, even after the adoption is finalized.

In all states the adoptive parents can pay for medical fees and their own legal fees, and in most states, the adoptive parents can also pay for some living expenses. However, the issue is subject to much interpretation. Often an attorney will, as required by some state laws, have all living expenses preapproved by the judge who will oversee the adoption. Because living expenses for a birth mother can be high (for example, if a birth mother lives at a fancy hotel), most judges place a cap on what is considered "reasonable."

Another rule of thumb for defining reasonable expenses is that after all adoption-related expenses are paid, the birth mother should not have a financial gain. In other words, she should not have extra money in her bank account or a new car in her driveway as a result of placing the baby for adoption.

Where does the final adoption take place?

In most states you and your baby will attend an adoption finalization. This usually takes place at your county courthouse. If your child was born in your state, your attorney may suggest that the adoption proceedings take place in the county where the child was born, depending upon the presiding judge. For example, one judge may define "reasonable" living expenses that can be paid to the birth mother more broadly than another judge. You may want the more lenient judge to finalize your adoption.

If you are finalizing the adoption in another state (usually the state where the baby was born), you will probably go to court in the county where the baby was born. NOTE: In some states you cannot finalize an adoption unless you are a resident.

How are familial and step-parent adoptions different from nonbiological adoptions?

When a relative or step-parent is adopting a child, the laws will often be more lenient and requirements such as the home study may be less stringent or waived altogether. In general, the legal process is much easier unless the adoption is contested.

Can a nonresident finalize an adoption in the state?

If you adopt a child who is born outside of your state, you may have the option of finalizing the adoption in that state. However, many states do not permit you to adopt unless you are a resident.

NOTE: If you plan to advertise in a state where you are not a resident and, because of your state adoption laws, you also need to finalize the adoption there, call an attorney or the ICPC in that state and make sure you are still permitted to finalize there. (For example, if you live in Georgia and you find a birth mother through advertising in another state, you cannot finalize the adoption in Georgia.) To spend the money on advertising only to find out that you cannot finalize in that state is a waste of time and money.

If you just moved to a state, the laws specifying how long you have to live in a state before you can adopt generally do not apply. You can usually proceed with your adoption plans, since by the time the adoption is finalized you will have lived in the state long enough to qualify for residency.

ADOPTION AGENCIES AND SUPPORT GROUPS

In an attempt to make this book a complete adoption resource we have included lists of private adoption agencies and support groups for each state. There are also numerous public adoption agencies, and the adoption specialist's office of each state can forward you a list or refer to the proper state office for more information about state-operated adoption agencies. Since there was no way for us to confirm the professionalism and competency of all the adoption agencies and support groups listed, check with a local adoption support group for references. Also, you or your attorney can call the state office responsible for licensing adoption agencies for background information on any particular agency. Your attorney can also call the person at your local family court who is responsible for processing adoption cases; this person can probably provide a reference to a particular agency.

ALABAMA

State Adoption Specialist
Shirley Scanlan
Alabama Department of Human
  Resources
Division of Family and Children's
  Services
50 North Ripley Street
Montgomery, AL 36130-1801
(205) 242-9500

Compact Administrator
P.L. Corely, Acting Administrator
Alabama Department of Human
  Resources
S. Gordon Persons Building, 2nd
  Floor
50 Ripley Street
Montgomery, AL 36130-1801
(334) 242-1160

Deputy Compact Administrator
Sharon Mintz, Consultant
Office of Protective Services
Alabama Department of Human
  Resources
S. Gordon Persons Building, 2nd
  Floor
50 Ripley Street
Montgomery, AL 36130-1801
(334) 242-9500

Adoption
Barbara Berg, Consultant
Office of Adoption
(address same as above)
(334) 242-9500

All correspondence and telephone
calls should be directed to the
Deputy Compact Administrator.

Office hours:
Monday-Friday
8:00 A.M.-4:30 P.M.
Central Time Zone

State Licensing Specialist
Virginia Gorman
Alabama Department of Human
  Resources
Division of Family and Children's
  Services
50 Ripley Street
Montgomery, AL 36130-4000
(334) 242-9500

**State Adoption Exchange and
  Photo Listing**
Alabama Adoption Resource
  Exchange
Alabama Department of Human
  Resources
Division of Family and Children's
  Services
50 North Ripley Street
Montgomery, AL 36310-4000
(334) 242-9500

Private Adoption Agencies

Alabama Baptist Children's Home
1404 16th Avenue, S.E.
P.O. Box 1805
Decatur, AL 35602
(205) 355-6892

Alabama Baptist Children's Home
6512 Grelot Road
P.O. Box 91294
Mobile, AL 36691
(334) 639-1022

Alabama Baptist Children's Home
715 Elm Street
P.O. Box 429
Troy, AL 36081
(334) 566-2840

Association for Guidance, Aid,
  Placement and Empathy
  (AGAPE)
P.O. Box 3887
Huntsville, AL 35810
(205) 859-4481

Association for Guidance, Aid,
  Placement and Empathy
  (AGAPE)
P.O. Box 850663
Mobile, AL 35810
(205) 859-4481

Association for Guidance, Aid,
  Placement and Empathy
  (AGAPE)
P.O. Box 230472
Montgomery, AL 36116
(334) 272-9466

Catholic Family Services
P.O. Box 745
Huntsville, AL 35801
(205) 536-0041

Catholic Family Services
733 37th Street East
Tuscaloosa, AL 35405
(205) 553-9045

Catholic Social Services
2164 11th Avenue South
Birmingham, AL 35265
(334) 324-6561

Catholic Social Services
P.O. Box 759
Mobile, AL 36601
(334) 438-1603

Catholic Social Services
P.O. Box 454
Montgomery, AL 36101
(334) 269-2387

Alabama State Bar Association
P.O. Box 671
Montgomery, AL 36101
(334) 269-1515

Adoption Attorneys

Maryon A. Allen
631 Beacon Parkway West, #102
Birmingham, AL 35209
(205) 290-0077

William Blanchard
505 South Perry Street
Montgomery, AL 36104
(205) 269-9691

David Patterson Broome*
McDonough and Broome
P.O. Box 1944
Mobile, AL 36633-1944
        or
107 St. Francis Street
First National Band Building
Suite 1408
Mobile, AL 36602

(334) 432-9933
fax (334) 432-9706
fax (205) 432-3300

* Mr. Broom has conducted
  about 100 independent
  adoptions and about five
  international adoptions.

R. A. Ferguson, Jr.
290 21st. Street North, #600
Birmingham, AL 35203
(205) 251-2823

Beth M. Lyons
28 North Florida Street
Mobile, AL 26607
(205) 476-7857

Bryant A. Whitmore, Jr.*
215 North Street, Suite 501
Birmingham, AL 35203
(205) 324-6631
fax (205) 324-6632

* Mr. Whitmore has completed
more than 200 independent
adoptions.

ALABAMA LAWS RELATED TO ADOPTION: QUESTIONS AND ANSWERS

Can an attorney serve as an intermediary?
Yes, but an attorney can only provide outreach services to birth mothers; he or she cannot directly place a child with the adoptive parents.

Is advertising permitted?
Yes.

Who must consent to the adoption?
1. The birth mother
2. The birth mother's husband, regardless of whether or not he is the birth father, if he and the birth mother were married and the baby was born during the marriage or within 300 days after the marriage ended; or before the child's birth if he and birth mother had tried to marry, even if the marriage is invalid
3. A man whose name is on the birth certificate, or one who openly admits that the child is his
4. The adoption agency that has legal custody of the adoptee, unless the court orders placement without the agency's consent
5. The presumed father, if he is known to the court and if he responds within thirty days to the notice he receives

If one or both of the biological parents is under the age of nineteen, a guardian must be appointed to represent the birth parents' interests.

When can consent be taken from the birth mother (father), and how long after the consent is signed can it be revoked?
Bryant Whitmore, an adoption attorney in Birmingham, states that consent can be taken before or after birth and can be revoked within five days after the date of the child's birth or of the signing of consent, whichever day is later. A birth mother has up to fourteen days to withdraw her consent if the court finds it is in the child's best interests.

Generally, independent adoptions are finalized ninety days after birth, and agency adoptions are finalized 180 days after birth.

What are the birth father's rights?
His rights are the same as the birth mother's, but it is essential to consult your attorney, as each case is different. The unwed birth father's consent can be dispensed if he signs an affidavit saying that he is not the father or indicating that he has no interest in the child. His consent is also not necessary if he has not provided support or communicated with the child for a period of six months; the birth father's rights are considered terminated after this six-month period by reason of abandonment. While it is not clear from case law whether the birth father must receive notice of the adoption hearing if he does abandon his parental rights, it is wise to ensure the receipt of such notice. The birth father's rights

are terminated if he does not respond within thirty days after being provided notice of the adoption proceeding. If he can not be located or if his identity is unknown, then he can be served by publication; that is, a notice of the adoption proceeding is placed in a newspaper in the town or county of his last known whereabouts. If he does not respond to such publication, then his rights are terminated.

What fees can adoptive parents pay?

Adoptive parents can pay reasonable fees such as medical, living, and legal expenses with court approval.

Where does the adoption hearing take place?

The hearing can take place in the county in which the adoptive parents live, the child lives, or where the agency that has custody of the child is located.

How are familial and step-parent adoptions different from nonbiological adoptions?

Home studies are very seldom required, and there is no requirement as to disclosure of fees and costs. There is a one-year waiting period for a child in the home before the adoption can proceed. In step-parent and relative adoptions, visitation rights for grandparents may be given at the discretion of the court.

Can a nonresident finalize an adoption in this state?

Yes. After the child is placed in the adoptive home, at least one adoptive parent must be able to be at home with the child for at least sixty days.

ALASKA

State Adoption Specialist
Suzanne Maxson
Alaska Department of Health and
 Social Services
Division of Family and Youth
 Services
P.O. Box 110630
Juneau, AK 99811-0630
(907) 465-3631

Compact Administrator
L. Diane Worley, Director
Alaska Department of Health and
 Social Services
Division of Family and Youth
 Services
P.O. Box H-05
Juneau, AK 99811-0630

Deputy Compact Administrator
DeeAnn Grummet
Division of Family and Youth
 Services
Dept. of Health and Social Services
P.O. Box H-05
Juneau, AK 99811-0630
 or
Alaska Office Building
350 Main Street, Room 411
Juneau, AK 99801

(907) 465-2105
fax (907) 465-3190

Direct correspondence and
telephone calls should be directed
to the Deputy Compact
Administrator.

Office hours:
Monday-Friday
8:00 A.M-4:30 P.M.
Alaska Time Zone

Private Adoption Agencies

Adoption Advocates
 International
218 Martin Drive
Fairbanks, AK 99712
(907) 457-3832

Alaska International Adoptions
3605 Arctic, #1177
Anchorage, AK 99503
(907) 276-8018

Catholic Social Services
225 Cordova Street, Building B
Anchorage, AK 99501
(907) 276-5590

Fairbanks Counseling and
 Adoption
753 Gaffney Road
Box 71544
Fairbanks, AK 99707
(907) 456-4729

Kawerak Adoption Agency
P.O. Box 948
Nome, AK 99762
(907) 443-5231

Western Association of
 Concerned Adoptive Parents
P.O. Box 81865
Fairbanks, AK 99708
(907) 479-2895

**Adoptive Parent Support
 Groups and Postadoption
 Services**

Anchorage Adoptive Parents
 Association
Attn.: Fred Getty
550 West 7th, Suite 1780
Anchorage, AK 99502
(907) 276-1680

North American Council on
Adoptable Children State
Representative
Attn.: Sue White
1018 26th Avenue
Fairbanks, AK 99701
(907) 452-5397

**Adopted Person and Birth
Relative Support Groups**

Adoptee Liberty Movement
Association (ALMA)
P.O. Box 104281
Anchorage, AK 99501
(907) 376-6344

Adoptee Liberty Movement
Association (ALMA)
P.O. Box 585
Douglas, AK 99824
(907) 364-3133

Concerned United Birthparents
7105 Shoresin Circle
Anchorage, AK 99504
(907) 333-2272

Alaska State Bar Association
P.O. Box 100279
Anchorage, AK 99510
(907) 272-7469
Referral Service
(907) 272-0352

Adoption Attorneys

Robert W. Finn
717 K Street
Anchorage, AK 99501
(907) 276-1592Sharon L. Gleason
360 K Street
Anchorage, AK 99501
(907) 276-5231

Chip Wagoner
204 North Franklin, Suite 3
Juneau, AK 99801
(907) 586-1867

Frederick T. Sloan*
3003 Minnesota Drive, Suite 301
Anchorage, AK 99503
907) 272-4471

* Mr. Sloan has completed about
fifty independent adoptions and
has also done some agency and
international adoptions.

R. Brock Shamberg
P.O. Box 110295
Anchorage, AK 99511
(907) 345-3855

Attorney fees in this state are
about $1,700 to $3,000.

ALASKA LAWS RELATED TO ADOPTION: QUESTIONS AND ANSWERS

Can an attorney serve as an intermediary?
Yes.

Is advertising permitted?
Yes.

Who must consent to the adoption?
The birth mother, and the birth father if he is married to the birth mother

**When can consent be taken from the birth mother (father), and how long after the
consent is signed can it be revoked?**
Consent can be taken at any time before or after the birth. The birth parents have up to
ten days after birth to withdraw the consent if it was signed prior to delivery. If the consent is signed after birth, then the ten-day revocation period begins from the date of
signing.

What are the birth father's rights?
The birth father's consent to the adoption is required if he has legitimized the child by
marrying the mother. It is doubtful that the requirement of marriage to assert birth father
rights would hold up in the state Supreme Court or in the U.S. Supreme Court. If the
birth father acknowledged the child as his, maintained contact with the child, and supported him or her monetarily, then marrying the birth mother to assert his rights would
not be necessary in view of the Supreme Court cases dealing with birth father rights. If the
birth father has not had contact with the child for six months, then it is presumed that he
has abandoned his parental rights and his consent is not necessary.

What fees can adoptive parents pay?

Adoptive parents must submit all expenses to the court. The report should include expenses for the child's birth and placement, the birth mother's medical care, and adoption services (agency adoption).

Where does the adoption hearing take place?

The hearing may take place in the district in which adoptive parents live, the child lives, or where the agency is located.

How are familial and step-parent adoptions different from nonbiological adoptions?

There are few requirements regarding birth parent notice and the home study. No disclosure of fees is required. Grandparents may have visitation rights if a step-parent or other grandparent has adopted the child.

Can a nonresident finalize an adoption in this state?

Yes.

In addition to state laws, rules must be followed that are written in the Alaska Rules of Court. An adoption attorney should have this rule book.

ARIZONA

State Adoption Specialist
Carole Linker
Arizona Department of Economic
Security
P.O. Box 6123, site code 940A
Phoenix, AZ 85005
(602) 542-2362

Compact Administrator
Linda Blessing, Director
Department of Economic Security
P.O. Box 6123
Phoenix, AZ 85005

Deputy Compact Administrator
Mike Chapman
Department of Economic Security
3225 North Central Avenue,
10th Floor
Phoenix, AZ 85007
(602) 235-9134, ext. 7102

**Administrative Assistant to the
Deputy Compact
Administrator**
Marilyn Whites
(602) 235-9134, ext. 7100

Office hours:
Monday-Friday
8:00 AM-4:30 PM
(All paperwork should be in by
3:30 P.M.)
Mountain Time Zone

State Adoption Exchange and
Photo Listing

Arizona Adoption Exchange Book
c/o Arizona Families for Children
P.O. Box 17951
Tucson, AZ 85731
(520) 327-3324

Private Adoption Agencies

Adopt a Special Kid (AASK) of
Arizona
234 North Central, Suite 127
Phoenix, AZ 85004
(602) 254-2275

Adoption Care Center
1845 South Dobson, Suite 202
Mesa, AZ 85202
(602) 820-1121

Arizona Children's Home
2700 South 8th Avenue
Tucson, AZ 85713
(520) 622-7611

Arizona Family Adoptive Services
112 North Central Avenue,
Suite 425
Phoenix, AZ 85001
(602) 254-2271

Birth Hope Adoption Agency
3225 North Central, Suite 1217
Phoenix, AZ 85012
(602) 277-2860

Black Family and Children
Services
2323 North 3rd Street, Suite 202
Phoenix, AZ 85004
(602) 256-2948

Catholic Community Services
of Southern Arizona
P.O. Box 5746
Tucson, AZ 85703-0746
(602) 623-0344

Catholic Community Services of
Western Arizona
1700 1st Avenue, Suite 1000
Yuma, AZ 85364
(602) 783-3308

Catholic Social Services
of Flagstaff
201 West University Drive
Flagstaff, AZ 86001-0814
(602) 774-9125

Catholic Social Services
of Phoenix
1825 West Northern Avenue
Phoenix, AZ 85021
(602) 997-6105

Catholic Social Services
of East Valley
610 East Southern
Mesa, AZ 85204
(602) 964-8771

Catholic Social Services
of Tucson
155 West Helen
P.O. Box 5746
Tucson, AZ 85703-5746
(602) 623-0344

Catholic Social Services
of Yavapai
116 North Summitt
Prescott, AZ 86301
(602) 778-2531

Christian Family Care Agency
3603 North 7th Avenue
Phoenix, AZ 85014
(602) 234-1935

Commonwealth Adoptions
International, Inc.
4601 E. Ft. Lowell, Suite 200
Tucson, AZ 85712
(520) 327-7574

Dillon Southwest
P.O. Box 3535
Scottsdale, AZ 85257
(602) 945-2221

Family Service Agency
1530 East Flower
Phoenix, AZ 85014
(602) 264-9891

Hand in Hand International
Adoptions
3102 North Country Club
Tucson, AZ 85716
(520) 743-3322

LDS Social Services
235 South El Dorado
Mesa, AZ 85204
(602) 968-2995

LDS Social Services
P.O. Box 3544
Page, AZ 86040
(520) 645-2489

LDS Social Services
P.O. Box 856
Snowflake, AZ 85937
(520) 536-4118

LDS Social Services
3535 South Richey
Tucson, AZ 85713
(520) 745-6459

**Adoptive Parent Support
Groups and Postadoption
Services**

Advocates for Single Adoptive
Parenting
Attn.: Dolly Bacher
1 East Camelback Road
Phoenix, AZ 85012
(602) 951-8310

Arizona Families for Children
Attn.: Kay Buckler
1011 North Craycroft, Suite 470
Tucson, AZ 85711
(520) 327-3324

Children With AIDS Project
of America
P.O. Box 83131
Phoenix, AZ 85061
(602) 973-4319
(800) 866-AIDS

Families with Children
from China
Attn.: Cheryl Allen
10105 E. Via Linda, #103-198
Scottsdale, AZ 85258
(602) 273-6055

Family and Adoption Counseling
Center
2211 E. Highland Avenue,
Suite 130
Phoenix, AZ 85016
(602) 224-9757

North American Council
on Adoptable Children
State Representative
Attn.: Rachel Oesterle
234 N. Central, Suite 127
Phoenix, AZ 85004
(602) 254-2275

**Adopted Person and Birth
Relative Support Groups**

Adoptee Liberty Movement
Association (ALMA)
P.O. Box 13334
Scottsdale Airpark Station
Scottsdale, AZ 85267
(602) 569-5071

Adoptee Liberty Movement
Association (ALMA)
P.O. Box 20583
Sedona, AZ 86341

Adult Adoptees Support Group
Attn.: Dee Davis
7757 E. Marquise Drive
Tucson, AZ 85715
(520) 885-6771

Arizona Confidential
Intermediary Program
Attn.: Torin Scott
Arizona Supreme Court
1501 W. Washington
Phoenix, AZ 85007
(602) 542-9580

Concerned United Birthparents
2613 N. Saratoga Street
Tempe, AZ 85381

Flagstaff Adoption Search and
Support Group
P.O. Box 1031
Flagstaff, AZ 86002
(520) 526-0525

Orphan Voyage
P.O. Box 8245
Scottsdale, AZ 85252
(602) 990-1890

Scottsdale Adoption Connection
Attn.: Julie Mara
Box 2512
Scottsdale, AZ 85251

Search Triad
Attn.: Dara Brown-Watkins
Box 10181
Phoenix, AZ 85064
(602) 834-7417

Trace
Attn.: Brenda Wilson-Hasty
Box 1541
Sierra Vista, AZ 85636
(602) 458-5509

Tracers Ltd.
Box 18511
Tucson, AZ 85730
(520) 885-5958

T.R.I.A.D.
Box 12806
Tucson, AZ 85732
(520) 881-8250

Arizona State Bar Association
363 North 1st Avenue
Phoenix, AZ 85003-1742
(602) 252-4804

Adoption Attorneys

Robert Budoff
1640 West Thomas Road
Phoenix, AZ 85015
(602) 285-1100

Bruce Cohen
2198 East Camelback, Suite 365
Phoenix, AZ 85016
(602) 955-1515

Robert W. Finn
1988 North Kalb
Tucson, AZ 85715
(602) 722-0185

Cori Leonard Ford
2 North Central Ave, Suite 1600
Phoenix, AZ 85004
(602) 262-5850

Macre S. Inabinet
40 East Virginia, Suite 202
Phoenix, AZ 85004
(602) 263-5771
fax (602) 279-5569

Denise Lowell-Britt
30 W. First Street
Mesa, AZ 85201
(602) 461-5300

Rita Meiser
1 Renaissance Square
2 North Central, Suite 1600
Phoenix, AZ 85004
(602) 262-5841
fax (602) 253-3255

Scott E. Myers*
3180 East Grant Road
Tucson, AZ 85716
(602) 327-6041
(602) 326-9097

* Mr. Myers has completed over
    100 independent adoptions.

Kerry Beth Moore
4041 North Central Avenue,
    Suite 1460
Phoenix, AZ
(602) 271-9899

Kathryn A. Pidgeon
8433 North Black Canyon
    Highway, #100
Phoenix, AZ 85201-4859
(602) 371- 1317

Lucille Rosenstock
4480 North Osage Drive
Tuscon, AZ 85719

Kelly Sifferman*
7000 North 16th Street
Phoenix, AZ
(602) 997-8831
(602) 331-1122

* Ms. Sifferman has conducted
    about 500 agency adoptions.

Lon Taubman*
3030 North Central Avenue,
    Suite 807
Phoenix, AZ 85012
(602) 266-9552
fax (602) 279-6651

* Mr. Taubman has conducted
    about 4,000 independent, about
    2,000 agency, and about 300
    international adoptions.

Terry Williams
4327 North Scottsdale Road,
    Suite 200
Scottsdale, AZ 85251
(602) 423-3838
fax (602) 371-1506

Daniel Ziskin*
3309 North Second Street
Phoenix, AZ 85012
(602) 234-2280
fax (602) 234-0013

* Mr. Ziskin has conducted about
    375 independent adoptions.

Attorney fees in this state are
about $1,000 to $2,500.

ARIZONA LAWS RELATED TO ADOPTION: QUESTIONS AND ANSWERS

Can an attorney serve as an intermediary?
Yes, attorneys may assist in direct placement adoptions. However, the birth parents must select the adoptive parents. Also, the adoptive parents must already have an approved home study filed with the court.

Is advertising permitted?
Yes.

Who must consent to the adoption?
1. Both the birth parents
2. The agency who has given consent to place the child for adoption

When can consent be taken from the birth mother (father), and how long after the consent is signed can it be revoked?
Consent cannot be taken until seventy-two hours after the baby's birth, and is irrevocable.

What are the birth father's rights?
According to Scott Meyers, an adoption attorney in Tuscon, the law permits the serving of a "Potential Father Notice" on any man identified by the birth mother. This notice can be served at any time that an adoption plan is being considered. The birth father has thirty days after being served the notice to proceed with paternity proceedings. If he fails to respond within thirty days, his consent is not required.

Arizona law also provides for a registry in which a putative father can file a claim as to his paternity of a child to be born. If he does not file a claim within thirty days after the child's birth, then he may not assert any parental interest in the child (unless he can show that he was unable to file such a claim and that he then did file within thirty days after being able to file). The fact that he was not aware of the birth mother's pregnancy is a valid excuse for not filing a claim.

If the birth father is married to the birth mother, his rights are the same as hers.

What fees can adoptive parents pay?
Reasonable medical and legal expenses can be paid. Living expenses can be paid with court approval. Expenses are reviewed by the court.

Where does the adoption hearing take place?
The adoption hearing takes place in the court in the county in which the adoptive parents live.

How are familial and step-parent adoptions different from nonbiological adoptions?
No home study is required, and according to Scott Meyers, a step-parent adoption can be expedited depending upon how long the step-parent has been married to the parent, and how long the child has been in the home.

Can a nonresident finalize an adoption in this state?
No.

ARKANSAS

State Adoption Specialist
June Flye
Arkansas Department
  of Human Services
P.O. 1437, Slot 808
Little Rock, AR 72203
(501) 682-8462

Compact Administrator
Patricia Dahlgren
Assistant Deputy Director
Arkansas Department
  of Human Services
P.O. Box 1437
Little Rock, AR 72203

Deputy Compact Administrator
Judy Miller
ICPC Unit
Arkansas Department
  of Human Services
P.O. 1437
Little Rock, AR 72203
  or
Donaghey Building, Room 817
7th and Main Streets
Little Rock, AR 72201
(501) 682-8556 or 8557

Direct all correspondence and
telephone calls to the Deputy
Compact Administrator.

Office hours:
Monday-Friday
8:00 A.M.-4:30 P.M.
Central Time Zone

State Adoption Exchange and
  Photo Listing
Department of Human Services
7th and Main Street
P.O. Box 1437, Slot 808
Little Rock, AR 72203-1437
(501) 682-8462

Private Adoption Agencies

Adoption Services, Inc.
2415 N. Tyler
Little Rock, AR 72207
(501) 664-0340

Bethany Christian Services
1100 N. University Avenue,
Suite 209
Little Rock, AR 72207
(501) 664-5729

Children's Home, Inc.
Church of Christ
5515 Old Walcott Road
Paragould, AR 72450
(501) 239-4031

Children's Home, Inc.
Church of Christ
190 Jan Drive, Suite 2
Sherwood, AR 72116
(501) 835-1595

Edna Gladney Home
P.O. Box 4615
N. Little Rock, AR 72116
(501) 791-3126

Families Are Special, Inc.
2200 Main Street
P.O. Box 5789
N. Little Rock, AR 72119
(501) 758-9184

Friends of Children, Inc.
2024 Arkansas Valley Drive,
Suite 804
Little Rock, AR 72212
(501) 224-5900

Highlands Child Placement
Services
P.O. Box 300198
Kansas City, MO 64130
(816) 924-6565

Holt International Children
Services
P.O. Box 2880
Eugene, OR 97402
(503) 687-2202

LDS Social Services of Oklahoma
4500 S. Garnett, Suite 425
Tulsa, OK 74146
(918) 665-3090

Searcy Children's Home
900 North Main Street
Searcy, AR 72143
(501) 268-3242

Small Miracles International
7430 S.E. 15th Street, Suite 204
Midwest City, OK 73110
(405) 732-7295

Southern Christian Home
P.O. Box 556
Morrilton, AR 72110
(501) 354-2428

Volunteers of America—
Shreveport
360 Jordan Street
Shreveport, LA 71101
(318) 424-9394

**Adoptive Parent Support
Groups and Postadoption
Services**

AFACT and North American
Council on Adoptable Children
State Representative
Attn.: Jean Dahms
17 McKee Circle
North Little Rock, AR 72166
(501) 758-7061

Miracles
Attn.: Connie Foster
1008 Barbara
Jacksonville, AR 72076
(501) 982-7134

PAR Project
Donaghey Plaza N., Suite 301
7th and Main Streets
P.O. Box 1437, Slot C
Little Rock, AR 72203
(501) 682-1882

River Valley Adoption
Support Group
Attn.: Elizabeth and Steve Franks
1005 West 18th Terrace
Russellville, AR 72801
(501) 967-1641

**Adopted Person and Birth
Relative Support Groups**

Adoptee Liberty Movement
Association (ALMA)
P.O. Box 145
Blytheville, AR 72316

Adoptee Liberty Movement
Association (ALMA)
P.O. Box 1402
Little Rock, AR 72203

Adoptee Liberty Movement
Association (ALMA)
P.O. Box 1409
Rogers, AR 72757
(501) 925-2866

Orphan Train Heritage Society
of America, Inc.
4912 Trout Farm Road
Springdale, AR 72764
(501) 756-2780

Arkansas Bar Association
400 West Markham
Little Rock, AR 72201
(501) 375-4605

Adoption Attorneys

Charles Dougan
7509 Cantrell Road, Suite 232
Little Rock, AR 72207
(501) 661-8086

Eugene T. Kelley*
Kelley Law Firm
222 West Walnut
Rogers, AR 72756
(501) 636-1051
fax (501) 636-1663

* Mr. Kelley has conducted more
than 200 independent
adoptions.

Kaye H. McLeod*
620 West 3rd Street
Riley Building
Little Rock, AR
(501) 372-1121
fax (501) 376-9614

* Ms. McLeod has conducted
more than 600 independent
adoptions, more than thirty
agency adoptions, and about
thirty international adoptions.

Attorney fees in this state are
about $2,000 to $6,000,
depending upon the type of
adoption.

ARKANSAS LAWS RELATED TO ADOPTION: QUESTIONS AND ANSWERS

Can an attorney serve as an intermediary?
Yes.

Is advertising permitted?
Yes.

Who must consent to the adoption?
1. The birth mother
2. An agency or court

When can consent be taken from the birth mother (father), and how long after the consent is signed can it be revoked?
According to Kaye McLeod, an adoption attorney in Little Rock, a relinquishment and termination can be obtained before or after the child's birth, and can be revoked up to ten days after birth. A written consent can only be taken after the baby is born. The consent forms must state the procedure for withdrawing consent. The birth mother (and possibly the father) has ten days from the date of signing to revoke the consent. The better practice appears to be to utilize a relinquishment and termination with a power to consent document, which involves the appointment of a guardian ad litem for the child to be born.

Ms. McLeod also states that rights can also be terminated by using the abovementioned documents by way of a judicial appearance or by a sworn affidavit in front of a notary.

What are the birth father's rights?
According to Eugene Kelley, an adoption attorney in Rogers, Arkansas, adoption law provides that if the birth father is not married to the birth mother his consent is not necessary, and he must file a claim of paternity with the putative father registry located at the Department of Vital Records; a birth father who files such a claim is entitled to notice of any adoption proceedings. The birth father's written consent for the adoption is needed if he was married to the birth mother at the time of conception or any time thereafter, or if he has legitimized the child.

What fees can adoptive parents pay?
Medical and legal fees can be paid, as well as living expenses. A listing of these expenses must be submitted to the court.

Where does the adoption hearing take place?
The hearing can take place in the county in which the adoptive parents live, the child lives, or where the agency that has custody of child is located.

How are familial and step-parent adoptions different from nonbiological adoptions?
No home study is required. The adoption process is less complicated, and, therefore, less expensive.

Can a nonresident finalize an adoption in this state?

Yes. According to Ms. McLeod, nonresidents can usually obtain a final decree of adoption within two weeks after the baby's birth, and, therefore, no Interstate Compact approval is required.

Arkansas now requires prospective adoptive parents to have FBI fingerprint clearance before an adoption hearing.

CALIFORNIA

State Adoption Specialist
James Brown
California Department
of Social Services
744 P Street, M.S. 19-69
Sacramento, CA 95814
(916) 445-3146

Compact Administrator
Jim Brown, Deputy Director
Adult and Family Division
California Department
of Social Services
744 P Street, M/S 17-18
Sacramento, CA 95814
(916) 657-2614
fax (916) 653-1695

Adoption Section
(916) 322-4228

Deputy Compact Administrator
California does not have this
office. Instead, the function is
provided by local, licensed public
and private adoption agencies,
probation departments, and the
Department of Social Service's
District Office. Direct
correspondence, including
overnight mail, and telephone
calls to the appropriate local
agency.

State Adoption Exchange and
  Photo Listing
California Waiting Children
  Photolisting Service
California Department
of Social Services
744 P Street, M.S. 19-68
Sacramento, CA 95814
(916) 323-0590

Private Adoption Agencies

ACCEPT
339 S. San Antonio Road
Los Altos, CA 94022
(415) 917-8090

Adopt A Special Kid (AASK)
  of Northern California
2201 Broadway, Suite 702
Oakland, CA 94612
(510) 451-1748

Adoption Center, Headquarters
391 Taylor Boulevard, Suite 100
Pleasant Hill, CA 94523
(510) 827-2229

Adoption Center
8616 La Tijera Boulevard,
  Suite 212
Los Angeles, CA 90045
(310) 215-3180

Adoption Center
6929 Sunrise Boulevard,
  Suite 102-I
Sacramento, CA 95610
(916) 723-6962

Adoption Center
2084 Walsh Avenue, Suite C-1
Santa Clara, CA 95050
(408) 986-8343

Other branches:
Modesto, (209) 577-3060
Stockton, (209) 952-2301

Adoption Horizons
302 4th Street, 2nd Floor
Eureka, CA 95501-0302
(707) 444-9909

Adopt International
121 Springdale Way
Redwood City, CA 94062
(415) 369-7300

Adoption Services International
2021 Sperry Avenue, Suite 41
Ventura, CA 93003
(805) 644-3067

Adoptions Unlimited
11800 Central Avenue, Suite 110
Chino, CA 91710
(909) 902-1412

Bal Jagat Children's World, Inc.
9311 Farralone Avenue
Chatsworth, CA 91311
(818) 709-4737

Bay Area Adoption Services, Inc.
465 Fairchild Drive, Suite 215
Mountain View, CA 94043
(415) 964-3800

Bethany Christian Services
Northern Region
3048 Hahn Drive
Modesto, CA 95350-6503
(209) 522-5121

Bethany Christian Services
Southern Region
9928 Flower Street, Suite 202
Bellflower, CA 90706-5453
(310) 804-3448

Black Adoption Placement and
  Research Center
1801 Harrison Street, 2nd Floor
Oakland, CA 94612
(510) 839-3678

Black Adoption Placement
  and Research Center
1722 J Street, Suite 7
Sacramento, CA 95814
(916) 443-1129

Catholic Charities Adoption
  Agency
349 Cedar Street
San Diego, CA 92101-3197
(619) 231-2828

Catholic Charities, San Francisco
2045 Lawton Street
San Francisco, CA 94122
(415) 665-5100

Children's Bureau of Los Angeles
3910 Oakwood Avenue
Los Angeles, CA 90004
(213) 953-7356

Children's Bureau of Los Angeles,
Inglewood District Office
610 North Eucalyptus
Inglewood, CA 90302
(310) 673-7830

Children's Bureau of Los Angeles,
Orange County Office
50 S. Anaheim Boulevard,
Suite 241
Anaheim, CA 92805
(714) 517-1900

Children's Bureau of Los Angeles,
Palmdale Office
1529 E. Palmdale, Suite 210
Palmdale, CA 93550
(805) 272-9996

Children's Home Society
of California
1300 West 4th Street
Los Angeles, CA 90017-1475
(213) 240-5900

Children's Home Society
of California
15535 San Fernando Mission
Boulevard
Mission Hills, CA 91345
(818) 837-8100

Children's Home Society
of California
3200 Telegraph Avenue
Oakland, CA 94609
(510) 655-7406

Children's Home Society
of California
550 Bercut Drive, Suite G
Sacramento, CA 95814
(916) 658-0100

Children's Home Society
of California
2444 Moorpark Avenue,
Suite 312
San Jose, CA 95128
(408) 293-8940

Children's Home Society
of California
300 South Sycamore Street
Santa Ana, CA 92701-5792
(714) 542-1147

Christian Adoption and Family
Services
1698 Greenbriar Lane, Suite 219
Brea, CA 92621
(714) 529-2949

Chrysalis House
2134 West Alluvial Avenue
Fresno, CA 93711
(209) 432-7170

El Centro Human Services
Corporation
5800 S. Eastern Avenue,
Suite 370
Commerce, CA 90040
(213) 887-1573

El Centro Human Services
Corporation
1200 North Main Street,
Suite 736
Santa Ana, CA 92701
(714) 836-9743

Families First
1909 Galileo Court
Davis, CA 95616
(916) 753-0220

Families for Children
3620 Auburn Boulevard,
Suite A-200
Sacramento, CA 95821
(916) 974-8744

Family Builders By Adoption
528 Grand Avenue
Oakland, CA 94610
(510) 272-0204

Family Connections
1528 Oakdale Road
Modesto, CA 95355
(209) 524-8844

Family Network
307 Webster Sreet
Monterey, CA 93940
(408) 655-5077

Future Families
3233 Valencia Avenue, Suite A-6
Aptos, CA 95003
(408) 662-0202

Future Families, Inc.
South Bay Region
1671 The Alameda
San Jose, CA 95126-2222
(408) 298-8789

Good Samaritan Homes
9276 Greenback Lane, Suite C
Orangevale, CA 95662
(916) 989-1157

Hand in Hand Foundation
2401 Robertson Road
Soquel, CA 95073
(408) 476-1866

Help the Children, Inc.
41 West Yokuts Avenue,
Suite 107
Stockton, CA 95207-5722
(209) 478-5585

Heritage Adoption Services
2214 Capital Avenue, Suite 2
Sacramento, CA 95816
(916) 442-5477

Holt International Children's
Services
3807 Pasadena Avenue, Suite 170
Sacramento, CA 95821
(916) 487-4658

Holy Family Services-Counseling
and Adoption
402 S. Marengo Avenue
Pasadena, CA 91101-3113
(818) 578-1156

Holy Family Services/Counseling
and Adoption
1403 South Main Street
Santa Ana, CA 92707-1790
(714) 835-5551

Indian Child and Family Services
28441 Rancho California Road,
Suite J
Temecula, CA 92590
(714) 676-8832

Infant of Prague
6059 North Palm Avenue
Fresno, CA 93704
(209) 447-3333

Institute for Black Parenting
9920 La Cienega Boulevard,
Suite 806
Inglewood, CA 90301
(310) 348-1400

Institute for Black Parenting
3233 Arlington Avenue,
Suite 202
Riverside, CA 92506
(714) 782-2800

International Christian Adoptions
41745 Rider Way, #2
Temecula, CA 92590
(909) 695-3336

Kinship Center
30 Ragsdale Drive, Suite 210
Monterey, CA 93940
(408) 649-3033

LDS Social Services
501 North Brookhurst, Suite 300
Anaheim, CA 92801
(714) 520-0525

LDS Social Services, California
North Agency
6060 Sunrise Vista Drive,
Suite 1160
Citrus Heights, CA 95610
(916) 725-5032

LDS Social Services
791 North Pepper Avenue
Colton, CA 92324
(714) 824-0480

LDS Social Services
2120 Diamond Boulevard,
Suite 120
Concord, CA 94520-5704
(510) 685-2941

LDS Social Services
17350 Mt. Herrmann Street
Fountain Valley, CA 92708
(714) 444-3463

LDS Social Services
1425 N. Rabe Avenue, Suite 101
Fresno, CA 93727
(209) 255-1446

LDS Social Services,
California South Agency
5675 Ruffin Road, Suite 325
San Diego, CA 92123
(619) 467-9170

LDS Social Services
4320 Stevens Creek Boulevard,
Suite 129
San Jose, CA 95129
(408) 243-1688

LDS Social Services
7100 Hayvenhurst Avenue,
Suite 102
Van Nuys, CA 91406
(818) 781-5511

Life Adoption Services
440 West Main Street
Tustin, CA 92680
(714) 838-5433

Lilliput Children's Services
1540 River Park Drive, Suite 107
Sacramento, CA 95815
(916) 923-5444

Lilliput Children's Services
525 Estudillo Avenue, Suite D
San Leandro, CA 94577
(510) 483-2030

Lilliput Children's Services
130 East Magnolia
Stockton, CA 95202
(209) 943-0530

North Bay Adoptions
9068 Brooks Road South
Windsor, CA 95492
(707) 837-0277

Partners For Adoption
4527 Montgomery Drive, Suite A
P.O. Box 2791
Santa Rosa, CA 95405
(707) 539-9068

Sierra Adoption Services
8928 Volunteer Lane, Suite 240
Sacramento, CA 95826
(916) 368-5114

Sierra Adoption Services
123 Nevada Street
P.O. Box 361
Nevada City, CA 95959
(916) 265-6959

Vista Del Mar Child Care
Services
3200 Motor Avenue
Los Angeles, CA 90034
(310) 836-1223

Adoptive Parent Support Groups and Postadoption Services

ACCEPT (singles group)
Attn.: Mary Nicholson
416 Chardonnay Drive
Fremont, CA 94539
(510) 490-4402

Adopt a Special Kid (AASK)
of Northern California
3530 Grand Avenue
Oakland, CA 94610
(510) 451-1748

Adopt a Special Kid (AASK)
of San Diego
Attn.: Sally Danover
544 Augusta Drive
San Marcos, CA 92069
(619) 741-5399

Adoption Assistance and Support
Group
Attn.: David Baum
16255 Ventura Boulevard,
Suite 704
Encino, CA 91436-2302
(818) 501-8355

Adoption Avenues
Attn.: Kim Foster
7945 Tucker Lane
Redding, CA 96002

Adoption Center
4141 State Street, Suite B-2
Santa Barbara, CA 93110
(805) 967-5133

Adoption Choice of America
716 North Ventura Road,
Suite 348
Oxnard, CA 93030
(805) 483-2551

Adoption Horizons
Attn.: Sherill Chand
630 "J" Street
Eureka, CA 95501
(707) 444-9909

Adoptive Parent Support
and Referral
Attn.: Sharyn Harrison
12065 Persimmon Terrace
Auburn, CA 95603
(916) 885-1944

Adoptive Parent Support Group
Attn.: Lee Ann Perry
1584 North Ferger Avenue
Fresno, CA 93728
(209) 486-2019

Bal Jagat Children's World, Inc.
Attn.: Hemlata Momaya
9311 Farralone Avenue
Chatsworth, CA 91311
(818) 709-4737

Bay Area Adoption Support
465 Fairchild Drive, Suite 215
Mountain View, CA 94043
(415) 964-3800

Bay Area Single Adoptive Parent
Group (South)
Attn.: Jan Johnson
385 South 14th Street
San Jose, CA 95112
(408) 292-1638

Bay Area Single Adoptive Parent
Group (North)
Attn.: Nancy Smythe
3816 Via Verde
El Sobrante, CA 94803
(510) 758-9431

BLAC
Attn.: Camilla Smith
3270 Cerritos Avenue
Long Beach, CA 90807
(213) 424-1281

Building Families
Through Adoption
Attn.: Peg Brown
19150 Gorstrom Lane
Ft. Bragg, CA 95437
(707) 964-3973

California Adoption Advocacy
Network
Attn.: Harvey and Nancy Ng
718 East Meadow
Palo Alto, CA 94303
(415) 494-3057

Faces
Attn.: June Davies
2510 Smith Grade Road
Santa Cruz, CA 95060
(408) 423-3870

Families Adopting in Response
(FAIR) and North American
Council on Adoptable Children
State Representative
Attn.: Lansing Wood
P.O. Box 51436
Palo Alto, CA 94303
(415) 328-6832

Families by Adoption
Attn.: Ann Elizabeth Fisher
1405 Marcelina Avenue,
Suite #101
Torrance, CA 90501
(213) 782-9161

Family Adoption Network
Attn.: Lois Knoll
5869 North Bethel
Clovis, CA 93612
(209) 298-1760

Family Network
Attn.: Carol Land
P.O. Box 1995
Studio City, CA 91614
(213) 650-3100

Foothill Adoptive Parent Support
Group
Attn.: Steve and Jan Hallam
12490 Erin Drive
Auburn, CA 95603
(916) 885-4617

For the Children
Attn.: Bob and Donna King
13074 Larkhaven Drive
Moreno Valley, CA 92553
(714) 656-4240

Hand in Hand
Attn.: Chris Winston
874 Phillip Court
El Dorado Hills, CA 95630
(916) 933-4562

Heartline
Attn.: Bonnie and Bruce Eddy
37680 Green Knolls Road
Winchester, CA 92396
(714) 677-1124

Holt San Diego Support Group
Attn.: Mary Lebedinski
8690 Via Del Luz
El Cajon, CA 92021
(619) 390-1487

Humbolt County Council on
Adoptable Children
Attn.: Kathleen Marks
P.O. Box 4767
Arcata, CA 95521
(707) 444-2565

Inter Country Adoption Network
Attn.: Jennifer Underwood
10419 Pearson Place
Sunland, CA 91040
(818) 352-0332

Kinship Alliance
513 East First Street
Tustin, CA 92680
(714) 573-8865

MICA
Attn.: Betty Factor
1744 North Damon
Simi Valley, CA 93063

North Coast Adoptive Families
Attn.: Colleen Morris
2136 Parrish Drive
Santa Rosa, CA 95404
(707) 575-8663

Open Door Society
of Los Angeles
Attn.: Donna Salisbury
12235 Silva Place
Cerritos, CA 90701
(213) 402-3664

Orange County Adoptive Parents
Attn.: Gerry Mazur
39 Foxboro
Irvine, CA 92714
(714) 752-8642

OURS Through Adoption
Attn.: Lisa Kirk
Box 85152-343
San Diego, CA 92138
(619) 578-5707

Pact, an Adoption Alliance
Attn.: Gail Steinberg or Beth Hall
3450 Sacramento Street,
Suite 239
San Francisco, CA 94118
(415) 221-6957

Parents of Adoptees in Crisis
Attn.: Patty Wills
1664 Springvale Road
Placerville, CA 95667
(916) 626-6891

Partners for Adoption
Attn.: Rose Marie Nielsen
3913 Mayette Avenue
Santa Rosa, CA 95405
(707) 578-0212

Patchwork Adoptive Families
Attn.: Joanne Green
P.O. Box 5153
Stockton, CA 95205
(209) 942-2812

Placer Adoption/Attachment
Attn.: Judy Lewis
P.O. Box 7155
Aubum, CA 95604
(916) 885-5258

Post Adoption Support Group
Attn.: Shirley Mayfield
3805 Regent Road
Sacramento, CA 95821
(916) 487-7243

Private Adoption:
Where to Begin?
P.O. Box 405
Boulder Creek, CA 95006

Romanian Club
702 16th Street
Santa Monica, CA 90402
(213) 393-2856

Single Adoptive Parent Group
Attn.: Marilyn Emett
4316 G Street
Sacramento, CA 95819
(916) 457-4278

Single Adoptive Parents
Attn.: Joanne Martinis
P.O. Box 1089
Del Mar, CA 91014
(619) 755-6331

Silver Spoon Adoptions
(facilitators)
28481 Rancho California Road,
Suite 206
Temecula, CA 92590-3619
(909) 699-3238

Solano County Adoption Group
Attn.: Cheryl Richno
212 Sunhaven Drive
Fairfield, CA 94533
(707) 429-5447

South Bay Adoption
Support Group
Attn.: Lil Snee
21405 Roaring Water Way
Los Gatos, CA 95030
(408) 353-2995

Stars of David
Attn.: Marcia and Herb Dietz
621 Pine Avenue
Sunnyvale, CA 94086
(408) 735-1846

Stars of David
Attn.: Nancy and Arnold
Birenbaum
2309 English Court
Walnut Creek, CA 94598
(510) 933-2133

Together Expecting a Miracle
(TEAM)
Attn.: Arlene Frietze
1300 Astoria Place
Oxnard, CA 93030
(805) 485-4677

**Adopted Person and Birth
Relative Support Groups**

Adoptee Liberty Movement
Association (ALMA)
P.O. Box 2341
Alameda, CA 94501

Adoptee Liberty Movement
Association (ALMA)
(Research Library)
P.O. Box 9425
Canoga Park, CA 91309

Adoptee Liberty Movement
Association (ALMA)
P.O. Box 5068
Fresno, CA 93755

Adoptee Liberty Movement
Association (ALMA)
P.O. Box 4572
Lancaster, CA 93539

Adoptee Liberty Movement
Association (ALMA)
P.O. Box 2538
Monterey, CA 93942

Adoptee Liberty Movement
Association (ALMA)
P.O. Box 714
Moorpark, CA 93021

Adoptee Liberty Movement
Association (ALMA)
P.O. Box 191514
Sacramento, CA 95817-7514
(916) 455-ALMA

Adoptee Liberty Movement
Association (ALMA)
P.O. Box 1233
Simi Valley, CA 93062
(805) 583-0965

Adoptee Liberty Movement
Association (ALMA)
P.O. Box 4318
Sunland, CA 91041
(818) 771-7585

Adoptee Liberty Movement
Association (ALMA)
P.O. Box 271
Vina, CA 96092
(916) 824-4790

Adoptee/Birthparent Connection
1365 Lesley Court
Santa Maria, CA 93454
(805) 922-4313

Adoptees Birthparents
Association
P.O. Box 33
Camarillo, CA 93011
(805) 482-8667

Adoptees Birthparents
Association
2027 Finch Court
Simi Valley, CA 93063
(805) 583-4306

Adoption Reality
2180 Clover Street
Simi Valley, CA 93065
(805) 526-2289

Adoption Reunion Support Group
1115 Sunset Drive
Vista, CA 92083
(619) 726-1924

Adoption Triad Support Group
1755 Diamond Mountain Road
Calistoga, CA 94515
(707) 943-5877

Adoption with Truth
66 Panoramic Way
Berkeley, CA 94704
(415) 704-9349

Adoption/Birth Family Registry
Dept. R, Box 803
Carmichael, CA 94303

Americans for Open Records
P.O. Box 401
Palm Desert, CA 92261

Bay Area Birthmothers
Association
1546 Great Highway #44
San Francisco, CA 94122

Birth Connection
P.O. Box 277434
Sacramento, CA 95827-0674
(916) 451-9868

Birthparent Connection/Adoption
Connection of San Diego
Attn.: Curry Wolfe
P.O. Box 230643
Encinitas, CA 92023-0643
(619) 753-8288

Birthparents in the Open
Attn.: Lesley Jon
3075 Stanley Avenue
Santa Cruz, CA 95065
(408) 464-7301

Central Coast Adoption
  Support Group
Box 2483
Goleta, CA 93117
(805) 682-5250 or 968-4351

Central Coast Adoption
  Support Group
1718 Longbranch
Grover City, CA 93433
(805) 481-4086

Central Coast Adoption
  Support Group
1365 Lesley Court
Santa Maria, CA 93454
(805) 922-4313

Concerned United Birthparents
2041 Willowood Lane
Encinitas, CA 92024
(619) 436-0892

Concerned United Birthparents
14769 Fairvilla Drive
La Mirada, CA 90638
(714) 521-4204

Concerned United Birthparents
1835 Casa Linda Circle
Orange, CA 92668

Concerned United Birthparents
5224 Caminito Aruba
San Diego, CA 92124
(619) 685-7673

Equality Nationwide/Unwed
  Fathers
4724 Lincoln Boulevard, #334
Marina del Rey, CA 90292
(310) 821-4581

Full Circle
Box 816
Lake Forrest, CA 92630
(714) 951-1689

Hand in Hand
391 Teasdale Street
Thousand Oaks, CA 91360
(714) 951-1689

Independent Search Consultants
P.O. Box 10192
Costa Mesa, CA 92627

Los Angeles County Adoption
  Search Association
P.O. Box 1461
Roseville, CA 95661
(916) 784-2711

Mendo Lake Adoption Triad
620 Walnut Avenue
Ukiah, CA 95482
(707) 468-0648

Post Adoption Center for
  Education and Research
  (PACER) of Marin
Box 826
Larkspur, CA 94977
(415) 924-7047

Post Adoption Center for
  Education and Research
  (PACER)
P.O. Box 309
Orinda, CA 94563
(510) 935-6622

PURE, Inc.
P.O. Box 638
Westminster, CA 92683
(714) 892-4098

Reconnections of California
41669 Zinfandel Avenue
Temecula, CA 92591
(909) 695-1152

R.O.O.T.S.
P.O. Box 40564
Bakersfield, CA 93384-0564
(805) 832-5549

Santa Cruz Birthmother Support
Box 1780
Freedom, CA 95019
(408) 728-3876

Search and Find
Box 8765
Riverside, CA 92515

Search Finders
P.O. Box 24095
San Jose, CA 95154
(408) 356-6711

Searchers Connection
7709 Skyhill Drive
Los Angeles, CA 90068
(213) 878-0630

Second Abandonment
2323 Eastern Canal
Venice, CA 90291
(805) 379-4186

South Coast Adoption
  Research and Support
P.O. Box 039
Harbor City, CA 90710
(213) 833-5822

Triad Research
300 Golden West
Shafter, CA 93262

Triple Hearts Adoption Triangle
Box 52017
Riverside, CA 92517
(909) 784-7358

Westside Adoption Support
4117 Overland Avenue
Culver City, CA 90230
(310) 470-9065

California State Bar Association
555 Franklin Street
San Francisco, CA 94102
(415) 561-8200

Adoption Attorneys

Lauren J. Abrams
Law Offices of Allen Hultquist
San Diego, CA 92108
(619) 233-3000
fax (619) 297-8564

G. Darlene Anderson
105 North Rose Street, #200
Escondido, CA 92027
(619) 743-4700

Edward Charles Ash*
9454 Wilshire Boulevard,
  Suite 907
Beverly Hills, CA 90212-2911
(213) 274-1990
fax (213) 858-9786

* Mr. Ash has conducted twenty
  independent and 150 agency
  adoptions.

David Baum*
16255 Ventura Boulevard,
  Suite 704
Encino, CA 91436-2312
(818) 501-8355
fax (818) 501-8465

* Mr. Baum has conducted over
  200 independent adoptions and
  more than fifty agency
  adoptions.

Barbara Bayliss
DBA Adoption Associates
4525 Wilshire Boulevard,
    Suite 201
Los Angles, CA 90010
(213) 664 5600

Timothy Blied
4100 Newport Place, Suite 800
Newport Beach, CA 92660
(714) 863-1644

James Bunker
620 Newport Center, 16th Floor
Newport Beach, CA 92660
(714) 760-0404

Alvin Coen*
Adoption Counseling Services
16152 Beach Blvd, Suite 101
Huntington Beach, CA 92647
(714) 841-3444
fax (714) 841-3595

* Mr. Coen has conducted more
  than 1,000 independent
  adoptions and about 200
  agency adoptions.

Durand Cook
8383 Wilshire Boulevard,
    Suite 750
Beverly Hills, CA 90211
(213) 655-2611
fax (213) 658-8126

Douglas Donnelly*
926 Garden Street
Santa Barbara, CA 93101
(805) 962-0988
fax (805) 966-2993

* Mr. Donnelly has conducted
  more than 1,200 independent
  adoptions and more than 100
  agency adoptions. He also won
  a major case involving birth
  father rights before the
  California Supreme Court.

Joan Flam
16133 Ventura Boulevard, #700
Encino, CA 91436-2440
(818) 986-6840

Jane Gorman*
513 East First Street, 2nd Floor
Tustin, CA 92680
(714) 731-3600
fax (714) 731-7760

* Ms. Gorman does adoption
  litigation exclusively.

Marc Gradstein*
1204 Burlingame Avenue, No. 7
Burlingame, CA 94010
(415) 347-7041
fax (415) 347-7048

* Mr. Gradstein has conducted
  about 2,000 independent
  adoptions and 200 agency
  adoptions.

Randall B. Hicks*
6608 Palm Avenue
Riverside,CA 92506
(909) 369-3342
fax (909) 628-2531

Satellite office
513 East First Street
Tustin, CA 92680
(714) 544-1289

* Mr. Hicks has completed more
  than 500 adoptions, 90 percent
  of which were independent
  adoptions. He is the author of
  the book Adopting in America:
  How to Adopt Within One
  Year.

Allen Hultquist
San Diego, CA 92108
(619) 233-3000
fax (619) 297-8564

Althea Lee Jordan
385 Sherman Avenue, Suite 1
Palo Alto, CA 94306
(415) 325-8800

Karen Lane
100 Wilshire Boulevard,
    20th Floor
Santa Monica, CA 90401
(213) 393-9802

David Laredo
606 Forest Avenue
Pacific Grove, CA 93950
(408) 646-1502

David Keane Leavitt
9454 Wilshire Boulevard,
    Suite 600
Beverly Hills, CA 90212
(213) 273-3151

Lynne Francis Mann
6500 Wilshire Boulevard,
    Suite 300
Los Angeles, CA 90048
(213) 655-8993
fax (213) 615-0801

George Maricie
800 North Haven Avenue,
    Suite 440
Ontario, CA 91764
(909) 945-9549

Diane Michelsen*
3190 Old Tunnel Road
Lafayette, CA 94549
(510) 945-1880
fax (510) 933-6807

* Ms. Michelsen has conducted
  more than 1,000 independent
  adoptions, as well as several
  hundred agency adoptions.

Judy Nesburn
11755 Wilshire Boulevard,
    Suite 1310
Los Angeles, CA 90025
(213) 575-5555

Linda Nunez*
513 E. First Street, 2nd Floor
Tustin, CA 92680
(714) 544-9921
fax (714) 544-5155

* Ms. Nunez has completed
  about 3,000 adoptions, most of
  them independent.

Julie E. O'Connor
1762 Columbia Street
San Diego, CA 92101

Susan Peck
Law Offices of Diane Michelsen
3190 Old Tunnel Road
Lafayette, CA 94549
(510) 945-1880
fax (510) 933-6807

David J. Radis*
1901 Avenue of Stars, 20th Floor
Los Angeles, CA 90067
(310) 552-0536
fax (310) 552-0713

* Mr. Radis has completed over
  1,500 independent adoptions
  and 300 agency adoptions.

Lesley A. Siegel
3018 Willow Pass Road, Suite 205
Concord, CA 94519
(510) 676-3961
(510) 676-6215

Lindsay K. Slatter
8501 Wilshire Boulevard, No. 305
Beverly Hills, CA 90211

Jed Somit
1440 Broadway, No. 910
Oakland, CA 94162
(510) 839-3215
800/JLSOMIT
fax (510) 839-7041

Janis K. Stocks
1450 Frazee Road, Suite 409
San Diego, CA 92108
(619) 296-6251

Ronald L. Stoddart*
1698 Greenbriar Lane, Suite 201
Rea, CA 92621
(714) 990-5100
fax (714) 671-7834

* Mr. Stoddart has conducted
over 700 independent
adoptions, 100 agency
adoptions, and ninety-five
international adoptions.

Felice Webster*
4525 Wilshire Boulevard, Suite
201
Los Angeles, CA 90010
(213) 664-5600
(800) 622-3678 (CA only)
fax (213) 664-4551

* Ms. Webster has completed
more than 300 independent
adoptions and 100 agency
adoptions.

M.D. Widelock
O'Neil and Widelock
5401 California Avenue, No. 300
Bakersfield, CA 93309
(805) 325-6950
fax (805) 325-7882

Beverly R. Williscroft
3018 Willow Pass Road, Suite 205
Concord, CA 94519
(510) 676-3961
(510) 676-6215

Nanci R. Worchster
210 Magnolia Avenue, No. 2
Auburn, CA 95603
(916) 888-1311

CALIFORNIA LAWS RELATED TO ADOPTION: QUESTIONS AND ANSWERS

Can an attorney serve as an intermediary?
Yes. In fact, many nonattorneys also serve as intermediaries and operate as independent facilitators.

Is advertising permitted?
No, only a licensed intermediary, attorney, or adoption agency can advertise. Many prospective adoptive parents simply advertise in other states or in national publications.

Who must consent to the adoption?
Both birth parents

When can consent be taken from the birth mother (father), and how long after the consent is signed can it be revoked?
The birth mother must be counseled twice by a state authorized adoption service provider (there are many in the state). The first advisement can occur before the child's birth; the birth mother must then be readvised at least ten days between the first and second session before she can sign a placement agreement that contains the consent. The maximum fee for being advised is $500; however, travel and counseling time can also be added to the fee.

According to David J. Radis, an adoption attorney in Los Angeles, the consent can be given any time after the baby is born and the mother is discharged from the hospital. In an agency adoption the relinquishment is binding, and in an independent adoption the birth parents can withdraw consent for ninety days or waive those ninety days.

The waiver must be signed in front of a state social worker, but finding such a social worker can sometimes be difficult. If a state social worker is not available because the birth mother lives in a remote area, she can go before a judge—but this very seldom is necessary. There is no charge for the social worker's service.

According to Linda Nunez, an adoption attorney in Tustin, because a preplacement home study is not required for an in-state placement, a social worker will not take a waiver until she knows more about the adoptive parents, and usually the social worker will want to meet the parties involved.

Ms. Nunez also says that if a child is born in another state, the taking of a consent must follow California procedure and there must be ten days in between the advisement of counsel and the second advisement before a consent can be taken. The birth mother's consent and waiver can be taken by an attorney who represents her exclusively in lieu of a State Authorized Adoption Placement Provider and a state social worker.

NOTE: Your adoption can become an identified agency adoption in which the agency conducts your home study and takes the birth mother's relinquishment seventy-two hours after the child is born. This process can be done without signing an Adoption Placement Agreement and without involvement of the Department of Social Services.

What are the birth father's rights?

According to Douglas Donnelly, an adoption attorney in Santa Barbara, the birth father's consent is not necessary unless he is married to the mother, received the child into his home, and publicly acknowledges his paternity or has done all he can to support the child as soon as he learned of the pregnancy or child. Diane Michelsen, an adoption attorney in Lafayette, states that the alleged father can halt an adoption if, upon learning of the pregnancy or of the birth of the baby, he takes responsibility and provides for the mother and/or child.

According to David J. Radis, the birth father has the right to a notice of the adoption hearing and the opportunity to be heard, unless he signs a pre- or post-birth waiver. The birth father has thirty days from being served or after the birth to respond—whichever is longer. His rights can be terminated thirty days after the birth if he fails to respond to the notice. The presumed father must sign a consent or have his rights terminated by court action. Fitness of the birth father is the test.

The alleged father can voluntarily end his rights before or after the child's birth by signing a denial of paternity or waiver of rights in front of a notary.

According to the law, the court must make efforts to identify the named (alleged) birth father (more than one can be named), and notify him of the adoption hearing. If he fails to appear in court, his rights are automatically terminated. If the birth father does appear in court and contests the adoption, the court will determine if he is the birth father and then determine if it is in the child's best interest to be placed with him or to be placed for adoption.

What fees can adoptive parents pay?

Adoptive parents can pay medical, legal, and reasonable living expenses, and must file with the court all expenses paid.

Where does the adoption hearing take place?

The hearing takes place in the county where the adoptive parents live.

How are familial and step-parent adoptions different from nonbiological adoptions?

The home study is more superficial and is conducted by the county. In a step-parent adoption, the parents must be married at least one year.

In a relative adoption, the birth parents' rights can be terminated by a citation hearing as well as by the same methods as an independent adoption. Consents are revocable, by court order, until the final adoption. No accounting report is required and no placement agreement is required. Also, there is no requirement for the birth parent to meet with an Adoption Service Provider.

Beverly R. Williscroft, an adoption attorney in Concord, states that in a step-parent adoption, there is no statutory time limit in which the adoption must be completed, so the process often takes a long time.

If a child is adopted by a step-parent or grandparent and one of child's parents is deceased, then the deceased parent's parents may be granted visitation rights if it is in the child's best interest.

Can a nonresident finalize an adoption in this state?
No.

NOTE: There are many facilitators who "find" birth mothers. They market themselves to look like agencies and try to recruit adoptive parents, and while doing so, also find birth mothers, although they cannot advertise to find birth mothers. The facilitators' fees can be very high—as much as $6,000—just to find a birth mother. If a facilitator finds a birth mother, you must also use an attorney and a counselor for the birth mother. Some facilitators do much for the birth mother and their fee includes making many arrangements such as finding an apartment, making health care visits, and so on.

According to David Keane Leavitt, an adoption attorney in Beverly Hills, birth mothers are often contacted through obstetricians. In California, this method of contacting birth mothers is very different from most states. Since physicians can serve as intermediaries, perhaps this is the reason why so many are willing to tell birth mothers and adoptive parents about each other.

COLORADO

State Adoption Specialists
Barbara Killmore/Charlotte Little
Colorado Department of Social
  Services
Child Welfare Services
1575 Sherman Street, 2nd Floor
Denver, CO 80203-1714
(303) 866-3209 or 866-3228

Compact Administrator
Karen Beye, Director
Department of Social Services
1575 Sherman Street
Denver, CO 80203-1714

Deputy Compact Administrator
Beverly Soholt, LCSW
Child Welfare Services
Department of Social Services
1575 Sherman Street, 2nd Floor
Denver, CO 80203-1714
(303) 866-5140
fax (303) 866-2214

Chantal Corr, ICPC Assistant
(303) 866-2998

Office hours:
Monday-Friday
8:00 A.M.-5:00 P.M.
Mountain Time Zone

State Adoption Exchange and
  Photo Listing
Colorado Adoption Resource
  Registry (CARR)
Colorado Department of Human
  Services
Child Welfare Services
1575 Sherman Street, 2nd Floor
Denver, CO 80203-1714
(303) 866-3209

Private Adoption Agencies

AAC Adoption and Family
  Network
307 Welch Avenue
P.O. Box W
Berthoud, CO 80513
(970) 532-3576

Adoption Advocacy
  and Alternatives
P.O. Box 270683
Ft. Collins, CO 80527
(970) 493-5868

Adoption Alliance
3090 South Jamaica Court,
  Suite 106
Aurora, CO 80014
(303) 337-1731

Adoption Center of America,
  Ltd./Adoption Choice
1119 North Wahsatch, Suite 2
Colorado Springs, CO 80903
(970) 444-0198

Adoption Centre
6535 South Dayton, Suite 1950
Englewood, CO 80111
(303) 799-6852

Adoption Consultants, Inc.
200 Union Boulevard, Suite G-16
Lakewood, CO 80228
(303) 988-4226

Adoption Option
2600 South Parker Road,
Suite 2-320
Aurora, CO 80014
(303) 695-1601

Adoption Services, Inc.
2212 West Colorado Avenue
Colorado Springs, CO 80904
(970) 632-9941

Bethany Christian Services of
Colorado
2140 South Ivanhoe, Suite 106
Denver, CO 80222
(303) 758-4484

Catholic Community Services
of the Diocese of Colorado
Springs
29 West Kiowa
Colorado Springs, CO 80903
(970) 636-2345

Catholic Social Services, Inc.
Family Counseling Center
302 Jefferson
Pueblo, CO 81005
(719) 544-4234

Chinese Children Adoption
International
1100 W. Littleton Boulevard
Littleton, CO 80120
(303) 347-2224

Christian Family Services
1399 South Havana Street,
Suite 204
Aurora, CO 80012
(303) 337-6747

Christian Home for Children, Inc.
1880 South Cascade Avenue
Colorado Springs, CO 80906-
2590
(970) 632-4661

Colorado Adoption Center
1136 East Stuart Street,
Suite 2040
Fort Collins, CO 80525
(970) 493-8816

Colorado Adoption Center
4175 Harlan
Wheatridge, CO 80033
(303) 467-3128

Colorado Christian Services
4796 South Broadway
Englewood, CO 80110
(303) 761-7236

Covenant International, Inc.
2055 Anglo Drive, Suite 104
Colorado Springs, CO 80918
(970) 531-5100

Creative Adoptions
2546 West Main Street, Suite 100
Littleton, CO 80120
(303) 730-7791

Denver Catholic
Community Services, Inc.
1020 Upham Street
Lakewood, CO 80215
(303) 238-0521

Designated Adoption Services
of Colorado, Inc.
1420 Vance Street, Suite 202
Lakewood, CO 80215
(303) 232-0234

Family Extension
525 3rd Avenue
P.O. Box 1458
Longmont, CO 80502
(303) 776-1224

Family Ties Adoption Agency
7257 Rogers Street
Golden, CO 80403
(303) 420-3660

Friends of Children
of Various Nations
1756 High Street
Denver, CO 80218
(303) 321-8251

Hand in Hand
1617 West Colorado Avenue
Colorado Springs, CO 80904
(970) 473-8844

Hope's Promise
309 Jerry Street, Suite 202
Castle Rock, CO 80104
(303) 660-0277

Innovative Adoptions, Inc.
1850 Race Street
Denver, CO 80206
(303) 355-2107

LDS Social Services
(Colorado Agency)
3263 Fraser Street, Suite 3
Aurora, CO 80111
(303) 371-1000

Littlest Angels, International
1512 Grand Avenue
Glenwood Springs, CO 81601
(970) 945-2949

Loving Homes
2406 North Grand Avenue
Pueblo, CO 81003-2406
(719) 545-6181

Lutheran Family Services
503 Remington
Ft. Collins, CO 80524
(970) 484-5955

Lutheran Social Services
of Colorado
3707 Parkmoor Village Drive,
Suite 101
Colorado Springs, CO 80917
(970) 597-0700

Lutheran Social Services
of Colorado, Inc.
363 South Harlan Street
Denver, CO 80226
(303) 922-3433

Parent Resource Center
7025 Tall Oak Drive
Colorado Springs, CO 80919
(970) 599-7772

Professional Adoption Services
1210 South Parker Road,
Suite 104
Denver, CO 80231
(303) 755-4797

Rainbow House International
547 Humboldt Street
Denver, CO 80218
(303) 830-2108

Small Miracles
6160 South Syracuse Way,
Suite 310
Englewood, CO 80111
(303) 220-7611

Top of the Trail
3760J 75 Road
Paonia, CO 81428
(970) 527-4385

Whole Family, The
190 East 9th Avenue, Suite 200
Denver, CO 80203
(303) 863-8443

Worldwide Children's
Connection
191 East Orchard Road, Suite 105
Littleton, CO 80121
(303) 798-5250

**Adoptive Parent Support
Groups and Postadoption
Services**

Adoptive Families of Denver
Attn.: Pat Kluck or Marge Moran
918 Clover Circle
Lafayette, CO 80026-1774
(303) 730-1044

Adoptive Families of Ft.
Collins/Welcome a Child
Attn.: Susan Elbinger
or Diana Shropshire
(303) 224-2924 or 224-3022

Adoptive Parent Support Group
for Developmentally Disabled
Attn.: Bev Milligan
Westminster, CO
(303) 428-4266

Adoptive Parents of Colorado
Springs
Attn.: Anita Walter
(719) 590-7126

Adoptive Support Group
Attn.: Jackie Gianunzio
Colorado Springs, CO
(719) 577-4527

Advocates for Black Adoption
Attn.: John Adams
4715 Crystal Street
Denver, CO 80239
(303) 375-1531

Attachment Center at Evergreen
P.O. Box 2764
Evergreen, CO 80439
(303) 674-1910

Attachment Disorder Network
Attn.: Gail Trenberth
Boulder, CO
(303) 443-1446

Boulder County Partners in
Adoption
Attn.: Carol Etter
Boulder County, CO
(303) 494-5361

Colorado Parents for All Children
Attn.: Cheryl Berce
4769 North Academy Boulevard
Colorado Springs, CO 80918
(719) 599-9099

Colorado Parents for All Children
Attn.: Linda Donovan
780 East Phillips Drive South
Littleton, CO 80122
(303) 794-4838

Colorado Parents for All Children
Attn.: Tina Tubbs-Oberheid
Mountain Area, CO
(303) 668-3780

Denver Adoptive Mothers Club
Attn.: Haroldyne Freeke
Denver, CO
(303) 935-3847

Evergreen Consultants
in Human Behavior
28000 Meadow Drive, Suite 206
Evergreen, CO 80439
(303) 674-5503

Family Attachment Institute
P.O. Box 1731
Evergreen, CO 80439
(303) 674-0738

HCC Adoption Link
9495 East Florida Avenue
Denver, CO 80231
(303) 369-8514

Innovative Adoption Solutions,
Inc.
Attn.: Naomi Reid
1850 Race Street
Denver, CO 80206
(303) 355-2107

International Concerns
Committee for Children
Attn.: Anne Marie Merrill
911 Cypress Drive
Boulder, CO 80303
(303) 494-8333

Jewish Children's Adoption
Network
Attn.: Vicki Krausz
P.O. Box 16544
Denver, CO 80216
(303) 573-8113

Longmont Adoptive Families
Attn.: Donna Pratt
Longmont, CO
(303) 776-1749

Loving Bonds
Attn.: Drive Patricia Olson
Fort Collins, CO
(303) 223-0239

Lucky Mothers Club
Attn.: Karen Stone
Denver, CO
(303) 690-8649

Multi-Racial Families of Colorado
Attn.: Cindy Fields
Denver, CO
(303) 399-5986

North American Council
on Adoptable Children
State Representative
Attn.: Violet Pierce
6660 S. Race Circle West
Littleton, CO 80121
(303) 795-2890

Parents of Adopted Teens
Attn.: Alice Levine
Boulder, CO
(303) 447-0799

Pikes Peak Foster Adoptive
Resources
Attn.: Kimm Bolding
1158 Kachina Drive
Colorado Springs, CO 80915
(719) 597-7797

Single Adoptive Families
Everywhere/Adoptive Families
of Denver
Attn.: Judy Stewart
6451 South Lakeview
Littleton, CO 80120
(303) 730-1044

South Suburban Mothers Club
Attn.: Chris Peterson
(303) 972-1471

Stars of David
Attn.: Milly Nadler
100 Julian Street
Denver, CO 80219
(303) 922-3037

Whole Family, Inc.
Attn.: Nancy Murray
190 East 9th Avenue, Suite 200
Denver, CO 80203
(303) 863-8443

**Adopted Person and Birth
Relative Support Groups**

Adoptees and Birthparents
Together
708 Garfield
Ft. Collins, CO 80524
(303) 226-2956

Adoptees in Search
P.O. Box 323
Lakewood, CO 80215
(303) 232-6302

Adoptees Support Group
420 N. Nevada
Colorado Springs, CO 80903
(719) 471-8522

Birthparents Group
Box 16512
Colorado Springs, CO 80935

Colorado Confidential
Intermediary Services
P.O. Box 260460
Lakewood, CO 80226-0460
(303) 237-6919

Colorado Voluntary Adoption
Registry
Colorado Department of Health
4300 Cherry Creek Drive South
Denver, CO 80222-1530
(303) 692-2188

Concerned United Birthparents
10511 West 104th Avenue
Bloomfield, CO 80020
(303) 825-3430

Concerned United Birthparents
2895 Springdale Lane
Boulder, CO 80303
(303) 825-3430 or 447-8112

Lambs in Search
35780 Parkmoor Village Drive
Colorado Springs, CO 80917
(719) 550-0453

Orphan Voyage
2141 Road 2300
Cedaredge, CO 81413
(303) 856-3937

Re-Unite
P.O. Box 7945
Aspen, CO 81612
(303) 927-2400

Search and Support of Denver
805 S. Ogden
Denver, CO 80209
(303) 778-8612

Colorado State Bar Association
1900 Grant Street # 950, 9th
Floor
Denver, CO 80203-1714
(303) 860-1115

Adoption Attorneys

Thomas Beltz*
Adoption Choice Center
316 North Tejon Street

Colorado Springs, CO 80903
(719) 473-4444
fax (719) 444-0186

* Mr. Beltz also directs an
adoption agency, enabling
independent adoptions to
become identified adoptions, as
is required in Colorado. He has
conducted about 400 agency
adoptions and 250 international
adoptions.

Adoption Choice Center will
complete a home study
conducted in another state so
that it complies with Colorado's
Interstate Compact regulations.

Pamela Gordon*
468 Corona Street
Denver, CO 80218
(303) 777-6051

* Ms. Gordon has conducted
about fifty agency adoptions.

Susan Price*
777 W. Littleton Boulevard
Littleton, CO 80120-5825
(303) 347-2004
fax (303) 347-2778

* Ms. Price has conducted about
fifty independent adoptions and
hundreds of agency adoptions,
as well as a few international
adoptions.

COLORADO LAWS RELATED TO ADOPTION: QUESTIONS AND ANSWERS

Whether independent adoption is legal or not in Colorado is debatable, as the statute is
unclear. However, Thomas Beltz, an adoption attorney in Colorado Springs, has outlined
a uniform code for family court judges to follow when interpreting the statute. Beltz also
states that an independent adoption must become a "designated" adoption, which is

essentially an identified adoption. A birth mother and adoptive parents can meet without the assistance of an agency, but an agency must become involved by providing counseling to the birth mother, conducting a home study for the prospective adoptive couple, and completing certain forms.

In Colorado, adoptive parents can seek a birth mother through an intermediary such as an attorney, physician, or member of the clergy, and can also advertise. (Intermediaries cannot be reimbursed for that specific service.)

If an out-of-state couple finds a birth mother in Colorado, the couple must have their home study comply with Colorado Interstate Compact regulations.

Can an attorney serve as an intermediary?
Yes, although the attorney is not licensed to place children with adoptive parents and cannot charge for such a service.

Is advertising permitted?
Yes.

Who must consent to the adoption?
Both parents must consent.

When can consent be taken from the birth mother (father), and how long after the consent is signed can it be revoked?
Consents cannot be given until after the child is born and a personal court appearance is required.

What are the birth father's rights?
He must have notice of the adoption proceedings if he has not consented to the adoption.

What fees can adoptive parents pay?
Attorney fees and other fees are permitted if approved by the court. Only an adoption agency can receive payment in locating or identifying a child for adoption. A statement of all fees must be submitted to the court.

Where does the adoption hearing take place?
The hearing takes place in the county where the adoptive parents live or where the child placement adoption agency is located.

How are familial and step-parent adoptions different from nonbiological adoptions?
No agency involvement is required. The adoption process for a step-parent adoption is very simple. In a familial adoption, the adoptive parents can be named as guardians at the time of placement.

Can a nonresident finalize an adoption in this state?
Yes, if they comply with Colorado law. The birth parents' rights must be terminated through a court hearing. This usually occurs about 30 days after the child is born.

CONNECTICUT

Although independent adoption is illegal in Connecticut, an identified adoption can be completed with the help of an agency. For example, if a Connecticut couple advertises in another state and then finds a birth mother, the couple must still use an agency in the state where the baby is born to finalize the adoption. The adoption would then be an agency identified adoption. The agency must be on Connecticut's "Approved Agency" list. To determine which out-of-state agencies are approved, contact the Connecticut Deputy Compact Administrator's office, which is listed below. An adoption attorney in the state where the baby is born should help you meet the requirements of Connecticut's Interstate Compact regulations if you plan to finalize the adoption in the other state.

State Adoption Specialist
Jean Watson
Connecticut Department of
    Children and Youth Services
Whitehall Building 2
Undercliff Road
Meriden, CT 06451
(860) 238-6640

Compact Administrator
Lina D' Amario Rossi,
    Commissioner
Department of Children
    and Youth Services
170 Sigourney Street
Hartford, CT 06105
(860) 566-3536

Deputy Compact Administrator
Polly U. Champ
Program Supervisor
Interstate Compacts
Department of Children and
    Youth Services
Whitehall Building #2, 3rd Floor
Undercliff Road
Meriden, CT 06450
(860) 238-6405, 6406, 6407

Direct all correspondence and telephone calls to the Deputy Compact Administrator.

Office hours: Monday-Friday
8:30 A.M.-4:30 P.M.
(Eastern Time Zone)

State Adoption Exchange and
    Photo Listing
Connecticut Adoption Resource
    Exchange (CARE)
Undercliff Road, White Hall
    Building, #2
Meriden, CT 06451
(860) 238-6640

Private Adoption Agencies

Adoption Services of Connecticut
769 Newfield Street, Suite 2
Middletown, CT 06457-1815
(860) 635-0003; (800) 537-6230

Casey Family Program East
    (administrative offices)
1 Corporate Drive, Suite 515
Shelton, CT 06484
(800) 332-6991 or (203) 929-
    3837

Bridgeport Division
2400 Main Street
Bridgeport, CT 06606
(203) 334-6991

Hartford Division
43 Woodland Street
Hartford, CT 06105
(860) 727-1030

Catholic Charities
    of Diocese of Norwich
11 Bath Street
Norwich, CT 06360
(860) 889-8346

Catholic Charities/Catholic
    Family Services
Archdiocese of
Catholic Charities
    of Fairfield County
238 Jewett Avenue
Bridgeport, CT 06606
(203) 372-4301

Child Adoption Resource
    Association, Inc.
7 Vauxhall Street
New London, CT 06320
(860) 442-2797

A Child Among Us/The Center
    for Adoption, Inc.
2410 New London Turnpike
So. Glastonbury, CT 06073
(860) 657-2467

Children's Center
1400 Whitney Avenue
Hamden, CT 06514
(203) 248-2116

Curtis Home Corporation,
    Children's Program
380 Crown Street
Meriden, CT 06450
(860) 237-9526

Downeyside
829 Wethersfield Avenue
Hartford, CT 06114
(860) 296-3310

Family and Children's Aid of Mid-
    Fairfield County, Inc.
9 Mott Avenue
Norwalk, CT 06850
(203) 855-8765

Family Life Center
Shady Brook Lane
Norwalk, CT 06850
(203) 698-1808

Family Services, Inc.
92 Vine Street
New Britain, CT 06052
(860) 223-9291

Franciscan Family Care
    Center, Inc.
271 Finch Avenue
P.O. Box 417
Meriden, CT 06450
(860) 237-8084

Hall Neighborhood House
52 Green Street
Bridgeport, CT 06608
(203) 334-3900

Highland Heights (St. Francis
    Home for Children, Inc.)
651 Prospect Street, Box 1224
New Haven, CT 06505
(203) 777-5513

International Alliance for
    Children, Inc.
23 South Main Street
New Milford, CT 06776
(860) 354-3417

Jewish Family Services Inc.
2370 Park Avenue
Bridgeport, CT 06604
(203) 366-5438

Jewish Family Services Infertility
Center
740 North Main Street
West Hartford, CT 06117
(860) 236-1927

Jewish Family Services
of New Haven
1440 Whalley Avenue
New Haven, CT 06515
(203) 389-5599

LDS Social Services
1000 Mountain Road
P.O. Box 108
Bloomfield, CT 06002
(800) 735-0149

Lutheran Social Services
2139 Silas Deane Highway, Suite
201
Rocky Hill, CT 06067
(860) 257-0303

New Haven Family Alliance
5 Science Park
New Haven, CT 06511
(203) 786-5970

Professional Counseling Center
1 Eliot Pl.
Fairfield, CT 06430
(203) 259-5300

Quinebaug Valley Youth
and Family Services
303 Putnam Road
P.O. Box 378
Wauregan, CT 06387
(860) 564-6100 or (800) 953-
0295

Thursday's Child, Inc.
227 Tunxis Avenue
Bloomfield, CT 06002
(860) 242-5941

The Village for Families
and Children, Inc.
1680 Albany Avenue
Hartford, CT 06105
(860) 236-4511

Northeast District Office
110 Main Street
Manchester, CT 06040
(860) 643-2761

Wheeler Clinic, Inc.
91 Northwest Drive
Plainville, CT 06062
(860) 527-1644 or 747-6801

Wide Horizons
34 Connecticut Boulevard,
Suite 7
E. Hartford, CT
(860) 291-8610

**Adoptive Parent Support
Groups and Postadoption
Services**

Adoption Connection
3 Hampden Circle
Simsbury, CT 06070

Adoptive Parent Exchange
Support Group
Attn.: Deborah Stroffolino
6 Putnam Park Road
Bethel, CT 06801
(203) 743-9283

Attachment Disorder Parents
Network of Connecticut
85 Westwood Avenue
Plainville, CT 06062

Casey Family Services
Attn.: Ms. Linda E. Robertson
2400 Main Street
Bridgeport, CT 06605
(203) 334-6991

Connecticut Friends
of Adopted Children
P.O. Box 3246
Waterbury, CT 06705

FAITH
60 Wells Avenue
Shelton, CT 06484

International Adoptive Families
Attn.: Christine Hamilton
433 Quarry Brook Drive
South Windsor, CT 06074
(203) 270-1424

Latin America Parents
Association of Connecticut,
Inc.
Attn.: Christine Hamilton
P.O. Box 523
Unionville, CT 06085
(203) 270-1424

National Adoption Foundation
100 Mill Plain Road
Danbury, CT 06811
(203) 791-3811

Open Door Society of
Connecticut and North
American Council on
Adoptable Children State
Representative
Attn.: Lynn Gabbard
P.O. Box 478
Hartford, CT 06101
(860) 248-9937

Single Parents for the Adoption
of Children Everywhere
Attn.: Betty Laliberte
52 Back Lane
Wethersfield, CT 06109
(860) 257-9331

Stars of David
Attn.: Joan Margolis
c/o Jewish Family Service
740 North Main Street
West Hartford, CT 06117
(860) 236-1927

**Adopted Person and Birth
Relative Support Groups**

Adoptees Search Connection
1203 Hill Street
Suffield, CT 06078
(860) 668-1042

Adoption Answers Support
Kinship (AASK)
Attn.: Judy Taylor
8 Homestead Drive
South Glastonbury, CT
06073-2804
(860) 657-4005

Adoption Crossroads
956 Broad Street
Stratford, CT 06497

Adoption Healing
Attn.: Barbara Wille
F2 Hadik Pkwy.
South Norwalk, CT 06854
(203) 866-6475

Birthparent Support Network
9 Whitney Road
Columbia, CT 06237
(860) 228-0076

Ties That Bind
P.O. Box 3119
Milford, CT 06460
(203) 874-2023

**Connecticut State Bar
 Association**
101 Corporate Place
Rocky Hill, CT 06067-1894
(860) 721-0025

Adoption Attorneys

Janet Stulting*
68 South Main Street
P.O. Box 270748
West Hartford, CT 06127-0748
(860) 561-4832
fax (860) 521-5560

* Ms. Stulting has conducted
 about 200 agency adoptions.
 Her usual fee is about $1,000.

CONNECTICUT LAWS RELATED TO ADOPTION: QUESTIONS AND ANSWERS

Can an attorney serve as an intermediary?
No.

Is advertising permitted?
Yes.

Who must consent to the adoption?
1. Birth parents
2. The adoptive parents

When can consent be taken from the birth mother (father), and how long after the consent is signed can it be revoked?
According to Janet Stulting, an attorney from West Harford, a consent can be taken forty-eight hours after the child's birth and is revocable until the court hearing (about thirty days later).

Because most birth mothers and adoptive parents do not want the baby in foster care, some agencies place the baby directly in the adoptive couple's home before the first court hearing. This is considered a "legal risk placement" (i.e., the birth mother can change her mind after the baby is in the adoptive parents' home).

What are the birth father's rights?
If he has been named or claims to be the birth father, he must be notified of the adoption proceedings. He must assert his rights or his rights will be terminated.

What fees can adoptive parents pay?
This issue is not addressed in the existing laws, but a couple can pay all reasonable living and medical expenses through an agency.

Where does the adoption hearing take place?
The hearing takes place in the county where the adoptive parents live or where the child placement adoption agency is located.

How are familial and step-parent adoptions different from nonbiological adoptions?
No agency involvement is required. If all necessary persons have consented, the court will waive the investigation and report by the Children and Youth Services.

Can a nonresident finalize an adoption in this state?
Yes.

DELAWARE

State Adoption Specialist
Bob Lindecamp
Delaware Department of Services
for Children and Their Families
1825 Faulkland Rd
Wilmington, DE 19805
(302) 633-2655

Compact Administrator
Mary Ball Morton, Service
    Administrator
Office of Case Management
Delaware Department of Services
for Children and Their Families
1825 Faulkland Rd, 2nd Floor
Wilmington, DE 19805
(302) 633-2676

Deputy Compact Administrator
Rose Marie Homquist
Office of Case Management
Delaware Department of Services
for Children and Their Families
1825 Faulkland Road, 2nd Floor
Wilmington, DE 19805
(302) 633-2698, 2683
fax (302) 633-2565

Direct all correspondence and
    telephone calls to the Deputy
    Administrator.

Office hours:
Monday-Friday
8:00 A.M.-4:30 P.M.
Eastern Time Zone

**State Adoption Exchange
    and Photo Listing**

Deladopt
Delaware Department of Services
    for Children, Youth,
    and Their Families
1825 Faulkland Road
Wilmington, DE 19805
(302) 633-2655

Private Adoption Agencies

Adoptions from the Heart
Suite 18A, Trolley Square
Wilmington, DE 19806
(302) 658-8883

Bethany Christian Services
308 Possum Park Road
Newark, DE 19711
(302) 737-2890

Catholic Charities
442 South New Street
Dover, DE 19901
(302) 674-1600

Catholic Charities
21 Chestnut Street
Georgetown, DE 19947
(302) 856-9578

Catholic Charities
4th Street and Greenhill Avenue
Wilmington, DE 19805
(302) 655-9624

Child and Home Study Associates
101 Stone Crop Road
Wilmington, DE 19810
(302) 475-5433

Children's Choice of Delaware
910 B Walker Road
Dover, DE 19901-2759
(302) 678-0404

Family and Children Services
    of Delaware, Inc.
611 South DuPont Highway
Milford, DE 19963
(302) 422-8013

Family and Children Services
    of Delaware, Inc.
2005 Baynard Boulevard
Wilmington, DE 19802
(302) 658-5177

LDS Social Services
502 West Chestnut Hill
Newark, DE 19711
(302) 456-3782

Madison Adoption Agency
1009 Woodstream Drive
Wilmington, DE 19810
(302) 475-8977

Welcome House, Inc.
910 Barley Drive
Wilmington, DE 19807
(302) 654-7683

**Adoptive Parent Support
    Groups and Postadoption
    Services**

Adoptive Families with
    Information and Support
Attn.: Mary Lou Edgar
2610 Northgate Road
Wilmington, DE 19810
(302) 475-1027

Delaware Coalition for Children
Attn.: Nancy McKenna
23 Arthur Drive, RD#1
Hockessin, DE 19707
(302) 239-7340

North American Council
    on Adoptable Children State
    Representative
Attn.: Barbara Bancroft
523 Ashland Ridge Road
Hockessin, DE 19707
(302) 239-0727

**Adopted Person and Birth
    Relative Support Groups**

Adoption Forum of Delaware
Attn.: Carolyn Hoard
20 Weates Drive
Penn Acres, DE 19720
(302) 325-2903

Finders Keepers
P.O. Box 748
Bear, DE 19701-0748
(302) 836-9888

Delaware State Bar Association
1225 North King Street
Wilmington, DE 19801
(302) 658-5278

Adoption Attorneys

Ellen S. Meyer
521 West Street
Wilmington, DE 19801
(302) 429-0344

Joel Tenenbaum
3200 Concord Pike
P.O. Box 7329
Wilmington, DE 19803
(302) 477-3200

DELAWARE LAWS RELATED TO ADOPTION: QUESTIONS AND ANSWERS

Independent adoption is illegal in Delaware. Identified adoptions are permitted, however, and most agencies are willing to conduct them.

If the fees for an agency are too high, it is suggested that a Delaware couple contact an attorney, then advertise and finalize an adoption in one of the following nearby states: New York, New Jersey, Pennsylvania, Maryland, Washington, D.C., Virginia, or South Carolina. (In New Jersey, Maryland, and D.C. an agency must be involved if an out-of-state couple finalizes there.) However, a Delaware agency must conduct your home study.

Can an attorney serve as an intermediary?
No.

Is advertising permitted?
No.

Who must consent to the adoption?
1. Both birth parents
2. A licensed agency or the Department of Services for Children, Youth and Their Families

When can consent be taken from the birth mother (father), and how long after the consent is signed can it be revoked?
Consent cannot be given by the birth mother until the child is born, but can be given by the birth father before the child's birth. The birth parents or agency can request the court to revoke the consent within sixty days after filing the adoption petition. The court will then decide what is in the best interest of the child.

What are the birth father's rights?
The presumed father's consent is required unless he has abandoned the child.

What fees can adoptive parents pay?
The agency can only charge for services rendered, court costs, and legal fees.

Where does the adoption hearing take place?
The hearing can take place in the county where the adoptive parents reside or where the child placement agency is located.

How are familial and step-parent adoptions different from nonbiological adoptions?
An agency adoption is not required, but a home study is required, and the child must be in the home for at least one year.

Can a nonresident finalize an adoption in this state?
No. You must be a resident. However, no specific length of time is required to establish residency.

DISTRICT OF COLUMBIA

State Adoption Specialist
Mae Best
District of Columbia Department
of Human Services
609 H Street, NE., Room 313
Washington, D.C. 20002
(202) 724-8602

Deputy Compact Administrator
Lucille Huff
Child and Family Services
Division
District of Columbia Department
of Human Services
609 H Street, N.E. 3rd Floor
Washington, D.C. 20002
(202) 724-2093
fax (202) 727-4782 (emergency
only)

Compact Assistant
Marilyn Dickenson, MSW
(202) 724-2093

Office hours:
Monday-Friday
8:15 A.M.-4:45 P.M.
Eastern Time Zone

Private Adoption Agencies

Adoption Center of Washington
1990 M Street, N.W., Suite 380
Washington, DC 20036
(202) 452-8278

Adoption Service Information
Agency (ASIA)
7720 Alaska Avenue, N.W.
Washington, DC 20012
(202) 726-7193

American Adoption Agency
1228 M Street, N.W., 2nd Floor
Washington, DC 20005
(202) 638-1543

Barker Foundation
1200 18th Street, N.W., Suite 312
Washington, DC 20036
(202) 363-7751

Catholic Charities - Archdiocese
of District of Columbia
1438 Rhode Island Avenue, N.E.
Washington, DC 20018
(202) 526-4100

Datz Foundation
4545 42nd Street, N.W.,
Suite 209
Washington, DC 20016
(202) 686-3400

Family and Child Services
of Washington, D.C.
929 L Street, N.W.
Washington, DC 20001
(202) 289-1510

Holy Cross Child Placement
Agency, Inc.
1915 I Street, N.W., Suite 500
Washington, DC 20006
(202) 332-1367

International Children's Alliance
1101 17th Street, N.W.,
Suite 1002
Washington, DC 20036
(202) 463-6874

International Families, Inc.
5 Thomas Circle, N.W.
Washington, DC 20005
(202) 667-5779

Lutheran Social Services
of the National Capital Area
4406 Georgia Avenue, N.W.
Washington, DC 20011
(202) 723-3000

New Family Foundation
3615 Wisconsin Avenue, N.W.
Washington, DC 20016
(202) 244-1400

·Progressive Life Center
1123 11th Street, N.W.
Washington, DC 20001
(202) 842-2016

World Child, Inc.
4300 16th Street, N.W.
Washington, DC 20011
(202) 829-5244

**Adoptive Parent Support
Groups and Postadoption
Services**

Adoption Resource Exchange
for Single Parents
P.O. Box 5782
Springfield, VA 22150
(703) 866-5577

Adoption Support Institute
Attn.: Karen Howze
1319 Geranium Street, N.W.
Washington, DC 20012
(202) 291-2290

American Adoption Agency
Adoptive Parent Support Group
1228 M Street, N.W., 2nd Floor
Washington, DC 20005
(202) 638-1543

ASIA Families and Friends
Attn.: Margie Perscheid
1906 Sword Lane
Alexandria, VA 22308
(703) 799-4945

Families Adopting Children
Everywhere
P. O. Box 28058,
Northwood Station
Baltimore, MD 21239
(410) 488-2656

Families for Private Adoption
P. O. Box 6375
Washington, DC 20015-0375
(202) 722-0338

Interracial Family Circle
P.O. Box 53290
Washington, DC 20009
(202) 393-7866 or (800) 500-
9040

Latin America Parents
Association of the National
Capital Region
Attn.: Sheila Mooney
P.O. Box 4403
Silver Spring, MD 20914-4403
(301) 431-3407

National Council for Adoption
1930 17th Street, N.W.
Washington, DC 20009
(202) 328-1200

Stars of David
Attn.: Ilene Gottfried
(301) 622-4757

Washington, DC Area
Association of Single Adoptive
Parents
Attn.: Letty Grishaw
P.O. Box 1704
Springfield, VA 22151
(703) 521-0632

Adopted Person and Birth
Relative Support Groups

Adoptee Birthparent
Support Network
3421 M Street, N.W., Suite 328
Washington, DC 20007
(202) 686-4611

Adoptees in Search
P.O. Box 41016
Bethesda, MD 20824
(301) 656-8555

American Adoption Congress
1000 Connecticut Avenue, N.W.,
Suite 9
Washington, DC 20036
(202) 483-3399

Barker Foundation Adult
Adoptee Support Group
7945 MacArthur Boulevard,
Suite 206
Cabin John, MD 20818
(301) 229-8300

Barker Foundation Birthparent
Support Group
7945 MacArthur Boulevard,
Suite 206
Cabin John, MD 20818
(301) 229-8300

District of Columbia Bar
Association
1819 H Street, N.W., 12th Floor
Washington, D.C. 20006-3690
(202) 223-6600
fax (202) 331-3883

Adoption Attorneys

Ellen Ann Callaham
12600 War Admiral Way
Gaithersburg, MD 20878
(301) 258-2664

Mark Eckman
4545 42 Street N.W.
Suite 209
Washington D.C. 20016
(703) 242-8801

Mark McDermott*
1300 19th Street, N.W., Suite 400
Washington, D.C. 20036
(202) 331-1955
fax (202) 293-2309

* Mr. McDermott has conducted
over 500 independent
adoptions and over 100 agency
adoptions.

Stanton Phillips*
2009 North 14th Street, Suite 510
Arlington, VA 22201
(703) 522-8800

* Mr. Phillips is the editor of the
Adoption Law Journal. He has
represented clients in more
than 600 adoption cases.

Nancy Poster
9909 Georgetown Pike
P.O. Box 197
Great Falls, VA 22066
(703) 759-1560

Leslie Scherr
1225 Eye Street, N.W., Suite 900
Washington, D.C. 20005
(202) 371-8900

James Shrybman
801 Wayne Avenue, Suite 400
Silver Spring, MD 20910
(301) 588-0040

Peter J. Wiernicki
1300 19th Street, N.W., Suite 400
Washington, DC 20036
(202) 331-1955

D. C. LAWS RELATED TO ADOPTION: QUESTIONS AND ANSWERS

Can an attorney serve as an intermediary?
No.

Is advertising permitted?
Yes.

Who must consent to the adoption?
1. Both birth parents
2. The child placement adoption agency, if involved

When can consent be taken from the birth mother (father), and how long after the consent is signed can it be revoked?
A relinquishment is given in an agency adoption and a consent is given in an independent adoption. These can both be signed seventy-two hours after the child's birth. A relinquishment can be revoked up to ten days after signing. A consent is irrevocable.

What are the birth father's rights?
As long the birth father has been given notice, if it can be proved during a hearing that he has abandoned the child or has not provided support to the child for at least six months, his consent is not required. Also, his consent is not required if the court determines after a

hearing that consent is withheld contrary to the best interests of the child. If the birth father cannot be located, the court will waive his consent after a detailed search is conducted.

What fees can adoptive parents pay?
There are no laws regarding permissible fees; however, medical and legal fees can be paid.

Where does the adoption hearing take place?
The Superior Court of D.C. has jurisdiction if the adoptive couple is a legal resident of D.C. or has lived there for one year, or if the child is in the legal custody of an agency licensed by D.C.

How are familial and step-parent adoptions different from nonbiological adoptions?
In a step-parent adoption, the court may waive the home study if the noncustodial parent consents to the adoption.

Can a nonresident finalize an adoption in D.C.?
Yes. However, the adoption must be an agency placement.

FLORIDA

State Adoption Specialist
Gloria Walker
Florida Department of Health
and Rehabilitative Services
2811-E Industrial Plaza Drive
Tallahassee, FL 32308
(904) 487-2383

Compact Administrator
Samuel G. Ashdown, Jr.
Children and Family Services
(PDCFI)
Florida Department of Health
and Rehabilitative Services
1317 Winewood Boulevard,
Building 8
Tallahassee, FL 32399-0700
(904) 487-2760

Deputy Compact Administrator
Linda Scott
HRS-PDCFI
Interstate Compact on
the Placement of Children
1317 Winewood Boulevard
Tallahassee, FL 32399-0700
(904) 487-2760
fax (904) 487-4337

Direct all correspondence and
telephone calls to the Deputy
Compact Administrator.

Office hours:
Monday-Friday
8:00 A.M.-5:00 P.M.
Eastern Time Zone

**State Adoption Exchange
and Photo Listings**

Florida's Waiting Children
Florida Department of Health
and Rehabilitative Services
2811-E Industrial Plaza Drive
Tallahassee, FL 32308
(904) 487-2383

Adoption Information Center
Daniel Memorial, Inc.
134 East Church Street
Jacksonville, FL 32202
(800) 962-3678
(904) 353-0679 (in FL)

Private Adoption Agencies

Adoption Advocates, Inc.
11407 Seminole Boulevard
St. Petersburg, FL 34648-3238
(813) 391-8096

Adoption Agency of Central
Florida
200 West Welbourne Avenue
Winter Park, FL 32789
(407) 644-2117

Adoption By Choice
4102 W. Linebaugh Avenue,
Suite 200
St. Andrew's Square
Tampa, FL 33624
(813) 960-2229

Adoption Centre, Inc.
341 N. Maitland Avenue,
Suite 260
Maitland, FL 32751
(305) 740-0044

Adoption Placement, Inc.
2734 East Oakland Park
Boulevard, Suite 104
Ft. Lauderdale, FL 33306
(305) 564-2950

Adoption Resources of Florida
2753 State Road 580
Clearwater, FL 34621
(813) 726-4555

Adoption Services, Inc.
3003 S. Congress Avenue,
Suite 1C/1F
Palm Springs, FL 33461
(407) 969-0591

Advent Christian Home
for Children
P.O. Box 4309
Dowling Park, FL 32062
(904) 658-3333

All About Adoptions
501A E. New Haven Avenue
Melbourne, FL 32901
(407) 723-0088

Bond of Love Adoption Agency,
Inc.
2520 South Tamiami Trail
Sarasota, FL 34239
(813) 957-0064

Catholic Charities
900 54th Street
West Palm Beach, FL 33407
(407) 842-2406

Catholic Charities, Inc.
6533 94th Avenue, N.,
    Suite 1-East
St. Petersburg, FL 33710
(813) 345-9126

Catholic Charities of the Diocese
    of Venice, Inc.
2210 Santa Barbara Boulevard
Naples, FL 33963
(813) 455-2655

Catholic Charities Bureau
134 E. Church Street, Suite 100
Jacksonville, FL 32202-3130
(904) 354-3416
(904) 372-0294 (Branch in
    Gainesville)

Catholic Community Services,
    Inc.
1300 South Andrews Avenue
Fort Lauderdale, FL 33316
(305) 522-2513

Catholic Foster Services
18601 S.W. 97th Avenue
Miami, FL 33157
(305) 238-1447

Catholic Social Service
    of Bay County
3128 East 11th Street
Panama City, FL 32024
(904) 763-0475

Catholic Social Services
319 Riveredge Boulevard,
    Suite 109
Cocoa, FL 32922
(407) 636-6144

Catholic Social Services
40 Beal Pkwy., S.W.
Fort Walton Beach, FL 32548
(904) 244-2825

Catholic Social Services
1771 North Semoran Boulevard
Orlando, FL 32807
(407) 658-1818

Catholic Social Services
855 West Carolina Street
Tallahassee, FL 32309
(904) 222-2180

Catholic Social Services
    of Pensacola
222 East Government Street
Pensacola, FL 32501
(904) 436-6410

Children's Home, Inc.
10909 Memorial Highway
Tampa, FL 33615
(813) 855-4435

Children's Home Society of
    Florida, North Coastal Division
201 Osceola Avenue
Daytona Beach, FL 32114
(904) 255-7407

Children's Home Society of
    Florida, Intercoastal Division
401 N.E. 4th Street
Fort Lauderdale, FL 33301
(305) 763-6573

Children's Home Society of
    Florida, Southwest Division
1524 Carson Street
Fort Myers, FL 33901
(813) 334-2008

Children's Home Society
    of Florida, FTP
2274 N. U.S. Highway 1
Fort Pierce, FL 34946
(407) 489-5601

Children's Home Society
    of Florida, Central
    Administrative Office
3027 San Diego Road
P.O. Box 10097
Jacksonville, FL 32207
(904) 398-3265

Children's Home Society of
    Florida, Rose Keller Division
842 Missouri Avenue, S.
Lakeland, FL 33801-4740
(813) 688-7968

Children's Home Society of
    Florida, Southeastern Division
800 N.W. 15th Street
Miami, FL 33136-1495
(305) 324-1262

Children's Home Society of
    Florida, Mid-Florida Division
403 S.E. 19th Avenue
Ocala, FL 32670
(904) 629-7597

Children's Home Society of
    Florida, Central Florida
    Division
212 Pasadena Place
Orlando, FL 32803-3828
(407) 422-4441

Children's Home Society of
    Florida, Western Division
875 Royce Street
Pensacola, FL 32503
(904) 494-5990
(904) 376-5186 (Branch in
    Gainesville)

Children's Home Society
218 Hardee Lane
Rockledge, FL 32955
(407) 636-0126

Children's Home Society of
    Florida, Gulf Coast Division
5700 54th Avenue, North
St. Petersburg, FL 33709-2095
(813) 546-4626 or 223-5383

Children's Home Society of
    Florida
1201 Hays Street, Suite 100
Tallahassee, FL 32301
(904) 877-5176

Children's Home Society of
    Florida, South Coastal Division
3600 Broadway
West Palm Beach, FL 33407-4844
(407) 844-9785

Chosen Children
3924 "A" Avenue
Lake Worth, FL 33461
(407) 964-2076

Christian Family Services, Inc.
2720 S.W. 2nd Avenue
Gainesville, FL 32607
(904) 378-6202

Clear Choice
2727 Ulmerton Road, Suite 2D
Clearwater, FL 34622
(813) 572-1557

Family Enrichment Center
6013 North 40th Street
Tampa, FL 33610
(813) 628-4432

First Coast Counseling
3601 Cardinal Point Drive
Jacksonville, FL 32257
(904) 448-1933

Florida Adoption and Children's
Center, Inc.
11410 N. Kendall Drive,
Bldg. B, Suite 306
Miami, FL 33176
(305) 274-2811

Florida Baptist Children's Home
7748 S.W. 95th Terrace
Miami, FL 33156
(305) 271-4121

Florida Baptist Children's Home
8415 Buck Lake Road
Tallahassee, FL 32311-9522
(904) 878-1458

Florida Baptist Family Ministries
1030 Central Avenue
P.O. Box 1870
Lakeland, FL 33802
(813) 688-4981

Gift of Life, Inc.
136 4th Street, North
St. Petersburg, FL 33701
(813) 920-6023

Gorman Family Life Center, Inc.,
dba Life for Kids
315 North Wymore Road
Winter Park, FL 32789
(407) 628-5433

Hearts and Homes for Children
858 North Xavier Avenue
Ft. Myers, FL 33919
(813) 481-4548

International Children's
Foundation
8620 N.E. Second Avenue,
Suite 207
Miami Shores, FL 33138
(305) 751-9600

Jewish Adoption
and Foster Care Options
300 South Pine Island, #246
Plantation, FL 33324
(305) 424-6734

Jewish Family Services
of Broward County
8358 W. Oakland Park
Boulevard, #304
Fort Lauderdale, FL 33321
(305) 749-1505

Jewish Family Services
of Broward County
6100 Hollywood Boulevard,
Suite 410
Hollywood, FL 33024
(305) 966-0956

Lake County Boys Ranch
P.O. Box 129
Altoona, FL 32702
(904) 669-3252

LDS Social Services
1020 N. Orlando Avenue, Suite F
Winter Park, FL 32789
(407) 628-8899

St. Vincent Adoption Center
18601 S.W. 97th Avenue
Miami, FL 33157
(305) 445-5714

Shepherd Care Ministries
9280-3 College Pkwy.
Fort Myers, FL 33919
(813) 433-1929

Shepherd Care Ministries
5935 Taft Street
Hollywood, FL 33021
(305) 981-2060

Shepherd Care Ministries
220 South Dixie Highway, #4
Lake Worth, FL 33460
(407) 588-3649

Shepherd Care Ministries
5200 Davison Highway, Suite B
Orlando, FL 32810
(407) 290-3286

Suncoast International
Adoptions, Inc.
14277 Walsingham Road
Largo, FL 34644
(813) 596-3135

Universal Aid for Children, Inc.
1600 S. Federal Highway, 2nd Flr.
Hollywood, FL 33020
(305) 925-7550

**Adoptive Parent Support
Groups and Postadoption
Services**

Adopt a Special Kid (AASK)
of Florida
P.O. Box 2173
Clewiston, FL 33440
(813) 983-8419

Adoption Resource Group
Attn.: Grace Ahlsen-Girard
3006 Northwood Boulevard
Orlando, FL 32803
(407) 644-9627

Bay Area Adoptive Families
Attn.: Drive Kathie Erwin
305 Orangewood Lane
Largo, FL 34640
(813) 581-6010

Families of Adopted Children
Together
Attn.: Jan Shoupe
234 S.E. Grove Avenue
Lucie, FL 34983
(407) 879-0668

Families Through Adoption
Attn.: Kathi Timmons
Box 420085
Naples, FL 33942-0085
(813) 591-4403

Gainesville Adoption Information
Network
Attn.: Susan Justus Weinstein
130 N.W. 28th Street
Gainesville, FL 32607-2511
(904) 377-6455

Gatherings of International
Adoptive Families
Attn.: Lori Stolt Bollman
2923 S.W. 5th Place
Cape Coral, FL 33914
(813) 574-4590

Harmony
P.O. Box 16996
West Palm Beach, FL 33416
(407) 439-4438

Hope: Share-N-Care
4062 Greenwillow Lane, E.
Jacksonville, FL 32211
(904) 743-9024

Lifeline for Children and North
American Council on
Adoptable Children State
Representative
Attn.: Gail Kreitz
611 N.W. 45th Avenue
Coconut Creek, FL 33066
(305) 972-2735

Parents Adoption Lifeline, Inc.
18 Cayman Place
Palm Beach Gardens, FL 33418
(407) 775-3092

People Adopting Children
Everywhere
P.O. Box 560293
Rockledge, FL 32956-0293
(407) 639-8895

Rainbow Families
11578 Tradewinds Boulevard
Largo, FL 34643
(813) 541-7084

Sarasota County Adoption
Support Group
Attn.: Carol Ann Davis
2570 Loma Linda Street
Sarasota, FL 34239
(813) 953-3426

Shepherd Care Ministries, Inc.
Attn.: Leigh Ann Johnson
5935 Taft Street
Hollywood, FL 33021

Stars of David
Attn.: Rabbi Michael Gold
Temple Beth Torah
9101-15 N.W. 57th Street
Tamarack, FL 33351
(305) 721-7660

Stressed Out Adoptive Parents
1403 N.W. 40th Avenue
Lauderhill, FL 33313
(305) 797-8368

Tapestry
Attn.: Mrs. Eileen Chin
3862 Marquise Lane
Mulberry, FL 33860
(813) 425-4112

Universal Aid for Children
Attn.: Ed and Norma Robinson
P.O. Box 610246
North Miami, FL 33261-0246
(305) 754-4886

**Adopted Person and Birth
Relative Support Groups**

Active Voices in Adoption
Box 24-9052
Coral Gables, FL 33124
(305) 667-0387

Adoptee Liberty Movement
Association (ALMA)
P.O. Box 4358
Fort Lauderdale, FL 33338
(305) 462-0958

Adoptee Liberty Movement
Association (ALMA)
P.O. Box 15343
West Palm Beach, FL 33416-5343

Adoption Connection
5524F Lakewood Circle
Margate, FL 33063
(305) 979-9351

Adoption Connection of Florida
3100 Hunter Road
Ft. Lauderdale, FL 33331
(305) 384-8909

Adoption Search and Support
of Tallahassee
P.O. Box 3504
Tallahassee, FL 32315
(904) 893-0004

Adoption Support and Knowledge
11646 N.W. 19th Drive
Coral Springs, FL 33071
(305) 753-3878

Adoption Triangle
1301 N.W. 2nd Avenue
Delray Beach, FL 33444
(407) 276-5737

ALARM Network
P.O. Box 6581
Fort Myers, FL 33911
(813) 542-1342

Birthparent Support Group
176 Harris Street, N.E.
Ft. Walton Beach, FL 32547
(904) 863-5877

Christian Adoptees
Support Exchange
2354 Willard Street
Ft. Myers, FL 33901

Circle of Hope
1125 N.W. 18th Avenue
Delray Beach, FL 33445
(407) 272-2930

Concerned United Birthparents
Box 1117
St. Augustine, FL 32085
(904) 829-9341

Florida Adoption Reunion
Registry
Florida Department of Health
and Rehabilitation Services
2811-E Industrial Plaza Drive
Tallahassee, FL 32301
(904) 353-0679
(800) 962-3678 (in FL)

Forever Families
130 N.W. 28th Street
Gainesville, FL 32607
(904) 377-6455

Mid-Florida Adoption Reunions
P.O. Box 3475
Bellview, FL 34421
(904) 237-1955

Mother and Child Reunion
2219 S.W. Mt. Vernon Street
Port St. Lucie, FL 34953
(407) 878-9101

National Organization for
Birthfathers and Adoption
Reform
P.O. Box 50
Punta Gorda, FL 33950
(813) 575-0948, 637-7477

Oasis
P.O. Box 530761
Miami Shores, FL 33153
(305) 948-8933

Orphan Voyage
1122 Marco Pl.
Jacksonville, FL 32207
(904) 398-4269

Orphan Voyage
13906 Pepperell Drive
Tampa, FL 33624
(813) 962-1620

People Searching News
Adoption Search National
Hotline and Reunion Registry
Adoptee-Birthparent Connection
P.O. Box 100444
Palm Bay, FL 32910-0444
(407) 768-2222

Search Light
1032 Veronica Street
Pt. Charlotte, FL 33952

Searches International
1600 W. 64th Street
Hialeah, FL 33012

Tallahassee Adoption
Support Group
275 John Knox Road, #F104
Tallahassee, FL 32303
(904) 385-8703

Triad Search and Support Group
3408 Neptune Drive
Orlando, FL 32804
(407) 843-2760

The Florida Bar
650 Apalachee Parkway
Tallahassee, FL 32399-1067
(904) 251-5600

Adoption Attorneys

Bennett Cohn
205 6th Street
West Palm Beach, FL 33401-4003
(407) 478-5292

Charlotte Danciu*
136 East Boca Raton Road
Boca Raton, FL 33432
(407) 392-5445
(407) 395-8002
fax (40) 393-0585

* Ms. Danciu has conducted
more than 1,000 independent
adoptions and more than 50
agency adoptions, as well as a
few international adoptions.

Donald Darrach
9350 S. Dixie Highway
Miami, FL 33156
(305) 670-9994

Helen Hope
6490 Griffin Road, Suite 100
Davie, FL 33314
(305) 791-9994

Linda McIntyre*
Coral Springs Professional
  Building
10239 West Sample Road
Coral Springs, FL 33065
(305) 344-0990

* Ms. McIntyre has conducted
more than 700 independent
adoptions and more than 200
agency adoptions.

Nancy S. Palmer*
213 Flame Avenue
Maitland, FL 32751
(407) 260-9786
(407) 648-9099

* Ms. Palmer has conducted
about 300 independent
adoptions, 100 agency
adoptions, and five
international adoptions.

Mary Ann Scherer
2734 E. Oakland Park Boulevard,
  #200
Fort Lauderdale, FL 33006
(305) 564-6900

Michael A. Shorstein
1660 Prudential Drive, #402
Jacksonville, FL 32207
(904) 348-6400

Laurie Slavin
17021 N.E. 6th
North Miami Beach, FL 33162
(305) 653-2474

Susan Stockham
P.O. Box 7092
Sarasota, FL 34278-7092
(813) 379-9290

Mary Ann Scherer*
2734 East Oakland Park
  Boulevard, Suite 200
Ft. Lauderdale, FL 33306
(305) 564-6900

* Ms. Scherer has conducted
about 500 independent
adoptions, 1,000 agency
adoptions, and 2,000
international adoptions.

Cynthia S. Swanson
500 E. University Avenue, #C
Gainesville, FL 32601
(904) 375-5602

Attorney fees in this state are
about $4,000 to $6,000.

FLORIDA LAWS RELATED TO ADOPTION: QUESTIONS AND ANSWERS

Can an attorney serve as an intermediary?
Yes. According to ICPC guidelines, an attorney or physician licensed in Florida can place children within the state. It is unlawful for an intermediary to accept a fee of more than $1,000.

Attorneys and agencies outside of Florida may place children in the state if they adhere to ICPC guidelines and the Florida Adoption Act. Birth parents who wish to place a child outside of the state must surrender the child to a licensed agency.

Is advertising permitted?
Yes. Technically only attorneys and agencies and obstetricians may advertise, but advertising is a well-accepted practice. The law requires that a license number be shown on all adoption-related advertisements in the state. However, in practice a couple can place an ad without an attorney. Many newspapers will require a letter from your attorney.

Who must consent to the adoption?
1. The birth mother
2. The birth father, if he has acknowledged in writing that he is the child's father or was married to the mother when the child was conceived or born, or if he has supported the child

When can consent be given by the birth mother (father), and how long after the consent is signed can it be revoked?
Consent cannot be given until the child is born. Once the consent is signed, it is irrevocable.

Unless excused by the court, the law requires an independent, licensed psychologist or social worker to interview the birth parents to ensure that consent was given on a voluntary basis. The same social worker would also conduct your home study before the baby is placed in your home.

What are the birth father's rights?
According to Charlotte Danciu, an adoption attorney in Boca Raton, the birth father may only challenge the adoption if he has provided meaningful emotional and financial support. The court must either excuse his consent or it must be obtained. The birth father's consent is not needed if he does not respond in writing to a request for his consent within sixty days.

What fees can adoptive parents pay?
All fees for an attorney or physician intermediary or out-of-state adoption agency must be submitted to the court for prior approval. Payment of living expenses is permitted up to six weeks after the baby's birth. Any fees over $1,000, except for medical, hospital or court costs, must be preapproved by the court. A final report of all fees associated with the adoption must be given to the court.

Where does the adoption hearing take place?
The adoption hearing takes place in the county where the adoptive parents reside, or where the child placement agency is located.

How are familial and step-parent adoptions different from nonbiological adoptions?
No home study is required unless requested by the court. If the grandparents have visitation rights, their rights continue if a relative or step-parent adopts the child.

Can a nonresident finalize an adoption in this state?
No. Only those whose primary residence and place of employment is Florida may adopt, unless a special-needs child is involved.

GEORGIA

State Adoption Specialist
Anne Jewett
Georgia Department
   of Human Resources
Two Peachtree Street, N.E. 13th
   Floor, Suite 317
Atlanta, GA 30303
(404) 657-3550

Compact Administrator
Douglas Greenwell, Director
Division of Family and Children
   Services
Georgia Department
   of Human Resources
Atlanta, GA 30303-3180

Deputy Compact Administrator
Janese Pullen, Acting Director
   Social Services
Department Of Human Resources
Atlanta, GA 30303-3180

Independent Placements
Edith Horne, Adoption
   Consultant
Division of Family
   and Children Services
Georgia Department
   of Human Resources
2 Peachtree Street, N.W., 12th
   Floor, Room 100
Atlanta, GA 30303-3180
(404) 894-3706
fax (404) 894-4672

Adoption Assistance
Gail Merlinger, Adoption
   Consultant
(404) 894-4469

Office hours:
Monday-Friday
8:00 A.M.-5:00 P.M.
Eastern Time Zone

State Adoption Exchange

Georgia State Adoption Exchange
Department of Human Resources
Two Peachtree Street N.W., 13th
   Floor, Suite 400
Atlanta, GA 30303
(404) 657-3550

State Photo Listing

My Turn Now
Two Peachtree Street, 12th Floor,
　Suite 204
Atlanta, GA 30303
(404) 657-3479

Private Adoption Agencies

Adoption Care
1447 Peachtree Street, Suite 511
Atlanta, GA 30309
(404) 897-1766

Adoption Planning, Inc.
17 Executive Park Drive,
　Suite 480
Atlanta, GA 30329
(404) 248-9105

Adoption Services, Inc.
P.O. Box 155
Pavo, GA 31778
(912) 859-2654

Bethany Christian Services
1867 Independence Square,
　Suite 201
Atlanta, GA 30338
(404) 396-7700

Bethany Christian Services
　of Tennessee, Inc.
4719 Brainerd Road, Suite D
Chattanooga, TN 37411
(615) 622-7360

Catholic Social Services, Inc.
Adoption Program
680 West Peachtree Street, N.W.
Atlanta, GA 30308
(404) 881-6571

Covenant Care Services, Inc.
363 Pierce Avenue, Suite 202
Macon, GA 31204
(912) 741-9829

Edgewood Baptist Church, Inc.
New Beginning Adoption
　and Counseling Agency
1316 Wynnton Court, Suite A
Columbus, GA 31906
(706) 571-3346

Families First
1105 West Peachtree Street
Atlanta, GA 30309
(404) 853-2800

Family Counseling
　Center/CSRA, Inc.
603 Ellis Street
Augusta, GA 30901
(706) 722-6512

Family Partners Worldwide, Inc.
1776 Peachtree Street N.W.,
　Suite 210 North
Atlanta, GA 30309
(404) 872-6787

Friends of Children, Inc.
5064 Roswell Road, N.E.,
　Suite B-201
Atlanta, GA 30342
(404) 256-2121

Georgia Association for Guidance,
　Aid, Placement and Empathy
　(AGAPE), Inc.
3094 Mercer University Drive,
　Suite 200
Atlanta, GA 30341
(404) 452-9995

Georgia Baptist Children's Home
　and Family Ministries
North Area (Palmetto)
Route 2, Box 4
Palmetto, GA 30268
(404) 463-3344

Greater Chattanooga
　Christian Services
400 Vine Street
Chattanooga, TN 37403
(615) 756-0281

Hope for Children, Inc.
1511 Johnson Ferry Road,
　Suite 100
Marietta, GA 30062
(404) 977-0813

Jewish Family Services, Inc.
Cradle of Love Adoption
　Counseling and Services
1605 Peachtree Street N.E.
Atlanta, GA 30309
(404) 873-2277

LDS Social Services
4832 North Royal Atlanta Drive
Tucker, GA 30084
(404) 939-2121

Lutheran Ministries of Georgia
726 West Peachtree Street, N.W.
Atlanta, GA 30308
(404) 607-7126

Open Door Adoption
　Agency, Inc.
403B N. Broad Street
P.O. Box 4
Thomasville, GA 31792
(912) 228-6339

Parent and Child
　Development Services
21 East Broad Street
Savannah, GA 31401
(912) 232-2390

Partners in Adoption, Inc.
1050 Little River Lane
Alpharetta, GA 30201
(404) 740-1371

ROOTS
5532G Old National Highway,
　Suite 250
College Park, GA 30349
(404) 209-8311

Adoptive Parent Support Groups and Postadoption Services

Adopted Kids and Parent Support
　Group (AKAPS)
Attn.: Marsha Kennedy
4137 Bellflower Court
Roswell, GA 30075
(404) 640-0031

Adoption Center
Atlanta Area
(404) 321-6900

Adoption Information Services
Attn.: Marsha Barker
Atlanta, GA
(404) 339-7236

Adoption Resource Exchange
Attn.: Norman Race
P.O. Box 6692
Americus, GA 31709
(912) 937-2591

Adoption Resource Exchange
　of Columbus
Attn.: Ivy Mallisham
P.O. Box 9304
Columbus, GA 31908-9304
(706) 569-9199

Adoption Services, Inc.
Parents Support Group
Attn.: Roxanne Walker
P.O. Box 155
Pavo, GA 31778
(912) 859-2654

Adoptive Families
of Gwinnett County
Attn.: Marjorie Thomaston
3980 Rocmar Drive
Lithonia, GA 30058
(404) 827-6114

Adoptive Families Support Group
Attn.: Nancy Sanderson
(706) 689-5562

Adoptive Parents Association
Attn.: Karen Turner
911 Moss Drive
Savannah, GA 31410
(912) 897-6840

All God's Children
Attn.: Garry Seitz
3621 Mars Hill Road
Watkinsville, GA 30677
(404) 725-7658

Alliance of Single
Adoptive Parents
Attn.: Sharyn Hilley
687 Kennolia Drive, S.W.
Atlanta, GA 30314
(404) 755-3280

American-Romanian Connection
Attn.: Mary Springer
(404) 978-0019

Augusta Adoption
League/Home Base
Attn.: Rick Derby
4245 Match Point Drive
Augusta, GA 30907-2712
(404) 863-0583

Augusta Adoption Agency
Special Needs Group
Attn.: Brenda Brown
(706) 541-1640

Bartow/Paulding Adoptive
Families
Attn.: Sylvia Baldwin
(404) 387-1008 or 387-3710

Cherokee County Adoptive
Parent Support Group
Attn.: Pam Collins
3075 Batesville Road
Woodstock, GA 30188
(404) 475-7410

Clarke County Adoption
Resource Exchange
Attn.: Susan Jones
P.O. Box 6311
Athens, GA 30604
(706) 353-8539
(706) 542-9800 (Special Needs
Group)

Clayton County Adoptive
Parent Support Group
Attn.: Drive Sherry Ramey
(404) 996-7622

Coffee County Adoption
Support Group
Attn.: Cheryl Cleveland
P.O. Box 422
Douglas, GA 31533

Decatur County Adoptive
Parents Support Group
Attn.: Brenda Reddick
(912) 248-2420

Douglas Region Adoptive
Families Together (DRAFT)
Attn.: Carol E. Jones
(404) 489-2239

Early Tri-County
Adoption Support Group
Attn.: Nancy Mock
(912) 723-4331

Emanuel County
Adoptive Parents Group
Attn.: Billie Scott
(912) 237-6494

Families Adopting Across Racial
Lines Support Group
Bethany Christian Services
Attn.: Karen Sievert
(404) 924-8645

Families By Choice
Attn.: Connie Sealy
(912) 474-8952

Families First Adoptive
Parent Support Group
1105 West Peachtree Street
Atlanta, GA 30309
(404) 853-2800

Families Forever
Post Adoption Project
Attn.: Noreen Horrigan
Two Peachtree Street, 13th Floor,
Suite 400
Atlanta, GA 30303
(404) 657-3556

Flint River Adoptive
Parent Support Group
Attn.: Jill Holder or Marsha
Raleigh
(404) 954-2354 or 954-2014

Fulton County Adoptive
Parent Support Group
Attn.: Drive McClellon Cox
3653 Rainbow Drive
Decatur, GA 30335
(404) 220-0210

Georgia Adoptive Parents
Attn.: Peggy Bethea
178 Sams Street
Decatur, GA 30030
(404) 658-7327 or 508-0081

Georgia Council
on Adoptable Children
Attn.: Linda Price
(404) 986-0760

Glynn County Adoptive Parents
Attn.: Mary Cira
(912) 638-8556

Gwinnett County Adoptive
Parents Support Group
Attn.: Barbara Sorenson
530 Northdale Road
Lawrenceville, GA 30245
(404) 995-2100

Houston County Adoptive
Parent Support Group
Attn.: Nancy McDowell
202 William John Lane
Bonaire, GA 31005
(912) 922-9699

Interracial Family Alliance
Attn.: Mark Lockhart
P.O. Box 20290
Atlanta, GA 30324
(404) 924-8453

Jenkins County
Adoptive Parents Group
Attn.: Billie Scott
(912) 237-6494

Lowndes Area
Adoption Support Group
Attn.: Claudia Benson
P.O. Box 3674
Valdosta, GA 31604
(912) 244-2852

Lutheran Ministries
Parent Support Group
Attn.: Joyce Hayes
(404) 607-7126

Lutheran Ministries
Parent Support Group
Attn.: Kari Manning
955 Ridgedale Drive
Lawrenceville, GA 30243
(404) 962-7370

Mid-Town
Adoptive Parent Group
Attn.: Susan Zoukis
(404) 892-0587

North American Council
on Adoptable Children
State Representative
Attn.: Kathryn Karp
P.O. Box 7727
Atlanta, GA 30357
(404) 657-3479

North Georgia OURS
Attn.: Barbara Gale
One Legion Drive
Lindale, GA 30147
(404) 232-2128

One Church,
One Child Program, Inc.
General L.M. Smoot
P.O. Box 115238
Atlanta, GA 30310
(404) 766-0383
(800) 662-3651

Prospective Adoptive Parent
and Adoptive Parent Group
of Marietta
Attn.: Kasey and Kimberly
Summer
225 Hamilton Court
Marietta, GA 30068

Screven County
Adoptive Parents Group
Attn.: Billie Scott
(912) 237-6494

Single Women
Adopting Children
Attn.: Lauri Lanning
(404) 730-4593

Soweta Six
Adoptive Parents Group
Attn.: Brenda Riddick
(912) 248-2420

Stars of David
Attn.: Jill Glass
3300 Arborwood Drive
Alpharetta, GA 30202

Statesboro Adoptive Families:
Action, Reassurance and Ideas
(SAFARI)
Attn.: Laurie Bradford
(912) 764-8130

Terrell Tri-County Adoption
Support Group
Attn.: Nancy Mock
(912) 723-4331

Warren, McDuffie, and Glascock
Counties Adoption Support
Group
Attn.: Brenda Brown
(706) 541-1640

White County Adoption Support
Group
Attn.: Kay Clinard
(706) 896-3524

Wilkes, Taliaferro, and Lincoln
Counties Adoption Support
Group
Attn.: Eloise Wood
(706) 678-2814

**Adopted Person and Birth
Relative Support Groups**

Adoptee Birthparent Connection
4565 Pond Lane
Marietta, GA 30062
(404) 642-9063

Adoptee Liberty Movement
Association (ALMA)
1344 Surrey Lane
Marietta, GA 30060

Adoptee's Search Network
3317 Spring Creek Drive
Conyers, GA 30208

Adoption Beginnings
P.O. Box 440121
Kennesaw, GA 30144
(404) 971-5263

Bridges in Adoption
665 Peach Creek Terr.
Alpharetta, GA 30302-4350
(404) 351-6779

Families First
1105 West Peachtree Street, N.E.
Atlanta, GA 30305
(404) 853-2800

State Bar of Georgia
800 The Hurt Building
50 Hurt Plaza
Atlanta, GA 30303
(404) 527-8700
(706) 456-2339

Adoption Attorneys

Adoption Planning, Inc.
Rhonda Fishbein*
17 Executive Park, Suite 480
Atlanta, GA 30329
(404) 248-9205
fax (404) 248-0419

* Ms. Fishbein has conducted
about sixty independent
adoptions, 175 agency
adoptions, and twenty-five
international adoptions.

Adoption Information Services,
Inc.*
558 Dovie Place
Lawrenceville, GA
(770) 339-7236

* Provides education and makes
referrals to domestic and
international adoption
programs.

Jerrold W. Hester
3941 Holcomb Bridge Road,
#200
Norcross, GA 30092
(404) 446-3645

Richard A. Horder
1100 Peachtree Street, #2800
Atlanta, GA 30309-4530
(404) 815-6538

Irene A. Steffas   Allan J. Tanenbaum
4187 Kindlewood Court   359 E. Paces Ferry Road, #400
Roswell, GA 30075-2686   Atlanta, GA 30305
(404) 642-6075   (404) 266-2930

GEORGIA LAWS RELATED TO ADOPTION: QUESTIONS AND ANSWERS

Can an attorney serve as an intermediary?

No.

Is advertising permitted?

No, and you may not post flyers either. Networking in Georgia is limited to those you know. We recommend getting out your school yearbook, and professional, church denomination, and volunteer membership directories and send letters to as many people as possible.

Georgia residents who advertise in another state cannot finalize the adoption in Georgia; they must finalize in the state where they advertised. Therefore, make sure non-residents can finalize in that state before you advertise.

Who must consent to the adoption?

1. The birth parents
2. The child placement agency, if involved

When can consent be taken from the birth mother (father), and how long after the consent is signed can it be revoked?

Consent cannot be obtained until twenty-four hours after the child's birth. In both an agency and independent adoption, the birth parents have ten days after signing the consent to withdraw consent.

What are the birth father's rights?

Georgia law requires that a known or unknown birth father has a right to a notice. The birth father of a child born out of wedlock must consent to the adoption if he is known, or be served with notice of the hearing. If he does not respond within thirty days to notice of adoption, his parental rights will be terminated, and he cannot legally object to the adoption. If his location is not known, a petition will be filed with the court to terminate his rights and allow the adoption to occur. The court will then make a decision to proceed with the adoption based on whether the birth father has established a familial bond with the child or if reasonable efforts were made to locate him. Publication for the unknown birth father must be done.

Judges very seldom permit a birth mother to *not* name the birth father. In one scenario, an adoption took more than a year to finalize because the birth mother would not name a birth father who had threatened her life.

Parental rights can also be terminated because of a felony and imprisonment that has a negative effect on the parent-child relationship.

What fees can adoptive parents pay?

Only medical and legal expenses for the birth mother and child are permitted. Any other payment is considered an inducement. Only in an agency adoption can living expenses be paid. A report of payments must be filed with the court. Every attorney must also file a report of all fees paid or promised to the attorney for all services rendered.

Where does the adoption hearing take place?

The hearing takes place in the court in the county where the adoptive parents reside.

How are familial and step-parent adoptions different from nonbiological adoptions?

Ms. Rhonda Fishbein, an adoption attorney in Atlanta, states that some courts do not require a home study. The child's biological parents must give written permission for a relative or step-parent to adopt the child.

If the grandparents have court-ordered visitation rights previous to an adoption, they may file an objection to an adoption by another blood relative. The court will then decide if the child should be adopted by the other relative. If the court approves the adoption, the grandparent's visitation rights remain.

Can a nonresident finalize an adoption in this state?

No. You must be a resident of Georgia for at least six months before filing to adopt.

HAWAII

State Adoption Specialist
Lynn Mirikidani
Hawaii Department
   of Human Services
810 Richard Street, Suite 400
Honolulu, HI 96813
(808) 586-5705

Compact Administrator
Beatrice Yuh
Hawaii Department
   of Human Services
810 Richard Street, Suite 400
Honolulu, HI 96813
(808) 586-5705

Office hours:
Monday-Friday
7:45 A.M.-4:30 P.M.
Hawaii Standard Time Zone

Direct all correspondence and
   telephone calls to the Compact
   Administrator.

State Adoption Exchange
   and Photo Listing
Central Adoption Exchange
   of Hawaii
810 Richards Street, Suite 400
Honolulu, HI 96813
(808) 586-5705

Private Adoption Agencies

Adopt International
900 Fort Street
Pioneer Plaza Building, #1700
Honolulu, HI 96813
(808) 523-1400

Catholic Services to Families
200 North Vineyard Boulevard,
   3rd Floor
Honolulu, HI 96817
(808) 537-6321

Child and Family Services
200 North Vineyard Boulevard,
   Suite 20
Honolulu, HI 96817
(808) 521-2377

Crown Child Placement
   International, Inc.
75-5851 Kuakini Highway
Kailua-Kona, HI 96740
(808) 326-4444

Hawaii International Child
   Placement and Family Services,
   Inc.
1208 Laukahi Street
Honolulu, HI 96821
(808) 377-0881

LDS Social Services
Hawaii Honolulu Agency
1500 South Beretonia Street,
   Suite 403
Honolulu, HI 96826
(808) 945-3690

**Adoptive Parent Support
   Groups and Postadoption
   Services**

Adoptive Families of Kauai
Attn.: Steve Soltysik
1702 Makoi Street
Lihue, Kauai, HI 96766
(808) 245-1711

**Adopted Person and Birth
   Relative Support Groups**

Access Hawaii and Concerned
   United Birthparents
Box 1120
Hilo, HI 96721
(808) 965-7185

Adoption Circle of Hawaii
Box 61723
Honolulu, HI 96839
(808) 625-1841

Concerned United Birthparents
Box 37838
Honolulu, HI 96837
(808) 239-5819

Family Court
Attn.: Supervisor, First Circuit
   Central Registry
Court Management Service
P.O. Box 3498
Honolulu, HI 96811
(808) 548-4601

Hawaii State Bar Association
Penthouse 1, 9th Floor
1136 Union Mall
Honolulu, HI 96813
(808) 537-1868

Adoption Attorneys

Laurie Loomis
Pacific Tower, Suite 2050
1001 Bishop Street
Honolulu, HI 96813
(808) 524-5066

HAWAII LAWS RELATED TO ADOPTION: QUESTIONS AND ANSWERS

Can an attorney serve as an intermediary?
Yes.

Is advertising permitted?
No. Only attorneys can advertise.

Who must consent to the adoption?
1. The birth mother
2. The presumed birth father

When can consent be taken from the birth mother (father), and how long after the consent is signed can it be revoked?
Consent can be taken at any time after the sixth month of pregnancy and is considered irrevocable once the child is placed, unless placement is not in the child's best interest.

    The birth parents may have to appear in court unless the consent is taken before the court hearing and is accepted by the court without a personal appearance.

What are the birth father's rights?
The birth father's consent is required if he was married to the birth mother (or attempted to marry her) at the time of child's birth or if the child was born within 300 days after their marriage ended; or if he has received the child in his home as his own child or acknowledges paternity in writing or agreed to his name being placed on the child's birth certificate; or, if by court order or written promise, he agrees to support the child.

    Also, a birth father's consent is required if he is not a "legal," "court approved," or a "presumed" father but is a father who has shown interest in the child's welfare within the first thirty days of the child's life, or before the birth mother consented to the adoption; or before the placement of the child with the adoptive parents (whichever time period is greater).

    A birth father's consent is not required if he was not married to the birth mother at time of conception or birth and has not met the preceding requirements. Nor is his consent required if the court determines he is not fit or able to provide the child with a proper home and education However, a birth father must still receive notice of an adoption proceeding.

What fees can adoptive parents pay?
The law does not address this matter.

Where does the adoption hearing take place?
The hearing may take place in the family court where the adoptive parents live, where the child was born or where the child placement agency is located.

How are familial and step-parent adoptions different from nonbiological adoptions?
    The law does not address this issue.

Can a nonresident finalize an adoption in this state?
Yes.

IDAHO

State Adoption Specialist
Mari Brennan
Family and Children's Services
    (FACS) Adoption Section
P.O. Box 83720, 3rd Floor
Boise, ID 83720-0036
(208) 334-5700

Compact Administrator
Roseann Hardin, J.D.
Division of Family
    and Children's Services
Idaho Dept. of Health
    and Welfare
Division of Family and
    Community Services
P.O. Box 83720, 3rd Floor
Boise, ID 83720-0036
(208) 334-5700

Deputy Compact Administrator
Carolyn K. Ayres
Division of Family
    and Children's Services
Idaho Dept. of Health
    and Welfare
Division of Family
    and Community Services
P.O. Box 83720, 3rd Floor
Boise, ID 83720-0036
(208) 334-5700
fax (208) 334-6699

Direct all telephone calls and
    correspondence to the Deputy
    Compact Administrator.

Office hours:
Monday-Friday
8:00 A.M.-5:00 P.M.
Mountain Time Zone

State Adoption Exchange

Meri Brennan
Idaho Department of Health
    and Welfare
P.O. Box 83720, 3rd Floor
Boise, ID 83720-0036
(208) 334-5700

Private Adoption Agencies

Casey Family Program
6441 Emerald
Boise, ID 83704
(208) 377-1771

Children's Aid Society of Idaho
2308 North Cole, Suite E
Boise, ID 83704
(208) 376-0558

Children's House International
1053 N. 1390 W.
Layton, UT 84041
(801) 546-6216

Christian Counseling Services
1920 E. 17th Street, Suite 109
Idaho Falls, ID 83404
(208) 529-4673

Community Counseling Services
    of Idaho, Inc.
6054 West Emerald
Boise, ID 83704
(208) 322-1262

Idaho Youth Ranch Adoption
    Services
P.O. Box 8538
Boise, ID 83707
(208) 377-2613

LDS Social Services
10740 Fairview, Suite 100
Boise, ID 83704
(208) 376-0191

LDS Social Services
255 North Overland Avenue
Burley, ID 83318
(208) 678-8200

LDS Social Services
1420 East 17th, Suite B
Idaho Falls, ID 83404
(208) 529-5276

LDS Social Services
1070 Hiline Road, Suite 200
Pocatello, ID 83201
(208) 232-7780

Lutheran Social Services
    of Washington and Idaho
2201 Government Way, #J
Coeur d'Alene, ID 83814
(208) 667-1898

New Hope Child and Family
    Agency
Attn.: Betsy Ohman
1810 W. State Street, #314
Boise, ID 83702
(208) 343-2945

New Hope Child and Family
    Agency
Attn.: Kim Huitt
P.O. Box 95
Caldwell, ID 83605
(800) 388-3603 or (208) 459-
    0050

New Hope Child and Family
    Agency
Attn.: Loraye Becker
700 West Riverview Drive
Idaho Falls, ID 83401
(208) 523-6930

**Adoptive Parent Support
Groups and Postadoption
Services**

Adoptive Families
    of Southeastern Idaho
Attn.: Beth McHugh
2356 Oak Trail Drive
Idaho Falls, ID 83404
(208) 529-3576

Families Involved
    in Adoption Northwest
Attn.: Dee Ann Brennan
Box 612
Priest River, ID 83856
(208) 448-1779

Idaho Post Adoption Project
Attn.: Linda Jenson
Family Wellness Center
420 W. Bannock
Boise, ID 83701
(208) 344-0094

Magic Valley Adoptive
    Parent Support Group
Attn.: Frannie McMahon
Department of Health and
    Welfare
601 Poleline Road, Suite 6
Turin Falls, ID 83301

North American Council
    on Adoptable Children
    State Representative
Attn.: Susan Smith
1301 Spokane Street
Post Falls, ID 83854
(208) 773-5629

Parents and Children Together
Attn.: Carol Day
7474 South Cloverdale
Boise, ID 83709
(208) 384-7965

Special Needs
  Adoptive Parents (SNAP)
Lutheran Social Services
420 West Bannock
Boise, ID 83701
(208) 344-0094

**Adopted Person and Birth
  Relative Support Groups**

Adopted Child
P.O. Box 9362
Moscow, ID 83843
(208) 882-1794

Adoptee Liberty Movement
  Association (ALMA)
P.O. Box 4281
Boise, ID 83711
(208) 362-2364

Adoption Support Group
Box 2316
Ketchum, ID 83340
(208) 726-8543

Helping Hands
Box 249
Pinehurst, ID 83850
(208) 682-4280

Search Finders of Idaho
P.O. Box 7941
Boise, ID 83707
(208) 375-9803

Search Light
Box 5341
Coeur d'Alene, ID 83814
(208) 689-3255

Idaho State Bar Association
P.O. Box 895
Boise, ID 83701
(208) 342-8958

Adoption Attorneys

Margaret Mary Lezamiz
447 West Myrtle
Boise, ID 83701
(208) 384-1627
Speaks Spanish

John R. Cocks
Scott M. Ludwig
Davison, Copple, Copple,
  Copple and Ludwig
205 North 10th Street, Office 530
Boise, ID 83701
(208) 342-3658

John T. Hawley, Jr.
1087 West River, #230
Boise, ID 83702
(208) 343-8880

Alan W. Schroeder
447 W. Myrtle
Boise, ID 83701
(208) 384-1627

Larry F. Weeks
2308 North Cole Road , Suite C
Boise, ID 83704
(208) 377-2721

IDAHO LAWS RELATED TO ADOPTION: QUESTIONS AND ANSWERS

Can an attorney serve as an intermediary?
Yes.

Is advertising permitted?
No.

Who must consent to the adoption?
The birth parents

**When can consent be taken from the birth mother (father), and how long after the
  consent is signed can it be revoked?**
The birth mother cannot give consent until forty-eight hours after the child's birth, and
the consent is irrevocable.

What are the birth father's rights?
The birth father may claim rights if he registers with the Registry of Vital Statistics of the
Department of Health and Welfare. This claim must occur before the child is placed with
an adoption agency. If he fails to file, he can never try to establish paternity, and his
parental rights may be terminated. The Department of Health and Welfare, the adoption
agency, or the adoption attorney must notify him of his need to register so that if he
desires, he can give his intent to support the child and exercise his rights. If the birth
father cannot be located, an attempt must be made to notify him through publication at
least ten days before parental rights are terminated or the child is placed with an agency.

What fees can adoptive parents pay?
Payment of medical, legal, and some living expenses is permitted.

Where does the adoption hearing take place?
The hearing usually takes place in the District Court in the county where the adoptive parents reside.

How are familial and step-parent adoptions different from nonbiological adoptions?
A home study may be required if requested by the court. There is no state residency requirement.

Can a nonresident finalize an adoption in this state?
No. You must live in the state for at least six consecutive months.

ILLINOIS

State Adoption Specialist
Gary Morgan
Illinois Department of Children and Family Services
100 West Randolph Street, Suite 6-211
Chicago, IL 60601
(312) 814-6864

Compact Administrator
Diana Clevenger
Interstate Compact Unit
Illinois Department of Children and Family Services
406 East Monroe, Mail Station #55
Springfield, IL 62701-1498
(217) 785-2680

Deputy Compact Administrator
(vacant)
Interstate Compact Unit
Illinois Department of Children and Family Services
406 East Monroe,
Mail Station #55
Springfield, IL 62701-1498
fax (217) 785-2454

Direct all telephone calls and correspondence to the Compact Administrator.

Office hours:
Monday-Friday
8:00 A.M.-4:00 P.M.
Central Time Zone

State Adoption Exchange and Photo Listing

Adoption Information Center of Illinois (AICI)
188 West Randolph, Suite 600
Chicago, IL 60606
(312) 346-1516
(800) 572-2390 (IL residents)

Private Adoption Agencies

Aunt Martha's Youth Services
4343 Lincoln Highway, #340
Matteson, IL 60443
(708) 747-2701

Baby Fold
108 East Willow Street
Normal, IL 61761
(309) 452-1170

Bensenville Home Society/Lifelink
331 South York Road
Bensenville, IL 60106
(708) 766-5800

Bethany Christian Services
9730 South Western, Suite 704
Evergreen Park, IL 60642
(708) 422-9626

Bethany Home Family Services
1606 Brady Street, Suite 309
Davenport, IA 52803
(319) 324-9169

Catholic Charities
Chicago Archdiocese
126 North DesPlaines
Chicago, IL 60661
(312) 655-7000

Catholic Charities
Chicago Archdiocese,
Lake County Division
116 North Lincoln Street
Round Lake, IL 60073
(847) 546-5733

Catholic Charities
Joliet Diocese
203 N. Ottawa Street,
2nd Flr., Suite A
Joliet, IL 60431
(815) 723-3053

Catholic Charities
Springfield Diocese
120 S. 11th Street
Springfield, IL 62704
(217) 525-0500

Catholic Social Services
Belleville Diocese
617 South Belt West
Belleville, IL 62220
(618) 277-9200

Catholic Social Services
Peoria Diocese
413 Northeast Monroe
Peoria, IL 61603
(309) 671-5720

Catholic Social Services
Rockford Diocese
921 West State Street
Rockford, IL 61102
(815) 965-0623

Central Baptist Family Services
2100 South Indiana, Suite 360
Chicago, IL 60616
(312) 326-7430

Chicago Child Care Society
5467 South University Avenue
Chicago, IL 60615
(312) 643-0452

Chicago Youth Centers
10 West 35th Street
Chicago, IL 60616
(312) 225-8200

Children's Home
  and Aid Society of Illinois
1002 College Avenue
Alton, IL 62002
(618) 462-2714

Children's Home
  and Aid Society of Illinois
1819 South Neil, Suite D
Champaign, IL 61820
(217) 359-8815

Children's Home
  and Aid Society of Illinois
1122 North Dearborn
Chicago, IL 60610
(312) 944-3313

Children's Home
  and Aid Society of Illinois
910 Second Street
Rockford, IL 61104
(815) 962-1043

Childserv
9415 Western Avenue
Chicago, IL 60620
(312) 233-5100

Christian Family Services
9955 Bunkham Road
Fairview Heights, IL 62208
(618) 397-7678

Counseling and Family Service
330 S.W. Washington
Peoria, IL 61602
(309) 676-2400

Cradle Society
2049 Ridge Avenue
Evanston, IL 60201
(847) 475-5800

Evangelical Child
  and Family Agency
1530 North Main
Wheaton, IL 60187
(708) 653-6400

Family Care Services of Illinois
234 South Wabash Avenue
Chicago, IL 60604
(312) 427-8790

Family Counseling Clinic, Inc.
19300 West Highway 120
Grayslake, IL 60030
(847) 223-8107

Family Resource Center
5820-30 North Clark
Chicago, IL 60660
(312) 334-2300

Family Resources, Inc.
852 Middle Road
Bettendorf, IA 52722
(319) 359-8216

Family Service Agency
  of Adams County
915 Vermont Street
Quincy, IL 62301
(217) 222-8254

Family Service Center
  of Sangamon County
1308 South Seventh Street
Springfield, IL 62703
(217) 528-8406

Glenkirk
2501 North Chestnut
Arlington Heights, IL 60004
(847) 394-2171

Hobby Horse House
208 S. Mauvaisterre Street
P.O. Box 1102
Jacksonville, IL 62651
(217) 243-7708

Illinois Baptist Children's Home
4243 Lincolnshire Drive
Mt. Vernon, IL 62864
(618) 242-4944

Illinois Children's Christian Home
P.O. Box 200
St. Joseph, IL 61873
(217) 469-7566

Jewish Children's Bureau
1 South Franklin Street
Chicago, IL 60606
(312) 346-6700, ext. 3024

LDS Social Services
1801 N. Mill Street, Suite F
Naperville, IL 60540
(708) 369-0486

Lutheran Child
  and Family Services
2408 Lebanon Avenue
Belleville, IL 62221
(618) 234-8904

Lutheran Child
  and Family Services
800 South 45th Street,
  Wells Bypass
Mt. Vernon, IL 62864
(618) 242-3284

Lutheran Child
  and Family Services
7620 Madison Street
P.O. Box 5078
River Forest, IL 60305
(708) 771-7180 or (312) 287-
  4848

Lutheran Child
  and Family Services
431 South Grand Avenue West
Springfield, IL 62704
(217) 544-4631

Lutheran Social Services
  of Illinois
701 Devonshire, Suite 204,
  Box C-9
Champaign, IL 61820
(217) 398-3011

Lutheran Social Services
  of Illinois
1144 Lake Street, 3rd Floor
Oak Park, IL 60301
(708) 445-8341

Lutheran Social Services of
  Illinois, Chicago South Office
11740 South Western
Chicago, IL 60643
(312) 239-3700

Lutheran Social Services
  of Illinois
610 Abington
Peoria, IL 61603
(309) 671-0300

PSI Services, Inc.
111 East Wacker Drive,
  Suite 2500
Chicago, IL 60601
(312) 946-0740, ext. 3386

Saint Mary's Services
717 West Kirchoff Road
Arlington Heights, IL 60005
(847) 870-8181

Sunny Ridge Family Center
2 South 426 Orchard Road
Wheaton, IL 60187
(708) 668-5117

Volunteers of America
224 North Desplaines, Suite 500
Chicago, IL 60661
(312) 707-9477

Volunteers of America
4700 State Street
East St. Louis, IL 62205
(618) 271-9833

**Adoptive Parent Support
Groups and Postadoption
Services**

Adopt-Ed
Attn.: Michallyn Sloan
301 Oregon
Frankfort, IL 60423
(815) 469-5190

Adopt a Special Kid (AASK)
AASK Field Representative
for Illinois
1025 North Reynolds
Toledo, OH 43615
(419) 534-3350

Adoption by Choice
435 Clavey Lane
Highland Park, IL 60035
(847) 432-2023

Adoption Information Center
of Illinois
188 West Randolph, Suite 600
Chicago, IL 60601
(312) 346-1516

Adoption Resources
Attn.: Tobi Ehrenpreis
1830 Sherman Avenue, Suite 302
Evanston, IL 60201
(847) 869-6979

Adoptive Families
of DeKalb Area
Attn.: Mary Fleming Kowalski
303 North 2nd Street
DeKalb, IL 60115-3236
(815) 758-4307

Adoptive Families Today
Attn.: Kathy Casey
P.O. Box 1726
Barrington, IL 60011-1726
(847) 382-0858

Adoptive Family Support Group
Attn.: Gretchen Forsythe
RR#2 Box 295F
Camp Point, IL 62320
(309) 828-2353

Adoptive Parents Together
Attn.: Susan Clukey
309 Pleasant Ridge Road
Fairview, IL 62208
(618) 394-0139

All-Dopt Support Group
Attn.: Marietta Bear
727 Ramona Place
Godfrey, IL 62035
(618) 466-8926

BHS International Reachout
Attn.: Barry Leitch
706 Morningside
Naperville, IL 60563
(708) 717-9306

Central Illinois Adoptive Families
Attn.: Mary Zunik
6 Graystone Court
Bloomington, IL 61704
(309) 663-1322

Chicago Area Families
for Adoption
Attn.: Carla Richards
1212 South Naper Boulevard,
Suite 119
Naperville, IL 60540
(708) 739-6576

Child International
Attn.: Maureen Kay
4121 Crestwood Drive
Northbrook, IL 60062
(847) 272-2511

Children's Advocate
Attn.: Chris Miller
900 West Jackson
Ottawa, IL 61350
(815) 434-5380

Christian Adoption Ministries
Attn.: Katrina Schmitz
327 North High
Carlinville, IL 62626
(217) 854-8871

Families of Adoption
Coming Together
Attn.: Paula Randant
524 E. Northwest Highway
Mt. Prospect, IL 60056
(847) 255-4055

Foster Another Child This Season
Attn.: Fran Nytco
OS628 Kirk
Elmhurst, IL 60126
(708) 941-7793

Fox Valley Adoption Group
Attn.: Cindy Schalk
3106 Royal Fox Drive
St. Charles, IL 60174
(708) 513-1370

Gifts Through Adoption
Attn.: Bernard Relph
P.O. Box 914
Morton, IL 61550-0914
(309) 266-5983

Hands Around the World
Attn.: Gail C. Walton
1417 East Miner
Arlington Heights, IL 60004
(847) 255-8309

Heart of Illinois
Adoptive Families
Attn.: Diane Dingleding
730 High Point Lane
East Peoria, IL 61611
(309) 698-6011

Illiana Adoptive Parents
Attn.: Linda Rich
4177 Oak Lane
Gary, IN 46408
(219) 884-7746

Illinois Council
on Adoptable Children
Attn.: Patricia Cooper
809 Laurel Avenue
Des Plaines, IL 60016
(847) 698-3668

Illinois Parents for Black
Adoptions and North
American Council on
Adoptable Children
State Representative
Attn.: Drucilla Fair
7930 South Colfax Avenue
Chicago, IL 60617
(312) 734-2305

International Families
Attn.: Pam and Ronald Capion
3296 Knox Drive
Freeport, IL 61032
(815) 232-7547

Little Egypt Adoptive Parents
Association
109 East 2nd Street North
Mount Olive, IL 62069-1309
(618) 695-3334

New Beginnings
Attn.: Ruth Ann Zwilling
606 West Butler
Olney, IL 62450
(618) 392-0336

North American Council
  on Adoptable Children
  State Representative
Attn.: Carla Richards
1777 Alan Deatherage Drive
Bolingbrook, IL 60440
(708) 378-5071

Ours for a United Response
  of East Central Illinois
Attn.: Jeanine Berlocher
109 W. Nevada
Urbana, IL 61801
(217) 328-7352

Ours for a United Response
  of Northern Illinois
Attn.: Janet Allen
P.O. Box 15332
Rockford, IL 61132
(815) 389-1030

Ours Through Adoption
Attn.: Jean Hess
2618 Arlington Avenue
Davenport, IA 52803
(319) 322-6469

Ours With Love
Attn.: Jeanne Wirth
303 N. Church
Newton, IL 62448
(618) 783-8393

Parents Adopting Children
  Together
Attn.: Kathy Jachna
4413 Chelsea
Lisle, IL 60532
(708) 963-4121

Quincy Adoption Support Group
Attn.: Deb Brink
1405 S. 24th Street
Quincy, IL 62301
(217) 222-4813

Resolve of Illinois
318 Half Day Road, #300
Buffalo Grove, IL 60089
(312) 743-1623

Saint Paul's
  Adoption Support Group
Attn.: Jon Widel
1508 Karin
Belleville, IL 62220
(618) 277-6422

Single Adoptive Parent
  Support Group
Attn.: Susan Weiss
1132 North Euclid
Oak Park, IL 60302
(847) 524-8908

South Central Illinois
  Adoptive Parents Assocation
Attn.: Susan Lael
P.O. Box 416
Edinburg, IL 62531
(217) 623-4494

Stars of David International,
  Chicago Area Chapter
Attn.: Susan Katz
3175 Commercial Avenue,
  Suite 100
Northbrook, IL 60062-1915
(847) 205-1200

Tapestry
Attn.: Sherry Blass
40 Francis Avenue
Crystal Lake, IL 60014
(815) 459-8548

Uniting Families
Attn.: Lynn Wetterberg
440 East Ogden
Hinsdale, IL 60521
(708) 654-0750

**Adopted Person and Birth
  Relative Support Groups**

Adoptee Liberty Movement
  Association (ALMA)
Attn.: Laverne
  and Gene Hoffman
P.O. Box 23255
Belleville, IL 62223
(618) 538-5599 or 537-2198

Adoptee Liberty Movement
  Association (ALMA)
Attn.: Susan Lentz
P.O. Box 81
Bloomington, IL 61702
(309) 828-2217

Adoptee Liberty Movement
  Association (ALMA)
P.O. Box 59345
Chicago, IL 60659
(312) 409-0273

Adoptee Liberty Movement
  Association (ALMA)
P.O. Box 74
Lebanon, IL 62254
(618) 537-2198

Adoptee Liberty Movement
  Association (ALMA)
Attn.: Joy Schneider
P.O. Box 1802
Skokie, IL 60076
(312) 409-0273

Adoption Search
  and Support Group
Attn.: Sharon Keeling
1701 Riverview Drive
Macomb, IL 61455
(309) 836-3809

Adoption Triangle
Attn.: Beth Duensing
Box 384
Park Forest, IL 60466
(217) 365-0574

Adoption Triangle
Attn.: Lydia Granda
512 Oneida Street
Joliet, IL 60435
(815) 722-4999

Adoption Triangle
Attn.: Mary Jo Jackson
P.O. Box 384
Park Forest, IL 60466
(219) 365-0574

Adoption Triangle
Attn.: Melinda Reitman
c/o Illinois Department
  of Children and Family Services
200 South Wyman, Suite 200
Rockford, IL 61101-1232
(815) 987-7117

American Adoption Congress
  and Concerned United
  Birthparents
Attn.: Bonnie Bis
835 Ridge Avenue, #208
Evanston, IL 60202
(847) 475-4095

American Adoption Congress
Attn.: Harold Bauer
1201 South First Street
Springfield, IL 62704
(217) 789-0796

Children Remembered
Attn.: John Lietzau
Box 1477
Northbrook, IL 60062
(847) 647-9856

Family Counseling Center
Birth Mother Support Group
Attn.: Renee Eifert
10 Henson Place, Suite C
Champaign, IL 61820
(217) 352-6565

Family Tree
Attn.: Sandy Kamen Wisniewski
P.O. Box 233
Libertyville, IL 60048
(847) 362-3721

Folk Finders
P.O. Box "H"
Neoga, IL 62447
(800) 277-3318

Healing Hearts
Attn.: Marilyn Strohkirch
P.O. Box 136
Stanford, IL 61774
(309) 379-5401

Heritage Finders
Attn.: Alice Lumbard
1102 Erie Street
Elgin, IL 60123
(847) 741-2189

Heritage Finders
Attn.: Barb Lollar
20955 S. Canterbury
Shorewood, IL 60436
(815) 725-8960

Illinois Department
of Public Health
Office of Vital Records
Adoption Registry
605 West Jefferson
Springfield, IL 62702

Informed Choice for Birthparents
Attn.: Sally Gantz
Rt. 1, Box 5
DeLand, IL 61839
(217) 664-3342

Lost Connection
Attn.: Karen Saunders
2661 North Illinois Street,
   Suite 147
Belleville, IL 62221
(618) 235-9409

Midwest Adoption Center
Confidential Intermediary Service
   of Illinois/Illinois Department
   of Children and Family Service
Post-Adoption Service
Attn.: Nancy Golden
3166 Des Plaines River Road,
   Suite 23
Des Plaines, IL 60018
(847) 298-9096

Midwest Adoption
   Center|Branch
5519 RFD
Long Grove, IL 60047

Missing Pieces
Attn.: Maggie Ruby
P.O. Box 7541
Springfield, IL 62791-7541
(217) 787-8450

Reflections
Attn.: Katrina Thomas
606 Shipley Street
Carmi, IL 62821
(618) 382-3142

Search Connection
Attn.: Michael Egan
9748 Roberts Road, Suite 11
Palos Hills, IL 60465
(708) 430-9133

Truth Seekers in Adoption
Attn.: Barbara Gonyo
P.O. Box 366
Prospect Heights, IL 60070-0366
(847) 342-8742

Illinois State Bar Association
424 S. Second Street
Springfield, IL 62701
(217) 525-1760
(800) 572-8916 (Illinois residents)

Adoption Attorneys

Daniel Azulay
35 E. Wacker Drive
Chicago, IL 60601
(312) 236-6965

Shelley Ballard Bostick
20 North Wacker Drive,
   Suite 3710
Chicago, IL 60606
(312) 541-1149
fax (312) 629-5499

Kirsten Crouse Buys
Deborah Crouse Cobb*
6100 Center Grove Road, Suite 5
Edwardsville, IL 62025
(618) 692-6300
fax (618) 692-9831
      or
655 W. Lincoln #8
Charleston, IL 61920
(217) 345-6099
fax (217) 345-6098

* Ms. Cobb has completed more
   than 200 independent
   adoptions, more than 100
   agency adoptions, and more
   than 100 international
   adoptions.

H. Joseph Gitlin
111 Dean Street
Woodstock, IL 60098
(815) 338-0021

Susan Grammer
P.O. Box 111
Bethalto, IL 62010
(618) 259-2113

Theresa Rabe Hardesty
7513 North Regent Place
Peoria, IL 61614
(309) 692-1087

John C. Hirschfeld*
306 West Church Street
P.O. Box 6750
Champaign, IL
(618) 264-6750
(217) 352-1800
fax (217) 352-1083

* Mr. Hirschfeld has completed
   1,000 independent adoptions,
   more than 100 agency
   adoptions and more than 100
   international adoptions. He has
   been conducting adoptions for
   more than thirty-four years.

Kathleen H. Morrison
120 North LaSalle Street, #2900
Chicago, IL 60602
(312) 236-7080

Richard Lifshitz*
120 North LaSalle Street,
Suite 2900
Chicago, IL 60602
(312) 236-7080
fax (312) 236-0781

* Mr. Lifshitz has completed
about 400 independent
adoptions, 2,000 agency
adoptions, and 200
international adoptions.

Lawrence M. Raphael
77 W. Washington Street,
No. 1018
Chicago, IL 60602

Carolyn Smoot
208 North Market
P.O. Box 1234
Marion, IL 62959
(618) 993-2700

Glenna Weith
306 West Church Street
P.O. Box 577
Champaign, IL 61824-0577
(217) 352-1800

Sally Wildman
180 North LaSalle, Suite 2401
Chicago, IL 60601
(312) 726-9214

Attorney fees for an independent
agency adoption in this state are
about $1,000 to $3,000.

ILLINOIS LAWS RELATED TO ADOPTION: QUESTIONS AND ANSWERS

Can an attorney serve as an intermediary?
Many attorneys do, but technically they should not.

Is advertising permitted?
Technically it is not permitted, but it is done extensively.

Who must consent to the adoption?
1. The birth mother
2. The birth father, if married to the birth mother, or if the child was born out of wedlock
   and he has lived with the child for six months and has openly stated that he is the
   child's father

**When can consent be taken from the birth mother (father), and how long after the
consent is signed can it be revoked?**
Consent cannot be given until seventy-two hours after the child's birth. However, the
birth father's consent can be given before the birth, and he can revoke his consent within
seventy-two hours of the birth if he notifies the representative to whom he had given consent. According to John Hirschfeld, an adoption attorney in Champaign, rights are terminated via written consents taken in the presence of a notary public or, preferably, in the
presence of a judge. Consent is irrevocable.

What are the birth father's rights?
Shelley Ballard Bostick, an adoption attorney in Chicago, states that Illinois has a putative
Father's Registry, and a birth father (generally) must register within thirty days of birth
and initiate a parentage action.

What fees can adoptive parents pay?
Any fees or expenses paid that exceed $3,500 must be filed with the court. If all costs are
less than $3,500, an affidavit must be submitted stating this. No fees can be paid for
placing a child.

Where does the adoption hearing take place?
The hearing may take place in the county where the adoptive parents reside, where the birth parents reside, where the baby was born, or where the child placement agency is located.

How are familial and step-parent adoptions different from nonbiological adoptions?
The process is faster (four to six weeks), and the home study and criminal check are not mandatory. If a home study is conducted, there is minimal investigation. Grandparents have visitation rights if the adoption is by close relatives and occurs after the death of both parents.

Can a nonresident finalize an adoption in this state?
Yes, but only if the child is placed by an agency; otherwise, you must have lived in the state for six months.

INDIANA

State Adoption Specialist
Lynn Arthur
Indiana Division
of Family and Children
Family Protection/Preservation
402 West Washington Street,
3rd Floor, W-364
Indianapolis, IN 46204-2739
(317) 232-4630

Compact Administrator
Suzanne Turner, Director
Division of Family and Children
Indiana Family and Social
Services Administrations
402 West Washington Street,
Room W-392
Indianapolis, IN 46204-2739

Deputy Compact Administrator
Bureau of Family
Protection/Development
Division of Family and Children
Indiana Family and Social
Services Administrations
402 West Washington Street,
Room W-364
Indianapolis, IN 46204-2739
(317) 232-4427

Adoption Consultant
Norma Farrar
(317) 232-4429

Address all correspondence
to the Deputy Compact
Administrator. Direct all
telephone calls to the Adoption
Consultant.

Office hours:
Monday-Friday
8:25 A.M.-4:45 P.M.
Eastern Time Zone

**State Adoption Exchange
and Photo Listing**

Indiana Adoption Resource
Exchange
Indiana Division of Family
and Children
Third Floor, W-364
402 West Washington Street
Indianapolis, IN 46204-2739
(317) 232-5613

Private Adoption Agencies

Adoption Alternatives
116 South Taylor
South Bend, IN 46601
(219) 232-5843

Adoption Center
500 East Washington, Suite 200
Muncie, IN 47305
(317) 741-9467

Adoption Resources Services, Inc.
724 West Bristol, Suite E
Elkhart, IN 46514
(219) 262-2499

Adoption Services, Inc.
3050 North Meridian Street
Indianapolis, IN 46208
(317) 926-6338

Adoption Support Center
6331 North Carrolton Avenue
Indianapolis, IN 46220
(317) 255-5916

Americans for African
Adoptions, Inc.
8910 Timberwood Drive
Indianapolis, IN 46234
(317) 271-4567

Baptist Children's Home
354 West Street
Valparaiso, IN 46383
(219) 462-4111

Bethany Christian Services
6144 North Hillside Avenue,
Suite 10
Indianapolis, IN 46220
(317) 254-8479

Bethany Christian Services
830 Cedar Pkwy.
Schererville, IN 46375
(219) 864-0800

Catholic Charities
315 East Washington
Fort Wayne, IN 46802
(219) 439-0242

Catholic Charities
120 South Taylor Street
South Bend, IN 46601
(219) 234-3111

Catholic Charities Bureau
603 Court Building
Evansville, IN 47708
(812) 423-5456

Catholic Family Services
973 West 6th Avenue
Gary, IN 46402
(219) 882-2723

Catholic Family Services
of Michigan City
1501 Franklin Street
Michigan City, IN 46360-3709
(219) 879-9312

Childplace, Inc.
2420 Highway 62
Jeffersonville, IN 47130
(812) 282-8248

Children's Bureau of Indianapolis
426 English Foundation Building
615 North Alabama Street
Indianapolis, IN 46204
(317) 264-2700

Chosen Children
Adoption Services
5227 Bardstown Road
Louisville, KY 40291
(812) 945-6021

Coleman Adoption Agency
419 English Foundation Building
615 North Alabama Street
Indianapolis, IN 46204
(317) 638-0965

Compassionate Care
Highway 64 West
Wilder Center, Rte. 3, Box 12B
Oakland City, IN 47660
(812) 749-4152
(800) 749-4153

Family and Children's Services
655 S. Hebron
Evansville, IN 47414
(812) 471-1776

G.L.A.D.
5000 First Avenue
Evansville, IN 47711
(812) 424-4523

Homes for Black Children
3131 East 38th Street
Indianapolis, IN 46218
(317) 545-5281

Indiana Agency
for LDS Social Services
5151 West 84th Street
Indianapolis, IN 46268
(317) 872-1749

Jeremiah Agency
P.O. Box 864
Greenwood, IN 46142-0864
(317) 887-2434

Loving Option
206 South Main Street
Bluffton, IN 46714
(219) 824-9077

Lutheran Child
and Family Services
1525 North Ritter Avenue
Indianapolis, IN 46219
(317) 359-5467

Lutheran Social Services
330 Madison Avenue
P.O. Box 11329
Fort Wayne, IN 46857-1329
(219) 426-3347

Lutheran Social Services,
Northwest Regional Office
1400 North Broad Street
Griffith, IN 46319
(219) 838-0996

St. Elizabeth's Home
2500 Churchman Avenue
Indianapolis, IN 46203
(317) 787-3412

St. Elizabeth's of Southern
Indiana
621 East Market
New Albany, IN 47150
(812) 949-7305

Shults-Lewis Child
and Family Services
P.O. Box 471
Valparaiso, IN 46383
(219) 462-0513

Sunny Ridge Family Center
900 Ridge Road
Munster, IN 46321
(219) 836-2117

Valley Children's Services
One Professional Centre
1801 North Sixth Street,
Suite 600
Terre Haute, IN 47804
(812) 234-0181

VIDA
Glendale Medical Center
1101 E. Glendale Boulevard
Valparaiso, IN 46383
(219) 322-9175

The Villages, Inc.
652 N. Girls' School Road, Suite
240
Indianapolis, IN 46214-3662
(800) 874-6880

**Adoptive Parent Support
Groups and Postadoption
Services**

Adopt a Special Kid (AASK)
Support Group
Attn.: Carol Keusch
2500 Old Orchard Place
Vincennes, IN 47591

Adopt a Special Kid (AASK)
Midwest
Attn.: Bonnie Henson
P.O. Box 402
Cicero, IN 46304-0402

Adoptive and Foster Parent
Support Group of Delaware
County
Attn.: Cindy Michael
RR 1, Box 60A
Daleville, IN 46334

Adoptive Parents Together
and North American Council
on Adoptable Children State
Representative
Attn.: Jeanine Jones
756 Woodruff Pl., Middle Drive
Indianapolis, IN 46201
(317) 638-0965

Association for the Rights
of Children
Attn.: Claire Coleman
1017 Foster Avenue
South Bend, IN 46617

Black Adoptive Parents Together
Attn.: Cynthia Diamond
3131 East 38th Street
Indianapolis, IN 46218
(317) 875-7066

Council on Adoptable
Children/Association
for the Rights of Children
Attn.: Mary Miller
10414 East 25th Street
Indianapolis, IN 46229

Council on Adoptable Children
Attn.: Peg Hurt
1021 Holly Drive
Lafayette, IN 47906

Council on Adoptable Children
of Grant County
Attn.: Tane Templin
503 East Washington Street
Fairmont, IN 46928

Delaware County
Foster Parent Association
Attn.: Helen Medaris
227 South Mississinewa
Albany, IN 47319

Families Adopting Children
Today
Attn.: Karen Scherringa
819 North Rensselaer
Griffith, IN 46319

Families Adopting Children
Together
Attn.: Robert and Connie Cramer
29746 CR 118
Elkhart, IN 46517

Families Adopting Children
Together
Attn.: Bobbe Stahl
RR#1 Box 151
Gentryville, IN 47537
(812) 925-3341

Illiana Adoptive Parents
Attn.: Linda Rich
4177 Oak Lane
Gary, IN 46408
(219) 884-7746

Indiana Foster Care
and Adoption Association
3901 North Meridian Street,
Suite 24
Indianapolis, IN 46208
(800) 468-4228 (Indiana only)
(317) 925-1320

Indiana Foster Care Association
R1, Box 102
Waveland, IN 47989

Indiana One Church
One Child Program, Inc.
850 North Meridian Street
Indianapolis, IN 46204
(317) 684-2181

OURS by Adoption
Attn.: Debbie Ford
4614 Morning Wind Place
Fort Wayne, IN 46806
(219) 436-3268

Ours of Central Indiana
Attn.: Denise Busch
8912 Keevers Drive
Indianapolis, IN 46234

Rainbow Families of OURS
Attn.: Linda Bontreger
3003 South Main Street
Goshen, IN 46526

**Adopted Person and Birth
Relative Support Groups**

Adoptee Identity
Doorway/Reunion Registry
of Indiana
P.O. Box 361
South Bend, IN 46624
(219) 272-3520

Adoptee Liberty Movement
Association (ALMA)
P.O. Box 5923
Bloomington, IN 47407

Adoptees Birthparents and
Siblings Enlightenment
Network of Thorntown
(A.B.S.E.N.T.)
211 E. Bow Street
Thorntown, IN 46071-1249
(317) 436-7257 or 436-2516

Adoption Searching with Love
Attn.: Sandi Fest
Spaeth Road
Mariah Hill, IN 47556
(812) 937-2485

Adoption Support Connection
Attn.: Larry Erhardt
21518 Burtzelbach Road
Guilford, IN 47022
(812) 487-2108

Adoption Triangle
Attn.: Pam Richardson
7158 E. State Road 45
Bloomington, IN 47408
(812) 332-9212

Adoption Triangle NW Indiana
Attn.: Kris Lucas
7361 Wilson Pl.
Merryillville, IN 46410
(219) 736-5515

Anonymous by Adoption
Attn.: Tina Miller
Box 12132
Ft. Wayne, IN 46862
(219) 744-1518

As I Am
Attn.: Laurie Lehman
Box 1123
Muncie, IN 47308
(317) 284-5473

Common Bond
Attn.: Diana Hunter
Box 833
Kendallville, IN 46755
(219) 636-2404

Connected by Adoption
Attn.: Judy Johnston
1817 Woodland Drive
Elkhart, IN 46514
(210) 262-0210

Coping with Adoption
61 Country Farm Road
Peru, IN 46970
(317) 472-7425

Double Heritage
Attn.: Cathy Miles
332 Briner Road
Marion, IN 46953
(317) 664-2116

Full Circle
Attn.: Susan Tooton
203 S. German Church Road
Indianapolis, IN 46229
(317) 897-3979

Indiana Adoption Coalition
P.O. Box 187
Sharpsville, IN 46068-0187
(317) 963-2835

Indiana Adoption
History Registry
Attn.: Registrar,
Vital Records Division
P.O. Box 1964
Indianapolis, IN 46206-1964

Lafayette Adoption
Search/Support Organization
5936 Lookout Drive
West Lafayette, IN 47906
(317) 567-4139

Search for Tomorrow
P.O. Box 441
New Haven, IN 46774
(219) 749-4392

Searching for Answers
Attn.: Lisa Mattingly
RR-4, Box 29A
Loogootee, IN 47553
(812) 295-4954

Seek
213 Breamwold MS
Michigan City, IN 46360
(219) 874-8415

Support of Search
P.O. Box 1292
Kokomo, IN 46903
(317) 453-4427

Indiana State Bar Association
230 East Ohio, 4th Floor
Indianapolis, IN 46204
(317) 639-5465

Adoption Attorneys

Todd I. Glass
330 E. Main Street, #4
Muncie, IN 47305
(317) 288-0207

John Q. Herrin
3400 Bank One Center Tower
Indianapolis, IN 46204-5134
(317) 636-3551

Timothy J. Hubert
P.O. Box 1287
Evansville, IN 47706-1287
(812) 426-1231

Joel Kirsh*
401 Pennsylvania Parkway, Suite
  370
Indianapolis, IN 46280
(317) 575-5555
(Exclusive adoption practice)

* Mr. Kirsh has conducted about
  1,000 independent adoptions,
  100 agency adoptions, and
  some international adoptions.

Steven M. Kirsh
401 Pennsylvania Parkway,
  Suite 370
Indianapolis, IN 46280
(317) 575-5555
(Exclusive adoption practice)

Franklin I. Miroff
251 E. Ohio Street, #1000
Indianapolis, IN 46204
(317) 264-1040

Charles P. Rice*
400 Plaza Building
210 South Michigan Avenue
South Bend, IN 46601
(219) 237-0904
fax (219) 237-0906

* Mr. Rice has completed over
  100 adoptions.

Attorney fees for an adoption
in this state are about $2,000
to $5,500.

INDIANA LAWS RELATED TO ADOPTION: QUESTIONS AND ANSWERS

Can an attorney serve as an intermediary?
Yes, intermediaries are permitted to place children for adoption.

Is advertising permitted?
Yes.

Who must consent to the adoption?
1. The birth mother
2. The birth father, if married to the birth mother, or if the birth father's paternity is established by the court
3. The parents of a birth parent who is under eighteen years old, if the court decides that it is in the adoptee's best interest to get their consent

When can consent be taken from the birth mother (father), and how long after the consent is signed can it be revoked?
Consent can be given twenty-four hours after the child's birth. It can be revoked up to the time the adoption is finalized if the court determines it is in the child's best interest (which is very difficult to prove). The adoption usually takes place three to four months after the consent is signed, but it can take up to a year. Every county is different.

What are the birth father's rights?
According to Joel Kirsh, an adoption attorney in Indianapolis, birth fathers are entitled to receive a notice of the adoption, either before or after the birth. If the birth mother identifies

the birth father and provides his address, he will receive the notice. If the birth mother does not name him or provide his address, he must file with the Putative Father Registry any time during the pregnancy or up to thirty days after the child's birth or the filing of the adoption petition in order to assert his rights.

What fees can adoptive parents pay?
Reasonable expenses are permitted for the birth mother's medical needs and legal fees. Reasonable costs for housing for the birth mother during her pregnancy and up to six weeks later can also be paid. Some other living expenses can be paid if approved by the court; however, what is permitted can vary depending upon the judge.

Where does the adoption hearing take place?
The hearing may take place in the county where the adoptive parents reside, where the adoptee lives, or where the child placement agency is located.

How are familial and step-parent adoptions different from nonbiological adoptions?
According to Joel Kirsh, these adoptions are handled the same way as nonrelative adoptions. Grandparents may be given visitation rights when adopted by a step-parent.

Can a nonresident finalize an adoption in this state?
No, unless they are adopting a special-needs child.

IOWA

State Adoption Specialist
Charlie Parish
Iowa Department
 of Human Services
Hoover State Building
Des Moines, IA 50319
(515) 281-5358

Compact Administrator
Charles M. Palmer, Director
Iowa Department
 of Human Service
Hoover State Office Building
Des Moines, IA 50319

Deputy Compact Administrator
Ms. Jane C. McMonigle, MJW
Bureau of Adult, Children
 and Family Services
Interstate Unit
Division of Social Services
Iowa Department
 of Human Services

Hoover Bldg, 5th Floor
Des Moines, IA 50319
(515) 281-5730

Direct all telephone calls and
 correspondence to the Deputy
 Compact Administrator.

Office hours:
Monday-Friday
6:30 A.M.-3:00 P.M.
Central Time Zone

**State Adoption Exchange
 and Photo Listing**

Iowa Adoption Resource
 Exchange
Bureau of Adults, Children,
 and Family Services
Hoover State Office Building
Des Moines, IA 50319
(515) 281-5358

Private Adoption Agencies

Alternative Services, Inc.
1228 3rd Avenue, S.E.
P.O. Box 2425
Cedar Rapids, IA 52406-2425
(319) 364-6185

American Home
 Finding Association
217 East Fifth Street
P.O. Box 656
Ottumwa, IA 52501
(515) 682-3449

Baptist Children's Home
 and Family Ministries
224-1/2 Northwest Abilene Road
Ankeny, IA 50021
(515) 964-0986

Bethany Christian Services
6000 Douglas, Suite 230
Des Moines, IA 50322
(515) 270-0824

Bethany Christian Services
123 Albany Avenue, S.E.
P.O. Box 143
Orange City, IA 51041
(712) 737-4831

Boys and Girls Home
 and Family Services, Inc.
2625 Nebraska Street
Sioux City, IA 51104
(712) 277-4031

Bethany Home
1606 Brady, Suite 309
Davenport, IA 52803
(319) 324-9169

Bremwood Lutheran
 Children's Home Society
106 16th Street, S.W.
Waverly, IA 50677
(319) 352-2630

Catholic Charities of the
  Archdiocese of Dubuque
1229 Mt. Loretta
P.O. Box 1309
Dubuque, IA 52004-1309
(319) 588-0558

Catholic Charities of Sioux City
1601 Military Road
Sioux City, IA 51103
(712) 252-4547

Catholic Social Service
601 Grand Avenue
Des Moines, IA 50303
(515) 244-3761

Cedar Valley Family Counseling
Rt. 1, Box 150
Swisher, IA 52338
(319) 857-4480

Children and Families of Iowa
1111 University Avenue
Des Moines, IA 50314
(515) 288-1981

Children's Square U.S.A.
Child Connect
Box 8-C, 541 6th Avenue
Council Bluffs, IA 51502-3008
(712) 322-3700

Crittenton Center
1105 28th Street
Sioux City, IA 51104
(712) 255-4321

Families, Inc.
P.O. Box 130
West Branch, IA 52358
(319) 643-2532

Families of Northeast Iowa
108 West Maple
P.O. Box 806
Maquoketa, IA 52060
(319) 652-4958

Family Resources, Inc.
115 West Sixth Street
P.O. Box 190
Davenport, IA 52803
(319) 323-1853

First Resources Corporation
109 E. Marion, P.O. Box 107
Sigourney, IA 52591
(515) 622-2543

Four Oaks, Inc.
5400 Kirkwood Boulevard, S.W.
Cedar Rapids, IA 52406-5216
(319) 364-0259

Francis Lauer Youth Services
17162 Kingbird Avenue
Mason City, IA 50401
(515) 423-2582

Gift of Love
  International Adoptions, Inc.
P.O. Box 447
5750 Columbine Drive
Johnston, IA 50131
(515) 276-9277

Healing the Children
2316 Olympia Drive
Bettendorf, IA 52722

Healing the Children
412 E. Church Street
Marshalltown, IA 50158
(515) 753-7544

Heart International
  Adoption Services
5335 Merle Hay Road, Suite B
Johnston, IA 50131
(515) 278-4053

Hillcrest Family Services
2316 Olympia Drive
Bettendorf, IA 52722

Hillcrest Family Services
205 12th Street, S.E.
Cedar Rapids, IA 52403-4028
(319) 362-3149

Holt Midwest Services
2200 Abbott Drive, Suite 203
Carter Lake, IA 51510
(712) 347-5911

Integrated Health Services, Inc.
118 S. Main, P.O. Box 277
North English, IA 52316
(319) 664-3278

Keys to Living
463 Northland Avenue, N.E.
Cedar Rapids, IA 52402-6237
(319) 377-2161

LDS Social Services
Iowa Des Moines Agency
3301 Ashworth Road
P.O. Box 65713
West Des Moines, IA 50265
(515) 226-0484

Lutheran Family Service
230 Ninth Avenue, North
Fort Dodge, IA 50501
(515) 573-3138

Lutheran Social Service of Iowa
3116 University Avenue
Des Moines, IA 50311
(515) 277-4476
(also has branch offices
  throughout the state)

New Horizons
  Adoption Agency, Inc.
Frost-Benco Building,
  Highway 254
Frost, MN 56033
(507) 878-3200

Ralston Adoption Agency
2208 S. 5th Avenue
Marshalltown, IA 50158-4515
(800) 304-0219

Tanager Place
724 N. 3rd, P.O. Box 845
Burlington, IA 52601
(319) 752-4000

Young House, Inc.
724 North Third
Burlington, IA 52601
(319) 752-4000

**Adoptive Parent Support
Groups and Postadoption
Services**

Adopt A Special Kid (AASK)
AASK Field Representative
  for Iowa
1025 N. Reynolds Road
Toledo, OH 43615
(419) 534-3350

Iowa City International
  Adoptive Families
Attn.: Chris Forcucci
248 Hawkeye Court
Iowa City, IA 52246
(319) 353-5219

Iowa Foster/Adoptive Parents
Attn.: Phyllis Nielsen
RR 1
Everly, IA 51338
(712) 834-2512

Iowans for International Adoption
Attn.: Donna Duvall
31496 Iron Bridge Road
Spragueville, IA 52074
(319) 672-3273

Iowa Parents
of (East) Indian Children
Attn.: Betty L. Dittrich
1805 - 11th Street
Eldora, IA 50627
(515) 858-5072

North American Council
on Adoptable Children
State Representative
Attn.: Karen Combs
Social Work Services
RR1, Box 24
McCallsburg, IA 50154
(515) 487-7832

North Iowa Adoption Group
Attn.: Sharon Clausen
408 - 28th, S.W.
Mason City, IA 50401
(515) 423-4224

Ours Through Adoption
Attn.: Jean Hess
2618 Arlington Avenue
Davenport, IA 52803
(319) 322-6469

**Adopted Person and Birth
Relative Support Groups**

Adoptee Liberty Movement
Association (ALMA)
P.O. Box 2071
Waterloo, IA 50703

Adoptees Quest
1513 Buresh Avenue
Iowa City, IA 52245

Adoption Experience
1105 Fremont
Des Moines, IA 50316

Adoption Experience
Route 5, Box 22
Osceola, IA 50213
(515) 342-4803

Concerned United Birthparents
130 33rd Avenue, S.W.
Cedar Rapids, IA 52404
(319) 363-6939

Concerned United Birthparents
RR2
Proscott, IA 50859

Concerned United Birthparents
2000 Walker Street
Des Moines, IA 50317
(515) 263-9558 or (800) 822-
2777

Family Search Services
P.O. Box 30106
Des Moines, IA 50310
(515) 255-0356

Heritage Finders
1330 Prodehl
Lockport, IA 50441
(815) 838-5801

Iowa Reunion Registry
P.O. Box 8
Blairsburg, IA 50034-0008

Origins
4300 Ashby Avenue
Des Moines, IA 50310-3540
(515) 277-7700

Iowa State Bar Association
521 E. Locust, Suite 300
Des Moines, IA 50309
(515) 243-3179

Adoption Attorneys

Larry E. Ivers
221 W. Broadway, P.O. Box C
Eagle Grove, IA 50533
(515) 448-3919

Lori L. Kiockau
402 S. Linn
Iowa City, IA 52240
(319) 338-7968

Ross S. Randall
3112 Broadway Road
P.O. Box 1287
Waterloo, IA 50704-1287
(319) 235-9507

Gerald Stambaugh
10 First Street, NW
Mason City, IA 50401
(515) 423-5154

Mark Young
800 Brick and Tile Building
Mason City, IA 50401
(515) 423-4264

IOWA LAWS RELATED TO ADOPTION: QUESTIONS AND ANSWERS

Can an attorney serve as an intermediary?
Yes, attorneys can place children in adoptive homes.

Is advertising permitted?
Yes.

Who must consent to the adoption?
The birth parents must consent.

**When can consent be taken from the birth mother (father), and how long after the
onsent is signed can it be revoked?**
The consent cannot be taken until seventy-two hours after the child's birth. The birth
parent can revoke consent within ninety-six hours after signing. This means the child
must be at least eight days old before the consent is irrevocable.

At least three hours of counseling must be made available to birth parents who request it.

What are the birth father's rights?
If a birth father cannot be located or refuses to give consent, the court will determine if the adoption is in the child's best interest without such a consent.

Iowa has a Putative Father's Registry, and a man seeking birth father rights must register before or after the child's birth.

What fees can adoptive parents pay?
The adoptive parents must file with the court a statement of all money paid.

Where does the adoption hearing take place?
The hearing takes place in the county where the adoptive parents reside.

How are familial and step-parent adoptions different from nonbiological adoptions?
Family relations may be distant and the adoption can still be considered a relative adoption. The parental rights do not always have to be terminated before an adoption can take place. The child does not necessarily have to live in the home for at least six months, as is the case with other adoptions.

Grandparents may be given visitation rights when a grandchild is adopted by a step-parent, as long as the grandparents already have a substantial relationship with the child and it is in the child's best interest.

Can a nonresident finalize an adoption in this state?
No.

KANSAS

State Adoption Specialist
Patricia Long
Kansas Department of Social
  and Rehabilitation Services
300 S.W. Oakley, West Hall,
  Room 226
Topeka, KS 66606

Compact Administrator
Carolyn Hill, Commissioner
  Youth Services
Kansas Department of Social
  and Rehabilitation Services

300 S.W. Oakley Street,
  Smith-Wilson Building
Topeka, KS 66606
(913) 296-3284

Deputy Compact Administrators
Debbie Alvey (913) 296-4656
Janet Davenport (913) 296-7030
Jan Knoll (913) 296-4210
Linda Perrier (913) 296-0913
Rosalie Sacks (913) 296-0510

Direct all telephone calls
  to the Deputy Compact
  Administrators.

Address correspondence to:

Youth and Adult Services
300 S.W. Oakley Street,
  Smith-Wilson Building
Topeka, KS 66606
fax (913) 296-4649

Office Hours Monday-Friday
8:00 A.M.- 4:30 P.M.
Central Time Zone

**State Adoption Exchange
  and Photo Listing**
Kansas Department of Social
  and Rehabilitation Services
West Hall, 300 S.W. Oakley,
  Room 226
Topeka, KS 66606
(913) 296-4661

Private Adoption Agencies

A.C.T. Adoption Services
  (Adoption, Counseling
  and Training)
612 Main
Lansing, KS 66043
(913) 727-2888

Adoption of Babies and Children
9303 W. 75th Street
Overland Park, KS 66204
(913) 385-2229

Adoption Centre of Kansas
1831 Woodrow
Wichita, KS 67203
(316) 265-5289

Adoption and Counseling
  Services for Families
10045 Hemlock
Overland Park, KS 66212
(913) 383-8448

Adoption and Fertility Resources
4600 College Boulevard,
Suite 105
Overland Park, KS 66211
(913) 338-2283

Adoption by Gentle Shepherd
6405 Metcalf, Suite 318
Overland Park, KS 66206
(913) 432-1353

Adoption Option
7211 W. 98 Terrace, #100
Overland Park, KS 66212
(913) 642-7900

Adoption Works, Inc.
400 N. Woodlawn, Suite 24
Wichita, KS 67208
(316) 687-4393

American Adoptions
11560 W. 95th, Suite 143
Overland Park, KS 66214
(913) 492-2229

Baumann, Powell and Stonestreet
   Independent Adoptions
5847 Southwest 29th Street
Topeka, KS 66614
(913) 273-7524

Catholic Charities,
   Diocese of Dodge City
2546 20th Street
Great Bend, KS 67530
(316) 792-1393
Branch in Garden City

Catholic Charities,
   Diocese of Kansas City
2220 Central Avenue
Kansas City, KS 66102
(913) 621-1504

Catholic Charities,
   Diocese of Salina
P.O. Box 1366
Salina, KS 67402
(913) 825-0208

Catholic Social Service
437 North Topeka
Wichita, KS 67202
(316) 264-8344

Childrens Foundation
   Adoption and Counseling
602 W. Amity
Louisburg, KS 66053
(913) 837-4303

Christian Family Services
   of the Midwest, Inc.
10550 Barkley, Suite 100
Overland Park, KS 66212
(913) 383-3337

Family Life Services
   Adoption Agency
305 S. Summit
Arkansas City, KS 67005-2848
(316) 442-1688

Hagar Associates, Inc.
3601 West 29th Street,
   Suite 129A
Topeka, KS 66614
(913) 271-6045

Heart of America
   Adoption Center
100 E. Poplar
Olathe, KS 66061
(913) 764-1888

Heart of America Family
   and Children's Services, Inc.
10500 Barkley, Suite 210
Overland Park, KS 66212
(913) 642-4300
(816) 753-5280 (Missouri)

Heartland International
1831 Woodrow Avenue
Wichita, KS 67203-2932
(316) 265-5289

Highlands Child Placement
   Service, Inc.
5506 Cambridge
Kansas City, KS 64132
(816) 924-6565

Inserco, Inc.
5120 East Central, #A
Wichita, KS 67208
(316) 681-3840

Kansas Children's Service League
P.O. Box 517
Wichita, KS 67201
(316) 942-4261

Kansas Children's Service League
2053 Kansas Avenue
Topeka, KS 66605
(913) 232-0543

Kansas Children's Service League,
   Black Adoptions Project
630 B Minnesota Street, Suite 310
Kansas City, KS 66117
(913) 621-2016

Kaw Valley Center
4300 Brenner Road
Kansas City, KS 66104
(913) 334-0294

Lighthouse of Kansas (under
   Youth for Christ Charter)
6900 College Boulevard,
   Suite 860
Overland Park, KS 66211
(913) 338-2100

Lutheran Social
   Services/Adoption
   for Black Children
1855 North Hillside
Wichita, KS 67214
(316) 686-6645

Maude Carpenter
   Children's Home
1501 North Meridian
Wichita, KS 67203
(316) 942-3221

Native American
   Family Services, Inc.
15880 K Road
Mayetta, KS 66509
(913) 966-2141

Special Additions
10985 W. 175th Street
Olathe, KS 66062
(913) 681-9604

Sunflower Family Services
1503 Vine, Suite E
P.O. Box 1384
Hays, KS 67601-8384
(913) 628-3692

The Villages, Inc.
2209 S.W. 29th Street
Topeka, KS 66611
(913) 267-5900

Wynne Services, Inc.
P.O. Box 171221
Kansas City, KS 66117
(913) 621-0665

**Adoptive Parent Support
   Groups and Postadoption
   Services**

International Families
   of Mid America
Attn.: Laura Hewitt
6708 Granada Road
Prairie Village, KS 66208
(913) 722-5697

North American Council
on Adoptable Children
State Representative
Attn.: Debbie Scheamann
10985 W. 175th Street
Olathe, KS 66062
(913) 681-9604

Ours Through Adoption
c/o Humana Hospital Education
Department
Attn.: Stacy M. Barnes
10500 Quivira
Overland Park, KS 66215
(913) 384-0459

Salina Adoptive Parents Group
Attn.: Betty Brown
Hope Center,
First Presbyterian Church
308 South Eighth
Salina, KS 67401

Special Needs Adoption Project
University of Kansas Medical
Center
Children's Rehabilitation Unit
39th and Rainbow Boulevard
Kansas City, KS 66103
(913) 588-5745

**Adopted Person and Birth
Relative Support Groups**

Adoption Concerns Triangle
411 S.W. Greenwood Avenue
Topeka, KS 66606
(913) 235-6122 or 266-3437

Adoption Support Group
1425 New York Street
Lawrence, KS 66044

Adoption with Wisdom
and Honesty
1333 Ranch Road
McPherson, KS 67460
(316) 241-6116

Reunions, Ltd.
2611 East 25th Street
Topeka, KS 66608

Tri-Adoption Search
and Support Group
2546 20th Street
Great Bend, KS 67530
(316) 792-1393

Wichita Adult Adoptees
4551 S. Osage Street
Wichita, KS 67217
(316) 522-8772

Kansas Bar Association
1037 Harrison Street
Topeka, KS 66606
(913) 296-4661

Kansas State Bar Association
1200 Harrison Street
P.O. Box 1037
Topeka, KS 66601
(913) 234-5696

Adoption Attorneys

The Adoption Centre Inc.
of Kansas
1831 Woodrow Avenue
Wichita, KS 67203

Martin W. Bauer
300 Page Court
            or
220 W. Douglas
Wichita, KS 67202
(316) 265-9311

Jill Bremyer-Archer
P.O. Box 1146
McPherson, KS 67460-1146
(316) 241-0554

Melinda L. Garvert*
Garvert Law Offices
2606 Fleming, Suite 6
Garden City, KS 67846
(316) 275-2300
fax (316) 276-8963

* Ms. Garvert has conducted
over 600 adoptions and
specializes in international
adoptions.

Allan A. Hazlett*
1622 S.W. Washburn
Topeka, KS 66601
(913) 232-2011
fax (913) 232-5214

Send correspondence to:
1608 S.W. Mulvane Street
Topeka, KS 66604

* Mr. Hazlett has conducted
more than 200 independent
adoptions.

Richard Macias*
901 North Broadway
Wichita, KS 67214-3531
(316) 265-5245
(800) 362-2909 in Kansas only
fax (316) 263-5105

* Mr. Macias had completed 250
independent adoption and 150
agency adoptions.

Joseph Vader*
Heart of America
Adoption Center
108 East Poplar
P.O. Box 1185
Olathe, KS 66051
(913) 764-5010

* Mr. Vader has completed
about 150 agency and 150
independent adoption.

Attorney fees for an adoption
in this state are about $2,500 to
$5,000.

KANSAS LAW RELATED TO ADOPTION: QUESTIONS AND ANSWERS

Can an attorney serve as an intermediary?
Yes.

Is advertising permitted?
Possibly. According to Allan Hazlett, an adoption attorney in Topeka, the current
Attorney General condones advertising, even though the existing statute forbids it. People
are advertising in Kansas newspapers.

By law, only adoption agencies can advertise in newspapers; however, attorneys can place ads in the yellow pages.

Who must consent to the adoption?
Both birth parents.

When can consent be taken from the birth mother (father), and how long after the consent is signed can it be revoked?
Richard Macias, an adoption attorney in Wichita, states that consents (for independent adoptions) and relinquishments (for agency adoptions) cannot be obtained until twelve hours after the baby's birth and are irrevocable. Consents must be acknowledged before a judge. The birth parents' rights in an independent adoption are terminated at a court hearing that takes place thirty to sixty days after the adoption petition is filed. The birth father can sign a consent or relinquishment before the birth.

What are the birth father's rights?
The birth father's consent is not necessary if he is not a "presumed" father, if his relationship has not been established by the court, or if he is not married to the birth mother. If he voluntarily agrees to place the child for adoption, the birth mother must file a petition to terminate his parental rights. A birth father's parental rights may be involuntarily terminated for failure to support the birth mother during the last six months of pregnancy, unfitness, abandonment of the child, abandonment of the mother despite knowledge of her pregnancy, rape, or nonsupport of the child for at least two years. (The proceeding terms, as appropriate, also apply to birth mothers.)

The court must make efforts to determine who the father is based on certain factors (e.g., if has provided for the child or was married to the mother at time of conception). If these factors cannot be found, and he does not claim his rights to the child, his rights can be terminated.

What fees can adoptive parents pay?
Legal, medical, living expenses, and counseling fees associated with the adoption can be paid, and these fees must be approved by the court.

Health insurers are required to offer adoptive parents the option to purchase coverage for the birth mother's delivery expenses.

Where does the adoption hearing take place?
The hearing can take place in the county where the adoptive parents live, the child lives, or where the adoption agency is located.

How are familial and step-parent adoptions different from nonbiological adoptions?
Home studies are not necessary in step-parent adoptions, and the court may waive the need for one when grandparents are adopting. Alan Macias states that all other issues remain the same.

Can a nonresident finalize an adoption in this state?
Yes.

KENTUCKY

State Adoption Specialist
Brooke Thomas
Kentucky Cabinet
for Human Resources
275 East Main Street,
6th Floor West
Frankfort, KY 40621
(502) 564-2147

Compact Administrator
Masten Childers II
Secretary
Kentucky Cabinet
for Human Resources
275 East Main Street,
4th Floor
Frankfort, KY 40621

Deputy Compact Administrator
Sue Howard
ICPC
Department for Social Services
275 East Main Street,
6th Floor West
Frankfort, KY 40621
(502) 564-4826
fax 502) 564-3096
(call before faxing)

Direct all telephone calls and
correspondence to the Deputy
Compact Administrator.

Office hours:
Monday-Friday
8:00 A.M.-4:30 P.M.
Central Time Zone

**State Adoption Exchanges
and Photo Listings**

Kentucky Adoption
Resource Exchange
Department of Social Services
275 East Main Street,
6th Floor West
Frankfort, KY 40621
(502) 564-2147

Department for Social Services
908 West Broadway
Louisville, KY 40203
(502) 595-4303

Special Needs Adoption Project
(SNAP)
Department for Social Services
710 West High Street
Lexington, KY 40508
(606) 252-1728

Private Adoption Agencies

Adoptions of Kentucky
One River Front Plaza, Suite 1708
Louisville, KY 40202
(502) 585-3005

Bluegrass Christian
Adoption Services
1309 S. Limestone
Lexington, KY 40503
(606) 276-2222

Catholic Charities
2911 South 4th Street
Louisville, KY 40208
(502) 637-9786

Catholic Social Service Bureau
3629 Church Street
Covington, KY 41015
(606) 581-8974

Catholic Social Service Bureau
1310 Leestown Road
Lexington, KY 40508
(606) 253-1993

Childplace
(South Central
Christian Family Services)
3248 Taylor Boulevard
Louisville, KY 40215
(502) 363-1633

Children's Home
of Northern Kentucky
200 Home Road
Covington, KY 41011-1942
(606) 261-8768

Chosen Children
Adoption Services, Inc.
5227 Bardstown Road
Louisville, KY 40291
(502) 491-6410 or (812) 945-
6021

Hannah's House
3198 Dupin Drive
Louisville, KY 40259
(502) 962-9664

Jewish Family
and Vocational Service
3640 Dutchmans Lane
Louisville, KY 40205
(502) 452-6341

Kaleidoscope Adoptions
International
1890 Lyda Avenue
Bowling Green, KY 42104
(502) 782-7555

Kentucky Baptist Homes
for Children
10801 Shelbyville Road
Middletown, KY 40243
(502) 245-2101

Kentucky One Church One Child
1730 W. Chestnut
Louisville, KY
(800) 248-8671
or (502) 561-6827

LDS Social Services, Inc.
1000 Hurstbourne Lane
P.O. Box 24487
Louisville, KY 40224
(502) 429-0077

Pathways Child Placement
Services, Inc.
1579 Bardstown Road
Louisville, KY 40205-1150
(502) 459-2320

United Methodist Childrens
Home Adoption Program
193 Phillips Court
Owensboro, KY 42301
(502) 683-3723

**Adoptive Parent Support
Groups and Postadoption
Services**

Adoptive Parents Guild
Attn.: Pamela Raidt
1888 Douglass Boulevard
Louisville, KY 40205
(502) 452-6578

Bluegrass Adoptive Parents
Support Group
Attn.: Emily Davis
3319 Ridgecane Road
Lexington, KY 40513-1127
(606) 271-3299

Families and Adoptive
Children Together
Attn.: Patty Klutts
150 Ridgemont Road
Paducah, KY 42003
(502) 554-0203

Kentuckiana Families
for Adoption
Attn.: Eileen Deren
10417 Scarlet Oak Court
Louisville, KY 40241
(502) 339-8412

North American Council
on Adoptable Children
State Representative
Attn.: Virginia Sturgeon
710 W. High Street
Lexington, KY 40508
(606) 252-1728

Northern Kentucky
for International Adoption
Attn.: Debbie Behle
728 Mill Valley Drive
Taylor Mill, KY 41015
(606) 431-3020

Parents and Adoptive Children
of Kentucky
Attn.: Carolyn Brown
139 Highland Drive
Madisonville, KY 42431
(502) 825-2158

Resolve of Kentucky
Adoptive Parents Support Group
Attn.: Peggy Moody
1401 Elkin Station Road
Winchester, KY 40391
(606) 745-4319

**Adopted Person and Birth
Relative Support Groups**

Adoptee Awareness
P.O. Box 23019
Anchorage, KY 40223
(502) 241-6358

Adoption Reunion
Registry/Adoption Education
of Lexington
P.O. Box 1218
Nicholasville, KY 40340
(800) 755-7954
(606) 885-1777

Concerned United Birthparents
4049 Edwards Street
Ft. Knox, KY 40121
(502) 943-9579

Concerned United Birthparents
P.O. Box 22795
Louisville, KY 40252-0795
(502) 423-1438

Department for Social Services
Attn.: Program Specialist,
Adult Adoptees
Sixth Floor West

275 East Main Street
Frankfort, KY 40621
(502) 564-2147

Kentucky Bar Association
514 W. Main Street
Frankfort, KY 40601
(502) 564-3795

Adoption Attorneys

Carolyn S. Arnett
1500 Kentucky Home Life Bldg.
Louisville, KY 40202

Mitchell Charney
2800 First National Tower
Louisville, KY 40202
(502) 589-4440

Elisabeth Goldman*
118 Lafayette AVenue
Lexington, KY 40502
(606) 252-2325
fax (606) 252-2325

* Ms. Goldman has conducted
more than 100 independent
adoptions, as well as some
agency and international
adoptions.

D. Bruce Orwin
P.O. Box 557
Somerset, KY 42502
(606) 678-4386
fax (606) 678-4672

Megan Lake Thornton
163 West Short Street, #300
Lexington, KY 40507
(606) 231-8780

W. Waverley Townes*
Mosley, Clare and Townes
730 W. Main Street, Suite 500
Louisville, KY 40202
(502) 583-7400
(502) 589-4997

* Mr. Townes has conducted
about 450 independent
adoptions and fifty agency
adoptions.

Attorney fees for adoptions in this
state are about $2,000 to $5,000.

KENTUCKY LAWS RELATED TO ADOPTION: QUESTIONS AND ANSWERS

Can an attorney serve as an intermediary?
Yes, with the Commissioner's permission

Is advertising permitted?
No. Prospective adoptive parents cannot advertise in newspapers or other publications,
but they can post flyers and distribute business cards.

Who must consent to the adoption?
1. The birth mother
2. The birth father, if he is married to birth mother

When can consent be given by birth mother (father), and how long after the consent is signed can it be revoked?

Consent cannot be given until seventy-two hours after birth. The consent can be only be revoked if done within twenty days after the adoptive parents have been appproved by the Cabinet for Human Resources. If a relinquishment is given, the birth parents' rights can be terminated within ten days by going to court with an aggressive attorney.

What are the birth father's rights?

The birth father's consent is needed if paternity has been determined by the court, or an affidavit of paternity is filed with the court. He generally must assert his paternity within sixty days after birth. The birth father loses his rights if he has not married or financially supported the birth mother, if he is not identified by the birth mother, if his name is not on the birth certificate, or if he is not living with the birth mother.

What fees can adoptive parents pay?

Adoptive parents can pay for medical, legal, counseling, and living expenses. An adoption agency is permitted to charge reasonable fees.

Where does the adoption hearing take place?

The hearing takes place in the county where the adoptive parents live.

How are familial and step-parent adoptions different from nonbiological adoptions?

Home studies may not be necessary in a step-parent or close relative adoption. The law does not specifically address these types of adoptions.

Can a nonresident finalize an adoption in this state?

No. Only residents and nonresidents who have lived in Kentucky for at least one year can adopt.

LOUISIANA

State Adoption Specialist
Ada White
Louisiana Department of Human
 Services, Office of Community
 Services
P.O. Box 3318
Baton Rouge, LA 70821
(504) 342-4086

Compact Administrator
Brenda Kelley, Assistant Secretary
Field Services Division
Division of Children,
 Youth and Families, DSS
P.O. Box 3318
Baton Rouge, LA 70804
(504) 342-4015

Deputy Compact Administrator
Leola McClinton
Field Services Division

Division of Children,
 Youth and Families, DSS
P.O. Box 3318
Baton Rouge, LA 70821
 or
333 Laurel Street
Baton Rouge, LA 70802

(504) 342-4034
fax (504) 342-4038

Office hours:
Monday-Friday
8:30 A.M.-4:30 P.M.
Central Time Zone

Direct all correspondence and
 telephone calls to the Deputy
 Compact Administrator.

State Licensing Specialist
Thalia Millican
Louisiana Department
 of Social Services

Office of the Secretary, Licensing
P.O. Box 3767
Baton Rouge, LA 70821
(504) 922-0015

**State Adoption Exchange
 and Photo Listings**
Louisiana Adoption Resource
 Exchange (LARE)
Louisiana Department
 of Social Services
Office of Community Services
P.O. Box 3318
Baton Rouge, LA 70821
(504) 342-4040
(800) 259-3428

Private Adoption Agencies

Adoption Options
1724 North Burnside, Suite 7
Gonzales, LA 70737
(504) 644-1033

Answered Prayer Adoption
Services, Inc.
1511 S. Sandra Avenue
Gonzales, LA 70737
(504) 647-8911

Associated Catholic Charities
of New Orleans, Inc.
1231 Prytania Street
New Orleans, LA 70130
(504) 523-3755

Beacon House, Inc.
750 Louisiana Avenue, Suite C
Port Allen, LA 70767
(504) 387-6365

Bethany Christian Services
of Louisiana
4854 Constitution Avenue,
Suite 1D
Baton Rouge, Louisiana 70808
(504) 927-3235

Catholic Community Services
Couseling, Maternity,
and Adoption Department
4884 Constitution Avenue
Baton Rouge, LA 70821
(504) 927-4930

Catholic Social Services
of Houma-Thibodaux
1220 Aycock Street
P.O. Box 3894
Houma, LA 70361
(504) 876-0490

Catholic Social Services
of Lafayette
708 West University, 2nd Floor
P.O. Box 2008
Laafayette, LA 70501
(318) 235-5218

Children's Bureau
of New Orleans, Inc.
1001 Howard Avenue, Suite 2800
Plaza Tower
New Orleans, LA 70113
(504) 525-2366

Gail House
8676 Goodwood Boulevard
Baton Rouge, LA 70806
(504) 926-0070

Gladney Center
2300 Hemphill Street
Fort Worth, TX 76110
(817) 926-3304

Holy Cross Child Placement
Agency, Inc.
929 Olive Street
Shreveport, LA 71104
(318) 222-7892

Jewish Children's
Regional Service
P.O. Box 15225
New Orleans, LA 70175
(504) 899-1595

Jewish Family Service
of Greater New Orleans
2026 St. Charles Avenue
New Orleans, LA 70130
(504) 524-8475

LDS Social Services
2000 Old Spanish Trail, Suite 115
Slidell, LA 70458
(504) 649-2774

Louisiana Baptist
Children's Home
7200 DeSiard Road
P.O. Box 4196
Monroe, LA 71211
(318) 343-2244

Louisiana Child Care
and Placement Services, Inc.
9080 Southwood Drive
Shreveport, LA 71118
(318) 686-2243

New Family
Adoption Services, Inc.
118 Ridgelake Drive
Metairie, LA 70001
(504) 833-5829

Special Delivery
Adoption Services, Inc.
7809 Jefferson Highway,
Suite D-1
Baton Rouge, LA 70809
(504) 924-2507

St. Elizabeth Foundation
8054 Summa Drive
Baton Rouge, LA 70809
(504) 769-8888

St. Gerard's
Adoption Network, Inc.
100 S. Vivian Street
P.O. Drawer 1260
Eunice, LA 70535
(318) 457-9048

Volunteers of America-
Alexandria
1756 Elliott Street
Alexandria, LA 71301
(318) 442-8026

Volunteers of America—
Greater New Orleans
3900 N. Causeway Boulevard,
#700
Metairie, LA 70002
(504) 836-5225

Volunteers of America-Ruston
210 W. Alabama
Ruston, LA 71270
(318) 254-8160

Volunteers of America-
Shreveport
354 Jordan Street
Shreveport, LA 71101
(318) 221-5000

**Adoptive Parent Support
Groups and Postadoption
Services**

Adopt Older Kids
Attn.: Ebrar Reaux
818 Briarwood Drive
New Iberia, LA 70560

Catholic Social Services Auxiliary
Attn.: Lynn Rogers
1106 Jenkins Street
Crowley, LA 70526

Korean-American
Resource Exchange
Attn.: Gerri Lattier
4107 Saint Elizabeth Drive
Kenner, LA 70065
(504) 455-9445

North American Council
on Adoptable Children
State Representative
Attn.: Cecile Tebo
3528 Vincennes Place
New Orleans, LA 70125
(504) 866-4449

Adopted Person and Birth Relative Support Groups

Adoptee Liberty Movement Association (ALMA)
P.O. Box 1340
Slidell, LA 70459

Adoptee Birthparents Committee
P.O. Box 9442
Metairie, LA 70005
(504) 888-7963

Adoptees Birthright Committee
Box 7213
Metairie, LA 70010

Adoption Connection
7301 W. Judge Perez, #311
Arabi, LA 70032
(504) 277-0030

Adoption Search Organization
8154 Longwood Drive
Denhan Springs, LA 70726
(504) 665-2030

Adoption Triad Network, Inc.
Attn.: Johnnie Kocurek
120 Thibodaux Drive
Lafayette, LA 70503
(318) 984-3682

Adoption Triad Network
511 Blue Bell
Port Allen, LA 70605

Adoption Triad Network
Box 324
Swartz, LA 71281

Adult Adoptee
Search and Support Group
Attn.: Peggy Ponder
195 Arthur Street
Shreveport, LA 71105
(318) 865-7784

Healing Hearts
Birth Mother Support Group
Volunteers of America
Attn.: Katie Sentilles
3900 N. Causeway Boulevard,
Suite 700
Metairie, LA 70002
(504) 836-5225

Lost and Found
18343 Weatherwood Drive
Baton Rouge, LA 70817
(504) 769-2456

Louisiana Department
of Social Services
Office of Community Services
Voluntary Registry
P.O. Box 3318
Baton Rouge, LA 70821
(504) 342-9922
(800) 259-2456

Volunteers of America
Birth Mother Support Group
Attn.: Pat Atkins
360 Jordan Street
Shreveport, LA 71106
(318) 865-7784

Louisiana State Bar Association
610 Street Charles Avenue
New Orleans, LA 70130
(504) 566-1600

Adoption Attorneys

Edith Henderson Morris*
1515 Poydras Street, Suite 1870
New Orleans, LA 70112
(504) 524-3781
fax (504) 561-0027

* Ms. Morris has completed
about 150 independent
adoptions.

Henri Louridans
P.O. Box 5089
915 Barksdale Boulevard
Bossier City, LA 71111
(318) 425-4710

David Painter*
P.O. Box 1586
Lake Charles, LA 70602
(318) 436-1415
fax (318) 436-2403

* Mr. Painter has conducted
more than 300 independent
adoptions and more than 50
agency adoptions.

Noel E. Vargas, II
526 Rue Street Louis, #302
New Orleans, LA 70130
(504) 561-8129

LOUISIANA LAWS RELATED TO ADOPTION: QUESTIONS AND ANSWERS

Can an attorney serve as an intermediary?
Yes.

Is advertising permitted?
Yes.

Who must consent to the adoption?
1. The birth mother
2. The birth father
3. The parents or guardian of any birth parents who are under the age of eighteen at the time of surrender (applies to independent adoptions only)

When can consent be taken from the birth mother (father), and how long after the consent is signed can it be revoked?
In both agency and private adoptions a consent cannot be given by a birth mother until the child is five days old. Consent is essentially irrevocable. A birth parent can attempt to

withdraw consent within thirty days of signing; however, the adoption will proceed if it is in the child's best interest.

David Painter, an adoption attorney in Lake Charles, states that a birth father can sign a consent before birth, and the consent is revocable until five days after birth. His rights may be terminated before the child's birth.

Birth parents' rights are terminated at a court hearing, but the birth parents' appearance is not required.

What are the birth father's rights?
The legal birth father or the birth father of a child born out of wedlock must consent to the adoption before the mother's termination or relinquishment, unless he has signed a valid surrender. In Louisiana, legal fathers, or fathers who have formally acknowledged or legitimized the child (even if they are not the biological father), or fathers who are named on the birth certificate must give consent to the adoption.

Any other "birth father" can oppose an adoption only if he can legally prove he is the father and has been responsible.

What fees can adoptive parents pay?
Medical, hospital, and legal fees can be paid. A statement of fees paid must be included in the adoption petition.

Where does the adoption hearing take place?
The hearing may take place in the county where the adoptive parents reside.

How are familial and step-parent adoptions different from nonbiological adoptions?
No home study is required. The adoption can be finalized quickly and no written termination of parental rights is necessarily required. In step-parent adoptions in which the former spouse has died, the grandparents may be granted limited visitation rights.

Can a nonresident finalize an adoption in this state?
Yes.

MAINE

State Adoption Specialist
Leonore Taylor
Maine Department
  of Human Services
State House, 221 State Street
Augusta, ME 04333
(207) 287-5060

Compact Administrator
Timothy Hickey
Bureau of Social Services
Department of Human Services
State House, Station 11
Augusta, ME 04333
(207) 289-5060

Direct all correspondence and
  telephone calls to the Compact
  Administrator.

Office hours:
Monday-Friday
8:00 A.M.-5:00 P.M.
Eastern Time Zone

State Adoption Specialist
Leonore Taylor
Maine Department
  of Human Services
State House, 221 State Street
Augusta, ME 04333
(207) 287-5060

State Licensing Specialist
Leonore Taylor
Department of Human Services
State House, 221 State Street
Augusta, ME 04333
(207) 287-5060

**State Adoption Exchange
  and Photo Listing**

Northern New England Adoption
  Exchange, Department
  of Human Services
State House, 221 State Street
Augusta, ME 04333
(207) 287-2971

Private Adoption Agencies

Good Samaritan Agency
450 Essex Street
Bangor, ME 04401
(207) 942-7211

International Adoption
  Services Centre
P.O. Box 55
Alna, ME 04535
(207) 586-5058

Maine Adoption
  Placement Service
P.O. Box 2249
Bangor, ME 04402-2249
(207) 941-9500

Maine Adoption
  Placement Service
Market Square
Houlton, ME 04730
(207) 532-9358

Maine Adoption
  Placement Service
306 Congress Street
Portland, ME 04101
(207) 772-3678

Maine Children's Home
  for Little Wanderers
34 Gilman Street
Waterville, ME 04901
(207) 873-4253

St. Andre Home, Inc.
283 Elm Street
Biddeford, ME 04005
(207) 282-3351

Sharing in Adoption
38 LaFayette Street
Yarmouth, ME 04096
(207) 781-3092

**Adoptive Parent Support
  Groups and Postadoption
  Services**

Adoptive Families of Maine
Attn.: Kitsie Claxton
129 Sunderland Drive
Auburn, ME 04210
(207) 784-3804

Adoptive Families of Maine
  and North American Council
  on Adoptable Children
  State Representative
Attn.: Judy Collier
156 Essex Street
Bangor, ME 04401
(207) 941-9500

Adoptive Families of Maine
Attn.: Cindy Jones
P.O. Box 340
Winterport, ME 04496
(207) 941-9500

Adoptive Parents
  of Aroostook County
Attn.: Susan Shaw
71 Barton Street
Presque Isle, ME 04769
(518) 561-0338

**Adopted Person and Birth
  Relative Support Groups**

Adoption Support Group
  of Penobscot Bay
Taylor's Point
Tenant's Harbor, ME 04860
(207) 372-6322

Maine State
  Adoption Reunion Registry
Division of Vital Records
221 State Street
Augusta, ME 04330
(207) 287-3181

Mira Bicknell
  Adoption Resource Center
Box 2793
South Portland, ME 04116
(207) 773-3378

Solomon's Mothers
RR #3, Box 1050
Wells, ME 04090
(207) 646-4258

Maine State Bar Association
P.O. Box 788
Augusta, ME 04332-0788
(207) 622-7523

Adoption Attorneys

Judith M. Berry
28 State Street
Gorham, ME 04038
(207) 839-7004

Susan E. Bowie
66 Pearl Street, Suite 321
Portland, ME 04101
(207) 774- 5621

MAINE LAWS RELATED TO ADOPTION: QUESTIONS AND ANSWERS

Can an attorney serve as an intermediary?
Yes.

Is advertising permitted?
Yes.

Who must consent to the adoption?
The birth mother, and the birth father (if married to the birth mother)

**When can consent be taken from the birth mother (father), and how long after the
  consent is signed can it be revoked?**
The law is not clear, but it appears consent can be given any time after the child's birth.
Parental consent in an independent adoption is executed before a probate judge. A birth

mother has until the first hearing (about ninety days after consent is given) to revoke her consent and the court may permit her to do so up until the final adoption if it is in the child's best interest. In an agency adoption, consents are not given until seventy-two hours after birth and are irrevocable.

What are the birth father's rights?
The birth father must provide a consent if his name is on the birth certificate, if his whereabouts are known, and he is involved in the child's life. Otherwise, his consent is not needed. If the birth father has been given notice of the adoption, he has twenty days to petition the court to establish his paternity. The judge will then decide whether to give the birth father parental rights.

What fees can adoptive parents pay?
Only reasonable fees for services can be charged by an agency or intermediary.

Where does the adoption hearing take place?
The hearing can take place in the county where the adoptive parents live, where the child lives, or where the adoption agency is located.

How are familial and step-parent adoptions different from nonbiological adoptions?
When a blood relative is adopting, no home study is required.

Can a nonresident finalize an adoption in this state?
Yes.

MARYLAND

State Adoption Specialist
Cassandra Fallin
Social Services Administrations
Maryland Department
 of Human Services
311 West Saratoga Street
Baltimore, MD 21201
(410) 767-7423

Compact Administrator
Joan Davis
Social Services Administration
Department of Human Resources
311 West Saratoga Street
Baltimore, MD 21201
(410) 767-7249
fax (410) 333-0392

Direct all correspondence and
 telephone calls to the Deputy
 Compact Administrator.

Office hours:
Monday-Friday
8:30 A.M.-5:00 P.M.
Eastern Time Zone

**State Adoption Exchange
 and Photo Listing**
Social Services Administration
Maryland Adoption Resource
 Exchange (MARE)
311 West Saratoga Street
Baltimore, MD 21201
(410) 767-7372

Private Adoption Agencies

Adoption Resource Center
6630 Baltimore National Pike,
 Suite 100B
Baltimore, MD 21228
(410) 744-6393

Adoption Resource Center
507 Midland Road
Silver Spring, MD 20904
(301) 989-0026

Adoption Service
 Information Agency (ASIA)
8555 16th Street, Suite 603
Silver Spring, MD 20910
(301) 587-7068

Adoptions Forever
5830 Hubbard Drive
Rockville, MD 20852
(301) 468-1818

Adoptions Together
6 Sudbrook Lane
Baltimore, MD 21208
(410) 653-3446

Adoptions Together
3837 Farragut Avenue
Kensington, MD 20895
(301) 933-7333

American Adoption Agency
3500 Bancroft Road
Baltimore, MD 21215
(410) 358-0554

Barker Foundation
7945 MacArthur Boulevard,
 Suite 206
Cabin John, MD 20818
(301) 229-8300

Bethany Christian Services
1641 Route 3 North, Suite 205
Crofton, MD 21114
(410) 721-2835

Board of Child Care
3300 Gaither Road
Baltimore, MD 21244
(410) 922-2100

Burlington United Methodist
  Family Services, Inc.
St. Paul's United Methodist
  Church
P.O. Box 477, 318 E. Oak Street
Oakland, MD 21550-1504
(301) 334-1285

Catholic Charities
1504 St. Camillus Drive
Silver Spring, MD 20903
(301) 434-2550

Catholic Charities of Baltimore
19 West Franklin Street
Baltimore, MD 21201
(410) 659-4050

Children's Choice
301 N. Charles Street, Suite 400
Baltimore, MD 21201
(410) 576-9225

Children's Choice
213-219 West Main Street,
  2nd Floor
Salisbury, MD 21801-4906
(410) 546-6106

Children's Choice
Island Professional Park,
  Suite 200-B
Stevensville, MD 21666
(410) 643-9290

Cradle of Hope
  Adoption Center, Inc.
8630 Fenton Street, Suite 310
Silver Spring, MD 20910
(301) 587-4400

Creative Adoptions
10750 Hickory Ridge Road,
  Suite 109
Columbia, MD 21044
(410) 596-1521

Datz Foundation
16220 Frederick Road, Suite 404
Gaithersburg, MD 20877
(301) 424-3911

Family and Children's Services
  of Central Maryland, Inc.
204 West Lanvale Street
Baltimore, MD 21217
(410) 669-9000

Family and Child Services
  of Washington, DC, Inc.
5301 76th Avenue
Landover Hills, MD 20784
(301) 459-4121, ext. 334

Holy Cross Child Placement
  Agency, Inc.
6701 Wisconsin Avenue
Chevy Chase, MD 20815
(301) 907-6887

Jewish Family Service
5750 Park Heights Avenue
Baltimore, MD 21215
(410) 466-9200

Jewish Social Services Agency
6123 Montrose Road
Rockville, MD 20852-4880
(301) 816-2700

LDS Social Services-East Coast
198 Thomas Johnson Drive,
  Suite 13
Frederick, MD 21702
(301) 694-5896

Lutheran Social Services
  of the National Capital Area
c/o Zion Evangelical Lutheran
  Church
7410 New Hampshire Avenue
Takoma Park, MD 20017
(301) 434-0080 or 434-0081

New Partners, Inc.
International Relief for Children
8905 Bradley Boulevard
Potomac, MD 20854
(301) 469-0476

Private Adoption Agency, Inc.
801 Wayne Avenue, 4th Floor
Silver Spring, MD 20910
(301) 495-9021

Tressler Lutheran Services
  of Maryland
5000 York Road
Baltimore, MD 21212-4437
(410) 532-9600

Welcome House Social Services
  of the Pearl S. Buck
  Foundation, Inc.
5407B Roland Avenue
Baltimore, MD 21210
(410) 435-6389

World Child-Frank Adoption
  and Assistance
1400 Spring Street, Suite 410
Silver Spring, MD 20910
(301) 589-3271

**Adoptive Parent Support
Groups and Postadoption
Services**

Adoption Resource Exchange
  for Single Parents
P.O. Box 5782
Springfield, VA 22150
(703) 866-5577

Adoptive Family Network
Attn.: Jennifer Geipe
P.O. Box 7
Columbia, MD 21045
Information lines:
(301) 984-6133
(410) 379-0891

Association of Single Adoptive
  Parents for DC Metro Area
Attn.: Letty Grishaw
P.O. Box 1704
Springfield, VA 22151
(703) 521-0632

Barker Foundation
Parents of Adopted Adolescents
  Group
7945 MacArthur Boulevard,
  Suite 206
Cabin John, MD 20818
(301) 229-8300

Black Adoptive Parents
  Support Group
Attn.: Georgette Brown
3110 Hardford Road
Baltimore, MD 21218
(410) 889-0568

Britt Adoption Services
P.O. Box 522
Bel Air, MD 21014
(410) 638-7886

Families Adopting Children
Everywhere (FACE)
and North American Council
on Adoptable Children
State Representative
P.O. Box 28058, Northwood
Station
Baltimore, MD 21239
(410) 488-2656

Families Adopting Children
Everywhere (FACE)
of Delmarva
Attn.: Jody Haltom
P.O. Box 193
Fruitland, MD 21826
(410) 546-5938

Families Adopting Children
Everywhere (FACE)
of Frederick County
Attn.: Marguerite Wilson
4426 Teen Barnes Road
Jefferson, MD 21755
(301) 371-4953

Families for Private Adoption
P. O. Box 6375
Washington, DC 20015-0375
(202) 722-0338

Harford County Parent Support
Group
(for parents of older adopted
children)
Attn.: Maureen Murawsky
(410) 575-2999

Info Adopt
Attn.: Margaret Lee
P.O. Box 3682
Salisbury, MD 21802
(410) 219-5971

Interracial Family Circle
P.O. Box 53290
Washington, DC 20009
(202) 393-7866 or (800) 500-
9040

Latin America Parents
Association,
National Capital Region
Attn.: Sheila Mooney
P.O. Box 4403
Silver Spring, MD 20914-4403
(301) 431-3407

Maryland League
of Foster/Adoptive Parents
1777 Reisterstown Road,
Building A, #220
Baltimore, MD 21208
(410) 486-4757

National Council for Single
Adoptive Parents
P.O. Box 15084
Chevy Chase, MD 20825
(202) 966-6367

Our Special Family
6 Autumn Wind Court
Reisterstown, MD 21136
(410) 561-1250

Parent Support for American
Adoption Agency
Attn.: Cheryl Adkins
250 Hereford Court
Millersville, MD 21108
(301) 544-1543

Rainbow Families
Attn.: Jim and Terri Cooney
128 East Lynnbrook Place
Bel Air, MD 21014
(410) 838-3858

Stars of David
Attn.: Ilene Gottfried
(301) 622-4757

Stars of David
Attn.: Lucy Steinitz
c/o Jewish Family
and Children's Service
5750 Park Heights Avenue
Baltimore, MD 21215
(410) 466-9200, ext. 233

Adopted Person and Birth
Relative Support Groups

Adoptee Birthfamily Connection
P.O. Box 115
Rocky Ridge, MD 21778
(301) 271-3037

Adoptee Birthparent
Support Network
3421 M Street, N.W., Suite 328
Washington, DC 20007
(202) 686-4611

Adoptees in Search
P.O. Box 41016
Bethesda, MD 20824
(301) 656-8555

Adoption Connection Exchange
204 W. Lanvale Street
Baltimore, MD 21217
(410) 669-9000

Adoptions Together Birthparent
Support Group
6 Sudbrook Lane
Baltimore, MD 21208
(410) 653-3446

Adoptions Together
Birthparent Support Group
3837 Farragut Avenue
Kensington, MD 20895
(301) 933-7333

Barker Foundation Adult
Adoptee Support Group
7945 MacArthur Boulevard,
Suite 206
Cabin John, MD 20818
(301) 229-8300

Barker Foundation Birthparent
Support Group
7945 MacArthur Boulevard,
Suite 206
Cabin John, MD 20818
(301) 229-8300

Concerned United Birthparents
P.O. Box 15258
Chevy Chase, MD 20825
(202) 966-1640

Concerned United Birthparents
Baltimore Area
Attn.: Margaret McMorrow
327 Dogwood Road
Millersville, MD 21108
(410) 544-0083

Maryland Mutual Consent
Voluntary Adoption Registry
311 West Saratoga Street
Baltimore, MD 21201
(410) 767-7423

Maryland State Bar Association
520 West Fayette Street
Baltimore, MD 21201
(410) 685-7878

Adoption Attorneys

Jeffrey E. Badger*
Long, Badger and Sullivan
124 E. Main Street
Salisbury, MD 21801
(410) 749-2356

* Mr. Badger had conducted twenty-six independent adoption and six agency adoptions.

Jeffrey Berman
5830 Hubbard Drive
Rockville, MD 20852
(301) 468-1818

Ellen Ann Callahan
12600 Admiral Way
Gaithersburg, MD 20878
(301) 258-2664

Nancy Davis-Loomis
Master in Chancery
Circuit Court, Anne Arundel
  County
Annapolis, MD 21404-2395
(410) 222-1284

Sara M. Donahoe
200A Monroe Street, #315
Rockville, MD 20850
(310) 294-0460

Anne Herrity Faust
2200 Defense Highway, #300
Crofton, MD 21114
(301) 261-6224
Rockville office (301) 231- 7225
Baltimore office (301) 793-0257

Mary G. Loker
30 E. Padonia Road, #404
Timonium, MD 21093
(410) 561-3000

Mark McDermott*
1300 19th Street, N.W., Suite 400
Washington, D.C. 20036
(202) 331-1955
fax (202) 293-2309

* Mr. McDermott has conducted more than 500 independent adoptions and more than 100 agency adoptions. He has served as past president of the American Academy of Adoption Attorneys.

Dawn Oxley Musgrave
6 Sudbrook Lane
Pikesville, MD 21208
(410) 486-9020

Stanton Phillips
2009 North 14th Street, Suite 510
Arlington, VA 22201
(703) 522-8800

Nancy D. Poster
9909 Georgetown Pike
P.O. Box 197
Great Falls, VA 22066
(703) 759-1560

Natalie H. Rees*
Mercantile-Toson Building., Suite 920
409 Washington Avenue
Baltimore, MD 21204-4903
(410) 494-8080
(410) 653-3033 (emergency nightline)
fax (410) 494-8082

* Ms. Rees has been an adoption attorney for more than eighteen years and has completed more than 1,000 independent adoptions. She also handles surrogacy and egg donor issues.

James Shrybman
801 Wayne Ave, No. 400
Silver Spring, MD
(301) 588-0040

Margaret E. Swain
21 W. Susquehanna Avenue
Towson, MD 21204
(410) 823-1250

Carolyn N. Thaler
29 W. Susquehanna Avenue,
  Suite 205
Towson, MD 21204
(410) 828-6627
fax (410) 296-3719

MARYLAND LAWS RELATED TO ADOPTION: QUESTIONS AND ANSWERS

Can an attorney serve as an intermediary?
No.

Is advertising permitted?
Yes.

Who must consent to the adoption?
Both birth parents and the child placement agency (if an agency adoption)

When can consent be taken from the birth mother (father), and how long after the consent is signed can it be revoked?
Consent cannot be taken until the child's birth. The birth parents can revoke their consent up to thirty days after signing. A final adoption decree can be challenged up to six months after finalization for reasons of fraud or duress.

Although a birth mother has nearly a month to change her mind, Natalie Rees, an adoption attorney in Baltimore, states that during the many years that she has practiced law, virtually no birth mothers have revoked the consent after placing the child for adoption. Rees attributes this fact to her awareness of potential "red flags" that indicate that a birth mother may change her mind, the birth mother's receiving counseling by a social worker, and the fact that each birth mother has her own attorney.

What are the birth father's rights?
His consent is needed regardless of whether he has financially supported the birth mother or not.

What fees can adoptive parents pay?
Payments for reasonable medical, hospital, and legal services are permitted. In an independent adoption, the birth parents will be advised of their right to receive legal counsel and adoption counseling; the court may order the adoptive parents to pay all or some of these costs. A description of all fees paid must be filed with the court.

Where does the adoption hearing take place?
The law does not address this issue. According to ICPC, the petition for adoption is filed in the county where the adoptive parents live.

How are familial and step-parent adoptions different from nonbiological adoptions?
Familial adoptions are treated just like an independent adoption, including a home study.

Can a nonresident finalize an adoption in this state?
Yes, but only if an agency receives consent from the birth parents.

MASSACHUSETTS

State Adoption Specialist
Mary Gambon
Massachusetts Department
 of Social Services
24 Farnsworth Street
Boston, MA 02210
(617) 727-0900

Compact Administrator
Deputy Commissioner
Massachusetts Department
 of Social Services
150 Causeway Street
Boston, MA 02114

Deputy Compact Administrator
Kenneth R. D'Ambrosia
Massachusetts Department
 of Social Services
24 Farnsworth Street
Boston, MA 02210
617) 727-0900, ext. 553

Direct all correspondence and
 telephone calls to the Deputy
 Compact Administrator.

Office hours:
Monday-Friday
9:00 A.M.-5:00 P.M.
Eastern Time Zone

**State Adoption Exchange and
 Photo Listing**
Massachusetts Adoption Resource
 Exchange, Inc. (MARE)
45 Franklin Street, 5th Floor
Boston, MA 02110-1301
(617) 542-3678
(800) 882-1176 (in MA)

Private Adoption Agencies

Adoption Center
55 Wheeler Street
Cambridge, MA 02138
(617) 864-5437

Adoption Center, Inc.
1105 Washington Street
West Newton, MA 02165
(617) 527-6171

Adoption Resource Associates
57 Russell Avenue
Watertown, MA 02172
(617) 923-1895

Adoption Resource Center
 at Brightside
2112 Riverdale Street
West Springfield, MA 01089
(413) 788-7366

Adoptions With Love, Inc.
188 Needham Street, Suite 220
Newton, MA 02164
(617) 964-4357

Alliance for Children, Inc.
40 William Street, Suite G80
Wellesley, MA 02181
(617) 431-7148

Beacon Adoption Center, Inc.
66 Lake Buel Road
Great Barrington, MA 01230
(413) 528-2749

Berkshire Center for Families
 and Children
480 West Street
Pittsfield, MA 01201
(413) 448-8281

Bethany Christian Services
1580 Turnpike Street
North Andover, MA 01845
(508) 794-9800

Boston Adoption Bureau, Inc.
14 Beacon Street, Suite 620
Boston, MA 02108
(617) 277-1336

Boston Children's Services
271 Huntington Avenue
Boston, MA 02115
(617) 267-3700

Cambridge Adoption and
  Counseling Associates, Inc.
Mail:
P.O. Box 190
Cambridge, MA 02142
Office:
111 Mt. Auburn Street
Watertown, MA 02172
(617) 923-0370

Cambridge Family
  and Children's Services
929 Massachusetts Avenue
Cambridge, MA 02139
(617) 876-4210

Catholic Charities
70 Lawrence Street
Lowell, MA 01852
(508) 452-1421

Catholic Charities
79 Elm Street
Southbridge, MA 01550
(508) 765-5936

Catholic Charities Center
  of the Old Colony Area
686 North Main Street
Brockton, MA 02401
(617) 587-0815

Catholic Charities, Merrimack
  Valley
430 North Canal Street
Lawrence, MA 01840
(508) 685-5930

Catholic Charities, North Shore
3 Margin Street
Peabody, MA 01960
(508) 532-3600

Catholic Charities
  of Cambridge and Somerville
270 Washington Street
Somerville, MA 02143
(617) 625-1920

Catholic Charities
  of the Diocese of Worcester,
  Inc.
53 Highland Avenue
Worcester, MA 01420
(508) 343-4879

Catholic Family Services of
  Greater Lynn
55 Lynn Shore Drive
Lynn, MA 01902
(617) 593-2312

Catholic Social Services
  of Fall River, Inc.
783 Slade Street
P.O. Box M, South Station
Fall River, MA 02724
(508) 674-4681

Children's Aid and Family
  Services of Hampshire County,
  Inc.
8 Trumbull Road
Northampton, MA 01060
(413) 584-5690

Children's Services
  of Roxbury, Inc.
2406 Washington Street
Roxbury, MA 02119
(617) 445-6655

Concord Family Service
  Society, Inc.
111 O.R.N.A.C.
Concord, MA 01742
(508) 369-4909

DARE Family Services
2 Electronics Avenue, Suite 7
Danvers, MA 01923
(508) 750-0751

DARE Family Services
17 Popular Street
Roslindale, MA 02131
(617) 469-2311

Downey Side Families for Youth
999 Liberty Street
Springfield, MA 01104
(413) 781-2123

Family and Children's Services
  of Catholic Charities
53 Highland Avenue
Fitchburg, MA 01420
(508) 343-4879

Family and Children's Services
  of Greater Lynn, Inc.
111 North Common Street
Lynn, MA 01902
(617) 598-5517

Florence Crittenton League
119 Hall Street
Lowell, MA 01854-3612
(508) 452-9671

Full Circle Adoptions
93 Franklin Street
Northampton, MA 01060-2038
(413) 587-0007

Gift of Love Adoption Services
1087 Newman Avenue
Seekonk, MA 02771
(401) 826-8470

Hope Adoptions, Inc.
71 Elm Street
Worcester, MA 01609
(508) 752-1456

Italian Home for Children, Inc.,
  Family Resource Program
1125 Centre Street
Jamaica Plain, MA 02130
(617) 524-3116

Jewish Family
  and Children's Service
Adoption Resources
1340 Centre Street
Newton, MA 02159
(617) 332-2218

Jewish Family Services
  of Metrowest
14 Vernon Street, Suite 104
Framingham, MA 01701
(617) 875-3100

Jewish Family Services
  of Greater Springfield, Inc.
15 Lenox Street
Springfield, MA 01108
(413) 737-2601

Jewish Family Services
  of the North Shore
324B Essex Street
Swampscott, MA 01907-1212
(617) 581-1530

Jewish Family Services
  of Worcester
646 Salisbury Street
Worcester, MA 01609
(508) 755-3101

La Alianza Hispana, Inc.
409 Dudley Street
Roxbury, MA 02119
(617) 427-7175

LDS Social Services
of Massachusetts, Inc.
Mail:
131 Route 101A
Amherst Plaza, Suite 204
Amherst, NH 03031
Office:
150 Brown Street
Weston, MA
(603) 889-0148 (New Hampshire)

Love the Children
of Massachusetts
2 Perry Drive
Duxbury, MA 02332
(617) 934-7025

Lutheran Child and Family
Services of New England
416 Belmont Street
Worcester, MA 01604
(508) 791-4488

New Bedford Child and Family
Services
1061 Pleasant Street
New Bedford, MA 02740
(508) 996-8572

New England Home
for Little Wanderers
161 South Huntington Avenue
Boston, MA 02130
(617) 232-8610

Protestant Social Service Bureau
776 Hancock Street
Quincy, MA 02170
(617) 773-6203

Southeastern
Adoption Services, Inc.
585 Front Street
P.O. Box 356
Marion, MA 02738
(508) 996-6683

Special Adoption Family Services
418 Commonwealth Avenue
Boston, MA 02215
(617) 572-3678

United Homes for Children
90 Cushing Avenue
Dorchester, MA 02125
(617) 825-3300

United Homes for Children
1147 Main Street, Suite 210
Tewksbury, MA 01876
(508) 640-0089

Wide Horizons for Children
38 Edge Hill Road
Waltham, MA 02154
(617) 894-5330

Worcester Children's Friend
Society
21 Cedar Street
Worcester, MA 01609
(508) 753-5425

**Adoptive Parent Support
Groups and Postadoption
Services**

Adoption Connection
Attn.: Susan C. Darke
11 Peabody Square, Room 6
Peabody, MA 01960
(508) 532-1261

Adoption Resource Center
20 Sacramento Street
Cambridge, MA 02138
(617) 547-0909

Adoption Support and
Enrichment Services
118 Union Avenue, Suite 203
Framingham, MA 01701
(508) 875-6603

Berkshire County
Open Door Society
Attn.: Carol and David
Weissbrod
Washington Mountain Road
Becket, MA 01223
(413) 623-6031

Berkshire Learning Center
823 North Street
Pittsfield, MA 01202
(413) 442-5531

Family Center
Pre and Post Adoption Consulting
Team
385 Highland Avenue
Somerville, MA 02144
(617) 628-8815

International Concerns
Committee for Children
Attn.: Betty Laning
130 Temple Street
West Newton, MA 02165
(617) 969-7025

Latin American
Adoptive Families
Attn.: Marilyn Rowland
211 Turner Road
Falmouth, MA 02536
(508) 457-4525

Nazarene Association
for Foster Care and Adoption
Attn.: Lora Wooster
167 Amesbury Road
Haverhill, MA 01830

Open Door Society
of Massachusetts
and North American Council
on Adoptable Children
State Representative
Attn.: Joan Clark
P.O. Box 1158
Westboro, MA 01581
(800) 932-3678

Pioneer Valley Open Door
Attn.: Karen Lutsky
40 Peabody Lane
Greenfield, MA 01301
(413) 773-5025

Single Parents for the Adoption
of Children Everywhere
Attn.: Betsy Burch
6 Sunshine Avenue
Natick, MA 01760
(508) 655-5426

Stars of David of Massachusetts
Attn.: Donna Davis
8 Brook Way
Westboro, MA 01581
(508) 752-2512

Worcester Area
Open Door Society
Attn.: Jane O'Toole
19 Omaha Avenue
Northboro, MA 01532
(508) 393-2893

**Adopted Person and Birth
Relative Support Groups**

Adoptee Liberty Movement
Association (ALMA)
P.O. Box 115
Townsend, MA 01469

Adoption Connection
O'Shea Building, # 6
11 Peabody Square
Peabody, MA 01960
(508) 532-1261

Adoption Search Coordinator for
  the Massachusetts Department
  of Social Service
Attn.: Sheila Frankel
24 Farnsworth Street
Boston, MA 02210
(617) 727-0900

Adoption Support
118 Union Avenue
Framingham, MA 01701
(508) 875-6603

Cape Cod Adoption Connection
P.O. Box 336
Brewster, MA 02631
(508) 896-7332

Center for Family Connections
Box 383246
Cambridge, MA 02238-3246
(617) 547-0909

Concerned United Birthparents
63 Mile Hill Road
Boylston, MA 01505

Concerned United Birthparents
P.O. Box 396, Harvard Square
Cambridge, MA 02138
(617) 328-3005

Family Ties Support Group
11 Alvanos Drive
Haverhill, MA 01830
(508) 373-7446

Love the Children
  (Korean born adoptees)
1 Burnham Lane
Danvers, MA 01923
(508) 373-7446

SAFE Harbor
Box 1666
Wellfleet, MA 02667
(508) 349-9895

Today Reunites Yesterday (TRY)
P.O. Box 989
Northampton, MA 01061-0989
(413) 584-6599

Massachusetts Bar Association
20 West Street
Boston, MA 02111
(617) 542-3602

Adoption Attorneys

Susan L. Crockin
One Gateway Center, #601 West
Newton, MA 02158
(617) 332-2020

Herbert Friedman
115 Broad Street, 6th Floor
Boston, MA 02110
(617) 451-0191

Julie E. Ginsburg
60 Walnut Street
Wellesley, MA 02181
(617) 237-8630

Karen Greenberg*
Knowitz and Greenberg
144 Gould Street, Suite 152
Needham, MA 02194
(617) 444-6611
fax (617) 449-3093

* Ms. Greenberg has been
  conducting adoptions since
  1989. She has conducted
  numerous agency adoptions and
  about ten international
  adoptions.

Jeffrey M. Kaye*
260 Haverhill Street
Lawrence, MA 02165
508) 682-4413
617) 720-0028
fax 617) 227-6308

* Mr. Kaye has conducted about
  fifty independent adoptions,
  more than 700 agency
  adoptions, and ten
  international adoptions.

Paula Mackin*
1 Prescott Street
Charlestown, MA 02129
617) 242-1689

* Ms. Mackin has conducted
  hundreds of adoptions,
  including fifty international
  adoptions. She handles cases
  involving complex disruptions
  and agency failures. She
  represents the adoptive parents
  and not the agency in
  adoptions.

Michele M. Modica
2 Kilburn Street
Revere, MA 02151
(617) 286-4936

Arthur Rosenberg
85 Wells Avenue, Suite 200
West Newton, MA 02159
(617) 928-3683
fax (617) 928-3699

Robert H. Weber
246 Walnut Street
Newton, MA 02160
(617) 964-7000
(617) 964-4025

MASSACHUSETTS LAWS RELATED TO ADOPTION: QUESTIONS AND ANSWERS

Independent adoption is illegal in Massachusetts; however an agency-identified adoption is permissible. According to Arthur Rosenberg, an adoption attorney in West Newton, adoptive parents may participate in independent adoptions in other states. The other state's laws and guidelines would then govern the process.

Can an attorney serve as an intermediary?
An attorney can serve as intermediary provided the adoptive family has a home study done by a Massachusetts agency, and the child is surrendered to an agency.

Is advertising permitted?
No.

Who must consent to the adoption?
Both birth parents and the child placement agency.

When can consent be taken from the birth mother (father), and how long after the consent is signed can it be revoked?
Consent cannot be taken until four days after the child is born and is irrevocable.

What are the birth father's rights?
His consent is needed regardless of whether he has supported the birth mother or not.

What fees can adoptive parents pay?
Payments for reasonable living, medical, hospital, and legal services are permitted.

Where does the adoption hearing take place?
The hearing takes place in the county where the child or the adoptive parents live.

How are familial and step-parent adoptions different from nonbiological adoptions?
No home study or agency involvement is required, thereby saving time and expenses.

Can a nonresident finalize an adoption in this state?
Yes, but only if an agency receives consent from the birth parents.

MICHIGAN

State Adoption Specialist
Richard Hoekstra
Michigan Department
of Social Services
P.O. Box 30037
Lansing, MI 48909
(517) 373-4021

Compact Administrator
Harold S. Gazen, Deputy Director
Office of Children's Services
Michigan Department
of Social Services
P.O. Box 30037
235 S. Grand Avenue,
5th Floor
Lansing, MI 48909
(517) 335-6158

Deputy Compact Administrator
Bryan Stewart
Office of Children's Services
Michigan Department
of Social Services

P.O. Box 30037
235 S. Grand Avenue, 5th Floor
Lansing, MI 48909
(517) 335-4652

Adoption Consultant
Dale L. Murray
Michigan Department
of Social Services
P.O. Box 30037
Lansing, MI 48909
(517) 373-6918
fax (517) 373-6177 (Limit 5
pages)

Direct all telephone calls and
correspondence to the
Adoption Consultant.

Office hours:
Monday-Friday
8:00 A.M.-4:30 P.M.
Eastern Time Zone

**Adoption Exchanges
and Photo Listings**

Spaulding for Children
Black Family Registry
16250 Northland Drive, Suite 120
Southfield, MI 48075
(810) 443-0306

Michigan Adoption Resource
Exchange
Family Service and Children's Aid
P.O. Box 6128
Jackson, MI 49204-6128
(517) 787-2738, 783-6273,
or (800) 589-6273

Private Adoption Agencies

Adoption Associates
6491 San Ru Avenue
Jenison, MI 49428
(616) 669-9696

Adoption Cradle
554 Capital Avenue, S.W.
Battle Creek, MI 49015
(616) 963-0794

Alternatives for Children
and Families
644 Harrison
P.O. Box 3038
Flint, MI 48502
(810) 235-0683

Americans for International Aid
& Adoption
877 South Adams Street,
Suite 106
Birmingham, MI 48009-7026
(810) 645-2211

Bethany Christian Services
6995 West 48th
P.O. Box 173
Fremont, MI 49412-9506
(616) 924-3390

Bethany Christian Services
901 Eastern Avenue N.E.
Grand Rapids, MI 49503
(616) 459-7836
or 459-7945

Bethany Christian Services
12048 James Street
Holland, MI 49424-9661
(616) 396-0623

Bethany Christian Services
4225 W. Main Street, Suite M
Kalamazoo, MI 49006
(616) 384-0202

Bethany Christian Services
32500 Concord Drive, Suite 250
Madison Heights, MI 48701-1140
(810) 588-9400

Bethany Christian Services
919 E. Michigan Avenue
Paw Paw, MI 49079
(616) 657-7096

D.A. Blodgett Services
for Children and Families
805 Leonard, N.E.
Grand Rapids, MI 49503
(616) 451-2021

Catholic Family Services
1819 Gull Road
Kalamazoo, MI 49001
(616) 381-9800

Catholic Family Services
of the Diocese of Saginaw
1008 South Wenona
Bay City, MI 48706
(517) 892-2504

Catholic Human Services
154 South Ripley Boulevard
Alpena, MI 49707
(517) 356-6385

Catholic Human Services
111 South Michigan
Gaylord, MI 49735
(517) 732-6761

Catholic Human Services
1000 Hastings Street
Traverse City, MI 49686
(616) 947-8110

Catholic Social Services/St.
Vincent Home
2800 West Willow Street
Lansing, MI 48917
(517) 323-4734

Catholic Social Services
of the Diocese of Muskegon
1095 Third Street, Suite 125
Muskegon, MI 49440
(616) 726-4735

Catholic Social Services of Flint
202 East Boulevard Drive,
Suite 210
Flint, MI 48503
(810) 232-9950

Catholic Social Services
of Kent County
1152 Scribner, N.W.
Grand Rapids, MI 49504
(616) 456-1443

Catholic Social Services
of Macomb County
235 South Gratiot Avenue
Mount Clemens, MI 48043
(810) 468-2616

Catholic Social Services
of Marquette
347 Rock Street
Marquette, MI 49855
(906) 228-8630; 786-7212

Catholic Social Services
of Monroe County
16 East Fifth Street
Monroe, MI 48161
(313) 242-3800

Catholic Social Services
of Oakland County
26105 Orchard Lake Road,
Suite 303
Farmington Hills, MI 48334
(810) 471-4140

Catholic Social Services
of Oakland County
50 Wayne Street
Pontiac, MI 48342
(810) 333-3700

Catholic Social Services
of St. Clair
2601 Thirteenth Street
Port Huron, MI 48060
(313) 987-9100

Catholic Social Services
of Washtenaw
117 North Division Street
Ann Arbor, MI 48104
(313) 662-4534

Catholic Social Services
of Wayne County
9851 Hamilton Avenue
Detroit, MI 48202
(313) 883-2100

Child and Family Services
of Michigan
4801 Willoughby Road, Suite 1
Holt, MI 48842
(517) 699-1600

Child and Family Services
of Michigan
2157 University Park Drive
P.O. Box 348
Okemos, MI 48805
(517) 349-6226

Child and Family Services
of Northeast Michigan
1044 U.S. 23 North
P.O. Box 516
Alpena, MI 49707
(517) 356-4567

Child and Family Services
of Northwestern Michigan
3785 Veterans Drive
Traverse City, MI 49684
(616) 946-8975

Child and Family Services
of Saginaw County
2806 Davenport
Saginaw, MI 48602
(517) 790-7500

Child and Family Services
of Southwestern Michigan
2000 South State Street
St. Joseph, MI 49085
(616) 983-5545

Child and Family Services
of the Upper Peninsula
104 Coles Drive
P.O. Box 706
Marquette, MI 49855
(906) 226-2516

Child and Family Services
of Western Michigan
412 Century Lane
Holland, MI 49423
(616) 396-2301

Child and Parent Services
30600 Telegraph, Suite 2215
Bingham Farms, MI 48025
(810) 646-7790

Children's Aid Society
7700 Second Avenue
Detroit, MI 48202
(313) 875-0200

Children's Hope Adoption
Services
7823 South Whiteville Road
Shepherd, MI 48883
(517) 828-5842

Christian Care Maternity
Ministries
Baptist Children's Home
214 North Mill Street
St. Louis, MI 48880
(517) 681-2172

Christian Cradle
416 Frandor, Suite 205
Lansing, MI 48912
(517) 351-7500

Christian Family Services
17105 West 12 Mile Road
Southfield, MI 48076
(810) 557-8390

Developmental Disabilities
Genessee County Community
Mental Health Board
420 W. Fifth Avenue
Flint, MI 48503
(810) 257-3714

Eagle Village
Family Living Program
4507 170th Avenue
Hersey, MI 49639
(616) 832-2234

Ennis Center for Children
20100 Greenfield Road
Detroit, MI 48235
(313) 342-2699

Ennis Center for Children
129 E. Third Street
Flint, MI 48502
(810) 233-4031

Ennis Center for Children
91 South Telegraph Road
Pontiac, MI 48341
(810) 333-2520

Evergreen Children's Services
10421 West Seven Mile Road
Detroit, MI 48221
(313) 862-1000

Evergreen Children's Services
15565 Northland Drive,
Suite 203 East
Southfield, MI 48075-5307
(810) 557-5800

Family Adoption Consultants
P.O. Box 50489,
421 West Crosstown Pkwy.
Kalamazoo, MI 49005
(616) 343-3316

Family Adoption Consultants
310 West University
Rochester, MI 48307
(810) 652-2842

Family and Children's Service of
Calhoun and Barry Counties
182 West Van Buren Street,
Suite 208
Battle Creek, MI 49017
(616) 965-3247

Family and Children's Service
of the Kalamazoo Area
1608 Lake Street
Kalamazoo, MI 49001
(616) 344-0202

Family and Children's Service
of Midland
1714 Eastman Avenue,
P.O. Box 2086
Midland, MI 48641-2086
(517) 631-5390

Family Counseling and Children's
Service of Lenawee County
213 Toledo Street
Adrian, MI 49221
(517) 265-5352

Family Service and Children's Aid
of Jackson County
115 West Michigan Avenue
P.O. Box 6128
Jackson, MI 49204
(517) 787-2738

Homes for Black Children
2340 Calvert
Detroit, MI 48206
(313) 869-2316

Huron Services for Youth
1952 S. Industrial Hwy., Suite J
Ann Arbor, MI 48104
(313) 994-4224

Huron Services for Youth
124 Pearl Street
Ypsilanti, MI 48197
(313) 480-1800

Jewish Family Services
24123 Greenfield Road
Southfield, MI 48075
(810) 559-1500

Judson Center
4410 W. 13 Mile Road
Royal Oak, MI 48073-6515
(810) 549-4339

Keane Center for Adoption
937 Mason
Dearborn, MI 48124
(313) 277-4664

LDS Social Services
37634 Enterprise Court
Farmington Hills, MI 48331
(810) 553-0902

Livingston Area Child
and Family Services, Inc.
3075 East Grand River Avenue
Howell, MI 48843
(517) 546-7530

Lutheran Adoption Service
P.O. Box 48
6019 West Side Saginaw Road
Bay City, MI 48707
(517) 686-3170

Lutheran Adoption Service
801 South Waverly, Suite 202
Lansing, MI 48917
(517) 321-7663

Lutheran Adoption Service
21700 Northwestern Hwy.,
Suite 1490
Southfield, MI 48075-4901
(810) 423-2770

Lutheran Social Service
1335 West Washington
Marquette, MI 49855
(906) 226-7410

Methodist Children's Home
Society
26645 West 6 Mile Road
Detroit, MI 48240
(313) 531-4060

Michigan Indian
Child Welfare Agency
1345 Monroe Avenue, N.W.,
Suite 220
Grand Rapids, MI 49505
(616) 454-9221

Michigan Indian
Child Welfare Agency
P.O. Box 5126
348 Davis Street
Kincheole, MI 49788
(906) 495-2900

Michigan Indian
Child Welfare Agency
6425 S. Pennsylvania Avenue,
Suite 3
Lansing, MI 48911
(517) 393-3256

Morning Star
Adoption Resource Services
2300 North Woodward Street,
Suite 9
Royal Oak, MI 48073
(810) 399-2740

Oakland Family Services
114 Orchard Lake Road
Pontiac, MI 48341
(810) 858-7766

Orchards Children's Services
2990 West Grand Boulevard,
Suite 400
Detroit, MI 48202
(313) 433-8695

Orchards Children's Services
30215 Southfield Road
Southfield, MI 48076-1360
(810) 258-0440

Sault Tribe Binogii
Placement Agency
2864 Ashmun Street
Sault St. Marie, MI 49783
(906) 632-5250

Spaulding for Children
16250 Northland Drive, Suite 120
Southfield, MI 48075
(810) 443-0300

Spectrum Human Services
34000 Plymouth Road
Livonia, MI 48150
(313) 552-8020

Spectrum Human Services
23077 Greenfield Road, Suite 500
Southfield, MI 48075
(810) 552-8020

St. Francis Family Services
17500 W. 8 Mile Road
Southfield, MI 48075
(810) 552-0750

St. Vincent-Sarah Fisher Center
27400 West 12 Mile Road
Farmington Hills, MI 48334
(810) 626-3025

Lula Belle Stewart Center
11000 W. McNichols, #116
Detroit, MI 48221
(313) 862-4600

Teen Ranch Family Services
2861 Main Street
Marlette, MI 48453
(810) 635-7511

Teen Ranch Family Services
15565 Northland Drive, Suite 300
East
Southfield, MI 48075-5307
(810) 443-2900

Touch of Hope Adoption Center
12 South Center Street
Hartford, MI 49057
(616) 621-2411

Whaley Children's Center
1201 North Grand Traverse
Flint, MI 48503
(810) 234-3603

Youth Living Centers
30000 Hiveley
Inkster, MI 48141
(313) 728-3400

**Adoptive Parent Support
Groups and Postadoption
Services**

A.D.O.P.T.
Attn.: James Berden
6939 Shields Court
Saginaw, MI 48603
(517) 781-2089

Adopt A Special Kid (AASK)
and North American Council
on Adoptable Children State
Representative
Attn.: Candee Bobalek
3051 Siebert Road
Midland, MI 48640
(517) 832-8117

Adoption Advocate Project/Child
& Family Services
Attn.: Bruce Falkconer
3785 North Townhall Road
Traverse City, MI 49684

Adoption Resources Group
Attn.: Micki Sliva
319 Mason
Hancock, MI 49930
(906) 482-5954

Adoptive Families
of Southwestern Michigan
Attn.: Don Grabemeyer
51558 Indian Lake Road
Dowagiac, MI 49047
(616) 424-3531

Building Families
Through Adoption
Attn.: Alice Grogan
4874 Meyer Street
Cadillac, MI 49601
(616) 775-6202

Children's Charter
of the Courts of Michigan
324 North Pine Street
Lansing, MI 48933
(517) 482-7533

Concerned Citizens for
International Adoption
Box 1083
Portage, MI 49082-1083

Community of Hope
Attn.: Robert and Ellen Van Eyck
544 Graafschap
Holland, MI 49423
(616) 396-1863

European Adoptive Families
of SW Michigan
Attn.: Deborah Lawless
47540 Saltz Road
Canton, MI 48187
(313) 981-6534

Families Adopting
Children Together
Attn.: Nancy Kohl
1015 Tomahawk
Niles, MI 49120
(616) 684-2091

Families for Adoption
Attn.: Pat Mucha
349 Adams Street
Plymouth, MI 48170
(313) 722-6163

Families for International
Children
Attn.: Jeff Gietzen
6475 28th Street, S.E., #124
Grand Rapids, MI 49546
(616) 676-2044
also Peggy Reed, (616) 247-1854

Families of Latin Kids
Attn.: Kathi Nelson
Box 15537
Ann Arbor, MI 48106
(313) 429-4312

Family Tree
Attn.: Janis Seikaly
27821 Santa Barbara
Lathrup Village, MI 48076
(810) 557-3501

FIAA of Ann Arbor
Attn.: Craig and Jane Waters
1503 Linwood
Ann Arbor, MI 48103
(313) 761-8265

Genesee County
Adoptive Parent Association
Attn.: Patti Heath
202 East Boulevard Drive, #210
Flint, MI 48504
(810) 232-9950

Greater Jackson Families
for Adoption
Attn.: Patricia Brown
6243 Mountie Way
Jackson, MI 49201
(517) 782-9023

Greater Lansing
OURS by Adoption
Attn.: Sue Rapier
P.O. Box 25161
Lansing, MI 48909

Hear My Voice
P.O. Box 2064
Ann Arbor, MI 48106
(313) 747-9669

International Families
Through Adoption
Attn.: Earl Geiger
1507 Marlboro
Muskegon, MI 49441
(616) 755-1484

Kinship
Attn.: Cheryl Kocsis
P.O. Box 62
Bay City, MI 48707
(517) 894-1068

Latin American Families
Through Adoption
Attn.: Sabina Seidel
608 Marcelletti Avenue
Paw Paw, MI 49079
(616) 657-6498

Marquette Adoption Group
Attn.: Joy Niemi
1702 Gray Street
Marquette, MI 49855
(906) 226-6208

Michigan Association
for Openness in Adoption
P.O. Box 5117
Traverse City, MI 49684
(616) 275-6221

Michigan Association
of Single Adoptive Parents
Attn.: Janet Way
7412 Coolidge
Centerline, MI 48015
(313) 758-6909

Michigan Foster and Adoptive
Parent Association
Attn.: Marylou Bax
4601 W. Saginaw Hwy., Suite J
Lansing, MI 48917
(517) 321-7554
or (800) 632-4180

National Coalition to End Racism
in America's Child Care System
22075 Koths
Taylor, MI 48180
(313) 295-0257

National Resource Center
for Special Needs Adoption
16250 Northland Drive, Suite 120
Southfield, MI 48075
(810) 443-7080

O.C.A.P.
Attn.: Linda Francisco
13660 Sherwood
Oak Park, MI 48237
(810) 546-8113

One Church,
One Child of Michigan
2929 Russell
Detroit, MI 48207
(313) 972-1360

One Church,
One Child of Michigan
1314 Ballard
Lansing, MI 48906
(517) 372-0184
or (800) 632-4180

Orchards Adoptive Parent
Support Group
Attn.: Catherine Katikos
30215 Southfield Road #100
Southfield, MI 48076
(810) 258-1278

OURS by Adoption
Attn.: Jeanne Revoir
4330 Van Vleet
Swartz Creek, MI 48473

People Adopting Children
Everywhere
Attn.: Lynn and Bill Uildriks
2948 160th Avenue
Holland, MI 49424
(616) 399-4096

Post Adoption Resources
21700 Northwestern Hwy.,
Suite 1490
Southfield, MI 48075-4901
(810) 423-2770

Post Adoption Support Services
1221 Minnesota Avenue
Gladstone, MI 49837
(906) 428-4861

Psychotherapy Center for
   Adoptive Families
7600 Grand River, Suite 290
Brighton, MI 48116
(810) 531-9659

Psychotherapy Center for
   Adoptive Families
17500 Northland Park Court
Southfield, MI 48075
(810) 531-9659

Singles for Adoption
Attn.: Carol Powell
619 Norton Drive
Kalamazoo, MI 49001
(616) 381-2581

Stars of David
Attn.: Elissa Rosenfeld
4458 Apple Valley Lane
West Bloomfield, MI 48323
(810) 737-3874

Support for Parents
   and Older Adopted Kids
Attn.: Betty Gorning
3666 Boulder
Troy, MI 48084
(810) 649-3469

Today's Families
18326 Middlebelt Road, #8
Livonia, MI 48152-5007
(313) 559-8310

West Michigan Friends
   of Adoption
Attn.: Pattie and Greg Mindock
7635 Yorktown Street
Richland, MI 49083-9637
(616) 629-9037

Yellin and Associates
   Adoption Consultants
27600 Farmington Road, Suite
107
Farmington Hills, MI 48334
(810) 489-9570

**Adopted Person and Birth
Relative Support Groups**

Adoptee Liberty Movement
   Association
P.O. Box 1804
Royal Oak, MI 48086-1804
(810) 542-2930

Adoptee's Search for Knowledge
Attn.: Jeanette Abronowitz
P.O. Box 762
East Lansing, MI 48823
(517) 321-7291

Adoption Circle Support Group
Attn.: Lois Plantefaber
117 North Division
Ann Arbor, MI 48104-1590
(313) 662-4534

Adoption Connections
Attn.: Julie Carter
Box 293
Cloverdale, MI 49035-0293
(616) 623-8060

Adoption Identity Movement
Attn.: Chris Spurr
1602 Cole
Birmingham, MI 48009
(810) 642-4029

Adoption Identity Movement
Attn.: Beth Johnson
Box 72
Ortonville, MI 48462
(810) 627-3275

Adoption Identity Movement
   of Grand Rapids
Attn.: Peg Richer
P.O. Box 9265
Grand Rapids, MI 49509
(616) 531-1380

Adoption Identity Movement
   of the Detroit Area
Attn.: Tina Caudill
P.O. Box 812
Hazel Park, MI 48030
(810) 548-6291

Adoption Identity Movement
   of Northern Michigan
Attn.: Martha Knapp
P.O. Box 134
Traverse City, MI 49685-0134
(616) 922-1976

Adoption Insight
Attn.: Elaine Meints
P.O. Box 171
Portage, MI 49081
(616) 327-1999

Adoption Reform Movement of
   Michigan/American Adoption
   Congress
Attn.: Bob Schafer
P.O. Box 9265
Grand Rapids, MI 49509
(616) 531-1380

Adoption Support Group
Attn.: Lori Gill
2008 Katherine Street
Port Huron, MI 48060
(810) 982-9774

Birth Parent Support Group
Attn.: Gayle Merkle
21700 N.W. Hwy. #1490
Southfield, MI 48075
(810) 423-2770

Birthbond
Attn.: Kay Silsby
738 Center t.
Mason, MI 48854

Bonding by Blood, Unlimited
4710 Cottrell Road, Rt. 5
Vassar, MI 48768
(517) 823-8248

Catholic Services of Macomb
Attn.: Joanne Ales
235 S. Gratiot Avenue
Mt. Clemens, MI 48043
(810) 468-2616

Central Adoption Registry
Michigan Department
   of Social Services
P.O. Box 30037
Lansing, MI 48909
(517) 373-3513

Concerned United Birthparents
Attn.: Mary Ahrens
524 Westchester Drive
Saginaw, MI 48603
(517) 792-5876

Informed Adoption Network
Attn.: Carol Taite
Box 6084
Ann Arbor, MI 48106
(313) 482-1697

Kalamazoo Birthparent
   Support Group
Box 2183
Kalamazoo, MI 49081
(616) 324-0634

Michigan Association
for Openness in Adoption
Attn.: Mike Spry
P.O. Box 5117
Traverse City, MI 49684
(616) 275-6221

Mid-Michigan Adoption Identity
Movement
13623 Podunk
Cedar Springs, MI 49319
(616) 754-4055

Missing in Adoption
Attn.: Joan Keller
4198 E. Cedar Lake Drive
Greenbush, MI 48738
(517) 739-4492

Post Reunion Support Group
Attn.: Linda Yellin
27600 Farmington Road
Farmington Hills, MI 48334
(810) 489-9570

Post Adoption Support Services
1221 Minnesota Avenue
Gladstone, MI 49837
(906) 428-4861

Retraced Roots
P.O. Box 892
Ludington, MI 49431
(616) 843-8409

Roots and Reunions
Attn.: Patti VanderBand
210 Barbeau Street
Sault St. Marie, MI 49783
(906) 635-5922

Tri-County Genealogical Society
21715 Brittany
East Pointe, MI 48021-2503
(810) 774-7953

Truth in the Adoption Triad
8107 Webster Road
Mt. Morris, MI 48454
(313) 686-3988

Truth in the Adoption Triad
Attn.: Marilyn Philips Jackson
2462 Kansas
Saginaw, MI 48601
(517) 777-6666

State Bar of Michigan
306 Townsend Street
Lansing, MI 48933
(517) 372-9030

Adoption Attorneys

Herbert Brail
930 Mason Street
Dearborn, MI 48124
(313) 278-8775

Monica Farris Linker
3250 Coolidge Highway
Berkeley, MI 48072
(810) 548-1430

Neal D. Nielsen
9812 E. Grand River Avenue
Brighton, MI 48116
(313) 227-7777

MICHIGAN LAWS RELATED TO ADOPTION: QUESTIONS AND ANSWERS

Can an attorney serve as an intermediary?
Yes, but the attorney cannot be reimbursed for this service.

Is advertising permitted?
Yes. Some newspapers may accept classified ads with a letter from an attorney or agency.

Who must consent to the adoption?
1. Both birth parents must consent unless they have released the child to an adoption agency.
2. If an agency has custody of the child, the agency must consent.

When can consent be taken from birth mother (father), and how long after the consent is signed can it be revoked?
A consent is not needed if the child is released to an adoption agency; the rights of the birth parents can then be terminated by court proceedings, notice of which they must receive. Consent must be given within a reasonable time frame; if this is not done, the court may determine if the withholding of consent is "arbitrary and capricious." If the birth parents select the adoptive parents, then approval must be granted by the probate court as to the placement.

What are the birth father's rights?
If the alleged birth father's consent cannot be obtained, the adoption cannot take place until his rights are terminated. The birth mother can terminate her own parental rights

while waiting for him to do so. The birth father's rights can be terminated if these requirements are met:

- he does not respond to notice of the adoption
- he denies interest in custody of the child
- he fails to appear at the adoption hearing and denies interest in the child
- his identity or location are unknown and reasonable efforts have been made to find him, and he has not provided for or cared for the child for at least ninety days
- If the birth father requests custody, the court shall determine his ability to care for the child if it is in the child's best interest.

What fees can adoptive parents pay?
Adoptive parents can pay for the birth mother's medical expenses, counseling, legal fees, travel, and reasonable living expenses. Fees and charges must be approved by the court.

Where does the adoption hearing take place?
The hearing can take place in the court of the county where the adoptive parents live or where the child lives.

How are familial and step-parent adoptions different from nonbiological adoptions? There are no specific provisions in the law for relative adoptions. In a stepparent adoption, a parent who does not have legal custody of the child but whose rights have not been terminated must consent to the adoption.

Can a nonresident finalize an adoption in this state?
Yes.

MINNESOTA

State Adoption Specialist
Robert DeNardo
Minnesota Department of Human
   Services
Human Services Building
444 Lafayette Road
St. Paul, MN 55155-3831
(612) 296-3740

Compact Administrator
Maria R. Gomez
Commissioner
Minnesota Department of Human
   Services
Human Services Building
444 Lafayette Road
St. Paul, MN 55155-3815

Deputy Compact Administrator
Luella J. Brelje
Minnesota Department
   of Human Services
Family and Children's Division
444 Lafayette Road
St. Paul, MN 55155-3832
(612) 296-2725

Direct all telephone calls and
   correspondence to:

Terre Wessels
Adoption and Guardianship
Minnesota Department of Human
   Services
Human Services Building
444 Lafayette Road
St. Paul, MN 55155-3831
(612) 296-3973
fax (612) 297-1949

Office hours:
Monday-Friday
8:00 A.M.-4:00 P.M.
Central Time Zone

**State Adoption Exchange
   and Photo Listing**

State Adoption Exchange
Ruth Weidell
Minnesota Department
   of Human Services
Human Services Building
444 Lafayette Road
St. Paul, MN 55155-3831
(612) 296-3740

Photo Listing
Minnesota Adoption
   Resource Network
P.O. Box 39722
Minneapolis, MN 55439
(612) 941-5146

Private Adoption Agencies

Bethany Christian Services
3025 Harbor Lane, Suite 223
Plymouth, MN 55447
(612) 553-0344

Caritas Family Services
305 7th Avenue, North, Suite 100
St. Cloud, MN 56303
(612) 252-4121

Catholic Charities of the
   Archdiocese of Minneapolis-St.
   Paul
1600 University Avenue,
   Suite 400
St. Paul, MN 55104
(612) 641-1180

Catholic Charities,
Diocese of Crookston
P.O. Box 610
Crookston, MN 56716
(218) 281-4224

Catholic Charities,
Diocese of Winona
903 W. Center Street, Suite 150
Rochester, MN 55902
(507) 287-2047

Catholic Charities
of the Diocese of Winona
11 Riverfront
Winona, MN 55987
(507) 454-2270

Children's Home Society
of Minnesota
2230 Como Avenue
St. Paul, MN 55108
(612) 646-6393

Christian Family Life Services,
Inc.
15 10th Street South
Fargo, ND 58102-3530
(701) 237-4473

Crossroads, Inc.
4620 West 77th Street, Suite 105
Minneapolis, MN 55435
(612) 831-5707

Downyside Adoption Agency
400 Sibley Street, Suite 560
St. Paul, MN 55101
(612) 228-0117

Family Alternatives, Inc.
416 East Hennepin Avenue
Minneapolis, MN 55414
(612) 379-5341

Forever Families International
Adoption Agency
2004 Hwy. 37
Eveleth, MN 55734
(218) 744-4734

Hope Adoption and Family
Services, Inc.
421 South Main Street
Stillwater, MN 55082
(612) 439-2446

International Adoption Services,
Inc.
4940 Viking Drive, Suite 288
Edina, MN 55435
(612) 893-1343

LDS Social Services
1813 North Mill Street, Suite F
Naperville, IL 60563
(708) 369-0486

Love Basket
3902 Minnesota
Duluth, MN 55802
(218) 720-3097

Lutheran Social Service
of Minnesota
2414 Park Avenue South
Minneapolis, MN 55404
(612) 871-0221

New Horizons Adoption Agency
Frost-Benico Building, Hwy. 254
P.O. Box 623
Frost, MN 56033
(507) 878-3200

New Life Family Services
1515 East 66th Street
Minneapolis, MN 55423-2674
(612) 866-7643

Reaching Arms International, Inc.
11409 Ridgemount Avenue West
Minnetonka, MN 55305
(612) 541-0370

Summit Adoption Home Studies,
Inc.
1389 Summit Avenue
St. Paul, MN 55105
(612) 645-6657

Adoptive Parent Support Groups and Postadoption Services

Adopción, Inc.
1901 Cape Cod Place
Minneapolis, MN 55305
(612) 545-7409

Adopt A Special Kid (AASK)
AASK Field Representative
for Minnesota
1025 North Reynolds Road
Toledo, OH 43615
(419) 534-3350

Adoption Action Network
Attn.: Sharon Struthers
or Jolene Garberich
(612) 254-3457 or 974-4052

Adoptive Families of America
Attn.: Susan Freivalds
3333 Hwy. 100 North
Minneapolis, MN 55422
(612) 535-4829

Adoptive Families Together
Attn.: Steve and Lois Merchant
Stumpf
Route 1, Box 248
Pierz, MN 56364
(612) 468-6032

Adoptive Families Together
Attn.: Jim and Maureen Dragseth
RR3, Box 189#
Sebeka, MN 56477
(218) 837-5145

Adoptive Family Counseling
Center
3338 18th Avenue, South
Minneapolis, MN 55407
(612) 722-5362

Adoptive Parent Support Group
Attn.: Vicky Lauer
856 Gull Rive Road N.W.
Brainerd, MN 56501
(218) 829-5379

Adoptive Parent Support Group
Attn.: Cathy Lattu
390 County Road 13 S
Moose Lake, MN 55767
(218) 485-8170

Adoptive Parent Support Group
Attn.: Donna Schiller
Box 367 Route 1
Richville, MN 56576
(218) 495-3239

Adoptive Parent Support Group
Attn.: Phyllis Collins
90 Riverside Drive S.E.
St. Cloud, MN 56304
(612) 252-1625

Adoptive Parent Support Group
Attn.: Barbara Steiner
HR 73-Box 337
Walker, MN 56484
(218) 547-3033

Children of Korean Heritage
Attn.: Jeff Mondloh
2230 Como Avenue
St. Paul, MN 55108
(612) 646-6393

Contact One-Plus
Attn.: Cheryl Schwichtenberg
1316 California Avenue
St. Paul, MN 55108
(612) 644-0728

Families Helping Families in
  Adoption
Attn.: Lynn Holter
6729 Jackson Street N.E.
Fridley, MN
(612) 574-0807

Families of Mixed Race Adoptions
Attn.: Roxanne Johnson
10 Woodview Drive
Mankato, MN 56001
(507) 345-1850

Families of Multi-Racial
  Adoptions
Attn.: Gary and Jean Sandstra
1125 Cross Street
North Mankato, MN 56033
(507) 345-4279

Families Supporting Adoption
Attn.: Joyce Anderson
11462 Crow Hassan Park Road
Rogers, MN 55374
(612) 498-7101

Families Under Severe Stress
Attn.: Maxine Walton
2230 Como Avenue
St. Paul, MN 55108
(612) 646-6393

Headwaters Adoption Support
  Group
Attn.: Karyl Hoeger
P.O. Box 460
Blackduck, MN 56630
(218) 835-4797

Heart and Seoul
Attn.: Roxanne West Johnson
10 Woodview Drive
Mankato, MN 56001
(507) 345-1850

Minnesota Adoption Resource
  Network and North American
  Council on Adoptable Children
  State Representative
P.O. Box 39722
Minneapolis, MN 55439
(612) 941-5146

Niños de Paraguay
Attn.: Jim and Jane Nichols
7801 Bush Lake Drive

Bloomington, MN 55438
(612) 829-0938

North American Council
  on Adoptable Children
970 Raymond Avenue, Suite 106
St. Paul, MN 55114-1149
(612) 644-3036

North Suburban Ours
  for a United Response
Attn.: Margaret Newmaster
2723 Crown Hill Court
White Bear Lake, MN 55110
(612) 429-0357

Northland Families
  Through Adoption
Attn.: Suzanne Kunze
2506 Branch Street
Duluth, MN 55812
(218) 724-1278

Northwest Minnesota Families
  Through Adoption
Attn.: Steve and Kathy Martin
Box 135
Crookston, MN 56716

Our Korean Kids
Attn.: Kelly DeRosier
1600 University Avenue,
  Suite 400
St. Paul, MN 55104
(612) 641-1180

Parents of (Asian) Indian
  Children
Attn.: Lynn Malfeld
1395 Simpson Street
St. Paul, MN 55108
(612) 645-9068

Parents of Latin American
  Children
Attn.: Bernice Tenquist
16665 Argon Street, N.W.
Anoka, MN 55304
(612) 427-6277

Partners for Adoption
Attn.: Theresa Salden
621 County Road 10 S.E.
Watertown, MN 55388
(612) 955-2046

Partners in Adoption
Attn.: Lola Jahnke
107 H Street
Marshall, MN 56258
(507) 532-6678

Peruvian Adoptive Families
Attn.: Tina Kush
2717 Cedar Lane
Burnsvile, MN 55337
(612) 890-8430

Resources for Adoptive Parents
Attn.: Peggy Meyer
P.O. Box 27373
Minneapolis, MN 55427
(612) 541-0088

Southwest Minnesota Adoptive
  Families
Attn.: Marilyn Bridgland
605 Kathyrn Avenue
Marshall, MN 56258
(507) 532-6474

Stars of David
Attn.: Amy Silberberg
15511 Afton Hills Drive South
St. Paul, MN 55001
(612) 436-2015

West Central Minnesota
  Adoptive Families
Attn.: Nancy Johnsrud
918 North 3rd Street
Montevideo, MN 56265
(612) 269-8620

**Adopted Person and Birth
  Relative Support Groups**

Adoptee Liberty Movement
  Association (ALMA)
P.O. Box 613
Excelsior, MN 55331
(612) 470-9544

Concerned United Birthparents
6429 Mendelssohn Lane
Edina, MN 55343-8424
(612) 938-5866

Independent Search Consultant
512 Wayside Avenue
Albert Lea, MN 56007
(507) 377-0517

Minnesota Department
  of Human Services
Adoption/Guardianship Section
444 Lafayette Road
St. Paul, MN 55155-3831
(612) 296-2795

Minnesota Reunion
Registry/Liberal Education
for Adoptive Families
23247 Lofton Court North
N. Scandia, MN 55073-9752
(612) 436-2215 or 433-5211

Support Group
Attn.: Belden Sadler
500 Fry Street, #10
Minneapolis, MN 55104

Adoption Attorneys

Jody O. DeSmidt
701 4th Avenue South, #650
Minneapolis, MN 55415-1606
(612) 340-1150

Steven L. Gawron
2850 Metro Drive, Suite 429
Bloomington, MN 55425
(612) 854-4483

Amy M. Silberberg
15511 Afton Hills Drive South
Afton, MN 55001
(612) 228-1455

Judith Vincent*
Mill Place, Suite 240
111 Third Ave South
Minneapolis, MN 55401
(612) 332-7772

* Ms. Vincent has conducted
about 500 independent
adoptions, 400 agency
adoptions, and 300
international adoptions.

Independent Adoption Resource
Center, Inc.
111 3rd Avenue S., No. 245
Minneapolis, MN 55401

Wright S. Walling
701 4th Avenue, Suite 650
Minneapolis, MN 55415
(612) 340-1150

MINNESOTA LAWS RELATED TO ADOPTION: QUESTIONS AND ANSWERS

Can an attorney serve as an intermediary?
No.

Is advertising permitted?
Yes.

Who must consent to the adoption?
1. The birth parents
2. If a birth parent is a minor, consent of the minor's parent or guardian is also required.

When can consent be taken from birth mother (father), and how long after the consent is signed can it be revoked?
Consent cannot be signed until seventy-two hours after birth. The consent can be revoked up to ten working days afterward. After that time frame, it is irrevocable. A consent must be signed before an agency or a judge. If a birth mother refuses counseling by an agency, Judith Vincent, an attorney in Minneapolis, states that the birth mother must sign the consent in front of a judge.

What are the birth father's rights?
The presumed birth father must have his rights terminated in court or through a consent or notice of the adoption hearing. If a nonpresumed birth father wants to retain his rights, he must file an affidavit within sixty days after the child is placed or ninety days after the child's birth, whichever is sooner.

The unwed birth father must be served a notice of the adoption placement and hearing, but this can be waived if the child was conceived as a result of rape or incest, or if locating him might cause physical or severe emotional harm to the birth mother or child.

What fees can adoptive parents pay?
Adoptive parents can pay for legal, medical, counseling, and reasonable living expenses.

Where does the adoption hearing take place?
The hearing takes place in the court of the county where the adoptive parents live.

How are familial and step-parent adoptions different from nonbiological adoptions?
Judith Vincent states that familial adoptions are not different from nonfamilial adoptions.
In step-parent adoptions the court can waive the home study requirement. Also, the consent requires just two witnesses and a notary public; no agency or judge is required to take
the consent. In a stepparent adoption, the residence requirement of living in Minnesota
for one year may also be waived.

Can a nonresident finalize an adoption in this state?
No. The adoptive parents must have lived in Minnesota for at least one year and with the
child for three months. This requirement can be waived by the court.

MISSISSIPPI

State Adoption Specialist
Patricia P. Jones
Mississippi Department
of Human Services
P.O. Box 352
Jackson, MS 39205
fax (601) 359-4981

Compact Administrator
(vacant)
Interim Executive Director
Mississippi Department
of Human Services
P.O. Box 352
Jackson, MS 39205
(601) 960-5242

Deputy Compact Administrator
Ann Pullum
Mississippi Department
of Human Services
P.O. Box 352
Jackson, MN 39205
(601) 334-6634
fax (601) 354-6660

Direct all telephone calls
and correspondence to:
Terry Varnado
P.O. Box 352
Jackson, MS 39205
        or
939 N. President Street
Jackson, MS 39202

(601) 354-6613

Office hours:
Monday-Friday
8:00 A.M.-5:00 P.M.
Central Time Zone

**State Adoption Exchange
and Photo Listing**

Mississippi Adoption Resource
Exchange
P.O. Box 352
Jackson, MS 39205
(601) 359-4407
(800) 821-9157 (MS residents)

Private Adoption Agencies

Adoption Ministries
of Misisippi, Inc.
P.O. Box 20346
Jackson, MS 39289
(601) 352-7888

AGAPE Child and Family
Services
P.O. Box 11411
Memphis, TN 38111
(901) 272-7339

Bethany Christian Services
2619 Southerland Drive
Woodland Hills Building
Jackson, MS 39216
(601) 366-4282

Catholic Charities
748 North President St.
P.O. Box 2248
Jackson, MS 39205
(601) 355-8634

Catholic Social
and Community Services
P.O. Box 1457
Biloxi, MS 39533
(601) 374-8316

Harden House Adoptions
P.O. Box 1573
Fulton, MS 28543
(601) 862-5315

Jewish Family Services
6560 Poplar Avenue
Memphis, TN 38138
(901) 767-8511

LDS Social Services
2000 Old Spanish Trail
Pratt Center, Suite 115
Slidell, LA 70458
(504) 649-2774

Lutheran Ministries of Georgia
756 W. Peachtree, N.W.
Atlanta, GA 30308
(404) 875-0201

Mississippi Band
of Choctaw Indians Agency
P.O. Box 6010
Philadelphia, MS 39350
(601) 656-5251, ext. 350

Mississippi Children's
Home Society
P.O. Box 1078
1801 North West Street
Jackson, MS 39205
(601) 352-7784

New Beginnings of Tupelo
P.O. Box 7055
Tupelo, MS 38802-7055
(601) 842-6752

Southern Adoption Agency
420 Crockett Avenue
Philadelphia, MS 39350
(601) 693-3933

Sunnybrook Children's Home
P.O. Box 4871
Jackson, MS 39296
(601) 856-6555

Adoptive Parent Support
  Groups and Postadoption
  Services

Adoption Foster Friends Support
  Group of Warren County, MS,
  and North American Council
  on Adoptable Children State
  Representative
Attn.: Deborah Sanders
209 Henry Road
Vicksburg, MS 39180
(601) 636-3962

Ministers For Adoption
Attn.: Linda West
P.O. Box 1078
Jackson, MS 39205
(601) 352-7784

Southwest Mississippi
  Adoption Support Group
Attn.: Sylvia Sessions
P.O. Box 470
McComb, MS 39648
(601) 684-0195

**Adopted Person and Birth
  Relative Support Groups**

Adoption Information Network
Attn.: Lee Sande
P.O. Box 4154
Meridian, MS 39304
(601) 482-7556

Mississippi State Bar
P.O. Box 2168
Jackson, MS 39225-2168
(601) 948-4471

Adoption Attorneys

Susan M. Brewer
P.O. Box 768
Southaven, MS 38671-0768
(601) 342-6000

Lisa Milner
P.O. Box 25
Jackson, MS 39205
(601) 948-8800

MISSISSIPPI LAWS RELATED TO ADOPTION: QUESTIONS AND ANSWERS

Can an attorney serve as an intermediary?
Yes.

Is advertising permitted?
Yes.

Who must consent to the adoption?
Both birth parents must consent if married to each other. Consent is not necessary if it can be shown that the parent has abandoned or deserted the child to be adopted. Also, no consent is needed if it can be established that the parent is mentally, morally, or otherwise unfit to raise the child.

When can consent be taken from birth mother (father), and how long after the consent is signed can it be revoked?
Consent cannot be given until child is three days old and is irrevocable.

What are the birth father's rights?
If the birth father is not married to the birth mother, he is not considered a parent.

What fees can adoptive parents pay?
Reasonable fees approved by the court may be charged for the preadoption investigation. Also, medical, legal, and in some instances, living expenses can be paid.

Where does the adoption hearing take place?
The hearing takes place in the court of the county where the adoptive parents live or where the child lives.

How are familial and step-parent adoptions different from nonbiological adoptions?
The residency requirement is waived.

Can a nonresident finalize an adoption in this state?
No. Adoptive parents must have resided in the state for ninety days before filing the adoption petition.

MISSOURI

State Adoption Specialist
(Vacant)
Missouri Department of Social
  Services
P.O. Box 88
Jefferson City, MO 65103-0088
(314) 751-2502

Compact Administrator
Carmen Schulze, Director
Missouri Division of Family
  Services
P.O. Box 88
Jefferson City, MO 65103-0088
(573) 751-4247

Deputy Compact Administrator
Charles Edwards
ICPC
Missouri Division of Family
  Services
P.O. Box 88
Jefferson City, MO 65103-0088
(573) 751-2981

Caseload Distribution
Relative, and private adoptions,
  A-H—Mary Kay Kliethermes
Relative and private adoptions, I-
  M, as well as all public and
  international adoptions—
  Charles Edwards
Relative and private adoptions,
  N-Z—Jim Cade

Direct all telephone calls
  and correspondence to:

Caseload Person
ICPC Unit
P.O. Box 88
Jefferson City, MO 65103-0088

Office hours:
Monday-Friday
8:00 A.M.-5:00 P.M.
Central Time Zone

**State Adoption Exchange
  and Photo Listing**

Missouri Adoption Exchange
Missouri Division of Family
  Services
P.O. Box 88
Jefferson City, MO 65103
(314) 751-2502
(800) 554-2222 in Missouri only

Private Adoption Agencies

A.C.T. Adoption Services
  (Adoption, Counseling
  and Training)
10102 N.W. 72nd Terrace
Weatherby Lake, MO 64152
(913) 682-7914

Adam's Child Placement &
  Counseling, Inc.
600 Broadway, Suite 430
Kansas City, MO 64105
(816) 471-2255

Adoption Advocate
3100 Broadway, Suite 218
Kansas City, MO 64111
(816) 753-1711

Adoption and Counseling
  Services
10045 Hemlock
Overland Park, KS 66212
(913) 383-8448

Adoption and Fertility Resources
144 Westwoods Drive
Liberty, MO 64068
(816) 781-8550

Adoption Option
200 S.E. Douglas
Lee's Summit, MO 64063
(816) 224-1525

Adoption Resource Center
10436 Gregory Court
St. Louis, MO 63128-1637
(314) 772-8041

Associates in Adoption
  Counseling
6915 N.W. 77th Terrace
Kansas City, MO 64152
(816) 452-0139

Bethany Christian Services
7700 Clayton Road, Suite 205
St. Louis, MO 63117-1346
(314) 644-3535

Catholic Charities of Kansas City
1112 Broadway
Kansas City, MO 64111
(816) 221-4377

Catholic Services for Children
  and Youth
4140 Lindell Boulevard
St. Louis, MO 63108
(314) 371-4980

Central Baptist Family Services
7750 Clayton Road, Suite 305
Richmond Heights, MO 63117
(314) 644-4548

Children's Foundation Adoption
  and Counseling, Inc.
930 Carondelet Drive, Suite 300
Kansas City, MO 64114
(913) 837-4303

Children's Home Society
  of Missouri
9445 Litzsinger Road
Brentwood, MO 63144
(314) 968-2350

Children's Hope International
dba China's Children
10245 Chaucer, Suite 4
St. Louis, MO 63114
(314) 890-0086

Christian Family Life Center
7700 Clayton Road, Suite 102
St. Louis, MO 63117
(314) 644-3700

Christian Family Services
  of the Midwest, Inc.
P.O. Box 9373
6000 Blue Ridge Boulevard
Raytown, MO 64133
(913) 383-3337

Christian Family Services, Inc.
8039 Watson Road, Suite 120
Webster Groves, MO 63119
(314) 968-2216

Family Network, Inc.
9378 Olive Street Road, Suite 320
St. Louis, MO 63122
(314) 567-0707

Family Therapy Center
  of the Ozarks
1345 E. Sunshine, Suite 108
Springfield, MO 65804
(417) 882-7700

Gentle Shepherd
  Child Placement Agency
6310 Lamar Avenue, Suite 140
Overland Park, KS 66202
(913) 432-1353

Heart of America Family Services
3217 Broadway
Kansas City, MO 64111
(816) 753-5280

Highlands Child Placement
  Services
P.O. Box 300198
Kansas City, MO 64130-0198
(816) 924-6565

James A. Roberts Agency
8301 State Line Road, Suite 216
Kansas City, MO 64114
(816) 523-4440

Jewish Family
  and Children's Services
9385 Olive Boulevard
Olivette, MO 63044
(314) 993-1000

Kansas Children's Service League
3200 Wayne, W-104
Kansas City, MO 64109
(913) 621-2016

LDS Social Services
517 West Walnut
Independence, MO 64050
(816) 461-5512

Love Basket, Inc.
4472 Goldman Road
Hillsboro, MO 63050
(314) 789-4100

Lutheran Family
  and Children's Services
4625 Lindell Boulevard, Suite 501
St. Louis, MO 63108
(314) 361-2121

Missouri Baptist Children's Home
11300 Street Charles Rock Road
Bridgeton, MO 63044
(314) 739-6811

Provident Counseling
2650 Olive Street
St. Louis, MO 63103
(314) 371-6500

Small World Adoption
  Foundation, Inc.
2203 Devonbrook
Chesterfield, MO 63005
(314) 536-1611

Universal Adoption Services
124 East High Street
Jefferson City, MO 64101
(314) 634-3733

Worldwide Love for Children
1601 West Sunshine, Suite L
Springfield, MO 65807
(417) 869-3151

**Adoptive Parent Support
Groups and Postadoption
Services**

Adoptees and Their Families
100 North Euclid, Suite 206
St. Louis, MO 63108

Adoption Today
Attn.: Mary Kay Helldoerfer
5350 Casa Royale Drive
St. Louis, MO 63129-3007
(314) 894-4586

Adoptive Family Support Group
Attn.: John and Molly Strickland
Rt. 1, Box 84
Millersville, MO 63701
(314) 266-3609

Adoptive Parents
  of Southwest Missouri
Attn.: Elizabeth Raidel
4925 Royal Drive
Springfield, MO 65804
(417) 887-5788

AMCH
Attn.: Angela Starky
2612 Annie Malone
St. Louis, MO 63113
(314) 531-1907

Families Through Adoption
Attn.: Al and Chris Thimbur
1350 Summit Drive
Fenton, MO 63026
(314) 343-7658

Friends of Adoption
Attn.: Janet Huber
5813 N. Kensington Avenue
Kansas City, MO 64119
(816) 459-7434

International Families
Attn.: Bob Henkel
P.O. Box 1352
St. Charles, MO 63302
(314) 423-6788

Missouri Foster Care
  & Adoption Association
Attn.: JoAnna O'Neill
303 Country Road 433
Rocheport, MO 65279
(314) 698-2052

Open Door Society of Missouri
  and North American Council
  on Adoptable Children
  State Representative
Attn.: Lauren Johnson
9417 Pine
St. Louis, MO 63144
(314) 968-5239

Parents Association of the
  Children's Home Society
  of Missouri
3511 Brookwood Circle
St. Charles, MO 63301
(314) 968-2350

Respond Black Adoption
  and Foster Care Citizen
  Support Group
4411 N. Newstead Avenue
St. Louis, MO 63115
(314) 727-3687

Single Adoptive Parents
  Support Group
Attn.: Buffy Atkins
1800 Fairview Road
Columbia, MO 65202
(314) 445-1262

World Children's Fund
1015 Barberry Lane
Kirkwood, MO 63122
(314) 822-3361

**Adopted Person and Birth
Relative Support Groups**

Adoptee Liberty Movement
  Association (ALMA)
P.O. Box 92
Montgomery City, MO 63361
(314) 564-2004

Adoption Connection
842 Country Stone Drive
St. Louis, MO 63021

Birthright
6309 Walnut
Kansas City, MO 64801

Connecting Adoptees Through
  Research and Education
P.O. Box 30252, Plaza Station
Kansas City, MO 64112
(816) 333-5656

Donors' Offspring
P.O. Box 37
Sarcoxie, MO 64862
(417) 548-3679

Kansas City Adult Adoptees
P.O. Box 11828
Kansas City, MO 64138
(816) 229-4075

National Adoption Registry, Inc.
6800 Elmwood Avenue
Kansas City, MO 64132-9963
(816) 361-1627
  or (800) 875-4347

Post Adoption Support Team
Box 1534
Ballwin, MO 63022
(314) 281-8921

Search for Life
Rt. 2, Box 93
Birchtree, MO 65438

Searcher's Forum
830 Marshall Avenue
Webster Grove, MO 63119

The Missouri Bar
P.O. Box 119
Jefferson City, MO 65102
(314) 635-4128

Adoption Attorneys

Mary Beck
206 Hulston Hall
Columbia, MO 65211
(314) 882-7872

Catherine Keefe
120 South Central, Suite 1505
Clayton, MO 63105
(314) 727-7050

Sanford P. Krigel
900 Harzfeld Building
Kansas City, MO 64105
(816) 474-7800

Allan F. Stewart
120 South Central, Suite 1505
Clayton, MO 63105
(314) 727-7050

Elizabeth Karsian Wilson
401 Locust Street, #406
P.O. Box 977
Columbia, MO 65205-0977
(314) 443-3134

MISSOURI LAWS RELATED TO ADOPTION: QUESTIONS AND ANSWERS

Can an attorney serve as an intermediary?
Yes.

Is advertising permitted?
Yes.

Who must consent to the adoption?
The birth parents and the court must consent.

When can consent be taken from birth mother (father), and how long after the consent is signed can it be revoked?
Written consent can be given either before or after birth, but is only valid when the consent is filed with the court. The consent should be filed immediately after it is signed. Judges will consider a birth parent who wants to revoke consent up to the first court hearing, which usually takes place about one to two weeks after the consent is filed.

According to Katherine Keefe, an attorney in Clayton, some judges require the child to be placed in foster care before being placed with the adoptive couple and before the parental rights are terminated. Because many birth mothers and adoptive parents are opposed to this, a court must be selected that will permit direct placement of the child into the couple's home. Keefe further states that using an experienced attorney to resolve this situation is critical.

What are the birth father's rights?
If the birth father's identity is unknown or cannot be determined, then his consent is not needed. Either birth mother or birth father can waive in writing the need to provide consent. Also, no consent is required if either birth parent willfully abandoned the child or

neglected to provide the child with care and protection for a period of sixty days (if the child is under one year of age) or for a period of six months (if the child is over one year of age).

What fees can adoptive parents pay?
Legal, medical, and reasonable living expenses can be paid. All statements of payment must be submitted to the court. The court may refuse to allow the adoption if payments were unreasonable or if adoptive parent did not report all expenses paid.

Where does the adoption hearing take place?
It can take place in the juvenile court in the county where the adoptive parents live or the child lives.

How are familial and step-parent adoptions different from nonbiological adoptions?
The court may waive the home study requirement in a step-parent adoption.

Can a nonresident finalize an adoption in this state?
Yes. According to Katherine Keefe, if you are not from Missouri but adopt a child there, a Missouri adoption agency must review your home study (conducted in your state) and the court must verify the home study. The cost for a Missouri agency to review your home study is usually about $2,000.

MONTANA

State Adoption Specialist
Betsy Stimatz
Montana Department
   of Family Services
P.O. Box 8005
Helena, MT 59604
(406) 444-1675

Compact Administrator
Kandice Morse
Montana Department
   of Family Services
P.O. Box 8005
Helena, MT 59604
(406) 444-5900

Deputy Compact Administrator
Betsey Stimatz
Montana Department
   of Family Services
P.O. Box 8005
Helena, MT 59604
(406) 444-1675
fax (406) 444-5956

Direct all telephone calls and
   correspondence to the Deputy
   Compact Administrator.

Office hours:
Monday-Friday
8:00 A.M.-12:00 P.M
   and 1:00 P.M-5:00 P.M.
Mountain Time Zone

Private Adoption Agencies

Catholic Social Services
25 South Ewing, P.O. Box 907
Helena, MT 59601
(406) 442-4130

LDS Social Services
2001 11th Avenue
Helena, MT 59601
(406) 443-1660

Lutheran Social Services
P.O. Box 1345
Great Falls, MT 59403
(406) 761-4341

**Adoptive Parent Support
   Groups and Postadoption
   Services**

Adopt a Special Kid (AASK)
   of Montana
Attn.: Penny Hauer
628 Hwy. 93 South
Conner, MT 59827
(406) 821-3654

Adoptive Families of Montana
Attn.: Becky MacDonald
1499 Cobb Hill Road
Bozeman, MT 59715
(406) 586-9788

Family Support in Adoption
   Association
   and North American Council
   on Adoptable Children State
   Representative
Attn.: April Horvath
7049 Fox Lane
Darby, MT 59829
(406) 349-2872

G.I.F.T.
6111 Birdseye
Helena, MT 59601
(406) 443-5099

Montana Adoption Resource
   Center
P.O. Box 634
Helena, MT 59624
(406) 449-3266

Montana State Foster
  and Adoptive Parents
  Association
Attn.: Chris Yde
7035 Jockey Drive
Helena, MT 59601

Northwest Montana
  Adoptive Parent Group
Attn.: Sandy Scull
629 5th Avenue East
Kalispell, MT 59102
(406) 257-8221

Yellowstone International
  Adoptive Families
Attn.: Vern Barkell
3433 Barley Circle
Billings, MT 59102
(406) 652-4654

**Adopted Person and Birth
  Relative Support Groups**

Montana Adoption
  Resource Center
P.O. Box 634
Helena, MT 59624
(406) 449-3266

State Bar of Montana
P.O. Box 577
Helena, MT 59624
(406) 442-7660

Adoption Attorneys

Cameron Ferguson
P.O. Box 1629
Great Falls, MT 59403
(406) 727-4020

MONTANA LAWS RELATED TO ADOPTION: QUESTIONS AND ANSWERS

Can an attorney serve as an intermediary?
No.

Is advertising permitted?
No. Nor is any public solicitation permitted, such as posting fliers or sending letters,
except to people that you know.

Who must consent to the adoption?
1. Both birth parents
2. The executive head of an agency (if an agency adoption)

When can consent be taken from birth mother (father), and how long after the consent is signed can it be revoked?
Consent cannot be given until seventy-two hours after the child's birth and is irrevocable.
If the birth mother changes her mind, the court will consider the best interests of the child
up until the time the adoption is finalized.

What are the birth father's rights?
If he is named, his consent is required. If he contests the adoption, he must present his
case to the court. A birth fathers rights may be terminated without his consent if he is
served with a notice thirty days before the child's expected date of delivery and fails to file
a notice of intent to claim paternity before the child's birth. If the birth father's whereabouts are not known, then his rights can be terminated if he has not provided support for
the mother or shown any interest in the child or otherwise provided for the child's care
during a time period of ninety days before the adoption hearing. If the birth father's identity is unknown, then his rights can be terminated if he has not supported the birth mother
during her pregnancy or provided support for the child after the birth.

What fees can adoptive parents pay?
Legal, medical, and other reasonable expenses can be paid. In an independent adoption,
all fees and expenses must be submitted in an itemized statement to the court.

Where does the adoption hearing take place?
The adoption hearing takes place in the District Court in the county where the adoptive
  parents reside.

How are familial and step-parent adoptions different from nonbiological adoptions?
The home study report may be waived by the court.

Can a nonresident finalize an adoption in this state?
No. You must be residing in the state at time of petition.

NEBRASKA

State Adoption Specialist
Mary Dyer
Division of Human Services
Nebraska Department
  of Social Services
P.O. Box 95026
Lincoln, NE 68509
(402) 471-9331

Compact Administrator
Chris Hanus-Schulenberg,
  Administrator
Division of Human Services
Nebraska Department
  of Social Services
301 Centennial Mall South
Lincoln, NE 68509
(402) 471-9308

Deputy Compact Administrator
Suzanne Schied
Interstate Placement Specialist
Nebraska Department
  of Social Services
P.O. Box 95026
Lincoln, NE 68509
(402) 471-9245
fax (402) 471-9455

Send all correspondence
  in triplicate to the Deputy
  Compact Administrator.

Office hours:
Monday-Friday
8:00 A.M.-5:00 P.M.
Central Time Zone

State Adoption Exchange
  and Photo Listing

Nebraska Adoption
  Resource Exchange
Division of Human Services
Department of Social Services
P.O. Box 95026
Lincoln, NE 68509
(402) 471-9331

Private Adoption Agencies

Adoption Links Worldwide
3528 Dodge Street, #28
Omaha, NE 68131
(402) 342-1234

Black Homes for Black Children
115 South 46th Street
Omaha, NE 68132
(402) 595-2912

Catholic Social Service Bureau
237 South 70th Street, Suite 220
Lincoln, NE 68510
(402) 489-1834

Child Saving Institute
115 South 46th Street
Omaha, NE 68132
(402) 553-6000

Holt International
  Children's Services
2200 Abbott Drive, Suite 203
Carter Lake, IA 51510
(712) 347-5911

Jewish Family Service
333 South 132nd Street
Omaha, NE 68154
(402) 330-2024

LDS Social Services
517 West Walnut
Independence, MO 64050
(816) 461-5512

Lutheran Family Services
  of Nebraska, Inc.
120 South 24th Street
Omaha, NE 68102
(402) 342-7007

Nebraska Children's
  Home Society
3549 Fontenelle Boulevard
Omaha, NE 68104
(402) 451-0787

Nebraska Christian Services, Inc.
11600 West Center Road
Omaha, NE 68144
(402) 334-3278

United Catholic Social Services
3300 North 60th Street
Omaha, NE 68104
(402) 554-0520

**Adoptive Parent Support
  Groups and Postadoption
  Services**

Families Through Adoption
Attn.: Lori Erickson
1619 Coventry Lane
Grand Island, NE 68801-7025
(308) 381-8743

Forever Families
Attn.: Carol Stolp
1115 North 130th Street
Omaha, NE 68154

Intercultural Families
Attn.: Nan Hutton
2312 South 88th
Omaha, NE 68124
(402) 390-0278

Kearney Area Adoption
  Association
Attn.: Marian Davis
14960 W. Cedarview Road
Wood River, NE 68883-9320
(308) 583-2402

Open Hearts Adoption
  Support Group
Attn.: Kay Lytle
4023 S. 81st Street
Lincoln, NE 68506
(402) 483-7634

Parents of Adopted Children
Attn.: Jari Houston
16562 Ontario Circle
Omaha, NE 68135
(402) 334-0386

United Thru Private Adoption
Attn.: Terrie Roberts Rauscher
1511 South 25th Street
Lincoln, NE 68502
(402) 477-3868

Voices for Children in Nebraska
and North American Council
on Adoptable Children State
Representative
Attn.: Kathy Moore
7521 Main Street
Omaha, NE 68127
(402) 597-3100

**Adopted Person and Birth
Relative Support Groups**

Adoptee Liberty Movement
Association (ALMA)
P.O. Box 5782
Lincoln, NE 68505

Adoption Identity Desire
1808 West F
North Platt, NE 69101

Adoption Triad Midwest
P.O. Box 37273
Omaha, NE 68137
(402) 895-3706 or 493-8047

Concerned United Birthparents
4075 W. Airport Road
Grand Island, NE 68803
(308) 384-3571

Nebraska State Bar Association
P.O. Box 81809
Lincoln, NE 68501-1809
(402) 475-7091

Adoption Attorneys

Lawrence Batt
209 S. 19th Street, #400
Continental Building
Omaha, NE 68102-1757
(402) 346-2000

Susan K. Sapp
Cline, Williams, Wright,
Johnson & Oldfather
1900 Firtier Bank Building
Lincoln, NE 68508
(402) 474-6900
fax (402) 474-5393

Michael Washburn
10330 Regency Parkway Drive
Omaha, NE 68114
(402) 397-2200

NEBRASKA LAWS RELATED TO ADOPTION: QUESTIONS AND ANSWERS

Can an attorney serve as an intermediary?
This is open to interpretation; the Attorney General opinion states that an attorney can legally assist birth parents and adoptive parents in meeting each other. Also, although it is unlawful for anyone to place a child for adoption without a license, this does not prevent an attorney from assisting a birth parent in selecting an adoptive couple.

Is advertising permitted?
Yes.

Who must consent to the adoption?
1. Both birth parents must consent if married to each other.
2. The birth mother must consent if the child was born out of wedlock.

When can consent be taken from birth mother (father), and how long after the consent is signed can it be revoked?
Consent in a private placement must be done in front of the birth mother's attorney and at least one other witness. The consent is irrevocable when signed; however, until the final adoption, the birth mother can revoke her consent, which then forces a judge to consider whether remaining with the adoptive couple or being returned to the birth mother is in the best interests of the child. Relinquishment to an agency is irrevocable after the agency accepts full responsibility for the child.

What are the birth father's rights?
The unmarried father's rights are not recognized unless he files a notice to claim paternity within five days after the baby's birth. If he wants custody of the child, the court will determine if he can properly care for the child and if it would be in the child's best interest. If it can be shown that the birth father has abandoned the child for at least six months, then his rights can also be terminated.

What fees can adoptive parents pay?

There are no special provisions in the law, but adoptive parents can pay for living, medical, counseling, and one-time legal expenses.

Where does the adoption hearing take place?

The hearing takes place in the court of the county where the adoptive parents live.

How are familial and step-parent adoptions different from nonbiological adoptions?

In stepparent adoptions the home study is sometimes waived.

Can a nonresident finalize an adoption in this state?

No.

NEVADA

State Adoption Specialist
Wanda Scott
Division of Child and Family
  Services
6171 West Charleston Boulevard,
  Building 15
Las Vegas, NV 87158
(702) 486-7650

Compact Administrator
John H. Sarb
Division of Child and Family
  Services
Department of Human Resources
711 E. Fifth Street
Capitol Complex
Carson City, NV 89710
(702) 687-4783

Deputy Compact Administrator
Rota Rosachi
Division of Child
  and Family Services
Department of Human Resources
711 E. Fifth Street
Capitol Complex
Carson City, NV 89710
(702) 687-4979

Address for Adoption
  correspondence:
Wanda Scott, Adoption Specialist
Division of Child
  and Family Services
610 Belrose Street
Las Vegas, NV 89158
fax (702) 687-4277

Office hours:
Monday-Friday
8:00 A.M.-5:00 P.M.
Pacific Time Zone

**State Adoption Exchange and
  Photo Listing**

Nevada Adoption Exchange
Division of Child and Family
  Services
610 Belrose Street
Las Vegas, NV 87158
(702) 486-7800

Private Adoption Agencies

Catholic Community Services
808 South Main
Las Vegas, NV 89101
(702) 385-2662

Catholic Community Services
P.O. Box 5415
Reno, NV 89513
(702) 322-7073

Jewish Family Services Agency
3909 S. Maryland Pkwy.,
  Suite 205
Las Vegas, NV 89119
(702) 732-0304

LDS Social Services
513 South Ninth Street
Las Vegas, NV 89015
(702) 385-1072

New Hope Child and Family
1601 E. Flamingo Road, Suite 18
Las Vegas, NV 89119
(702) 734-9665

New Hope Child and Family
955 S. Virginia Street
Reno, NV 89502
(702) 861-5128

**Adoptive Parent Support
  Groups and Postadoption
  Services**

Families for Adoption
1858 Citation
Las Vegas, NV 89118

Southern Nevada Adoption
  Association
Attn.: Margaret Dunn
2300 Theresa Avenue
Las Vegas, NV 89101
(702) 649-8464

Special Needs Adoptive Parents
  of Northern Nevada
Attn.: Roberta Simon
3 Audrey Drive
Carson City, NV 89706
(702) 246-5373

**Adopted Person and Birth
  Relative Support Groups**

Adoptee Liberty Movement
  Association (ALMA)
P.O. Box 34211
Las Vegas, NV 89133

Adoptee Liberty Movement
  Association (ALMA)
P.O. Box 40644
Reno, NV 89504

International Soundex Reunion
  Registry
P.O. Box 2312
Carson City, NV 89702
(702) 882-7755

Division of Child and Family
    Services Adoption
    Registry (Search)
711 East Fifth Street,
    Capitol Complex
Carson City, NV 89710-1002
(702) 687-5982

T.A.S.S.
Attn.: Sharon L. Borzelleri
1810 N. Decatur Boulevard,
    #204
Las Vegas, NV 89108
(702) 631-7101

State Bar of Nevada
201 Las Vegas Boulevard,
    Suite 200
Las Vegas, NV 89101
(702) 382-2200

Adoption Attorneys

Israel L. Kunin
612 South 10th Street
Las Vegas, NV 89101
(702) 384-8489

Rhonda Mushkin
930 South Third Street, Suite 300
Las Vegas, NV 89101
(702) 386-3999
fax (702) 388-0617

NEVADA LAWS RELATED TO ADOPTION: QUESTIONS AND ANSWERS

If you live in Nevada but adopt in another state, or if you live in another state and adopt a child from Nevada, you must pay the ICPC fee of $1,000.

Can an attorney serve as an intermediary?
Yes, but no fee can be charged for the service.

Is advertising permitted?
Yes.

Who must consent to the adoption?
1. Both birth parents
2. An agency, if involved

When can consent be taken from birth mother (father), and how long after the consent is signed can it be revoked?
The birth father can sign a consent before the child's birth if he is not married to the birth mother. The birth mother's consent cannot be given until seventy-two hours after birth. Consent cannot be revoked. Rhonda Mushkin, an attorney in Las Vegas, states that consents must be taken in front of a licensed social worker, preferably a Department of Child and Family Services' caseworker.

What are the birth father's rights?
His consent is required. If he wants to parent the child and comes forward in a timely fashion, he has the right to parent unless it can be shown that it would not be in the child's best interests.

What fees can adoptive parents pay?
Reasonable living expenses can be paid, and an affidavit of all medical fees and other expenses paid must be submitted to the court.

Unlike other states, Nevada has a law that makes it illegal for the birth parent to receive money for medical expenses or other necessary expenses from an adoptive parent if she has no true intention of placing the child for adoption. Certainly every birth mother has the right to change her mind; she just cannot use adoption plans as a means of having her bills paid for by an adoptive couple.

Where does the adoption hearing take place?
The hearing takes place in the district court where the adoptive parents live or where the child lives.

How are familial and step-parent adoptions different from nonbiological adoptions?
The court may waive the home study requirement.

Can a nonresident finalize an adoption in this state?
No. You must have resided in Nevada for six months before the adoption.

NEW HAMPSHIRE

State Adoption Specialist
Catherine Atkins
New Hampshire Department
  of Health and Human Services
6 Hazen Drive
Concord, NH 03301
(603) 271-4707

Compact Administrator
Lorrie Lutz
New Hampshire Department
  of Health and Human Services
Division for Children
  and Youth Services
6 Hazen Drive
Concord, NH 03301-6522
(603) 271-4451

Deputy Compact Administrator
New Hampshire Department
  of Health and Human Services
Division for Children and
Youth Services
6 Hazen Drive
Concord, NH 03301
(603) 271-4708

Direct all elephone calls and
  correspondence to the Deputy
  Compact Administrator.

Office hours:
Monday-Friday
8:00 A.M.-4:00 P.M.
Eastern Time Zone

**State Adoption Exchange and
  Photo Listing**

New Hampshire Division for
  Children, Youth and Families
6 Hazen Drive
Concord, NH 03301
(603) 271-4721

Private Adoption Agencies

Adoptive Families for Children
26 Fairview Street
Keene, NH 03431
(603) 357-4456

Bethany Christian Services
1538 Turnpike, Route 114
North Andover, MA 01845
(508) 794-9800
(800) BETHANY

Casey Family Services
6 Chennel Drive, Suite 100
Concord, NH 03301
(603) 224-8909

Child and Family Services
  of New Hampshire
99 Hanover Street
P.O. Box 448
Manchester, NH 03105
(603) 668-1920
(800) 642-6486

Creative Advocates
  for Children and Families
P.O. Box 1703
Manchester, NH 03105
(603) 623-5006

LDS Social Services
  New Hampshire Agency
131 Route 101A
Amherst Plaza, Suite 204
Amherst, NH 03031
(603) 889-0148

Lutheran Child and Family
  Services of New Hampshire
85 Manchester Street
Concord, NH 03301
(603) 224-8111

New Hampshire Adoption Bureau
71 West Merrimack Street
Manchester, NH 03103
(800) 338-2224

New Hampshire Catholic
  Charities, Inc.
215 Myrtle Street
P.O. Box 686
Manchester, NH 03105
(603) 669-3030
(800) 562-5249

New Hope Christian Services
210 Silk Farm Road
Concord, NH 03301
(603) 225-7400

Vermont Children's
  Aid Society, Inc.
79 Weaver Street
Winooski, VT 05404
(802) 655-0006

Wide Horizons for Children
282 Moody Street
Waltham, MA 02154
(617) 894-5330

**Adoptive Parent Support
  Groups and Postadoption
  Services**

Manchester Concern
  for Adoption
Attn.: Rose Devoe
11 Davis Road
Merrimack, NH 03054
(603) 429-2751

New Hampshire Division for
  Children, Youth and Families
Attn.: Gail Snow
40 Terrill Park
Concord, NH 03301
(603) 271-6202

Open Door Society
of New Hampshire, Inc.
and North American Council
on Adoptable Children State
Representative
Attn.: Betty Todd
40 Gerrish Drive
Nottingham, NH 03290
(603) 679-8144

Ours for a United Response
of New England
Attn.: Karen Needham
347 Candia Road
Chester, NH 03036
(617) 967-4648

**Adopted Person and Birth
Relative Support Groups**

Adoption Bonding Circle
RR2, Box 125
Claremont, NH 03743
(603) 542-5917

Circle of Hope
P.O. Box 127
Somersworth, NH 03878
(603) 692-5917

Living in Search of Answers
Box 215
Gilsum, NH 03448
(603) 357-3762

**New Hampshire Bar
Association**
112 Pleasant Street
Concord, NH 03301
(603) 224-6942

Adoption Attorneys

Joseph Dubiansky
740 Chestnut Street
Manchester, NH 03104
(603) 669-7880

Marlene Lein
694 Pine Street
Manchester, NH 03104
(603) 666-4140

Jeffrey M. Kaye
14 Beacon Street, #616
Boston, MA 02108
(508) 682-4413

Ann McLane Kuster
Two Capital Plaza
P.O. Box 854
Concord, NH 03302-1500
(603) 226-2600

Barry Martin Scotch
Scotch and Zalinsky
Elm Street
Manchester, NH 03104
(603) 668-8100

NEW HAMPSHIRE LAWS RELATED TO ADOPTION: QUESTIONS AND ANSWERS

Can an attorney serve as an intermediary?
Yes.

Is advertising permitted?
Yes.

Who must consent to the adoption?
1. Both birth parents must consent if married to each other.
2. The involved agency must consent.

When can consent be taken from birth mother (father), and how long after the consent is signed can it be revoked?
Consent cannot be taken until seventy-two hours after the child's birth. Consent can be withdrawn until the final decree if the court finds that it is in the best interests of the child not to remain with the adoptive couple but to be returned to the birth parent.

What are the birth father's rights?
A birth father has the right to a hearing to prove paternity if he is named by the birth mother, has filed a notice with the Office of Child Support and Enforcement that he is the father, or if he is living with the birth mother or child and providing support. He must request such a hearing within thirty days after receiving notice of the adoption proceeding.

If the birth father is not married to the birth mother and has not met the above paternity requirements, then his consent is not required.

What fees can adoptive parents pay?

The adoptive parents must file a statement with the court listing all legal fees and medical expenses paid, as well as living expenses paid for the birth parents.

Where does the adoption hearing take place?

The hearing takes place in the Probate Court where the adoptive parents or adoptee lives.

How are familial and step-parent adoptions different from nonbiological adoptions?

The court may waive the home study requirement.

Can a nonresident finalize an adoption in this state?

No. There is a six-month residency requirement for the adoptive parent or the child, unless the child is in the legal care of a licensed adoption agency in New Hampshire. If that is the case, then the adoption can be finalized in the county in which the agency maintains its main office.

NEW JERSEY

State Adoption Specialist
Joanne Fillimon
New Jersey Division
of Youth and Family Services
50 East State Street, 5th Floor,
C.N. 717
Trenton, NJ 08625
(609) 292-9139

Deputy Compact Administrator
Betsey Rigel
Interstate Services Unit
New Jersey Division of Youth
and Family Services
Department of Human Services,
DYFS, CN-717
Trenton, NJ 08625
(609) 292-0010
fax (609) 633-6931

Call the Deputy Compact
Administrator's office to
determine to whom to address
correspondence and direct
telephone calls.

Address correspondence to:
NJ D.Y.F.S.
Interstate Services Unit
Capital Center, 7th Floor, F1 N.E.
50 East State Street
Trenton, NJ 08625
(overnight delivery services)
or
NJ D.Y.F.S.
Interstate Services Unit, CN 717
Trenton, NJ 08625
(U.S. Postal Service)

Office hours:
Monday-Friday
9:00 A.M.-5:00 P.M.
Eastern Time Zone

**State Adoption Exchange
and Photo Listing**

Adoption Exchange
Division of Youth and Family
Services
Operations Support Unit
50 East State Street, C.N. 717
Trenton, NJ 08625
(609) 984-5453

Private Adoption Agencies

Adoptions from the Heart
18-20 Washington Avenue
Haddonfield, NJ 08033
(609) 795-5400

AMOR Adoptions
12 Grenoble Court
Matawan, NJ 07747
(908) 583-0174

Bethany Christian Services
1120 Goffle Road
Hawthorne, NJ 07506
(201) 427-2566

Better Living Services, Inc.
735 East Broad Street
P.O. Box 2969
Westfield, NJ 07091-2969
(908) 654-0277

Black Adoption Consortium
5090 Central Hwy., Suite 6
Pennsauken, NJ 08109
(800) 552-0222 or (609) 486-
0100

Catholic Charities,
Diocese of Metuchen
P.O. Box 358
Millington, NJ 07946
(908) 604-6992

Catholic Charities,
Diocese of Trenton
115 West Pearl Street
Burlington, NJ 08016
(609) 386-6221

Catholic Community
Services of Newark
499 Belgrove Drive
Kearny, NJ 07032
(201) 991-3770

Catholic Family
and Community Services
476 17th Avenue
Paterson, NJ 07501
(201) 523-2666

Catholic Social Services of the
Diocese of Camden, Inc.
810 Montrose Street
Vineland, NJ 08360
(609) 691-1841

Children of the World
685 Bloomfield Avenue, Suite 201
Verona, NJ 07044
(201) 239-0100

Children's Aid
  and Family Services
575 Main Street
Hackensack, NJ 07601
(201) 487-2022

Children's Aid
  and Family Services
196 Speedwell Avenue
Morristown, NJ 07960
(201) 285-0165

Children's Aid
  and Family Services
439 Main Street
Orange, NJ 07050
(201) 673-6454

Children's Choice, Inc.
115 Fries Mill Road
728 Blackhorse Pike, Suite D-4
Turnersville, NJ 08012
(609) 228-5223

Children's Home Society
  of New Jersey
51 Main Street
Clinton, NJ 08809
(908) 852-5825

Children's Home Society
  of New Jersey
929 Parkside Avenue
Trenton, NJ 08618
(609) 695-6274

Christian Homes of Children
275 State Street
Hackensack, NJ 07601
(201) 342-4235

Downey Side
1610 South Broad Street
Hamilton Township, NJ 08610
(609) 392-7300

Family and Children's Services
40 North Avenue
P.O. Box 314
Elizabeth, NJ 07207
(908) 352-7474

Family Options
43 Main Street
Holmdel, NJ 07738
(908) 946-0880

Golden Cradle
1080 North Kings Hwy.
Suite 201
Cherry Hill, NJ 08034
(609) 667-2229

Growing Families, Inc.
178 South Street
Freehold, NJ 07728
(908) 431-4330

Holt International
  Children's Services
340 Scotch Road, 2nd Floor
Trenton, NJ 08628
(609) 882-4972

Homestudies, Inc.
1182 Teaneck Road
Teaneck, NJ 07666
(201) 833-9030

Jewish Family Services
100 Park Boulevard
Cherry Hill, NJ 08002
(609) 662-8611

Jewish Family Services
  of Central New Jersey
655 Westfield Avenue
Elizabeth, NJ 07208
(908) 352-8375

Jewish Family Services
  of Metro West
256 Columbia Turnpike,
  Suite 105
Florham Park, NJ 07932-0825
(201) 674-4210

Jewish Family Services
  of Monmouth County
705 Summerfield Avenue
Asbury Park, NJ 07712
(908) 774-6886

Jewish Family Services
  of Southern Middlesex
517 Ryders Lane
East Brunswick, NJ 08816
(908) 257-4100

Lutheran Social Ministries
  of New Jersey
120 Route 156
Yardville, NJ 08620
(609) 585-0303

Seedlings, Inc.
1 Tall Timber Drive
Morristown, NJ 07060
(201) 605-1188

Spaulding for Children
707 Market Street
Camden, NJ 08102
(609) 964-3838

Branches:
Plainfield
(908) 226-0445
East Orange
(201) 678-4975

Today's Adoption
399 Clove Road
P.O. Box 1744
Montague, NJ 07827
(201) 293-8660

United Family
  and Children's Society
305 West Seventh Street
Plainfield, NJ 07060
(908) 755-4848

**Adoptive Parent Support
Groups and Postadoption
Services**

Adoption Information
  Service, Inc.
12 Roberts Street
Rockaway, NJ 07866
(201) 586-1552

Adoptive Mothers
  of Essex County
Attn.: Lili Hartman
40 Burnett Terrace
Maplewood, NJ 07040
(201) 763-9220

Adoptive Parents
  for Open Records
Attn.: Joan and John Crout
625 St. Marks Avenue
Westfield, NJ 07090
(908) 233-2768

Adoptive Single Parents
  of New Jersey
Attn.: Joan Jacobs
73 Tristan Road
Clifton, NJ 07013
(201) 742-9441
                    or
Lea Wait
79 Old Army Road
Bernardsville, NJ 07924
(908) 766-6281

Camden County FACES
Attn.: Susan Grella
130 South Mansfield Boulevard
Cherry Hill, NJ 08034
(609) 784-1081

Camp Se Jong
Attn.: Lindy Gelber
79 South Street
Demarest, NJ 07627
(201) 784-1081

Central New Jersey Singles
Network of Adoptive Parents
Attn.: Carol Perlmutter, Esq.
P.O. Box 1012
Flemington, NJ 08822
(908) 782-5500

Comprehensive Mental Health
Services
2480 Pennington Road
P.O. Box 591
Pennington, NJ 08534
(609) 737-7797

Concerned Parents for Adoption
and North American Council
on Adoptable Children
State Representative
Attn.: Bernette Berman
P.O. Box 179
Whippany, NJ 07981
(609) 799-3269

Familes United by Adoption
Attn.: Darlane Woodworth
245 Prospect Drive
Brick, NJ 08724
(908) 840-2277

Jersey Shore Families by Adoption
Attn.: Jan A. Devaney
507 Laurelwood Drive
Lanoka Harbor, NJ 08734
(609) 693-4387

Latin America Parents
Association
Attn.: Leslie Brookes
P.O. Box 2013
Brick, NJ 08723-1074
(908) 249-5600

Latin America
Parents Association,
Northern New Jersey
Attn.: Connie Violante
Box 762
Lyndhurst, NJ 07071

Links
Attn.: Sally Vroom
91 Carlton Avenue
Washington, NJ 07882
(908) 689-5932

New Jersey Adoptive
Parents Support Group
20 Jonathan Drive
Sewell, NJ 08080
(609) 863-1166

New Jersey Friends of Holt
Attn.: Peggy Overton
43 Fairfield Road
Princeton, NJ 08540

New Jersey Friends
Through Adoption
Attn.: Cynthia V.N. Peck
30 Endicott Drive
Great Meadows, NJ 07838
(908) 637-8828

Rainbow Families
Attn.: Kathleen Becker
670 Oakley Place
Oradell, NJ 07649
(201) 261-1148

Roots & Wings
P.O. Box 638
Chester, NJ 07930
(908) 637-8828

Singles Network
of Adoptive Parents
Attn.: Lois Cowen
8 North Whittesbog Road
Browns Mills, NJ 08015
(609) 893-7875

Stars of David
Attn.: Ilene and Stuart Schwartz,
Acting National Presidents
#2 Wenonah Avenue
Rockaway, NJ 07866
(201) 627-7752

Stars of David,
Central New Jersey Chapter
Attn.: Stephanie Safdieh
P.O. Box 471
Holmdel, NJ 07733

Stars of David
of the Delaware Valley
Attn.: Laurie and Sid Katz
(609) 424-6280

Stars of David,
Northern New Jersey Chapter
Attn.: Jamie Moscowitz
P.O. Box 1023
Denville, NJ 07834
(908) 789-2906

Today's Adoptive Families
Attn.: Carol and Ted Eiferman
30 Manchester Way
Burlington, NJ 08016
(609) 386-7237

**Adopted Person and Birth
Relative Support Groups**

Adoptee Liberty Movement
Association (ALMA)
P.O. Box 153
South Orange, NJ 07079
(201) 762-2151

Adoptee Liberty Movement
Association (ALMA)
P.O. Box 1825
West Caldwell, NJ 07007
(201) 762-2151

Adoption Crossroads
85 Paramus Road
Paramus, NJ 07652
(201) 843-3550 or (201) 358-
0976

Adoption Reunion Coalition
of New Jersey
15 Fir Place
Hazlet, NJ 07730
(908) 739-9365

Adoption Support Group
of Central New Jersey
500-4B Auten Road
Somerville, NJ 08876
(908) 874-8983

Adoption Support Group
of Southern New Jersey
32 Trotters Lane
Smithville, NJ 08201
(609) 748-8126

Adoption Support Network
505 West Hamilton Avenue,
#207
Linwood, NJ 08221
(609) 653-4242

Adoptive Parents
for Open Records
9 Marjorie Drive
Hackettstown, NJ 07840
(908) 850-1706

ALARM Network
55 High Oaks Drive
Watchung, NJ 07060
(908) 754-0013

Angles and Extensions
Box 7247
Sussex, NJ 07461
(201) 875-9869

Birthparent Support Group,
   Golden Cradle Adoption
   Services
1101 N. Kings Hwy., Suite G-102
Cherry Hill, NJ 08034
(609) 667-2229

Division of Youth & Family
   Services, Adoption Unit
Attn.: Adoption Registry
   Coordinator
CN 717
Trenton, NJ 08625-0717
(609) 292-8819

New Jersey Coalition for
   Openness in Adoption
3 Harding Terrace at Fenwick
Morristown, NJ 07960-3252
(201) 267-8698

New Jersey Coalition for
   Openness in Adoption
189 Cosman Street
Township of Washington, NJ
   07675
(201) 267-8698

Origins
289 E. Halsey Road
Parsippany, NJ 07054
(201) 884-1695

Origins
8509 Tammaron Drive
Plainsboro, NJ 08536
(609) 936-1267

Origins
P.O. Box 556
Whippany, NJ 07981
(201) 428-9683

**New Jersey State Bar
   Association**
1 Constitutional Square
New Brunswick, NJ 08901-1500
(908) 249-5000

Adoption Attorneys

Craig Bluestein
200 Old York Road
Jenkinstown, PA 19046
(215) 576-1030

Robin Fleischner*
159 Millburn Avenue
Millburn, NJ 07052
(201) 376-6623

* Ms. Fleischner practices in New
   York and New Jersey. She
   completes about forty adoptions
   per year.

Raymond W. Godwin*
409 East North Street
Greenville, SC 29601
(800) 238-1003
(864) 271-4525
fax (864) 242-5902

* Mr. Godwin practices in New
   Jersey and South Carolina. He
   has completed about 400
   independent adoptions and 150
   agency adoptions.

Jerry Kaminsky
3084 State Highway 27, Suite 3
Kendall Park, NJ 08824
(908) 821-2889

James Miskowski
24 North Broad Street
Ridgewood, NJ 07450
(201) 445-4600

Suzanne Nichols
420 Chestnut Street
Union, NJ 07083
(908) 964-1096

Steven B. Sacharow
950 Kings Highway North, Box
   8484
Cherry Hill, NJ 08002-0484
(609) 667-1111

Toby Solomon*
354 Eisenhower Parkway
Livingston, NJ 07068
(201) 533-0078
fax (201) 533-0466

* Ms. Solomon is the Chair of the
   Adoption Subcommittee,
   Family Law Section, New Jersey
   Bar Association. She received
   the Distinguished Legislative
   Service Award for work on
   Adoption Amendments.

Deborah Steincolor
281 Liberty Street
Bloomfield, NJ 07003
(201) 743-7500

NEW JERSEY LAWS RELATED TO ADOPTION: QUESTIONS AND ANSWERS

Can an attorney serve as an intermediary?
Yes, but he or she cannot be paid for such services.

Is advertising permitted?
Yes.

Who must consent to the adoption?
Both birth parents must consent.

When can consent be taken from birth mother (father), and how long after the consent is signed can it be revoked?
In an agency adoption, a surrender of parental rights can be taken seventy-two hours after the child's birth and is irrevocable. In a nonagency independent adoption, the birth

mother can appear before a judge and have her rights terminated. If she does not do that, then her parental rights are not terminated until the first court hearing, which is usually held sixty to ninety days after the adoption petition is filed. Each birth parent must receive notice of this first hearing. During this time the birth parents can revoke their consent and have the child returned to them. New Jersey, unlike other states, does not consider whether it would be in the child's best interests to remain with the adoptive couple unless the parental rights have been terminated.

What are the birth father's rights?
If the birth father cannot be determined or if the birth mother refuses to name him, and the court is unable to determine who he is, his consent is not needed and his parental rights are terminated at the first hearing held two to three months after the adoption is filed. In an independent adoption, notice must be sent by certified mail to a known birth father of the adoption hearing. Some judges want the birth father served with the notice by a process server. If the known birth father does not respond within thirty days and does not appear at the first hearing, then his rights are terminated. The adoption is finalized approximately seven months after the first hearing.

In an agency adoption, the adoption complaint is filed six months after placement and a final hearing is held within thirty days after filing of the complaint. If the birth father has not signed an agency surrender, then his rights can be terminated at the final hearing if he has received notice of the hearing and not responded. An agency can terminate his rights sooner by scheduling a termination hearing at any time after the birth and providing him notice of the hearing. As long as he does not object in writing or appear at the hearing, his rights are terminated.

In both an agency or private adoption, a birth parent's rights can be terminated by the court if it can be established that the birth parent hadd abandoned his or her rights to the child. This can be established by showing that the birth parent had no contact with or provided no emotional or monetary support for the child during the six-month period prior to placement.

What fees can adoptive parents pay?
Legal, medical, counseling, and living expenses can be paid. However, all expenses must be submitted to the court before the final adoption. In an independent adoption, judges only permit limited expenses to be paid, and may not approve certain items.

Where does the adoption hearing take place?
The hearing take place in the court of the county where the adoptive parents or birth parents reside, or where the agency is located.

How are familial and step-parent adoptions different from nonbiological adoptions?
The court can waive a home study if the child has resided with the adoptive parent for a period of at least six months.

Can a nonresident finalize an adoption in this state?
Yes, but only through an agency.

NEW MEXICO

State Adoption Specialist
Jan Stanley
New Mexico Children,
    Youth and Families
    Department
Placement Services
P.O. Drawer 5160, PERA
    Building
Santa Fe, NM 87502-5160
(505) 827-8456

Compact Administrator
Heather Wilson, Secretary
Children, Youth
    and Families Department
P.O. Drawer 5160
PERA Building
Santa Fe, NM 87504-5160
(505) 827-7602

Deputy Compact Administrator
Elizabeth M. Findling
Protective Services Division -
    ICPC
Children, Youth
    and Families Department
P.O. Drawer 5160
PERA Building, Room 254
Santa FE, NM 87504-5160
(505) 827-8457

Direct all telephone calls and
    correspondence to the Deputy
    Compact Administrator.

Office hours:
Monday-Thursday
7:00 A.M.-5:00 P.M.
Friday 7:00 A.M.-11:00 A.M.
Mountain Time Zone

**State Adoption Exchange
    and Photo Listing**

New Mexico Adoption Exchange
New Mexico Children,
    Youth and Families
    Department
P.O. Drawer 5160
Santa Fe, NM 87502
(505) 827-8422

Private Adoption Agencies

Association for Retarded Citizens
    of Albuquerque
1515 4th Street, N.W.
Albuquerque, NM 87102
(505) 247-0321

Catholic Social Services, Inc.
1234 San Felipe Avenue, #B
Santa Fe, NM 87505-3339
(505) 982-0441

Chaparral Maternity and
    Adoption Services
1503 University Boulevard, N.E.
Albuquerque, NM 87102
(505) 243-2586

Child-Rite/Adopt a Special Kid
    (AASK) of New Mexico
120 Madiera N.E., Suite 308
Albuquerque, NM 87108
(505) 764-9438

Child-Rite/Adopt a Special Kid
    (AASK) of New Mexico
2008 Rosina, #6
Santa Fe, NM 87505
(505) 988-5177

Child-Rite/Adopt a Special Kid
    (AASK) of New Mexico
P.O. Box 1448
Taos, NM 87571
(505) 758-0343

Christian Child Placement
    Services
West Star Route, P.O. Box 48
Portales, NM 88130
(505) 356-8414

Families for Children (A Division
    of New Mexico Boys' Ranch)
6209 Hendrix, N.E.
Albuquerque, NM 87110
(505) 881-4200

Healing the Children
502 Georgenne, N.E.
Albuquerque, NM 87123
(505) 298-7841

Hogares
P.O. Box 6342
Albuquerque, NM 87197
(505) 345-8471

La Familia Placement Services
707 Broadway N.E., Suite 103
Albuquerque, NM 87102
(505) 766-9361

LDS Social Services
3811 Atrisco, N.W., Suite A
Albuquerque, NM 87120
(505) 836-5947

LDS Social Services
925 Canary Court
Farmington, NM 87401
(505) 327-6123

Methodist Home Services
7920 Mountain Road, N.E.
Albuquerque, NM 87110
(505) 255-8740

Rainbow House International
19676 Hwy. 85
Belen, NM 87702
(505) 865-5550

Triad Adoption Services, Inc.
2811 Indian School Road, N.E.
Albuquerque, NM 87106
(505) 266-0456

**Adoptive Parent Support
    Groups and Postadoption
    Services**

Adoptive Families of Resolve
P.O. Box 13194
Albuquerque, NM 87192
(505) 242-4420

Families for Children
Attn.: Nikki Cull
6209 Hendrix Road, N.E.
Albuquerque, NM 87110
(505) 881-4200

North American Council on
    Adoptable Children State
    Representative
Attn.: Gail Neher
88 Manzano Spring Road
Taijeras, NM 87059
(505) 281-6537

Parents Helping Parents
Attn.: Cathy Keinigs
1307 Avenida Aliso
Santa Fe, NM 87501
(505) 988-1621

Parents of Intercultural Adoption
Attn.: Susan Rogers
P.O. Box 91175
Albuquerque, NM 87199
(505) 296-6782

Santa Fe Rainbow Families
Attn.: Stephanie Garcia
2215 Rancho Siringo #3
Santa Fe, NM 87505
(505) 473-0649

Adopted Person and Birth
    Relative Support Groups

Adoptee Liberty Movement
    Association (ALMA)
P.O. Box 1346
Astec, NM 87410
(505) 334-2654

Concerned United Birthparents
358 Joya Loop
Los Alamos, NM 87544

Geborener Deutscher
805 Alvarado Drive N.E.
Albuquerque, NM 87108
(505) 268-1310

Open Circle
RR3, Box 107-3
Santa Fe, NM 87505

Operation Identity
13101 Blackstone, N.E.
Albuquerque, NM 87111
(505) 293-3144

Survival Strategies
10909 Apache, N.E.
Albuquerque, NM 87111
(505) 293-0706

State Bar of New Mexico
P.O. Box 25883
Albuquerque, NM 87125
(505) 842-6132

Adoption Attorneys

Michael J. Collopy
P.O. Box 2297
Hobbs, NM 88241-2297
(505) 397-3608

Jane Printz*
1200 Pennsylvania NE
Albuquerque, NM 87110
(505) 266-8787
fax (505) 255-4029

* Ms. Printz has completed about
    150 independent adoptions and
    thirty agency adoptions.

Attorney fees for an adoption in
this state are about $1,500.

NEW MEXICO LAWS RELATED TO ADOPTION: QUESTIONS AND ANSWERS

A home study must be conducted thirty days before a child can be placed in your home in an interstate independent adoption. If you plan to advertise outside of the state, be sure to have a home study very near completion before placing an ad. Also, your attorney must obtain a court order that permits a child from another state to come into your home.

Can an attorney serve as an intermediary?
No.

Is advertising permitted?
Yes.

Who must consent to the adoption?
1. The birth mother
2. The birth father if he is married to or attempted to marry the birth mother, or if the child was born within 300 days after the marriage ended, or if he has stated he is the father and established a personal and financial relationship with the child.
3. The adoption agency involved, if applicable. Consent is not required if either birth parent has left the child with a third party (the adoptive couple, for example) and has not supported the child or communicated with her for a period of three months if the child is under the age of six years. If the child is over the age of six years then the time period is six months.

When can consent be taken from birth mother (father), and how long after the consent is signed can it be revoked?
Consent cannot be given until forty-eight hours after child's birth and must be taken in front of a judge. Consent cannot be withdrawn unless it was obtained by fraud.

What are the birth father's rights?
His rights are limited, as described above. If he has not registered with a putative father registry within ninety days of the child's birth, then his consent is not needed.

What fees can adoptive parents pay?
Medical, legal, and living expenses can be paid. All expenses paid must be filed by the adoptive parents with the court.

Where does the adoption hearing take place?
The hearing takes place in the court of the county where the adoptive parents live, where the child lives, or where the agency is located.

How are familial and step-parent adoptions different from nonbiological adoptions?
If the child has lived with a relative (up to the fifth degree of relation) for at least one year, then the home study can be waived. Grandparent visitation rights apply to adoption by a step-parent or relative, a person designated in the deceased parent's will, or a person who served as a godparent.

Can a nonresident finalize an adoption in this state?
No. A minimum residency of six months is required.

NEW YORK

State Adoption Specialist
Anne Furman
New York State Department
    of Social Services
40 North Pearl Street
Albany, NY 12243
(518) 474-9447

Peter Winkler
New York State Department of
    Social Services
40 North Pearl Street
Albany, NY 12243
(518) 474-2868

Compact Administrator
Kevin Leyden
New York State Department of
    Social Services
40 North Pearl Street
Albany, NY 12243
(518) 474-9447
fax (518) 486-6326

Direct all correspondence to the
    Compact Administrator. Direct
    telephone calls to:

Jim Keeler (518) 473-1591
Gwen Pope (518) 474-9582
Barbara Lynch (518) 474-9702

Office hours:
Monday-Friday
8:30 A.M.-4:30 P.M.
Eastern Time Zone

**State Adoption Exchange
    and Photo Listing**
Judy Goldman
New York State Adoption Service
40 North Pearl Street
Albany, NY 12243
(518) 473-1512
(800) 345-KIDS (nationwide)

Private Adoption Agencies

Abbott House
100 North Broadway
Irvington, NY 10533
(914) 591-7300

Adoption and Counseling
    Services, Inc.
One Fayette Park
Syracuse, NY 13202
(315) 471-0109

Angel Guardian Home
6301 12th Avenue
Brooklyn, NY 11219
(718) 232-1500, ext. 352

Association to Benefit Children's
    Variety House
404 East 91st Street
New York, NY 10128
(212) 369-2010

Astor Home for Children
13 Mt. Carmel Place
Poughkeepsie, NY 12601-1714
(914) 452-4167

Bethany Christian Services
16 Maple Avenue
Warwick, NY 10990
(914) 987-1453

Brookwood Child Care
25 Washington Street
Brooklyn, NY 11201
(718) 596-5555, ext. 510

Cardinal McCloskey School
    and Home
2 Holland Avenue
White Plains, NY 10603
(914) 997-8000

Catholic Charities of Buffalo
525 Washington Street
Buffalo, NY 14203
(716) 856-4494

Catholic Charities of Ogdensburg
105 West Main Street
Malone, NY 12953
(518) 483-1460

Catholic Charities of Ogdensburg
716 Caroline Street
P.O. Box 296
Ogdensburg, NY 13669-0296
(315) 393-2660

Catholic Charities of Ogdensburg
380 Arlington Street
Watertown, NY 13601
(315) 788-4330

Catholic Charities
of Ogdensburg/Plattsburgh
151 South Catherine Street
Plattsburgh, NY 12901
(518) 561-0470

Catholic Charities of Syracuse,
Family Division
1654 West Onondaga Street
Syracuse, NY 13204
(315) 424-1871

Catholic Charities of
Syracuse/Rome
212 West Liberty Street
Rome, NY 13440
(315) 337-8600

Catholic Family Center
25 Franklin Street
Rochester, NY 14604
(716) 546-7220

Catholic Guardian Society
of New York
1011 First Avenue
New York, NY 10022
(212) 371-1000, ext. 2340

Catholic Home Bureau
1011 First Avenue
New York, NY 10022
(212) 371-1000

Catholic Social Services
of Broome County
232 Main Street
Binghamton, NY 13905
(607) 729-9166

Catholic Social Services
of Utica/Syracuse
1408 Genesee Street
Utica, NY 13502
(315) 724-2158

Central Brooklyn Coordinating
Council
1958 Fulton Street, 4th Floor
Brooklyn, NY 11233
(718) 778-1400

Child and Family Services
678 West Onondaga Street
Syracuse, NY 13204
(315) 474-4291

Child and Family Services of Erie
107 Statler Towers
Suite 555, 5th Floor
Buffalo, NY 14202
(716) 856-3802

Child Development Support
Corporation
1119 Bedford Avenue
Brooklyn, NY 11216
(718) 398-2050

Children's Aid Society
150 East 45th Street
New York, NY 10017
(212) 949-4955

Children's Home of Kingston
26 Grove Street
Kingston, NY 12401
(914) 331-1448

Children's Home of Poughkeepsie
91 Fulton Street
Poughkeepsie, NY 12601
(914) 452-1420

Children's Village
Dobbs Ferry, NY 10522
(914) 693-0600

Coalition for Hispanic Family
Services
315 Wyckoff Avenue, 4th Floor
Brooklyn, NY 11237
(718) 497-6090

Community Maternity Services
27 North Main Avenue
Albany, NY 12203
(518) 438-2322

Concord Family Services
1313 Bedford Avenue
Brooklyn, NY 11216
(718) 398-3499

Downey Side Families for Youth
Southgate Tower, Hudson Room
371 Seventh Avenue
New York, NY 10001-3984
(212) 629-8599

Edwin Gould Services for
Children
41 East 11th Street
New York, NY 10003
(212) 598-0051, ext. 279

Episcopal Mission Society
18 West 18th Street
New York, NY 10011-4607
(212) 675-1000, ext. 377

Family and Children's Services
of Broome County
257 Main Street
Binghamton, NY 13905
(607) 729-6206

Family and Children's Services
of Ithaca
204 North Cayuga Street
Ithaca, NY 14850
(607) 273-7494

Family and Children's Services
of Schenectady
246 Union Street
Schenectady, NY 12305
(518) 393-1369

Family Focus
54-40 Little Neck Pkwy., Suite 3
Little Neck, NY 11362
(718) 224-1919

Family Service of Utica
401 Columbia Street, Suite 201
Utica, NY 13502
(315) 735-2236

Family Service of Westchester
One Summit Avenue
White Plains, NY 10606
(914) 948-8004

Family Support Systems
Unlimited
2530 Grand Concourse
Bronx, NY 10458
(212) 220-5400

Family Tree
1743 Route 9
Clifton Park, NY 12065
(518) 371-1336

Forestdale, Inc.
67-35 112 Street
Forest Hills, NY 11375
(718) 263-0740

Friendship House of Western
New York, Inc.
90 Dona Street
Lackawanna, NY 14218
(716) 826-1500

Graham-Windham
33 Irving Place
New York, NY 10013
(212) 529-6445

Green Chimneys
Putnam Lake Road,
 Caller Box 719
Brewster, NY 10509-0719
(914) 279-2996, ext. 231

Harlem Dowling Children's
 Services
2090 Seventh Avenue
New York, NY 10027
(212) 749-3656

Heartshare Human Services
186 Joralemon Street
Brooklyn, NY 11201
(718) 330-0639

Hillside Children's Center
1337 East Main Street
Rochester, NY 14609
(716) 654-4529

International Social Service
 American Branch, Inc.
390 Park Avenue South
New York, NY 10016
(212) 532-6350

Jewish Board of Family
 and Children Services
120 West 57th Street
New York, NY 10019
(212) 582-9100

Jewish Child Care Association
575 Lexington Avenue
New York, NY 10022
(212) 371-1313

Jewish Family Services
 of Erie County
70 Barker Street
Buffalo, NY 14209
(716) 883-1914

Jewish Family Service
 of Rochester
441 East Avenue
Rochester, NY 14607
(716) 461-0110

LDS Social Services of New York
2 Jefferson Street, #205
Poughkeepsie, NY 12601
(914) 485-2755

Leake and Watts Children's
 Home
463 Hawthorne Avenue
Yonkers, NY 10705
(914) 963-5220

Little Flower Children's Services
186 Remsen Street
Brooklyn, NY 11201
(718) 260-8840, ext. 640

Louise Wise Services
12 East 94th Street
New York, NY 10128
(212) 876-3050

Lutheran Service Society
 of New York
P.O. Box 1963
Williamsville, NY 142310-1963
(716) 631-9212

Lutheran Social Services, Inc.
27 Park Place, 4th Floor
New York, NY 10007
(212) 406-9110

McMahon Services for Children
305 Seventh Avenue
New York, NY 10001
(212) 243-7070

Mercy Home for Children
310 Prospect Park West
Brooklyn, NY 11215
(718) 467-2564

Miracle Makers, Inc.
33 Somers Street
Brooklyn, NY 11233
(718) 342-2250

Mission of the Immaculate Virgin
6581 Hylan Boulevard
Staten Island, NY 10309
(718) 317-2627

New Alternatives for Children
37 West 26th Street
New York, NY 10010
(212) 696-1550

New Beginnings Family and
 Children's Services, Inc.
141 Willis Avenue
Mineola, NY 11501
(516) 747-2204

New Hope Family Services
3519 James Street
Syracuse, NY 13206
(315) 437-8300

New Life Adoption Agency
430 E. Genesee Street
Syracuse, NY 13202|1103
(315) 422-7300

New York Foundling Hospital
590 Avenue of the Americas
New York, NY 10011
(212) 727-6828

Ohel Children's Home
 and Family Services
4510 16th Avenue, 4th Floor
Brooklyn, NY 11204
(718) 851-6300

Our Lady of Victory
790 Ridge Road
Lackawanna, NY 14218
(716) 827-9611

Parsons Child and Family Center
60 Academy Road
Albany, NY 12208
(518) 426-2600

Pius XII Youth/Family Services
188 W. 230 Street
Bronx, NY 10463
(718) 562-7855

Praca Child Care
853 Broadway
New York, NY 10003
(212) 673-7320

Richard Allen Center on Life
1872 Amsterdam Avenue
New York, NY 10031
(212) 862-7160

St. Augustine Center
1600 Filmore
Buffalo, NY 14211
(716) 897-4110

St. Christopher Ottilie
3rd Avenue and 8th Street
P.O. Box Y
Brentwood, NY 11717
(516) 273-2733

St. Christopher Ottilie
570 Fulton Street
Brooklyn, NY 11217
(718) 855-0330

St. Christopher Ottilie
90-04 161st Street
Jamaica, NY 11432
(718) 526-7533

St. Christopher Ottilie
99 North Village Avenue
Rockville Centre, NY 11570
(517) 764-4499

St. Christopher Ottilie
12 Main Avenue
Sea Cliff, NY 11579
(516) 759-1844

St. Christopher's/Jennie Clarkson
71 South Broadway
Dobbs Ferry, NY 10522
(914) 693-3030, ext. 209

St. Dominics
535 East 138th Street
Bronx, NY 10454
(718) 402-5900

St. Joseph's Children's Services
540 Atlantic Avenue
Brooklyn, NY 11217-1982
(718) 858-8700

St. Mary's Child
and Family Services
Convent Road
Syosset, NY 11791
(516) 921-0808

St. Vincent's Services
66 Boerum Place
P.O. Box 174
Brooklyn, NY 11202
(718) 522-3700, ext. 251

Salvation Army Foster Home
132 West 14th Street
New York, NY 10011
(212) 807-6100, ext. 579

Sheltering Arms Children
Services
122 East 29th Street
New York, NY 10016
(212) 679-4242, ext. 735

Society for Seamen's Children
25 Hyatt Street, 4th Floor
Staten Island, NY 10301
(718) 447-7740

Spence-Chapin Adoption
Services
6 East 94th Street
New York, NY 10028
(212) 369-0300

Talbot-Perkins Children Services
116 West 32nd Street, 12th Floor
New York, NY 10001
(212) 736-2510

Voice for International
and Domestic Adoptions
(VIDA)
345 Allen Street
Hudson, NY 12534
(518) 828-4527

**Adoptive Parent Support
Groups
and Postadoption Services**

Adopt a Special Kid (AASK)
of New York
Attn.: Geri Hecox
216 Lawrence Street
Rome, NY 13440
(315) 336-9148

A.D.O.P.T.
Attn.: Candice Dayton
RR 1, Box 430
Jeffersonville, NY 12748
(914) 482-5339

Adopted Children
of Romania Network
Attn.: Karen LoGrippo
299 Oak Street
Patchogue, NY 11772
(516) 298-9274

Adoption Advocacy Network
Attn.: Vicki Pratt
425 Oak Orchard Estates
Albion, NY 14411
(716) 589-5433

Adoption Group
of Orange County
Attn.: William Merritt
P.O. Box 156
Chester, NY 10918
(914) 469-7015

Adoption Resource Center
177 Flatbush Avenue
Brooklyn, NY 11217
(718) 789-9783 or 789-9793

Adoption Resource Network, Inc.
Attn.: Cindy Fleischer
and Lisa Maynard
P.O. Box 178
Pittsford, NY 14534
(716) 924-5295

Adoptive Families Association
of Tompkins County
Attn.: Nancy Lazarus
Howland Road
Spencer, NY 14883
(607) 589-4938

Adoptive Families Network
Attn.: Gail Nachimson
48 Hillcrest Avenue
Kingston, NY 12401
(914) 339-3191

Adoptive Families
of Chemung County
Attn.: Lucinda Wakeman
5702 State Route 414
Beaver Dams, NY 14812
(607) 936-4706

Adoptive Families of Westchester
Attn.: Ann Marie McFarland
11 Bristol Place
Yonkers, NY 10710
(914) 779-1509

Adoptive Family Network
Attn.: Kathy Costa
3 Turnpike Boulevard
Middle Island, NY 11953
(516) 924-5829

Adoptive Family Network
of Central New York
Attn.: Linda Peressini
Box 6256 6256
Syracuse, NY 13217-6256
(315) 424-3934

Adoptive/Foster Families
of Long Island
831 Montauk Avenue
Islip Terrace, NY 11752
(516) 277-7149

Adoptive Parents Committee,
Albany Area
Attn.: Barbara Amarando
4356 Buckingham Drive
Schenectady, NY 12304
(518) 372-2874

Adoptive Parents Committee,
Hudson Region
Attn.: Ken Hettinger
P.O. Box 245
White Plains, NY 10605|0245
(914) 997-7859

Adoptive Parents Committee,
Long Island
Attn.: Suzanne and Chuck Cryda
Box 71
Bellmore, NY 11710
(516) 326-8621

Adoptive Parents Committee,
New York City
Attn.: Sam Pitkowsky
254 Seaman Avenue
New York, NY 10034
(212) 304-8479

Adoptive Parents Committee,
New York State
Attn.: Felix Fornino
Box 3525
Church Street Station
NY, NY 10008-3525
(718) 259-7921

Albany County Foster
and Adoptive Parents
Association
RR1, Box 5
Elm Lane
Greenville, NY 12083
(518) 966-0649

Allegany County
Adoption Support Group
Attn.: Rebecca Hodgson
62 South Street
Bolivar, NY 14715
(716) 928-1491

Allegany County Foster Parent
Association
Attn.: Mary Barnes
7388 Wellsville Street, Rt. 417E
Bolivar, NY 14715
(716) 928-2441

American Information Center
for Eastern European Orphans
1758 61st Street
Brooklyn, NY 11204-2257
(718) 232-3486

Association of Black Social
Workers
Child Adoption, Counseling
and Referral Service
1969 Madison Avenue, #6DFL
New York, NY 10035-1549
(212) 831-5181

Bed-Stuy Foster
& Adoptive Parent Association
Attn.: Marissa Singletary
593 Halsey Street
Brooklyn, NY 11233
(718) 455-2483

Black Homes for Black Children
Attn.: Emma Holley
Main P.O. Box 2193
Niagara Falls, NY 14302
(716) 282-4471

Camillus West Support Group
Attn.: Carole Smith
117 Clark Lane
Camillus, NY 13031
(315) 487-0484

Capital District Foster
and Adoptive Parents
Attn.: Markia Sloan
312 Sullivan Road
Schenectady, NY 12304
(518) 377-1012

Catholic Adoptive Parents
Association
Attn.: Paul McCabe
Two Park Lane
North Salem, NY 10560
(914) 277-4156

Catholic Home Bureau
Foster and Adoptive Parents
Association
Attn.: Victoria Torres
4048 Hill Avenue
Bronx, NY 10466
(718) 994-4623

Cayuga County Foster and
Adoptive Parents Association
Attn.: Betty Graff
1 1/2 Chestnut Street
Auburn, NY 13021
(315) 255-2416

Center Kids
Attn.: Wayne Steinman
1171 Fr. Capodanno Boulevard
Staten Island, NY 10306
(718) 987-6747

Center Kids Gay/Lesbian Foster
Parent Support Group
Attn.: Robert McNamara
Morningside Gardens
501 W. 123rd Street, #18D
New York, NY 10027-5062
(212) 678-8661

Central New York Friends
of Love the Children
Attn.: Louis Girolamo
4324 Carrigan Circle
Syracuse, NY 13217
(315) 468-4170

Champlain Valley
Adoptive Families
Attn.: Mary Ward
6 Grace Avenue
Plattsburgh, NY 12901
(518) 563-5224

Chemung County Adoptive
and Foster Parent Association
Attn.: Linda Kasper
404 Locust Street
Elmira, NY 14904
(607) 732-8517

Children Awaiting Parents
Attn.: Peggy Soule
700 Exchange Street
Rochester, NY 14608
(716) 232-5110

Clinton County Foster
& Adoptive Parent Support
Group
Attn.: Norma Homburger
RFD 2, Box 214B
Morrisonville, NY 12962
(518) 563-8620

Concerned Foster and Adoptive
Parents Support Group
Attn.: Clifton and Pauline Griffin
1256 Ocen Avenue
Brooklyn, NY 11230
(718) 421-3247

Committed Parents
for Black Adoption
Attn.: Alma Smith
900 Baychester, Bldg. 1B, #8A
Bronx, NY 10475
(718) 671-6772

Cortland County Foster
and Adoptive Parents
Attn.: Joyce Zelsnack
Box 120, RD 2
Marathon, NY 13803
(607) 849-6145

Council of Adoptive Parents
Attn.: Terry Savini
1724 Five Mile Line Road
P.O. Box 964
Penfield, NY 14526
(716) 383-0947

Dare to Care Fund, Foster Parent
Association of Broome County
Attn.: Bonnie Bergman
2 Pease Road
Harpersville, NY 13787
(607) 693-1790

A Different Direction
Attn.: Joanne Colangelo
4 Fabbri Court
Mahopac, NY 10541
(914) 628-9387

Division of Adoption and Foster
Care Services
Foster and Adoptive Parents
Association
Attn.: Cora Williams
413 Clermont Avenue
Brooklyn, NY 11238
(718) 636-1829

Erie County Foster Parents
Support Group
Attn.: Linda Rhodes
75 North Brier Road
Amherst, NY 14228
(716) 691-4872

Essex County Foster/Adoptive
Parent Support Group
Attn.: Debbie Egglefield
Box 731
Elizabethtown, NY 12932
(518) 873-6649

Families Adopting Need Support
Attn.: Mary Grace Morris
768 Richmond Avenue
Buffalo, NY 14222
(716) 882-0867

Families for the
Children/Adirondack Region
Attn.: Diana Bixler
303 Coy Road
Greenfield Center, NY 12833
(518) 893-7699

Families Interested in Minority
Adoption (FIMA)
Attn.: Emily Eisenbaum
2316 Delaware Avenue, #101
Buffalo, NY 14216
(716) 827-7845

Families Through Adoption
Attn.: Cheryl Anderson
301 Middle Road
Oneida, NY 13421
(315) 363-4634

Families With Children
From China
Attn.: Susan Caughman
or Laurie Heineman
255 West 90th Street, Apt. 11C
New York, NY 10024
(212) 595-8007 or 496-8063

Family Services of Westchester
1 Summit Avenue
White Plains, NY 10606
(914) 948-8004

Finger Lakes Adoption Group
Attn.: Ann DeBolt
15 Ridge Street
Seneca Falls, NY 13148
(315) 789-4560

Forestdale Foster and Adoptive
Parents Association
Attn.: Marion Bennett
235 Montana Avenue.
Brooklyn, NY 11706

Foster and Adoptive Parents
Advisory Committee of Edwin
Gould Services for Children
382 East 52nd Street
Brooklyn, NY 11203
(718) 346-2234

Foster & Adoptive Parents
Association of Cattaraugus
County
Attn.: Robert McClure
141 North 9th Street
Olean, NY 14760
(716) 372-5267

Foster and Adoptive Parents
Association of Episcopal
Mission Society
Attn.: Debra Smith
P.O. Box 930|335
Rockaway Beach, NY 11693
(718) 945-1666

Foster and Adoptive Parents
Association of Erie County
Attn.: Kathy Sullivan
164 Broadmoor Drive
Tonawanda, NY 14150
(716) 694-8170

Foster and Adoptive Parents
Association of Jefferson County
Attn.: Ed Robbins
903 Franklin Street
Watertown, NY 13601
(315) 786-0970

Foster & Adoptive Parents
Association of Oneida County
Attn.: Dawn Corrigan
3 Symphony Place
Whitesboro, NY 13492
(315) 724-5753

Foster and Adoptive Parents
Association of Society
for Seamen's Children
Attn.: Helen Cunningham
159 Tyson Street
Staten Island, NY 10301
(718) 720-5907

Foster and Adoptive Parents
Group of Angel Guardian
Home
134-39 224th Street
Laurelton, NY 11413
(718) 712-6990

Foster and Adoptive Parents
Network
Attn.: Margie Burnham
166 Marion Street
Staten Island, NY 10310
(718) 273-3005

Foster and Adoptive Parents
of Otsego County
Attn.: Marcie Frampton
RD 2, Box 237
Worcester, NY 12197
(607) 397-8600

Foster and Adoptive Parents
Organization of New York
Attn.: Ruby Watson
536 East 37th Street, #7
Brooklyn, NY 11203
(718) 282-7413

Foster Parents Advisory Council
of Suffolk County
Attn.: Lois Winiavski
177 43rd Street
Lindenhurst, NY 11757
(516) 957-8294

Foster Parents Association of
Oswego County
Attn.: Ray and Nancy Clark
4193 South Railroad Street
Parish, NY 13131
(315) 625-7107

Foster Parents Organization of
Madison County
Box 242, South Main Street
Munnsville, NY 13409
(315) 495-6556

Fostering Friendships
9555 Roberts Road
Sauquoit, NY 13456
(315) 737-8016

Friends in Adoption Post
  Placement Group
Attn.: Carol Bianco-Gray
16 Winey Street
Albany, NY 12203
(518) 452-0271

Friends of Children Everywhere
Attn.: Margaret Wilkie
3379 Weidner Avenue
Oceanside, NY 11572
(516) 536-4229

Friends of Foster and Adopted
  Children
Attn.: Betty Wesley
65 Leslie Street
Buffalo, NY 14211
(716) 892-7859

Friends of Voices for International
  and Domestic Adoption
Attn.: Charlotte Jakubiec
Box 351 RD 4
Rome, NY 13440
(315) 865-8637

Fulton County Adoptive and
  Foster Parent Support Group
Attn.: Malinda Argotsinger
Fulton County
  DSS|P.O. Box 549
Johnstown, NY 12095
(518) 762-0615

Gateway Youth & Family Services
  Foster Parents
Attn.: Ron Sprague
202 N. Barry Street
Olean, NY 14760
(716) 373-0139

Gathering International Families
  Together
Attn.: Sara Lavner
2229 Walnut Avenue
Ronkonoma, NY 11779
(212) 978-9524

Genesee County Foster and
  Adoptive Parents Association
Attn.: Joanne Pangrazio
9374 South Street Road
LeRoy, NY 14482
(716) 768-7464

Graham Windham Foster Parent
  Association
Attn.: Gladys Garcia
4144 Gunther Avenue
Bronx, NY 10466
(212) 325-9154

Grandparents Reaching Out
Attn.: Mildred Horn
141 Glen Summer Road
Holbrook, NY 11741
(516) 472-9728

Greater Rochester Committee for
  Single Adoptive Parents
Attn.: Linda Abee
35 West Canon Drive
Rochester, NY 14624
(716) 594-2755

Harlem Dowling Foster Parents
  Association
Attn.: Ann Purnell
100 Alcott Place
Bronx, NY 10475
(718) 379-2038

Heartshare Foster and Adoptive
  Parents Association
291 Nostrand Avenue
Brooklyn, NY 11216
(718) 230-8084

Hillside Emergency Foster Parents
  Group
Attn.: Pam and Tony Gregorio
40 Pacer Drive
Henrietta, NY 14467
(716) 359-1038

Holt Families Unlimited
Attn.: Hope and Richard
  VanScoy
Box 25
Candor, NY 13743
(607) 659-7540

International Adoptive Families
Attn.: Sharon Burgess
9 Rudder Lane
Latham, NY 12110
(518) 783-6786

Jason's Helping Hands
  Memorial Fund
219 Edgewater Avenue
Bayport, NY 11705
(516) 472-2686

Kids Adopted Overseas
12 North Main
Cohocton, NY 14826
(716) 384-5989

A K.I.D.S. Exchange
Attn.: Janet Marchese
56 Midchester Avenue
White Plains, NY 10606
(914) 428-1236

Latin America Parents
  Association
Attn.: Epy Scrivano
P.O. Box 339
Brooklyn, NY 11234
(718) 236-8689

Latin American Families
104 Cooper Road
Rochester, NY 14617
(716) 342-4247

Livingston County Foster and
  Adoptive Parent Association
Attn.: Judy Faulkner
4626 Main Street
Hemlock, NY 14466
(716) 367-3383

Louise Wise Foster and Adoptive
  Parents Association
116-32 220th Street
Cambria Heights, NY 11411
(718) 712-0702

Love the Children of Rochester
Attn.: Ellen Calkins
29 Bridgewood Drive
Fairport, NY 14450
(716) 425-7609

Love the Children
  of Western New York
Attn.: Jim and Linda Glose
347 Huntington Avenue
Buffalo, NY 14214
(716) 833-6282

Matanya of Rochester
Attn.: Ellen Bloom
441 East Avenue
Rochester, NY 14607
(716) 461-0110, ext. 121

McMahon Foster/Adoptive
  Parents
Attn.: Delia Ortiz
550 West 125th Street, # 1 H
New York, NY 10027
(212) 865-5961

Minority Adoptive Parent
  Organization
Attn.: Velvia Benjamin
71 Aberdeen Street
Rochester, NY 14619
(716) 328-3596

Minority Foster & Adoptive
Parents
Support Group of Monroe
County
Attn.: Evelyn Bagley
141 Columbia Avenue
Rochester, NY 14608
(716) 328-6756

Minority Foster and Adoptive
Parents of Tompkins County
Attn.: Gail Davis
P.O. Box 304
Freeville, NY 13068
(607) 844-3825

Minority Homes for Minority
Children
Attn.: Mary Brinson
510 Memorial Pkwy
Niagara Falls, NY 14301
(716) 285-1487

Miracle Makers Foster and
Adoptive Parents Association
Attn.: Mary Ray
201 Linden Boulevard, #A20
Brooklyn, NY 11226
(718) 469-7311

Monroe County Foster and
Adoptive Parents Association
Attn.: Lillian Babcock
30 Trowbridge Trail
Pittsford, NY 14534
(716) 381-2584

Montgomery County Foster &
Adoptive Parents Association
Attn.: Irene Kearns
12 Prospect Street
Fultonville, NY 12072
(518) 853-4477

Network of Families for Adoption
Attn.: Paul Hipworth
153 Brixton Road
Garden City, NY 11530
(516) 294-5149

New Alternatives for Children
Foster/Adoptive Parents
Association
Attn.: Faye Bailey
34|40 107th Street
Corona, NY 11368
(718) 476-2682

New Life for Black Children
Attn.: Thomasena Newton
P.O. Box 11164
Rochester, NY 14611
(716) 436-6075

New York Council on Adoptable
Children
Attn.: Ernesto Loperena
666 Broadway, 8th Floor
New York, NY 10012
(212) 475-0222

New York Singles Adopting
Children
Attn.: Andrea Troy
220 East 94th Street, 2 B
New York, NY 10128
(212) 289-1705

New York Singles Adopting
Children - Long Island
Attn.: Leslie Kizner
54-44 Little Neck Pkwy.
Little Neck, NY 11362
(718) 229-7240

New York State Citizens Coalition
for Children and North
American Council on
Adoptable Children State
Representative
Attn.: Judith Ashton
614 West State Street, 2nd Floor
Ithaca, NY 14850
(607) 272-0034

New York State Foster and
Adoptive Parents Association
177 Flatbush Avenue
Brooklyn, NY 11217
(718) 789-9783

Niagara County Foster Parents
Attn.: George M. Mayer
2470 Youngstown Lockport Road
Ransomville, NY 14131
(716) 791-3321

Open Door Society of Long Island
Attn.: Judy Mole
40 Pennsylvania Avenue
Medford, NY 11763
(516) 758-5571

Organization of Foster Families
for Equality & Reform
Attn.: Jean Ring
88 Plymouth Drive North
Glen Head, NY 11545
(516) 224-1919

Orleans County Foster and
Adoptive Parents Association
Attn.: Kathy Foss
178 Gulf Street
Medina, NY 14103
(716) 798-0722

Otsego Adopt
Attn.: Barbara Field
RD 1, Box 1
Mt. Vision, NY 13810
(607) 432-0988

Otsego County Special Needs
Adoption Information &
Referral
Attn.: Brigid Sullivan
Box 26
Morris, NY 13808
(607) 263-5093

Our Children Adoptive Families
Attn.: Shari Bartlett
9976 Route 19
Pavilion, NY 14525
(716) 768-7915

OURS Through Adoption
Attn.: Peggy Metzger
P.O. Box 2054
Buffalo, NY 14240

Parents and Children Together
Attn.: Helene Gershowitz
9 Arnold Road
Poughkeepsie, NY 12601
(914) 473-4123

Parents and Children Together,
Columbia County
Attn.: Albert and Kathy Stumph
Route 2, Box 2007
Chatham, NY 12037
(518) 392-2618

Peer Adoption Support Group
Attn.: Kathy and Mike Riley
984 Danby Drive
Webster, NY 14580
(716) 671-0326

Pius XII Foster and Adoptive
Parents Association
66 Judith Drive
Stormville, NY 12582
(914) 221-0753

Positively Peds and Adolescents
Attn.: Diane Donovan
17 Prospect Drive
Queensbury, NY 12804
(518) 798-8940

Post Adoption Support Services
Jewish Community Center
1200 Edgewood Avenue
Rochester, NY 14618
(716) 244-4133

Private Adoption Support
Group/Western New York
Attn.: Glenn and Mary Ellen
Ferguson
152 Kinsey Avenue
Kenmore, NY 14217
(716) 873-6347

Protection for Foster Children
Attn.: Kathy Boyle
140 Roberts Lane
Yonkers, NY 10701
(914) 423-1216

Proud Parents, Inc.
Attn.: Deidre Brown
35 Baker Road
Hoepwell Junction, NY 12533
(914) 223-7663

Putnam County Foster Parent
Association
Attn.: Marion Gierner
Marie Road RD 7
Carmel, NY 10512
(914) 225-5708

Rensselaer County Foster Parents
RR 1, Box 116A Wyomanock
Road
Stephentown, NY 12168
(518) 733-6393

Richmond Adoptive Parents
Attn.: Joan Immitti
P.O. Box 020665
Staten Island, NY 10302
(718) 370-2905

Rochester Adoptive Parents
Attn.: Raymond and Terry Pease
120 Milton Street
Rochester, NY 14619
(716) 235-0172

Rockland County Foster &
Adoptive Parents Association
Attn.: Suzanne Peters
One Jacqueline Road
Chestnut Ridge, NY 10952
(914) 356-0922

Saratoga County Foster Parents
Support Group
Attn.: Vena Reynolds
Box 91
Victory Mills, NY 12884
(518) 695-4174

Schenectady County Adoptive
Parents
Attn.: Paul Starson
37 Cooks Court
Waterford, NY 12188
(518) 383-9151

Schorarie County Foster Parents
Attn.: Suzanne Skelly
HCR1-Box 37 South Gilboa Road
Gilboa, NY 12076
(607) 588-9824

Seneca County Foster and
Adoptive Parent Group
(forming)
Attn.: Cynthia Swarthout
1 DiPronio Drive
P.O. Box 690
Waterloo, NY 13165
(315) 539-5609

Single Parents for Adoption
Attn.: Nancy Kresge
73 Cleveland Avenue
Buffalo, NY 14223
(716) 851-3356

Single Parents Network of Long
Island
Attn.: Maureen Reichardt
P.O. Box 563
Bethpage, NY 11714
(516) 420-0347

Skaneatles Foster Parent Group
Attn.: Peg Gilmour
3110 Falls Road
Marcellus, NY 13108
(315) 673-2890

Skip Generations
Attn.: Shirley Wilmoth
196 Kenwood Avenue
Rochester, NY 14611
(716) 464-9466

Southern Chautauqua County
Foster Parents Association
Attn.: Kathy Pisarek
RD 1, Edson Road, Box 287
Sinclairville, NY 14782
(716) 962-8220

Southern Tier Adoptive Families
Attn.: Tom Lasarso
3617 Lorne Drive
Endwell, NY 13760
(607) 722-9212

Spence-Chapin Families
Attn.: Sandra Ripbergen
6 East 94th Street
New York, NY 10128
(212) 369-0300

Stars of David
Attn.: David Gersh
70 Barker Street
Buffalo, NY 14209-2013
(716) 883-1914

Stars of David/Albany Area
Attn.: Alan Krieger/Judy Prest
RD1, Box 88
Duanesburg, NY 12056
(518) 895-8001

St. Catherine's Foster Parents
Support Group
Attn.: Roberta Jeracka
RD 2 Rarick Road, Box 114
Selkirk, NY 12158
(518) 767-3090

St. Christopher/J. Clarkson Foster
and Adoptive Parents
Association
Attn.: Dorothy Rutherford
4 Dennison Street
White Plains, NY 10606
(914) 328-0848

St. Christopher - Ottilie Foster
and Adoptive Parents Group
Attn.: Doris Moore
80 East Pennywood Avenue
Roosevelt, NY 11575
(516) 378-5507

St. Joseph's Foster and Adoptive
Parents Association
Attn.: Genovia Wheeler
540 Atlantic Avenue
Brooklyn, NY 11217
(212) 222-7865

St. Lawrence County Foster
and Adoptive Parents
Attn.: Nancy Welch
RD 2 Box 194
Governor, NY 13642
(315) 287-3826

St. Vincent's Foster and Adoptive
Parents Association
237 East 93rd Street
Brooklyn, NY 11212
(718) 346-3615

Steuben County Foster Parent
Support Group
Attn.: Barbara Peraldo
Rt.1 Box 25
Jasper, NY 14855
(607) 792-3855

United Metropolitan Foster &
Adoptive Parents Association
Attn.: Janice Hafele
151 Main Street
Staten Island, NY 10307
(718) 317-8761

Sullivan County Foster and
Adoptive Parents Association
Attn.: Ed Hernandez
1181 Horseshoe Lake Road
Swan Lake, NY 12783
(914) 583-5037

Tioga County Adoptive and
Foster Parents Group
24 Smith Street
Candor, NY 13743
(607) 659-7504

Tompkins County Foster
and Adoptive Parents
Association
Attn.: Coraleen Rooney
108 Homestead Road
Ithaca, NY 14850
(607) 272-5746

Tri County Families of Korean
Children
54 Benney Water Road
Port Jervis, NY 12771
(914) 355-3711

Ulster County Foster Parents
and Adoptive Parents
Association
Attn.: Gail Bodie
CPO Box 1262
Kingston, NY 12401
(914) 246-7436

United Metropolitan Foster
and Adoptive Parents
Association
Attn.: Janice Hafele
151 Main Street
Staten Island, NY 10307
(718) 317-8761

Upstate New York Singles
Adopting Children
21 Concord Drive
Saratoga Springs, NY 12866
(518) 581-0891

Washington County Foster
Parents
Attn.: Janet Donaldson
Box 2159 RD 2
Fort Ann, NY 12827
(518) 632-5496

Wayne County Foster
and Adoptive Parents (forming)
Attn.: Terry and Jennifer Bertou
2201 Palmyra - Marrion Road
Palmyra, NY 14522
(315) 597-9025

We Care Foster
and Adoptive Parents
Association
Attn.: Awilda Cirino
45 Storey Lane
Yonkers, NY 10710
(914) 963-8469

Westchester Foster and Adoptive
Parents Association
Attn.: Rosetta Mingo
20 East 4th Street
Mt. Vernon, NY 10550
(914) 699-4167

Westchester Singles Adopting
Children
Attn.: Sally Shore
26 Riverview Avenue
Tarrytown, NY 10591
(914) 631-1473

Western New York Foster Parents
Association
Attn.: Dorothy Durham
2190 Main Street
Buffalo, NY 14214
(716) 835-6851

Western New York Single Parents
for Adoption
Attn.: Nancy Kresge
73 Cleveland Drive
Kenmore, NY 14223
(716) 873-4173

Wyoming County Foster Parents
Attn.: Lucille Powers
4760 Java Road
North Java, NY 14113
(716) 457-9366

**Adopted Person and Birth
Relative Support Groups**

Adoptee Liberty Movement
Association (ALMA)
P.O. Box 727, Radio City Station
New York, NY 10101-0727
(212) 581-1568

Adoptee Liberty Movement
Association (ALMA)
485 Magee Street
Southampton, NY 11968

Adoptee Liberty Movement
Association (ALMA)
P.O. Box 53
Union Hill, NY 14563

Adoptees Connection
P.O. Box 492
Northville, NY 12134
(518) 863-6793

Adoptees Information
Service, Inc.
19 Marion Avenue
Mount Vernon, NY 10552

Adoptees Political Action
Coalition
P.O. Box 2807
Glenville, NY 12302

Adoption Alliance
17 Colton Avenue
Sayville, NY 11782

Adoption Crossroads
7 Cheryl Road
Massapequa, NY 11758

Adoption Crossroads
P.O. Box 9025
Schenectady, NY 12309
(518) 377-5936

Adoption Crossroads
Box 311
Shenorock, NY 10587
(914) 248-6644

Adoption Crossroads Chapter 11,
Western NY
28 A Windwood Court
Cheektowaga, NY 14225
(716) 894-4117

Adoption Crossroads/Council
  for Equal Rights in Adoption
401 East 74th Street
New York, NY 10021
(212) 988-0110

Adoption Friendship Circle
Box 125
Bible School Park, NY 13737
(607) 772-6793

Adoption Group of Orange
  County
Box 156
Chester, NY 10918

Adoption Information Registry,
  Department of Health
Attn.: Public Health
  Representative
Corning Tower, Room 208
Albany, NY 12237
(518) 474-1746

Adoption Kinship
817 Taylor Drive
Vestal, NY 13850
(607) 772-6793

Adoption Support Group
57 Little Neck Road
Centerport, NY 11721

Adoption Support Network
  of Long Island
194 Old Country Road
Mineola, NY 11501
(516) 248-1929 or 678-4068

Always Support for Adopted
  People
12 Sunset Avenue South
Farmingdale, NY 11735
(516) 694-4289

Birth Mothers of Minors
  (B.M.O.M.S.)
Cherokee Station
P.O. Box 20510
New York, NY 10021
(212) 532-4104

Birthmoms in Recovery
  Through Healing
7 Cheryl Place
Massapequa, NY 11758
(516) 735-0941

Birthmothers, Adoptees,
  Adoptive Parents United
  in Support
P.O. Box 299
Victor, NY 14564
(716) 924-0410

Birthparent Support Network
669 Coney Island Avenue
Brooklyn, NY 11218
(718) 284-0666

Birthparent Support Network
P.O. Box 120
North White Plains, NY 10603
(914) 682-2250

Birthparent Support Network
P.O. Box 34
Old Bethpage, NY 11804
(516) 785-0886 or 931-5925

Birthparent Support Network
93 Main Street
Queensbury, NY 12804
(518) 370-5392

Birthparents/Adoptees in Support
39 Tidd Avenue
Farmington, NY 14425

Birthparents and Kids in
  Desperate Search (B.K.I.D.S.)
P.O. Box 43
Erin, NY 14838
(607) 739-2957

Blood Roots
620 Central Chapel Road
Brooktondale, NY 14817
(607) 539-7401

Candid Adoption Talk
175A Fawnhill Road
Tuxedo, NY 10987
(914) 351-3306

Center for Reuniting Families
51 Burke Drive
Buffalo, NY 14215

Concerned United Birthparents
64 Ames Avenue
Jamestown, NY 14701

Concerned United Birthparents
215 Edgemont Drive
Syracuse, NY 13214

Concerned United
  Birthparents/Adoption
  in Recovery
Route 1, Box 224A
Petersburg, NY 12138
(518) 658-2972

Help Us Regain the Children
235 Dover Street
Brooklyn, NY 11235
(718) 332-0860

Independent Search Counselor
116 Pinehurst Avenue, Apt. C62
New York, NY 10033
(212) 280-2878

Jamestown Adoption Triad
Box 95
Falconer, NY 14733

KinQuest, Inc.
89 Massachusetts Avenue
Massapequa, NY 11758
(516) 541-7383

Lost & Found People Connection
P.O. Box 2222
Ballston Spa, NY 12020
(518) 899-2468

Manhattan Birthparents Group
P.O. Box 20137, Cherokee
  Station
New York, NY 10028-0051
(212) 289-6782

Missing Connection
Attn.: Sue Boyce
P.O. Box 712
Brownville, NY 13615
(315) 782-6245

Missing Pieces
Rt. 4, Box 389
Potsdam, NY 13676
(315) 265-7598

Origins
216 Carroll Street
Brooklyn, NY 11231

Post Adoption Center of NWY
Box 1223
Amherst, NY 14226
(716) 823-2044

Right to Know
P.O. Box 52
Old Westbury, NY 11568

Searchline of New York
Route 2, Whitaker Road
Fulton, NY 13069

Springer Registry
Attn.: Linda King
4426 Murphy Road
Binghamton, NY 13903
(607) 772-9514

Triangle of Truth
P.O. Box 2039
Liverpool, NY 13089
(315) 622-9010

Variable Media Link, Inc.
P.O. Box 884
Pleasant Valley, NY 12569
(914) 635-5244

W.A.I.F.
201 E. 28th Street
New York, NY 10016

New York State Bar Association
One Elk Street
Albany, NY 12207
(518) 463-3200

Adoption Attorneys

Aaron Britvan*
7600 Jericho Turnpike
Woodbury, NY 11797
(516) 433-1555
(516) 496-2222
fax (516) 496-3450

* Mr. Britvan has completed
more than 2,500 adoptions,
including more than 300
agency adoptions and about
500 international adoptions. He
has served as the chair of the
New York State Bar
Association Committee on
Adoption.

Anne Reynolds Copps
279 River Street
P.O. Box 1530
Troy, NY 12181
(518) 272-6565

Robin Fleischner
11 Riverside Drive, Suite 14 MW
New York, NY 10023
(212) 362-6945

Gregory A. Franklin
95 Allens Creek Road,
 Building 1, #104
Rochester, NY 14618
(716) 442-0540

Blanche Gelber
215 West 98th Street, Suite 7D
New York, NY 10025
(212) 866-9306

Laurie B. Goldheim
One Blue Hill Plaza
Pearl River, NY 10965
(914) 735-9650

Michael Goldstein*
62 Bowman Avenue
Rye Brook, NY 10573
(914) 939-1111
fax (914) 939-1111
 or
121 Derby Drive
Freehold, New Jersey 07728
(908) 866-0110

* Mr. Goldstein has conducted
over 1,000 independent
adoptions, 300 agency
adoptions, and fifteen
international adoptions.

Flory G. Herman
338 Harris Hill Road, #110
Williamsville, NY 14221
(716) 631-9971

Jane Iacobellis*
19 Highway Park Place
Rye, NY 10580
(914) 967-7763
fax (914) 967-7763

* Ms. Iacobellis has completed
about 100 independent
adoptions.

Carolyn Kalos
62 Bowman Avenue
Rye Brook, NY 10573
(914) 939-1111

Stephen Lewin
845 Third Avenue, Suite 1400
New York, NY 10022
(212) 759-2600

Frederick J. Magovern*
111 John Street, Suite 1509
New York, NY 10038
(212) 962-1450
ax (212) 385-0235

* Mr. Magovern has conducted
more than 100 independent
adoptions, and 1,000 agency
adoptions, as well as some
international adoptions.

Cynthia Peria Meckler
83 Blue Heron Court
Buffalo, NY 14051
(716) 688-1540

Christine Mesberg
28 Hilltop Road
Waccabuc, NY 10597
(914) 669-5401

Suzanne Nichols
1991 Broadway
New York, NY 10023
(212) 769-9000

Brendan C. O'Shea
11 N. Pearl Street
Albany, NY 12207
(518) 432-7511

Douglas H. Reiniger
630 Third Avenue
New York, NY 10017
(212) 972-5430

Lucille S. Rosenstock
4480 N. Osage Drive
Tucson, AZ 85718
(602) 529-1005

Benjamin Rosin
501 Fifth Avenue
New York, NY 10017
(212) 972-5430

Deborah Steincolor
One Blue Hill Plaza
P.O. Box 1706
Pearl River, NY 10965
(914) 735-9650

Joel Tenenbaum
89-91 Independence Mall
1601 Concord Mall
P.O. Box 7329
Wilmington, DE 19803
(302) 477-3200

Stephen Wise Tulin
350 Fifth Avenue, Suite 1229
New York, NY 10018
(212) 643-3737

Golda Zimmerman
430 E. Genesee Street, Suite 203
Syracuse, NY 13202
(315) 475-3322
fax (315) 475-7727

NEW YORK LAWS RELATED TO ADOPTION: QUESTIONS AND ANSWERS

In New York a birth mother must have separate representation from the adoptive parents; therefore, she must have her own attorney whose fees are paid by the adoptive parents.

Can an attorney serve as an intermediary?
No. Michael Goldstein, an attorney in Rye Brook, states that it is considered an illegal placement under Social Services Law. It does not matter if the attorney located the birth mother in or out of state.

Is advertising permitted?
Yes.

Who must consent to the adoption?
1. The birth mother
2. The birth father if the child is born or conceived in wedlock

When can consent be taken from birth mother (father), and how long after the consent is signed can it be revoked?
Consent cannot be signed until the child is born. Aaron Britvan, an attorney in Woddbury, explains that in a private placement in which the consent is not taken in court, a birth parent has up to forty-five days to revoke a consent. The parent must attempt to revoke the consent by notification to the court where the adoption proceedings takes place. If the attempt is timely, then it will open the door legally for the Court to conduct a "best interests" hearing to determine whether the child should remain with the adoptive couple or returned to the objecting birth parent. If consents are taken by an agency the birth parents have up to thirty days to revoke a consent. However, in an independent adoption, if a judge receives consent from the birth parents, their rights are terminated at that point and are irrevocable even if it is only a few days after placement.

The birth father can also sign an irrevocable consent before the birth.

What are the birth father's rights?
If the child is born in wedlock, the birth father has the same rights as the birth mother. If a child is born out of wedlock, and the birth father has maintained substantial and continuous contact with the child and has financially supported the child, then his consent is needed. If the birth father was not involved during the six months before placement and is named by the birth mother, he must receive a notice. He is then entitled to a "best interests" hearing if he contests the adoption. Aaron Britvan states that in New York State the best interestsof the child is paramount, and if the birth father has not shown the prerequisite concern for the child, he may not upset the adoption placement. It is not sufficient for him to suggest that he was not aware of the pregnancy or birth of the child.

What fees can adoptive parents pay?

In a private adoption, the adoptive parents must give the court a statement of all fees and expenses paid. (New York judges usually permit the adoptive parents to pay more living expenses than is generally permitted in other states.) The attorney must also give an affidavit of all fees received.

The adoptive parents' health insurer company must cover the baby's medical expenses as soon as he is born.

Where does the adoption hearing take place?

The hearing takes place in the Family Court or Surrogate court in the county where the adoptive parents reside or where the placement agency is located.

How are familial and step-parent adoptions different from nonbiological adoptions?

Legally, they are handled in the same way. In a step-parent adoption, if the noncustodial birth parent is unwilling to consent, then you need to be able to prove that they abandoned the child for at least six months before the adoption can proceed.

Can a nonresident finalize an adoption in this state?

Yes, if the child is born in the state and the adoptive parents are certified as approved parents by the court.

NORTH CAROLINA

State Adoption Specialist
Esther High
N.C. Department
  of Human Services
Division of Social Services
325 North Salisbury Street
Raleigh, NC 27603-5905
(919) 733-3801

Compact Administrator
Kevin FitzGerald, Director
N.C. Department
  of Human Services
Division of Social Services
325 North Salisbury Street
Raleigh, NC 27603

Deputy Compact Administrator
Elsie Roane
Child Welfare Standards
  Interstate Services Unit
Division of Social Services
325 North Salisbury Street
Raleigh, NC 27603
(919) 733-9464
fax (919) 733-7058

Direct all telephone calls
  and correspondence to:

Dawn Rochelle
Child Welfare Standards
  Interstate Services Unit
Division of Social Services

325 North Salisbury Street
Raleigh, NC 27603
(919) 733-3801

Office hours:
Monday-Friday
8:00 A.M.-5:00 P.M.
Eastern Time Zone

**State Adoption Exchange and
  Photo Listing**

Amelia Lance
North Carolina Adoption
  Resource Exchange
Division of Social Services
325 North Salisbury Street
Raleigh, NC 27603 - 5905
(919) 733-3801

Private Adoption Agencies

Another Choice for Black
  Children
713 Wall Street
Sanford, NC 27330
(919) 774-3534 or (800) 774-
  3534

Association for Guidance, Aid,
  Placement and Empathy
  (AGAPE)
302 College Road
Greensboro, NC 27410
(910) 855-7107

Bethany Christian Services, Inc.
P.O. Box 15569
Asheville, NC 28813-0569
(704) 274-7146

Caring for Children
P.O. Box 19113
Asheville, NC 28815
(704) 253-0241

Carolina Adoption Services, Inc.
106 E. Northwood Street, Suite 7
Greensboro, NC 27401
(910) 275-9660

Catholic Social Ministries of the
  Diocese of Raleigh, Inc.
400 Oberlin Road, Suite 350
Raleigh, NC 27605
(919) 832-0225

Catholic Social Services of the
  Diocese of Charlotte, Inc.
1524 East Morehead Street
P.O. Box 36776
Charlotte, NC 28236
(704) 343-9954

Children's Home Society of North
  Carolina, Inc.
740 Chestnut Street
P.O. Box 14608
Greensboro, NC 27415-4608
(910) 274-1538

Christian Adoption Services
624 Matthews-Mint Road,
Suite 134
Matthews, NC 28105
(704) 847-0038

Datz Foundation of North
  Carolina
875 Walnut Street, Suite 275
Cary, NC 27511
(919) 319-6635

Family Services, Inc.
610 Coliseum Drive
Winston-Salem, NC 27106-5393
(919) 722-8173

Gladney Center
1811 Sardis Road North,
  Suite 207
Charlotte, NC 28270
(704) 849-2003

International Adoption Society
3803B Computer Drive, Suite 201
Raleigh, NC 27609
(919) 510-9135

LDS Social Services
5624 Executive Center Drive,
  Suite 109
Charlotte, NC 28212-8832
(704) 535-2436

Lutheran Family Services
  in the Carolinas, Inc.
505 Oberlin Road
P.O. Box 12287
Raleigh, NC 27605
(919) 832-2620

**Adoptive Parent Support
Groups and Postadoption
Services**

Adoptive Families Heart to Heart
Attn.: Sandy and Mark Voigt
456 NC Hwy. 62 E
Greensboro, NC 27406
(919) 674-5024

Adoptive Families of Piedmont
Attn.: Mary Ann Bills
4125 Sewanee Drive
Winston-Salem, NC 27106
(910) 924-0074

Adoptive Parents Together
Attn.: Pegg Southerland
107 Glenwood Trail
Southern Pines, NC 28387

Capital Area Families
  for Adoption
Attn.: Pauline McNeill
24616 Thendara Way
Raleigh, NC 27612
(919) 571-8330

Carolina Adoptive Families
Attn.: Kristin Blank
3200 Mill Pond Road
Charlotte, NC 28226
(704) 598-9632

Coastal Hearts of Adoption
Attn.: Deborah Lillie
6002 McClean Drive
Emerald Isle, NC 28549
(919) 354-5826

Family Resources
Attn.: Joan and Bernard
  McNamara
1521 Foxhollow Road
Greensboro, NC 27410
(919) 852-5357

Iredell County Adoptive Families
Attn.: Debbie Haney
327 Shoreline Loop
Mooresville, NC 28115
(704) 664-6026
Mountain Area Adoptive Parent
  Group
Attn.: Nancy Gilligan
109 Robin Lane
Waynesville, NC 28786

THE LINK
(Adoption Consultants)
P.O. Box 103
Concord, NC 27402-3112
(888) 272-2229
(704) 792-2229

North Carolina Friends
  of Black Children
Attn.: Ruth Amerson
610 West Main Street
Sanford, NC 27330
(919) 774-4880

Rowan/Cabarrus Adoption
  Support Group
Attn.: Amy Sloop Miller
405 Arcadia Road
Chinagrove, NC 28023

Southern Piedmont Adoptive
  Families of America
Attn.: Sara Lynne and Rich
  Roettger

P.O. Box 221946
Charlotte, NC 28222
(704) 541-3614

Special Needs Adoption Parents
  Support Group
Attn.: Nan Poplin
1220 Onslow Drive
Greensboro, NC 27408
(919) 855-8006

SPICE & TIKA
Attn.: Lynn Beard
604 Rollingwood Drive
Greensboro, NC 27410
(919) 295-5385

Tri-Adopt
Attn.: Anne Nashold
P.O. Box 51331, Shannon Plaza
Durham, NC 27717-1331
(919) 286-2891

Triad Adoptive Parent Support
  Group and North American
  Council on Adoptable Children
  State Representative
Attn.: Liz and Jac Grimes
133 Penny Road
High Point, NC 27260
(910) 886-8230

Triangle Area Ours for a United
  Response
Attn.: Judith Geyer
6609 Chantilly Place
Bahama, NC 27503
(919) 471-9693

Western Carolina Ours for a
  United Response
Attn.: Paula Wells
29 Griffing Boulevard
Asheville, NC 28804

**Adopted Person and Birth
Relative Support Groups**

Adoptee Liberty Movement
  Association (ALMA)
P.O. Box 20351
Greenville, NC 27858
(919) 756-5777

Adoptees in Search of
  Enlightenment
365 W. Illinois Avenue
Southern Pines, NC 28387
(910) 695-0603

Adoption Information Exchange
8539 Monroe Road
Charlotte, NC 28212
(704) 532-6827

Adoption Information
Exchange/Adoption Search
Consultants
P.O. Box 1917
Matthews, NC 28106
(704) 537-5919

Birthmothers Easing the Hurt
Box 266
Dobson, NC 27017
(910) 386-4274

Carolina Adoption Triangle
Support
116 West Queen Street
Hillsborough, NC 27278
(919) 732-2751
Branches in Burlington and
Raleigh

Concerned United Birthparents
2906 Plantation Road
Charlotte, NC 28226

National Adoption Awareness
Convention
P.O. Box 2823
Chapel Hill, NC 27515-2823
(919) 967-5010

North Carolina Adoption
Connections
P.O. Box 4153
Chapel Hill, NC 27515
(919) 967-5010
Ashville: (704) 254-8248
Raleigh: (919) 876-85641

North Carolina Bar Association
P.O. Box 25908
Raleigh, NC 27611
(919) 828-4620
Referral Service
(919) 828-1054

Adoption Attorneys

Ellis Bragg
500 East Moorehead Street, Suite
210
Charlotte, NC 28202
(704) 334-0888

Phil Bottoms
Salisbury, NC
(704) 633-3344

Carol Brooke
P.O. Box 103
China Grove, NC 28023
(704) 857-6121

Randall Combs
P.O. Box 2
Kannapolis, NC 28082-0002
(704) 932-3167
fax (704) 932-9597

Donna Ambler Davis
143 West Franklin Street.
Suite 202
Chapel Hill, NC 27516
(919) 929-0386
James Early
1320 Westgate Center Drive
Winston-Salem, NC 27103
(919) 768-2546

Nancy Gaines
416 W. Kerr Street
Salisbury, NC 28144
(704) 633-1723

Sharon Jumper
1351 Moorehead Street, Suite 201
Charlotte, NC 28202
(704) 376-6527

Bob McLaughlin
122 N. Ellis St.
Salisbury, NC 28144
(704) 633-2020

W. David Thurman
801 E. Trade Street
Charlotte, NC 28202
(704) 377-4164

Brinton D. Wright
P.O. Box 3112
Greensboro, NC 27402-3112
(910) 373-1500
fax (910) 272-8258

NORTH CAROLINA LAWS RELATED TO ADOPTION: QUESTIONS AND ANSWERS

Can an attorney serve as an intermediary?

In a direct placement, a parent must personally select the prospective adoptive parent, but the parent may obtain assistance from another person or entity or an adoption facilitator in locating or evaluating a prospective adoptive parent. Information about the adoptive parent must be given to the birth parent by the adoptive parent or the adoptive parent's attorney. This information must include the home study, and may include additional information if requested by the birth parent. An intermediary is allowed as long as that person is not compensated for their services.

Is advertising permitted?

No. You may not post fliers either. Networking is limited to those you know.

Who must consent to the adoption?
1. The birth mother
2. The birth father, if he is married to the birth mother or has established paternity

When can consent be taken from birth mother (father), and how long after the consent is signed can it be revoked?
A consent to adopt an unborn child or one who is less than three months' old may be revoked within twenty-one days. A consent to the adoption of an older child may be revoked within seven days.

What are the birth father's rights?
If named, the birth father must consent to the adoption. If the birth father has not consented to the adoption and fails to respond to a notice of adoption proceedings within thirty days after being notified, his consent is not required.

If the birth father wants to contest the adoption of a child born out of wedlock, he must establish paternity by filing a petition for legitimization. Paternity can also be established if he has provided substantial financial support or consistent care to the child and mother.

What fees can adoptive parents pay?
Adoptive parents can pay for medical, traveling, and counseling services that are directly related to the adoption, as well as ordinary living expenses (for no longer than six weeks after delivery) and legal expenses during the pregnancy. An affidavit of all moneys paid in connection with the adoption must be presented to the court.

Where does the adoption hearing take place?
The adoption hearing takes place in the court of the county where the adoptive parents live, where the child lives, or where the child placement agency is located.

How are familial and step-parent adoptions different from nonbiological adoptions?
The child must have resided primarily with the stepparent and the legal parent for at least six months. The state residency and probationary period are waived in step-parent and grandparent adoptions. Grandparents' visitation rights are still in effect after the adoption. Grandparents may also seek visitation rights if it is in the child's best interest.

Can a nonresident finalize an adoption in this state?
No. Only those who have lived in North Carolina for at least six months can adopt.

NORTH DAKOTA

State Adoption Specialist
Linda Schell
North Dakota Department
   of Human Services
State Capitol Building
600 East Boulevard
Bismarck, ND 58505
(701) 328-4805

Compact Administrator
Donald L. Schmid, ACSW,
   Director
Children and Family Services
   division
North Dakota Department
   of Human Services
State Capitol Building-Judiciary
   Wing
600 East Boulevard
Bismarck, ND 58505
(701) 224-4811
fax (701) 224-2359

Direct all telephone calls and
   correspondence to:

Linda Schell, LCSW
Adoption Services
North Dakota Department
   of Human Services
State Capitol Building
600 East Boulevard
Bismarck, ND 58505
(701) 224-4805

Office hours:
Monday-Friday
8:00 A.M.-5:00 P.M.
Central Time Zone

**State Adoption Exchange
and Photo Listing**

Department of Human Services,
Children and Family Services
State Capitol Building
600 East Boulevard
Bismarck, ND 58505
(701) 328-2316

Private Adoption Agencies

Catholic Family Service
1223 S. 12th Street
Bismarck, ND 58504-6633
(701) 255-1793

Catholic Family Service
2537 South University
Fargo, ND 58103
(701) 235-4457

Catholic Family Service
505 University Avenue, Suite #1
Grand Forks, ND 58203
(701) 775-4196

Catholic Family Service
400 22nd Avenue, N.W.
Minot, ND 58701
(701) 852-2854

Christian Family Life Services
1202 12th Avenue North
Fargo, ND 58102
(701) 237-4473

LDS Social Services
P.O. Box 3100
Bismarck, ND 58502
(605) 342-3500 (Rapid City)

Lutheran Social Services
616 Capital Way
Bismarck, ND 58501
(701) 223-1510

Lutheran Social Services
211 S. 3rd Street
Grand Forks, ND 58201
(701) 772-7577

Lutheran Social Services
12 Main Street South, #204
Minot, ND 58701
(701) 838-7800

Lutheran Social Services
of North Dakota
1325 South 11th Street
P.O. Box 389
Fargo, ND 58107-0389
(701) 235-7341

New Horizons Foreign Adoption
Service
2823 Woodland Place
Bismarck, ND 58504
(701) 258-8650

Village Family Service Center
415 Avenue A East
Bismarck, ND 58501
(701) 255-1165

Village Family Service Center
1201 25th Street, South
P.O. Box 9859
Fargo, ND 58106-9859
(701) 235-6433

Village Family Service Center
Riverview Center
215 N. 3rd
Grand Forks, ND 58201
(701) 746-8062

Village Family Service Center
308 2nd Avenue S.W.
Minot, ND 58701
(701) 852-3328

Village Family Service Center
P.O. Box 1029
Williston, ND 58801
(701) 774-3328

**Adoptive Parent Support
Groups
and Postadoption Services**

Adoption Forum
Attn.: Warren Granfor
1609 Porter Avenue
Bismarck, ND 58501
(701) 223-5055

Adoption in Our Heart
Attn.: Jan Kearns
1341 1st Street N.
Fargo, ND 58102-2720
(701) 298-3052

Adults Adopting Special Kids
Lutheran Social Services
of North Dakota (coordinating
agency)
Attn.: Kathy Thoreson
P.O. Box 389
Fargo, ND 58107-0389
(701) 237-0610

**Adopted Person and Birth
Relative Support Groups**

Adoptee Liberty Movement
Association (ALMA)
P.O. Box 802
Fargo, ND 58107

Adoption Search/Disclosure
ND Department of Human
Services
600 East Boulevard
Bismarck, ND 58505
(701) 328-4805

Lutheran Social Services
of North Dakota
P.O. Box 389
Fargo, ND 58107-0389
(701) 235-7341

**State Bar Association of North
Dakota**
515 1/2 East Broadway, Suite 101
Bismarck, ND 58502
(701) 255-1404

Adoption Attorneys

Gregg Runge
418 East Rosser Avenue,
Suite 102
Bismarck, ND 58501
(701) 222-1808

Mel Webster
418 East Rosser Avenue,
Suite 115
Bismarck, ND 58501
(701) 255-3523

NORTH DAKOTA LAWS RELATED TO ADOPTION: QUESTIONS AND ANSWERS

According to the staff at the State Adoption Specialist's office, if you adopt a child in a state in which independent adoption is legal, to finalize the adoption there, you must use an agency in that state to meet North Dakota's ICPC regulations. However, check with an attorney to confirm this information, as North Dakota does use The Uniform Adoption Act as its adoption statute, which does not require you to use an agency.

Can an attorney serve as an intermediary?
No.

Is advertising permitted?
No.

Who must consent to the adoption?
Both birth parents

When can consent be taken from birth mother (father), and how long after the consent is signed can it be revoked?
Consent can be withdrawn before the adoption decree is final if it is in the child's best interests.

What are the birth father's rights?
He must give consent if he receives the child into his home and claims the child as his biological child, or if he acknowledges paternity in a document filed with the Division of Vital Statistics. Consent is not needed from either birth parent if it can be shown that the child to be adopted has been abandoned by a birth parent; or that a birth parent has not communicated with or supported the child for at least one year. Also, consent is not necessary if the birth parent is unavailable, absent with no explanation, incapable, or has failed to establish a substantial relationship with the child. A court that finds these conditions will terminate the birth parent's parental rights.

What fees can adoptive parents pay?
A full accounting must be given to the court of all fees paid for medical care (both pre- and postnatal care of the birth mother and child) as well as placement and agency fees.

Where does the adoption hearing take place?
The adoption hearing takes place in the court of the county where the adoptive parents live or the child lives, or where the child placement agency is located.

How are familial and step-parent adoptions different from nonbiological adoptions?
In a step-parent adoption, the court does not need an accounting of expenses.

Can a nonresident finalize an adoption in this state?
Yes.

OHIO

State Adoption Specialist
Rhonda Abban
Ohio Department
    of Human Services
65 East Broad Street, 5th Floor
Columbus, OH 43266-0423
(614) 466-9274

Compact Administrator
Terry Wallace, Director
Ohio Department
    of Human Services
30 East Broad Street, 32nd Floor
Columbus, OH 43266-0423

Deputy Compact Administrator
Ohio Department
    of Human Services
ICPC Unit
65 E. State Street, 5th Floor
Columbus, OH 43215
(614) 466-8520
fax (614) 466-0164

Direct all telephone calls and
    correspondence to the Deputy
    Compact Administrator.

Office hours:
Monday-Friday
8:00 A.M.-5:00 P.M.
Eastern Time Zone

**State Adoption Exchange
and Photo Listing**

Wynn Hollingshead
Ohio Adoption Photo Listing
    (OAPL)
Bureau of Children Services
Adoption Services Section
65 East State Street, 5th Floor
Columbus, OH 43266-0423
(614) 466-9274

Southwest Ohio Adoption
    Exchange
Department of Human Services
628 Sycamore Street
Cincinnati, OH 45202
(513) 632-6366

Private Adoption Agencies

Adopt a Special Kid (AASK)
    of the Midwest
1025 N. Reynolds Road
Toledo, OH 43615-4753
(419) 534-3350

Adoption Circle
2500 E. Main Street, Suite 103
Columbus, OH 43215
(614) 237-7222

Agape for Youth, Inc.
914 Senate Drive
Dayton, OH 45459
(513) 439-4406

Bair Foundation
5249 Belmont Avenue
Youngstown, OH 44505-1023
(216) 545-0435

Baptist Children's Home
    and Family Ministries, Inc.
1934 South Limestone Street
Springfield, OH 45505
(513) 322-0006

Beacon Agency
743 S. Byrne Road
Toledo, OH 43690
(419) 382-3572

Beech Acres
6881 Beechmont Avenue
Cincinnati, OH 45230
(513) 231-6630

Beech Brook/Spaulding
    for Children
3737 Lander Road
Pepper Pike, OH 44124
(216) 831-2255

Berea Children's Home
202 East Bagley Road
Berea, OH 44017
(216) 234-2006

Catholic Community Services
625 Cleveland Avenue, N.W.
Canton, OH 44702
(216) 455-0374

Catholic Community Services,
    Inc., of Trumbull County
175 Laird Avenue, N.E., 3rd Flr.
Warren, OH 44483
(216) 369-4254

Catholic Service Bureau
    of Lake County
544 Ameritrust Building
8 North State Street
Painesville, OH 44077
(216) 946-7264

Catholic Service League
    of Ashtabula County
4436 Main Avenue
Ashtabula, OH 44004
(216) 992-2121

Catholic Service League
    of Summit County
640 North Main Street
Akron, OH 44310
(216) 762-7481

Catholic Service League
    of Western Stark County, Inc.
1807 Lincoln Way, East
Massillon, OH 44646
(216) 833-8516

Catholic Service League
    of Youngstown, Inc.
4495 Market Street
Youngstown, OH 44512
(216) 788-8726

Catholic Social Services
    of Lorain County
2136 North Ridge Road
Elyria, OH 44035
(216) 277-7228

Catholic Social Service
    of Southwest Ohio
100 East Eighth Street
Cincinnati, OH 45505
(513) 241-7745

Catholic Social Service
    of Cuyahoga County
7800 Detroit Avenue
Cleveland, OH 44102
(216) 687-0000

Catholic Social Services
140 N. 5th Street
Hamilton, OH 45011
(513) 863-6129

Catholic Social Services
641 E. High Street
Springfield, OH 45505
(513) 325-8715

Catholic Social Services, Inc.
197 East Gay Street
Columbus, OH 43215
(614) 221-5891

Catholic Social Services
    of the Miami Valley
922 West Riverview Avenue
Dayton, OH 45407
(513) 223-7217

Catholic Social Services of Toledo
1933 Spielbusch Avenue
Toledo, OH 43624
(419) 244-6711

Children's Home
of Cincinnati, Ohio
5050 Madison Road
Cincinnati, OH 45227
(513) 272-2800

Children's Services
1001 Euclid Road, 3rd Floor
Cleveland, OH 44115
(216) 781-2043

Clearcreek Valley of Ohio
94 S. Paint Street
Chillicothe, OH 45601

Cooper Care, Inc.
5820 Seybold Road
Brookville, OH 45309
(513) 837-8029

European Adoption Consultants
9800 Boston Road
North Royalton, OH 44133
(216) 237-3554

Family Adoption Consultant
Macedonia Professional Building
8536 Crow Drive
Macedonia, OH 44056
(216) 468-0673

Family and Community Services,
Inc., of Catholic Charities,
Columbiana County
966 1/2 North Market Street
P.O. Box 413
Lisbon, OH 44432
(216) 424-9509

Family and Community Services
of Catholic Charities
302 North Depeyster Street
Kent, OH 44240
(216) 678-3911

Family Counseling and Crittenton
Services
1414 E. Broad Street
Columbus, OH 43205
(614) 221-7608

Family Counseling and Crittenton
Services
185 South Fifth Street
Columbus, OH 43215
(614) 221-7608

Family Counseling Services
of Central Stark County
101 Cleveland Avenue, N.W.
Canton, OH 44702
(216) 454-7066

Family Counseling Services of
Western Stark County, Inc.
325 3rd Street SE
Massillon, OH 44646-6703
(216) 832-5043

Family Resources Centers
DBA Focas Network
799 S. Main Street
Lima, OH 45804
(419) 222-1168

Family Service Agency
535 Marmion Avenue
Youngstown, OH 45502
(216) 782-5664

Family Service Association
P.O. Box 1027
Steubenville, OH 43952
(614) 283-4763

Family Service Association
1704 North Road, S.E.
Heaton Square
Warren, OH 44484
(216) 856-2907

Family Services of Summit
County
212 East Exchange Street
Akron, OH 44304
(216) 376-9494

Gentle Care Adoption
Service, Inc.
17 Brickel Street
Columbus, OH 43215
(614) 469-0007

Hannah Neil Center for Children
301 Obetz Road
Columbus, OH 43207
(614) 491-5784

HARAMBEE,
Services for Black Families
11811 Shaker Boulevard,
Suite 420
Cleveland, OH 44120
(216) 791-2229

Helping Hands
for Black Adoption
226 Middle Avenue
Elyria, OH 44035

Jewish Children's Bureau
22001 Fairmount Boulevard
Shaker Heights, OH 44118
(216) 932-2800

Jewish Family and Children's
Services of the Youngstown
Area Jewish Federation
505 Gypsy Lane
Youngstown, OH 44501
(216) 746-3251

Jewish Family Service
83 N. Miller Road, Suite 202
Akron, OH 44333
(216) 867-3388

Jewish Family Service
Adoption Connection
1710 Section Road
Cincinnati, OH 45237
(513) 351-3680

Jewish Family Service
2831 East Main Street
Columbus, OH 43209
(614) 231-1890

Jewish Family Service
4501 Denlinger Road
Dayton, OH 45426
(513) 854-2944

Jewish Family Service of Toledo
6525 Sylvania Avenue
Sylvania, OH 43560
(419) 885-2561

KARE, Inc.
(Kids Are Really Essential)
3453 W. Siebenthaler
Dayton, OH 45406
(513) 275-5715

LDS Social Services
4431 Marketing Place
P.O. Box 367
Groveport, OH 43125
(614) 836-2466

Lutheran Children's Aid
and Family Services
4100 Franklin Boulevard
Cleveland, OH 44113
(216) 281-2500

Lutheran Social Services
11370 Springfield Pike
Cincinnati, OH 45246
(513) 326-5430

Lutheran Social Services
74 W. Main Street
Springfield, OH 45502
(513) 325-2898

Lutheran Social Services
of Central Ohio
57 East Main Street
Columbus, OH 43215
(614) 228-5209

Lutheran Social Service
of the Miami Valley
1563 E. Dorothy Lane
Dayton, OH 45429
(513) 643-2227

Lutheran Social Services
of Northwestern Ohio, Inc.
2149 Collingwood Boulevard
Toledo, OH 43620
(419) 243-9178

Mid-Western Children's Home
4581 Long Spurling Road
P.O. Box 48
Pleasant Plain, OH 45162
(513) 877-2141

New Start Foundation
119 Main Street
Chardon, OH 44024

Northeast Ohio Adoption
Services
8031 East Market Street
Warren, OH 44484
(216) 856-5582

NWOARE/Ottawa CDHS
8444 W. State Route 163
Oak Harbor, OH 43449
(419) 898-3688

Ohio Human Society
2300 Reading Road
Cincinnati, OH 45202

Ohio Youth Advocate Program,
Inc.
3780 Ridge Mill Drive, #100
Hilliard, OH 43026-9231
(614) 221-0895

Regional Family Counseling, Inc.
635 West Spring Street
Lima, OH 45805
(419) 225-1040

St. Joseph's Children's Treatment
Center
650 St. Paul Avenue
Dayton, OH 45410
(513) 275-0762

SEOARE/Athens County CSB
P.O. Box 1046
Athens, OH 45701
(614) 592-3061

Southern Ohio Pregnancy Center
P.O. Box 4
Hillsboro, OH 45133
(513) 393-2990

SWOARE/Hamilton County
DHS
628 Sycamore Street
Cincinnati, OH 45202
(513) 946-1000

United Methodist Children's
Home
West Ohio Conference
of the United Methodist
Church
1045 North High Street
Worthington, OH 43085
(614) 885-5020

Youth Engaged for Success
3930 Salem Avenue
Dayton, OH 45406

**Adoptive Parent Support
Groups and Postadoption
Services**

Adopt a Special Kid (AASK)
of Ohio
Attn.: Tom Isabel
340 Bank Street
Painesville, OH 44077
(216) 352-3780

Adopt A Special Kid (AASK)
Parent Group
AASK Field Representative
1025 N. Reynolds Road
Toledo, OH 43615
(419) 534-3350

Adopting Older Kids
Attn.: Rita and George Rich
7626 Harshmanville Road
Huber Heights, OH 45424
(513) 236-8788

Adoption Support Group
Attn.: Aileen Maslinski
4902 Mapleview Drive
Vermillion, OH 44089
(216) 967-5995

Adoptive Families of Greater
Cincinnati
Attn.: Peggy Schramm
4 Revel Court
Cincinnati, OH 45217
(513) 821-6392

Adoptive Families Support
Association
Attn.: John Seavers
Box 91247
Cleveland, OH 44101
(216) 491-4638

Adoptive and Foster Parents
Together
Attn.: David and Julianna
Scheaffer
190 Jeanne Drive
Springboro, OH 45066
(513) 748-9299

Adoptive Parent Support Group
Attn.: Linda Wilburn
2272 Harrisburg Pike
Grove City, OH 43123
(614) 871-1164

Adoptive Parents Support
Organization
Attn.: Jeff and Lynn Stacy
2638 Ridgecliffe Avenue
Cincinnati, OH 45212-1324
(513) 631-2883

Adoptive Parents Together
Attn.: Erika Gross
P.O. Box 112
Sandyville, OH 44671

Ashtabula County Adoptive
Parent Support Group
Attn.: Denise Smith
P.O. Box 458
Ashtabula, OH 44004
(216) 998-1811

Athens County Children
Foster Parent Group
Attn.: Jackie Fokes
14 Stoneybrook Drive
P.O. Box 1046
Athens, OH 45701
(614) 592-3061

Attachment Disorders Parents
Network
Attn.: Marli Bonner
P.O. Box 176
Cortland, OH 44410

Black Adoption Recruitment
Committee
1882 Nason Avenue
Columbus, OH 43208
(614) 228-5209

Black Adoptive Parent Outreach
Attn.: Carolyn Rucker
1564 Thruston
Akron, OH 44320

Children/Teen Adoption Support
Group
c/o Lucas County Children's
Services
Attn.: Laura Linthicum
2500 River Road
Maumee, OH 43537
(419) 891-3495

Cincinnati Multiracial Alliance
Attn.: Barb Slavinski
P.O. Box 17163
St. Bernard, OH 45217
(513) 281-7071

Clearcreek Valley of Ohio
Adoptive Parent Group
Attn.: Ralph and Wilma Mets
P.O. Box 338
Amanda, OH 43102-0338
(614) 969-4475

Comprehensive Psychological and
Psychiatric Services
1660 N.W. Professional Plaza
Columbus, OH 43220
(614) 442-0664

Concern for Children, Inc.
Attn.: Lynne Berkley
10440 Hawke Road
Columbia Station, OH 44028
(216) 748-2506

Connections
c/o Jewish Family Services
Attn.: Virginia Salander
6525 Sylvania Avenue
Toledo, OH 43560
(419) 885-2561

Dayton Area Minority Adoptive
Parents, Inc. and North
American Council
on Adoptable Children
State Representative

Attn.: Raymond Moore
191 Coddington Avenue
Xenia, OH 45385
(513) 372-4720

Down Syndrome Association
of Cincinnati
Attn.: David and Robin Steele
5741 Davey Avenue
Cincinnati, OH 45224
(513) 542-3286

Families Forever
Attn.: Denise Renollet
15903 Road133
Cecil, OH 45821
(419) 399-2134

Families Through Adoption
Attn.: Mary Ellen Pyke
Box 2521
Akron, OH 44309
(216) 922-0987

Families Thru Adoption
Attn.: Debbie Bibart
426 Goosepond Road
Newark, OH 43055-3137
(614) 745-1427

Families thru World Adoption
Attn.: Donna Morris
2933 Lower Bellbrook Road
Spring Valley, OH 45370

Families United by Adoption
Attn.: Linda and Donald James
2112 Sherwood Forest Drive
Miamisburg, OH 45342
(513) 866-1337

Families United
for Adoption, Inc.
Attn.: Colleen A. Roberts
P.O. Box 82
Swanton, OH 43558
(419) 825-1308

Family Defense Fund
Attn.: Eleanor Green
702 South Main Street
Ada, OH 45810

Foreign Adoptive Children
Eastern Suburbs
Attn.: Tony and Kate Strazisar
11875 Laurel Road
Chesterland, OH 44026
(216) 729-2535

Foster Parent Association
Attn.: Brenda and Gale Schaile
8729 Peter Hoover Road
New Albany, OH 43054
(614) 855-9785

Friends Through Intercultural
Adoption
Attn.: Melissa Sweeney
4113 Cedarbluff Circle
Dayton, OH 45415
(513) 890-3600

Geauga County Adoptive Family
Group
Attn.: Mary Klepac
303 North Hambden
Chardon, OH 44024
(216) 285-3274

Group of Black Adoptive Parents
Attn.: Robert Simpson
1055 Grayview Court
Cincinnati, OH 45224
(513) 541-4166

Harambee Adoption Support
Group
Attn.: Dederick Barer
11811 Shaker Boulevard,
Suite 420
Cleveland, OH 44120
(216) 791-2229

Korean Family Connection
Attn.: Diane Gersten
5067 Lakeside Drive
Mason, OH 45040-1767
(513) 459-8266

Lake County Catholic Services
Attn.: Beth Brindo
8 North State Street, Suite 455
Painesville, OH 44077
(216) 946-7264

Limiar: USA
Attn.: Nancy Cameron
2373 Brunswick Lane
Hudson, OH 44236
(216) 653-8129

New Roots Adoption Support
Group
P.O. Box 14953
Columbus, OH 43214
(614) 470-0846

Northeast Ohio Adoption
Services
8029 East Market Street
Warren, OH 44484-2229
(216) 856-5582

Ohio Family Care Association
Attn.: Dot Erickson
2931 Indianola Avenue
Columbus, OH 43202
(614) 299-9261 or 262-1297

Open Adoption Support Group
Attn.: Eric and Debbie Sykes
541 Brandywynne Court
Dayton, OH 45406
(513) 275-9628

Parenthesis Adopted Adolescent
  Program
P.O. Box 02265
Columbus, OH 43202
(614) 236-2211

Parenthesis Adoptive Parents'
  Support Organization
Attn.: Karen Boyd
P.O. Box 02265
Columbus, OH 43202
(614) 236-2211

Parents of Adopted Children
Attn.: Mariann Weeks
773 Andover Road
Mansfield, OH 44907-2236
(419) 756-5301

Parents Supporting Parents
Attn.: Jane Nicol
19306 Boerger Road
Marysville, OH 43040
(513) 349-7105

Project Orphans Abroad
Attn.: Kathy Berman
P.O. Box 91247
Cleveland, OH 44101
(216) 526-3618

Rainbow Connection
Attn.: Sue Gerwig
1065 CR 1600 Rte. 7
Ashland, OH 44805
(419) 281-3837

Rainbow Families of Toledo
Attn.: Nancy Shanks
1920 South Shore Boulevard
Oregon, OH 43618
(419) 693-9259

Single Adoptive Parents
Attn.: Peggy Sorenson
1185 Franklin Avenue
Columbus, OH 43205
(614) 253-4318

Southeast Ohio Adoptive Family
  Support Group
Box 1046
Athens, OH 45701
(614) 592-3061

Stars of David
Attn.: Paula Reshotko
26001 South Woodland
Beachwood, OH 44122
(216) 831-0700, ext. 375

Trumbull County Foster Parent
  Association
Attn.: Melanie Jones
2282 Reeves Road, N.E.
Warren, OH 44483
(216) 372-2010

Western Reserve Adoptive
  Parents
Attn.: Candace Catheline
2787 Citadel, N.E.
Warren, OH 44483
(216) 372-2060

**Adopted Person and Birth
Relative Support Groups**

Adoptees (Irish-Born Americans)
  Search
c/o Catherine O'Dea
18460 Bishop Lane
Strongville, OH 44136
(216) 238-1004

Adoptees Search Rights
  Association
P.O. Box 8713
Toledo, OH 43613
(419) 691-3463 or 474-5430

Adoption Connection
4495 Market Street
Youngstown, OH 44512
(216) 792-2154

Adoption Network Cleveland
291 E. 222nd Street, Room 229
Cleveland, OH 44123-1751
(216) 261-1511

Adoption Option
P.O. Box 429327
Cincinnati, OH 45242
(513) 793-7268

Adoption Triad
5900 S.O.M. Center Road, #273
Cleveland, OH 44094
(216) 943-2118

Adoption Triad Support
980 Main Street
Wellsville, OH 43968
(216) 532-4990

Adoption Triangle Unity
4144 Packard Road
Toledo, OH 43613
(419) 244-7072

Aftermath
2547 Loris
W. Carollton, OH 45449
(513) 848-2668

Akron Adoption Support Group
7385 Herrick Park Drive
Hudson, OH 44236
(216) 656-4153

ALARM/Sunshine Reunions
1175 Virginia Avenue
Akron, OH 44306
(216) 773-4691

Birthmothers Support Group
856 Pine Needles Drive
Centerville, OH 45458
(513) 436-0593

Birthparent Support
3423 Bluerock Road
Cincinnati, OH 45239

Birthright
6779 Manchester Road
Clinton, OH 44216

Chosen Children
311 Springbrook Pl.
Dayton, OH 45405
(513) 274-8017

Circle of Love
409 W. Machanic Street
Wapakoneta, OH 45895-1050
(419) 738-8862

Concerned United Birthparents
6340 Aspen Way
Cincinnati, OH 45224
(513) 761-3894

Concerned United Birthparents
P.O. Box 39185
Cincinnati, OH 45239
(513) 741-4536

Concerned United Birthparents
10040 Carlisle Park
Germantown, OH 45327

The Complete Adoption Book

Concerned United Birthparents
Attn.: Lisa Dinges
6704 Inglewood
Holland, OH 43528
(419) 865-9604

Concerned United Birthparents
2544 Bonnie Lane
Maumee, OH 43537

Concerned United Birthparents
240 South Fulton
Wauseon, OH 43567

Full Circle
318 Albright Drive
Loveland, OH 45140
(513) 683-7923

Insight to the Adoption Triad
P.O. Box 14217
Columbus, OH 43214
(614) 267-9311

Lost and Found
P.O. Box 1033
Cuyahoga Falls, OH 44223-0033

Mum's the Word
381 Bartley Avenue
Mansfield, OH 44903
(419) 524-0564

Reconnections
Attn.: Marjalie Schaaf
3782 Skyline Drive
Beavercreek, OH 45432
(513) 426-0646

Reunite
P.O. Box 694
Reynoldsburg, OH 43068
(614) 861-2584

Southeastern Ohio Searchers
(S.O.S.)
4 Cook Drive
Athens, OH 45701
(614) 592-1070

Sunshine Reunions
1175 Virginia Avenue
Akron, OH 44306
(216) 773-4691

Support Adoption Triad
P.O. Box 723
Stryker, OH 43557-0723
(419) 682-1808

Support for Birthparents
1983 Sitterly Road
Canal Winchester, OH
43110-9522
(614) 833-1647

Swirls
132 East South Street
Fostoria, OH 44830
(419) 435-0325

Ohio State Bar Association
P.O. Box 6562
Columbus, OH 43216
(614) 487-2050

Adoption Attorneys

James Albers*
88 North Fifth Street
Columbus, OH c43215
(614) 464-4414
(614) 464-0604

* Mr. Albers has completed
  about 300 independent
  adoptions, 1,000 agency
  adoptions, and fifty
  international adoptions.

Margaret L. Blackmore
536 South High Street
Columbus, OH 43215

Susan G. Eisenman
338 South High Street
Columbus, OH 43215
(614) 222-0540

Ellen Essig
105 E. 4th Street, #900
Cincinnati, OH 45202
(513) 721-5151

Carolyn M. Franke*
3411 Michigan Avenue
Cincinnati, OH 45208

* Ms. Franke completed more
  than 300 independent
  adoptions.

David Garretson
110 Old Street
Monroe, OH 45050
(513) 534-7334

Jerry M. Johnson
400 W. North Street
Lima, OH 45801
(419) 222-1040

Mary E. Smith
711 Adams Street
Toledo, OH 43624
(419) 243-6281

James Edwin Swaim*
Flanagan, Lieberman,
   Hoffman & Swaim
318 West Fourth Street
Dayton, OH 45402
(513) 223-5200
fax (513) 223-3335

* Mr. Swaim has conducted
  about 500 independent and
  1,000 agency and step-parent
  adoptions, as well as about fifty
  international adoptions.

Attorney fees for an adoption in
this state are about $3,500.

OHIO LAWS RELATED TO ADOPTION: QUESTIONS AND ANSWERS

Can an attorney serve as an intermediary?
Yes.

Is advertising permitted?
No. If a prospective adoptive parent does advertise, the Department of Human Services will
contact you and ask you not to do so, although they will not prosecute. It is recommended

that you advertise instead in newspapers along the Pennsylvania and West Virginia borders, as these publications are often available in Ohio.

Who must consent to the adoption?
1. The birth mother
2. The birth father, if child was conceived or born while he was married to the birth mother, or if he claims to be the father and establishes a relationship with the child before placement, or if he has acknowledged the child in writing before placement, signed the birth certificate, or filed an objection to the adoption before the placement

When can consent be taken from birth mother (father), and how long after the consent is signed can it be revoked?
Consent can be taken seventy-two hours after the child's birth and is irrevocable unless the birth parents attempt to withdraw before the final adoption decree; any such withdrawal will be successful only if the court finds it is in the child's best interest. An adoption cannot be finalized until the child has lived in the adoptive parents' home for at least six months.

What are the birth father's rights?
If the birth father has abandoned the birth mother during the pregnancy or if he has failed to provide for the child, his consent is not required. If after thirty days of the child's placement, he does not file a paternity case or an objection to the adoption, his parental rights are terminated. As with all birth fathers, he must receive notice of the adoption proceedings.

What fees can adoptive parents pay?
Only medical and legal expenses and agency fees are permitted. The adoptive parents must submit a statement to the court of all fees and expenses paid.

Where does the adoption hearing take place?
The adoption hearing takes place in the court of the county where the adoptive parents live, where the child was born, where the birth parents live, or where the placement agency is located.

How are familial and step-parent adoptions different from nonbiological adoptions?
If a child is adopted by a step-parent, this does not curtail the court's power to award visitation rights to grandparents. A home study is not required in a step-parent or grandparent adoption.

Can a nonresident finalize an adoption in this state?
Yes.

OKLAHOMA

State Adoption Specialist
Jane Morgan
Oklahoma Department of Human
  Services
P.O. Box 25352
Oklahoma City, OK 73125
(405) 521-2475

Compact Administrator
Benjamin Demps
Oklahoma Department of Human
  Services
P.O. Box 25352
Oklahoma City, OK 73125
(405) 521-3646

Deputy Compact Administrator
Mike Swepston
Oklahoma Department of Human
  Services
Division of Children and Youth
  Services
P.O. Box 25352
Oklahoma City, OK 73125
(405) 521-4077

Direct all telephone calls and
correspondence to:

Boston Anderson
Oklahoma Department of Human
    Services
Division of Children and Youth
    Services
P.O. Box 25352
Oklahoma City, OK 73125
(405) 521-4375
fax (405) 521-6684

Office hours:
Monday-Friday
8:00 A.M.-5:00 P.M.
Central Time Zone

Private Adoption Agencies

Adoption Affiliate
6136 East 32nd Place
Tulsa, OK 74135
(918) 665-6400

Adoption Center of Northeastern
    Oklahoma
121 South Creek
Bartlesville, OK 74003
(405) 521-2475

Appletree
Box 52697
Tulsa, OK 74152
(918) 747-9998

Baptist Children's Home
16301 South Western
Oklahoma City, OK 73170
(405) 691-7781
(918) 272-2233 (Owasso)

Baptist General Convention
3800 North May Avenue
Oklahoma City, OK 73112
(405) 942-3800

Bethany Adoption Service
3940 North College
Bethany, OK 73008
(918) 789-5423

Catholic Charities
1501 NW Classen Boulevard
Oklahoma City, OK 73106
(405) 523-3000

Catholic Charities
P.O. Box 6429
Tulsa, OK 74106
(918) 585-8167

Chosen Child Adoption Agency
P.O. Box 55424
Tulsa, OK 74155-5424
(918) 298-0082

Cradle
7901 Terrace Hill Boulevard
Lawton, OK 73105
(405) 355-1730

Deaconess Home
5401 North Portland
Oklahoma City, OK 73112
(405) 942-5001

Dillon International, Inc.
7615 East 63rd Place South
Tulsa, OK 74133
(918) 250-1561

Edna Gladney Center
2300 Hemphill
Fort Worth, TX 76110
(817) 926-3304

Hannah's Prayer Adoption
    Agency
2651 East 21st, Suite 409
Tulsa, OK 74114
(918) 743-5926

LDS Social Services
4500 S. Garnett, Suite 425
Tulsa, OK 74146-5201
(918) 665-3090

Lutheran Social Services
3000 United Founders Boulevard,
    #141
Oklahoma City, OK 73112-4279
(405) 848-1733

Lutheran Social Services of Tulsa
1244 South Utica
Tulsa, OK 74104
(918) 582-0910

Metrocenter for Family Ministries
4500 East 2nd
P.O. Box 2380
Edmond, OK 73083
(405) 359-1400

Project Adopt (Neighborhood
    Services Organization)
3000 United Founders Boulevard,
    #141
Oklahoma City, OK 73112
(405) 848-0592

Small Miracles International
7430 S.E. 15th Street, Suite 204
Midwest City, OK 73110
(405) 732-7295

**Adoptive Parent Support
Groups and Postadoption
Services**

Adopt A Special Kid, Oklahoma
    Field Representative
448 Claremont
Norman, OK 73068
(405) 364-4956

Adopt A Special Kid, Oklahoma
    Field Representative
3517 N.W. 66th
Oklahoma City, OK 73116

Adopt A Special Kid of
    Oklahoma (AASK OK) and
    North American Council on
    Adoptable Children State
    Representative
Attn.: Rita Laws
5150 North Harrah Road
Harrah, OK 73045
(405) 454-2913

Adoptive Families Support
    Organization
Attn.: Judy Smith
2009 West Dena Drive
Edmond, OK 73034
(405) 359-0812

Adoptive Parents of Central
    Oklahoma
Attn.: Lonna Yeary
1237 Mountain Brook Drive
Norman, OK 73072-3446
(405) 364-8488

Adoptive Parents of Northeast
    Oklahoma
Attn.: Vince and Karen Griffin
2939 South 95th East Avenue
Tulsa, OK 74129
(918) 665-7778

Adoptive Parents Support Group
Meadowlake Hospital
Enid, OK
(800) 522-1366

Attachment Network
Attn.: Kathy Miller
P.O. Box 532
Broken Arrow, OK 74013
(918) 251-7781

Chickasha Support Group
Attn.: Vicki Streber, DHS
217 North 3rd
Chickasha, OK 73018
(405) 224-2733

Citizen Band Potawatomi Tribe
Attn.: Rick Short
1901 South Gordon Cooper Drive
Shawnee, OK 74801
(405) 275-3121

Concerned Families Reaching
Out
Attn.: Lola Bivens
615 East First Street
Watonga, OK 73772
(405) 623-8622

Cradle of Lawton
Attn.: Jan Howenstine
902 N.W. Kingswood Road
Lawton, OK 73505
(405) 536-2478

Families and Friends of Southeast
Oklahoma
Attn.: Joyce K. Meddock
P.O. Box 188
Broken Bow, OK 74728
(405) 536-2478

Families by Choice
Attn.: Connie Dennis
P.O. Box 879
Apache, OK 73006
(405) 588-3348

Families Helping Families
Attn.: Betty Stout
Route 1, Box 58
Mead, OK 73449
(405) 920-0188

Lake County Adoptive Families
Attn.: Patti Smith
614 "Q" Street, S.W.
Ardmore, OK 73401
(405) 223-1037

North Central Oklahoma New
Beginnings in Adoption
Attn.: Sharon Stephens
Route 5, Box 740
Ponca City, OK 74601
(405) 762-7213

Northwest Aware
Attn.: Jeanne Weber
Route 1, Box 325
Sharon, OK 73857
(405) 256-8741

Oklahoma Adoption Support
Association
5721 South Cedar
Broken Arrow, OK 74011
(918) 455-7771

Oklahoma Council on Adoptable
Children and North American
Council on Adaptable Children
State Representative
Attn.: Dwe Williams
2609 N.W. 38th Street
Oklahoma City, OK 73112
(405) 942-0810

Parents of Unattached Kids
Tulsa, OK
(918) 272-6250

Siblings Support Group
Ardmore, OK
(405) 226-1838

Southeast Oklahoma Adoptive
Parent Society
Attn.: Warren and Laverda
Johnson
Route 1, Box 815
Antlers, OK 74523
(405) 298-3995

Urban League Support Group
Oklahoma City, OK
(405) 424-5243

**Adopted Person and Birth
Relative Support Groups**

Adoptee Liberty Movement
Association (ALMA)
P.O. Box 1421
Edmond, OK 73083-1421

Adoptees As Adults
7908 Hemingford Court, #A
Oklahoma City, OK 73120

Adoption Tree of Support
3703 S. Nogales Avenue
Tulsa, OK 74107
(918) 445-1493

ALARM Network
909 Bell Avenue
Lawton, OK 73507
(405) 355-5535

AR Adoption Connections
Rt.1, Box 54
Roland, OK 74954
(918) 427-0453

Family Tree
3500 W. Robinson Street, #102
Norman, OK 73072
(405) 360-8134

Oklahoma Adoption Triad
Box 471008
Tulsa, OK 74147
(918) 254-1014

Shared Heartbeats
P.O. Box 12125
Oklahoma City, OK 73157
(405) 943-4500

Shepherds Heart
2401 Slagle Road
Newalla, OK 74857
(405) 391-4308

Oklahoma Bar Association
P.O. Box 53036
Oklahoma City, OK 73152
(405) 524-2365

Adoption Attorneys

Cynthia C. Butler
2109 Cache, #C
Lawton, OK 73505
(405) 248-1511

William R. Cubbage
P.O. Box 550
Cushing, OK 74023-0550
(918) 225-2464

John M. O'Connor
Newton & O'Connor
15 West 6th Street, Suite 2900
Tulsa, OK 74119
(918) 587-0101
fax (918) 587-0102

Jack H. Petty
6666 N.W. 39th Expressway
Bethany, OK 73008
(405) 787-6911

Peter K. Schaffer
204 N. Robinson, Suite 2600
Oklahoma City, OK 73102
(405) 239-7707

Phyllis Zimmerman*
15 West 6th Street
Suite 1220
Tulsa, OK 74119-5444
918) 582-6151
fax 919) 582-6153

* Ms. Zimmerman has completed about 1,000 independent adoptions about 4,000 agency adoptions and about 250 international adoptions.

Attorney fees for adoptions in this state are about $500 to $2,000.

OKLAHOMA LAWS RELATED TO ADOPTION: QUESTIONS AND ANSWERS

Can an attorney serve as an intermediary?
Yes.

Is advertising permitted?
Yes.

Who must consent to the adoption?
1. Both birth parents, if sixteen years or older
2. If the birth mother or father is younger than 16, then a guardian or parent must also give written consent
3. The child placement agency, if it has custody of the child

When can consent be taken from birth mother (father), and how long after the consent is signed can it be revoked?
The birth parents can appear before the judge and consent in writing to the adoption and a termination of their parental rights seventy-two hours after the birth of the child. The consent can be withdrawn up to thirty days after signing if the court finds it is in the child's best interest. An agency surrender can be signed in front of the agency caseworker and the birth parent need not go to court. The surrender is irrevocable at the time of signing.

What are the birth father's rights?
The birth father's consent is not required if he fails to acknowledge his paternity and does not support the mother during pregnancy; or if he fails to prove that he is the father or fails to exercise parental duties toward the child; or if he waives his right to notice of the adoption hearing; or if he does not appear at the adoption hearing after receiving notice.

What fees can adoptive parents pay?
Medical and legal expenses are permitted. Living expenses can be paid in a private adoption with court preapproval.

Where does the adoption hearing take place?
The hearing can take place in the court of the county where the adoptive parents live, where the birth parents live, or where the placing agency is located.

How are familial and step-parent adoptions different from nonbiological adoptions?
Phyllis Zimmerman, an attorney in Tulsa, states that in a step-parent adoption no home study is required. A step-parent adoption can be finalized in about three to four weeks. Grandparent visitation rights are permitted in step-parent adoptions or relative adoptions only if at least one of the biological parents is deceased and it is in the child's best interest.

Ms. Zimmerman states that in a relative adoption, a home study is required and the steps for a nonbiological adoption are followed.

Can a nonresident finalize an adoption in this state?
Yes, but only if the child is a resident of Oklahoma.

OREGON

State Adoption Specialist
Kelly Shannon
Adoption Programs
Oregon State Offices for Services
  to Families and Children
2nd Floor, South Mailroom
500 Summer Street, N.E.
Salem, OR 97310
(503) 945-6616

Compact Administrator
Mr. William Carey
Oregon Department of Human
  Resources
Children's Services Division
198 Commercial Street, S.E.
Salem, OR 97310
(503) 378-4374

Deputy Compact Administrator
Lea Goodman
Joann Noffsinger
Interstate Compact on the
Placement of Children
Children's Services Division
500 Summer Street, N.E., 2nd
  Floor
Salem, OR 97310-1017
Joann, (503) 378-2026 (A-K)
Lea, (503) 378-4468 (L-Z)

Direct all telephone calls and
  correspondence to the Deputy
  Compact Administrator.

Office hours:
Monday-Friday
8:00 A.M.-5:00 P.M.
Pacific Time Zone

State Adoption Exchange and Photo Listing

Oregon Adoption Exchange
Oregon State Office for Services
  to Families and Children
500 Summer Street, N.E.
Salem, OR 97310
(503) 945-5998

Private Adoption Agencies

Adventist Adoption and Family
  Services Program
6040 Southeast Belmont Street
Portland, OR 97215
(503) 232-1211

Albertina Kerr Center for
  Children
424 Northeast 22nd Avenue
Portland, OR 97232
(503) 239-8101

Boys and Girls Aid Society of
  Oregon
018 S.W. Boundary Court
Portland, OR 97201-3985
(503) 222-9661

Caring Connection
5439 S.E. Bantam Court
Milwaukie, OR 97267
(505) 282-3663

Casey Family Program
3910 S.E. Stark Street, Suite 230
Portland, OR 97214
(503) 239-9977

Catholic Community Services
231 S.E. 12th Avenue
Portland, OR 97214
(503) 231-4866

China Adoption Services Agency
P.O. Box 19764
Portland, OR 97280
(503) 245-0976

Columbia Counseling, Inc.
1445 West Rosemont Drive
West Linn, OR 97068
(503) 655-9470

Dove Adoption International,
  Inc.
3735 S.E. Martins
Portland, OR 97202
(503) 775-0469

First American Adoptions
P.O. Box 69622
Portland, OR 97201
(503) 243-5576

Give Us This Day, Inc.
P.O. Box 11611
Portland, OR 97211
(503) 288-4335

Heritage Adoptions
516 S.E. Morrison, Suite 714
Portland, OR 97214
(503) 233-1099

Holt International Children's
  Services
P.O. Box 2880
Eugene, OR 97402
(503) 687-2202

Journeys of the Heart
905 East Main Street
Hillsboro, OR 97123
(503) 681-3075

LDS Social Services
530 Center Street, Suite 706
Salem, OR 97301
(503) 581-7483

Lutheran Family Services
605 S.E. 39th Avenue
Portland, OR 97214
(503) 231-7480

Northwest Adoptions and Family
  Services
2695 Spring Valley Lane, N.W.
Salem, OR 97304
(503) 581-6652

Open Adoption and Family
  Services, Inc.
239 East 14th Avenue
Eugene, OR 97401
(503) 343-4825

Open Adoption and Family
  Services
2950 S.E. Stark Street, Suite 230
Portland, OR 97214
(503) 233-9660

Orphans Overseas
P.O. Box 249
Beaverton, OR 97075-0245
(503) 297-2006

Plan International Adoption
  Services
P.O. Box 667
McMinnville, OR 97128
(503) 472-8452

Waverly Children's Center
3550 S.E. Woodward
Portland, OR 97202
(503) 234-7532

**Adoptive Parent Support
  Groups and Postadoption
  Services**

Adoption Network
Attn.: Linnie Sohler
2251 Dry Creek Road
Mosier, OR 97040
(503) 478-3496

Adoptive Families Unlimited
Attn.: Lynn Stevens
Box 40752
Eugene, OR 97404
(503) 688-1654

Adoptive Parent Support Group
Attn.: Claudia Hutchison
018 S.W. Boundry Court
Portland, OR 97201-3985
(503) 222-9661

Coos County Adoptive Parents
Attn.: Sharon Howell
P.O. Box 4052
Coos Bay, OR 97420
(503) 572-5938

North American Council on
  Adoptable Children State
  Representative
Attn.: Kathie Stocker
5737 S.W. Pendleton
Portland, OR 97122-1762
(503) 245-2195

Northwest Adoptive Families
  Association
Attn.: Kathy Johnson
P.O. Box 25355
Portland, OR 97225-0355
(503) 243-1356

Single Adoptive Parents Support
  Group
Attn.: Pam Taylor
5621 S.E. Oak Street
Portland, OR 97215
(503) 234-7042

Southern Oregon Adoptive
  Families
Attn.: Maryjo Regula
P.O. Box 332
Medford, OR 97501
(503) 779-8494

**Adopted Person and Birth
  Relative Support Groups**

Adoptee Birthfamily Connection
Box 50122
Eugene, OR 97405
(503) 345-6710

Adoptee Liberty Movement
  Association (ALMA)
P.O. Box 1892
Beaverton, OR 97075

Adoptee Liberty Movement
  Association (ALMA)
P.O. Box 52
Umpqua, OR 97486

ALARM Network
11505 S.W. Dutchess
Beaverton, OR 97005

Family Ties
3355 N. Delta Road, #99
Eugene, OR 97408-5913

Footprints
Box 643
Talent, OR 97540

Medford Adoption Rights
  Association/ALARM
3413 Corey Road
Central Point, OR 97502

Oregon Adoptive Rights
  Association
P.O. Box 882
Portland, OR 97207
(503) 235-3669

Southern Oregon Adoptive
  Rights
1605 S.W. K Street, P.O. Box 882
Grants Pass, OR 97526
(503) 479-3143

The Circle
635 Elkader
Ashland, OR 97520
(503) 482-5554

The Circle
1090 Ellendale Sp. 14
Medford, OR 97504
(503) 773-7554

Oregon State Bar
P.O. Box 1689
Lake Oswego, OR 97035
(503) 620-0222

Adoption Attorneys

John Chally
825 NE Multnomah, #1125
Portland, OR 97232
(503) 238-9720

Catherine Dexter*
921 Southwest Washington, Suite
  865
Portland, OR 97205
503) 222-2474

* Ms. Dexter has completed more
  than 350 independent
  adoption, more than 250
  agency adoptions, and at least
  twenty international adoptions.

Lawrence Evans
1211 Southwest Fifth Avenue
Pacwest Center, 30th Floor
Portland, OR 97204
(503) 241-0570

John Hassen
129 North Oakdale, Suite 1
Medford, OR 97501
(503) 779-8550

Susan Moffet
921 Southwest Washington, Suite
  865
Portland, OR 97205
(503) 222-2474

Larry Spiegel*
4040 Southwest Douglas Way
Lake Oswego, OR 97035
(503) 635-7773

* Mr. Spiegel has completed
  about 200 independent
  adoptions, 400 agency, and 100
  international adoptions.

Attorney fees for adoptions in this
state range from $1,000 to $4,000.

OREGON LAWS RELATED TO ADOPTION: QUESTIONS AND ANSWERS

Can an attorney serve as an intermediary?
Yes.

Is advertising permitted?
Yes, if the adoptive parents have an Oregon-approved home study.

Who must consent to the adoption?
The birth parents

When can consent be taken from birth mother (father), and how long after the consent is signed can it be revoked?
A birth parent can sign the consent before birth, but it is not effective until afterward. It can be signed after birth once the birth mother has recovered from the effects of delivery. Once signed it is irrevocable if these five conditions have been met:
1. The adoptive couple has completed a home study, and it is filed with the court.
2. Once consent is given, the attorney files a petition for adoption with the court and appoints the adoptive couple guardians of the child. At the time of appointment a Certificate of Irrevocability is issued by the court. (You need an attorney who will file this immediately.) After the adoptive parents take the child home from the hospital, the consent is irrevocable.
3. The child is in the physical custody of the adoptive family.
4. The birth mother and, if possible, the birth father's social, medical, and genetic history is taken by an agency or an attorney who is not representing the adoptive couple.
5. The consequences of signing the consent are explained to the birth parents by the Children's Services Division, an adoption agency, or the birth mother's attorney. (You should use an attorney, if possible.)

What are the birth father's rights?
Catherine Dexter, an attorney in Portland, states that if he is not married to the birth mother and no paternity is established, his rights may be terminated when the birth mother signs an affidavit and the child is placed with the adoptive couple.

Unless the birth father has supported the birth mother and the child (by monetary means or\and emotional relationship) or he files with the Putative Father's Registry indicating that he is the father, he is not entitled to notice of any adoption proceedings and cannot contest the adoption.

What fees can adoptive parents pay?
Medical, legal, and reasonable living expenses can be paid. The adoptive parents must submit to the court an itemized list stating all fees and expenses paid.

No fees can be paid or accepted for finding a child or an adoptive parent, unless it is the reasonable fee of a licensed adoption agency. The Children's Services Division may charge up to $750 for a home study.

Where does the adoption hearing take place?

The adoption hearing can take place in the court of the county where the adoptive parents live, where the child's birth parents live, or where the agency is located.

How are familial and step-parent adoptions different from nonbiological adoptions?

Catherine Dexter states that no home study is required in a step-parent adoption or a relative adoption if the child has resided with the step-parent or relative for six months before filing the petition.

Can a nonresident finalize an adoption in this state?

Yes, if the birth mother is a resident. The adoptive parent, birth parent, or child must reside in Oregon continuously for six months prior to the date of the adoption petition.

PENNSYLVANIA

State Adoption Specialist
Robert Gioffre
Pennsylvania Department of
  Public Welfare
Office of Children, Youth and
  Families
P.O. Box 2675
Harrisburg, PA 17105
(717) 787-7756

Compact Administrator
John F. White, Jr. Secretary
Pennsylvania Department of
  Public Welfare
P.O. Box 2675
Harrisburg, PA 17105

Deputy Compact Administrator
Division of State Services
Pennsylvania Department of
  Public Welfare
P.O. Box 2675, Lanco Lodge, 2nd
  Floor
Harrisburg, PA 17105
(717) 772-7016
        or
Division of State Services
Harrisburg State Hospital
Lanco Lodge, 2nd Floor
Harrisburg, PA 17103

Direct all telephone calls and
  correspondence to:

Vilma Dornell
(717) 772-5503
fax (717) 783-6354

Office hours:
Monday-Friday
8:00 A.M.-5:00 P.M.
Eastern Time Zone

**Statewide Adoption
  System/Exchange**

Jewel McCliment
Statewide Adoption Network
Pennsylvania Office of Children,
  Youth and Families
P.O. Box 2675
Harrisburg, PA 17105
(717) 787-7756 or 787-5010

Private Adoption Agencies

Adopt-A-Child
6403 Beacon Street
Pittsburgh, PA 15217
(412) 421-1911

Adoption Arc, Inc.
30 Pelham Road, P.O. Box 18804
Philadelphia, PA 19119
(215) 844-1082

Adoption Horizons
403 Roxbury Road
Shippensburg, PA 17257
(717) 530-5363

Adoption Services, Inc.
28 Central Boulevard
Camp Hill, PA 17011
(717) 737-3960

Adoption Services International
Swede and Airy Streets
Norristown, PA 19401
(610) 270-9980

Adoption Unlimited
2770 Weston Road
Lancaster, PA 17603
(717) 872-1340

Adoptions from the Heart
1244 Hamilton Street
Allentown, PA 18102
(610) 740-0200

Adoptions from the Heart
76 Rittenhouse Place
Ardmore, PA 19003
(610) 642-7200

Adoptions from the Heart
P.O. Box 60093
Harrisburg, PA 17106
(717) 691-9686

Adoptions from the Heart
1525 Oregon Pike
Oregon Commons, Suite 501
Lancaster, PA 17601
(717) 399-7766

Adoptions International
601 South 10th Street
Philadelphia, PA 19147
(215) 238-9057

Aid for Children International
403 Roxbury Road
Shippensburg, PA 17257
(717) 530-5363

Best Nest
1335-37 Pine Street
Philadelphia, PA 19107
(215) 546-8060

Bethanna
1030 Second Street Pike
South Hampton, PA 18966
(215) 355-6500

Bethany Christian Services
550 Pinetown Road, Suite 205
Fort Washington, PA 19034
(215) 233-4626

Bethany Christian Services
113 North Lime Street
Lancaster, PA 17602
(717) 399-3213

Bethany Christian Services of
   Western Pennsylvania
694 Lincoln Avenue
Pittsburgh, PA 15202
(412) 734-2662

A Better Chance, Inc.
275 Glen Riddle Road, H-12
Glen Riddle, PA 19037
(610) 459-0454

Capital Area Adoption Services
514 Landsvale Street
Marysville, PA 17053
(717) 957-2513

Catholic Charities Agency of the
   Diocese of Greensburg
115 Vannear Avenue
Greensburg, PA 15601
(412) 837-1840

Catholic Charities Counseling
   and Adoption Services
Deposit Bank Building, Room 242
DuBois, PA 15801
(814) 371-4717

Catholic Charities Counseling
   and Adoption Services
329 West Tenth Street
Erie, PA 16502
(814) 456-2091

Catholic Charities Counseling
   and Adoption Services
786 East State Street
Sharon, PA 16146
(412) 346-4142

Catholic Charities of the Diocese
   of Harrisburg
4800 Union Deposit Road
P.O. Box 3551
Harrisburg, PA 17105
(717) 657-4804

Catholic Charities of the Diocese
   of Pittsburgh, Inc.
212 9th Street
Pittsburgh, PA 15222-3507
(412) 471-1120
Catholic Social Agency of the
   Diocese of Allentown
2141 Downyflake Lane
Allentown, PA 18103
(610) 791-3888

Catholic Social Services of the
   Archdiocese of Philadelphia
222 North 17th Street
Philadelphia, PA 19103
(215) 587-3900

Catholic Social Services of the
   Diocese of Altoona-Johnstown
1300 12th Avenue
P.O. Box 1349
Altoona, PA 16603
(814) 944-9388

Catholic Social Services of the
   Diocese of Scranton
400 Wyoming Avenue
Scranton, PA 18503
(717) 346-8936

Catholic Social Services of
   Luzerne County
33 East Northhampton
Wilkes-Barre, PA 18701-2406
(717) 822-7118

Child and Home Study Associates
1029 Providence Road
Media, PA 19063
(610) 565-1544

Children's Adoption Network
245 Bradley Court
Holland, PA 18966
(215) 860-3353

Children's Aid Society in
   Clearfield County
1004 South Second Street
Clearfield, PA 16830
(814) 765-2685

Children's Aid Society of Franklin
   County
225 Miller Street
P.O. Box 353
Chambersburg, PA 17201-0353
(717) 263-4159

Children's Aid Society of Mercer
   County
350 West Market Street
Mercer, PA 16137
(412) 662-4730

Children's Aid Society of
   Montgomery County
1314 DeKalb Street
Norristown, PA 19401
(215) 279-2755

Children's Aid Society of
   Somerset County
574 East Main Street
Somerset, PA 15501
(814) 445-2009

Children's Choice
Scott Plaza II
Philadelphia, PA 19113
(215) 521-6270

Harrisburg
(717) 541-9809

Pottstown
(610) 326-7103

Selinsgrove
(717) 743-0505

West Chester
(610) 430-7735

Branches also in Delaware,
   Maryland, and New Jersey

Children's Home of Pittsburgh
5618 Kentucky Avenue
Pittsburgh, PA 15232
(412) 441-4884

Children's Services
311 South Juniper Street
Philadelphia, PA 19107
(215) 546-3503

Choices—An Adoption Agency
1265 Drummers Lane
Building 3, Suite 101
Wayne, PA 19087
(215) 997-5059

Common Sense Adoption
   Services
208 West Main Street
Mechanicsburg, PA 17055
(717) 766-6449

Concern
1 West Main Street
Fleetwood, PA 19522
(610) 944-0447

Council of Three Rivers
Native American
Adoption Resource Exchange
200 Charles Street
Pittsburgh, PA 15238
(412) 782-4457

Counseling and Care Services
RD 3
Watsontown, PA 17777
(717) 538-2760

Eckels Adoption Agency
915 Fifth Avenue (Rear)
Williamsport, PA 17701
(717) 323-2520

Families Caring for Children
Mercy Medical Arts
P.O. Box 1311
8 Church Street
Wilkes-Barre, PA 18703
(717) 822-6288

Family Adoption Center
1201 Allegheny Tower
625 Stanwix Street
Pittsburgh, PA 15222
(412) 288-2138

Family Service
630 Janet Avenue
Lancaster, PA 17601
(717) 397-5241

Family Service of Beaver/Butler
   County
401 Smith Drive
Evans City, PA 16033
(412) 775-8390

Family Services and Children's
   Aid Society of Venango County
716 East Second Street
Oil City, PA 16301
(814) 677-4005

Family Services, Inc.
670 West 36th Street
Erie, PA 16508
(814) 864-0605

Genesis of Pittsburgh
185 Dakota Street
Pittsburgh, PA 15202
(412) 766-2693

Infant Care
P.O. Box 300
Montandon, PA 17850
(717) 522-8291

International Adoption
   Assistance
3118 Plymouth Rock Road
Norristown, PA 19401
(610) 292-9420

International Assistance Group
21 Brilliant Avenue
Pittsburgh, PA 15215
(412) 781-6470

International Families
518 South 12th Street
Philadelphia, PA 19147
(215) 557-7797

Jewish Family and Children's
   Agency
10125 Verree Road
Philadelphia, PA 19116
(215) 698-9950

Jewish Family and Children's
   Service
The Adoption Center
234 McKee Place
Pittsburgh, PA 15213
(800) 841-5894 or (412) 683-
   4900

Juvenile Justice Center
100 West Coulter Street
Philadelphia, PA 19144
(215) 849-2112

Kaleidoscope of Family Services,
   Inc.
355 West Lancaster Avenue
Haverford, PA 19041
(610) 642-3322

La Vida Adoption Agency
900 East 8th Avenue, Suite 300
King of Prussia, PA 19406
(610) 647-8008

La Vida Adoption Agency
9 Birch Road
Malvern, PA 19355
(610) 296-7699

LDS Social Services
46 School Street
Greentree, PA 15205
(412) 921-8303

Love the Children
221 West Broad Street, 2nd Floor
Quakertown, PA 18951
(215) 536-4180

Lutheran Children and Family
   Services
101 East Olney Avenue, 5th Floor
Philadelphia, PA 19120
(215) 951-6850

Lutheran Home at Topton
One South Home Avenue
Topton, PA 19562
(215) 682-1504

Lutheran Service Society of
   Western Pennsylvania
1011 Old Salem Road, Suite 107
Greensburg, PA 15601
(412) 837-9385

Marion Adoption Services
3138 Butler Pke
Plymouth Meeting, PA 19462
(610) 941-0910 or (800) 585-
   9944

Medical Adoption Services
721 Willow Run Road
Spring House, PA 19002
(215) 482-9423

National Adoption Network, Ltd.
223 Gypsy Lane
Wynnewood, PA 19096
(610) 649-5046

PAACT
703 North Market Street
Liverpool, PA 17045
(717) 444-3629

Pearl S. Buck Foundation
   (Welcome House Social
   Services)
Green Hills Farm
P.O. Box 181
Perkasie, PA 18944
(215) 249-0100

Project STAR of Permanency
   Planning Advocates of Western
   Pennsylvania
6301 Northumberland Street
Pittsburgh, PA 15217
(412) 521-9000, ext. 215

Rainbow Project
200 Charles Street
Pittsburgh, PA 15238
(412) 782-4457

St. Joseph's Center
2010 Adams Avenue
Scranton, PA 18509
(717) 342-8379

Tabor Children's Services
601 New Britain Road
Doylestown, PA 18901-4248
(215) 348-4071

Tabor Children's Services
4700 Wissahickon Avenue
Philadelphia, PA 19144
(215) 842-4800

Three Rivers Adoption
Council/Black Adoption
Services
307 4th Avenue, Suite 710
Pittsburgh, PA 15222
(412) 471-8722

Today's Adoption Agency
P.O. Box G
Hawley, PA 18428
(717) 226-0808

Tressler Lutheran Services
960 Century Drive
P.O. Box 2001
Mechanicsburg, PA 17055
(717) 795-0300

Tressler Lutheran Services
1139 Chester Street
Williamsport, PA 17701
(717) 327-9195

Tressler Lutheran Services
836 South George Street
York, PA 17403
(717) 845-9113

Wiley House
1650 Broadway
Bethlehem, PA 18015
(610) 867-5051

Women's Christian Alliance
1610 North Broad Street
Philadelphia, PA 19121
(215) 236-9911

**Adoptive Parent Support
Groups and Postadoption
Services**

Adoption Center of the Delaware
Valley
1500 Walnut Street, Suite 701
Philadelphia, PA 19102
(215) 735-9988

Adoption Connection, Inc.
Attn.: Adrienne Ward
P.O. Box 28030
Philadelphia, PA 19131
(215) 927-5144

Adoption Forum
Attn.: Sophie Janney
525 South Fourth Street, Suite
3465
Philadelphia, PA 19147
(215) 238-1116

Adoption Information Services
Attn.: Abby Ruder
901 B East Willow Grove Avenue
Wyndmoor, PA 19118
(215) 233-1380

Adoption Support Group State
College
Attn.: Debbie Riesterer
146 Meadow Lane
State College, PA 16801
(814) 237-5568

Adoption World
3246 Birch Road
Philadelphia, PA 19154
(215) 632-4479

Adoptive Families Together
Attn.: Christine M Braho
712 Herman Road
Butler, PA 16001
(412) 285-1594

Adoptive Families Together
Attn.: Rita Neu
2510 Elkridge Drive
Wexford, PA 15090
(412) 935-9607

Adoptive Family Rights Council
239 Fourth Avenue, Suite 1403
Pittsburgh, PA 15222
(412) 232-0955

Adoptive Parents Group of
Delaware Valley
Attn.: Mary Fossett
1147 Myrtlewood Avenue
Upper Darby, PA 19082
(610) 853-1042

Adoptive Parents of Delaware
County
Attn.: Nancy Urban
5129 Palmers Mill Road
Clifton Heights, PA 19018
(610) 622-3890

After Adoption and Parenting
Services for Families
5500 Wissahickon Avenue
Alden Park Manor | #A-202
Philadelphia, PA 19144
(215) 844-1312

Common Sense Associates
5021 E. Trindle Road
Mechanicsburg, PA 17055
(717) 766-6449

Concerned Adoptive Parents
Attn.: Jim Sacco
2803 East Kings Highway
Coatesville, PA 19320
(610) 383-4260

Council on Adoptable Children of
Allegheny County
Attn.: Ross Fullen
807 Sleepy Hollow Road
Pittsburgh, PA 15234
(412) 561-1603

Council on Adoptable Children of
Southwestern Pennsylvania and
North American Council on
Adoptable Children State
Representative
Attn.: Sherry Anderson
224 South Aiken Avenue
Pittsburgh, PA 15206
(412) 471-8722

Elizabeth S. Cole Associates
286 Thompson Mill Road
New Hope, PA 18938
(215) 598-0414

Families Together
Attn.: Susan Pedaline
Apollo Lane
Rochester, PA 15074
(412) 772-7260

Family Serv Adoptive Parent
Attn.: Sandy Ross
401 Cranberry Professional Park
Evans City, PA 16033
(412) 772-1773

FCVN/Open Door Society-
Pennsylvania
Attn.: Pat Sexton
1835 Troxell Street
Allentown, PA 18103
(610) 865-1882

Foreign Adoption Network
Attn.: Marcia Hirster Moll
1 East Main Street
Fleetwood, PA 19522
(610) 944-0445

Foreign Adoption Network
Attn.: Susan Kegerise
286 Levan Street
Reading, PA 19606
(215) 779-O727

International Adoptive Families
Attn.: Lynne Jennings
402 Pebblecreek Drive
Cranberry Township, PA 16066
(412) 772-5787

International Families of Somerset
County
Attn.: Mrs. Mary Forney
875 Hemlock Road
Warmister, PA 18974-4122

Keystone Adoptive Families
Attn.: Debbie Kelly
2708 West Chestnut Avenue
Altoona, PA 16001
(814) 943-4767

Korean Konnection
Attn.: Bobbie Duffey
2390 Deep Hollow Road
Dover, PA 17315-2512
(717) 292-4983

Lehigh Valley Adoptive Parents
Group
Attn.: Donna Yurko
1710 Monroe Street
Bethlehem, PA 18017-6439
(215) 896-1549

Love the Children Support Group
Attn.: Geoff Hurd
384 Tampa
Pittsburgh, PA 15228
(412) 563-4931

Love the Children of Western
Pennsylvania
Attn.: Andy Marcinko
539 Greenspire Court
Evans City, PA 16033
(412) 452-0294

National Adoption Center
1500 Walnut Street, Suite 701
Philadelphia, PA 19102
(215) 735-9988

Our Children
Attn.: Maureen Bahr
1305 Joan Drive
Southampton, PA 18966
(215) 364-7675

Parent Network for the Post-
Institutionalized Child
Attn.: Thais Tepper
Box 613
Meadow Lands, PA 15347
(412) 222-1766 or 222-6009

Parents and Adopted Children's
Organization of Lawrence
County
Attn.: John and Sandy Wilson
RD#4 Box 397
New Castle, PA 16101

Parents and Adopted Children's
Organization of the Midwest
Attn.: Kathy Hamilton
330 Winters Road
Butler, PA 16001
(412) 586-9316

Parents and Adopted Children's
Organization of Mercer County
Attn.: Amy Phillips
105 Wasser Road
Greenville, PA 16125
(412) 962-1039 or 588-2167

Parents and Adopted Children's
Organization of Washington
County
Attn.: Becky Tomasiak
551 McCrea Avenue
Donora, PA 15033
(412) 379-5716

Parents and Adopted Children's
Organization of Westmoreland
Attn.: Donna Forys
3550 Meadowgate Drive
Murrysville, PA 15668
(412) 327-4798

Parents of Adopted African
Americans
Attn.: Barb Lewis
544 West 31st Street
Erie, PA 16508-1743
(814) 455-2149

Parents of Adopted International
Children of Chester County
Attn.: Donna Kneisly
5 Clover Lane
Downingtown, PA 19335
(610) 269-3724

Philly Kids Play It Safe
1650 Arch Street, 17th Floor
Philadelphia, PA 19103
(215) 686-3966

Pre and Post Adoption
Consultation and Education
47 Marchwood Road, Suite 1E
Exton, PA 19341
(610) 524-9060

Single Adoptive Parent Group
Attn.: Geri Searight
3811 Wilkes-Barre Avenue
Pittsburgh, PA 15212
(412) 766-7895

Single Adoptive Parents of
Delaware Valley
Attn.: Judy Volk
45 West Stratford Avenue
Lansdowne, PA 19050
(215) 626-6624

Stars of David
Attn.: Carol R. Halper
Jewish Community Center
702 North 22nd Street
Allentown, PA 18104
(610) 435-3571

Stars of David
Attn.: Alan Iszauk
P.O. Box 322
Export, PA 15632

Stars of David of the Delaware
Valley
Attn.: Laurie and Sid Katz
(609) 424-6280

Tabor Adoptive Parents and
North American Council on
Adoptable Children State
Representative
Attn.: Phyllis Stevens
478 Moyers Road
Harleysville, PA 19438-2302
(215) 256-6438

Today's Adoptive Families
Attn.: Carol and Ted Eiferma
30 Manchester Way
Burlington, NJ 08016
(609) 386-7237

Tremitiere, Ward and Associates
122 West Springettsbury
York, PA 17403
(717) 845-9113

Welcome House Adoptive
Parents Group
Attn.: Carole Nebhut
275 Glen Riddle Road, Apt. C-1
Media, PA 19063
(215) 358-3894

Welcome House Adoptive
Parents Group
Attn.: Penny Fishman
604 Hasting Street
Pittsburgh, PA 15206
(412) 665-1458

Adopted Person and Birth Relative Support Groups

Adoptee Liberty Movement
Association (ALMA)
P.O. Box 53735
Philadelphia, PA 19105
(215) 561-2525

Adoption Forum
525 South Fourth Street, Suite
3465
Philadelphia, PA 19147
(215) 238-1116
Branches in Lehigh Valley,
Harrisburg, and Bucks County

Adoption Healing
3329 Pennysville
Pittsburgh, PA 15214
(412) 322-5607

Adoption Lifeline of Altoona
414 28th Avenue
Altoona, PA 16601

Lansdale Adoption Connection
1167 Hill Drive
Lansdale, PA 19446|2125
(215) 361-9679

Lost Loved Ones
621 W. Crawford Street
Edensberg, PA 15931

NW Pennsylvania Adoption
Connection
632 N. Michael Street
St. Mary's, PA 15857
(814) 781-7312

Origins
Box 1032, Hemlock Farms
Hawley, PA 18428
(717) 775-9729

Parents/Adoptees Support
Together (PAST)
8130 Hawthorne Drive
Erie, PA 16509
(814) 899-1493

Pittsburgh Adoption Connection
37 Edgecliff Road
Carnegie, PA 15106
(412) 279-2511

Pittsburgh Adoption Lifeline
P.O. Box 52
Gibsonia, PA 15044
(412) 443-3370

Searching
P.O. Box 7446
Harrisburg, PA 17113-0446
(717) 939-0138

Pennsylvania Bar Association
100 South Street
P.O. Box 186
Harrisburg, PA 17108
(717) 238-6715

Adoption Attorneys

Richard J. Armhelm
70 E. Beau Street
Washington, PA 15301
(412) 222-4520

Craig Bluestein
200 Old York Road
Jenkinstown, PA 19046
(215) 576-1030

Harry L. Bricker, Jr.
407 N. Front Street
Harrisburg, PA 17101
(717) 233-2555

Barbara L. Binder Casey
527 Elm Street, P.O. Box 399
Reading, PA 19603
(610) 376-9742

Steven Dubin*
The Benson Manor, Suite 110
101 Washington Lane
Jenkinstown, PA 19046
(215) 745-1210
(800) 745-1210
fax (215) 885-1217

* Mr. Dubin has completed over
200 independent adoptions and
about fifty agency adoptions as
well as some international
adoptions.

Debra M. Fox*
Kaleidoscope of Family Services,
Inc.
355 W. Lancaster Avenue
Haverford, PA 19041
(215) 896-4832
fax (215) 642-7731

* Ms. Fox has conducted about
100 independent adoptions
about 500 agency adoptions,

Tara E. Gutterman
3900 City Line Avenue, #A-603
Philadelphia, PA 19131
(215) 844-1082

Deborah Lesko
5032 Buttermilk Hollow Road
West Miffin, PA 15122
(412) 469-3500

Martin Leventon
355 W. Lancaster Avenue
Haverford, PA 19041
(215) 642-3322

William P. Rosen, III
Station Square Three, #202
Paoli, PA 19301
(610) 647-8800

Samuel J. Totaro, Jr.*
Four Greenwood Square, Suite
100
Bensalem, PA 19020
(215) 244-1045
fax (215) 244-0641

* Mr. Totaro has completed more
than 1,300 independent
adoptions, 700 agency
adoptions, and 250
international adoptions.

Attorney fees for adoptions in this
state are about $1,500 to $5,000.

PENNSYLVANIA LAWS RELATED TO ADOPTION: QUESTIONS AND ANSWERS

Can an attorney serve as an intermediary?
Yes. However, he or she cannot accept any fees or charge on an hourly basis for this service.

Is advertising permitted?
Yes.

Who must consent to the adoption?
1. The birth parents
2. The birth mother's husband, if he was married to her at any time within one year before the child's birth, unless he proves not to be the child's biological father

When can consent be taken from birth mother (father), and how long after the consent is signed can it be revoked?
Consents can be given seventy-two hours after the child's birth. All consents must be confirmed by a court hearing, which occurs at least fifty days after the consents are taken. The consents are filed with the court at least forty days after they are signed; the court then schedules a hearing to confirm consents at least ten days later. The birth parents must receive notice of this hearing, and they can revoke their consents up until the court hearing. Debra M. Fox, an attorney in Haverford, states that this hearing usually occurs two to four months after the baby's birth, making Pennsylvania a "legal risk" state.

Birth fathers can sign consents, even before birth.

What are the birth father's rights?
He can sign a consent before or after birth, and his rights essentially end when the birth mother's rights are terminated, at the termination hearing. Debra Fox states that if the birth father does not sign a consent, his rights can be terminated as a "putative father" as long as he is not married to the birth mother and has failed to acknowledge paternity, and as long as he has not appeared in court to oppose the adoption.

What fees can adoptive parents pay?
No living expenses can be paid in an agency or independent adoption. In an independent adoption, only medical and hospital expenses are permitted. In an agency adoption, reasonable administrative costs and counseling fees are permitted.

The court may also require the adoptive parents to pay for the birth parents' legal fees and the child's guardian, but these fees may be capped at $150. An itemized statement of all money paid must be made in the adoption report.

Where does the adoption hearing take place?
The hearing can take place in the court of the county where the adoptive parents live, where the birth parents live, or where the placement agency is located.

How are familial and step-parent adoptions different from nonbiological adoptions?
They are handled the same way other adoptions are conducted, except that a home study may be waived in a step-parent adoption. The attorney can request that the hearing to confirm the consent also be the final hearing, instead of waiting for the final hearing to be held at a later date.

Can a nonresident finalize an adoption in this state?
Yes. For nonresidents to finalize in Pennsylvania, they must have proof that they have no history of child abuse or child-related crimes.

RHODE ISLAND

State Adoption Specialist
Patricia Keogh
Rhode Island Department for
  Children and their Families
610 Mt. Pleasant Avenue
Providence, RI 02908
(401) 457-4548

Independent Adoption
  Information
Donna Pariseau
(401) 277-2186

Compact Administrator
Joseph V. Castaldi
Rhode Island Dept for Children
  and Their Families
101 Dyer Street, Suite 300
Providence, RI 02903
(401) 277-6167
fax (401) 277-6100

Direct all telephone calls and
  correspondence to the Compact
  Administrator.

Office hours:
Monday-Friday
8:30 A.M.-4:30 P.M.
Eastern Time Zone

Private Adoption Consultant
Deborah Siegel
School of Social Work
Rhode Island College
Providence, RI 02908
(401) 456-8617

State Adoption Exchange and Photo Listing

Ocean State Adoption Resource
  Exchange, Inc. (OSARE)
500 Prospect Street
Pawtucket, RI 02860
(401) 724-1910

Private Adoption Agencies

Alliance for Children
500 Prospect Street
Pawtucket, RI 02860
(401) 725-9555

Bethany Christian Service
P.O. Box 618
Barrington, RI 02806
(401) 245-2960

Give of Life Adoption Services
P.O. Box 40864
Providence, RI 02940
(401) 353-6715

International Adoptions, Inc.
259 Eddie Dowling Highway
North Smithfield, RI 02895
(401) 765-8200

Jewish Family Services
229 Waterman Avenue
Providence, RI 02906
(401) 331-1244

Urban League of Rhode Island,
  Inc.
246 Prairie Avenue
Providence, RI 02905
(401) 351-5000

Wide Horizons
116 Andre Avenue
Wakefield, RI 02879
(401) 783-4537

Adoptive Parent Support Groups and Postadoption Services

Adoption Rhode Island, Inc. and
  North American Council on
  Adoptable Children State
  Representative
Attn.: Donna Caldwell
P.O. Box 1495
Kingston, RI 02881
(401) 792-3240

AGAND USA
Attn.: Joseph Di Martino
621 Wakefield Street
W. Warnick, RI 02893
(401) 821-2220

Getting
  International/Transcultural
  Families Together (GIFT)
11 Baneberry Drive
Cranston, RI 02921
(401) 944-6517

GIFT of Rhode Island
Attn.: Susan Round
9 Shippee School House Road
Foster, RI 02825
(401) 647-2021

GIFT
c/o Lynn Sheridan
144 Old North Road
Kingston, RI 02881

Jewish Family Services Adoptive
  Parent Support Group
229 Waterman Avenue
Providence, RI 02906
(401) 331-1244

Minority Adoptive Support
  Group, Inc.
Attn.: Rev. Robert Carter
246 Prairie Avenue
Providence, RI 02905
(401) 351-5000

Adopted Person and Birth Relative Support Groups

Jewish Family Services
Birth Parent Support Group
229 Waterman Avenue
Providence, RI 02906
(401) 331-1244

PALM
Box 15144
E. Providence, RI 02915
(401) 433-4692

Yesterday's Children
77 Homer Street
Providence, RI 02903

Rhode Island Bar Association

115 Cedar Street
Providence, RI 02903
(401) 421-5740

Adoption Attorneys

Robert Brennan
188 Benefit
Providence, RI 02903
(401) 274-1700

David McKenna*
941 Chalkstone Avenue
Providence, RI
(401) 421-1044
fax (401) 421-1053

* Mr. McKenna has completed
  forty-five agency adoptions and
  fourteen independent
  adoptions.

William Gallogly
6 Canal Street
Westerly, RI 02981
(401) 596-0183

Charles Greenwood*
333 Westminster Street
Providence, RI 02903
(401) 273-8202
fax (401) 521-9280

* Mr. Greenwood has completed
about 100 agency adoptions,
and 30 independent adoptions.

Allen Kirshenbaum
67 Jefferson Boulevard
Warwick, RI
(401) 467-5300

Lou Pulner
2 Williams Street
Providence, RI 02903
(401) 455-0040

Carol Saccucci
1350 West Main Road
Middletown, RI 02840
(401) 847-8168

Drew Thomas
1100 Aquidneck Avenue
Middletown, RI 02840
(401) 849-6200

Jill Votta
Smith Street
Providence, RI 02903
(401) 331-5555

RHODE ISLAND LAWS RELATED TO ADOPTION: QUESTIONS AND ANSWERS

In an independent adoption, even if the child is brought into the state, the Department of Children and their Families must be notified within fifteen days. Failure to notify could result in the court ordering the child to be removed from the adoptive parents' home.

A home study must be conducted within fifteen days of a child's placement. If you plan to advertise in another state, you may not have to have a home study completed at time of placement; however, the state in which the child is born will require a completed home study, as well as Interstate Compact approval, before the child is permitted to leave the state. If you have identified a birth mother, contact Donna Pariseau at (401) 277-2186, who will conduct a home study at no charge.

The religious preference of the biological parents is honored, as much as is practically possible, when placing a child.

Can an attorney serve as an intermediary?
Yes.

Is advertising permitted?
Technically not, but ads are placed.

Who must consent to the adoption?
1. The birth parents
2. The birth parents' guardian or court-appointed guardian if the birth parent is a minor

When can consent be taken from birth mother (father), and how long after the consent is signed can it be revoked?
Consent cannot be given sooner than fifteen days after the child's birth. No law discusses revocation, but case law suggests it is only possible due to fraud, duress, or misrepresentation.

What are the birth father's rights?
Unless the birth father has neglected to provide care for the child for at least one year, is excessively using drugs or alcohol, is unfit based on conduct or mental illness, or has abandoned or deserted the child, his consent is required.

What fees can adoptive parents pay?
The law does not address this issue. However, paying legal, medical, and reasonable living expenses is permitted.

Where does the adoption hearing take place?
The law does not address where the adoption hearing takes place, but it is usually conducted in the county where the adoptive parents live.

How are familial and step-parent adoptions different from nonbiological adoptions?
A specific statute deals with step-parent adoption. Relative adoptions are not significantly different from nonbiological adoptions.

Can a nonresident finalize an adoption in this state?
Yes, but only in an agency adoption.

SOUTH CAROLINA

Out-of-Home Care
Romona Foley, MSW
Director of Family Preservation
  and Child Welfare Services
P.O. Box 1520
Columbia, SC 29202-1520
(803) 734-5670
(800) 922-2504 (in South
  Carolina only)

Assistant Director
  of Out-of-Home Care
Carolyn Orf
ICPC Supervisor
South Carolina Department of
  Social Services
1530 Confederate Avenue, Room
  421
P.O. Box 1520
Columbia, SC 29202
(803) 734-6095
fax (803) 734-6285

Direct telephone calls and
  correspondence to the ICPC
  Supervisor, Carole Henderson
  (803) 734-6078.

Office hours:
Monday-Friday
8:30 A.M.-5:00 P.M.
Eastern Time Zone

**State Adoption Exchange and
  Photo Listing**

South Carolina Seedlings
P.O. Box 1453
Greenville, SC 29602-1453
(803) 239-0303

Private Adoption Agencies

Adoption Center of South
  Carolina
1600 Marian Street
P.O. Box 7788
Columbia, SC 29202
(803) 771-2272

A Loving Choice Adoption
  Agency
1535 Sam Rittenburg Boulevard
Charleston, SC 29407
(803) 556-3391
  or
1501 Readville Road
Spartanburg, SC 29306
(803) 576-7033

Bethany Christian Services
712 Richard Street, Suite I
Columbia, SC 29202
(803) 779-0541

Catholic Charities of Charleston
1662 Ingram Road
Charleston, SC 29407
(803) 769-4466

Children Unlimited, Inc.
1825 Gadsden Street
Columbia, SC 29211
(803) 799-8311

Christian Family Services
5072 Tara Tea Drive
Tega Cay, SC 29715
(803) 548-6030

Christian World Adoption, Inc.
270 W. Coleman Boulevard, Suite
  100
Mount Pleasant, SC 29464
(803) 856-0305

Epworth Children's Home
2900 Millwood Avenue
P.O. Box 50466
Columbia, SC 29250
(803) 256-7394

LDS Social Services
5624 Executive Center Drive,
  #109
Charlotte, NC 28212-8832
(704) 535-2436

Lutheran Family Services
1329 Atlantic Drive
P.O. Box 21728
Columbia, SC 29221
(803) 750-0034

Shekinah Life Ministries
1671 N. Cherry Road, Suite 105
Fort Mill, SC 29732
(803) 366-0707

Southeastern Children's Home,
  Inc.
155 Children's Home
Duncan, SC 29334
(803) 439-0259

World Wide Adoptions
205 Overland Drive
Spartanburg, SC 29307
(803) 583-6981

Adoptive Parents Support Groups and Postadoption Services

Center for Child and Family
Studies
Post-Legal Adoption Education
and Training
University of South Carolina
Columbia, SC 29208
(803) 777-9408

G.I.F.T. (Guiding Interracial
Families Together)
Attn.: Mike and Carrie Uram
(864) 288-0965

North American Council on
Adoptable Children State
Representative
Attn.: Jennifer Mayo
P.O. Box 14553
Greenville, SC 29602

Piedmont Adoptive Families
Attn.: Karen Kearse
P.O. Box 754
Spartanburg, SC 29304
(803) 578-3571

Single Adoptive Parents of South
Carolina
Attn.: J. Kirk Mason
P.O. Box 407
Norway, SC 29113

South Carolina Council on
Adoptable Children/South
Carolina Seedlings
Attn.: Linda R. Williams
P.O. Box 1453
Greenville, SC 29602
(803) 239-0303

Adopted Person and Birth Relative Support Groups

Adoptees and Birthparents in
Search
P.O. Box 5551
West Columbia, SC 29171
(803) 791-1133 or (803) 796-
4508
Branches in Greer, Charleston,
and Florence

Adoption and Family Reunion
Center
126 Brown Log Road
Pacolet, SC 29302
(803) 474-3934

Adoption Reunion Connection

P.O. Box 239
Moore, SC 29369
(803) 574-0681

Adoption Reunion Connection
263 Lemonade Road
Pacolet, SC 29372
(803) 474-3479

Adoption Search for Life
303 Brighton Road
Anderson, SC 29621
(803) 224-8020

Bits and Pieces
Box 380
Norris, SC 29667
(803) 639-3850

Home BASE
Box 7966
N. Augusta, SC 29841
(803) 279-0536

Triad, Inc.
1725 Atascadero Drive
Columbia, SC 29206
(803) 787-3778 or (803) 787-
4192

South Carolina Bar
950 Taylor Street
Columbia, SC 29202
(803) 799-6653

Adoption Attorneys

Richard C. Bell*
1535 Sam Rittenberg Boulevard
#E
Charleston, SC 29407
(803) 556-3391
fax (803) 556-3496
or
1501 Reidville Road
Spartanburg, SC 29306
(854) 576-7033
fax (854) 576-6435

* Mr. Bell has completed more
than 300 independent
adoptions, as well as about 100
agency and twenty-five
international adoptions.

Raymond W. Godwin*
135 South Main Street, 9th Floor
Greenville, SC 29601
(800) 238-1003
(864) 271-4525
fax (864) 242-5902

* Mr. Godwin practices in New
Jersey and South Carolina. Mr.
Godwin has completed over
300 independent adoptions and
about 150 agency and
international adoptions. He
also accepts referrals for
contested adoption cases,
andhas written and spoken
extensively on adoption
matters.

Thomas P. Lowndes, Jr.*
128 Meeting Street
Charleston, SC 29401
or
P.O. Box 214
Charleston, SC 29402
(803) 723-1688

* Mr. Lowndes has been an
adoption attorney for nearly 30
years and has conducted several
hundred adoptions. He has
served as the president of the
American Academy of
Adoption Attorneys.

James Fletcher Thompson*
P.O. Box 1853
Spartanburg, SC 29304-1853
(864) 573-7575

* Mr. Thompson has completed
more than 500 independent
adoptions, 150 agency
adoptions, and fifteen
international adoptions.

Stephen A. Yacobi
408 N. Church Street, #B
Greenville, SC 29601
(864) 242-3271

Attorney fees for adoption in this
state are about $2,500 to $4,500.

Adoption and Home Study Services

Laura Beauvais
(home studies, birth family
background reports, and
counseling)
307 Sassafras Drive
Taylors, SC 29687
(864) 268-0570

SOUTH CAROLINA LAWS RELATED TO ADOPTION: QUESTIONS AND ANSWERS

If you advertise in South Carolina and are not a state resident, you must petition the South Carolina Family Court to take a child out of state.

Nonresidents may adopt a child who has special needs or in cases where there has been pubic notoriety concerning the child or the child's family. They may also adopt if they are a relative; or if one of the adoptive parents is in the military in South Carolina; or there are unusual or exceptional circumstances making adoption by a nonresident in the child's best interest. If you personally meet with a birth mother and she selects you as the adoptive parent, then the courts will usually permit adoption under the "unusual or exceptional circumstances" clause. (See discussion below.)

Can an attorney serve as an intermediary?
Yes. A person who facilitates an adoption is not required to be licensed.

Is advertising permitted?
Yes.

Who must consent to the adoption?
1. The birth mother
2. The birth father, if he is married to the birth mother, or if he states that he is the biological parent and has either lived with the birth mother for six months or more before the child was born or has paid medical and other expenses during the mother's pregnancy

When can consent be taken from birth mother (father), and how long after the consent is signed can it be revoked?
Consent cannot be given until the child is born and the birth mother has basically recovered from the effects of delivery; once given, it cannot be withdrawn unless it was given involuntarily or obtained under duress or through coercion. The final adoption decree is irrevocable.

What are the birth father's rights?
Essentially, the birth father must have supported the birth mother during her pregnancy if his consent is to be required. If he has not done so for at least the last six months during her pregnancy, or if he has not supported the child during the last six months before placement, he must only be given notice of the adoption; his surrender is not required.

According to the Interstate Compact on the Placement of Children, if a parent has not surrendered his rights, or his rights have not been terminated, documented attempts to locate him must be presented to the Deputy Compact Administrator.

What fees can adoptive parents pay?
The following expenses can be paid: medical expenses, reasonable living expenses for a limited period of time, fees for investigation and report, fees for those required to take the surrender, reasonable attorney fees and the fee of the guardian appointed by the court, and reasonable fees to a child-placing agency.

Where does the adoption hearing take place?
The adoption hearing may take place in the court of the county where the adoptive parents live, where the child was born, or where the child placement agency is located.

How are familial and step-parent adoptions different from nonbiological adoptions?
A home study is not required.

Can a nonresident finalize an adoption in this state?
The law states that only a resident of South Carolina can adopt a child. Yet, according to Interstate Compact on the Placement of Children guidelines, nonresidents may adopt at the discretion of the court in state.

SPECIAL NOTE:
South Carolina was know for years as the "adoption capital" of the nation; its laws were not highly structured or restrictive. It was not until Time Magazine put South Carolina on its front cover and intimidated that it was the country's baby market that the South Carolina legislature enacted the "special needs" requirement. Now, South Carolina law states that a child cannot be placed with an out-of-state adoptive parent unless there are unusual or exceptional circumstances. However, what has developed since the 1989 enactment of the law is a flexible approach in allowing out-of-state couples to adopt children born or residing in South Carolina.

    The ambiguous nature of the law in South Carolina is an example that demonstrates the need for an experienced adoption attorney.

SOUTH DAKOTA

State Adoption Specialist
DiAnn Kleinsasser
South Dakota Department of
  Social Services
Richard F. Kneip Building
700 Governor's Drive
Pierre, SD 57501
(605) 773-3227

Compact Administrator
Judith Hines, Program
  Administrator
Child Protection Services
South Dakota Department of
  Social Services
Richard F. Kneip Building
700 Governor's Drive
Pierre, SD 57501-2291
(605) 773-3227

Deputy Compact Administrator
Duanne Jenner
South Dakota Department of
  Social Services
Richard F. Kneip Building
700 Governor's Drive
Pierre, SD 57501-2291
(605) 773-3227
fax (605) 773-4855

Direct all telephone calls and
  correspondence to the Deputy
  Compact Administrator.

Office hours:
Monday-Friday
8:00 A.M.-5:00 P.M.
Central Time Zone

Private Adoption Agencies

Bethany Christian Services
2100 South 7th Street
Rapid City, SD 57701
(605) 343-7196

Catholic Family Services
3200 West 41st Street
Sioux Falls, SD 57016
(605) 336-3326

Child Protection Program
Sisseton Wahpeton Sioux Tribe
Sisseton, SD 57262
(605) 698-3911

Christian Counseling Services
231 South Phillips, Suite 255
Sioux Falls, SD 57102
(605) 336-6999

LDS Social Services
2525 West Main Street
Rapid City, SD 57702
(605) 342-3500

Lutheran Social Services
600 West 12th Street
Sioux Falls, SD 57104
(605) 336-3347

Office of Social Concerns
918 5th Street
Rapid City, SD 57701
(605) 348-6086

Yankton Sioux Tribal Social
  Services
P.O. Box 248
Marty, SD 57361-0248
(605) 384-3804

**Adoptive Parent Support
  Groups and Postadoption
  Services**

Adoptive Families of Black Hills
Attn.: Claire Vig
3701 Reder Street
Rapid City, SD 57702-2242
(605) 348-7391

Families Through Adoption
Attn.: Twyla Baedke
Box 851
Sioux Falls, SD 57101
(605) 371-1404

North American Council on
　Adoptable Children State
　Representative
Attn.: James Cadwell
c/o Native American Child and
　Family Resource Center
29758 202nd Street
Pierre, SD 57501
(605) 224-9045

Tiwahe Olota Adoption and
　Foster Care Support Group
Attn.: Jean Anderson
Box 565
Reliance, SD 57569
(605) 476-5610

**Adopted Person and Birth
　Relative Support Groups**

Adoptee Liberty Movement
　Association (ALMA)
1325 South Bahnaon
Sioux Falls, SD 57103

State Bar of South Dakota
222 East Capitol
Pierre, SD 57501
(605) 224-7554

Adoption Attorneys

Lee R. Burd
101 S. Main, Suite 201
Sioux Falls, SD 57102
(605) 332-4351

Craig and Nichols
427 N. Minnesota Avenue #101
Sioux Falls, SD 57102
(605) 332-4321

SOUTH DAKOTA LAWS RELATED TO ADOPTION: QUESTIONS AND ANSWERS

Can an attorney serve as an intermediary?
No.

Is advertising permitted?
Yes.

Who must consent to the adoption?
1. The birth mother
2. The birth father, if he married to the birth mother, or if he states the child is his and asserts paternity within sixty days after the birth

When can consent be taken from birth mother (father), and how long after the consent is signed can it be revoked?
Consent can be taken any time before or after the child's birth but is not valid until after birth. Birth parents can revoke consent up until termination of their parental rights. This occurs about five days later when the birth mother goes to court. The birth father does not have to go to court but can have his rights terminated by power of attorney.

What are the birth father's rights?
If he is known and identified by the birth mother, his consent is required. If he is unknown, newspaper notices must be placed in an effort to locate him as a "John Doe" birth father. If a known birth father has abandoned the child for a period of one year, then his rights can be terminated without his consent.

What fees can adoptive parents pay?
Only fees and expenses approved by the court and fees charged by a child placement agency are permitted. If any other adoption-related moneys are paid without approval from the court, you could be charged with a felony.

Where does the adoption hearing take place?
The adoption hearing takes place in the court of the county where the adoptive parents live or where the child lives.

How are familial and step-parent adoptions different from nonbiological adoptions?
In a step-parent adoption, a judge may, but is not compelled to, order a home study.

Can a nonresident finalize an adoption in this state?
Yes.

TENNESSEE

State Adoption Specialist
Jane E. Chittick
Tennessee Department of Human
  Services
Citizens Plaza, 14th Floor
400 Deaderick Street
Nashville, TN 37248-9000
(615) 313-4743

Compact Administrator
Robert Grunow, Commissioner
Tennessee Department
  of Human Services
Citizens Plaza
400 Deaderick Street, 15th Floor
Nashville, TN 37248-9100
(615) 741-3241

Deputy Compact Administrator
Cheri Stewart, Program Specialist
Social Services Division
Tennessee Department of Human
  Services
Citizens Plaza
400 Deaderick Street, 14th Floor
Nashville, TN 37248
(615) 641-5941
fax (615) 741-4165

Direct all telephone calls and
  correspondence (in triplicate)
  to the Deputy Compact
  Administrator.

Office hours:
Monday-Friday
8:00 A.M.-4:30 P.M.
Central Time Zone

**State Adoption Exchange and
  Photo Listing**

Resource Exchange for Adoptable
  Children in Tennessee
201 23rd Avenue North
Nashville, TN 37203-9000
(615) 321-3867

Private Adoption Agencies

Adoption Resource Center
8529 Timberlock
Memphis, TN 38018
(901) 754-7902

Associated Catholic Charities of
  the Diocese of Memphis-
  St. Peter Home
1805 Poplar Avenue
Memphis, TN 38104
(901) 725-8240

Associated Catholic Charities
  of East Tennessee
119 Dameron Avenue
Knoxville, TN 37917
(423) 971-3555

Association for Guidance, Aid,
  Placement and Empathy
  (AGAPE)
4555 Trousdale Drive
Nashville, TN 37204-4513
(615) 781-3000

Association for Guidance, Aid,
  Placement and Empathy
  (AGAPE) Child and Family
  Services
1881 Union Avenue,
  P.O. Box 1141
Memphis, TN 38104
(901) 272-7339

Bethany Christian Services
4719 Brainerd Road, Suite D
Chattanooga, TN 34711
(423) 622-7360

Bethany Christian Services
2200 21st Avenue South,
  Suite 404
Nashville, TN 37212
(615) 297-5229
Branches in Knoxville:
(423) 588-5283 and Memphis:
(901) 454-1401

Catholic Charities
  of Tennessee, Inc.
30 White Bridge Road
Nashville, TN 37205
(615) 352-3087

Child and Family Services
  of Knox County
114 Dameron Avenue
Knoxville, TN 37917-9981
(423) 524-7483

Christian Counseling Services
515 Woodland Street
P.O. Box 60383
Nashville, TN 37206
(615) 254-8336

Church of God Home
  for Children
P.O. Box 4391
449 McCarn Circle
Sevierville, TN 37864
(423) 453-4644

East Tennessee Christian
  Services, Inc.
4638 Chambliss Avenue
Knoxville, TN 37919
(423) 584-0841

Family and Children's Services
201 23rd Avenue, North
Nashville, TN 37203
(615) 320-0591

Family and Children's Services
  of Chattanooga, Inc.
300 East 8th Street
Chattanooga, TN 37403
(423) 755-2822

Greater Chattanooga
  Christian Services
P.O. Box 4535
Chattanooga, TN 37405
(423) 756-0281

Happy Haven Homes, Inc.
225 North Willow Avenue,
  Route 4
Cookeville, TN 38501
(615) 526-2052

Holston United Methodist Home
  for Children, Inc.
P.O. Box 188, Holston Drive
Greeneville, TN 37743
(423) 638-4172

Jewish Family Services, Inc.
6560 Poplar Drive
P.O. Box 38268
Memphis, TN 38138
(901) 767-8511

Life Choices, Inc.
3297 Park Avenue
P.O. Box 11245
Memphis, TN 38111
(901) 323-5433

Madison Children's Home
106 Gallatin Road, North
P.O. Box 419
Madison, TN 37116-0419
(615) 860-3240

Mid-Cumberland Children's
Services, Inc.
106 N. Mountain Street
Smithville, TN 37166
(615) 597-7134

Mid-South Christian Services
3100 Walnut Grove Road,
Suite 104
Memphis, TN 38111
(901) 454-1401

Porter-Leath Children's Center
868 North Manassas Street
P.O. Box 111229
Memphis, TN 38107
(901) 577-2500

Small World Ministries, Inc.
P.O. Box 290185
401 Bonnaspring
Nashville, TN 37076
(615) 883-4372

Tennessee Baptist Children's
Homes, Inc.
P.O. Box 728
Brentwood, TN 37024
(615) 371-2000

Tennessee Children's Home
P.O. Box 10
Main Street
Spring Hill, TN 37174
(615) 486-2274

Tennessee Conference
Adoption Services
900 Glendale Lane
Nashville, TN 37204
(615) 292-3500

West Tennessee Children's Home
P.O. Box 3261
#20 Redbud
Jackson, TN 38301
(901) 423-4851

Williams-Illien Adoptions, Inc.
3439 Vinson Drive
Memphis, TN 38315
(901) 386-2166

Adoptive Parent Support Groups and Postadoption Services

BRAG
Attn.: Vickie Nelson
1104 Hunter's Trail
Franklin, TN 37901
(615) 370-5846

Council on Adoptable Children
and North American Council
on Adoptable Children State
Representative
Attn.: Joyce Maxey
7630 Luscomb Drive
Knoxville, TN 37919
(423) 693-8001

Family and Children Services
210 23rd Avenue North
Nashville, TN 37203
(615) 320-0591

Forever Families
Attn.: Melissa Adkisson
6151 Ashley Road
Arlington, TN 38002
(901) 377-8867

Mid-South Families
Through Adoption
Attn.: Regina Fausett
3559 Oak Limb Cove
Memphis, TN 38135
(901) 388-2095

Mountain Region Adoption
Support Group
Attn.: Jim and Linda Samples
4428 Fieldstone Drive
Kingsport, TN 37664
(703) 523-7206

Ours of Middle Tennessee
Attn.: Charles and Wanda Beck
3557 Bethlehem Road
Springfield, TN 37172
(615) 643-3426

Pappoos
Attn.: David and Hannah Prosser
7856 Harpeth View Drive
Nashville, TN 37221
(615) 646-8144

West Tennessee AGAPE
Parents Group
Attn.: Janie Branden
P.O. Box 11411
Memphis, TN 38111

Adopted Person and Birth Relative Support Groups

Adoptee Liberty Movement
Association (ALMA)
P.O. Box 15064
Chattanooga, TN 37415

Adoptees and Birth Parents
in Search
P.O. Box 901
Cleveland, TN 37364

Birthparents Search for Answers
2750 Ward Road
Millington, TN 38053

Concerned United Birthparents
2601 Holston Drive
Morristown, TN 37814

F.A.I.T.H.
P.O. Box 294
Kingsport, TN 37662
(423) 3780-4679

Family Finders
122 Bass Drive
Mt. Juliet, TN 37122
(615) 758-8685

Group for Openness in Adoption
518 General George Patton Road
Nashville, TN 37221
(615) 646-8116

Rights of Origin
7110 Westway Cr.
Knoxville, TN 37919
(423) 691-7412

R.O.O.T.S.
P.O. Box 9662
Knoxville, TN 37940
(423) 573-1344

Tennessee Department of Human
Services
Attn.: Postadoption Specialist
400 Deaderick Street
Nashville, TN 37248-9000
(615) 741-5935

Tennessee Searches for Truth
7721 White Creek Pike
Joelton, TN 37080

Tennessee's Right to Know
P.O. Box 34334
Memphis, TN 38134
(901) 373-7049

Tennessee Bar Association
3622 West End Avenue
Nashville, TN 37205
(615) 383-7421

Adoption Attorneys

Paul M. Buchanan
P.O. Box 3375
Nashville, TN 37219-0375
(615) 256-9999

S. Dawn Coppock
2101 Doane Lane
Strawberry Lane, TN 37871
(423) 933-8173
fax (423) 933-3272

Robert Tuke*
Tuke Yopp & Sweeney
Nations Band Plaza, Suite 1100
Nashville, TN37219
(615) 313-3320
fax (615) 313-3310

* Mr. Tuke has completed more
than 200 independent
adoptions, and about thirty
agency adoptions, and has also
done refinalizations for
international adoptions. He
served as Chairman of the
Drafting Committee to rewrite
the new Tennessee adoption
statute that was effective
January 1, 1996.

Attorney fees for an adoption in
this state are about $2,000 to
$2,500.

TENNESSEE LAWS RELATED TO ADOPTION: QUESTIONS AND ANSWERS

Can an attorney serve as an intermediary?
Yes, but no fee can be charged.

Is advertising permitted?
Yes.

Who must consent to the adoption?
1. The birth mother
2. The birth father, if he is married to the birth mother, or if he listed on the birth certificate or named by the birth mother and has claimed paternity

When can consent be taken from birth mother (father), and how long after the consent is signed can it be revoked?
Robert Tuke, an attorney in Nashville, states that surrender is given before a judge three days or more after birth (unless the judge waives the time requirement) and is revocable for ten days. Surrenders or consents can be given before the birth if done in conformity with the laws of another state.

Tuke also states that the birth father can waive his rights by a sworn statement before or after the birth, and that this statement is irrevocable.

In cases of conflict, the courts are instructed to favor (not merely consider) the child's best interest.

What are the birth father's rights?
If the birth father is named by the birth mother and his whereabouts are unknown, a diligent search must be made to find him and notify him of the adoption. If he cannot be found, then he must be informed of the adoption through public notice (usually placed in a newspaper).

The court is allowed to exclude the birth father if the child is born out of wedlock and the birth father has failed to register with the putative father registry within thirty days of the child's birth and to file change of address information within ten days of any such change. If he is registered, this will subject him to court-ordered child support and medical payments. If he fails to register, his rights can be terminated. After receiving notice of the birth, the birth father must file a legitimation complaint and if he does not, then his rights can be terminated.

The birth father is also required to pay pregnancy-related expenses and child support as soon as he is informed of the birth mother's pregnancy or the child's birth. If he does not do so, then his rights can be terminated.

What fees can adoptive parents pay?
Only an adoption agency can receive fees for serving as an intermediary. Reasonable medical and legal fees and living expenses can be paid. The adoptive parents must give the court a statement of any fees paid or received.

Where does the adoption hearing take place?
The adoption hearing takes place in the court of the county where the adoptive parents live, where the adoptee lives, or where the child placement agency is located.

How are familial and step-parent adoptions different from nonbiological adoptions?
The home study and the six-month waiting period before finalization are waived.

Can a nonresident finalize an adoption in this state?
No. You must have lived in Tennessee for at least one year before filing the petition to adopt. This requirement is waived for those serving in the military who were residents of Tennessee for one year before entering the military.

The birth parents must be given notice of the availability of counseling. If the birth parent cannot afford counseling, the adoptive couple must pay for the counseling.

TEXAS

State Adoption Specialist
Janis Brown
Texas Department of Protective
and Regulatory Services
P.O. Box 149030 M.C.E.- 558
Austin, TX 78717-9030
(512) 438-3412

Compact Administrator
Burton F. Raiford
Interim Commissioner
Texas Department of Human
Services
P.O. Box 149030
Austin, TX 78714-9030

Deputy Compact Administrator
Clarence Timmermann, Jr.
Texas Interstate Placement
Section
Texas Department of Human
Services

P.O. Box 149030
Austin, TX 78714-9030
(512) 450-3314
or
701 West 51st Street, E-505
Austin, TX 78751

Administrative Assistant
Charlotte Howell
(512) 450-3295

Direct all telephone calls and
correspondence to the Deputy
Compact Administrator.

Office hours:
Monday-Friday
8:00 A.M.-5:00 P.M.
Central Time Zone

**State Adoption Exchange and
Photo Listing**

Texas Adoption Resource
Exchange
Texas Department of Protective
and Regulatory Services
P.O. Box 149030, M.C.E.-559
Austin, TX 78717-9030
(512) 438-3357

Private Adoption Agencies

AAA-Alamo Adoption Agency
1222 North Main, Suite 804
San Antonio, TX 78212
(210) 226-4124

AAMA Host Home Project
204 Clifton
Houston, TX 77011
(713) 926-4756

ABC Adoption Agency, Inc.
417 San Pedro Avenue
San Antonio, TX 78212
(210) 227-7820

Abrazo Adoption Associates
10010 San Pedro, Suite 540
San Antonio, TX 78216
(210) 342-5683 or (800) 454-5683

Adopt!, Inc.
3500 Overton Park West
Fort Worth, TX 76109
(817) 923-8874

Adopt a Special Kid (AASK) of
 Texas
1060 Pipeline Road, Suite 106
Hurst, TX 76053
(817) 595-0497

Adoption Access
8330 Meadow Road, Suite 222
Dallas, TX 75231
(214) 750-4847

Adoption Advisory, Inc.
3607 Fairmount
Dallas, TX 75219
(214) 520-0004

Adoption Advocates
GPM South Tower
Suite 355 800 N.W.
San Antonio, TX 78216
(210) 344-4838

Adoption Affiliates, Inc.
215 West Olmos Drive
San Antonio, TX 78212
(210) 824-9939

Adoption—A Gift of Love
P.O. Box 50384
Denton, TX 76206
(817) 387-9311

Adoption Alliance
7303 Blanco Road
San Antonio, TX 78216
(210) 349-3991

Adoption As An Option
3350 Highway 6
Sugarland, TX 77478
(713) 468-1053

Adoption, Inc.
2775 Villa Creek, Suite 240
Dallas, TX 75234
(214) 243-0808

Adoption Information and
 Counseling
2020 Southwest Freeway, Suite 3
Houston, TX 77098
(713) 529-5125

Adoption Resource Consultants
P.O. Box 1224
Richardson, TX 75083
(214) 517-4119

Adoption Services Associates
8703 Wurzbach Road
San Antonio, TX 78240
(210) 699-6094

Adoption Services, Inc.
3500 Overton Park West
Fort Worth, TX 76109
(817) 921-0718

All-Church Home for Children
1424 Summit Avenue
Fort Worth, TX 76102
(817) 335-4041

Alternatives In Motion
20619 Aldine Westfield Road
Humble, TX 77338
(713) 821-6508

Andrel Adoptions
3908 Manchaca
Austin, TX 78704
(512) 448-4605

Baptist Children's Home
7404 Highway 90 West
San Antonio, TX 78227
(210) 674-3010

Blessed Trinity Adoptions, Inc.
8503 Havner Court
Houston, TX 77037
(713) 855-0137

Buckner Baptist Benevolences
P.O. Box 13398
San Antonio, TX 75213
(210) 344-8351

Buckner Baptist Children's Home
5200 South Buckner Boulevard
Dallas, TX 75227
(214) 321-4506

Buckner Baptist Children's Home
129 Brentwood
Lubbock, TX 79416
(806) 795-7151

Care Connection, Inc.
400 Harvey Street
San Marcos, TX 78666
(512) 396-8111

Caring Choices
11559 Bellspring
Houston, TX 77072
(713) 722-8100

Caring Family Network
1223 N. FM 620, Suite 108
Austin, TX 78750
(512) 918-2992

Catholic Charities
3520 Montrose
Houston, TX 77006-4350
(713) 526-4611

Catholic Counseling Services
3845 Oak Lawn
P.O. Box 190507
Dallas, TX 75219
(214) 526-2772

Catholic Family and Children's
 Services, Inc.
2903 West Salinas Street
San Antonio, TX 78207
(210) 433-3256

Catholic Family Service
P.O. Box 15127
Amarillo, TX 79105
(806) 376-4571

Catholic Social Services
2669 Burchill Road
Fort Worth, TX 76105
(817) 536-6857

Catholic Social Services of Laredo
P.O. Box 3305
Laredo, TX 78044
(210) 724-5051

Children's Enterprises
3305 66th
Lubbock, TX 79413
(806) 723-6323

Children's Home of Lubbock
P.O. Box 2824
Lubbock, TX 79408
(806) 762-0481

Chosen Heritage
1331-A West Airport Freeway,
 Suite 311
Euless, TX 76040
(817) 267-7013

Christian Homes of Abilene, Inc.
242 Beech Street
Abilene, TX 79601
(915) 677-2205

Christian Services of East Texas
807 West Glenwood Boulevard
Tyler, TX 75701
(903) 592-3850

Christian Services of the
  Southwest
6320 LBJ Freeway, Suite 122
Dallas, TX 75240
(214) 960-9981

Christ's Haven for Children
P.O. Box 467
Keller, TX 76248
(817) 431-1544

Cradle of Hope
311 North Market Street,
  Suite 300
Dallas, TX 75202
(214) 747-4500

Cradle of Life Adoption Agency
245 North Fourth Street
Beaumont, TX 77701
(409) 832-3000

DePelchin Children's Center
100 Sandman Street
Houston, TX 77007
(713) 861-8136

El Paso Adoption Services
604 Myrtle
El Paso, TX 79901
(915) 542-1086

El Paso Center for Children
3700 Altura Boulevard
El Paso, TX 79930
(915) 565-8361

Family Counseling and Children's
  Services
5020A Lakeland Circle
Waco, TX 76710
(817) 751-1777

Fundacion Ascencio-Pine
P.O. Box 8225
Horseshoe Bay, TX 78654
(512) 598-2604

Gift of Love Adoption Agency
1420 West Mockingbird,
  Suite 395
Dallas, TX 75247
(214) 819-2424

Gladney Center
2300 Hemphill
Fort Worth, TX 76110
(817) 922-6000

Harmony Family Services
1626 North 3rd
Abilene, TX 79601
(915) 672-8820

Heart International Adoption
  Services
1317 Alabama Road
Wharton, TX 77488
(713) 532-1774

High Plains Children's Home
  and Family Services, Inc.
P.O. Box 7448
Amarillo, TX 79114-7448
(806) 355-6588

His Kids Adoptions
P. O. Box 5988
Amarillo, TX 78763
(512) 474-9661

Homes of Saint Mark
1302 Marshall
Houston, TX 77006
(713) 522-2800

Hope Cottage, Inc.
Circle of Hope
4209 McKinney Avenue,
  Suite 200
Dallas, TX 75205
(214) 526-8721

Jester Adoption Services
P.O. Box 280
Denton, TX 76202
(817) 380-1010

Jewish Family Service
7800 Northaven Road
Dallas, TX 75230
(214) 696-6400

Jewish Family Service
P.O. Box 20548
Houston, TX 77225
(713) 667-9336

LDS Social Services-Texas
1100 West Jackson Road
Carrollton, TX 75006
(214) 242-2182

Lee and Beulah Moor
  Children's Home
1100 Cliff Drive
El Paso, TX 79902
(915) 544-8777

Life Anew Adoption Agency
2635 Loop N.E. 286
Paris, TX 75460
(903) 785-7701

Los Niños International
  Adoption Center
1600 Lake Front Circle
The Woodlands, TX 77380-3600
(713) 363-2892

Loving Alternatives Adoptions
P.O. Box 131466
Tyler, TX 75713
(903) 581-2891

Lutheran Social Services
  of Texas, Inc
P.O. Box 49589
Austin, TX 78765
(512) 459-1000

Lutheran Social Services
  of Texas, Inc.
3001 LBJ Freeway, Suite 107
Dallas, TX 75234
(214) 620-0581

Lutheran Social Services
  of Texas, Inc.
3131 West Alabama, Suite 124
Houston, TX 77098
(713) 521-0110

Marywood Maternity
  and Adoption Services
510 West 26th Street
Austin, TX 78705
(512) 472-9251 or (800) 251-
  5433

Methodist Home
1111 Herring Avenue
Waco, TX 76708
(817) 753-0181

New Life Children's Services
1911 Tomball Pkwy.
Houston, TX 77070
(713) 955-1001

PAC Child Placing Agency
Box 826, Route 2
Amarillo, TX 79101
(806) 335-9138

Placement Services Agency
P.O. Box 797365
Dallas, TX 75739
(214) 387-3312

Quality of Life, Inc.
10242 Crestover Drive
Dallas, TX 75229
(214) 350-1637

Read Adoption Agency, Inc.
718 Myrtle
El Paso, TX 79901
(915) 533-3697

Smithlawn Maternity Home and
  Adoption Agency
711 76th Street
P.O. Box 6451
Lubbock, TX 79413
(806) 745-2574

Southwest Maternity
  Center/Methodist Mission
  Home
6487 Whitby Road
San Antonio, TX 78240
(210) 696-2410

Spaulding for Children
710 North Post Oak Road,
  Suite 500
Houston, TX 77024-3832
(713) 681-6991

Texas Baptist Children's Home
P.O. Box 7
Round Rock, TX 78664
(512) 255-3668

Texas Baptist Home for Children
P.O. Drawer 309
Waxahachie, TX 75165
(214) 937-1370

Texas Cradle Society
8600 Wurzbach Road, Suite 1110
San Antonio, TX 78240-4334
(210) 614-0299

Therapeikos, Inc.
2817 North Second
Abilene, TX 79603
(915) 677-2216

Triad
2212 Sunny Lane
Killeen, TX 76541
(817) 690-5959

Trinity Adoption Services
  International
7610 Club Lake Drive
Houston, TX 77095
(713) 463-3585

Worldwide Adoptions, Inc.
13430 Northwest Freeway
Houston, TX 77040
(713) 462-6573

**Adoptive Parent Support
  Groups and Postadoption
  Services**

Adopted Friends
Attn.: Traudel Meyer
6610 Sharpview
Houston, TX 77074
(713) 777-5461

Adopting Children Together, Inc.
Attn.: Debbie Sanders
P.O. Box 120966
Arlington, TX 76012-0966
(817) 461-5022

Adoptive Families Together
P.O. Box 272963
Houston, TX 77277
(713) 668-9733

Adoptive Families
  of Romanian Children
Attn.: Gloria C. Smith
1403 Nails Creek Drive
Sugarland, TX 77478-5360
(903) 763-4683

Alamo Association
  of Adoptive Parents
Attn.: Lori Felix
7806 Falcon Ridge
San Antonio, TX 78239
(210) 656-5633

APT
Attn.: Joyce Zachman
3035 Green Fields Drive
Sugar Land, TX 77479
(713) 980-4814

Aries Center
5025 N. Cental Expressway
Suite 3040
Dallas, TX 75205
(214) 521-4560

Austin Kids from All Cultures
Attn.: Pam and Ron Mathews
4508 Sinclair Avenue
Austin, TX 78756
(512) 467-9177

Circle of Hope
c/o Hope Cottage
4209 McKinney
Dallas, TX 75205
(214) 526-8721

Council on Adoptable Children
  of Abilene
Attn.: Stanley Morton
P.O. Box 2236
Granite Shoals, TX 78654-2699

Council on Adoptable Children
  of Austin
Attn.: Jerry and Sandra Dush
6600 Bradley
Austin, TX 78723
(512) 928-0702

Council on Adoptable Children
  of Dallas
Attn.: Bobbie T. Kerr
Box 141199, Dept. 366
Dallas, TX 75214
(214) 823-5047

Council on Adoptable Children
  of East Texas
Attn.: Chris and Ken Smith
601 Harvard
Tyler, TX 75703
(214) 534-1221

Council on Adoptable Children
  of Houston
Attn.: Glen Lingo
P.O. Box 1554
Houston, TX 77251
(713) 957-1148

Council on Adoptable Children
  of Texas
Attn.: Clara Flores
Route 2, Box 177-F
Edinburg, TX 78539
(512) 383-2680

Council on Adoptable Children
  of the Texas Panhandle
Attn.: Sandra Penn
P.O. Box 3700
Amarillo, TX 79116
(806) 358-6211

Council on Adoptable Children
  of Tip-O'-Tex
Attn.: Daniel Van Coppendale
3409 Hackberry Lane
Brownsville, TX 78521
(210) 544-7703

Families Through Adoption
Attn.: Bill Betzen
P.O. Box 190507
Dallas, TX 75219-0507
(214) 526-2772

Family Counseling Service
1635 N.E. Loop 410, Suite 601
San Antonio, TX 78209
(210) 821-5980

Forever Families of El Paso
Attn.: Cheryl Bowman
P.O. Box 3182
El Paso, TX 79925
(915) 594-2427

Friends and Families of Adoption
Attn.: Pam Heins
4117 Norcross
Plano, TX 75024
(214) 335-2311

Friends and Families of AGAPE
Attn.: Joan Bartels
2004 Aspen Drive
Lewisville, TX 75067

Heart Words
4054 McKinney Avenue,
  Suite 302
Dallas, TX 75204
(214) 521-4560

Maple, Inc.
Attn.: Hoagy and Cathy Powell
R#1 Box 52UB
Rosenberg, TX 77471
(713) 342-1952

National Adoption Network
P.O. Box 2130
Coppell, TX 75019
(800) 246-4237 or (214) 335-
  0906

North American Council on
  Adoptable Children State
  Representative
Attn.: Marye Lou Mauldin
2111 N. Copper Street
Arlington, TX 76011
(817) 265-3496

North American Council on
  Adoptable Children State
  Representative
Attn.: Johnny Wilson
808 Woodlawn Drive
Harker Hights, TX 76543
(817) 690-3317

North Texas Families
  for Adoption
Attn.: Patti Sorsby
Box 29903
Dallas, TX 75229
(817) 267-7545

Open Arms
Attn.: Lisa Archer
1306 Hitherfield Drive
Sugar Land, TX 77478-2486

Parents Aiding
  and Lending Support
Attn.: Donna Thompson
3709 Canterbury
Baytown, TX 77521
(713) 427-7293

Post Adoption Center
  of the Southwest
8600 Wurzbach Road, Suite 1110
San Antonio, TX 78240
(210) 614-0299

Romanian Cousins
Attn.: Cheryl Long
2208 Eastwood Drive
Richardson, TX 75080-2609
(817) 448-8002

Single Adoptive Parent Support
  Group
Attn.: Deborah Webne
12751 Whittington, Apt. 136
Houston, TX 77077
(713) 496-2855

Stars of David
Attn.: Janet Glasofer
P.O. Box 35181
Houston, TX 77235-5181
(713) 980-4634

**Adopted Person and Birth
Relative Support Groups**

Adoptee Liberty Movement
  Association (ALMA)
P.O. Box 200392
Austin, TX 78720|0392
(512) 335-8982

Adoptee Liberty Movement
  Association (ALMA)
P.O. Box 11273
Killeen, TX 76547

Adoptee Liberty Movement
  Association (ALMA)
P.O. Box 720301
McAllen, TX 78502
(210) 682-8748

Adoptee Liberty Movement
  Association (ALMA)
P.O. Box 1424
Plainview, TX 79072

Adoptee Liberty Movement
  Association (ALMA)
P.O. Box 831172
Richardson, TX 75083

Adoptee Liberty Movement
  Association (ALMA)
P.O. Box 468
Riverside, TX 77367

Adoptee Liberty Movement
  Association (ALMA)
P.O. Box 191
Spring Branch, TX 78070

Adoptees, Adoptive/Birth Parents
  in Search
4208 Roxbury
El Paso, TX 78704
(915) 581-0478

Adoption Knowledge Affiliates
P.O. Box 402033
Austin, TX 78704
(512) 442-8252

Adoption Search
  and Reunite, Inc.
Box 371
Pasadena, TX 77501
(713) 477-0491

Adoption Triad Forum
Box 832161
Richardson, TX 75081

Birthparents/Adoptees Support
  Group
4038 Clayhead Road
Richmond, TX 77469

Child and Family Resources
2775 Villa Creek, #240
Dallas, TX 75234

Hope Cottage Adoption Center
4209 McKinney Avenue, #200
Dallas, TX 75205
(214) 526-8721

Love Roots Wings
10432 Achilles
El Paso, TX 79924
(915) 821-7253

Marywood Post Adoption
  Services
510 W. 26th Street
Austin, TX 78705
(512) 472-9251

Orphan Voyage of Houston
5811 Southminster
Houston, TX 77035
(713) 723-1762

Post Adoption Center of the
    Southwest
8600 Wurzbach Road, Suite 1110
San Antonio, TX 78240-4334
(210) 614-0299

Search and Support Group of
    DePelchin Center
100 Sandman
Houston, TX 77007
(713) 802-7724

Searchline of Plano
3944 E. Bark Boulevard
Plano, TX 75074

Searchline of Texas
1516 Old Orchard
Irving, TX 75061
(214) 445-7005

State Bar of Texas
P.O. Box 12487
Austin, TX 78711-2847
                or
1414 Colorado Street
Austin, Texas 78701-1627
(512) 463-1400
fax (512)-463-1475

Adoption Attorneys

Vika Andrel
3908 Manchaca Road
Austin, TX 78704
(512) 448-4605

Gerald A. Bates
500 Throckmorton Street, #1404
Fort Worth, TX 76102
(817) 338-2840

Karla J. Boydston
2300 Hemphill
Fort Worth, TX 76110
(817) 922-6010

C. Harold Brown
Brown and Thompson
500 Throckmorton Street,
    # 3030
Fort Worth, TX 76102
(817) 338-4888
fax (817) 338-0700

Mary W. Clark
10 Eighth Street S.E.
Paris, TX 75460

Heidi B. Cox
2300 Hemphill
Fort Worth, TX 76110
(817) 922-6043

Dale R. Johnson*
7303 Blanco Road
San Antonio, TX 78216
(512) 349-3761

* Mr. Johnson had completed
more than 400 agency
adoptions and more than fifty
independent adoptions. He is
the executive Director of The
Adoption Alliance. He and the
staff of his licensed agency will
work with birth mothers
throughout Texas.

Michael R. Lackmeyer
1201 South W.S. Young Drive
Killeen, TX 76543
(817) 690-2223

Susan I. Paquiet
1701 River Run Road, Suite 1021
Fort Worth, TX 76107

Irv. W. Queal
8117 Preston Road, Suite 600
Dallas, TX 75225
(214) 373-9100
fax (214) 373-6688

Donald R. Royall
13430 Northwest Frwy. , #650
Houston, TX 77040
(713) 462-6500

Melody B. Royall
13430 Northeast Frwy. , #650
Houston, TX 77040
(713) 462-6500

Mel W. Shelander
245 N. Fourth Street
Beaumont, TX 77701
(409) 833-2165

Ellen A. Yarrell
1980 Post Oak Boulevard, #1720
Houston, TX 77056
(713) 621-3332

Linda Zuflacht
8703 Wurzbach Road
San Antonio, TX 78240
(512) 699-6088

TEXAS LAWS RELATED TO ADOPTION: QUESTIONS AND ANSWERS

In Texas, a preadoption report is given to the adoptive parents, which provides the health, social, educational, and genetic history of the child and the child's biological family.

Can an attorney serve as an intermediary?
No.

Is advertising permitted?
Yes.

Who must consent to the adoption?
1. Both birth parents
2. A managing conservator, if appointed; a conservator is a person or agency who retains all the rights and powers of a parent to the exclusion of other parents

When can consent be taken from birth mother (father), and how long after the consent is signed can it be revoked?
Consent cannot be taken until forty-eight hours after birth and is irrevocable if the consent designates the Department of Human Services as managing conservator.

The consent must specifically state that it is irrevocable for a certain time period, up to sixty days. During this period of time the adoptive couple or adoption agency must file the adoption petition in order that the birth parents' rights be terminated. It is in the adoptive couple's best interests to include the entire sixty days on the consent form, so that there is plenty of time for the court to terminate the birth parents' rights.

Termination of rights can also be done by court appearance by the birth parents within ten days of filing.

What are the birth father's rights?
There is no consent required of a birth father who has abandoned the child with no means of identification or who does not file an admission of paternity within a reasonable time frame. If the birth father cannot be found, his rights can be terminated by publication of notice of the adoption proceedings; termination will occur after a certain time period has elapsed if he does not respond. Texas law also states that if a birth parents leaves a child in custody of another with no intent to return and without providing adequate support for the child, then consent is not required and that birth parent's rights can be terminated.

If a birth father is out of the picture, you may want to file his termination of parental rights before the birth. Also, his rights cannot be terminated until five days after publication of the notice begins. This way, once the child is born, the paperwork is completed.

What fees can adoptive parents pay?
Medical, legal fees, and reasonable counseling fees are permitted. In an independent adoption, no living expenses can be paid.

Where does the adoption hearing take place?
The adoption hearing may take place in the court of the county where the adoptive parents live, the child lives, or where the agency is located.

How are familial and step-parent adoptions different from nonbiological adoptions?
In a relative or stepparent adoption, the preadoption report on the child's background and status is not required.

Can a nonresident finalize an adoption in this state?
Yes.

UTAH

State Adoption Specialist
Olivia Moreton
Utah Department of Human
    Services
Division of Family Services
120 North 200 West, #419
Salt Lake City, UT 84103
(801) 538-4084

Compact Administrator
Barbara Thompson
Division of Family Services
150 West North Temple,
    Room 360
P.O. Box 45500
Salt Lake City, UT 84145-0500
(801) 533-7107

Deputy Compact Administrator
Stacy Brubaker
Division of Family Services
150 West North Temple,
    Room 360
P.O. Box 45500
Salt Lake City, UT 84145-0500
(801) 533-4526
fax (801) 538-4016

Direct all telephone calls and correspondence to the Compact Administrator.

Office hours:
Monday-Friday
8:00 A.M.-5:00 P.M.
Mountain Time Zone

State Adoption Exchange and Photo Listings

Department of Human Services
Division of Family Services
P.O. Box 45500
Salt Lake City, UT 84145
(801) 538-4100

Private Adoption Agencies

Alternative Options
11638 High Mountain Drive
Sandy, UT 84092
(801) 572-6360

Catholic Community Services
2300 West 1700 South
Salt Lake City, UT 84104
(801) 977-9119

Children's Aid Society of Utah
652 26th Street
Ogden, UT 84401
(801) 393-8671

Children's Service Society
12450 400 East, Suite 400
Salt Lake City, UT 84111
(801) 355-7444

Families for Children
P.O. Box 521192
Salt Lake City, UT 84152
(801) 487-3916

LDS Social Services
350 East 300 North, Suite B
American Fork, UT 84003
(801) 756-5217

LDS Social Services
563 West 500 South
Bountiful, UT 84010
(801) 298-5700

LDS Social Services
1001 West, 535 South
Cedar City, UT 84720
(801) 586-4470

LDS Social Services
85 East 400 North
Price, UT 84501
(801) 637-2991

LDS Social Services
780 West 800 South
Salt Lake City, UT 84104
(801) 566-2556

LDS Social Services
625 East 8400 South
Sandy, UT 84070
(801) 566-2556

LDS Social Services
95 West 100 South
Logan, UT 84321
(801) 752-5302

LDS Social Services
1525 Lincoln Avenue
Ogden, UT 84404
(801) 621-6510

LDS Social Services
1190 North 900 East
Provo, UT 84601
(801) 3788-7620

LDS Social Services
55 West 100 North
P.O. Box 827
Richfield, UT 84107

Utah Adoption Service
3450 Highland Drive, Suite 102
Salt Lake City, UT 84106
(801) 466-9975

West Sands Adoption and Counseling
461 East 2780 North
Provo, UT 84604
(801) 377-4379

Adoptive Parent Support Groups and Postadoption Groups

Adoptive Parent Group of Utah
645 E. 4500 South
Salt Lake City, UT 84107
(801) 468-5493

Families Involved in Adoption
Attn.: Shelly Phillips
911 Walden Hills Drive
Salt Lake City, UT 84123
(801) 292-1062

HOPE of Utah/Parents for Attachment
Attn.: Margo and Nolan Fugal
1241 Wasatch Drive
Provo, UT 84604
(801) 373-7228

North American Council on Adoptable Children State Representative
Attn.: Suzanne Stott
1219 Windsor Street
Salt Lake City, UT 84105
(801) 487-3916

Utah State Adoption Support Group
Attn.: Carol Stenger
645 East 4500 South
Salt Lake City, UT 84117
(801) 264-7598

Adopted Person and Birth Relative Support Groups

Adoptee Liberty Movement Association (ALMA)
P.O. Box 11383
Salt Lake City, UT 84147

Adoption Connection of Utah
1349 Mariposa Avenue
Salt Lake City, UT 84106
(801) 278-4858

LAMBS
672 East 2025 South
Salt Lake City, UT 84010
(801) 298-8520

Utah Department of Health
Attn.: Director, Vital Statistics
288 North 1460 West
Salt Lake City, UT 84145
(801) 538-6105

Utah State Bar
645 South 200 East, Suite 300
Salt Lake City, UT 84111
(801) 531-9077

Adoption Attorneys

Paul Barton*
345 East 400 South, Suite 201
Salt Lake City, UT 84111
(801) 322-2300
fax (801) 322-2303

* Mr. Barton has completed ten independent and twenty agency adoptions.

Robert L. Moody
Marilyn M. Brown
2525 North Canyon Road
Provo, UT 84604
(801) 373-2721
fax (801) 375-6293

Les F. England*
Sutherland & England
P.O. Box 680845
Park City, UT 84068
(801) 649-1945
fax (801) 649-1956

* Mr. England has conducted
more than 500 independent
adoptions, 1,000 agency
adoptions, and fifty
international adoptions.

David Friel
2120 S. 1300 East, Suite 301
Salt Lake City, UT 84106
(801) 486-3751
fax (801) 487-9889

Frederick Green
10 East Exchange Place, Suite 622
Salt Lake City, UT 84111
(801) 363-5650

Robert MacDonald
459 East 500 South, Suite 200
Salt Lake City, UT 84111

UTAH LAWS RELATED TO ADOPTION: QUESTIONS AND ANSWERS

Can an attorney serve as an intermediary?
Yes.

Is advertising permitted?
Yes.

Who must consent to the adoption?
1. The birth parents mother
2. The birth father, if he is married to the birth mother, or if he has demonstrated a significant commitment to the child
3. The child placement agency, if involved

When can consent be taken from birth mother (father), and how long after the consent is signed can it be revoked?
Consent cannot be taken until at least twenty-four hours after birth through court appearance. The consent is irrevocable once signed.

What are the birth father's rights?
Although 1995 legislation reduced birth fathers' rights, their rights must still be terminated by court. No consent is needed if the birth father has not established paternity by filing an action in court, provided support for the birth mother during her pregnancy or for the child after delivery, or made an effort to maintain a parental relationship with the child.

What fees can adoptive parents pay?
Attorneys or other intermediaries cannot charge for locating a birth mother. A statement of all fees for legal and medical and living expenses paid must be filed with the court before the final adoption.

Where does the adoption hearing take place?
The hearing may take place in the court of the county where the adoptive parents live.

How are familial and step-parent adoptions different from nonbiological adoptions?
Les F. England, an attorney in Park City, states that no home study is usually required in stepparent and familial adoptions. In a step-parent adoption, the child must reside with

the petitioning parent for more than twelve months, instead of the six months required in other adoptions.

Can a nonresident finalize an adoption in this state?
No. However, residency can be established.

VERMONT

State Adoption Specialist
Diane Dexter
Division of Social and
  Rehabilitative Services
103 South Main Street
Waterbury, VT 05671
(802) 241-2131

Vermont Bar Association
P.O. Box 100
Montpelier, VT 05601
(802) 223-2020

Compact Administrator
Frederick Ober, MSW
Social Services Division
of Department of Social and
  Rehabilitative Services
103 South Main Street
Waterbury, VT 05671-2401
(802) 241-2131

Deputy Compact Administrator
Joan D. Steele
Social Services Division
of Department of Social and
  Rehabilitative Services
103 South Main Street
Waterbury, VT 05671-2401
(802) 241-2141

Direct all telephone calls and
  correspondence to the Deputy
  Compact Administrator.

Office hours:
Monday-Friday
8:00 A.M.-4:30 P.M.
Eastern Time Zone

State Adoption Exchange and Photo Listing

Northern New England Adoption
  Exchange
Department of Human Services
221 State Street
Augusta, ME 04333
(207) 289-2971

Private Adoption Agencies

Adoption Center, Inc.
278 Pearl Street
Burlington, VT 05401
(802) 862-5855

Adoption Resource Services, Inc.
1904 North Avenue
Burlington, VT 05401
(802) 863-5368

Bethany Christian Services
1538 Turnpike Street
North Andover, MA 01845
(508) 794-9800

Casey Family Services
7 Palmer Court
White River Junction, VT
  05001-3323
(802) 649-1400

Friends in Adoption
P.O. Box 1228
Middletown Springs, VT 05757
(802) 235-2373

LDS Social Services
131 Route 101A Amherst Plaza,
  Suite 203
Amherst, NH 03031
(603) 889-0148

Lund Family Center
P.O. Box 4009
Burlington, VT 05406-4009
(802) 864-7467

Vermont Catholic Charities
351 North Avenue
Burlington, VT 05401
(802) 658-6110

Vermont Children's Aid Society
P.O. Box 127
Winooski, VT 05404-0127
(802) 655-0006

Wide Horizons for Children
282 Moody Street
Waltham, MA 02154
(617) 894-5330
(802) 658-2070

Adoptive Parent Support Groups and Postadoption Services

Casey Family Services
7 Palmer Court
White River Junction, VT
  05001-3323
(802) 649-1400

Department of Mental Health
Children's Services for Respite
  Care
Waterbury, VT 05671

Friends in Adoption
Box 7270
Buxton Avenue
Middletown Springs, VT 05757

Future in Vermont
Attn.: Shirley Hammond
1904 North Avenue
Burlington, VT 05401
(802) 863-5368

North American Council on
  Adoptable Children State
  Representative
Attn.: Susan Correia
8 Aspen Drive
Essex Junction, VT 05452
(802) 878-5971

Vermont Children's Aid Society
Lifetime Adoption Project
P.O. Box 127
Winooski, VT 05404|0127
(802) 655-0006 or (800) 479-
  0015

Vermont Families Through
  Adoption
Attn.: Judy LeMay
16 Aspen Drive
Essex Junction, VT 05452
(802) 878-1753

Adopted Person and Birth Relative Support Groups

Adoptee Liberty Movement
  Association (ALMA)
P.O. Box 257
Milton, VT 05468

Adoptee Liberty Movement
  Association (ALMA)
RD#2, Box 2997
Vergennes, VT 05491

Adoption Alliance of Vermont
91 Court Street
Middlebury, VT 05753
(802) 388-7569

Adoption Alliance of Vermont
17 Hopkins Street
Rutland, VT 05701
(802) 773-7078

Adoption Alliance of Vermont
104 Falls Road
Shelburne, VT 05482-0641
(802) 985-2462

Adoption Alliance of Vermont
107 Twin Oaks
South Burlington, VT 05403
(802) 863-1727

Adoption Crossroads
Box 424
Concord, VT 05824

Adoption Resource Service, Inc.
1904 North Avenue
Burlington, VT 05401
(802) 863-5368

Adoption Search/Support
  Network
RR1, Box 83
East Calais, VT 05650
(802) 456-8850

B & C Search Assistance of
  Vermont
P.O. Box 1451
St. Albans, VT 05478
(802) 524-9825

Beacon of Vermont
Box 152
Bakersfield, VT 05441
(802) 758-2369

Beacon of Vermont
5 Calo Court
St. Albans, VT 05478
(802) 527-7507

Friends in Adoption
P.O. Box 1228
Middletown Springs, VT 05757
(802) 235-2373

Vermont Bar Association
P.O. Box 100
Montpelier, VT 05601
802) 223-2020

Adoption Attorneys

Norman Blais
289 College Street
Burlington, VT 05401
(802) 865-0095

Julie Frame
100 Main Street
Burlington, VT 05402
(802) 864-4531

Michael Gadue
110 Main Street
Burlington, VT 05401
(802) 658-6417

Barry Griffith
98 Merchants Row
Rutland, VT 05701
(802) 773-7638

Lindsey Huddle
72 Hungerford Terrace
Burlington, VT 05401
(802) 658-0888

Kurt Hughes
131 Main Street
P.O. Box 363
Burlington, VT 05402
(802) 864-9811

Peter Langrock
15 South Pleasant Street
P.O. Box 351
Middlebury, VT 05753
(802) 388-6356

Pam Marsh
62 Court Street
Middlebury, VT 05753
(802) 388-4026

Susan Murray
15 South Pleasant Street
P.O. Box 351
Middlebury, VT 05753
(802) 388-6356

Alan Rome
137 Elm Street
Montpelier, VT 05602
(802) 229-5060

Jeffrey Taylor
P.O. Box 349
Bradford, VT 05033
(802) 222-5705

Nancy Veresan
P.O. Box 231
Hanover, NH 03755
(603) 643-5178

VERMONT LAWS RELATED TO ADOPTION: QUESTIONS AND ANSWERS

Can an attorney serve as an intermediary?
Yes.

Is advertising permitted?
Yes.

Who must consent to the adoption?
1. The birth parents, if married to each other, or
2. The birth mother, if the child is born out of wedlock or if the husband is not the child's biological father
3. The child placement agency, if involved

When can consent be taken from birth mother (father), and how long after the consent is signed can it be revoked?
Consent cannot be taken until seventy-two hours after birth. If it is taken in court and if stated on the consent, it is irrevocable. If irrevocability is not stated, the birth parents have fifteen days to revoke their consent. According to a staff person at the Interstate Compact office, the birth parents can go to court for termination of their rights within days after the child's birth. The court prefers the birth father to be present; however, this is often not possible, or he may refuse.

What are the birth father's rights?
A birth father has full paternal rights. His rights cannot be terminated unless he provides a consent or it can be shown that he has abandoned his rights to the child to be adopted. Vermont law also states that a birth father's rights can be waived if he does not acknowledge paternity at the time of the adoption hearing.

What fees can adoptive parents pay?
Payment of medical, legal and some living expenses are permitted. The Department of Social and Rehabilitation Services may charge a fee of up to $535 for conducting a home study.

Where does the adoption hearing take place?
The adoption hearing takes place in the court of the county where the adoptive parents live. If they do not live in the state, the hearing takes place where the child placement agency is located.

How are familial and step-parent adoptions different from nonbiological adoptions?
In a stepparent adoption, the process is simple and an out-of-court consent is permitted. In a relative adoption, no home study is required the under present law.

Can a nonresident finalize an adoption in this state?
Yes, but only an agency adoption.

VIRGINIA

State Adoption Specialist
Brenda Kerr
Virginia Department of Social
    Services
730 East Broad Street
Richmond, VA 23219-1849
(804) 692-1290

Compact Administrator
Larry D. Jackson
Virginia Department of Social
    Services
Blair Building
8007 Discovery Drive
Richmond, VA 23229-8699

Deputy Compact Administrator
Suzanne Ashford
Virginia Department of Social
    Services

ICPC Office
8007 Discovery Drive
Richmond, VA 23229-8699
(804) 662-9434
fax (804) 662-9742

Direct all telephone calls and
    correspondence to the Deputy
Compact Administrator.

Office hours:
Monday-Friday
8:00 A.M.-5:00 P.M.
Eastern Time Zone

**State Adoption Exchange and
    Photo Listing**

Adoption Resource Exchange of
    Virginia (AREVA)
Virginia Department of Social
    Services

730 East Broad Street
Richmond, VA 23219-1849
(804) 692-1280 or
    (800) DO-ADOPT

Private Adoption Agencies

ABC Adoption Services, Inc.
4725 Garst Mill Road
Roanoke, VA 24018
(540) 989-2845

Adoption Service Information
    Agency, Inc. (ASIA)
7659 Leesburg Pike
Falls Church, VA 22043
(202) 726-7193

American Adoption Agency, Inc.
9070 Euclid Avenue
Manassas, VA 22110
(202) 638-1543

Barker Foundation, Inc.
1495 Chain Bridge Road,
Suite 201
McLean, VA 22101
(703) 536-1827

Bethany Christian Services, Inc.
11212 Waples Mill Road, #101
Fairfax, VA 22030
(703) 385-5440

Bethany Christian Services, Inc.
1406 Princess Anne Street
Fredericksburg, VA 22401
(540) 373-5165

Bethany Christian Services, Inc.
291 Independence Boulevard,
Suite 542
Virginia Beach, VA 23462
(804) 499-9367

Catholic Charities of the Diocese
of Arlington, Inc.
3838 North Cathedral Lane
Arlington, VA 22203
(703) 841-2531

Catholic Charities of the Diocese
of Arlington, Inc.
5294 Lyngate Court
Burke, VA 22015
(703) 425-0100

Catholic Charities of the Diocese
of Arlington, Inc.
612 Lafayette Boulevard, Suite 50
Fredericksburg, VA 22401
(540) 371-1124

Catholic Charities of the Diocese
of Arlington, Inc.
1011 Berryville Avenue, Suite 1
Winchester, VA 22601
(540) 667-7940

Catholic Charities
of Richmond, Inc.
1512 Willow Lawn Drive
Richmond, VA 23230
(804) 285-5900

Catholic Charities
of Hampton Roads, Inc.
Churchland Medical and
Professional Center
3804 A&C Poplar Hill Road
Chesapeake, VA 23321
(804) 484-0703

Catholic Charities
of Hampton Roads, Inc.
Windsor West Professional
Center
12829-A Jefferson Avenue, Suite
101
Newport News, VA 23602
(804) 875-0060

Catholic Charities
of Hampton Roads, Inc.
1301 Colonial Avenue
Norfolk, VA 23517
(804) 625-2568

Catholic Charities
of Hampton Roads, Inc.
4855 Princess Anne Road
Virginia Beach, VA 23462
(804) 467-7707

Catholic Charities
of Hampton Roads, Inc.
1300 Jamestown Road
Williamsburg, VA 23185
(804) 253-2847

Catholic Charities of
Southwestern Virginia, Inc.
St. Mary's Catholic Church
706 Harding Avenue, N.E.
Blacksburg, VA 24060
(540) 552-0664

Catholic Charities of
Southwestern Virginia, Inc.
820 Campbell Avenue, S.W.
Roanoke, VA 24016
(540) 344-5107

Children's Home Society
of Virginia, Inc.
4200 Fitzhugh Avenue
Richmond, VA 23230
(804) 353-0191

Children's Home Society of
Virginia, Inc.
1620 Fifth Street, S.W.
Roanoke, VA 24016
(540) 344-9281

Coordinators/2
5204 Patterson Avenue
Richmond, VA 23226
(804) 288-7595

Datz Foundation
404 Pine Street, Suite 202
Vienna, VA 22180
(703) 242-8800

Families United Through
Adoption
4609 Heather Court
Charlottesville, VA 22911
(804) 978-2861

Family and Child Services of
Washington, D.C., Inc.
5249 Duke Street, #308
Alexandria, VA 22304
(703) 823-2656

Family Life Services
1000 Villa Road
Lynchburg, VA 24503
(804) 384-3043

Family Services of Tidewater, Inc.
222 19th Street, West
Norfolk, VA 23517
(804) 622-7017

Jewish Family Service of
Tidewater, Inc.
United Jewish Community Center
of the Virginia Peninsula
2700 Spring Road
Newport News, VA 23606
(804) 489-3111

Jewish Family Service of
Tidewater, Inc.
7300 Newport Avenue
P.O. Box 9503
Norfolk, VA 23505
(804) 489-3111

Jewish Family Service of
Tidewater, Inc.
403 Boush Street, Suite 350.
Norfolk, VA 23510
(804) 622-0094

Jewish Family Service of
Tidewater, Inc.
5520 Greenwich Road, Suite 202
Virginia Beach, VA 23462
(804) 473-2695

Jewish Family Services, Inc.
6718 Patterson Avenue
Richmond, VA 23226
(804) 282-5644

Jewish Social Service Agency, Inc.
7345 McWhorter Place, Suite 100
Annandale, VA 22003
(703) 750-5400

LDS Social Services
of Virginia, Inc.
8110 Virginia Pine Court
Richmond, VA 23237
(804) 743-0727

Lutheran Family Services, Inc.
Route 1, Box 417
McGaheysville, VA 22804
(540) 289-6141

Lutheran Social Services of the
National Capital Area, Inc.
Family and Children's Services
7401 Leesburg Pike
P.O. Box 3363
Falls Church, VA 22043
(703) 698-5026

New Family Foundation
3615 Wisconsin Avenue, N.W.
Washington, DC 20016
(202) 244-1400 or (703) 273-
5960

Nurturing Family Growth
207 Pearson Drive
Lynchburg, VA 24502
(804) 237-4195

Pearl S. Buck Foundation, Inc.
(Welcome House Social Services)
5905 West Broad Street, Suite
300
Richmond, VA 23230
(804) 288-3920

Rainbow Christian Services, Inc.
P.O. Box 9
6004 Artemus Road
Gainesville, VA 22065
(703) 754-8516

Shore Adoption Services, Inc.
113 Holly Crescent
Virginia Beach, VA 23451
(804) 422-6361

United Methodist Family Services
of Virginia, Inc.
6335 Little River Turnpike
Alexandria, VA 22312
(703) 941-9008

United Methodist Family Services
of Virginia, Inc.
3900 West Broad Street
Richmond, VA 23230
(804) 353-4461

United Methodist Family Services
of Virginia, Inc.
715 Baker Road, Suite 201
Virginia Beach, VA 23462
(804) 490-9791

Virginia Baptist Children's Home
and Family Services
7100 Columbia Pike
Annandale, VA 22003
(703) 750-3660

Virginia Baptist Children's Home
and Family Services
8309 Orcutt Avenue
Newport News, VA 23605
(804) 826-3477

Virginia Baptist Children's Home
and Family Services
700 East Belt Boulevard
Richmond, VA 23224
(804) 231-4466

Virginia Baptist Children's Home
and Family Services
Mount Vernon Avenue
P.O. Box 849
Salem, VA 24153
(540) 389-5468

**Adoptive Parent Support
Groups and Postadoption
Services**

Adoption Resource Exchange
for Single Parents
P.O. Box 5782
Springfield, VA 22150
(703) 866-5577

Adoptive Families of Central
Virginia
Attn.: Lisa Landsverk
111 Cavalier Drive
Charlottesville, VA 22901
(804) 978-2835

Adoptive Families Hand in Hand
Attn.: Melissa Tiffany
P.O. Box 1175
Culpeper, VA 22701
(540) 937-3006

Adoptive Families
of Northern Virginia
P.O. Box 3408
Merrifield, VA 22116-3408
(703) 242-1125

Adoptive Family Group
of Central Virginia
Attn.: Thomas Spahn
6404 Westchester Circle
Richmond, VA 23225
(804) 775-4348

Adoptive Parent Resource
Network of Virginia
10261 Queensgate Road
Midlothian, VA 23113
(800) 772-3253

ASIA Family & Friends
Attn.: Noreen Hannigan
957 N. Patrick Henry Drive
Arlington, VA 22205
(703) 536-7918

Association of Single
Adoptive Parents
Attn.: Vicki Bascom
408 Henry Clay Road
Ashton, VA 23005
(804) 798-2673

Association of Single Adoptive
Parents of the DC Area
Attn.: Letty Grishaw
P.O. Box 1704
Springfield, VA 22151
(703) 521-0632

Blue Ridge Adoption Group
Attn.: Terry Cornwell
7887 Hollins Court Drive
Roanoke, VA 24019
(540) 890-5813

Fairfax Adoption Support Team
(F.A.S.T.)
Attn.: Shirley Green
12011 Government Center Pkwy.
Fairfax, VA 22035
(703) 324-7639

Families Adopting Children
Together of Southwestern
Virginia
Attn.: Bonnie Sue Walker
Route 4, Box 248
Forest, VA 24551
(804) 525-5370

Families for Private Adoption
P. O. Box 6375
Washington, DC 20015-0375
(202) 722-0338

Families for Russian/Ukranian
  Adoptions
P.O. Box 2944
Merrifield, VA 22116
(703) 560-6184

Families Through Adoption
Attn.: Carolyn Crosby
1420 Cobble Scott Way
Chesapeake, VA 23322
(804) 482-8330

Families With Children from
  China
Attn.: Mike Feazel
9803 Clyde Court
Vienna, VA 22181
(703) 281-9188

Friends of Children Services
Attn.: Mia Schulte
2312 North Wakefield Street
Arlington, VA 22207
(703) 528-6159

Heartwise Adoption Consulting
  Services
P.O. Box 10180
Alexandria, VA 22310
(703) 550-8011

Latin America Parents
  Association of the National
  Capital Region
Attn.: Sheila Mooney
P.O. Box 4403
Silver Spring, MD 20914-4403
(301) 431-3407

North American Council on
  Adoptable Children State
  Representative
Gwendolyn Ricks-Haskett
400 Farmer Street
Petersburg, VA 23804
(804) 861-4720

People for the Adoption of
  Children
Attn.: Harriet Thomas
7908 Chowning Circle
Richmond, VA 23294
(804) 747-6633

Romanian Children's Connection
Attn.: Mary Thomas
1206 Hillside Terr.
Alexandria, VA 22302
(703) 548-9352

Stars of David
Attn.: Ginny Fried
(703) 569-7148

United Methodist Family Services
  Adoptive Parent Support
  Group
6335 Little River Tpke.
Alexandria, VA 22312
(703) 941-9008

Virginia One Church, One Child
1214 West Graham Road, Suite 2
Richmond, VA 23220
(804) 329-3420

Virginia Peninsula Adoptive
  Parents Group
Attn.: Jewell Schaefer-Hanbury
17385 Warwick Boulevard
Lee Hall, VA 23603
(804) 599-8962

**Adopted Person and Birth
Relative Support Groups**

Adoptee and Birth Parent
  Support Group
#2 Hill Circle
Round Hill, VA 22141
(540) 338-5266

Adoptee Birthparent Support
  Network
3421 M Street N.W., Suite 328
Washington, DC 20007
(202) 686-4611

Adoptee Liberty Movement
  Association (ALMA)
P.O. Box 4328
Glen Allen, VA 23058
(804) 750-2335

Adoptees and Natural Parents
949 Lacon Drive
Newport News, VA 23602
(804) 874-9091

Adoptees in Search
P.O. Box 41016
Bethesda, MD 23602
(301) 656-8555

Adoptees/Birthparents Self-Help
  Group
603 14th Street
Virginia Beach, VA 23451

Adoptees Support for
  Birthmothers
8630 Granby Street
Norfolk, VA 23503
(804) 480-1571

Adoption Resource Group
Attn.: Monica Woropoj
8094 Rolling Road, Suite 125
Springfield, VA 22153
(703) 440-5771

Adoption Reports Unit
Virginia Department of Social
  Services
730 East Broad Street
Richmond, VA 23219
(804) 692-1285

Adult Adoptees in Search
P.O. Box 203
Ferrum, VA 24088
(540) 365-0712

Barker Foundation Adult
  Adoptee Support Group
7945 MacArthur Boulevard,
  Suite 206
Cabin John, MD 20818
(301) 229-8300

Barker Foundation Birth Parent
  Support Group
7945 MacArthur Boulevard,
  Suite 206
Cabin John, MD 20818
(301) 229-8300

Catholic Charities of the Diocese
  of Arlington
Birthparent Support Group
5294 Lyngate Court
Burke, VA 22015
(703) 425-0100

Parents and Adoptees In Search
2500 Lauderdale Drive
Richmond, VA 23233
(804) 744-2244

Virginia State Bar
801 East Main, Suite 1500
Richmond, VA 23219-2900
fax (804) 786-2061

Virginia Bar Association
701 E. Franklin Street, Suite 1515
Richmond, VA 23219
(804) 644-0041

Virginia State Bar
801 East Main, Suite 1500
Richmond, VA 23219
(804) 775-0500

Adoption Attorneys

Gary B. Allsion
1092 Laskin Road # 112
Virginia Beach, VA 23451

Teresa L. Ball
2800 Patterson Avenue, #100
Richmond, VA 23221
(804) 358-6669

Patricia Barton
700 North Fairfax Street,
    Suite 304
Alexandria, VA 22314
(703) 836-2728

Jennifer Brust
2000 North 14th Street, Suite 100
Arlington, VA 22201
(703) 525-400C

Mark Eckman
404 Pine Street
Vienna, VA 22180
(703) 242-8801

Wayne Glass
P.O. Box 235
Staunton, VA 24401
(703) 885-1205

Barbara C. Jones
5265 O'Faly Road
Fairfax, VA 22030
(703) 278-8072

Jonathan Kinney
2000 North 14 Street, Suite 100
Arlington, VA 22201
(703) 525-4000

Robert Klima*
9257 Lee Avenue, Suite 201
Manassa, VA 22110
(703) 361-5051
fax (703) 330-2090

* Mr. Klima has conducted about
    fifty independent adoptions,
    150 agency adoptions, and ten
    international adoptions.

Reilly Marchant
1205 East Main Street
4th Floor West
Richmond, VA 23219
(804) 648-9255

Mark McDermott
1300 19th Street, N.W., Suite 400
Washington, DC 20036
(202) 331-1955

Darlis E. Moyer
One Court Square
P.O. Box 136
Harrisonburg, VA 22801-1368
(703) 434-9947

Rosemary O'Brien
109 S. Fairfax Street
Alexandria, VA 22314
(703) 549-5110

Betsy H. Phillips
Route 4, Box 179P
Rustburg, VA 24588
(703) 821-5022

Stanton Phillips*
2009 North 14th Street, Suite 510
Arlington, VA 22201
(703) 522-8800

* Mr. Phillips has completed
    more than 900 adoptions. He
    has authored many adoptions
    articles, including the only
    national treatise on adoption
    law and practice. He also
    drafted the Uniform Adoption
    Act.

Rodney M. Poole
2800 Patterson Avenue, Suite 100
Richmond, VA 23221
(804) 358-6669

Nancy Poster*
9909 Georgetown Pike
P.O. Box 197
Great Falls, VA 22066
(703) 759-1560
fax (703) 759-6512

* Ms. Poster has conducted about
    250 independent adoptions,
    259 agency adoptions, and fifty
    international adoptions.

Colleen Marea Quinn
823 E. Main Street, 16th Floor
Richmond, VA 23204
(804) 644-1440

Teresa L. Temple
2800 Patterson Avenue, # 100
Richmond, VA 23221

Ellen Weinman
36 C East Main Street
Salem, VA 24153
(703) 389-3825

Richard Wexell
3975 University Drive, Suite 410
Fairfax, VA 22030
(703) 385-3858

James E. Wilcox, Jr.
8996 Burke Lake Road, # 301
Burke, VA 22015

Attorney fees for an adoption in
this state are about $700 to
$3,500.

VIRGINIA LAWS RELATED TO ADOPTION: QUESTIONS AND ANSWERS

In Virginia in a private placement adoption, the birth family and the adoptive family must exchange identifying information.

Can an attorney serve as an intermediary?
Yes.

Is advertising permitted?
Yes.

Who must consent to the adoption?
1. Both birth parents
2. The child placement agency, if involved

When can consent be taken from birth mother (father), and how long after the consent is signed can it be revoked?
In an agency adoption, consent can be taken ten days after the child's birth and can be revoked fifteen days after signed or twenty-five days after birth, or until adoptive placement, whichever is later.

In an independent adoption, a consent hearing takes place within ten days of filing the petition, or as soon as is practical. The hearing can take place in the county where the adoptive parents live, where the birth mother lives, or where the child was born. If the birth parents live outside of Virginia, the consent hearing may take place in the birth parents' state of residence, as long as the proceedings are first instituted in a Virginia court so that the Virginia court has jurisdiction over them.

Parental consent is revocable before the final adoption if it was given under fraud or duress, or if both the adoptive parents and birth parents agree to revoke it.

A birth father who is not married to the birth mother at the time of the child's conception or birth does not need to give a consent in court. He must be provided notice of the adoption proceedings, or he can sign a consent that waives further notice of adoption proceedings.

If the birth parents place a child and both birth mother and father do not show up in court (without good cause and after being given notice), the court may grant the adoption petition without their consent if the court finds it is in the child's best interests to do so. (Virtually all birth mothers do go to court, however.)

What are the birth father's rights?
When a birth father's consent is required and he has not consented, he must be given notice of the termination hearing and/or the adoption hearing. The hearing may be held after the birth mother's hearing. If the birth father does not respond within twenty-one days after personal notice of the hearing or ten days after an Order of Publication (notice of the adoption proceedings placed in the legal notices section of the newspaper), then the hearing can be held and his rights can be terminated.

If the birth father's consent is required but the court can also determine that the consent is withheld contrary to the child's best interests or cannot be obtained, the court will approve of the adoption as long as notice was provided to the birth father. Many judges will not permit a birth mother to refuse to name the birth father except in extreme situations such as rape.

What fees can adoptive parents pay?
Medical, legal, and transportation costs are permitted. Reasonable living expenses, including maternity clothes, can be paid if the birth mother's physician states that she cannot work. All fees must be disclosed to the court.

Where does the adoption hearing take place?

The adoption hearing takes place in the court of the county where the adoptive parents live or where the child placement agency is located.

How are familial and step-parent adoptions different from nonbiological adoptions?

Stanton Phillips, an attorney in Arlington, states that in a step-parent adoption, a hearing may not be required and is up to the court's discretion. In consensual step-parent adoptions, home studies are not necessarily required.

Stanton Phillips also states that relatives up to the fourth degree are now given special relative adoption status. These include the child's great aunt and uncle. Nancy Poster, an attorney in Great Falls, states that in a familial adoption no post-placement supervision is required. Also, no hearing is required before the court for qualified relative adoptions.

Can a nonresident finalize an adoption in this state?

Yes, but only in an agency or agency-identified adoption.

WASHINGTON

State Adoption Specialist
Lois Chowen
Washington Department of Social
   and Health Services
P.O. Box 45713
Olympia, WA 98504
(360) 753-4965

Compact Administrator
Jean Soliz, Secretary
Washington Department of Social
   and Health Services
14th and Jefferson, OB-2
Olympia, WA 98504-5710
(360) 753-3395

Deputy Compact Administrator
Anne Lundeen
Division of Children and Family
   Services
Washington Department of Social
   and Health Services
P.O. Box 45711
Olympia, WA 98504-5711
(360) 586-2612

Overnight mailing address:

OB-2 3rd Floor
14th and Jefferson
Olympia, WA 98504-5722
fax (360) 586-1040

Direct all telephone calls and
   correspondence to the Deputy
   Compact Administrator.

Office hours:
Monday-Friday
8:00 A.M.-5:00 P.M.
Pacific Time Zone

**State Adoption Exchange and
   Photo Listing**

Washington Adoption Resource
   Exchange
Washington Department of Social
   and Health Services
P.O. Box 45713
Olympia, WA 98504
(360) 753-2178

Private Adoption Agencies

Adoption Advocates
   International
401 East Front Street
Port Angeles, WA 98362
(360) 452-4777

Adoption Services of WACAP
P.O. Box 88948
Seattle, WA 98188
(206) 575-4550

Adventist Adoption and Family
   Services
1207 East Reserve Street
Vancouver, WA 98661
(360) 693-2110

Americans Adopting Orphans
12345 Lake City Way, NE,
   Suite 2001
Seattle, WA ᴐ8125

Americans for International Aid
   and Adoption (AIAA)
P.O. Box 6051
Spokane, WA 99207
(509) 489-2015, (206) 782-4251

Bethany Christian Services
103 East Holly Street, #316
Bellingham National Bank
   Building
Bellingham, WA 98225
(360) 733-6042

Black Child Adoption Program
123 16th Avenue
P.O. Box 22638
Seattle, WA 98122
(206) 329-3933 or 324-9470

Catholic Children and Family
   Services of Walla Walla
418 Drumheller Building
Walla Walla, WA 99362
(509) 525-0572

Catholic Children's Services of
   Northwest Washington
P.O. Box 5704
Bellingham, WA 98227-5704
(360) 733-5800

Catholic Children's Services of
   Tacoma
5410 North 44th
Tacoma, WA 98407
(206) 752-2455

Catholic Community Service,
   King County
100 23rd Avenue S.
Seattle, WA 98144
(206) 323-6336

Catholic Community Service,
Snohomish County
Commerce Building, Room 510
Everett, WA 98201
(206) 259-9188 or 622-8905

Catholic Family and Child Service
of Ephrata, Columbia Basin
Branch
121 Basin, N.W.
P.O. Box 191
Ephrata, WA 98823
(509) 754-2211

Catholic Family and Child Service
of Grandview
302 Division
P.O. Box 22
Grandview, WA 98930
(360) 882-3050

Catholic Family and Child Service
of Wenatchee
23 S. Wenatchee, #209
Wenatchee, WA 98801
(509) 662-6761

Catholic Family and Child Service
of Yakima
5301-C Tieton Drive
Yakima, WA 98908
(509) 453-8264

Catholic Family and Child
Services
518 West Clark
Pasco, WA 99301
(509) 545-6145

Catholic Family and Child
Services
P.O. Box 1504
Richland, WA 99352
(509) 946-4645

Catholic Family Counseling
Center
410 W. 12th
Vancouver, WA 98860
(360) 694-2631

Children's Home Society of
Washington, Central Area
321 E. Yakima Avenue,
Room 204
Yakima, WA 98901
(509) 457-8139

Children's Home Society of
Washington, Northeast Area
4315 Scott Street
P.O. Box 8244, Manito Station
Spokane, WA 99203
(509) 747-4174

Children's Home Society of
Washington, Northwest Area
3300 N.E. 65th Street
Box 15190
Seattle, WA 98115-0190
(206) 524-6020

Children's Home Society of
Washington, Southeast Area
405 Denny Building
6 West Alder
Walla Walla, WA 99362
(509) 459-2130

Children's Home Society of
Washington, Southwest Area
1105 Broadway
Vancouver, WA 98660
(360) 695-1325

Children's Home Society of
Washington, West Central
Area
201 South 34th
Tacoma, WA 98408
(206) 472-3355

Church of Christ Homes for
Children
30012 South Military Road
Auburn, WA 98003
(206) 839-2755

Family Foundation
1229 Cornwall Avenue, Suite 202
Bellingham, WA 98225
(360) 676-KIDS

Family Foundation
424 North 130th
Seattle, WA 98133
(206) 367-4600

International Children's Care
P.O. Box 4406
Vancouver, WA 98662
(360) 573-0429

International Children's Services
of Washington, Inc.
3251 107th, S.E.
Bellevue, WA 98004
(206) 451-9370

Jewish Family Services
1214 Boylston Avenue
Seattle, WA 98101
(206) 447-3240

LDS Social Services
220 South Third Place
Renton, WA 98055
(206) 624-3393

Lutheran Social Services of
Washington (Admin. Office)
4040 South 188th
Seattle, WA 98188
(206) 246-7650

Lutheran Social Services of
Washington and Idaho
S. 7 Howard, Suite 200,
Symons Bldg.
Spokane, WA 99204
(509) 327-7761

Lutheran Social Services of
Washington, Southeast Area
Plaza I, Suite 700
320 North Johnson Street
Kennewick, WA 99336
(509) 783-7446

Lutheran Social Services of
Washington, Southwest Area
223 North Yakima
Tacoma, WA 98403
(206) 272-8433

Lutheran Social Services of
Washington and Idaho
6920 220th Street, S.W.
Mountlake Terrace, WA 98043
(206) 672-6009

Medina Children's Services
P.O. Box 22638
Seattle, WA 98111
(206) 461-4520

New Hope of Washington
2611 N.E. 125th Street, Suite 146
Seattle, WA 98126
(206) 363-1800

Open Adoption and Family
Services
(206) 254-7236

Regular Baptist Child Placement
Agency
P.O. Box 16353
Seattle, WA 98116
(206) 938-1487

Seattle Indian Center
Infant Adoption and Family
Services Center
611 Twelfth Avenue, S., Suite 30
Seattle, WA 98144
(206) 329-8700

The Adoption of Special Children
(TASC)
123 16th Avenue
Seattle, WA 98122
(206) 461-4520

**Adoptive Parent Support
Groups and Postadoption
Services**

Adopt a Special Kid (AASK) of
Washington
Attn.: Wendy Badgley
P.O. Box 44
Langley, WA 98260
(206) 221-8957

Adoption Resource Center of
Children's Home Society of
Washington
3300 N.E. 65th Street
P.O. Box 15190
Seattle, WA 98133
(206) 524-6020

Adoption Resource Center of
Children's Home Society
4315 Scott Street
Spokane, WA 99203
(509) 747-4174

Adoption Facilitators, Inc.
8624 N.E. Juanita Drive
Kirkland, WA 98034
(206) 823-3060

Adoption Information Service
Attn.: Sandy Barnes
P.O. Box 55183
Seattle, WA 98155
(206) 364-8270

Adoption Support Group of
Kitsap County
Attn.: Leanne Biggs
11869 Olympic Terrace Avenue,
N.E.
Bainbridge Island, WA 98110
(206) 842-7122

Adoptive Families Network of
South Puget Sound
Attn.: Josie Silver
P.O. Box 112188
Tacoma, WA 98411-2188
(206) 759-0284

Adoptive Parents of Walla Walla
Attn.: Janet Narum
103 East Main Street
Walla Walla, WA 99362
(509) 529-8557

Advocates for Single Adoptive
Parents
Attn.: Esther Harmon
11634 S.E. 49th Street
Bellevue, WA 98006
(206) 644-4761

Americans for International Aid
and Adoption (AIAA)
Adoptive Parent Support Group
Attn.: Kristi Greene
S. 2711 Manito Boulevard
Spokane, WA 99203
(509) 624-2617

Cascade Adoptive Family Support
Group
Attn.: Linda Kellar
P.O. Box 12304
Mill Creek, WA 98012
(206) 355-8483

Circle of Love
Attn.: Donna Crowley
East 2423 Fifth Avenue
Spokane, WA 99202
(509) 534-2000

Families Through Adoption of
Washington
Attn.: Lori Guilfoyle
25310 217th Place S.E.
Maple Valley, WA 98038
(206) 432-4543

Friends Through Adoption
Attn.: Deanna Holroyd
3310 S.E. 168th Court
Camas, WA 98607
(206) 892-7911

Families with Children from
China
Attn.: Sarah Young
12224 210 Place S.E.
Issaquah, WA 98027
(206) 271-9932

Goldendale Adoptive Parent
Group
Box 404
Goldendale, WA 98620

Interracial Family Association of
Seattle
Attn.: Stephen and Sally Graves
2802 33rd Avenue South

Seattle, WA 98144
(206) 764-2746

KIN
Attn.: Peggy Hartup
14803 Ash Way
Lynnwood, WA 98037
(206) 743-3049

Kitsap Adoption Group
11869 Olympic Terrace Avenue
NE
Bainbridge Island, WA
98110- 4293
(206) 842-7122

Mt. Vernon Friends of WACAP
Attn.: Joanne Lynn
1598 McLean Road
Mt. Vernon, WA 98273

North American Council on
Adoptable Children State
Representative
Attn.: Jackie Erholm
1229 Cornwall Avenue, #206
Bellingham, WA 98225
(206) 676-5437

Okanogan Valley Adoptive
Parents
Attn.: Cozette Buzzard
P.O. Box 3002
Omak, WA 98841
(509) 826-2820

One Church, One Child
6419 Martin Luther King, Jr.
Way, South
Seattle, WA 98118
(206) 723-6224

Precious Connections
7989 N.E. Walden Lane
Bainbridge, WA 98110
(206) 842-6658

Spokane Consultants
in Family Living
South 1220 Division
Spokane, WA 99202
(509) 328-6274

SSAFE
Attn.: Teresa Burt
3325 Agate Height Road
Bellingham, WA 98226
(360) 671-6516

Stars of David
Attn.: Shelly Black
Seattle, WA
(206) 722-3134

WACAP Parent Group
Attn.: Sue Koentopp
South 509 Union Road
Spokane, WA 99206
(509) 924-0624

**Adopted Person and Birth
Relative Support Groups**

Adoptee Liberty Movement
Association (ALMA)
P.O. Box 23683
Federal Way, WA 98093-0683
(206) 927-1856

Adoptee Liberty Movement
Association (ALMA)
P.O. Box 597
Onalaska, WA 98570-0597
(509) 978-6033

Adoptee Liberty Movement
Association (ALMA)
P.O. Box 1823
Seattle, WA 98111
(206) 290-9876

Adoption Resource Center of
Children's Home Society of
Washington
3300 N.E. 65th Street
P.O. Box 15190
Seattle, WA 98133
(206) 524-6020

Adoption Resource Center of
Children's Home Society of
Washington
Attn.: Suzanne Apelskog
4315 Scott Street
Spokane, WA 99203
(509) 747-4174

Adoption Search and Counseling
Consultants
6201 15th Avenue, N.W., #P210
Seattle, WA 98107
(206) 782-4491

Adoption Search and
Reconciliation
9226 Beall Road, SW
Vashon Island, WA 98070
(206) 463-3292

B.I.R.T.H.
3018 28th Avenue, SE
Olympia, WA 98501
(360) 754-6249

Healing Circle
4125 Olympic Boulevard W.
Tacoma, WA 98466
(206) 565-1899

Lost and Found
3232 Laurel Drive
Everett, WA 98201
(206) 339-1194

Touched by Adoption
1105 Colonial Drive
College Place, WA 99324
(509) 529-1245

WARM
1119 Peacock Lane
Burlington, WA 98233

WARM
5950 6th Avenue S., #107
Seattle, WA 98108-2317
(206) 767-9510

WARM
20 Hall Avenue
Yakima, WA 98902

Adoption Attorneys

Rita Bender*
1301 5th Avenue, 34th Floor
Seattle, WA 98101
(206) 623-6501

* Ms. Bender has completed
about six hundred independent
adoptions, fifty agency
adoptions, and twenty
international adoptions.

Caroline Davis
1200 5th Avenue, Suite 1925
Seattle, WA 98101-1127
(206) 628-0890

Mark M. Demaray
1201 3rd Avenue, Suite 1400
Seattle, WA 98101-3017
(206) 682-4000

J. Eric Gustafson*
222 North 3rd Street
Yakima, WA 98901
(509) 248-7220
fax (509) 575-1883
or
P.O. Box 1689
Yakima, WA 98907

* Mr. Gustafson has completed
about 350 independent
adoptions and about 200
agency adoptions, some of
which include international
adoptions.

Michele Gentry Hinz
1420 5th Avenue, #3650
Seattle, WA 98101-2387
(206) 682-4000

Albert G. Lirhus
2200 6th Avenue, #1122
Seattle, WA 98121
(206) 728-5858

Attorney fees for an adoption in
this state are about $2,500 to
$4,500.

WASHINGTON LAWS RELATED TO ADOPTION: QUESTIONS AND ANSWERS

Can an attorney serve as an intermediary?
Yes.

Is advertising permitted?
Yes, but only through a Washington licensed attorney or agency and with verification of a
completed home study in compliance with Washington law. Those outside of Washington
cannot advertise in Washington newspapers.

Who must consent to the adoption?
1. Both birth parents
2. The child placement agency, if involved

When can consent be taken from birth mother (father), and how long after the consent is signed can it be revoked?
Rita Bender, an attorney in Seattle, states that consents can be taken before birth but the order terminating rights cannot be entered with the court until forty-eight hours after birth or signing, whichever is later. The birth mother must appear in court to testify as to her consent. The birth father does not have to appear, but his consent can be brought before the court. Once entered into the court, the birth mother's and the birth father's consents are irrevocable.

What are the birth father's rights?
Eric Gustafson, an attorney in Yakima, states that the birth father must consent or be given notice by serving him with summons or notice personally, or by publishing a notice of the adoption proceedings in the legal notices of a newspaper if his whereabouts are unknown. He does have an opportunity to object and have a hearing on his parenting abilities to show the court that it would be in the child's best interests to be parented by him. His rights can be terminated if it can be shown that he failed to perform his parental obligations.

What fees can adoptive parents pay?
The legal and agency fees must be reasonable and should be based on time spent in conducting preadoption home studies and preparing the report. Living expenses must be approved by the court. At the adoptive parent's request, this fee can be reviewed.

Where does the hearing take place?
The hearing takes place in the court of the county where the adoptive parents live or the child lives.

How are familial and step-parent adoptions different from nonbiological adoptions?
They are essentially the same, except that the home study may be streamlined or waived.

Can a nonresident finalize an adoption in this state?
Yes.

WEST VIRGINIA

State Adoption Specialist
Gwen Bridges
West Virginia Department of
  Health and Human Resources
Capital Complex, Building 6,
  Room B-850
Charleston, WV 25305
(304) 558-7980

Compact Administrator
Ruth Panepinto
West Virginia Department of
  Health and Human Resources

Capital Complex, Building 3,
  Room 206
Charleston, WV 25305
(304) 558-0684

Deputy Compact Administrator
Nancy Chalhoub
West Virginia Department of
  Health and Human Resources
Bureau of Community Support
Office of Social Services
Capital Complex, Building 6,
  Room B-850
Charleston, WV 25305
(304) 558-7980
fax (304) 558-8800

Direct all telephone calls and
  correspondence to the Deputy
  Compact Administrator.

Office hours:
Monday-Friday
8:30 A.M.-4:30 P.M.
Eastern Time Zone

State Adoption Exchange and Photo Listing

West Virginia Adoption Resource Network
Capitol Complex, Bldg. 6, Rm. B-850
Charleston, WV 25330
(304) 558-2891

Private Adoption Agencies

Adoption Services, Inc.
115 South St.
John's Drive
Camp Hill, PA 17011
(717) 737-3960

Burlington United Methodist Family Services
Rt. 3, Box 346A
Grafton, WV 26354
(305) 265-1338

Burlington United Methodist Family Services
Rt. 4, Box 240B
Keyser, WV 26726
(304) 788-2342

Burlington United Methodist Family Services
P.O. Box 370
Scott Depot, WV 25560-0370
(304) 757-9127

Catholic Charities of S.W. Virginia, Inc.
820 Campbell Avenue, S.W.
Roanoke, VA 24016
(703) 342-0411

Childplace, Inc.
1602 Stonehenge Road
Charleston, WV 25314
(304) 344-0319

Childplace, Inc.
2420 Highway 62
Jeffersonville, IN 47130
(812) 282-8248
or (304) 344-0319

Children's Home Society
432 Oakland Street, Suite A
Morgantown, WV 26505
(304) 599-6505

Children's Home Society of WV
1145 Greenbriar Street
Charleston, WV 25311
(304) 345-3894

Children's Home Society of WV
316 Oakvale Road
P.O. Box 5533
Princeton, WV 24740
(304) 425-8438

Family Services Association
248 North Fifth Street
P.O. Box 1027
Steubenville, OH 43952
(614) 836-2466

LDS Social Services
4431 Marketing Place
P.O. Box 367
Groveport, OH 43125
(614) 836-2466

Voice for International and Domestic Adoptions (VIDA)
354 Allen Street
Hudson, NY 12534
(518) 828-4527

Adoptive Parent Support Groups and Postadoption Services

Adoptive Parent Support Group
Attn.: Jamie Shuman and Betsy Pyles
1465 Dogwood
Morgantown, WV 26505
(304) 599-0598

Appalachian Families for Adoption
P.O. Box 2775
Charleston, WV 25330-2775
(304) 744-4067, 744-6028, or 756-9146

North American Council on Adoptable Children State Representative
1511 Byng Drive
South Charleston, WV 25303
(304) 744-9602

Parents Adopting and Learning to Support
Attn.: Drive and Mrs. H.D. Milem
301 High Street
Belington, WV 26250
(304) 823-3015

Adopted Person and Birth Relative Support Groups

ALARM Network
37 21st Street
McMechen, WV 26040
(304) 232-0747

Society's Triangle
411 Cabell Court
Huntington, WV 25703

West Virginia Adoption Resource Network
DHHR Capitol Complex
Bldg. 6, Rm. 850
Charleston, WV 25305
(304) 558-2891

West Virginia Bar Association
P.O. Box 346
Charleston, WV 25322
(304) 342-1474

West Virginia State Bar
2006 Kanawha Boulevard, East
Charleston, WV 25311
(304) 558-2456

Lawyer Referral Service
(304) 558-2880
(304) 558-7991

Adoption Attorneys

Heidi Kossuth
McDonald and Rotecker
P.O. Box 2151
Charleston, WV 25328
(304) 344-5046

WEST VIRGINIA LAWS RELATED TO ADOPTION: QUESTIONS AND ANSWERS

Can an attorney serve as an intermediary?
Yes, as long as fees are related to services rendered.

Is advertising permitted?
Yes.

Who must consent to the adoption?
1. Both birth parents
2. If a birth parent is under eighteen, the court must approve the consent and appoint a guardian.

When can consent be taken from birth mother (father), and how long after the consent is signed can it be revoked?
Consent cannot be given until seventy-two hours after the child's birth and may be revoked within ten days if the adoptive parents are in-state residents or up to twenty days if they are from out of state, unless the term "irrevocable" is written onto the consent.

The consent shall be before a county clerk and two witnesses. If the birth parent is a minor the consent shall be executed before a judge.

Heidi Kossuth, an adoption attorney in Charleston, recommends that if an out-of-state adoptive couple adopts a child born in West Virginia, then documentation, such as consents, should comply with both West Virginia law and the state laws of the adoptive parents.

What are the birth father's rights?
Notice of the adoption proceedings is given to any birth father who has exercised parental duties, unless the child is more than six months old and the birth father has not asserted his parental rights.

What fees can adoptive parents pay?
Payment of legal, medical, and adoption agency fees or fees to other persons is limited to cover fees-for-services only. All fees must be approved by the court.

Where does the adoption hearing take place?
The adoption hearing takes place in the court of the county where the adoptive parents live.

How are familial and step-parent adoptions different from nonbiological adoptions?
The preadoption home study is not required in a relative adoption. Closeness in age cannot be the sole factor in denying an adoption in stepparent adoptions.

In some stepparent adoptions, some grandparent visitations may be granted.

Can a nonresident finalize an adoption in this state?
No.

WISCONSIN

State Adoption Specialist
Christopher Marceil, Adoption
  Services Planner
Wisconsin Department of Health
  and Social Services
P.O. Box 7851
Madison, WI 53707-7851
(608) 266-3595

Compact Administrator
Bureau for Children Youth and
  Families
Wisconsin Department of Health
  and Social Services
Division of Community Services
P.O. Box 7851
Madison, WI 53707-7851
(608) 266-3595

Direct all telephone calls and
  correspondence to:

Adoption Placements
Karen Oghalai
Bureau for Children, Youth and
  Families
Bureau of Human Resources
Wisconsin Department of Health
  and Social Services
Division of Community Services
P.O. Box 7851, One West Wilson
Madison, WI 53707-7851
(608) 266-0690

Office hours:
Monday-Friday
7:45 A.M.-4:30 P.M.
Central Time Zone

State Adoption Exchange and Photo Listing

Wisconsin Adoption Information
Exchange
Special Needs Adoption Network
P.O. Box 10176
Milwaukee, WI 53210-0990
(414) 475-1246

Private Adoption Agencies

Adoption Advocates, Inc.
2601 Crossroads Drive
Madison, WI 53704
(608) 246-2844

Adoption Choice
924 East Juneau Avenue, #813
Milwaukee, WI 53202
(414) 276-3262

Adoption Option
1804 Chapman Drive
Waukesha, WI 53186
(414) 544-4278

Adoption Services of Green Bay
529 South Jefferson, Room 105
Green Bay, WI 54301
(414) 432-2030

Bethany Christian Services
of Wisconsin
W255 N477 Grandview
Boulevard, Suite 207
Waukesha, WI 53188
(414) 547-6557

Catholic Charities, Inc.
128 South 6th Street
P.O. Box 266
La Crosse, WI 54601
(608) 782-0704

Catholic Social Services,
Green Bay
P.O. Box 23825
Green Bay, WI 54305-3825
(414) 437-6541

Catholic Social Services, Madison
4905 Schofield Street
Monona, WI 53716
(608) 221-2000

Catholic Social Services,
Milwaukee
2021 North 60th Street
Milwaukee, WI 53208
(414) 771-2881

Center for Child
and Family Services
4456 N. 28th Street
Milwaukee, WI 53209
(414) 442-4702

Children's Home Society
of Minnesota
2230 Como Avenue
St. Paul, MN 55108
(612) 646-6393

Children's Service Society
of Wisconsin
1212 South 70th Street
West Allis, WI 53214
(414) 453-1400

Community Adoption Center
3701 Kadow Street
Manitowoc, WI 54220
(414) 682-9211

Evangelical Child and Family
Agency
2401 North Mayfair Road,
Suite 302
Milwaukee, WI 53226
(414) 476-9550

Family Service Association
of Sheboygan
2020 Erie Avenue
Sheboygan, WI 53081
(414) 458-3784

Hope International Family
Services, Inc.
421 South Main Street
Stillwater, MN 55082
(612) 439-2446

Institute for Child and Family
Development
4206 West Capital Drive
Milwaukee, WI 53216
(414) 449-2274

LDS Social Services
1711 University Avenue
Madison, WI 53705
(608) 238-4844

Lutheran Counseling
and Family Services
3800 North Mayfair Road
Wauwatosa, WI 53222-2200
Mailing Address:
P.O. Box 13367
Wauwatosa, WI 53213
(414) 536-8333

Lutheran Social Services of
Wisconsin and Upper Michigan
4143 South 13th Street
Milwaukee, WI 53221
(414) 281-4400

Pauquette Children's
Services, Inc.
315 West Conant Street
P.O. Box 162
Portage, WI 53901-0162
(608) 742-8004

Special Beginnings
237 South Street, #101
Waukesha, WI 53186
(414) 896-3600

Special Children, Inc.
910 N. Elm Grove Road, Office 2
Elm Grove, WI 53122
(414) 821-2125

Van Dyke, Inc.
515 Shady Lane
Sheboygan, WI 53081-8285
(414) 452-5358

Adoptive Parent Support Groups and Postadoption Services

Adoption Is Forever
Attn.: Joan Morecki
3305 West Justin Street
Appleton, WI 54914

Adoptive Families
of Greater Milwaukee
14900 West Woodview Court
New Berlin, WI 53151
(414) 789-8030

Adoptive Families
of Western Wisconsin
Attn.: Kurt Leichtle
N8207 970th Street
River Falls, WI 54022-4402

Adoptive Families of Wisconsin
Attn.: Jan Herold
Box 575, Route 3
Galesville, WI 54630

Adoptive Moms Discussion
  Group
Attn.: Susan Roth
Jewish Community Center
6255 North Santa Monica
  Boulevard
Whitefish Bay, WI 53217
(414) 964-4444

Adoptive Parent Group of South
  Wisconsin
4206 Mariton Way
Madison, WI 53711-3704
(608) 271-6815

Adoptive Parent Group of
  Southern Wisconsin
Attn.: Marilyn Holschuh
1408 Vilas Avenue
Madison, WI 53711
(608) 251-0736

Adoptive Parents Association of
  Greater Milwaukee
Attn.: Jane Pollock
4335 South Lake Drive
Cudahy, WI 53110
(414) 744-5049

Adoptive Parents of Superior
Attn.: Ron Gustafson
911 Clough Avenue
Superior, WI 54880

Black Adoptive Families
Attn.: Marie Granberry
3267 North 47th Street
Milwaukee, WI 53216

Central Wisconsin Adoption
  Support Group
Attn.: Karen Toepel
134 Ash Street
Montello, WI 53949

Chippewa Valley Adoptive
  Families
Attn.: Lynda Blakely-Koehn
7221 South Shore Drive
Altoona, WI 54720
(715) 834-4102

Clark County Support Group
Route 3, Box 79A
Neillsville, WI 54456

Families Through Adoption
Attn.: Karel Voss
2040 White Pine Lane
Sheboygan, WI 53083
(414) 457-3473

Family United of Southeast
  Wisconsin
Attn.: Jo Smirl/DCS
141 N.W. Barstow Street
Waukesha, WI 53188

Fox Valley Friends in Adoption
1032 Forestedge Drive
Kaukauna, WI 54130-2958
(414) 766-3213

Friends of Adoption
Attn.: Carol Jones
1702 Old A Road
Spooner, WI 54801
(715) 468-2881

Inter-Racial Families Network
2120 Fordem Avenue
Madison, WI 53704

Love Through Adoption
Attn.: Virginia Heckett
2288 Esker Road
Hartley, WI 54440

NAMASTE, Children from India
Attn.: Nancy Gamble
1735 North 14th Avenue
Sturgeon Bay, WI 54235

NAMASTE, Foreign and Indian
  Adoption
Attn.: Nancy Reinbold
546 Black Earth Court
Wales, WI 53183
(414) 968-4564

Ours of Greater Milwaukee
Attn.: Pat Henkels
14900 West Woodview Court
New Berlin, WI 53151
(414) 546-3340 or 355-3970

Ours Through Adoption
Attn.: Carol O'Neal
9041 15th Avenue
Kenosha, WI 53143
(414) 697-9181

Ours Through Adoption of
  Southeastern Wisconsin
Attn.: Judy Joosse
4232 Garden Drive
Racine, WI 53403
(414) 554-9351

Ours Through Adoption of
  Northeast Wisconsin
Attn.: Mary Freberg
990 Hickory Hill Drive
Green Bay, WI 54304-2581
(414) 498-8948

Resolve of Southern Wisconsin
Attn.: Ann Bahr
P.O. Box 23406
Milwaukee, WI 53223
(414) 521-4590

Rock County Adoptive Parent
  Group
Attn.: Marian McFall
7800 S. Butterfly Road
Beloit, WI 53511
(608) 365-9279

Special Needs Adoption Network
  and North American Council
  on Adoptable Children State
  Representative
Attn.: Colleen Ellingson
P.O. Box 10176
Milwaukee, WI 53210
(414) 475-1246

Special Needs Adoptive Parents
Attn.: Dave and Cara Leitner
Route 1, Box 230C
Scandinavia, WI 54977

St. Croix Valley Korean-
  American Cultural Society
Attn.: Kelly Guerkink
383 North Glover Road
Hudson, WI 54016
(715) 425-6208

They Adopt Special Kids
Attn.: Mary Cissoko
825 East Washington Street, #9
West Bend, WI 53095

The Ties Program
Attn.: Becca Piper
11801 Woodland Circle
Hales Corner, WI 53130
(800) 398-3676

United Families Organization
909 River Street
Rhinelander, WI 54501

United States Chilean Adoptive
  Families
1239 East Broadway
Waukesha, WI 53186

Unity
Attn.: Patty Henn
N290 Golden Eagle Court
Appleton, WI 54915-8701

Up Connection
Attn.: Jennifer Payne
725 American Avenue
Waukesha, WI 53188

Wisconsin Association of Single
Adoptive Parents
Attn.: Laurie Glass
4520 North Bartlett Avenue
Shorewood, WI 53211-1510
(414) 962-9342

Wisconsin Federation of Foster
Parents
Attn.: Cora White
2706 Badger Lane
Madison, WI 53713

Wisconsin Single Parents of
Adopted Children
Attn.: Anne Handschke
403 Vilas Avenue
Nekoosa, WI 54457
(715) 886-5572
or
Diane Karrow
127 St. Louis Drive
Prairie du Chien, WI 53821
(608) 326-6657

**Adopted Person and Birth
Relative Support Groups**

Adoption Information and
Direction
11 Sunny Slope Court
Appleton, WI 54914

Adoption Information and
Direction
P.O. Box 875
Green Bay, WI 54305-0875
(414) 336-3005

Adoption Information and
Direction
610 Hintze Road
Madison, WI 53704
(608) 241-8023

Adoption Information and
Direction
280 N. Campbell Road, #D
Oshkosh, WI 54901
(414) 233-6487

Adoption Information and
Direction
P.O. Box 516
Stevens Point, WI 54481-0516
(715) 345-1290

Adoption Resource Network
P.O. Box 174
Coon Valley, WI 54623
(608) 452-3146

Adoption Resource Network
Box 8221
Eau Claire, WI 54702
(715) 835-6695

Adoption Roots Traced
N. 6795 Highway A, #44
Lake Mills, WI 53551
(414) 648-2917

ALARM Network
530 N. 109th Street
Milwaukee, WI 53226
(414) 771-4000

Children's Service Society of
Wisconsin
Birth Parent Support Group
1212 South 70th Street
West Allis, WI 53214
(414) 453-0403

Lutheran Social Services of
Wisconsin and Upper Michigan
Birth Parent Support Group
4143 South 13th Street
Milwaukee, WI 53221
(414) 342-7175

On the Vine
P.O. Box 1852
Appleton, WI 54913|1852

Open Ends of Adoption
1220 Hobart Drive
Green Bay, WI 54304
(414) 496-8801

Orphan Voyage
Box 45754
Madison, WI 53744
(608) 845-3463

Reunions, The Magazine
P.O. Box 11727
Milwaukee, WI 53211-1727
(414) 263-4567

S.E.A.R.C.H.
617 Grove Street
Neenah, WI 54956

UP Connection
725 American Avenue
Waukesha, WI 53188

Wisconsin Division of
Community Services, Bureau
for Children, Youth and
Families
Attn.: Adoption Search
Coordinator
P.O. Box 7851
Madison, WI 53707
(608) 266-7163

State Bar of Wisconsin
402 West Wilson
Madison, WI 53703
(608) 257-3838

Adoption Attorneys

Carol M. Gapen
P.O. Box 1784, 3 S. Pickney
Madison, WI 53701-1784
(608) 256-0226

Stephen Hayes*
411 East Wisconsin Avenue
Milwaukee, WI 53202
(414) 287-1220
fax (414) 276-6281

* Mr. Hayes has conducted
several hundred independent,
agency, and international
adoptions.

Judith Sperling Newton*
Tenny Plaza, Tenth Floor
3 South Pinckney Street
P.O. Box 1784
Madison, WI 53701-1784
(608) 256-0226
fax (608) 259-2601

* Ms. Newton has completed
about 1,000 independent
adoptions and 500 agency
adoptions.

Victoria Schroeder*
383 Williamstowne
Delafield, WI 53018
(414) 646-2054
fax (414) 646-2075

* Ms. Schroeder has conducted
more than 200 independent
adoption, more than 50 agency
and over 25 international
adoptions.

WISCONSIN LAWS RELATED TO ADOPTION: QUESTIONS AND ANSWERS

Private adoption is allowed in Wisconsin, but an agency must conduct a home study and provide counseling to the birth parents.

In an interstate independent adoption, an agency must serve as the child's guardian from the time the child is placed with the adoptive couple to the time the adoption is finalized (about six months after consent is signed). Also, an agency must provide counseling to a birth mother in an independent adoption. Contact the ICPC office for written procedural information.

Can an attorney serve as an intermediary?
No, but the attorney is allowed to pass names along such as a friend might do, as long as no fees are charged.

Is advertising permitted?
Yes.

Who must consent to the adoption?
The birth parents must consent.

When can consent be taken from birth mother (father), and how long after the consent is signed can it be revoked?
A birth mother must have her rights terminated in court after the birth; there is no revocation period. A birth father who is not married to the birth mother and who does not appear in court with her may sign a written consent in front of a notary, and his consent is thereafter filed with the court at the time of the birth mother's hearing. Once the hearing takes place, he cannot revoke his consent.

What are the birth father's rights?
Victoria Schroeder, an attorney in Delafield, states that a birth father has the right to be notified of the court hearing. This can be done by notifying him personally or by publication of the adoption proceedings in the legal notice section of the newspaper if his whereabouts are unknown. If he appears and contests the adoption, he can be represented by an attorney at public expense.

What fees can adoptive parents pay?
Judith Sperling Newton, an attorney in Madison, states that the birth mother can be reimbursed for medical, legal, and agency expenses. With court approval, a birth mother may also be reimbursed for maternity clothing, travel, and child care. Sometimes the court has also permitted the birth mother to be compensated for lost wages due to medical necessity. She must get a statement from her employer and her physician stating that she cannot work.

If an adoptive parent or adoptee requests nonidentifying information about the birth mother, the fee for this service may not exceed $150.

Where does the adoption hearing take place?
The adoption hearing take places in the court of the county where the adoptive parents live or where the child lives.

How are familial and step-parent adoptions different from nonbiological adoptions?
A child may be placed with a relative without a court order. Stephen Hayes, an attorney in Milwaukee, states that in a step-parent or relative adoption, the termination of parental rights and adoption can take place at the same hearing; in other adoptions there is a six-month waiting time from termination of rights to the adoption finalization. Also, a screening is conducted instead of a full home study.

Can a nonresident finalize an adoption in this state?
No.

WYOMING

State Adoption Specialist
Ed Heimer
Wyoming Department of Family
 Services
Hathaway Building, 3rd Floor
Cheyenne, WY 82002-0710
(307) 777-5878

Compact Administrator
K. Gary Sherman, Director
Wyoming Department of Family
 Services
Hathaway Building, 3rd Floor
Cheyenne, WY 82002-0710
(307) 777-5831

Deputy Compact Administrator
Kathleen Petersen
Wyoming Department of Family
 Services
Hathaway Building, 3rd Floor
Cheyenne, WY 82002-0710
(307) 777-6789
fax (307) 777-7747

Direct all telephone calls and
 correspondence to the Deputy
 Compact Administrator.

Office hours:
Monday-Friday
8:00 A.M.-5:00 P.M.
Mountain Time Zone

State Adoption Exchange and Photo Listing

Wyoming Department of Family
 Services
Hathaway Building, Room #320
Cheyenne, WY 82002-0710
(307) 777-6890

Private Adoption Agencies

Bethany Christian Services
3001 Henderson Drive, Suite C
Cheyenne, WY 82001
(307) 635-2032

Catholic Social Services
P.O. Box 1026
Cheyenne, WY 82003-1026
(800) 788-4606 or (307) 638-
 1530

LDS Social Services
7609 Santa Marie
Cheyenne, WY 82009
(307) 637-8929

Wyoming Children's Society
P.O. Box 105
Cheyenne, WY 82003-0105
(307) 632-7619

Wyoming Parenting
P.O. Box 3774
Jackson, WY 83001
(307) 733-7771 or 733-6357

Adoptive Parent Support Groups and Postadoption Services

Northern Wyoming Adoptive
 Parents and North American
 Council on Adoptable Children
 State Representative
Attn.: Irene Tate
P.O. Box 788
Basin, WY 82410
(307) 568-2729 or 754-5355

Adopted Person and Birth Relative Support Groups

Adults Affected By Adoption
1203 E. 6th Street
Cheyenne, WY 82003
(307) 635-6843

Wyoming Confidential Adoption
 Intermediary Services
P.O. Box 5393
Cheyenne, WY 82003

Wyoming State Bar
P.O. Box 109
Cheyenne, WY 82003-0109
(307) 632-9061

Adoption Attorneys

Larry Bancourt
1807 Capitol Avenue, Suite 108
Cheyenne, WY 82001
(307) 635-2881

Peter J. Feeney
P.O. Box 437
Casper, WY 82602
(307) 266-4422

Anthony Ross
1712 Pioneer Avenue
Cheyenne, WY 82001
(307) 632-8957

Mark Stewart
1712 Carey Avenue
Cheyenne, WY 82001
(307) 634-1525

Al Wieberspahn
2020 Carey Avenue, Suite 700
Cheyenne, WY 82001
(307) 638-6417

WYOMING LAWS RELATED TO ADOPTION: QUESTIONS AND ANSWERS

Can an attorney serve as an intermediary?
Yes. However, attorneys generally do not bring birth parents and adoptive parents together. Because the population of Wyoming is only 400,000 and it is the ninth largest state, such a service is difficult to offer in such a sparsely populated area.

Is advertising permitted?
Yes.

Who must consent to the adoption?
1. Both birth parents if the birth father is known
2. The head of the child placement agency if involved

When can consent be given by birth mother (father), and how long after the consent is signed can it be revoked?
Consent cannot be given until the child is born. Once signed, the consent is irrevocable.

What are the birth father's rights?
The birth father's consent is not needed if the birth mother does not know his name, or if he has been given notice of the hearing and has not responded within thirty days after receiving notice of the child's birth, or if he has abandoned or deserted the child, or if he has failed to contribute to the support of the child for one year or more, or if he has failed to pay at least 70 percent of court-ordered support for a period of two years. A putative father also has no right to contest the adoption unless he has asserted paternity or registered with the birth father registry.

If he does object to the adoption and has shown an interest and responsibility in the child within thirty days after being notified of the birth, then the court will decide whether his objections are valid, and his assertions of paternity timely, as well as what would be in the best interests of the child.

What fees can adoptive parents pay?
Medical, legal and living expenses can be paid. An accounting of them must given to the court.

Where does the adoption hearing take place?
The adoption hearing takes place in District Court. Adoptions are usually finalized in about six months.

How are familial and step-parent adoptions different from nonbiological adoptions?
A medical report is not required in a step-parent adoption.

Can a nonresident finalize an adoption in this state?
No. According to ICPC guidelines, a petitioner must be a resident of Wyoming for at least sixty days.

Chapter 2: Agency Adoption

1. Flango, Victor E., and Karen R. Flango. "How Many Children Were Adopted in 1992?" *Child Welfare*, Vol. LXXIV, No. 5, Sept./Oct. 1995. We also gained some information from a personal interview with Karen Flango, who, with Victor Flango, is with the National Center for State Courts in Virginia. The Center is currently collecting data from the states to record the number of adoptions per year. Also, see "FactSheet on Adoption," a publication of the National Council for Adoption, 1930 Seventeenth Street, N.W., Washington, D.C. 20009-6297 202/238-1200. This organization collects and publishes adoption data.

Chapter 6: Who Are Typical Birth Mothers, Fathers, and Grandparents?

1. Cocozzeli, Carmelo. "Predicting the Decision of Biogical Mothers to Retain or Relinquish Their Babies for Adoption: Implications for Open Adoption." *Child Welfare League of America* Vol. LXVIII, No. 5, Jan/Feb 1989.
2. "FactSheet on Adoption." National Council for Adoption, pp. 1–2. Also, see Resnick, Michael D. "Studying Adolescent Mothers' Decision-Making About Adoption and Parenting" in *Social Work*, Jan/Feb 1984.
3. "FactSheet on Adoption," National Council for Adoption, pp. 1–2.
4. "Black Women Are Not More or Less Likely To Place a Child for Adoption: An Empirical Analysis of Adoption." *Economic Inquiry*, Vol XXXI, Jan. 1993, pp. 59–70.

Chapter 9: Openness in Adoption

1. Kraft, Adrienne D., et al. "Some Theoretical Considerations on Confidential Adoptions." *Human Services Press*, 1985 pp. 13–21.

2. *Ibid*, p. 150.

3. Blanton, Terril L., and Jeanne Buckner Deschner. "Biological Mother's Grief: The Post-adoptive Experience in Open Versus Confidential Adoption." *Child Welfare*, Vol 69, No. 6, Nov./Dec. 1990, pp. 525–535.

4. Phillips, B. Lee. "Open Adoption: A New Look at Adoption Practice and Policy in Texas." *Baylor Law Review*, Vol 43:407, 1991, pp. 407–429.

Chapter 10: Single-Parent Adoption

1. Mattes, Jane. *Single Mothers By Choice*. New York: Random House, 1994, p. 10.

2. *Ibid*, pp. 22–23.

3. Crain, Connie, and Janice Duffy. *How to Adopt a Child*. Nashville, Tenn.: Thomas Nelson, 1994, pp. 121–137.

4. Gilman, Lois. *The Adoption Resource Book*. New York: HarperCollins, 1992, p. 29.

5. Crain, Connie, and Janice Duffy. *How to Adopt a Child*. Nashville, Tenn.: Thomas Nelson, 1994, p. 126–127.

Chapter 11: Relative and Step-parent Adoption

1. Flango, Victor E., and Karen R. Flango. "How Many Children Were Adopted in 1992?" *Child Welfare*, Vol. LXXIV, No. 5, Sept./Oct. 1995. We also gained some information from a personal interview with Karen Flango, who, with Victor Flango, is with the National Center for State Courts in Virginia. The Center is currently collecting data from the states to record the number of adoptions per year. Also, see "FactSheet on Adoption," a publication of the National Council for Adoption, 1930 Seventeenth Street, N.W., Washington, D.C. 20009-6297 202/238-1200. This organization collects and publishes adoption data.

2. Melina, Lois. "Relative Adoptions Have Benefits, But Also Have Unique Challenges." *Adopted Child*, Vol. 12, No. 2, February 1993, pp. 1–4.

3. Sawyer, Richard J., and Howard Dubowitz. "School Performance of Children in Kinship Care." Academy for Educational Development, Washington, D.C., published in *Child Abuse and Neglect*; Vol. 18, No. 7, July 1994, pp. 587–597.

4. Personal interview with Ann Sullivan of the Child Welfare League.

5. Foster, Maurice Esq. "Adoption by Grandparents." *State Court Journal*. Vol 18, No. 1, Summer 1994, pp. 27–31.

6. Downey, Douglas B. "Understanding Academic Achievement Among Children in Step-Households: The Roles of Parental Resources, Sex of Stepparent, and Sex of Child." *Social Forces*, Vol. 73, March 1995, p. 875.

7. Adamec, Christine, and William L. Pierce. *Encyclopedia of Adoption*. Facts on File, New York, 1991, p. 272.

8. Downey, Douglas B. "Understanding Academic Achievement Among Children in Step-Households: The Roles of Parental Resources, Sex of Stepparent, and Sex of Child." *Social Forces*, Vol. 73, March 1995, p. 875.

9. Schur, William M. "Adoption Procedure." *Adoption Law and Practice*, Vol. 4, No. 1, December 1994, pp. 26–27.

Chapter 13: International Adoption

1. Personal interview with Melinda Garvert.

2. Jenista, Jerri Ann. "Adoptions from Africa." *Adoption Medical News*, Vol. I, No. 2. Nov./Dec 1995, p. 2.

3. Verhulst, Frank C., Monika Althaus, Versluis den Bieman, and Sophia J. Herma. "Damaging Backgrounds: Later Adjustment of International Adoptees." Children's Hospital, Dept of Child Psychiatry, Rotterdam, Netherlands. Printed in *Journal of the American Academy of Child and Adolescent Psychiatry*, Volume 31, No. 3, May 1992, pp. 518–524.

4. Reynolds, Nancy Thalia. *Adopting Your Child*. North Vancouver, Canada: Self-Counsel Press, 1993.

5. Verhulst, Frank C., Monika Althaus, Versluis den Bieman, and Sophia J. Herma. "Damaging Backgrounds: Later Adjustment of International Adoptees." Children's Hospital, Dept of Child Psychiatry, Rotterdam, Netherlands. Printed in *Journal of the American Academy of Child and Adolescent Psychiatry*, Volume 31, No. 3, May 1992, pp. 518–524.

6. Boer, Frits, Versluis den Bieman, J. M. Herma, and Frank C. Verhulst. "International Adoption of Children with Siblings: Behavioral Outcomes." Leiden University, Dept of Child and Adolescent Psychiatry, Netherlands. Published in *American Journal of Orthopsychiatry*, Vol. 62, No. 2, April 1994, pp. 252–262.

7. Van Gulden, Holly and Lida M. Bartels-Rabb. *Real Parents, Real Children: Parenting the Adopted Child*. New York: Crossroads, 1994, pp. 177–180.

8. *Ibid*, p. 179.

9. Kirkland, Judy. *Washington Metroplitan Area RESOLVE Newsletter*, March 1987.

Chapter 13: Adopting in Canada

1. Wine, Judith. *The Canadian Adoption Guide: A Family at Last*. Toronto: McGraw-Hill Ryerson, 1995.

2. *Ibid.*

3. Personal interview with spokesperson at the British Columbia Adoptive Parents Association.

4. Daly, Kerry J. and Michael Sobol. "Adoption In Canada: A Profile." Taken from a study prepared for the Royal Commission on New Reproductive Technologies. *Transition*, September 1992, pp. 4–5.

5. Wine, Judith. *The Canadian Adoption Guide: A Family at Last*. Toronto: McGraw-Hill Ryerson, 1995.

6. Shinyei, Marilyn E., and Linda Edney. "Open Adoption in Canada." *Transition*, September 1992, pp. 8–10.

7. Wine, Judith. *The Canadian Adoption Guide: A Family at Last*. Toronto: McGraw-Hill Ryerson, 1995.

8. Personal interview with Claire-Marie Gagnon, formerly of the Federation des parents adoptants du Quebec.

9. Wine, Judith. *The Canadian Adoption Guide: A Family at Last*. Toronto: McGraw-Hill Ryerson, 1995.

10. *Ibid.*

11. Personal interview with Claire-Marie Gagnon, formerly of the Federation des parents adoptants du Quebec.

12. *Ibid.*

Chapter 14: Special Needs Adoption

1. Kroll, Joe. "Waiting Children Still Wait." *Adoptalk*, Summer 1995, p 1.

2. Glidden, Laraine M. "Adopted Children with Developmental Disabilities: Post-placement Family Functioning." *Children and Youth Services Review*, Vol. 13, No. 5–6, 1991, pp. 363–377.

3. Rosenthal, James A., and Victor Groze. "Behavioral Problems of Special Needs Adopted Children." *Children and Youth Services Review*, Vol. 13, No. 5–6, 1991, pp. 343–361.

4. Fahlberg, Vera. *Common Behavioral Problems*, Michigan Department of Social Services, 1987.

5. Keck, Gregory C. *Adopting the Hurt Child*.

6. *Ibid.*

7. *Ibid.*

8. Kroll, Joe. "Waiting Children Still Wait." *Adoptalk*, Summer 1995, p 1.

9. Crain, Connie. " 'What I Need is a Mom': The Welfare State Denies Homes to Thousands of Foster Children." *Policy Review*, Vol. 10, No. 73, Summer 1995, p. 40.

10. McDonald, Thomas P., Alice A. Lieberman, Susan Partridge, and Helaine Hornby. "Assessing the Role of Agency Services in Reducing Adoption Disruptions." *Children and Youth Services Review*, Vol. 13, No. 5–6, 1991, pp. 425–438.

11. Adamec, Christine. "Rip-offs." *The Adoption Advocates NEWSletter* Vol. 3, No. 9, September 1995, p. 5.

12. Kroll, Joe. "Waiting Children Still Wait." *Adoptalk*, Summer 1995, p 1.

13. Groze, Victor, Simeon Haines, Mark Barth, and Richard P. Case. "Barriers in Permanency Planning for Medically Fragile Children: Drug Affected Children and HIV Infected Children." Case Western Reserve University, Mandel School of Applied Social Sciences. *Child and Adolescent Social Work Journal*; Vol. 11, No. 1, February 1994, pp. 63–85.

14. Lewert, George. "Children and AIDS." Columbia Presbyterian Medical Center, Dept of Social Work Services. *Social Casework*; Vol. 69, No. 6, June 1988, pp. 348–354.

15. Laws, Rita. "Between the Lines: How to Read a Waiting Child Description." *Adoptive Families*, Sept/Oct 1995, pp 34–35.

16. Chamberlain, Patricia, Sandra Moreland, and Cathleen Reid. "Enhanced Services and Stipends for Foster Parents: Effects on Retention Rates and Outcomes for Children." Oregon Social Learning Center. *Child Welfare*, Vol. 71, No. 5, September/October 1992, pp. 387–401. See also Tim O'Hanlon. *Adoption Subsidy: A Guide for Adoptive Parents*, published by New Roots, An Adoptive Families Support Group. February, 1995.

17. Bussiere, Alice and Ellen C. Sega. "Children With Special Needs." *Adoption Law and Practice*. Matthew Bender and Company, 1994.

18. *Ibid.*

19. *Ibid.*

20. Widermeier, Jeannette. "Adoption Subsidy Q & A." *Adoptalk*, Winter '96 pp. 7, 12

21. O'Hanlon, Tim. *Adoption Subsidy: A Guide for Adoptive Parents*, published by New Roots, An Adoptive Families Support Group. February, 1995.

22. *Ibid.*

23. *Ibid.*

24. McKelvey, Carol, and JoEllen Stevens. *The Adoption Crisis: The Truth Behind Adoption and Foster Care*. Golden, Colorado: Fulcrum Publishing, 1994.

25. Woodmansee, Carol. "Life Book." *Foster Care Connection*, Vol. 1, No. 5, October 1995.

26. Goetting, Ann, and Mark G. Goetting. "How Parents Fare After Placement." Western Kentucky University, *Journal of Child and Family Studies*, Vol. 2, No. 4, December 1993, pp. 353–369.

27. Bussiere, Alice and Ellen C. Sega. "Children With Special Needs." *Adoption Law and Practice*. Matthew Bender and Company, 1994.

Chapter 15: Transracial Adoption

1. Personal interview with Beth Hall of Pact, An Adoption Alliance and Pact Press, in San Francisco, California.

2. "All In the Family." *The New Republic*, January 24, 1994, p. 6.

3. Hayes, Peter. "Transracial Adoption: Politics and Ideology." Iowa State University, *Child Welfare*, Vol. 72, No. 3, May/June 1993, pp. 301–310.

4. Bartholet, Elizabeth. "Where Do Black Children Belong? The Politics of Race Matching in Adoption." University of Pennsylvania Law Review. Volume 139, No. 5, May 1991, pp. 1163–1256.

5. Kennedy, Randall. "Orphans of Separtism: The Politics of Transracial Adoption." *The American Prospect*, Spring 1994, pp. 38–45.

6. Bartholet, Elizabeth. "Where Do Black Children Belong? The Politics of Race Matching in Adoption." University of Pennsylvania Law Review. Volume 139, No. 5, May 1991, pp. 1163–1256.

7. *Ibid.*

8. *Ibid.*

9. Vroegh, Karen S. "Transracial Adoption: How It Is 17 Years Later." Paper published by Chicago Child Care Society, pp. 55.

10. Bowen, James S. "Cultural Convergences and Divergences, The Nexus Between Putative Afro-American Family Values and the Best Interests of the Child." *Journal of Family Law*, Vol. 26, 1988, pp. 487, 502.

11. Forde-Mazrui, Kim. "Black Identity and Child Placement: The Best Interests of Black and Biracial Children." *Michigan Law Revue*, No. 4, February 1994, pp. 925–967.

12. Mahoney, Joan. "The Black Baby Doll: Tranracial Adoption and Cultural Preservation." *UMKC Law. REV.* Vol. 59, No. 85, 1991, pp. 487–501.

13. Kallgren, Carl A., and Pamela J. Caudill. "Current Transracial Adoption Practices: Racial Dissonance or Racial Awareness?" Pennsylvania State U, *Psychological Reports*, Vol. 72, No. 2., April 1993, pp. 551–558.

Chapter 16: The Home Study

1. Johnston, Patricia Irwin. *Adopting After Infertility*. Indianapolis: Perspective Press, 1992, pp. 186-187.
2. Adamec, Christine. *There ARE Babies to Adopt*. New York: Kensington Press, 1996.
3. *Ibid.*
4. *Adoptalk*, publication of the North American Council on Adoptable Children, St. Paul, Minn., Fall 1996, p. 5.
5. *National Adoption Reports*, newsletter from the National Council for Adoption, Washington, D.C., July 1996.

Chapter 17: Adoption Expenses

1. "The New Adoption Tax Credit." From *Adoptalk*, publication of the North American Council on Adoptable Children, St. Paul, Minn., Fall 1996, p. 5.
2. "Common Questions on The Adoption Tax Credit." from *National Adoption Reports*, newsletter from the National Council for Adoption, Washington, D.C., Sept/Oct 1996, pp. 8, 9.

Chapter 18: Healthy Mothers, Healthy Babies

1. "Recommendations of the U.S. Public Health Service Task Force on the Use of Zidovudine (AZT) to Recuce Perinatal Transmission of Human Immunodeficiency Virus." The Center for Disease Control and Prevention, *Morbidity and Mortality Weekly Report*, Vol. 43, August 5, 1995, p. 194.
2. *Ibid.*
3. Hotchner, Tracie. *Pregnancy and Childbirth*. New York: Avon Books, 1984. p. 117.
4. Melina, Lois. "Prenatal Drug Exposure Affects School-Age Child's Behavior." *Adopted Child*, Vol. 15, No. 1, January 1996.
5. Chasnoff, Ira. "Guidelines for Adopting Drug-Exposed Infants and Children." Published by the National Association of Perinatal Addiction, Dept. of Research and Education, 1994.
6. Yolton, Kimberly A., and Rosemary Bolig. "Psychosocial, Behavioral, and Developmental Characteristics of Toddlers Prenatally Exposed to

Cocaine." University of Tennessee, Dept of Pediatrics, *Child-Study-Journal*, Vol. 24, No. 1, 1994, pp. 49–68.

7. Cook, Paddy Shannon, et al. "Alcohol, Tobacco, and Other Drugs May Harm the Unborn." Published by the U.S. Department of Health and Human Services, 1990.

8. Gonzalez, Nilda M., and Magda Campbell. "Cocaine Babies: Does Prenatal Exposure to Cocaine Affect Development?" *Journal of the American Academy of Child and Adolescent Psychiatry*, Vo. 33, No. 1, 1994, pp. 16–19.

9. Melina, Lois. "Prenatal Drug Exposure Affects School-Age Child's Behavior." *Adopted Child*, Vol. 15, No. 1, January 1996.

10. Schneider, Jane "Assessment of Infant Motor Develpments." Presentation at NAPARE conference in New York City, Aug 10, 1988.

11. Yolton, Kimberly A., and Rosemary Bolig. "Psychosocial, Behavioral, and Developmental Characteristics of Toddlers Prenatally Exposed to Cocaine." University of Tennessee, Dept of Pediatrics, *Child-Study-Journal*, Vol. 24, No. 1, 1994, pp. 49–68.

12. Barth, Richard P. "Adoption of Drug-Exposed Children." University of California School of Social Welfare, Child Welfare Research Center, *Children and Youth Services Review*; Vol 13., 1991, pp. 323–342.

13. Chasnoff, Ira. "Guidelines for Adopting Drug-Exposed Infants and Children." Published by the National Association of Perinatal Addiction, Dept. of Research and Education, 1994.

14. Cook, Paddy Shannon, et al. "Alcohol, Tobacco, and Other Drugs May Harm the Unborn." Published by the U.S. Department of Health and Human Services, 1990.

15. Abrams, Richard S. *Will It Hurt the Baby?* Reading, Mass.: Addison-Wesley, 1990, pp. 168–169.

16. Cook, Paddy Shannon, et al. "Alcohol, Tobacco, and Other Drugs May Harm the Unborn " U.S. Department of Health and Human Services Rockville, MD 1990.

17. *Ibid.*

18. Abrams, Richard S. *Will It Hurt the Baby?* Reading, Mass.: Addison-Wesley, 1990, pp. 168–169.

19. Cook, Paddy Shannon, et al. "Alcohol, Tobacco, and Other Drugs May Harm the Unborn " U.S. Department of Health and Human Services Rockville, MD 1990.

20. *Ibid.*

21. *Ibid.*

22. *Ibid.*

23. *Ibid.*

24. Jenista, Jerrri Ann. "Health Status of the 'New' International Adopted Child. *Adoption Medical News*, Vol. II, No. 6, June 1996, p. 3.

25. Jenista, Jerrri Ann. "Chronic Heptatitis B: Medical Mangagement Issues." *Adoption Medical News*, Vol. I, No. 2. November/December 1995.

26. Nelson-Erichsen, Jean, and Heino R. Erichsen. *How to Adopt Internationally.* The Woodlands, Texas: Los Ninos Inernational Adoption Center, 1993, p. 58.

27. Hostetter, Margaret, and Dana Johnson. "Medical Concerns for International Adoptees." *Report on Intercountry Adoption*, 1996, pp. 50–51.

28. Sweet, O. Robin, and Patty Bryan. *Adopt International.* New York: Farrar, Straus and Giroux, 1996, pp. 107–108.

Notes

Notes

Notes

The Everything™ Baby Names Book

by Lisa Shaw

$12.00, 352 pages, 8" x 9 ¼"

Everything you need to know to pick the perfect name for your baby! *The Everything™ Baby Names Book* features over 25,000 names for boys and girls from all over the world. Every entry is complete with clear definitions, country of origin, variations, and interesting anecdotes. There are dozens of sidebars and helpful hints to make choosing a name more fun, including names of saints, angels, world leaders, singers, celebrities, characters from movies and literature, and more!